ALL MY ROAD
BEFORE ME

ALL MY ROAD

⬩ BEFORE ME ⬩

The Diary of C. S. Lewis

1922–1927

Edited by Walter Hooper

Foreword by Owen Barfield

A Harvest/HBJ Book
Harcourt Brace Jovanovich, Publishers
SAN DIEGO   NEW YORK   LONDON

HBJ

Copyright © 1991 by C. S. Lewis Pte. Ltd.
Foreword copyright © 1991 by Owen Barfield

Requests for permission to make copies of
any part of the work should be mailed to:
Permissions Department,
Harcourt Brace Jovanovich, Publishers, 8th Floor,
Orlando, Florida 32887

Library of Congress Cataloging-in-Publication Data
Lewis, C. S. (Clive Staples), 1898–1963.
All my road before me: the diary of C. S. Lewis, 1922–1927/
edited by Walter Hooper: foreword by Owen Barfield.—1st U. S. ed.
p.   cm.
"First published in Great Britain in 1991 by Collins Religious Division,
part of the Harper Collins Publishing Group."
Includes bibliographical references and index.
ISBN 0-15-104609-3   ISBN 0-15-604643-1 (pbk.)
1. Lewis, C. S. Lewis (Clive Staples), 1898–1963—Diaries.
2. Authors, English—20th century—Diaries. I. Hooper, Walter. II. Title.
PR6023.E926Z463   1991
828'.91203—dc20   91-406
[B]

Printed in the United States of America

First Harvest/HBJ edition 1992
A B C D E

Contents

List of Illustrations   vii

Foreword by Owen Barfield   ix

Introduction by Walter Hooper   1

The Diary   13

Epilogue   458

Biographical Appendix   459

The Magdalen College Appendix   475

Index   489

List of Illustrations
(Between pages 272 and 273)

Little Lea, 1905

C.S. Lewis (Jack) with his father

C.S. Lewis after returning from the war

C.S. Lewis and his friend Paddy Moore

Arthur Greeves

Warnie Lewis at Glenmachan House

University College from the High

University College Freshmen of January 1919

28 Warneford Road, where C.S. Lewis
and the Moores lived

"Hillsboro", 14 Holyoake Road, Headington

Jack, Maureen and Mrs Moore

C.S. Lewis at Stonehenge

The Fellows of Magdalen College in 1928

Magdalen College and Magdalen Bridge

Foreword

Lewis himself has answered the first question: why devote the substantial tale of hours it must consume to perusing this meticulous record of a few years when he was still on the threshold of his career? Though admittedly interspersed with occasional shrewd comments on life and literature, by far the greater part of it is a factual, often repetitive, catalogue of endless household and domestic chores, academic studies and job-hunting. Well, in the entry dated 20 June 1923, he observed:

> I think the day to day continuity helps one to see the larger movement and pay less attention to each damned day in itself.

Such, I believe, will be the experience of those readers, and they are likely to be the majority, who feel a special interest not only in the whole or some part of his literary legacy but also in the personal being of C.S. Lewis. They will have got inside the skin, so to speak, of the young man he was between 1922 and 1927 to an extent that no other information or reflection could have enabled.

The second question is more difficult: why, since he himself was already inside that skin, did he find time to keep it up throughout (with only a few gaps) the exceptionally numerous and heavy other burdens he was carrying? Did he have it in mind that at some later stage in this life he would read it in order to "see the larger movement"? I doubt it very much. Entries here and there record his having read the diary to Mrs Moore, and on at least one occasion she rebuked him for having let it drop for some days. My guess therefore, and it is no more, is that these contemporary readings aloud were his main motive in sustaining it.

I find it strange to recall that during those early years I was given no hint of all of that household background. He was simply a fellow undergraduate and later a literary and philosophical friend. I remember his telling me on one occasion that he had to get back in order to clean out the oven in the gas cooker, and I took it to be something that would happen once in a blue moon. It is only from the Diary that I have learnt what a substantial part of his time and energy was being consumed in helping to run Mrs Moore's household, and also how much of that was due to the shadow of sheer poverty that remained hanging over them both until at last he obtained his fellowship. Perhaps it is relevant here to recall that it was not until some time in the 'forties that we used Christian names. Before that it was Lewis and Barfield. When he did suggest the change, I was able to remind him that I myself had done so some years previously and he had judiciously demurred on the ground that our friendship was intellectual rather than domestic!

It is of course not only in connection with domestic work and financial worries that Mrs. Moore's name – "D", as he called her and in the Diary names her – occurs so frequently. One of the things that make me welcome its appearance in print is, that it will do much to rectify the false picture that has been painted of her as a kind of baneful stepmother and inexorable taskmistress. It is a picture that first appeared as early as 1966 in the introductory Memoir to W.H. Lewis's *Letters to C.S. Lewis*, and it has frequently reappeared in the prolific literature on C.S. Lewis which has since been published here and there. If she imposed some burdens on him, she saved him from others by taking them on herself even against his protestations. Moreover she was deeply concerned to further his career. Such was the case at all events during the five or six years the Diary covers. They were followed by more years of what, at all events to friends and visitors, looked like a normal and reasonably happy family life. I recall more than one quite jolly social evening at Hillsboro with the three of them, Lewis, Mrs. Moore and her daughter Maureen; and here I can perhaps be of some technical help to the reader. There is more than one mysterious reference to a parlour game called "Boys' Names", which was sometimes played on these occasions. It was a pencil-and-paper game. Someone chose a letter from the alphabet and everyone was given a minute or two to write down as many boys' names as he or she could think of, beginning with that letter. At least that had presumably been the programme the first time the game was played. Boys' names, however, were soon exhausted and the practice was to select some other category: famous writers, capital cities, rivers, artists, patent foods or whatever. I once suggested that a more satisfactory name for the pastime would be "Categories", but tradition was too strong and the old label stuck.

Perhaps I have overstated the diarists' preoccupation with his personal problems whether academic or familial. There is much else. The love of nature, for instance, that transpired through the numberless descriptions of his daily walk at home and of others on holiday visits. Some of these reminded me of similar detailed accounts of walks in Coleridge's early Notebooks. It was a landscape painter's or a poet's love rather than a naturalist's, a delight in the prospect, in the impact of nature on his sense, rather than any intimate participation in her secret goings on, such as we find in a Richard Jefferies, a W.H. Hudson or a Konrad Lorenz. But it was none the less a deep love, and one not unconnected with that elusive experience of which he was to write later in *Surprised by Joy*:

> Beyond the fence was a deep rich brown. I got a very good touch of the right feeling.

> The stone seemed softer everywhere, the birds were singing, the air was deliciously cold and rare. I got a sort of eerie unrest and dropped into the real joy.

> I turned up to the left and so through the bracken to my favourite fir grove where I sat down for a long time and had the "joy" – or rather came just within sight of it but didn't arrive.

Nor was sight the only one of the five senses through which that love could surface:

> Walked over the fields to Stowe Woods after lunch, to see if any flowers were up there, but found none. It was all I could do on the way back to walk against the wind or keep my eyes open against the sun. How one enjoys nature's violences up to the very moment at which they become painful or dangerous.

I confess to some surprise at finding no reference to his long argument with myself, later referred to in *Surprised by Joy* as "the great war", since he makes it so clear there that he was a good deal preoccupied by it in the latter part of the diary years. The nearest he comes to it is an entry for 18 January 1927:

> Was thinking about imagination and intellect and the unholy muddle I am in about them at present: undigested scraps of anthroposophy and psychoanalysis jostling with orthodox idealism over a background of good old Kirkian rationalism. Lord what a mess! And all the time (with me) there's the danger of falling back into most childish superstitions, or of running into dogmatic materialism to escape them.

Perhaps it is no accident that the previous day reports "A letter from Barfield to say he is at Air Hill and will come over – always good news."

There is indeed plenty of readable metal in the large lump of ore besides its value as personal revelation: pithy comments on friends, colleagues, pupils; his continuing struggle with his narrative poem *Dymer* and his hopes and fears for its intrinsic quality as well as for its possible success; numerous critical observations both on contemporary writers and on the many books from different periods that he was reading or re-reading for his coming degree in English Language and Literature. For example:

After this I read Macdonald's *Phantastes* over my tea, which I have read many times and which I really believe fills for me the place of a devotional book. It tuned me up to a higher pitch and delighted me.

I also read some Dryden in the attempt to find out what he meant by wit. But he means something different each time. He's a rum case of a man who was just a poet and nothing else – no magnanimity, no knowledge, no power of thought: just rhythm and gusto.

I re-read some of the best stories in H.G. Wells' *Country of the Blind*. One never re-reads an old favourite without finding that it has contributed more than one suspected to one's habitual stock in trade.

That day I bought Fielding's *Amelia* and began to read it. It is odd how such a monotonous succession of misfortunes – in which the continual assaults on Amelia's impregnable virtue become ludicrous – ballasted with such shoddy rhetoric in the dialogue can be made palatable by dint of sheer narrative powers. The born story teller can really do what he likes in literature.

For a certain kind of humour, the prose Milton beats anyone I know. He abuses like an inspired coster – like Falstaff.

Or, more generally:

In the pressures of conversation I discovered a new idea of my own which I think true: what we call the "philosophy" of these modern novelists is a habit they have of attaching their characters to what they assume to be big movements of the Zeitgeist – as for example the revolt of youth in [Hugh] Walpole's novels. But this is really a literary device: parallel to the King and Queen setting of tragedies or the supernatural – a means to avoid the purely private and individual, who we don't really like.

These are only a few examples out of a great many that could equally well have been chosen. They suffice, I hope, to show that, interspersed with the humdrum reportage, the reader will find in the ensuing pages plenty of writing where, if it is not yet "vintage Lewis", we can already discern through the abundant foliage the glimmer of ripening clusters.

Owen Barfield
Forest Row, Sussex
May 1990

ALL MY ROAD
BEFORE ME

Introduction

C.S. Lewis made a number of attempts to keep a diary when he was a boy, but all were short lived. Then, at the age of 23, when an undergraduate at Oxford, he began a new diary which runs to over a quarter of a million words and covers the years 1922–27. This was the pre-Christian Lewis, an atheist whose objections to the Faith were ventilated in this attempt. He persevered because it was meant to be not just about his life, but that of his friend Mrs Moore. Several times he records how he fell behind and how Mrs Moore insisted that he pick it up again. Much of its documentary content was dictated by her interest in recording the pleasures and disappointments caused by the many visitors to their house. And, as the diary makes clear, Mrs Moore was its primary audience. Lewis often read it aloud to her, and she could have looked at it at any time. Thus, we do not get an entirely unguarded account of Mrs Moore by Lewis, but we do learn very much about his day to day life.

When C.S. Lewis came up to Oxford in April 1917 Europe was at war. He could have claimed exemption from military service by being Irish. But Jack Lewis, as his friends called him, believed he should earn his right to be in the University by passing through the Officers' Training Corps (O.T.C.) into the Army. Lewis, who was eighteen at the time, was a Scholar of University College and, despite the fact that most of the buildings were being used as an army hospital, he greatly enjoyed the company of the twelve men still left there. Though Lewis was at the stage of loving Oxford, he cared very little for England as a whole. It wasn't, then, surprising that he should be especially attracted to another Irishman in his college, Theobald Butler. One of the effects of being around the colourful Butler, other than getting "royally drunk", was that Lewis became nostalgic.[1] Writing to his Belfast friend, Arthur Greeves,[2] on 27 May about a conversation with Butler he said, "Like all Irish people who meet in

---

[1] *They Stand Together: The Letters of C.S.Lewis to Arthur Greeves (1914–1963)*, ed. Walter Hooper (1979), letter of 10 June 1917, p. 191.

[2] See Biographical Appendix.

England we ended by criticisms on the invincible flippancy and dulness of the Anglo-Saxon race. After all, there is no doubt, ami, that the Irish are the only people: with all their faults I would not gladly live or die among another folk."[3]

In this he was certainly to get what he wanted. After only one term the O.T.C. required Lewis to give up his rooms in University College and join a cadet battalion in Keble College. This was 8 June 1917 and here again he found himself with another of his countrymen. His roommate was Edward Francis Courtenay "Paddy" Moore who was born in Dublin and came to Keble from Clifton College in Bristol. Lewis made a number of good friends in the O.T.C., but from the first he preferred Paddy and his Irish family. Paddy's mother, Mrs Janie King Moore, who was 45 at this time, had come down from Bristol with her eleven year-old daughter, Maureen, to be with her son for as long as possible before he went overseas. Lewis seems to have met the entire family during his first week in Keble College and his first mention of Mrs Moore comes in a letter to his father, Albert Lewis,[4] of 18 June: "Moore, my room mate, comes from Clifton and is a very decent sort of man: his mother, an Irish lady, is staying up here and I have met her once or twice." Following a week of army manoeuvres in Warwick, he wrote to his father on 27 August saying, "We came back on Saturday, and the following week I spent with Moore at the digs of his mother who, as I mentioned, is staying at Oxford. I like her immensely and thoroughly enjoyed myself."[5]

When the course at Keble College was over the men were given a month's leave (18 September-18 October) before joining their regiments. By this time Lewis and Paddy's family were so mutually fond of one another that he disappointed his father greatly by spending a disproportionate three weeks of it with the Moores and only the last week at home. Lewis had come down with a feverish cold, and as soon as they were in his friends' house in 56 Ravenswood Road, Bristol, Mrs Moore insisted that he remain in bed till she could nurse him back to health. "It was during this period," Warren ("Warnie") Lewis[6] was to write later, "that a relationship first began

---

[3] *They Stand Together*, p. 187.

[4] See Biographical Appendix.

[5] *Letters of C. S. Lewis*, edited with a Memoir by W. H. Lewis (1966). Revised and Enlarged Edition edited by Walter Hooper (1988), p. 64.

[6] See *Brothers and Friends: The Diaries of Major Warren Hamilton Lewis*, ed. Clyde S. Kilby and Marjorie Lamp Mead.

that had a huge and determining effect upon the pattern of his subsequent life."[7]

Mrs Moore was the eldest child of a Church of Ireland clergyman, The Reverend William James Askins (1842–95), and his wife Jane King Askins (1846–90). She was born on 28 March 1872 in Pomeroy, County Tyrone, where her father was a curate (1869–72). Mr Askins became Vicar of Dunany, County Louth, in 1872 and his daughter was baptised Janie King in the church of Dunany on 21 July 1872. It was in Dunany, a small village on the east coast of Ireland, midway between Belfast and Dublin, that Janie grew up. Her father was the Vicar there until his death in 1895, and he and Mrs Askins had three sons, William, John and Robert, and two more daughters, Edith and Sarah.

On 1 August 1897 Janie married Courtenay Edward Moore, who, like herself, came from an Irish ecclesiastical family. He was the son of Canon Courtenay Moore (1840–1922), Rector of Mitchelstown in County Cork, and Jessie Mona Duff (1843–1936). Courtenay was born in Dublin on 26 June 1870 and, after four years (1884–88) at Haileybury College in Hertford, he took a B.A. from Trinity College Dublin in 1893. After he and Janie married they lived in Dublin where he was a Civil Engineer. Paddy was born on 17 November 1898 and Maureen on 19 August 1906. Not long after this they separated, under circumstances and causes entirely unknown to us. At this time divorce was granted in Ireland for only the gravest of causes, and it is unlikely that the Moores ever applied for one. What happened was that Mrs Moore went to live in Bristol where her brother Dr Robert Askins was a government medical officer, and where Paddy was admitted to Clifton College in May 1908. Mrs Moore thereafter usually referred to her husband as "The Beast", but for all her ill words for him, he came from two good families. It was through his mother that Maureen inherited a baronetcy and became Lady Dunbar of Hempriggs with a castle and an estate in Caithness, Scotland.

Of that three-week stay in 56 Ravenswood Road it is evident that Lewis savoured to the full the hospitality afforded by Mrs Moore. They all knew it could not be like this again for a long time because Lewis had already been gazetted into the 3rd Somerset Light Infantry and Paddy into the Rifle Brigade. And if the young men didn't come

---

[7] *Letters of C.S. Lewis*, p. 28.

back from the war? Maureen was twelve at the time, and she told me some years ago that she remembered hearing Lewis and her brother promise one another that if only one survived the war he would look after Paddy's mother and Lewis's father.

Lewis joined his regiment at Crownhill in South Devon on 19 October 1917. It was rumoured that they would be sent to Ireland to fight the Sinn Féin and they were very surprised when, on 15 November, they were ordered to the front following a 48-hour leave. It would have taken every one of those hours to make a round trip to Ireland, so on 15 November Lewis rushed to Mrs Moore's home in Bristol.

From here he sent the following telegram to his father: "Have arrived Bristol on 48 hours leave. Report Southampton Saturday. Can you come Bristol. If so meet at Station. Reply Mrs Moore's address 56 Ravenswood Road, Redlands, Bristol. Jack." To anyone in this country a soldier reporting to Southampton in 1917 could only mean that he was being sent overseas. But Albert Lewis wired back: "Don't understand telegram. Please write." In desperation, Jack wired back the following morning: "Orders France. Reporting Southampton 4 p.m. Saturday. If coming wire immediately."[8] Mr Lewis did not come. And Jack, after being transferred to the 1st Battalion of the Somerset Light Infantry, crossed to France on 17 November.

Lewis arrived at the front line trenches on 29 November, his nineteenth birthday. In February 1918 he "had the good luck," as he said, "to fall sick with what the troops call 'trench fever' and the doctors P.U.O. (Pyrexia, unknown origin)."[9] This meant a delightful three weeks in a hospital at Le Tréport, during which he wrote some of the poems which appeared in *Spirits in Bondage* (1919). From the letters he wrote to Arthur while in hospital it is clear that he believed his old friend needed to know that he had not been replaced in his affections by Mrs Moore. "I must admit fate has played strange with me since last winter", Lewis wrote on 2 February. "I feel that I have definitely got into a new epoch of life and one feels extraordinarily helpless over it . . . As for the older days of real walks far away in the hills . . . Perhaps you don't believe that I want all that again, because other things more important have come in: but after all there is room for other things besides love in a man's life."[10]

[8] *Lewis Papers*, vol. V, pp. 241-2.
[9] C.S. Lewis, *Surprised by Joy: The Shape of My Early Life* (1955), ch. XII.
[10] *They Stand Together*, p. 206.

Lewis rejoined his battalion at Fampoux on 28 February. He was one of those who faced the final German attack on the Western Front, and on 15 April he was wounded at Mount Bernenchon during the Battle of Arras. The casualties were very great, and after he reached the Liverpool Merchants Mobile Hospital at Etaples he learned that several of his friends had been killed. Jack was still at Etaples when he wrote to his father on 14 May saying: "My friend Mrs Moore is in great trouble – Paddy has been missing for over a month and is almost certainly dead. Of all my own particular set at Keble he has been the first to go, and it is pathetic to remember that he at least was always certain that he would come through."[11]

Lewis was transferred to the Endsleigh Palace Hospital in London on 25 May. From the time he got back to England he began begging his father to come and visit him. Here, again, Warren Lewis's "Memoir", the best thing ever written about C.S. Lewis, is very helpful. "My father was a very peculiar man in some respects," he said, "in none more than in an almost pathological hatred of taking any step which involved a break in the dull routine of his daily existence."[12] Even so, it is hard to see how Albert Lewis could resist the entreaties of a son just back from such a bloody war. Writing to Mr Lewis on 20 June 1918 Jack said: "I know I have often been far from what I should in my relations to you, and have undervalued an affection and a generosity which . . . an experience of 'other people's parents' has shown me in a new light. But, please God, I shall do better in the future. Come and see me. I am homesick, that is the long and the short of it . . . This week Mrs Moore has been up on a visit to her sister who works at the War Office, and we have seen a good deal of each other. I think it some comfort to her to be with someone who was a friend of Paddy's and is a link with the Oxford days: she has certainly been a very, very good friend to me."[13]

On 25 June Lewis was transferred to a hospital at Clifton, near Bristol, which he had chosen so that he could have the society of Mrs Moore. Again he remained unvisited by his father. In the middle of September it was confirmed that Paddy was dead and when Lewis was moved to Perham Down Camp in Ludgershall, Hampshire, on 4 October Mrs Moore went with him. The last part of Jack's convalescence was spent at a hospital at Eastbourne, and from there

[11] *Letters of C.S.Lewis*, p. 79.
[12] *Ibid.*, p. 30.
[13] *Ibid.*, p. 84.

he wrote to his father on 8 December saying: "At my suggestion Mrs Moore has come down here and is staying in rooms near the camp, where I hope she will remain until I go on leave."[14]

Armistice was signed on 11 November 1918. Jack, however, was given to understand that he would not be given leave before Christmas. Nevertheless, Warnie was able to write in his diary of 27 December: "A red letter day. We were sitting in the study about eleven o'clock this morning when we saw a cab coming up the avenue. It was Jack! He had been demobilized, thank God. Needless to say there were great doings. He is looking pretty fit . . . In the evening there was bubbly for dinner in honour of the event: the first time I have ever had champagne at home."[15]

Jack returned to Oxford on 13 January 1919 and took up residence in University College. He was reading the most celebrated of the arts courses at Oxford which is known as Literae Humaniores, or "Greats" to give it its slang name. "It was a great return and something to be very thankful for," he wrote to his father on 27 January. "There is of course already a great difference between this Oxford and the ghost I knew before: true, we are only twenty-eight in College, but we *do* dine in Hall again, the Junior Common Room is no longer swathed in dust sheets, and the old round of lectures, debates, games, and what not is getting under weigh. The re-awakening is a little pathetic: at our first J.C.R. Meeting we read the minutes of the last – 1914. I don't know any little thing that has made me realize the absolute suspension and waste of these years more thoroughly."[16]

In 1919 the average cost of living in one of the twenty colleges which made up Oxford University was about £60 a term. (At this time £1 was worth about 5 US dollars.) Lewis's scholarship from University College was worth £80 a year, but after all his college expenses were paid he was left with about £11 per term. Mr Lewis was giving him £67 per term, as well as paying incidental expenses. Besides this, Mr Lewis worked very hard to get his son a "wounds gratuity" from the army, and Jack received £145 in March 1919 and a further £104 in July. This £234 (excluding the wounds gratuity) would have allowed for some luxury for a man living in College – Albert Lewis was indeed very generous with his son. But as Warnie

[14] *Ibid.*, p. 98.
[15] Roger Lancelyn Green and Walter Hooper, *C.S. Lewis: A Biography* (1974), ch. II.
[16] *Letters of C.S.Lewis*, p. 100.

Lewis observed in his "Memoir": "since an allowance calculated to suit a bachelor living in college was by no means enough for a householder, Jack found himself miserably poor."[17]

Of course Lewis's father and brother didn't know Jack's new "family", as he called Mrs Moore and Maureen, had followed him to Oxford. They were living two miles east of the centre of town at the home of Miss Featherstone in 28 Warneford Road – the same house they were in when the Diary opens – and not far from Headington School where Maureen became a day pupil soon after they arrived in Oxford. Jack confided to Arthur Greeves in a letter of 26 January: "After breakfast I work (in the library or a lecture-room which are both warm) or attend lectures until 1 o'clock when I bycycle out to Mrs Moore's. They are installed in our 'own hired house' (like St Paul only not daily preaching and teaching). The owner of the house has not yet cleared out and we pay a little less than the whole for her still having a room."[18] We don't know how much money Mrs Moore was receiving from her husband, but it does not seem to have stretched far.

Jack lived in University College for three terms as he was required to do by the statutes of the University. After that he was allowed to "reside and keep term in lodgings situated within three miles of Carfax" – that is, from the centre of town. It is surely proof of their mutual dependency and Lewis's love of domesticity that he was able to take three first class degrees even while being constantly uprooted. They were all so poor that they were forced to live in a number of vile places. Between 1917 and 1930 they lived in nine different houses.

Lewis concealed all this from his father. Even before his first term at Oxford had ended, when of course his father expected him home, Jack was setting the pattern for years to come by fabricating some excuse for remaining in Oxford with his new family. "I shall be staying up for a week more following [his tutor's] instructions", Jack wrote to his father on 15 March 1919. "After that I shall go down to help Mrs Moore with her move at Bristol: she has had to come back to clear out the house. There seems to be considerable difficulty about getting anywhere else. London and Bristol are both hopeless: I have suggested here, but that seems equally impossible."[19] The truth is that "the family" had been in Oxford since January. The same

[17] *Ibid.*, p. 33.
[18] *They Stand Together*, p. 241.
[19] *Letters of C.S. Lewis*, pp. 103-4.

thing was to happen again when Lewis wrote to his father from Somerset on 4 April 1920 saying "I thought it a good opportunity of paying off an engagement with a man who has been asking me for some time to go and 'walk' with him."[20] But in his letter to Arthur of 11 April we learn that he was really with the Moores.

It is hard to say how much Albert Lewis ever knew about Jack's joint establishment with the Moores. He was certainly aware that Jack was seeing Mrs Moore during his first term back in Oxford and he wrote to Warnie about this. And Warnie, who was in Belgium, said in a letter of 10 May: "The Mrs. Moore business is certainly a mystery but I think perhaps you are making too much of it. Have you any idea of the footing on which he is with her? Is she an intellectual? It seems to me preposterous that there can be anything in it. But the whole thing irritates me by its freakishness."[21] Albert replied on 20 May: "I confess I do not know what to do or say about Jack's affair. It worries and depresses me greatly. All I know about the lady is that she is old enough to be his mother – that she is separated from her husband and that she is in poor circumstances. I also know that Jacks has frequently drawn cheques in her favour running up to £10 – for what I don't know. If Jacks were not an impetuous, kind hearted creature who could be cajoled by any woman who has been through the mill, I should not be so uneasy. Then there is the husband whom I have always been told is a scoundrel – but the absent are always to blame – some where in the background, who some of these days might try a little amiable black mailing. But outside all these considerations that may be the outcome of a suspicious, police court mind, there is the distraction from work and the folly of the daily letters. Altogether I am uncomfortable."[22] Apart from this there is very little in Albert's letters to Warnie about Mrs Moore. What I feel it would be a pity to forget about this good man – something Jack and Warnie mentioned often – is that he supported his son through all his undergraduate years and up to his being made a Fellow of Magdalen College.

More presciently than anyone, Albert Lewis suspected the presence of elements in the liaison that were profoundly unhealthy. A surrogate mother-son relationship is not among these: Jack and Mrs Moore had suffered reciprocal losses, so to speak, and a symbiotic

[20] *Ibid.*, p. 111.
[21] *Lewis Papers*, vol. VI, p.118.
[22] *Ibid.*, p. 123.

solution to that problem is neither unnatural, nor uncommon, nor morally troublesome. But the rapidity and depth of Jack's involvement, the initiatives taken by Mrs Moore to assure it, her acquiescence in Jack's lies and his readiness to lie in the first place – Albert Lewis is the only person with whom we know Jack to have broken faith – together invite such words as "affair", "mischief", and "blackmail", all used by Albert in discussing the liaison.

The notion of sexual intimacy between the two must be regarded as likely. The sensual young atheist lives with a not unattractive woman, still in early middle age, who is not only available to him but very likely possessed of an agenda of her own: the young man is, as his father points out, fundamentally good-natured and easily manipulated, and the woman – in that society, at that time – would surely benefit from the presence of a man in the household. This combination of motive, means, and opportunity invites, though it does not demand, the conclusion that Janie King Moore and C.S. Lewis were lovers.

Lewis himself must have implied as much in a conversation with Arthur Greeves during the visit to Belfast in October 1917, and about which he later expressed regret. When he wrote to Arthur on 28 October he said: "Since coming back & meeting a certain person I have begun to realize that it was not at all the right thing for me to tell you so much as I did. I must therefore try to undo my actions as far as possible by asking you to try & forget my various statements & not to refer to the subject."[23] And taboo it probably remained for the rest of Lewis's life.

Thus it is unwise to overinterpret. The nature of their intimacy, its duration, and the circumstances under which it ended are largely unknown to us. What is known is the day-to-day devotion shown by C.S. Lewis to Mrs Moore until her death, after a long mental and physical decline, at the age of 78. Life is more richly-textured – or as Lewis would put it, "thicker" – than we expect it to be. None of us is either this or that; rather we and all the "ordinary" people we meet and know are many things at once, full of shading and nuance. This story may have begun in self-indulgence, cynicism and sin, but it ended as an enduring exemplum of Christian charity – and of Divine Economy.

After Albert Lewis died on 25 September 1929, aged 66 years, the

[23] *They Stand Together*, p. 200.

family papers were brought to Oxford. Warnie Lewis spent much of the next few years editing those papers as well as his and Jack's diaries, and in the end they filled eleven bound volumes. After his own diary was in typescript Jack went through it and supplied footnotes where he thought they were needed. Both brothers' notes have been retained in this edition. Warnie's magnificent achievement is usually referred to as the *Lewis Papers*, the original of which is in Wheaton College in Illinois with a copy in the Bodleian Library. The *Lewis Papers* is the major source of the diary. Another source is a notebook Warren Lewis gave me in 1964 and which contains, amongst other things, the original of Lewis's diary for the period 27 April 1926 – 2 March 1927.

Neither of the brothers were good spellers, and Warnie used to say that he could never remember whether he kept a "diary" or a "dairy". His most characteristic mistake was altering such contractions as "can't" to "ca'nt". Besides errors such as this in the *Lewis Papers*, there were others which were the inevitable result of typing several thousand pages with two fingers. Because I could not distinguish between Warnie's and Jack's spelling errors I corrected that portion of the diary found only in the *Lewis Papers*. From 27 April 1926 onwards I have followed C.S. Lewis's original spelling as found in his notebook.

Those who have read a typescript version of the diary in the *Lewis Papers* will have noticed that throughout it Lewis refers to Mrs Moore as "D". I discovered from that portion of the diary in the notebook that the abbreviation Lewis used throughout his diary, and which Warnie Lewis could not reproduce with his typewriter, was the Greek letter Δ (Delta). I have retained the letter "D" because both brothers had approved the use of it. Jack and Warnie called Mrs Moore "Minto", and I am unable to say whether Δ has any meaning other than being a useful abbreviation.

Lewis brought his diary to an end with the entry of 2 March 1927. And although they were not copied into the *Lewis Papers*, the notebook contains several more pages of diary. Lewis wrote entries for 19-22 January and 2-3 June 1928 in Old English and an entry for 4 June 1928 in Latin. The notebook also contains "portraits" or written descriptions of nine of Lewis's colleagues at Magdalen College during the time the last portion of his diary was being written. I believe they were meant to accompany the diary and I have included them in an appendix.

Introduction

The most significant difference between this book and what is in the *Lewis Papers*, is that this is a good deal shorter. The whole diary runs, as I've said, to over a quarter of a million words and the Lewis Estate and the publishers felt it would be acceptable to more readers if it were cut by about a third. I have tried to do this in such a way that none of Lewis's main interests – friends, books, domestic life – would be lost. There was a great deal of repetition in the complete diary, and I have mainly cut out some of the many details of domestic chores which I dare say Lewis was happy to forget when they were written down.

I thank all those who have helped with the editing of this book. I have particular reason to be grateful to Mr Owen Barfield, Miss Nan Dunbar of Somerville College, Mr and Mrs Colin Hardie, Mr George Sayer, Professor James Como and Brother Paul Browne OSB. The editing of this book was made especially pleasurable because of the help I received from Miss Lesley Walmsley of Collins Publishers and John Ferrone of Harcourt Brace Jovanovich and I thank them both.

21 August 1990   Walter Hooper
Oxford

THE DIARY

You stranger, long before your glance can light
Upon these words, time will have washed away
The moment when I first took pen to write,
With all my road before me—yet to-day,
Here, if at all, we meet . . .

—C. S. Lewis, *Dymer*, I, 1

1922

At this time Lewis was sharing a house with Mrs Moore and her daughter, Maureen, in 28 Warneford Road, two miles from the centre of Oxford.[1] Maureen was a day pupil in Headington School. In 1920 Lewis had taken a First Class Degree in Classical Moderations – Greek and Latin Classical writers. Now he was preparing for his examination (8–14 June) in Literae Humaniores or "Greats" – Greek and Latin historians and philosophers. He was hoping to find a Fellowship in one of the Oxford colleges, and for this he would have a better chance with another First. "D" was Mrs Moore.

Saturday 1 April: I walked to Iffley in the morning and called in at the Askins.[2] The Doc has foolishly knocked himself up by walking too far and wd. not come to Headington in the afternoon. He talked about Atlantis, on which there is apparently a plentiful philosophical literature: nobody seems to realise that a Platonic myth is fiction, not legend, and therefore no base for speculation. We also spoke of the Old Testament and anthropology: ridiculous remarks by Mary. A fine day.

Went to the show at Headington School after tea . . . They did a scene from *Nicholas Nickelby* wh. was not badly acted and for a moment made me remember the Wynyard terrors – a high, but subjective tribute to amateurs.[3] They also did Arnold's *Tristram* (v. badly) and Yeats' *Land of Heart's Desire*: even school girl acting could not quite spoil its wonderful beauty.

Sunday 2 April: A beautiful spring day. D busy cutting oranges for marmalade. I sat in my own bedroom by an open window in bright sunshine and started a poem on "Dymer" in rhyme royal. I walked on Shotover in the afternoon, much disturbed by all the boys and

---

[1] Since Lewis returned to Oxford in 1919 with the Moores they had lived in a good many places, of which 28 Warneford Road was the one they liked best. It was owned by Miss Featherstone who had moved out for a while to give them more room, and was now thinking of returning.

[2] See **John Hawkins Askins** in the Biographical Appendix.

[3] When he was nine years old Lewis was sent to Wynyard School in Watford, Hertfordshire. It's the school referred to as "Belsen" in *Surprised by Joy* (1955).

girls out for their Sunday walk. In the evening we played bridge – very dull hands all round, and Maureen talking all the time. I read Colonel Repington's book aloud, which we are enjoying very much.[4] Late getting to bed. Still very worried by the non-arrival of D's pass book.[5]

Monday 3 April: Got a letter from home in the morning . . . My father seems in good form. It snowed hard all day: in the afternoon I had good fun shovelling and trying to get the roof clear, as it was sending down sudden drifts in front of the hall door, with a noise like thunder. I worked at Roman history notes all the morning and at Adamson's chapters on Aristotle after lunch.[6] A rather depressing day: in the evening more history and more Repington. Maureen in wonderful spirits.

Tuesday 4 April: I walked into Oxford and left two poems ("Misfire" and the "Offa" one) to be typewritten. Remembering yesterday, I set out in a coat and suffered from heat – the day turning out sunny and beautiful – all the more so for the drifts of snow lying under the hedges etc.

Worked at Adamson before lunch: I am beginning to get the hang of Aristotle's theory of *eidee*. Form and matter are almost the same as actuality and potentiality . . . This leads to Soul as the realisation of organic potentialities: the "living body", a great advance on the old Animism of Body plus Ghost, tho' seemingly fatal to immortality. Can't see why *nous* whd. be on a different footing.

A letter came from Arthur today asking me to spend a few days with him in London: wh. wd. be rather pleasant but is not possible.[7] Roman History all afternoon and some in evening, besides Bk. II of the *Republic*. In bed shortly after 12.

Wednesday 5 April: Started revising Greek History today. At first I found my notes etc. in great confusion, but when that was straightened out I worked with more interest and pleasure than I had expected.

A pretty woman called this morning with the enlargement of Paddy's photo:[8] it is not "finished" yet and (perhaps for that reason)

---

[4] Charles à Court Repington, *After the War: A Diary* (1922).
[5] The pass book to Mrs Moore's bank account in Ireland, into which account her husband was expected to make regular payments.
[6] Robert Adamson, *The Development of Greek Philosophy*, ed. W.R. Sorley and R.P. Hardie (1908).
[7] See **Arthur Greeves** in the Biographical Appendix.
[8] "Paddy" is Mrs Moore's son Edward Francis Courtenay Moore (1898–1918) who died in the War. See the Introduction.

seems to me to be more lively and interesting than the old one. After lunch I called on Miss Baker to get the details about a performance at Cumnor in which Masefield is to act as Lear: she did not know, and Maureen is to find out from the O'Maleys.

I also got the two poems (typed v. accurately for 1/-) and saw Stead in order to get the address of the *London Mercury*.[9] He told me with a solemn face and admirable naivety how he had got his accepted. Two or three were sent back by return post, whereupon he went up to London and called on the Editor, saying, "Look here Mr Squire, you haven't taken these poems of mine and I want to know what's wrong with them!!"[10] If the story ended there, it would be merely a side light on Stead, but the joke is that Squire said, "I'm glad you've come to talk it over: that's just what I want people to do" and actually accepted what he'd formerly refused. Truly the ways of editors are past finding out!

Stead gave me the proof of his new book, *The Sweet Miracle*, wh. I took away. So far it seems rather dull. Worked for the rest of the day, except for a nightcap of Repington.

Thursday 6 April: D woke me up with alarming news from Ireland. It appears that "Hi"[11] has called at the bank and that the bank's letters to D have been returned, once more by the stupidity of the Bristol post office. It is therefore very probable that the Beast[12] has been informed, and the bank's mention of letters (as opposed to pass book) suggests that D is overdrawn. Of course we have the wind up, since, if the Beast ceases payment it will be very hard to see our way: Maureen's school, for instance, must go to blazes: our joint incomes will hardly suffice for bare rent and food.

We move today to Red Gables, which Lady Gonner has very kindly lent us during her fortnight's absence (it only needs a few more such kindnesses to land us in the workhouse!).[13]

A day disturbed with packing, besides mental anxiety, yet I managed to do a fair morning's work. It was a strange, lurid

---

[9] See **William Force Stead** in the Biographical Appendix.

[10] John Collings Squire (1884–1958), poet and man of letters, founded and edited the *London Mercury* 1919–34.

[11] Mrs Moore's sister, Mrs Sarah Horan, was married to a Dublin solicitor.

[12] Mrs Moore's name for her husband, Courtenay Edward Moore, from whom she was separated.

[13] Lady Gonner (*née* Nannie Ledlie) was the widow of Sir Edward Carter Kersey Gonner (1862–1922) who had been Economic Adviser to the Ministry of Food and Professor of Economic Science in the University of Liverpool. Their one child, Sheila, was at Headington School with Maureen. "Red Gables" was on Headington Road, the first house on the right side of "The White Horse" public house.

afternoon, ready to thunder. We reached Red Gables at 6 p.m. by taxi. It is a very charming house with an excellent library, where I found and started Mallock's *New Republic*. After supper I had meant to do History Notes but was very tired: so read the 4th Bk. of the *Republic* instead. Maureen has got tomorrow's post. D rather done up by the move and the wind up: only Maureen, thro' stupidity or heroism, remains in excellent spirits . . .

Friday 7 April: Nothing from Ireland by this morning's post – only my two poems returned by the *Mercury*. Settled down after breakfast and had done two hours very satisfactory work memorising Gk. History notes up to date, when I was interrupted by the arrival of Joy Whicher and her mother . . .

I went to Warneford Rd. in the hope of letters, but there was no one in the house. I find that Maureen tried again after supper and very foolishly burgled the house from the back: it is to be hoped that Miss Featherstone will not mind. D and I propounded the strongest letter we could to the Bristol P.O. thro' whose bungling the whole situation has come about. With the absence of news, the wind up continues. D is very worn out with the move and indigestion.

I woke up with a sore throat but it seems to have gone. As I said this afternoon, I wish life and death were not the only alternatives, for I don't like either: one could imagine a *via media* . . .

Saturday 8 April: D woke me up this morning coming into my room with the joyful news that the pass book had come: no financial or personal crisis having materialised. I went to town immediately after breakfast for meat: got back shortly before eleven and put in good work on Gk. History till lunch, and after lunch again until tea time . . .

Maureen tells me that while she was in a shop today an unknown undergraduate entered and announced to all and sundry that he had taken his degree – this beats "Corsica" Boswell!

Heard from Dorothy that Miss Featherstone is talking of coming back to Warneford Rd., which is serious news. After supper I read most of the 5th Bk. of the *Republic*. A beastly headache and feeling generally fagged: D rather better, but not as well as before we left. As an intellectual nightcap have been puzzling over our accounts, which come out to a different figure each time. Not a pleasant day, but thank God for this morning's news.

(Finished *The Everlasting Mercy*, in my opinion much the poorest thing of Masefield that I have read yet – nearly all of it could have been composed extempore; but perhaps I was a dull reader today.)

Have just remembered to record that Pasley and "Johnnie" Hamber were married today. It must be one of the horrors of marriage to reflect at such a time how many kind friends know exactly what you are doing.[14]

Sunday 9 April: Today I finished Masefield's *Pompey the Great*, with very great pleasure: it has the merit of forcing you to ACT each speech as you go along, it is finely realistic and moving. Next to *Dauber* and parts of *Reynard*, the best thing of his I have read. Afterwards I walked on Shotover, getting back before lunch.

I tried very hard to write something today, but it was like drawing blood from a stone. In spite of promising myself not to be influenced by the decision of the *Mercury* – and I know from what they publish that their canon is wrong – the rejection of my things has made me rather despond . . .

Monday 10 April: A letter from Pasley written on the second day of his honeymoon – the eighth he had written that afternoon. D considers it a curious way of spending such a time, but he sounds pleased.

Put in a very satisfactory morning's work, going over Roman Hist. (the wars of AD 69, I'm glad to find the Gk. hasn't put them out of my head) and then Gk. notes up to date. Went out a little before lunch to enjoy the sunshine and drink a bottle of Guinness next door in the "White Horse".

After lunch I copied out the poem beginning "The last star of the night" meaning with it to try the *Mercury* again, and to send the *Mercury's* refusals to the *English Review*. I accordingly walked into Oxford: a beautiful warm day. Left the poem at the typists and sent off the two others: looking in a copy of the *English Review* for its address, I was disgusted by the poetry in it – all in the worst modern tradition – and half thought of not sending mine. But I decided I need not be nice, as I shall almost certainly be rejected anyway . . .

Tuesday 11 April: We were all much amused by the arrival of Maureen's report today, in which she is marked as "improving" in two subjects she doesn't do – a good example of the methods of this school.

Put in a good morning's work on Gk. History and read most of

---

[14] See Rodney Pasley in the Biographical Appendix.

the 6th Bk. of the *Republic* after lunch. Went into Oxford after tea . . .

Found the Doc here when I came back, looking very much better: he soon goes to Clevedon. He stayed for supper: afterwards we talked of the Napoleonic wars, a subject on which he has funds of information . . . I walked to the bus with him afterwards: we began on Christina dreams, but, as always with him, ended on immortality.[15] . . .

Friday 14 April: Last night I had a ridiculous dream of Squire's sending back my poem and saying he could not accept it because I spelt the word "receive" wrongly: and sure enough, the first post brought the poem back! I intend to hammer away for a bit at him yet.

Did Gk. History until lunch time – rather a slow morning. In the afternoon I walked up the field path which represents the Roman road, along the road which skirts Stowe Woods, and back by the footpath starting through Elsfield church . . .

Put in good work after tea and again after supper. Another beautiful day, with a very fine sunset at supper time: a wind was just rising then, soon followed by rain, and there is a glorious storm now. D has a wonderful Dundalk newspaper from one of her "gens" in Ireland called the *Democrat*: among other treasures, we found someone in the Deaths column described as "a thoroughly decent woman" . . .

Saturday 15 April: D reminds me that it was this day four years ago I was wounded at Mt. Bernenchon. Worked in the morning. After lunch I walked into Oxford to call in College and buy some things. A beautiful sunny and windy day, but in town detestable on account of the dust and crowds of holiday makers. College looking very deserted and dismal. I took from the library Grundy's *Persian War* which is indispensable . . .

Tried to work at "Dymer" and covered some paper: but I am very dispirited about my work at present – especially as I find it impossible

---

[15] In the Preface to the second edition of *Dymer* of 1950 Lewis defined "Christina Dreams": "In those days the new psychology was just beginning to make itself felt in the circles I most frequented at Oxford. This joined forces with the fact that we felt ourselves (as young men always do) to be escaping from the illusions of adolescence, and as a result we were much exercised about the problem of fantasy or wishful thinking. The 'Christina Dream', as we called it (after Christina Pontifex in Butler's novel), was the hidden enemy whom we were all determined to unmask and defeat . . . By the time I wrote *Dymer* I had come, under the influence of our common obsession about Christina Dreams, into a state of angry revolt against that spell. I regarded it as the very type of the illusions I was trying to escape from. It must therefore be savagely attacked."

to invent a new opening for the "Wild Hunt". The old one is full of clichés and will never do. I have leaned much too much on the idea of being able to write poetry and if this is a frost I shall be rather stranded.

Another fine sunset. I see I have never yet mentioned the cat in this house: it is very large, and bleats like a sheep in the most irritating way. Read some more Repington. A dissatisfying day, but, praise God, no more headaches. (This stay at Lady Gonner's is, as we expected, proving terribly expensive: while Miss Featherstone is turning the other house upside down in our absence.)

Sunday 16 April: Today being Easter Sunday I was somehow persuaded to go with Maureen to Highfield Church. I was struck with the extraordinary sternness of Mr Clarke in his official capacity – he looked a regular fighting priest. He preached a good little sermon with a flavour of metaphysic wh. one would not expect from his conversation – but perhaps it was out of a book. He is a jerky little man, like a wagtail, and it is surprising that he is not more popular with the Demos.[16]

After lunch I worked at "Dymer" and made some progress: but it will need more guts soon than I can at present put into it . . .

Monday 17 April: . . . Miss Brayne, Maureen's violin teacher, came to tea. I went to another room and worked at memorising and afterwards did some walking in the garden. D had a long talk with Miss Brayne, whom she likes. She (Miss B.) says that London or Brussels is absolutely necessary for serious music. Unless I happen to get a London job funds will never run to it.

After supper I finished the 7th and began the 8th book of the *Republic*. A most amusing and encouraging letter came to me today from Aunt Lily, telling me how she had put several people on to *Spirits in Bondage* and recording many nice things said.[17] Also a piece of wedding cake from the Pasleys.

Tuesday 18 April: Worked in the morning. In the afternoon I walked into Oxford and looked up Civil Service examination papers in the Union. "Greats" is child's play compared with them . . .

Before supper I called and saw Arthur Stevenson and his mother, hoping to hear something of the Civil Service.[18] He has however

---

[16] The Rev. Alured George Clarke became the Vicar of All Saints, Highfield, Headington in 1920.

[17] See Lily Suffern in the Biographical Appendix.

[18] Arthur Stevenson and his two sisters, Sylvia and Sydney, lived on Headington Hill with their mother of whom we hear much in the diary.

given it up. He tells me there is no vacancy this year in the Home Civil, and that probably there will be none next. This is owing partly to Geddism, partly to the nominations of so many ex-officers without examination. It was in this way that "Diz" got his post. Stevenson thought that the slackness of life in the C.S. was greatly exaggerated, and that people were often kept late at their offices. Thus ends the dream of a Civil Service career as suddenly as it began: I feel at once that I have been in alien territory – not mine, and deep down, impossible.

In the evening I copied out "Joy" and worked a new ending: it is now ready to be typed. D in poor form . . .

Wednesday 19 April: . . . We were not best pleased at the unexpected appearance of Cranny.[19] His bald head steamed (he had walked up in an overcoat from Warneford Rd.) but he refused my offer of a wash . . . Cranny and I talked theology. I asked him why people in his position, who didn't believe that Jesus was a God, spent their time in patching up a sinking ship instead of setting to work on the new one. He said he didn't think there was going to be anything new. He thought that evolution had first of all tried successive types, then settled down to the development of one type, MAN: in the same way we had first had successive religions and would now settle down to the development of one. I wonder if the mastodon talk in the same way.

He told me that Stead, after discussing various people, had said "Lewis, of course, is inclined to Roman Catholicism". Amazing man, Stead! Cranny is very keen on the Doc's becoming ordained: but there are many difficulties. He stayed for an interminable time and broached every conceivable subject: D and I were exhausted. He said that the present distress was rather exaggerated and that many of the unemployed at Childrey were living at the cinema. I don't think he has much real sympathy. I had a bad headache before he went . . .

Thursday 20 April: A somewhat dull morning's work. Went to the White Horse before lunch. In the afternoon I went into Oxford to try and get back "Joy" but found (wh. I knew already if I had remembered) that it was early closing day. We left Lady Gonner's by taxi at three o'clock. The maids have grown very fond of D and would hardly let us go: they are Dorothy and Beatrice (pronounced

---

[19] See Frederick Walker Macran in the Biographical Appendix.

Beetrus), both v. ill trained country girls, lazy, noisy and inefficient, but warm hearted and great fun.

We found Miss Featherstone in good form, but looking wretchedly ill. She made no proposal to come back. I think, and D agrees with me, that she has decided to put up with us and is playing out her part thro' pure virtue. Very busy settling in from tea to supper time. D has stood the move and the packing well, and is much stronger than when we went away. Maureen very sick at leaving: D and I miss the garden but on the whole find the change (as someone said "Warneford Rd. isn't even suburban") less unpleasant than we expected. Dorothy (Broad) still away. I shouldn't mind being back to my plates and dishes if it weren't for work: I am hoping to lose less by taking tomorrow as Sunday and working on the real Sunday.

After supper I began to copy out "Nimue" with many corrections: I am pleasantly satisfied with it. Whether I succeed or fail, how ridiculous that will read some day! . . .

Friday 21 April: Got up shortly before seven, cleaned the grate, lit the fire, made tea, "did" the drawing room, made toast, bathed, shaved, breakfasted, washed up, put the new piece of ham on to boil, and was out by half past ten . . .

I got "Joy" at last from the typist for 1/9d. In all the things they have typed so far, I have not found a single error . . .

Got back about 12 o'c: found to my disgust that Maureen was out and left D cooking – the first time since her illness. Washed up after lunch. Worked at Gk. History notes until tea when Miss Baker came. Had got settled to work when D called me down "for five minutes" to talk about Maureen's programme for next term. This would not have mattered, but before I could make my escape, Miss Baker began to be "just going" and continued so. When she finally got away it was time to get supper and to clear the tea things which Maureen had kindly left in status quo. A good hour thus wasted altogether . . . Worked again after supper, leaving washing up to Maureen. D keeping much better.

Saturday 22 April: Got up about 6.30 and did the same jobs as yesterday. Was settled to work by 9.5 o'clock and put in an excellent morning . . .

Sheila Gonner – jolly child – came to tea. Dorothy is to come back tomorrow: so we shall no longer be servantless. At her request I lent her my crib to Tacitus' History for her sister Rose – I wonder what makes her imagine that she wd. like it? Possibly early Christian novels of the *Quo Vadis* type.

Worked again after tea, and from supper till ten o'clock, finishing Herodotus. The last few pages of the IXth Bk. I now read for the first time, having got tired of it on my first reading . . .

Sunday 23 April: In the morning I finished fair copying "Nimue": if "Joy" is accepted I shall use the resulting money to type it . . .

In the afternoon I called on Mrs Stevenson to talk houses. The man Raisin (or Rayson) is building two more which he may let, and while Mrs St. assails the existing house, we are to try for one of the new ones. They are all at the foot of Shotover on the Roman Road and under Professor Jack's wood . . .

Monday 24 April: Yesterday I finished my notes to Herodotus and started to memorise them en masse today. Put in good work from 9 to 11 in the morning, then went in to town with Maureen to see her off for Bristol, where she will stay for some days . . .

I then called at the office of Rayson the architect, 15 Broad St. He is a chatty and cheerful little man and may be honest. He told me that his project of building two new houses near the one Mrs Stevenson is after is still in the vague future. He wd. not begin them until he had disposed of the present one. I explained our own position and asked him to tell me frankly if anyone was before us on the waiting list. He said there was no one and took D's name down. He tells me the roof of the Bodleian was made of copper: we both commented on the beautiful colour.

Worked after lunch: after tea I walked on Shotover. A boisterous day with fierce showers and bright sunshine. I stayed some time looking out over the plain to the Chilterns and watching the clouds. For some reason I was specially struck today by the *enormous scale* of the cloud landscape, especially from a hill. Worked after supper: earlier to bed.

A cheerful letter from my father today, announcing that Warnie has been at home (from Sierra Leone) for twelve days and is well: also that he has paid in my allowance for the coming term.

Tuesday 25 April: A hard day's work. The woman-with-the-false-eyebrows-who-tells-lies called today for Dorothy who is becoming one of her customers: she confided to her some details about us which were the subject of conversation among our next door neighbours. Dorothy told D as soon as the woman was gone. It was most illuminating: and how the dogs can know so many facts about me as they do, passes my comprehension. D said it was the worst part of being poor – to have to live among them . . .

D hung today a curtain we have made for the drawing room door. The base was an army blanket: on a design of mine D worked a tree (unknown to naturalists) and storks and lilies and a moon with stars. All in wool, bright flat colours. It goes admirably with the walls, and I am very pleased with it . . .

Wednesday 26 April: Having finished the Herodotus period I am now making up the Pentekontaetia:[20] a hard and enjoyable days work. If I had only a few months more I could manage well.

A card from Maureen to say that after an hour with Miss Whitty she finds her music "hopeless" and a letter from Miss W. saying that her technique has been disgracefully neglected.[21] After putting in some well deserved curses against the thorough inefficiency of the school in every branch, D and I discovered to our surprise that we did not know what technique was in music . . .

Thursday 27 April: Term began today. Worked hard on the Athenian politics of the Pentekontaetia: very hard to find out the facts. Grundy full of learning but writes abominably and it is almost impossible to see the connection of thought between some of his paragraphs. Before lunch I went into Oxford and got Whibley's book out of the Union: but I find it was written before the discovery of the Ath. Pol. and is therefore useless.[22] Worked again from lunch till tea. It is really rather hard not only to have to learn history but to write it first! . . .

Friday 28 April: Went into College early and found that we had collections in hall at 9.30.[23] Philosophy papers, but Stevenson handed them round, saying that Carritt had mumps.[24] He implored us to take them seriously, but everyone remained very cheerful: Blunt, Wyllie, Watling, P.O. Simpson, Montagu, Hastings, Haig, and Salvesen – the latter "a steady rumble in the distance" as Haig said.[25] Everyone talked and ragged and talked. Everyone always appeals to

---

[20] This is a term given the fifty years of Greek history between the Persian and Peloponnesian Wars (480–430 BC), the period in which Athens realised her greatest literary and artistic eminence.

[21] Miss Kathleen Whitty had been Maureen's music teacher in Bristol before they moved to Oxford in 1917.

[22] Leonard Whibley, *Political Parties in Athens during the Peloponnesian War*(1889).

[23] "Collections" is a college examination held at the end or the beginning of every term in Oxford and some other universities.

[24] See **George Hope Stevenson** and **Edgar Frederick Carritt** in the Biographical Appendix.

[25] Henry Pyot Blunt, Basil Platel Wyllie, Edward Fairchild Watling, Philip Overend Simpson, John Eric Montagu, John Maurice Hastings, Edward Felix Gray Haig and Harold Keith Salvesen – all of University College – were reading Greats, except for Salvesen who read Philosophy, Politics and Economics.

the rest for any fact he has forgotten, and gets a dozen suggestions: but I doubt if anyone writes down the varied and often irreconcilable information thus obtained. Blunt said that Plato was born too soon and was fitted by nature for an orthodox English parson. I said I didn't think we was as bad as that. Got out about 12.30. Looked into Wadham to see if Baker was up yet, but no sign of him.[26]

After lunch went on with Gk. History. Stead came in, obviously wanting to have his new proofs praised. Luckily the *Sweet Miracle* in its quiet way has considerable merits, and I told him so . . . He had a letter from Yeats who is now living in a tower at Gort on Lady Gregory's estates: it all sounds very well chosen as a setting for the great man . . . He also talked of Bridges. Either Stead is a much better man than he seems to me or else he has pushed like a true American in the literary world . . . D very busy making some "nighties" which Mrs Raymond is going to buy. Letter from Cox's acknowledging £67 from my father.

Saturday 29 April: Up betimes and into college where we did a general ancient history paper for Stevenson. I was interviewed by him as usual and arranged to do no lectures this term: he warned me "not to work too hard". All the usual people there. Wrote a good deal, but not of high quality . . . Simpson described collections as the effort to write journalese in the tower of Babel . . .

A long letter for D from Miss Whitty today. She says that a serious music career is hopeless for Maureen and that the fault is entirely in the teaching: she has been left to all the original sin that any child will indulge in if allowed, and taught inaccurate, emotional drawing room playing. Her fingers are too old to go back and learn technique now. So her dream has ended as suddenly as mine of the Civil Service: mine was killed by the Geddes Committee, hers by sheer inefficiency at the school. It is very regrettable: apart from the question of a career (and if she marries that doesn't matter) the immediate psychological effect on her will be very bad. Miss Whitty is furious, and I don't wonder.

Sunday 30 April: Called for Baker at Wadham and we walked over the fields to Marston, starting through Mesopotamia. A splendid morning. Baker is very busy with rehearsals for a Wycherley play in which he is to appear as a heavy father: it is at the Palace, got up by [Edith] Craig (Ellen Terry's daughter) and he is one of two or

---

[26] See Leo Baker in the Biographical Appendix.

three amateurs in an otherwise professional cast. He has had a good deal of encouragment and has met Mrs Asquith and Princess Bibesco. He described Mrs A. as a horrible old woman with queer garters.

He has had a poem accepted by the *Beacon*: he says that Barfield is now as good as sub-editor. So probably my "Joy" has gone to him. I don't much envy Barfield his job of refusing all his friend's poems for the next year or so![27]. . .

After lunch worked at "Dymer". D writing off arrears of letters. Miss Featherstone called while I was out: D says she was in wretched health. After tea put up curtains in D's room with the new gadget called Rawlplugs: their advertisement claims are untrue, but a clever idea.

After supper finished and fair copied the first canto of "Dymer" . . .

[27] See Owen Barfield in the Biographical Appendix.

Monday 1 May: This morning the fates tried to infuriate me but carried it too far, so that it became merely funny. D got at breakfast time an answer from a house agent, telling of a bungalow called Waldencot to let in Headington. So rushed off after swallowing a meal, only to find that it was the "stable" . . .

Worked all afternoon at Thucydides, an author I love. A letter from Barfield accepting "Joy" for the *Beacon* and saying nice things: he describes himself as "acting, unpaid, sub lance-editor" . . .

Tuesday 2 May: Worked in the morning memorising notes on the Pentecontaetia and reading Thucydides.

Maureen went up to Headington and got into the "stable", since we think it worth trying for. Maureen got in with a lady, another prespective tenant and rival, and did good work in pointing out to her all the disadvantages of the place.

After lunch I called to try and see Jenkin, but he was out.[1] Left "Nimue" to be typed. I walked slowly and pleasantly thro' Mesopotamia and by rope ferry to Marston, thence up the lane to Headington via the small cemetary. A beautiful day and plenty of cuckoos. Thinking for once – and free from Christina dreams . . .

Got back in time to put in some more work before supper. Concocted with D a letter to Dr Ley of Christ Church asking him to recommend a good music teacher for Maureen:[2] she has been removed from Miss Ploughman under some euphemism about "times not fitting in" – if Miss Ploughman will ever notice whether she turns up or not! . . .

Wednesday 3 May: A wet morning. Worked on the Thucydides text, with great interest, but finding many passages which, for the mere translation, it is wise to go over.

Went into town after lunch, and after looking in vain for Jenkin in Merton St., met him in the High. It had now cleared and

---

[1] See Alfred Kenneth Hamilton-Jenkin in the Biographical Appendix.
[2] Henry George Ley (1887–1962) was Organist and Choirmaster of Christ Church Cathedral 1909–26, and Precentor and Director of Music at Eton College 1926–45.

we walked down St Aldate's and over the waterworks to Hincksey.

I talked of staying up for another year and lamented that all my friends would be down: he said he had not got to know any new people of interest since his first year. We both agreed that to find people who had any interest in literature and who were not, at the same time, dam'd affected dillettanti talking "l'art pour l'art" etc., etc., was almost impossible – in fact he put Baker, Barfield and me as the only exceptions in his own circle: and even the "hearty" men were preferable to the usual literary sort . . .

We talked about religion, on which his views are traditional and quite different to mine. He quoted a good (and true) perversion of an old platitude – "To the pure all things are impure" . . .

D, after trying a new cure for indigestion, presented by Miss Featherstone, is very poorly, with a bad head. Worked at Thucydides again in the evening. Early to bed.

Thursday 4 May: A bright, windy, and beautiful day. D very sick as a result of Miss Featherstone's vile drug (heaven save us from our friends) and finding her sight queer – seeing the paper which I was reading at breakfast as if blue. This wore off to some extent during the day. Miss Featherstone, as an old nurse, ought to know better than to give this sort of drug to a patient without medical advice.

Went into town early. Called on Baker in Wadham. He asked me several questions about the Sophists. He said he wd. probably see Barfield today and I asked him to get Barfield to leave some message saying when he and I could meet. He showed me the May number of the *Beacon*: it is slowly improving from month to month.

Went to college at 10.30 for Stevenson's class: Watling, Wyllie, Blunt, Montagu, Haig, and (later) Hastings. Stevenson had marked my paper A minus. Blunt was a great nuisance, keeping us relentlessly to some damned chronological problem about intercalary months and eclipses, partly I think because Stevenson does not shine on these subjects . . .

Went to Cornmarket and got back "Nimue" accurately typed for 3/6: sent it to Squire in the afternoon, not so much in any hope that he will accept it, but "in order that he may fill up the measure of his iniquities".

Worked at an English text of the *Politics* in the afternoon, with some interest, and went for a short stroll up Headington before supper. Thucydides (note making) in the evening . . . Worried today by shooting pains in my left armpit near the old wound, but very slight.

Friday 5 May: . . . Met Barfield at 2.30 by Headington Post Office. A bright day: we walked over Bayswater brook (where I saw the snake) and had tea in a little house on the London Rd. We talked of Baker and the mysterious fragments of his previous life that one got, and compared our knowledge . . . He said Baker's mystifying way of referring to things was quite unconscious, and we had a good laugh over it.

We talked over old times: then of Barfield's fortnight in Italy last vac. Partly in Florence, partly walking in the Appenines. He told of how in a restaurant he had a call of nature and after peevishly hunting his phrase book found that the Italian (literally) was "Where can she make a little water please?" In answer to this the garçon replied "Wherever she likes."

We talked of the *Beacon* and he told me how Appleton had come to take him on.[3] One day Appleton showed him a poem and asked his opinion. "Filthy," said Barfield. Appleton showed him another: "Bloody," said Barfield. After that they became fast friends. Barfield seemed perfectly miserable and hoping for nothing. This wretched love affair has gone very deep tho' it has made him a real poet. I am sure he is going to be great . . .

Saturday 6 May: Went into town after breakfast to see Dr Allchin of 15 Beaumont St. about lessons for Maureen: found he was engaged till twelve.[4]

Tried to work on "Psyche" in the Union (not in the new metre wh. I think almost hopeless) with no success.

Met Wallis,[5] P.O. Simpson, and Blunt. Carritt appears to have been worried over everyone's collections. Wallis and Watling got $\Gamma =$. Went back to Allchin at 12: it was arranged that Maureen shd. go to him at 4.15 on Tuesday next and that after hearing her he was to come and see D. A nice little man.

I reminded him of summer 1917 when he was an officer in the O.T.C. and I was a Cadet: he laughed over the "mad things one had to do" – lecturing on subjects that no one knew anything about etc . . .

---

[3] E.R. Appleton was the editor of *The Beacon*.
[4] See **Basil Charles Allchin** in the Biographical Appendix.
[5] Edward John Wallis was reading Greats at University College and took his BA in 1923.

Sunday 7 May: A leap into summer. Sat in the garden, writing a passage for a new version of "Psyche" in blank verse, not without some success . . .

I found my way out to 14 Chadlington Rd., through the horror of North Oxford on a hot Sunday: villas, gardens, dazzle and Sunday clothes. Stevenson, his wife, his child Helen and a dummy called Mackay from Magdalen:[6] quite a pleasant lunch. Stevenson told me – what I never heard before – that the Master in his youth had lost a studentship at the House for writing a modernist essay on the Resurrection: that was in the days of Pusey.[7]

We sat in the garden after lunch. Stevenson talked of his job at Le Touquet during the war where they had a whole mess of code interpreting experts. He said that in the end, after the duds had been eliminated, it came to consist entirely of classical scholars. As a similar example of strange abilities used for war purposes, Mrs. S. mentioned a futurist painter who was employed on doing "dazzled" ships . . .

Came home to find D in the garden with the Doc, Mary, and the Brat [Peony Askins] . . . We sat in the garden after supper, D writing letters by moonlight: an evening of extraordinary beauty, but an exhausting day. The Doc looks much better, and in khaki shirt, belted slacks, pudding bason hat, tie pin acting as a stud (he is always studless) was an eloquent and characteristic figure.

While at the Walkers I had an amusing conversation with Ziman who now has my old rooms, telling me how much he dislikes my distemper and how old George encouraged him for Mods. by saying that "Mr Lewis got a fust sir, and he never worked at all: he was always out fust thing after breakfast."[8]

Monday 8 May: A blazing day with a light wind. I got to work in the garden at 8.45 and continued, making notes and memorising, till one o'clock.

Went into town after lunch to Jenkin's rooms. Robson-Scott was with him when I arrived.[9] After his departure J. told me that he had

---

[6] Roy McKay who read Law at Magdalen and took his BA in 1923.

[7] Reginald Walter Macan (1848–1941), was a Fellow and Tutor of History at University College 1884–1906 and Master of the College 1906–23. Something of the "modernist essay" may have gone into his book *The Resurrection of Jesus Christ* (1877).

[8] Herbert David Ziman (1902–83) took a second in Greats and received his BA in 1924. He was leader-writer for *The Daily Telegraph* 1934–39, and literary editor 1956-68.

[9] See **William Douglas Robson-Scott** in the Biographical Appendix. Lewis and Robson-Scott were both members of a literary society in University College called the Martlets. As Lewis had not been to a meeting in some time, there was a question of whether or not he was still entitled to go.

been quite surprised to hear of my removal from the Martlets: he had missed a meeting and he wondered whether the young men had us all degommed by now. Jenkin said he would go to any meeting he cared for, whether he was a member or not. He took me out in his canoe for a short time . . .

Got home about 4 o'clock: tea in the garden and made an analysis of Kant, getting as far as the "Anticipations of Experience". Memorised this after supper, and also my Gk. History notes.

A beautiful day. D very wretched, whether from psychological causes or that the effects of Miss Featherstone's poison still remain.

Tuesday 9 May: "Nimue" returned from Squire (they call him Jehovah C. I find), with the usual printed refusal. All this is done in order that the Scriptures might be fulfilled.

Another glorious day. Got to work at 8.45 in the garden: did some more of my analysis of Kant and some Thucydides notes. As soon as the sun gets on my bedroom window, I am trying the plan of shutting window and door and drawing curtains so as never to admit hot air: I think it is an improvement . . .

Wednesday 10 May: Back to cold weather and fires. Worked on Gk. History for part of the morning and then went in to town and did two questions in the Union under Schools conditions, one from a Roman History and one from a Logic Paper. I also bought a sham panama hat at Lane's in Queen St. for 5/11. It is cool and comfortable and the best solution of the sunstroke problem.

Met Watling who tells me that our schools begin on 8 June. I got Jowett's translation of the Sophists from the library and worked on it after lunch. It is about Nothing and most interesting: beautifully translated, but in his introduction where he talks philosophy, Jowett seems a fool and a self pleasing fool.

Miss Featherstone called today and said that she had been invited to stop with a friend for the summer, and that we need not move unless we chose, which is excellent news. I walked on Shotover after tea: it is gorgeous now and a mass of blackthorn. I was thinking seriously of how I could face the prospect of having to give up poetry, if it came to that . . .

Thursday 11 May: The weather continued wintry. In to town betimes and called to see Baker. I told him about the return of "Nimue" and cursed Jehovah C. I confessed to a fear that there must be something wholly wrong in our attitude: that though we were always ready to admit faults in the things that J.C. returned, perhaps we were really blind to the merits of what he accepted, much of which seems contemptible. Baker said he did not think it was likely.

He gave me back the first Canto of "Dymer" which I had left with him. He spoke encouragingly of most of it, especially the end. He thought some of the flippant parts weak and the first two stanzas tedious, in which I agreed with him. I found that besides the performance with professionals at the Palace, the Wycherley play is being given tonight, Friday and Saturday in the Corn Exchange with amateurs.

I then went to Univ. and saw Carritt. I made him explain what he meant by "atmosphere" in an exam paper and asked him when he had done, "In fact, sir, you mean bluff?" He agreed. Then I went to Stevenson's class. Watling, Wyllie, Blunt, Montagu, Hasting and Haig. A desperately dull but not a useless morning.

Got home about twelve thirty. Found the Doc here and Maureen very ill. The Doc told D that Cranny had been moving heaven and earth about his (the Doc's) ordination: but that the idea of his really wishing to be ordained was mainly a fiction of Cranny's. How typical!

After lunch I did, under school's conditions, a logic paper which Carritt had given me, greatly to my own satisfaction, and found that three hours gave me plenty of time to spare . . .

Friday 12 May: . . . I worked on my analysis of Kant and then on Gk. History until shortly before lunch: then went into town to see if Jenkin would come to the show tonight. Worked again after lunch, but dully and finding it hard to concentrate.

Lady Gonner and her niece called and I went into another room. The Doc was here twice today: the first occasion – before lunch – he told D a yarn about an undergraduate and an undergraduette living together somewhere in the neighbourhood. As the story is only one of those which "everybody knows" it need not be believed. It is to be hoped that it is untrue, as, when the crash came, it would lead to a lot of silly new statutes for the rest of us . . .

I came back for supper and then returned to wait in the queue at the Corn Exchange. It consisted chiefly of girls: we waited while the ticket holders went in. All the world was there: I noticed Cyril Bailey, Lindsay, Joachin, Carritt, Curtis, Mary and

Stead.[10] Great excitement was caused by the arrival of the Asquiths: it was rather a political allegory – everyone whispering "Here's Mrs Asquith" and nobody taking any notice of poor old Asquith himself, a fat, flabby figure, with a suggestion of John Bunny, flopping out of the car behind her. She had a crone's face, with thin, very bright lips, wagged her boney figers at someone, and was kittenish.[11]

The show was, on the whole, good. I had to stand. Allen conducted.[12] The music of the first ballet was from an old virginal book. The second by Purcell round the theme of a Wycherley play: this was the best of the three – a wonderful mad marionette like thing – completely carried one away. Baker capital as Mr Formal: during an interval I heard his performance praised by a theatrical looking stranger. The music was delightful. The third, by Bach, I did not care for quite so much. What struck me particularly was Barfield's dancing in the rowdier passages: a terrific, infectious gaiety about him and you'd think he cd. never be tired . . .[13]

Sunday 14 May: . . . Caught a bus into town and returned home shortly after lunch, having got G.K. Chesterton's *Magic* and Jones' *Road to Endor* from the Union.

Maureen got up before lunch. D and I sat in the little alley way behind the French windows after lunch. I read *Magic* through. A pleasant little play – I am not sure that I understand it. Afterwards I began to read *The Road to Endor* aloud, and continued it for the

[10] This group contains many of the great men whose books and lectures Lewis had read or heard during his years in Oxford. Cyril Bailey (1871–1957), a well-known teacher of the Classics and notable Oxford personality, was a Fellow of Balliol College; Alexander Dunlop Lindsay (1879–1952) was Fellow and Classical Tutor at Balliol 1906–22, and Master of Balliol 1924–49; Harold Henry Joachim (1868–1938) was Wykeham Professor of Logic 1919–35; Geoffrey William Seymour Curtis read Greats at University College and took a BA in 1925.

[11] This was Herbert Henry Asquith (later Earl of Oxford and Asquith, 1852–1928), a statesman who had been Prime Minister 1908–16. Margot Asquith (1864–1945), his second wife, had a magnetic personality which was sometimes a political liability.

[12] Sir Hugh Allen (1869–1946) was the Professor of Music at Oxford 1918–46, and obtained the creation of the music faculty.

[13] "The Oxford Musical Festival ended in a blaze of colour . . . The chief novelty of the Festival, three historical ballets, took place in the Corn Exchange on Thursday, Friday and Saturday evenings. The ballets were entitled 'A Masque at the Court of Queen Elizabeth', with music from the Fitzwilliam Virginal Book, 'The Gentleman Dancing Master', with music by Henry Purcell and 'J.S. Bach and Frederick the Great', set to music taken from the orchestral suites of Bach . . . The Music for the dances was selected from the works of Marchant, Byrd, Robert Johnson, and Giles Faranby, who took the B.Mus. degree at Oxford in 1592. 'The Gentleman dancing Master', arranged by F.R. Harris, is based on Wycherley's play of the same name . . . The . . . third ballet . . . illustrated a meeting between Frederick and the composer and the festivities given at the Court in Bach's honour. The several dances were gone through with a joyous abandon that was very inspiring and made a lively finish to a really enjoyable programme." *The Oxford Times* (19 May 1922), p. 8.

rest of the day.[14] It is the account (now famous) of two British officers' escape from Yosgad in Asia Minor by means of faked spiritualism. We both enjoyed it greatly. The irony of reading this and *Magic* on the same day was quite unintentional . . .

Monday 15 May: Got to work at 9.30 and put in a good morning on the Sicilian Expedition, and memorising.

After lunch D read me from the *Times* the memorial article on Sir Walter Raleigh who has just died: Jenkin was always singing his praises.[15] . . .

I memorised afterwards. While in town I met Poynton, and he gave me a Latin Prose to do, "as a trial ball".[16] He said he would only have time for one and so "you might as well put all your howlers into that". After supper I worked on the Sophist and started the prose which is interesting.

D rather poorly this evening.

Tuesday 16 May: An idle day. Started work after breakfast but soon walked into town to get Freeland's *History of Sicily*.

Called on Baker and drank some sherry. He had been rehearsing in London on Saturday and lunched with Ellen Terry: afterwards he had a good talk with Edith Craig at her flat and she said she could get him a job at the Old Vic. He has also been promised a part in M. Harvey's next play. I asked whether it was not necessary to go through a technical school: he said this applied more to girls. We also talked a good deal about "Dymer". I arranged to walk with him this afternoon . . .

Baker called for me soon after lunch, and we pushed our bikes up Shotover and sat there. He is trying to persuade Barfield to go on the music hall stage. I laughed heartily at the thought of my two chief literary friends ending both on the boards . . .

After tea, until nearly 7 o'clock, Baker and I had a close and good conversation again about "Dymer". We agreed that the great thing was to keep the MYTH true and intrude as little invention or conscious allegory as might be. He is particularly keen on the darkness in the passage where Dymer finds the girl, and opposed to anything like a dialogue. We struck out between us the excellent idea of making the witch a "matriarch". It all made me very keen, and anxious for power to do what needs to be done . . .

---

[14] By Elias Henry Jones (1920).
[15] See **Sir Walter Raleigh** in the Biographical Appendix.
[16] See **Arthur Blackburne Poynton** in the Biographical Appendix.

Wednesday 17 May: Worked at Gk. History – without much energy or interest – all morning.

A soft, wet day, such as I rather like. The Doc came to see Maureen for a few minutes before lunch. Worked again until tea time. Mrs Raymond came to tea.

I went into town for my tutorial with Carritt: he said there was no vancancy suitable for me and strongly advised me to stay up another year. I read the paper which I had done for him and he approved of it. He made some interesting remarks on Croce's theory of universals. The true concepts (Truth, Beauty, etc.) are immanent, transcendant: the mathematical are *only* transcendent – that is, they have no particulars: the pseudo-concepts are only immanent, that is they are mere arbitrary groupings of particulars. He also drew my attention to the difference between Kant's early and later views of the Noumena, which I must look up. I met Blunt, who tells me that he is starting to read Thucydides for the first time!

Forgot to mention a curious dream I had in the small hours of this morning: – Baker and I were walking in a field when suddenly there appeared from nowhere a huge bull with exaggerated sexual charac-teristics, going very fast. We leaped over a high wire fence and I hurt my leg. Sounds truly psychoanalytic . . .

Thursday 18 May: Today and yesterday D has had breakfast in bed, as the legs are not getting on well and need still more rest . . .

Worked in the dining room from lunch until tea . . . I then walked through Iffley, crossed the lock, and went along the meadows. Became wonderfully happy for a short time. A boisterous windy day: the river full of brisk waves and everything of an unusual brightness.

After supper I wrote a long letter home, explaining my position and proposing to stay up for another year.[17]

Friday 19 May: A damp morning: I worked on the Revolution of the 400, comparing Thucydides with Aristotle.

After lunch I walked into Oxford with a vague idea of sending off a new venture to a periodical. Calling on Baker to get the address of *Youth* I found him anxious for my advice. He is to go to the Old

[17] In the letter to his father of 18 May Lewis said: "The actual subjects of my own Greats school are a doubtful quantity at the moment: for no one quite knows what place classics and philosophy will hold in the educational world in a year's time . . . What is wanted everywhere is a man who combines the general qualification which Greats is supposed to give, with the special qualifications of any other subjects. And English Literature is a 'rising' subject. Thus if I cd. take a First or even a Second in Greats, *and* a First next year in English Literature, I should be in a very strong position indeed."

Vic. for an audition some day soon, and was trying to choose what lines he will spout . . .

After tea I bussed back to College and called on the Mugger.[18] He had just had a letter from "Mr Wyllie" asking him to recommend some one for a studentship tenable for one year in Cornell University (New York State). He said I was the only person he would care to offer: but as the money, tho' adequate for the year out there, did not include the travelling expenses, it was hardly to be considered. We then talked of my plans. He said the days were past when one could walk out of the Schools into a Fellowship: even in minor universities there was a demand for men who had done something, and this had been intensified at Oxford by the Royal Commission.

He advised me however to take the extra year. He said that College was very hard up, but that he thought that they could manage to continue my scholarship. I asked him whether if I "came a cropper in Greats" he would still advise the extra year, and he said he would. He said that I should try to pick up another University prize: and that there were possibilities in the University Extension jobs. I thanked him for his kindness. A dear old man, but the inexhaustible loquacity of educated age drove me to the "City and University" to recoup on a Guinness.

A long conversation with D after supper, telling her about old times, Tubbs, Miss Cowie etc.[19]

Afterwards I made a start on my next paper for Carritt and did 45 min . . . An outbreak of feminism from Maureen during supper about the "easier life" of men: D thinks there was no knowledge behind it – but interesting.

Saturday 20 May: Worked in the morning on early Attica and Solon. After lunch I rode to the Union and took out *The Admirable Crichton*:[20] thence rode beyond Marston with the idea of going to Beckley and seeing Barfield.

I met him, however, just beyond the village, riding in with a suit case, as he was going to the All Soul's dance. After trying vainly to get into a pub, we went into a field and sat. He has lately seen *Peer Gynt* at the Old Vic. Archer's translation in a loose kind of Hiawatha metre, which he says is very effective in dialogue. I congratulated

[18] The Master of University College.

[19] Mr Tubbs was one of the Masters, and Miss Cowie the Matron, at Cherbourg School, Malvern, when Lewis was a pupil there in 1910–12.

[20] By Sir James Barrie (1902).

him on his dancing: he is quite seriously thinking of the "Halls". He did not know when I should get the proofs of "Joy". Arranged to lunch with him at the Old Oak at 1 o'clock next Wednesday.

Home for tea, where I found the Doc and Mary who soon went to school sports with Maureen. For the rest of the day I worked on the second Canto of "Dymer", with wonderful enjoyment. A very warm evening with a silver mackerel sky: we had supper in the garden.

Sunday 21 May: A blazing hot day. Rode to Merton St. after breakfast and called for Jenkin. We then cycled through Marston to Elsfield and Beckley, where we called at Bee Cottage. Barfield was out, but Harwood gave us water and we rested for a while.[21] Jenkin arranged to go back there for lunch and I left the 1st Canto of "Dymer" for Barfield's criticism.

We continued our ride down hill from Beckley, the objective being Joseph's Stone: but after riding through some very bad marsh country, over ruts of petrified mud, we came to an evil, low lying swamp, and had to stop. Jenkin climbed an oak tree.

He said he never could bring himself to like Harwood – he always found something condescending in his manner. I said it was merely an unlucky voice and face. Baker had had the same trouble, and Barfield used to be very angry with him about it.

Today, for the first time since I have known him, Jenkin complained bitterly of the ill health which is always checking every physical and mental activity he takes up. I hardly knew how to answer him, but congratulated him, in spite of it all, on having refused to become a valetudinarian . . .

Monday 22 May: A stiflingly hot day. Bussed into College, in accordance with a note which arrived at breakfast, and paid Farquharson £5 entrance fee for Schools.[22] Went on and saw Allchin, arranging for Maureen to see him at 3.30 on Friday next. Came home and worked, finishing my notes on Solon. The Doc was in the garden with D most of the morning.

After lunch I bussed out to Wadham and saw Baker. He has had two hours with Bernice de Bergerac preparatory to his audition and is doing Romeo's speeches before the entrance of the apothecary . . .

---

[21] See **Cecil Harwood** in the Biographical Appendix.
[22] See **Arthur Spenser Loat Farquharson** in the Biographical Appendix.

I then told him my dream about the bull and this led to a long talk on psychoanalysis . . .

I arrived home to find a wire from P[apy] saying "Stay on" in answer to my letter. This is really very decent good form . . .

Tuesday 23 May: Worked all morning in the alley way, memorising Gk. History notes. Mary and the Doc called.

After lunch I bussed into Oxford, took Croce's *Essence of Aesthetic* out of the Union and walked to bathe at Parson's Pleasure.[23] As I went in, I met Wyllie coming out: we regretted to have missed each other and arranged to bathe together in future. A beautiful bathe (water 63 degrees) but very crowded. Amid so much nudity I was interested to note the passing of my own generation: two years ago every second man had a wound mark, but I did not see one today.

Came home and had tea in the garden, and then finished the paper for Carritt, time compelling me to end in the middle of a sentence. I finished the Croce: a difficult and provocative book. The different activities of the spirits apparently grow out of one another in a cycle. Emotion leads to image, and when we have made the image we want to understand: from understanding we turn to action which leads to new emotion and the cycle repeats. He assumes the unreality of matter, regarding it as we regard the news Queen Anne is dead.

D better today. Early to bed. After coming in from the garden I wrote one "gastronomic" stanza of "Dymer".

Wednesday 24 May: . . . I left home at about 12.45 and bussed into Oxford, meeting Barfield outside the Old Oak. After finding a table we decided to go to the Good Luck instead. An excellent lunch, the ices being particularly good and having, as Barfield says, the true butter like consistency.

From here we walked to Wadham gardens and sat under the trees. We began with Christina dreams: I condemned them – the love dream made a man incapable of real love, the hero dream made him a coward. He took the opposite view and a stubborn argument followed.

We then turned to "Dymer" which he had brought back: to my surprise, his verdict was even more favourable than Baker's. He said it was "by streets" the best thing I had done, and "Could I keep it up?" He did not feel the weakness of the lighter stanzas. He said

---

[23] There is a small area just north-east of Magdalen College where two branches of the River Cherwell come together. It is called "Mesopotamia" after the ancient country between the Tigris and the Euphrates, and on one of the branches is a pool reserved for men where the custom is to bathe nude – "Parson's Pleasure".

Harwood had "danced with joy" over it and had advised me to drop everything else and go on with it. From such a severe critic as Barfield the result was very encouraging. We then drifted into a long talk about ultimates. Like me, he has no belief in immortality etc., and always feels the materialistic pessimism at his elbow.

He is most miserable. He said however that the "hard facts" which worried us, might to posterity appear mere prejudices de siècle, as the "facts" of Dante do to us. Our disease, I said, was really a Victorian one. The conversation ranged over many topics and finally died because it was impossible to hold a court between two devil's advocates.

The gardens were ripping – lilac and chestnut magnificent. I find Wadham gardens fit my image of Acrasia's island very well. I walked with him as far as Magdalen, took a turn in the cloisters, and then came home for tea.

This we had in the garden, being suddenly put to flight by a thunderstorm. Went in again to Carritt at 5.45, and read him my paper. Interesting discussion: he was on his usual line of right unrelated to good, which is unanswerable: but so is the other side.

Found a short letter from P. in College confirming his wire. I don't know why, but something in it was uneasy to me.

Came home to find that the Doc had been here. There appears to be some danger that the pain in D's arm may be the veins breaking out out in a new place. Horrible news! . . .

Thursday 25 May: . . . worked hard on memorising in the morning. The Doc came shortly before lunch and examined D's arm and shoulder which are very swollen, tho' less painful than yesterday. He said he would not undertake the case of his own sister, and that if it was not better in a few days, we must get a doctor. He admitted that it might be a lot of unpleasant things. He and D were most afraid of thrombosis or a "benign" tumour. On the other hand it might be merely muscular. This is our iron ration of hope . . .

D and Baker were discussing my going to Ireland when I came in. Baker at first deprecated "putting my head in the lion's mouth". I said I didn't omit my stay on account of danger, when my father and my brother were there: especially as nasty things beginning "I had hoped" and ending up "far be it from me" not only might, but would be said. It is of course true that I have had my share of being shot at in greater measure than they – but what can one do? Baker

finally agreed with me. He said I shd. go to the Mugger and Truslove
if I wanted some tutoring work in September . . .

Friday 26 May: Much cooler today. Bussed into Oxford after
breakfast and did a Gk. History translation paper under schools
conditions in the Union. Came home shortly after twelve. Maureen
out for lunch (which by the by was one of our best, fried sole, new
potatoes, and asparagus.) Read Bosanquet's *Theory of the State* in
the afternoon: an attractive book on the whole.

The Doc and Mrs Stevenson came to tea. She was as lively as a
tennis ball on a hard court, and singing the praises of Mr Clarke. D
advised her to marry him, chiefly for the house.

An excited conversation between the Doc and Mrs S. on spiritualism. D retired as she felt she couldn't refrain from sceptical
interruptions. I was less kind and asked why ghosts always spoke as
though they belonged to the lower middle classes. We talked a little
of psychoanalysis, condemning Freud . . .

After supper I started reading Strachey's *Queen Victoria* to D. A
very beautiful sky this evening. D's arm was much less swollen today
and very little pain: the Doc seemed to take an encouraging view of
it. Sat up late talking: a memorable conversation.

Saturday 27 May: . . . I called on Stevenson and asked him to let me
know of any tutorial work for the vac, which he might hear of. I
then called on Carritt and made the same request of him. He also
promised to give my name to the *Manchester Guardian* for some
reviewing. In the course of the morning I met Blunt who said he was
sure he could get me a school boy to coach from Lynham's, as he is
an O.D. and often there.

I also visited Williams, who is the local agent for Trueman &
Knightley: he gave me a form and said that by narrowing the field
to Oxford I reduced my chances, but that if there was anything my
qualifications would get it. He advised me also to put an advertisement in the *Oxford Times* . . .

After lunch I worked on "Dymer" in the garden: bicycled to town
after tea and bathed (water 68 degrees). Some pups there, who, even
naked, I divined to be either Sandhurst cadets or very young officers.
They conducted the sort of conversation which proceeds theoretically
on the principle that it doesn't matter how many damned civilians
are listening, but of which every word, in practice, is uttered for the
benefit of the spectators.

As Harwood, whom I met just outside, said, "You can see them looking out of the corners of their eyes to see whether you're admiring them." . . . He praised "Dymer" rather extravagantly . . .

Monday 29 May: After lunch I cycled into town and went to Baker: we at once adjourned to Wadham gardens . . . I at once began talking of my difficulties with the erotic passage in "Dymer". I told him I was putting broad leaves and damp stems in it: he said this altered the symbolism from his point of view and made it auto-erotic. He was reassured when I told him about the smell.

He told me a good story about how he had woken Pasley up in hospital one night and said "I've thought of a good line". Pasley grunted and said good lines were a damned nuisance as one was always trying to write poems round them. A few days later Baker showed him a poem. "Capital," said Pasley, "but I'd leave that bit out." "That bit", was of course the good line . . .

After tea I had to go and see Miss Wiblin of 43, Hamilton Rd. Allchin had sent us a letter recommending her to teach Maureen technique until he had a vancancy for her. He spoke encouragingly of her natural talents.[24]. . .

Supper of boiled eggs, plums and cream in the garden. We all decided that it was the only meal for this weather. Afterwards Mary and the Doc called. I went indoors and worked on my Latin prose. We are sitting in the dining room tonight.

[24] See 3 June 1922.

Thursday 1 June: . . . In College I found a note from Carritt telling me that Farquharson thought he could get me a job in Oxford for the vac. and also drawing my attention to a Fellowship at Magdalen by examination, in today's *Gazette*.

I then called on Baker and gave him the new "Dymer". He described the usual blind with which Wadham had celebrated the end of Eights – all the wooden seats removed from the latrines of course, and burned. He agreed with me that this represented stopped energy and lack of originality.

I then came back and saw Farquharson: he thinks he can get me some good tutoring with some people on Boar's Hill. We discussed my plans. He said he would like College to send me to Germany for a year. I wish this man wasn't so oily. When I asked if he had some minutes to spare he said he was never too busy to see *me*. Silly old man!

I left him, had my hair cut, came home, and took a cold bath. Worked in the drawing room, which was coolest, after lunch. Tea in the garden and in to Parson's Pleasure for a bathe – disturbed by people with a football. I notice that the chestnut bloom is nearly over now.

After supper I read Heitland, going to my own room when Mary and the Doc appeared. When it was dark I went out and talked with him alone in the garden. Starting from sexual cannibalism in insects (which he compared with Sadism) and thence passing to perversion in general, we ended up on "blinds" and anecdotes and the general philosophy of getting drunk . . .

Friday 2 June: Cooler in the morning. I put in good work on Gk. History and started revising Roman – which I seem to retain well – from breakfast to lunch. D busy making cakes: Maureen out for lunch.

I changed and went in to Baker's tea fight at about 3.45.[1]

---

[1] By "tea fight" Lewis meant those occasions in which, just as you are getting to the intersting part of a conversation with someone, all the guests are shuffled about.

Had some talk before his guests arrived. He was very pleased with the new canto on the whole, but said that "feeding on vain fancy" was inexcusable, and that the two stanzas before the last were "simply awful" . . .

Saturday 3 June: . . . I read, in the Union, the preface and some of the poems in Hardy's new book: the preface written in such strained involved sentences that I could hardly understand it – one or two of the poems magnificent.

I also looked into a copy of Freud's *Introductory Lectures* which lay among the new books: got quite a new point of view about perversion, wh. has stuck in my head: i.e. that it is always the substitution of some minor detail for the act itself. Query – from the comparatively naturalistic point of view, is all human love, as opposed to mere appetite, one huge perversion? . . . Took Havelock Ellis's *World of Dreams* from the Union and returned home.

In the garden after lunch I read Spenser – the beautiful canto about Phaedria. Sheila Gonner came to tea: Jenkin arrived rather late. We had all sat down to tea and were, as Bozzy says, in extraordinary spirits when Miss Wiblin arrived – a fat, plain, shy, giggling woman.[2] A most insane meal – what the stranger thought of us I cannot imagine.

When things quieted down Jenkin asked me to come on the river: so walked to Magdalen Bridge and thence up the Cher in his canoe. River pretty empty and delightfully cool with a soft evening light. He quoted with approval the remarks of Mr Scrogan in Huxley's *Chrome Yellow* on modern "serious" sexuality. We spoke of *Don Juan*: he was ecstatic in praise of the Haidée cantos – said it was bound to collapse after them. He said that no one had lived who hadn't been on Haidée's island. I said in the same way no one had lived who hadn't done a thousand other things and one had to omit some. He is strongly obsessed by the modern – and ancient – ideal of having every experience. We also spoke of the horrors of marriage. He was also concerned to uphold the difficulties of the English school against the exaggerated prestige of Greats . . .

Sunday 4 June: . . . I read Havelock Ellis's dream book. He works it out chiefly as physiological events symbolised in image – or rather the physical causes the emotion, which then invents a symbol and the higher centre procedes to "logicalise" these symbols into a world,

---

[2] See **Vida Mary Wiblin** in the Biographical Appendix.

and so the dream is made. He is by no means a Freudian. (Memo reference to a footnote to Ellis's *Studies in Psychology of Sex* vol. III, Chapter on "Love and Pain".)

Maureen very much depressed today. After supper sat for a long time outside talking over old 1917 days: of Somerville, and why he was a strict Anglo-Catholic and yet joined in scoffing at religion – of Brand in the room below Paddy and me, and his loathsome friend – of Sutton etc.[3]...

Monday 5 June: ... I ... walked into the Cornmarket ... and ran into Mrs McNeill and Janie, who are staying at Oxenford Hotel. I promised to go to them on Wednesday afternoon.[4]...

Lady Gonner came to tea. Some interesting talk about parents and children: she and D agreed that when things went wrong it was nearly always the parent's fault. Lady Gonner said that her daughters had always treated her not as "an elder sister" as the sentimentalists would have it, but as a younger sister. We also discused Strachey: she thinks *Eminent Victorians* better than *Queen Victoria*. One cannot describe Lady G. better than by saying that tho' she is very deaf, we do not easily get tired of talking to her ...

Tuesday 6 June: ... Jenkin returned "Dymer" which I had lent him on Saturday: he was much less pleased with it than either Baker or Barfield. He says he cannot quite stomach the slang etc., and he has a constitutional inability to like psychological soliloquy. He found the Byronic element very pronounced – but praised one or two passages.

Watling returned, having been round to College: brought me a note from Carritt saying that Wadham wanted a Greats man to act as junior dean and would "press" him to read law and become a law tutor. Would this suit me?

We all repaired to Magdalen Bridge and took Jenkin's canoe: we went up the Thames, past Folly Bridge and the gas works, into a narrow side stream, and finally to Ferry Hinksey. Here we had a good tea (1/2d a head) in the garden of the pub, which runs down to the water ... nothing said all afternoon that's worth recording, but a very pleasant and cheery time. Cool on the

---

[3] These were some of the other members of the O.T.C. which Lewis came to know when he was billeted in Keble College. He shared a room with Paddy Moore, but the one he admired most was Martin Ashworth Somerville (1898–1918) of King's College, Cambridge, who served in Egypt and Palestine and died of wounds received in action.

[4] See Jane "Janie" McNeill in the Biographical Appendix.

water and the river full of beauty – natural and human . . .

Wednesday 7 June: . . . To College to see Carritt about the proposed job at Wadham. He was away for the day . . . I then called on Baker in Wadham and asked his advice about the Wadham job. He described the duties of the junior dean. Could I descend among a crowd of junior blues and say "Put out the bonfire!" in a voice that would command obedience from tight men? We both laughed at the picture, tho' I was rather depressed with the realisation of what I lack . . . Had a talk with D who quite agrees with Baker's view of my inability ever to be a junior dean . . .

I worked in the garden till about 3.45 and then went to the McNeills at Oxenford Hall Hotel, and took Janie to the Good Luck. Tolerable tea for two, with ices, for 3/-. I found her desperately boring – tho' in Ireland I have often regarded her as a bit of the larger world. She went over ancient stories and explained W[arnie]'s psychology to me with a lavish display of ignorance. She is stagnating like the rest, and falling back on matter which has been used over and over again – I am really very sorry for her. She tells me that Aunt Lily goes about saying that I have been promised a Fellowship . . .

Thursday 8 June: Began Greats today: D reminds me that this day five years ago was my first in the army. No sun, and cool out of doors whenever the wind blew, but very oppressive under cover.

Left home early and went to College: saw old George and recovered my mortar board, left there ever since I lived on his staircase. Tried to see Carritt, but he was out.

Repaired to the Schools at 9.30 with Blunt and Montagu. We did Roman History questions until 12.30: not a very nice paper, but my general impression is negative – nothing very hard or very easy and in me, no brilliance, no débâcle. Noticed an amusing affectation on the part of Joan Biggs who brought in – and used – an enormous and perfectly scarlet quill pen.

We all went to see Stevenson afterwards: he was unable to answer most of the gobbets, which were indeed a poor selection. Wyllie has unfortunately got some kind of internal chill, but is carrying on. Lunched in Hall with P.O. Simpson, Blunt, Montagu, Mackenzie, Currie and others, and lay on the grass in the quad afterwards.[5]

Returned to the Schools for Unseens at two o'clock. The Greek – a passage about dreams from Philostratus – was extraordinarily easy:

[5] Charles Wilfred Mackenzie took his BA in 1922, and John Alexander Currie took a B.Sc. in 1924.

the Latin (from the *De Natura Deorum*) rather harder. Finished at about 3.45 and came home feeling very tired and with a headache . . .

Friday 9 June: . . . Schools from 9.30 till 12.30, paper on philosophical books. I was quite pleased with my work. It became surprisingly cold during the morning and whether from that or some other reason, I found myself positively staggering when I came out. Lunch in Hall with Montagu, P.O.Simpson, Blunt etc.

Translation of Roman History texts from 2 till 4 – quite satisfactory so far as I can judge.

Coming home I found Miss Featherstone and D in the garden. D tells me that Miss F. has been undergoing horrible tortures with her ear of which the drum is now altogether gone. She is wonderfully cheerful. I was much less tired this afternoon than yesterday.

After reading a little Plato I returned to town. I met Wyllie in the High . . . [he] said that girls were not allowed to take Juvenal or Catullus for Schools, which I never knew before . . .

Found Mr Taylor – a nice old boy – with D on my return: some homespun but very sensible conversation. Letter from P. in the afternoon: also a notice from Truslove, drawing my attention to a philosophical lectureship at Bangor, N. Wales, with £300 a year.

Saturday 10 June: In the Schools at 9.30 as usual for Gk. History (questions) paper. This was my bête noir and I was very gratefully surprised to find gobbets – which I dreaded more than anything – excellently suited to me. The rest of the paper was very tolerable and I think I have managed it much better than I have any right to hope.

I came out shortly before time and went with Baker to Wadham: he has been overworking and is going out to Bee Cottage to recoup before his Schools. He showed me one of the finest modern poems I have seen, by an unknown American, in the *London Mercury*.[6] We lunched together at the Old Oak (plaice with sauce, bread, an ice and coffee, 2/7d). Harwood came over from another table and spoke to us. A very jolly meal, tho' I remember nothing that was said.

The town was full of people in strange costumes collecting money and selling programmes for the Rag Regatta. No one attacked me – perhaps they thought that a man in a white tie had troubles enough.

Back to the Schools at two o'clock for a paper on translation from

---

[6] This was Edwin Arlington Robinson's "For a Dead Lady" quoted in Conrad Aiken's "A Letter from America", *The London Mercury*, vol. VI (June 1922), pp. 196-8.

Plato and Aristotle which suited me down to the ground and could hardly have been better . . .

After supper I read through the two Cantos of "Dymer": felt fairly satisfied – I don't think the end of Canto II is half so bad as I imagined. It also occurred to me that a sensual stanza of the kind I have been trying to write would really be rather an anti-climax.

D and I then fell into conversation about ways and means – the summer vac. being always a problem, as my two allowances come so far apart . . . A notice from Truslove today about a Classical Lectureship at Durham, £300 a year.

Sunday 11 June: Rather late getting up; a very beautiful morning. I cycled into Oxford, leaving my bike in College: from there I walked through Christ Church down into Luke St., over the waterworks and up the fold in the hill from Hinksey to the top. Sat down in the patch of wood – all ferns and pines and the very driest sand and the landscape towards Wytham of an almost polished brightness. Got a whiff of the real joy, but only momentary.

I strolled back into the wood and home again: called at the Union to wash my hands which I had torn badly on a wire and to take out Wm. James's *Varieties of Religious Experience*. I have been reading this most of the afternoon, a capital book: particularly was I pleased to find for the first time Carlyle's remark about the lady who said she accepted the universe – "Gad! she'd better", and also to find an account of the rise and scope of Bostonese. The more I read the more I see that the sayings of the Doc and his like are simply taken from a tradition which is as much a ready made orthodoxy to them as the Bible and Prayer Book are to old fashioned people.

D very busy – much too busy in my opinion – on her dress making. Have been looking over some of my old philosophy essays as a refresher for tomorrow. Maureen out to tea at the Gonners.

Monday 12 June: . . . In College I found Poynton . . . in tremendous spirits and [he] began in his aged and tremulous falsetto to expound a theory of punishment which no one could understand. The main jist of it was that murderers ought to be let loose and shot by the local farmers because, tho' Poynton "had a vague belief in a future life" he thought it was a mistake to shut people up and let parsons on them as a preparation: and that they should rather be "sent off, shoo!" (here a magnificent gesture).

Stevenson kept up a gurgling titter and was suppressed by Poynton whenever he tried to speak. Before I came in Poynton had told them that if a man got A Plus on the Logic paper, he had to have a First: this was one of the *Arcana Imperii.*

We then repaired to the Schools for our Logic paper: I was greatly disappointed in it, and tho' I certainly did not do a bad one, I have often done very much better ones for Carritt . . .

Went back to Schools at two o'clock and did a pretty easy translation paper. Came home to tea. D (according to the superstition) said she had been afraid I'd get a bad paper this morning because I had been so looking forward to it . . .

I then went to Carritt and talked about the job at Wadham. He said everyone felt shy of being a dean at first, but that there was really very little unpleasantness to face. I said I was no good at ticking people off: he said mysteriously that he thought I was. He said I should see Allen to find out what Law was like.[7] He also told me that Ewing will probably come back from Switzerland to compete for the Magdalen Fellowship, which is unpleasing news . . .

Tuesday 13 June: Went into College and thence to Schools at 9.30 where I found an agreeable General Ancient History paper. I wrote steadily all through the time and I believe did good work.

Heavy rain began to fall during the morning. At 12.30 I rushed through it up to Queen's Lane to Wadham and called for Baker . . . We talked of Pasley and of the gulf which separates the married from the unmarried: on the same subject in the evening D said she thought it was the one who remained unmarried who unconsciously created the gulf.

Back to Schools at two o'clock for Latin Prose: not a bad piece – a criticism by J.R. Lowell on Carlyle. I came out at about 4.45: it was now so cold that I found myself shivering . . .

Wednesday 14 June: It continued very cold. In to Schools at 9.30 and did a pretty decent paper on Moral and Political philosophy . . .

Lunched in Hall with Montagu, Fasnacht, Currie and others. Greek prose in the afternoon – very few turned up and many stayed only half an hour.

I then came home and had tea: read a little of Wm. James and talked with D on a number of subjects.

Went in again at 7.45 to dine in Senior Common Room with Carritt and Stevenson . . . A very pleasant evening. Stevenson told us that a

---

[7] Carleton Kemp Allen (1887–1966) was Praelector in Jurisprudence at University College 1920-9, Professor of Jurisprudence 1929-31, and Warden of Rhodes House 1931-52.

Univ. man – Zumagrinoff (?) I think his name was – had been the murderer of Rasputin. He was fabulously rich and had brought Carritt an essay on socialism in which he said, "A man may haf one motor car or two or three, but ten – No!" . . .

Carritt described someone's – Smith perhaps – going for a walk with Bradley the philosopher.[8] Bradley kept rushing off to scold little boys who were throwing papers about or were "just going to write their names on walls." After these painful episodes he would ask "Do you like children?" in a voice which led you, if you were wise, to reply "Not very much." Then in a tender and encouraging voice, "Do you like *dogs?*"

Carritt, Haig and I then got into a long and interesting conversation on the subconscious which Carritt utterly denies, taking an extreme view and holding that the self literally ceases to exist during sleep. He allowed some force in my argument that a changeling subject might conceivably slip into your particular content next morning. Haig was on the "extreme left" and talked of Coué and Badouin . . .

Thursday 15 June: A free day, at last. I went out walking at 10 o'clock. It was the most delightful, cool, grey skied summer day. I went up Shotover and down the other side to Wheatley, thence to my right over the railway bridge and up past the old windmill where I once went with Jenkin on bicycles. I was in capital form, getting "thrills" from everything, full of unspecified memories and, for some time, almost free from thought.

Got home about quarter to one. Lunch very late. Wrote five stanzas for the third canto of "Dymer" in the afternoon. Miss Wiblin came to give Maureen a lesson and stopped to tea. Desperately plain but quite sensible – except that she remembered herself and had to giggle now and then . . .

Read Wm. James in the afternoon and evening: got as far as the chapter on Mysticism which is the most interesting so far. D in very good form but frightfully busy with her work. We are sitting in the drawing room tonight with a fire. My two poems back from the *English Review*.

Friday 16 June: . . . A note from Carritt was left for me in the lodge enclosing a ticket for the annual Greek play at Bradfield tomorrow week: went to the bus bureau but they had no details about a bus to Bradfield and I am thinking of biking . . .

---

[8] Francis Herbert Bradley (1846–1924).

Saturday 17 June: A notice from Truslove came by the early post about a classical lectureship for a year at Reading, £300, "apply E.R. Dodds, head of their Classical department". I wondered if this might not be Eric Dodds, the drunken Sinn Féiner and friend of Theobald Butler's who had been at Univ.[9] Going into town I met Carritt in the library and found that this was so – as he had met Dodds yesterday and my name had been mentioned. He also told me that it was quite possible to bike to Bradfield . . .

I then called on Poynton. He said he thought it very unlikely that my failure to do verse would stick me for the Reading job. I asked for a testimonial whereupon he threw up his hands in horror and exclaimed "Oh, my dear boy!" but promised to write one if Dodds asked for it. I also called on Stevenson who promised me another. He thought a job at Reading for a year would help me to one at Oxford and approved of my idea of taking a season ticket and continuing to live at Oxford if I got it.

I went into the J.C.R. and wrote two letters to Dodds, one a formal application, the other in a jovial strain reminding him of myself and when we had met . . .

Came home. Maureen had been on the river all day with the Rowells . . . Poor D terribly busy finishing a bit of work . . . Supper at 10 o'clock: we then discussed ways and means. It appears that we shall be put to the pin of the collar to get through this long vac . . .

Sunday 18 June: I woke up late this morning in such a state of misery and depression as I never remember to have had. There was no apparent reason. Really rather ridiculous – found myself in tears, for the first time for many a long day, while dressing. I concealed this as well as I could and it passed off after breakfast. I suppose it is some sort of pathological reaction by which I pay for not having had conscious wind up or exhaustion during schools.

Wrote a few stanzas for "Dymer" in the morning and then read Hume's *Of Morals*. This contains nearly all my own fallacies in ethics – which look more fallacious in another person's language.

After lunch I walked up Shotover and went on to the grove of firs

---

[9] Lewis came up to University College in the Hilary Term of 1917 when Butler and Dodds (both Irish) were taking Schools.

Theobald Butler (1894–1976) achieved distinction as a lawyer. He was called to the Bar, Inner Temple, in 1921, became Master of the Bench in 1960.

Eric Robertson Dodds (1893–1979) was Lecturer in Classics at University College, Reading, 1919–24, Professor of Greek in the University of Birmingham 1924–36, and Regius Professor of Greek in the University of Oxford 1936–60.

at the far end which overlooks the lane to Horspath. Here I was quite out of reach of the Sunday crowds and sat for some time . . .

After supper I continued the *Antigone*. Who can have invented the theory that the Greeks were great craftsmen in subordinating the parts to the whole? As a matter of fact they will sell their souls to bring in myths, "gnomes" and purple patches. I notice Creon's long digression on money, and the Πολλὰ τὰ δεινα chorus and the beautiful Niobe passage in Antigone's duet with chorus . . .

Monday 19 June: After breakfast I set out determined to waste no money on smokes or busses, leaving my tobacco behind and taking a halfpenny in my pocket . . .

A hot clammy day with much sun. I had a slight toothache but it went away after lunch. D and I sat in the garden, the first time for many days. I wrote some more of the IIIrd Canto of "Dymer" and two political stanzas for a later canto, with some self satisfaction . . .

After tea . . . I walked up to Headington again and [saw] Mrs Hinckley . . . We had an interesting conversation on parents and children and the "revolt of youth". I was inclined to think it was necessary and occurred in every generation: she held strongly that it was peculiar to our own . . . D very bad with sickness and headache but became better after sal volatile.

A letter from Aunt Lily containing a violent and rather silly attack on Sir W. Raleigh and announcing that she is coming to stay at Broadway: also telling me that I should eat at least "six or eight oranges a day"! . . .

Wednesday 21 June: Warmer today. Sat in the alley way and wrote Tan's speech for the IIIrd Canto of "Dymer": then wrote to P and Aunt Lily.

After lunch I bicycled to Beckley and called at Bee Cottage where I found Harwood alone and reading in a pleasant, stumpy 18th Century Bible. He quoted from Genesis "Whatever Adam called anything, that *was* the name of the thing", as an excellent definition of poetry. He told me that the Chancellor's prize had not been awarded this year. He put the wind up me by telling me that he thought he had got A on all his translation papers in Greats last year, but really got Γ. He showed me De la Mare's new book, *The Veil* which is very fine: the "Monologue" expecially concentrates all misery into the likeness of a nursery rhyme.

After tea he brought out Barfield's "Tower" and some new pieces of his own, while I gave him the new Canto of "Dymer" to read.

The "Tower" is full of magnificent material and never a dead phrase: the new part strong and savage – "Big Bannister" is splendid – but very hazy at present. The story is (to me) as hard to follow as *Sordello*.[10] But what genius! The metre *too* eccentric for me, but on that subject Barfield has probably forgotten more than I ever knew.

Harwood's pieces original, quaint and catchy – he has improved: the Dresden China bit about Nausika and "nous n'irons plus au bois" are the two best.[11] He surprised me by saying that Canto II of "Dymer" was better than Canto I: he thinks the end "really great".

We then went out for a walk, through a wood, down to Otmoor. He led me through the poppied garden of a Tudor Manor house with a stagnant moat, tall chimneys and narrow windows. It was still and uncanny. It was said that an eccentric American millionaire and his wife live there alone and do their own work. Got back to Bee Cottage about 7.15. Supped off home cured ham (the best that ever I ate in my life) which they get very cheap in the village.

Left – after a very pleasant afternoon – at 7.45 and biked in to the Martlets in 25 minutes. The first meeting I have been to for ages. Allen, Carritt, Watling, Robson-Scott, Curtis, Ziman, Fasnacht, E. F. Simpson, and unknown, and a dreadful old bore called Dr Counsell. Allen read a paper on Joseph Conrad: very good, tho' rather aggressively manly. Pretty good discussion afterwards, but was amazed at the stupidity of Allen in a theoretical argument against Carritt and me.

Heard from Carritt that one of the examiners had said to him "One of your men seems to think that Plato is always wrong." Carritt guessed several people. Finally the other said "No: – Lewis. Seems an able fellow anyway" – wh. I suppose is good news . . .

Thursday 22 June: Went into Oxford and left an advertisement at the *Oxford Times* office for tutoring work in the Vac., at the ridiculous charge of 7/6d for three appearances.[12] . . .

Became convinced today that Canto II of "Dymer" as written up to date will not do. Having now left the myth and being forced to use fiction I find new difficulties springing up and doubt if "Tan" and his revolutionaries are really advisable.

---

[10] By Robert Browning (1840).

[11] "Nous n'irons Plus" is found in *The Voice of Cecil Harwood*, ed. Owen Barfield (1979).

[12] The advertisement appeared in *The Oxford Times* of 23 June, 30 June and 7 July and reads: "Undergraduate, Classical Scholar, First-class in Honour Moderations, University Prizeman will give TUITION, Philosophy, Classics, to Schoolboy or Undergraduate in Oxford, August, September. Highest references – Write, D.3, 183, 'Times' Office, Oxford."

After supper I read the first volume of my diary aloud to D and we both got a laugh or two out of it. D troubled with a sore throat and swollen gland: the Doc calls it neuritis.

Friday 23 June: Letter from Arthur in the morning suggesting that he might come up on the 28th, and would we care to see him.

A bleak and blowing day. I went into town in the morning: first to Blackwell's where I sold for 25/- my *History of Persia*, the *History of Seventeenth Century France*, Joseph's *Logic*, two volumes of Sellar, and a volume of the Loeb Euripides. I seem almost to have lost the possessive love of books and shall henceforward be content with very few provided that I am within reach of a library.

I then went to Wadham and was almost alarmed to find a notice on Baker's door saying he had been moved to the Acland Nursing Home. I walked to the home in Banbury Rd. and saw him. He has had a break down and came in on Thursday with a temperature of 104. The last day of his Schools was a nightmare to him. I noticed that he asked me the same questions several times, forgetting what was said: yet he was able to imitate Dr Counsell to the life, who is attending him and who at that moment came in . . .

I then got a letter in College from Dodds, summoning me to an interview in Reading at 11 a.m. tomorrow – which will alter my route to Bradfield . . .

D suggested that Baker ought to come out and stay here, if he was fit to be moved, as they are rooking him £7-7-0 a week at the Acland: I therefore went back to town after lunch to make this proposal. I was admitted with difficulty. Baker now much worse, having gone up to 103 again. He thinks he may be able to move on Sunday . . .

Saturday 24 June: Breakfasted before 8 and cycled to the station to catch the 9.10 to Reading: I read the *Antigone* during the journey. Arriving at Reading I found my way to University College and left my bike at the Lodge. I saw a great many undergraduates of both sexes walking about: a nice looking lot. I then stolled until 11 o'clock when I was taken to the Principal's room.

Childs, de Burgh and Dodds were present.[13] All very very nice to me, but Childs very firmly ruled out my idea of living anywhere else

---

[13] William Macbride Childs (1869–1939) was Principal of University College, Reading, 1903–26, and Vice-Chancellor of the University of Reading 1926–29.

William George de Burgh (1866–1943) was Professor of Philosophy at the University of Reading 1907–34.

than at Reading. I was told that most of my pupils would be girls. I had seen so much beauty in the corridors that one born under a less temperate star would have wanted to enter on his duties at once. They seemed anxious to meet me half way (the dons not the girls) and said that "no verse" and Roman history confined to the third period would not matter.

Dodds then took me to his room and we talked for a while. I gather he is no longer a friend of Butler's. He said Carritt had examined me in 1916 when I got my scholarship and had been "astonished at my wide reading". Dodds does philosophy at Reading (tho' pure scholarship is his natural line) and is strong on Plotinus. Their staff includes Ure the Historian and Holts the composer. He then showed me round the college which is pleasant and unpretentious, and left me in the Senior Common Room, to wait for lunch, coming back at 1 o'c.

At lunch he introduced me to Miss Powell who is one of their dons. She smoked through a thing like a lorgnette. She discussed the nakedness of pigs. The contempt which her affectation and cheap Sitwellian artistic cynicism provoked in me is best described by saying that she is the sort of woman in whose presence one thinks it worth while to try and make epigrams. Thank God I've been through that once and come out the other side.

I left the College at 2 and cycled to Bradfield [to see Sophocles' *Antigone* performed in Greek at Bradfield College]: it was raining and blowing. Met Watling and Jenkin outside the theatre. It is perfectly Greek – simple stone steps to sit on and incense burning on the altar of Dionysus in the orchestra. Unfortunately the weather was perfectly English.

It was not well done: most of the actors were inaudible and as the rain increased (beating on the trees) it completely drowned them. The Carritts were there, his Cambridge daughter sitting beside me. Watling and Jenkin left me to find more shelter and when their places were taken by people who talked, I moved too and found that I could see nothing of the stage. The audience were spectacle enough: rows of unhappy people listening to inaudible words in an unknown language and sitting hunched up on stone steps under a steady downpour. If only P[apy] cd. be taken to this show!

I then noticed that Jenkin was standing on the last tier where the amphitheatre merged into the hillside – a steep bank of ivy overhanging the stone work. Crept up to join him – "Oh, think of a cup of steaming hot tea," said he. We exchanged a pregnant glance: then I led the way and in a trice we had plunged into the bushes, plugged our way on all fours up the ivy bank, and dropped into a lane beyond. Never shall I forget J. shaking streams off his hat and repeating over and over again, "Oh, it *was* a tragedy!" We then repaired to a marquee and had tea . . .

Came home: D and I had for supper the sandwiches she had made up for my lunch and discussed the Reading job. To live at Reading means my living there alone while the others live at Oxford, or else changing Maureen's school for a year. The first alternative I don't care about, the second would be a thousand pities. Also, from the commercial point of view, it is undesirable to lose touch with the dons here . . .

Sunday 25 June: Late getting up. After breakfast, at ten exactly, I set out and walked to Beckley. A beautiful, windy morning with blue sky and great colours. Calling at Bee Cottage where I found Harwood's brother and Barfield with a game leg, I arranged that Barfield and Harwood should come to tea on Tuesday, and continued my walk . . .

After lunch, while D was practising with Maureen, I wrote seven stanzas of a new canto III for "Dymer" in my own room. I think I have got back to the right track again . . . Jenkin arrived and we all had tea. D and I were amused to notice again how in his conversation all roads lead to Cornwall. A good talk afterwards on books. I showed him the American poet Robinson's poem in the *Mercury* and he agreed with me in praising it.

Baker arrived by taxi, with his Aunt, in a bright blue dressing gown and was put to bed in the back room. His Aunt left almost at once. Jenkin stayed till 7 o'clock. After supper I talked with Baker. He tells me that Beckett sat the *Antigone* out yesterday and thought it splendid.[14] . . .

Monday 26 June: . . . We had today our first dish of green peas this year – always a moment to be treasured up. After lunch I continued "Dymer" with considerable satisfaction, bringing him to the second view of the "matriarch". Baker got up and came down stairs for tea . . .

After supper while I was doing Latin with Maureen, D appears to have had a long conversation upstairs with Baker on a variety of

[14] See **Eric Beckett** in the Biographical Appendix.

subjects, including the possibility of my getting married. I sat with him for some time afterwards. He remarked that Harwood was playing Watts Dunton to Barfield's Swinburne. We talked of H.G. Wells.

A letter from Arthur today: funnily enough he is coming to Waldencote to stay with a Mrs Taunton, a painter. D reminded me that Pasley had seen her and taken a very different view of her profession – and Arthur is paying "only 4/- a night"!

Tuesday 27 June: Another close, drizzling day. Most of the morning worked on "Dymer", Canto III, with varying success. After lunch went out for a stroll through St Clement's and up the old London Rd. A most unpleasant day.

Harwood turned up at about 4 o'clock and Baker came down shortly afterwards. We discussed Doughty. Harwood thought his manner was no more difficult than Milton's would be if you had not come to it from the Classics and one might have as much survival power as the other. He supported Barfield's view that there was no essential difference between the Christina and art: Baker and I opposed this. Harwood accepted my suggestion that imagination was "disinterested fancy" . . .

D repeated to me some amusing details of her talk with Mrs Raymond . . . We then spoke of Baker: we quite agree about a certain lack of kindliness in him, and easy acquiescence in the fence which intellect tends to make between a man and the "solid folk", and that this is a great and dangerous fault . . .

Wednesday 28 June: . . . A wire came from Arthur saying that he would arrive by the 5.55. Wrote a little more "Dymer" and went in to meet him thro' a steady drizzle.

He turned up with many pieces of luggage and in much indecision, but finally taxied out here. D persuaded him to stay with us, after a long and cataclysmic argument wh. amused Baker immensely. Baker and Arthur seemed to take to each other. Arthur is tremendously improved: nearly all the nonsense is gone and he talked interestingly.

Supper, with Miss Wiblin, was a pandemonium: everyone in great form, but Maureen shouting them all down. Afterwards Miss W. played – delightfully: D and I were specially struck with Debussy's *Cathedral*. Miss Wiblin discovered that there were two poets present and asked someone to write words for her exercise, which is to be in the manner of Stravinsky: Baker knew Stravinsky and said at once that neither of us could do it. Whitman or a psalm was suggested.

It was arranged that Miss Wiblin – who is frightfully overworked – was to come to me for Latin tuition on Friday evenings. We were all late in getting to bed after an enjoyable evening. Arthur occupied my camp bed in my room.

Thursday 29 June: A bright morning. Arthur had been disturbed by my snoring during the night and had got up to plug his ears with India rubber! This was quite like old times.

When I brought Baker his shaving water I showed him "Misfire" which he had not seen before: he was interested in my taking that line, but did not approve. I then settled down to finish and fair copy Canto III of "Dymer". Baker and Arthur spent most of the morning in the drawing room talking psychoanalysis. Just before lunch Arthur and I walked as far as Magdalen to get a taxi, and were rather late in getting back. A very amusing time at lunch . . .

At five to three we said goodbye to Baker. He had to go in order to see Lilian Bayliss about his contract at the Old Vic., tho' he is not really fit to move. During the last two days he has been more human, less of the "spiritual aristocrat" than I ever knew, and, in that way, I really believe his stay has done him good.

Arthur and I then walked to Waldencote through Mesopotamia and the green lane: it was a cool and showery afternoon – curiously tiring. At Waldencote we saw Mrs Dawes the caretaker. She also hates Hall. The house has a certain attraction – it is nicely furnished – but it is dark and inconvenient.

We then came home to tea. D in very poor form and depressed by the shrieking wind which has a bad effect on her, as on some other people. Arthur read James' *Turn of the Screw* while I finished my canto. In the evening D, Arthur and I had started three handed bridge when Mary came in and made a fourth. We had a good evening of it, enough to make D and me sleepy. Arthur moves into the back room tonight. Dorothy came down in the evening with a present of flowers for D, the first thing she had bought out of Baker's tip.

Friday 30 June: It was another winding and tiring day. After breakfast Arthur and I bussed into Oxford. I called first at the *Times* office where I found one answer to my advertisement, apparently from a very illiterate person . . .

We went to College. Arthur went off to look for Bryson of Oriel while I saw Farquharson.[15] He made it pretty plain that he had now

---

[15] John Norman Bryson (1896–1976) was also from Northern Ireland. He was a lecturer at Balliol, Merton and Oriel Colleges 1923–40, and Fellow and Tutor in English Literature at Balliol 1940–63.

no tutoring job up his sleeve for me and hastened to talk about mathematics in the Greek philosophers. I showed him my answer to the advertisement and he advised me to ask Poynton what I should charge. I then showed Arthur the Library, Chapel and the Shelley memorial.

In Chundry's we saw a curious book of drawings by un nommé Austin Osmond, spare, affected, grotesque and foul, after the manner of Beardsley.

We returned home very tired, buying strawberries in Cowley Road. When lunch was just ready a woman called Malcomson of Islip, to whom Arthur had written, turned up. Arthur, instead of saying that he was staying in digs with me, or simply that he was in Oxford, had volunteered some yarn about "friends". It all seemed so gratuitous that I positively lost my temper. I was made to go into the drawing room for a few minutes and speak to her. She is a grey haired woman with a shrill voice: in her conversation everything in "killing" and "no end of a lark". She stayed an unconscionable time. I think that she wanted to be asked to lunch, but of course it was better that D and she should not meet. It was arranged that Arthur should spend Sunday and Sunday night at Islip.

After lunch I packed up my things for the night and biked into Oxford: failing to see Poynton in College I went on to Beckley through wind and rain. I was warmly welcomed by Barfield and Harwood. M.L. Jacks (brother of Stopford, late Dean of Wadham, headmaster elect of Mill Hill) and his jolly wife came for tea.[16] He was one of the strangers with whom I travelled from Pangbourne last Saturday: a pleasant man, laughs a lot. He tells me Stopford is now in business.

After their departure we got into conversation on fancy and imagination: Barfield cd. not be made to allow any essential difference between Christina dreams and the material of art. In the end we had to come to the conclusion that there is nothing in common between different people's ways of working, and, as Kipling says, "every single one of them is right".

At supper I drank Cowslip Wine for the first time in my life. It is a real wine, green in colour, bittersweet, as warming as good sherry,

---

[16] Maurice Leonard Jacks (1894–1964) was a Fellow and Dean of Wadham College 1919–22, Headmaster of Mill Hill School 1922–37, and Director of the Department of Education, Oxford University, 1938–57.

but heavy in its results and a trifle rough on the throat – not a bad drink however.

After supper we went out for a walk, into the woods on the edge of Otmoor. Their black and white cat, Pierrot, accompanied us like a dog all the way. Barfield danced round it in a field – with sublime lack of self consciousness and wonderful vigour – for our amusement and that of three horses. There was a chilling wind but it was quite warm in the wood. To wander here, as it got dark, to watch the cat poising after imaginary rabbits and to hear the wind in the trees – in such company – had a strange de la Mare-ish effect. On the way back we started a burlesque poem in *terza rima* composing a line each in turn: we continued it later, with paper, by candle light. It was very good nonsense. We entitled it "The Button Moulder's story" and went to bed.

Saturday 1 July: Woke early with a dry and sore throat. Thinking that I heard the others stirring in the next room, I got up. From my small window (framed in thatch) I looked out on Brill Hill. Going downstairs I found nothing doing and walked to the pub to buy a packet of cigarettes. I had to wait a long time for the others and read a *Study of Metre* – I think by a man called Ormond.[1] A badly written book. We breakfasted at about 9.30.

Afterwards they read the new (IIIrd) Canto of "Dymer" while I read the IIIrd part of Barfield's "Tower". His hero has got to France by now, and he describes waking up in billets. I thought it very fine. In the IInd part I was quite reconciled to the part about the telephone wires on a second reading.

Barfield and Harwood both approved of the new canto, but found the position of things obscure and could not always make out exactly what was happening. This is an unpardonable sort of offence in this sort of poem. They promised to try and come here before they went down next week.

I left at 12.15 and biked home through hurricanes of wind, feeling rather poorly. At lunch D reminded me that Miss Wiblin was coming, so I went into town to look up "Higher Certificate" papers, but cd. find none . . . Arthur had met the Doc yesterday evening, and (of course) used him as a father confessor.

After tea I went into College and again failed to see Poynton: walked home in torrents of rain under an umbrella lent by Frank. D making strawberry jam – a fine fruity smell pervading the house. Miss W. came for supper and afterwards I did Latin Unseens with her in the drawing room. I think my first "tutorial" went off alright. She wanted to pay but D and I would not allow this.

Sunday 2 July: My sore throat was much better this morning but my cold continued very heavy all day. I read Bernard Shaw's *Irrational Knot* which I bought in June 1917 and have never read. Arthur, to

[1] By Thomas Stewart Omond (1903).

whom I had lent it when last at home, brought it back. A crude, silly book, but rather interesting.

The Malcomson woman, in a Ford car, called for Arthur soon after breakfast and he went off to Islip ... In the evening D and I discussed our plans. It was hard to decide yes or no about the Reading job and D was so anxious not to influence me that I cd. not be quite sure what her wishes were – I am equally in the dark as to what my own real wishes are, apart from the mood of the moment ...

Monday 3 July: My cold was so heavy in the morning that I "allowed myself to be persuaded" by D to stop in bed – i.e. I accepted her advice as a confirmation of my own sneaking wishes. I finished *The Irrational Knot* and read Dr Miller's *The New Psychology and the Teacher*: a good little book, all about psychoanalysis really, and touching education in the first and last chapters. At about 12.30 I got up, shaved and dressed.

Arthur now re-appeared and we had lunch. He was very full of his visit to Islip which he appears to have enjoyed: he had been taken to see Robert Graves. He went up to see Mrs Taunton in the afternoon. After tea it cleared up and I walked up and down Warneford Rd. in the sunshine.

A letter arrived from Dodds to say that the Reading job has been given to someone with a name like Mabbot at Exeter.[2] Our discussion of the problem must have nearly coincided with their decision which removed the problem. On the whole it is rather a relief to have the difficult alternative out of our minds.

After supper we had an uproarous evening over Maureen's, Arthur's and my attempts to do a rider in Geometry. Later I read James' *Turn of the Screw* aloud to D and Arthur in his edition. We all liked it immensely, though D called it "absurd". The style certainly is wonderfully unnatural, but it gets there.

Tuesday 4 July: I dreamed that I was in our room at Little Lea and Warnie was in bed, when my mother (or someone I called my mother) came in and announced with malicious triumph her arrangement of some marriage either for W. or for "my sister". I was angry and said "God damn you". P shortly afterwards came in and told me I was to be "prosecuted for scandal" but I laughed at him and said "fiddlesticks".

---

[2] John David Mabbott (1898–) was Asst. Lecturer in Classics at Reading University 1922, after which he became a Fellow of St John's College, Oxford, 1924–63, and then the President of St John's College 1963–9.

After breakfast Arthur and I went into town: I called in College, while he went into Blackwells, in the hope of seeing Poynton, but found he was out of Oxford. I then went to the Union and looked round for a while. It began to rain heavily: when it was a little brighter I went to Blackwells and rejoined Arthur.

Returning to the Union, I took out for him Jung's *Analytical Psychology* and Rivers' *Instinct and the Subconscious* at his own request, but of course he won't read them. In the Corn he saw the Malcomson party and rushed after them: he is very anxious for me to follow up this acquaintance. We got home at about one o'clock.

D had had a "board and lodging" letter from Baker, describing his interview with Lilian Bayliss. She, apparently, is a "spiritual" woman who regards her career as an actress-manageress [of the "Old Vic"] in the light of a divinely appointed mission: she had a soulful conversation with Baker. But she is also, he says "a very, very good business woman" and "doesn't always clearly distinguish between the temporal and the spiritual".

After lunch Arthur retired to his room with Dr Miller, Jung, Rivers and "Dymer" to read. Later on he went to tea with the Gonners. D and I had a good deal of talk in the afternoon. After supper I continued reading out *The Turn of the Screw*. We were all much excited but held different views as to what had happened. This led to a general argument between Arthur and me about "obscurity" in art. I couldn't quite understand his point, nor cd. he explain it . . .

Wednesday 5 July: Arthur was late in getting up and hestitated for a long time whether to go out in the morning or not. At last he made up his mind and we went out for a walk together. I took him up Shotover.

We discussed Ireland, home, and fathers. He finds the thought of going home more intolerable each time and dreads, above all, business talks with the old man. The same old man has been trying to get him to make a will and seems to tell a good many lies.

We first sat down on the nearer slope of the first valley: Arthur was in raptures over the flat plain towards Sinodin Hills and the Chilterns. We then went on to the gate on the left looking towards Forest Hill, where we surprised the usual congregation of rabbits. Next we went to within sight of my favourite grove above Horsepath Lane, and returned home by the path over the fields by the wood's edge to Cowley Barracks. It was a fine morning with a soft air, rather windy, grey skied and a little warm at one time when the sun tried to break through. Arthur enjoyed the country immensely and it was quite like old times: he was collecting ideas for his competition picture under the title of "The Picnic".

After lunch he went into town. I read a little in Rivers' *Instinct and the Unconscious* and chatted with D who is in good form. It now began to rain and continued for the rest of the day. Arthur returned for tea, having found no more answers for me at the *Times* office.

We then settled down to draw pictures for the school sale. It became very dark. Furniture got moved into wrong places. The dining room does not comfortably hold four people. A lot of ragging. Arthur made a ghastly failure of a comic drawing in the Heath Robinson style: I made an equal mess of a symbolic thing in Indian ink.

At eight o'clock Miss Wiblin arrived and we had supper. She gave Maureen a lesson and I looked over her Latin Prose. D and I very late in getting to bed. We talked over the awful time we had had the term before last: I said again that the Askins were not ultimately forgivable.

Thursday 6 July: A grey and damp day. I took Arthur out for a walk, going as far as Carfax by bus: thence down St Aldate's and by Lake St. over the water works. The dampness of the air began to thicken into rain. Beyond Hinksey the mud on the field path was almost continental. Arthur was very tired from the first, and soon began to lag, tho' resisting for some time my suggestions that we should turn. Near the farm the rain became so heavy that we beat a retreat. Very tiring, but the tremendous wind, among so many fields of corn and trees, made it beautiful.

I put Arthur on a bus at Carfax, did some shopping, and called in College. Here I found a notice saying that candidates for the Magdalen Fellowship might send in a dissertation in addition to doing the exam. I was so engrossed in this news that I cannot remember whether I walked or bussed home. After lunch Arthur retired to "lie down" according to his usual practice: D was hard at work for the sale: I began a "dissertation" on the hegemony of the moral value . . .

After supper we all settled down to work for the sale. I drew an Indian ink drawing of which Arthur approved parts. D slaving away at some wretched work for the same sale, and we were not in bed till nearly 2 o'clock.

Friday 7 July: Another damp cold day. Set to work on a prose for

Miss Wiblin after breakfast: as we had been very late in getting up, this took me until lunch time. Just before we sat down, Barfield appeared to ask if he and Harwood might come to tea. I of course gladly agreed – then realised that I must be in town and at the Sale before their arrival.

Gobbled down some lunch and bussed into Oxford: left Livy back in College and took out a volume of Cicero for Miss Wiblin. Then, by bus to Headington where Arthur was to meet me. He turned up very late, a rather ridiculous figure on my bicycle with his knees coming up to his chin at each stroke of the pedal. We entered the sale – a very dull show, tho' some of the paintings by the girls were interesting . . .

Barfield and Harwood turned up, both tired with packing and distressed at leaving Bee Cottage, where a S. African lady is now installed. *Sic transit gloria.* D and Barfield hit it off splendidly and he remained with her while Harwood came into the drawing room and looked over the version I had done for Miss Wiblin. Coming back to the others we were joined by Arthur, who began to sketch Barfield, and fell into a long and strangely heartfelt conversation on happiness. We were rather pessimistic.

It rained hard. D now found out that Harwood was sleeping at the House, and that Barfield was looking for a room for the night. He accepted her invitation to stay with us, and I put up the camp bed in my room. A 8 o'clock Miss Wiblin arrived, and we sat down seven strong to supper: all in good spirits now, and plenty of ragging. Afterwards the others played bridge, while I retired with Miss W. to the drawing room. We had about an hour and a half and stopped because she was dead beat: this plain and therefore unnoticed girl has all the pluck in the world and works for at least eight hours a day teaching, while reading for exams as well. After the lesson we had some tea and she and Arthur played to us. Barfield went to bed at about 12.30 and I at about 1.30. Harwood had to leave early.

Saturday 8 July: We were all late getting up. Harwood turned up during breakfast to speak to Barfield for a minute and then went on to ride through wind and rain beyond Dorchester. We had some good talk over the breakfast table, but I cannot remember what it was about.

A letter from Pasley offering to come here for £2-10-0 a week while we are at Mrs Raymond's house which she is lending us for August. I did not notice his language much at the time and replied at once offering it for £2. Afterwards D drew my attention to a curious tone in Pasley's letter which suggested that they were coming merely as a kindness to us and that with an ill grace. We decided to write another letter tomorrow explaining ourselves.

Arthur went off to sketch on Shotover and Barfield left us at about 11.30. I did not go out, my cold being very heavy. We had lunch alone, leaving cold things for Arthur who was out till nearly four o'clock. In the afternoon I read Cicero's *De Finibus* – a not very inspired work. Supper at about 8 o'clock, when Harwood came. A variety of subjects were raised. Harwood made a statement about blancs manges which D and I found very amusing. Afterwards, he, Arthur and Maureen played. Rather earlier to bed, thank goodness.

Sunday 9 July: Set to work after breakfast to write a letter to Pasley explaining that we had meant to draw attention merely to the possible coincidence of his convenience and ours, not to ask him for a favour. D vetoed my first draft as offensive and likely to cause a quarrel – it reflected, tho' not deliberately, the tone of Pasley's letter, which I like less the more I read it. A friend dead is to be mourned: a friend married is to be guarded against, both being equally lost. I then wrote again in a more genial style and we let the second version go.

I read the IVth Book of *Paradise Lost* through in the morning, with much enjoyment. It stopt raining at about noon and I walked up Shotover, where Arthur had gone earlier, but couldn't meet him and came back to lunch at 1. Maureen was rather poorly with rheumatic pains. It was so cold that we lit the fire in the drawing room and sat there. A slack afternoon, D not in good form. Arthur came back for late lunch just before tea time and soon retired to his room. I tried my hand at a lyrical epilogue to "Dymer" but with no success.

Just as we were sitting down to supper, in came Jenkin who is up till Wednesday for his viva. We were delighted to see him. He has been bicycling in the Forest of Dean with Watling and goes from there to Cornwall. We discussed *The Turn of the Screw*: he agrees with me that the boy is "saved" in the last scene. We talked of *Emma*: he liked it, but parts of it made him "writhe". We then listened to him on mining. He said that 50 years ago when mines were beginning to be deep but before lifts were introduced, men, after eight hours work, used to climb up naked lengths of ladder in the shaft, to four times the height of St Paul's, often hanging on their arms when the angle of ascent was this side of perpendicular. He went off, borrowing "Dymer", at 10.30.

Arthur said he enjoyed Jenkin's conversation more than the others because it was about things you could understand. D and I were astonished, for Barfield and Co. had talked no literary shop at all, but general talk on subjects of interest to all men and women. Arthur is an incorrigible baby after all.

D and I sat up late. She said it was strange that I liked Baker more than the Bee Cottage people: we concluded it must be because Baker liked *me* more than they did, also he is my equal, while Barfield towers above us all. D liked him and Harwood exceedingly . . .

Monday 10 July: . . . After lunch (Arthur was out painting as usual) came Jenkin and we cycled together up Shotover, going as far as a gate on the bridlepath to Horsepath where we sat. It was a warm, miraculously quiet afternoon – sounds muffled by dampness, flies humming, and a hint of possible thunder in the air. The landscape eastwards over Wheatley to the Chilterns was very fine in the sunshine. We talked at random and most pleasantly, of the "stability" of the English countryside, of philosophy, of 17th Century prose.

On the way home Jenkin observed that there was more real humanity in the atmosphere of the 18th Century than in the "humanitarian" romantics that came after Rousseau, for these first began to regard . . . the man in the street, the bourgeois as an alien to be shocked and mocked or disregarded . . . Such a view made my heart warm toward Jenkin, tho' I pointed out that the man in the street was so much stronger than we and so ready to hit that one could not indulge one's sympathy too much.

Arthur was here when we came back, tired from his morning's work. Jenkin departed soon after tea. I read River's book with great interest, though many of the technicalities were Greek to me. I was struck with the idea that the "subconscious" might sometime be an "alternate consciousness" such as we get in dual personality and that such alternative consciousness might be normal say in amphibian animals . . .

Tuesday 11 July: It was a perfect, pearly grey morning, cool and dewy, with a promise of much heat to come, and the strangest touch of autumn in the air, unseasonable but delightful . . .

Arthur and I left at 11.30 and proceeded – after some hesitation – to the first gap on Shotover, where he settled down to paint. It was all delightful. I had Shelley with me and read some of the best parts of the IVth Act of *Prometheus*. Later I walked round the whole amphitheatre of the first gap, penetrating many bits where I have not been before. Arthur had brought sandwiches but I left him at 12.30 and came home to lunch . . .

Arthur came home at about 6.30 in a state of exhaustion, having worked on Shotover all day and had no tea. This is a fine advance on anything he wd. have dreamed of two years ago. He had done a landscape in oils, which we all admired, unintelligently enough no doubt.

After supper I read Ovid's *Metamorphoses* in the garden. Miss Wiblin called and left a Latin prose – better style than the last, but shocking grammar howlers, poor girl. A letter from Pasley making it plain that it is all O.K. about his coming here . . .

Wednesday 12 July: . . . It was a warm day. D hard at work on a petticoat for Lady Gonner. I worked on my dissertation in the garden until suddenly informed that it was 4.35 and that we must be at Meadowlands at 5.

I dashed off on foot while Arthur followed on my bicycle: I finally arrived in good time. Mrs Hinckley, Veronica, Arthur and I had tea in the shrubbery beyond her hill – quite a pleasant time. Veronica is going to teach French at Maureen's school next term. Mrs H. gave us a wonderful account of her cousin aged 78. This redoubtable old woman arrived before lunch, having biked from London, sleeping the night at High Wycombe. She then (after lunch) biked in to see a friend in Woodstock Rd., returned, had tea, walked all round Mrs Hinckley's wilderness, and biked twenty miles next morning. She told them that she had enjoyed the last twenty years of her life more than any period which had gone before . . .

Miss Wiblin came and we did about half an hour's lesson before supper, to which Jenkin came. A jolly meal, improved by mushroom stew. Afterwards I finished Miss Wiblin's lesson and we came back and all had tea and cakes in the dining room. Jenkin had told D about his father who died suddenly while riding with him, so that he had the awful job of telling his mother. He spoke very bitterly about the uselessness of his friends once they get married. He invited me to come and stay with him at St Ive's, but of course railway fares make that impossible . . .

Thursday 13 July: . . . I worked all morning on my dissertation with great enjoyment, and again after lunch until Miss Wiblin came for Maureen.

Just at that moment a bulky figure loomed in sight and Cranny entered the hall. D at once asked him if he had been ill – and indeed he looked shrunk and changed. He said he had been worried and came into the dining room with D and me. His story came out by degrees. He was utterly changed. He said his effort to exchange with a London parish had fallen through and his wife had been "very much upset". Further, they had invited a girl down to distract his son from an undesirable girl, but the decoy had worked too well and the son was distracted to the extent of getting engaged to the girl provided by the family.

Cranny said he lived among mad people and he thought he was going mad himself. It can't be his son's engagement, for he's used to trouble with the son: more probably his wife has nagged him half dead. He kept repeating that he wanted a change. D said "a change from his family" and he did not contradict her. He said his time was done: he had nothing to live for. He was quite unable to talk in his old style – soon tired of his own troubles, yet incapable of changing to other topics. I never saw a man so utterly at sea: yet even so, poor devil, he didn't forget his invariable little present of cigarettes for D.

Miss Featherstone, who came for tea, thought that there was a touch of madness about him. After the meal she and D foregathered in D's room: Arthur, Cranny and I remained in the dining room and talked a little about spiritualism, but it was all constrained and miserable. He departed at about 6.

Arthur and I walked to Headington, turned right along the Barracks Rd., thence by the Green Lane to the Horsepath Rd., and home via the golf links. We joyously compared an evening walk under these conditions to one which brought us back to our respective fathers . . .

Friday 14 July: A wet morning. Sat in the drawing room and wrote a few stanzas for the IVth Canto of "Dymer". Arthur went out to the Gonners, taking Maureen's violin with him.

It cleared up later and I went into College and saw Farquharson. He gave me some Latin proses and good advice, recommending Rivington's "Class Books" of Latin Unseens for Miss Wiblin. I then went for a short time to the Union and then returned home. Arthur in, Maureen out, for lunch.

Afterwards Arthur and I went up Shotover . . . I took him over the stile to the left to show him the "crab apple" landscape. We then proceeded to the bracken ridge above Horsepath. He had brought sandwiches and milk. I left him to paint and returned for tea – very strong sun by now and a plague of flies.

Found D and Dorothy making jam and joined then in snagging red currants – a beastly job – till tea at five. Did a little more snagging afterwards and read Hingley's *Psychoanalysis*: he seems to belong to a different school from River: it is a better written book . . .

Saturday 15 July: A beautiful morning. After breakfast I foolishly trusted to Arthur's timing, who was characteristically sitting down to the piano when I found we had only 20 min. in which to reach the Parks. We hastened into town and met Veronica – Sylvia Stevenson whom I seem happily fated not to meet had gone up to town. We walked to L.M.H.[3] and there took a canoe. Veronica and I paddled while Arthur made himself comfortable with the cushions.

We first went down as far as Parson's Pleasure, then up again a longish way between pleasant banks and under a fine sky – hard stony blue, veined with white showing through fleet after fleet of puffy clouds, some of them very large. We landed for a few minutes in a field where horses were pulling raking machines over new mown hay. We sat on the hay: there were ticks in it: Arthur tried to draw Veronica.

Embarking again, we continued upstream to the Cherwell Hotel: I was struck with the delightful little formal gardens coming down to the water. Here we had ginger beer through straws – unhappily Arthur considered it humorous to make a bubbling nose and Veronica followed suit, I think from sheer devilment, divining my shudder. She made one good remark – that an educational career is a school of hypocrisy in which you spend your life teaching others observances which you have rejected yourself.

On the return journey we yielded to Arthur's request to paddle, but he always desisted after three strokes until spurred into activity again. His violent and impulsive movements were near to having us over and once gave me a real fright. The river was perfectly empty and we might have been in a lost continent.

On the way back we looked into L.M.H. (which from the gardens is very jolly). I was amused by the stiff little J.C.R. with its irredeemably drawing room air.

Got home at about 2: found jam making still in progress and D

---

[3] Lady Margaret Hall.

looking very tired – for which I cd. willingly have every fruit tree in England burnt down . . .

Arthur told us today how he and all his brothers and sisters were baptised in bathing suits by immersion in the bath of the Bernagh bathroom when he was about 12 – in the presence of a gathering of the faithful.[4] I begin to see that his father is not at all temperamentally devout – goes to theatres when away from home – is religious from a sense of duty only – is cold and sullen by his own nature . . .

Sunday 16 July: . . . I found Miss Wiblin here and we settled to work. First we did grammar: I do not seem to shine in teaching this even where I know it, but I think she is fairly sound. We then went to Unseens for the rest of the morning: she stayed for lunch. D rather poorly these days but I think earlier hours make some difference. Afterwards we discovered that Miss W. had to go somewhere to tea from here and might as well stay. She asked to be allowed to work and I gave her some more Latin till four o'c.

I was rather fagged after my morning and afternoon session – but after Maureen's stupidity, devilment, and amazing faculty for forgetting, it is rather a relief to work with anyone who moves. Arthur went to tea at the Gonners. Later Maureen and I bussed into New College where we met Arthur and went to chapel. I enjoyed the music immensely, especially the psalms and Stanford's *Magnificat*: I wondered why I had never troubled to go before – the last time I was there was with Cherry Robbins in 1917 . . .

Monday 17 July: . . . After lunch Arthur and I set off with baskets of food and thermoi. We found Veronica at L.M.H. who greeted us with the cheerful news that she was bringing "two other females". As we had provided tea for only four, I thought this rather cool. The two parasites turned out to be Miss Wigg (who is recovering from paratyphoid, and anyhow seems a nonentity) and Miss Hugon - a grey faced, broad shouldered, slow spoken Frenchwoman, after the style of Miss Powell at Reading, over educated, affected, vain, flippant and insufferable. Yet she would have impressed me once. She said Masefield "took himself too seriously" this being a form of words applied indifferently to everyone by fools of her type.[5]

Arthur punted us up the river with some success. We had tea under

---

[4] The Greeves family were Plymouth Brethren.

[5] Marianne Cecile Gabrielle Hugon (1881–1952) had been an undergraduate at Somerville College, and in 1923 she became Tutor in French at the Society of Oxford Home-Students (St Anne's College). She was the author of *Social France in the XVII Century* (1911).

the trees opposite the Cherwell Hotel during a shower. We dropped the Hugon woman at the L.M.H. landing stage at five o'clock: then proceeded to a suitable place beside the Parks and tied up. Arthur began painting Veronica, with lavish burlesque criticism and encouragement from us.

All very merry till 7 o'clock when we came home. Getting back, we were surprised to find Baker who had been there since 2 o'clock. He had his viva this morning and swears that he is ploughed. He also gave us a further account of Lilian Bayliss: they sat with their knees touching and agreed to share their joys and sorrows while she addressed him as "dear boy". After she had been talking for some minutes he felt it obligatory to make noises in his throat: after quarter of an hour he laid aside his gloves and took out his handkerchief, pulling up his trousers in momentary expectation that he might have to kneel with her in prayer. He is up here for a fortnight to rehearse and act in a melodrama by Bernice de Bergerac at the House.[6] . . .

Tuesday 18 July: I forgot to call Arthur this morning and going late into his room was privileged to see the pellet of India rubber *in situ* in his hither ear. D and I with some difficulty persuaded him to postpone his departure till tomorrow.

D much better today. Shortly after breakfast Baker arrived: the three of us sat in the drawing room where he read out some of the more absurd passages in the melodrama. Later on we were joined by the Doc, who has been in London. He has spent most of his time at the Coué Institute and had *ça passe* treatment on his rheumatic arm. He said it did stop the pain: but when we asked for how long, he had to admit "for about twenty minutes".[7] This naturally led to a conversation on kindred subjects and in a few minutes the Doc was expounding his philosophy of the primal One and its objectification. My suggestion that people of his ilk really ignored the antithesis of mind and body proved an excellent hare wh. we followed all morning. I thought the Doc confused − but was delighted at his description of solipsism as "that old gag". It was very good talk anyway. We walked out for a short while before lunch.

At 2.30 came Miss Wiblin. I understood that she was to give

---

[6] Bernice de Bergerac's *Glorious England* (1922) was performed in the Priory gardens of Christ Church on 31 July.

[7] Émile Coué (1857–1926), a French chemist, developed a system of psychotherapy by which he claimed that auto-suggestion could be used to cure disease. His formula, which had a wide vogue, was "Every day, in every way, I am becoming better and better".

Maureen a lesson but it appeared that she was to have one from me instead: so we set to our Latin prose until nearly five o'clock, having tea brought to us.

It was now a glorious evening. I walked over to Iffley where I found Arthur with the Doc: Mary was also there, having come from London by a later train. We all walked to Iffley church and admired the Norman tower and arches: while we were inside, the parson – Clarendon, possibly a Ewart connection – came in and said that a service was about to begin: whereupon we all went out shamelessly and sat above the weir on the Lincoln bridge. The Doc gave us a vivid description of his sail 1500 miles up the Amazon. Speaking of the project of exploring central Brazil, Arthur said "That's the sort of thing I'd like to do!!"

We then returned home. Jam making still continued and I helped D to snag currants in the kitchen. Even when this was done, we had a long wait for supper, as the mushroom stew was not quite cooked. Seeing Arthur's misery I could not refrain from remarking on the gluttony which so demoralised my father if a meal were late. Whereupon he replied "Oh but some people do really get sick if they don't have their meals at the regular times. Mother does. *I'm just the same*!" So we gave him bread and butter and he struggled on somehow.

The reference to his mother reminds me of his reply which I forgot to put down the other day. After D had left the breakfast table and while he was still feeding, I ventured to say something about the sucking, squeaking, crunching noises he makes in eating, from which D and I suffer tortures. "I know. Sorry. It's in the family. Mother does it too!" . . .

Wednesday 19 July: Up betimes and a fine morning. Arthur took to his packing and I wrote a storm passage for the beginning of "Dymer" IV. He departed with many and I think true regrets: I accompanied him in his taxi to the station.

Came back and found that jam making had set in with unusual severity. After helping for a little longer I began to be afraid that Baker wd. arrive before we had lunch, and had a cold meal alone. The result was that he did not come till half past two.

We walked up Shotover. Not much serious conversation. He spoke of an American woman whom he had recently met, whose ruling passion for twenty years had been astrology. She had taken his horoscope: tho' ignorant of his circumstances she had said that teaching was not his real job, begged him to go on the stage and prophesied an early success. He would not get fame by writing. He would never have much domestic happiness: and if he married or had an affair before he was thirty, it would cause great trouble. His health would always be bad. We came back here for tea. D and I, after the charm of Barfield, were struck by the unfortunate brusqueness of his manners.

Not long after tea – Baker being gone – the Doc and Mary arrived. I had a few words alone with him: he admitted that he had suffered from what I call Arthur's "mania for confession" . . .

Saturday 22 July: We think that it will never stop raining again. In all morning, working on my dissertation. I was in poor form and seemed to be writing nonsense. Afterwards I read the *Chanson de Roland*. The Doc was here in the morning. After lunch came Baker: he must be royally bored in his digs if he finds us, in our present state, diverting. It is high time we were in Headington. After tea Maureen and I made him play "boy's names" which he did with great gusto – he is certainly improving. Miss Wiblin came in the evening for Latin . . .

Sunday 23 July: Another wet day. After lateish breakfast I settled down in the drawing room and read more than half of *Henry VI*, Part I, at first with great pleasure, but later I grew tired of the too wide field of action, the monotony of the verse and the continual intrusion of merely "public" interests on the real play.

Between this, chatting, sauntering and reading the *Sunday Times*, I got to luncheon. D rather poorly with rheumatism and indigestion – both results of the weather. After lunch I read Bradley's *Appearance and Reality* – the chapter on Reality. It is most difficult: he seems to do the very thing he protests against, namely, pass from the necessary consistency of the Absolute for *thought* to its harmony for *feeling*, using the word "inharmonious" in an ambiguous sense. But probably I do not understand him . . .

At six o'clock came Miss Wiblin and I did Latin with her until supper time. After she was gone, D and I talked. The question is whether Maureen is to leave school and give all her time to music or not: certainly there is no education, musical or otherwise, to be had at Headington . . .

Monday 24 July: . . . At about 2.30 Baker came. He had been at Tetsworth yesterday with the Kennedys, who took him to see Vaughan Williams. As if by arrangement, he was at work on his new symphony when they arrived, and was quite ready to talk of music. He is the largest man Baker has ever seen – Chestertonian both in figure and habits. He eats biscuits all the time while composing. He said that after he had written the first bar on the page of a full score, the rest was all mechanical drudgery and that in every art there was 10% of real "making" to 90% of spadework. He has a beautiful wife who keeps a pet badger – Baker saw it playing both with the dog and the kittens and it licked his hand . . .

Tuesday 25 July: . . . Allchin had been to see D in the morning and the whole question of Maureen's schooling had been discussed, the general result being that she must choose between music and school. The Doc, Baker and I sat like a jury on the sofa while D summed up: by some curious freak the conversation took only two minutes to degenerate in a really preposterous dialogue between Baker and the Doc on the educational merits of Holy Scripture, in which neither got on to the other's line of argument for a moment . . .

Miss Wiblin came as usual after tea. Her exam starts tomorrow and there is no doubt she has knowledge enough for a sporting chance, but with overwork and wind up she has got into a state in which anything may happen.

. . . the school problem was of course left entirely to Maureen: and she definitely decided to leave, tho' doubtless with regrets.

Wednesday 26 July: Fair weather. Went over my books and papers and made a few notes for the viva. Having waited till 11 o'clock did a little more gardening and went in to the Union, where I could not find anything of much use. What I did find was the VIth volume of Havelock Ellis's *Psychology of Sex* which is curious. The most interesting part was quotation expecially from Hindu and Persian books. Apropos of the ignorance of girls he quotes an amazing case of an American girl who was homosexual and was twice married (in disguise) to other women, neither of whom ever realised that she was not a man. Memo to look up Oneida where Plato's Communism seems to have been practised with some success.

Came back for lunch. D very much better, but busy. Baker came shortly after lunch and I persuaded him to accompany me to the show at Headington School. It was a dreadful business. The first item was a Latin play about H. Coccles, including a battle on the stage at which everyone, including the performers, roared with laughter. Who can have been the idiot who allowed them to do this? Next came a kind of fairy play, cheap mysticism from beginning to end, an undigested mass of Shelley, Maeterlinck, Walt Whitman, Trine, Barrie and Algernon Blackwood. I writhed at it. Lastly we had the murder scene from *Macbeth* . . .

Before supper – which was very late on account of D's work – I nailed up the peeling paper in various parts of the house. In the evening wrote to P, whose letter arrived this morning with an enclosure of £30.

Thursday 27 July: Did some work after breakfast, but with incredible reluctance. A lovely morning and I have seven devils in me. Baker came at about 10.30. He is now thoroughly depressed about *Glorious England* of which he showed us an absurd bill in the most ignorant attempt at mediaeval English, with "ye" for "the" and other tomfoolery. He is also worried by the girl who plays daughter to him and who has to "cling passionately" to his dead body: she is so shy that she is afraid to come near his face - the result being that she clings to his waist with embarrassing effect.

We walked to Headington by the cemetery and sat on a stone wall. The sun was intensely strong. We talked of group marriage as a remedy for monogamy. I pleaded that it was better than prostitution and a thousand times better than [an] *affaire de coeur*, but he didn't think much of it.

He said very truly of Mrs Hinckley that the only thing about her was her sincerity: she said things that ought to make you writhe but in a way that made them all right. They had talked of the school, and to Baker's onslaught she had replied "Don't you think that Mrs Moore is rather prejudiced?": to which absurdity Baker replied "Yes, she is. But what's the origin of the prejudice?" I'm afraid my opinion of Mrs Hinckley sinks steadily . . .

Friday 28 July: Heaven, to do it justice, granted me my prayer. Up betimes in white tie and "subfusc" and in to my viva. We all presented ourselves (I knew none of the others) at 9.30. Myers, looking his most piratical, called over our names and read out the times at which we were to come, but not in alphabetical order.[8] Two others and myself were told to stay and I was immediately called out, thus being the first victim of the day.

My operator was Joseph.[9] He was very civil and made every effort

---

[8] John Linton Myers (1869-1954) of New College was Wykeham Professor of Ancient History 1910-39, and Examiner in Final Classical School 1920-23.

[9] Horace William Brindley Joseph (1867-1943) was the Senior Philosophical Tutor of New College 1895-1932.

to be agreeable. He asked what I meant by the contradiction of the pleonexia, why I applied the word "disgusting" to my quotation from Pater, how I wd. distinguish a schoolmaster's from a state's right to punish, and if I cd. suggest any way of making "poor old Plato" less ridiculous than he appeared in my account, of "the lie in the Soul'. I showed some forgetfulness of the text in answering this, but I don't think it was serious. The whole show took about 5 minutes. From the phrase "poor old Plato" I fancy Joseph must have been Carritt's informant (v. June 21st) . . .

Saturday 29 July: . . . Baker came again after lunch and I sat with him in the garden. We talked of reincarnation. He now thinks that most of his youthful "reincarnation experiences" and visions were fancy, with three exceptions which he still regards as objective. He thought his faculty of seeing the aura had been merely a hallucination accompanying (by way of bluff) a real intuition of character. I remarked that his sketches of character tended to caricature, that he had a faculty for getting the worst out of people. He admitted that he had a tendency to exaggerate. We came indoors and had tea. Conversation turned to international politics, and this meant a rather perilous argument between D and Baker – dogmatisms on both sides and no hope of an issue.

. . . D being far from well, already overworked, and a move hanging over us, it has seemed to her a suitable moment to make gooseberry jam. Maureen and I picked all the ripe ones. After that I sat on the steps with D and read Hamilton's book. It was swelteringly hot. Supper very late.

Sunday 30 July: Up rather late to find D already dressed, breakfasted, and at work. After my own breakfast I repaired to the drawing room and started re-writing Canto IV of "Dymer", with which I am finding great difficulties.

Presently came Baker in a state of great indignation at having an extra performance put on tomorrow evening. I walked with him up Shotover – a fine cool morning. We sat on a stile above the descent to Quarry, talking about the probable symbolism of Maureen in a dream of his, about "*anima*" in general, and later about "Dymer".

Came home to lunch here. Baker and Maureen played duets afterwards. He stayed till about quarter to four and I must confess I was glad when he went. There are of friends, very few, whose visits if daily repeated, do not pall in a week. It is quite different if even the same friends are stopping in the house: there a sort of *modus vivendi* is established: they are digested and assimilated . . .

D was a good deal better today, tho' still far from well. In discussing Baker and boredom we decided that the great trouble was his lack of "chat". Humour of the best kind, uproarious farce, he has: serious discussion he has: but mere chat you can't get from him.

We are all surprised at hearing no news from Mlle Cahen and begin to wonder if she has taken fright.

Monday 31 July: . . . At 2.30 Miss Wiblin came: Maureen and I had decided to bike despite the weather, as if we bussed Miss W. would leave her bike here: if she left it, she would call for it afterwards: if she did that, she would stay till midnight.

Luckily it cleared up and was a glorious blue and white sky when the three of us reached Christ Church. We waited at the steps outside hall till Baker appeared, dressed but not made up, and led us through Dr Locke's door into the Priory gardens where the show was to be. A long wait was worth the free seats we thus obtained, and pleasant too for the extreme beauty of the garden. Baker had warned me that *Glorious England* was bad: he had not overstated it. The dialogue was contemptible, the fable childish, and all continually interrupted by interminable bad dances, ill danced to wretched music. The high wind often carried away the voices of the actors: in fact this and the *Antigone* have convinced me that outdoor theatricals in this country are a mistake. Some of the performers were professionals, but they were all bad. Baker was in a different sphere. His part was the crudest melodrama. (Ha! The mann must die-ie etc.!) But it was surprising how well he carried it off. The part of Saracen villain had a certain grotesque suitability.

As soon as we had got out we hastened to College where our bikes were left. I then found the History lists up and returned, as arranged, to tell Baker his fate . . . As he had expected to be ploughed he was delighted to hear that he had taken a third. I was introduced to Mlle de Bergerac – she looked a fit authoress for such tripe as *Glorious England* . . .

Lewis and Mrs Moore were offered the chance to live free of charge in "Hillsboro", 14 Holyoake Road, Headington, during the period 1 August-4 September. The property was owned by Mr Raymond, who planned to be away part of this time. They sub-let 28 Warneford Road to Mr and Mrs Rodney Pasley during part of August, and Lewis and Mrs Moore economised further by taking in a Paying Guest – Mlle Andrée Cahen, from Paris.

Tuesday 1 August: . . . Up betimes and to our packing. Hard at it all morning and afternoon, everyone busy, but all in good form. A letter from [Mlle] Cahen by second post: she is to arrive on Thursday and we shall know her by her "brown costume and brown hat with coloured ribbon round it" . . .

We were in great confusion through not knowing when the Pasleys would turn up until a wire came fixing their arrival for 6 . . . I went to buy some things in Cowley Rd. Coming back I found Pasley and his wife already here and talking to D in the kitchen while they unloaded their kitten from a basket. Pasley was plump and in good form. D and I remarked afterwards how old the girl looks, though she is really his junior. I think she is a decent sort.

It began to rain just as our taxi arrived. Maureen and I biked as D and the luggage completely filled the car. Tibbie in her basket was forgotten and this delayed D so that we arrived here as soon as she did. A busy evening settling in. A well earned supper at 8.30 after which Miss Wiblin and I washed up – Dorothy, who is to sleep in while we are here, having a headache and being dead beat. All of us pretty tired but I think D is none the worse. I am very favourably impressed with the house and the nice little garden: but the gas is poor and there are no good books.

Wednesday 2 August: I was wakened at 2 o'c by noises and getting up found that D's bed and herself had been soaked, as I seem – for the first time in my life – not to have screwed up her hot water bottle securely. I only hope that there will be no ill results. Later I dreamed that I had got a 2nd.

Immediately after breakfast I bussed into College and called on Farquharson. Apparently I am not too late to take my B.A. on Saturday. He kept me a long time, talking about the edition of Cooke Wilson's various writings which he is bringing out. He also discussed exams and kept saying that everyone knew my abilities and would not change their opinions if I happened to get a second. From a don, such talk has its uncomfortable side – I hope there is nothing behind it more than his general desire of flattery.

I then returned and took my share of getting things straight. Miss Wiblin came and helped. This house is full of unnecessary ornaments in the sitting rooms: beyond them, in the kitchen etc., we found a state of indescribable filth: bottles of cheap champagne in the cellar. Trash for the drawing room, dirt for the kitchen, second rate luxury for the table – an epitome of a "decent English household".

After lunch a note came from Mrs Stevenson asking us to entertain her French boy for the afternoon as all her people were going out. This is impertinence: if she is taking money for him, why can she not play fair? Answer, because she is a spiritualist, an idealist, an enthusiast, a new thought-ist, not of the common clay.

The boy was quite nice. I went with him to watch Miss W. ("Smudge" as we have christened her), Mary, Maureen, and Helen Rowell playing tennis on the school court. He knows very little English.

All back for tea here. Afterwards the others returned to their tennis while D and I had a little peace – dog tired by now. Supper at about 8.15. We are greatly afraid that Dorothy may be geting ill as she has a bad headache and dissolved into tears on misunderstanding a most innocent remark of mine. Heaven help us if she does.

We were just preparing to go to bed when three figures and one suitcase appeared at the hall door. We held our breath. It turned out to be the Pasleys and Mlle Cahen who had arrived a day before we expected her and gone to Warneford Rd. She had eaten nothing since 1 o'c., so it was all hands on deck again to feed her. When we cast our net we little thought that we should catch such odd fish. She is a Jewess, very striking in appearance, speaking the best English I have ever heard from a foreigner. She is going to "translate for the lawcourts" as soon as she has got her degree. One of her sisters is a Doctor, the other an engineer. She *may* be 18 as she says: has the self assurance of 50. D and I agree that we should be sorry to pit our wits against this young woman. Altogether a formidable and stimulating if somewhat unlovable character . . .

Thursday 3 August: Up betimes and a fair morning. At her request I went with Andrée into town and showed her the sights. I liked her better than on the previous evening. We talked of various things, largely of books. She told me – as I had always suspected - that French people could get no music out of Latin verse. We returned for a late-ish lunch.

The Pasleys came shortly afterward. I had a good deal of talk with Johnnie. It was tiring to shout, but she seemed alright – an oldish face and lined, though she is supposed to be younger than Pasley.

After tea I hastened into town and met Warnie at the Roebuck; dined with him at Buols with a bottle of Heidsieck. He has certainly grown enormously fat. He was in excellent form. I mooted the proposal of his coming out here: he did not seem inclined to take it up. I left my diary to read to put him en rapport with the life.

Friday 4 August: Bussed into town with Andrée and left her at Carfax. I then met W and we strolled to the Schools to see if my lists would be out in the evening. It gave me rather a shock to find them already up. I had a first: Wyllie a second: everyone else from College a third. The whole thing was rather too sudden to be as pleasant as it sounds on paper. I wired at once to P and went to lunch with W at Buols.

During the meal I thought I had arranged for him to come and meet the family at tea: but quite suddenly while sitting in the garden of the Union he changed his mind and refused pertinaciously either to come to tea or to consider staying with us. I therefore came back to tea alone. The Pasleys were here and Smudge. An amusing game of croquet followed after which I returned to W, and dined. He was now totally changed. He introduced the idea of coming to stay off his own bat and promised to come out tomorrow. Late home and straight to bed.

Saturday 5 August: Went to College after breakfast and saw Poynton about money matters. Found to my surprise and delight that after paying all fees I had a balance in my favour – but I shall not see it until September . . .

I then bussed out to Headington, changed rapidly into white tie and subfusc suit, and returned to lunch with W at Buols. At 2 o'clock I assembled with the others at Univ. porch to be taken under Farquharson's wing for degrees. A long and very ridiculous ceremony making us B.A.s – as Watling said, we felt no different beyond being "hot and bothered".

I met W again at the Roebuck and came up here. Everyone present for tea and got on well. Maureen formulated her first impressions of W. epigramatically by saying "he looks as if he were a good swimmer." Back to town for dinner.

Sunday 6 August: We had arranged to go on the river today but it rained. W came out with his luggage. Bridge in the afternoon. A wet night.

Tuesday 8 August: Owing to rush of events and having lent my diary to W., regular entry has become all but impossible. Yesterday was chiefly remarkable for the behavior of Smudge, whose condition is a cause of uneasiness to both D and me. It is strange that such a thing should have happened to me – of all people least desirous, least able to cope with such a situation. But I hope it is chiefly nerves. I also had tea with the Stevensons.

Today, despite a morning that opened with teeming rain, W and I proceeded to carry out a long treasured project of visiting Watford.[1] We started by bus and it was fine before we reached the station. Caught the 11.30 for Bletchley . . .

Reaching Bletchley we found that the 1.30, by which we had hoped to go on, was not running. We had an excellent lunch at the station and caught the 2.40, arriving pretty late at Watford. With curious sensations, oppressive but by contrast delicious, we went up to Wynyard. it is now called Northfield and is a girls' school. An absurd woman showed us round – pointing out improvements and telling us that the house looked "prettier in the front"!!

Vindictive memories and Christina dreams of hate were brought before my mind. We both remarked how absolutely right the school boy is in his envy of "grown ups". It was a hot day. Same old flinty roads, same old dusty town. We had tea in the garden of a hotel near the station and caught the 6.9 back.

Changed at Bletchley where we had a sandwich and a whiskey and soda. A pleasant return journey in evening sunlight through country which I like for our jolly stay at Crendon last year. We had supper at Buols. Here I had an interesting talk with W, but I don't know how much he weighed his words. He said he supposed he wd. grow

[1] Their intention was to visit Wynyard School, which both had attended and hated about equally. Their story is told in the chapter entitled "Concentration Camp" in Lewis's *Surprised by Joy*.

up some day. Then home by bus in glorious moonlight.

The others met us at the terminus where they were seeing Smudge off – who, says D, has been much better today. Letters of congratulation from the Ainley-Walkers, Carritt, Lionel Lord, Stevenson and Benecke. Carritt says I got A = for all the Philosophy papers, Aß for ancient history, ß = for the other histories, and ß = for classics, which is a shock. He also recalls Stock's dictum that "I am not a real philosopher, but quite brilliant". As consolation for all this, Stevenson tells me that I am one of the very few firsts who didn't get a serious viva.

Wednesday 9 August: . . . We were rather late for lunch at which Smudge was present. Afterwards I had intended to do a little work, but was beguiled into playing with W at pingpong which we continued very strenuously till tea time. Then came the Pasleys and Helen Munro. Pasley gave me a very poor account of the lectures for teachers which he is attending. They talk to them like babies and it must give strangers an odd impression of Oxford.

The rain, wh. had been heavy all afternoon, had now cleared and while I washed up the others played croquet. I managed a little reading of Bradley, alone in the drawing room with D, and then played myself. During the game I amused Helen and Maureen by surreptitiously clipping nearly all the clothes pegs on to the tail of W's coat . . .

Thursday 10 August: . . . At about 2 o'c. Smudge, Andrée, W, and I set out with tea baskets etc. and proceeded to Magdalen Bridge. In spite of Smudge's advice I insisted on taking a canoe, which was very foolish of me. For four of us it was too cramped and the state of the river after the recent rains made it rather dangerous. At the rollers[2] the landing stage was completely under water and in many places the current defied my poor skill in steering. I paddled alone all the time with occasional emergency help from Smudge. W. in the bow, wedged tightly into a small space with legs apart and a flybutton showing, dressed in a suit of P's, was rather a funny sight. It was a beautiful afternoon. We landed in a meadow on the left bank just above the Parks, and had tea in the hay. Plenty of ragging. Back to Magdalen bridge about seven, where the man said he was very glad to see us again!

---

[2] A weir divides the upper Cherwell from the lower: near it there is an inclined concrete ramp, furnished with steel rollers, by which device punts and canoes can be landed and hauled up to the upper river. – W.H.L.

The girls went home: W and I to College to look for post, thence to drink in the yard of the Mitre. Here he urged me definitely to say whether I would be home in September and I said probably not. This resulted in a complete cessation of talk.

Just before mounting our bus I met Beckett and agreed to lunch with him tomorrow. Home for supper and Smudge played for us. D in rather poor form. I am a little sick of our present life and specially of the work it makes for her and the total lack of privacy. Oh for a day alone.

Friday-Monday 11-14 August: These days I can hardly manage my diary. After we had gone to bed on Thursday W continued to sulk and presently announced his intention of returning home next Monday. Wishing to keep things on a friendly basis I made some conventional question of "why", to which he replied at once, "Oh, I can bore myself for nothing at home." I am now convinced that this was mere temper and not seriously to be resented from one who habitually lives (with me) in a thoroughly schoolboy atmosphere. At the time, though I only answered "that's true", it delivered me up to the usual circle of foolish and angry anti-Christinas.

In the morning discussion was renewed. He continued to sulk and I was so disgusted at this childish sort of compulsion that I was tempted to reject all thought of going home. His argument that I had to go sooner or later and that it was a pity not to acquire merit by being there when his presence made it easier, seemed to carry some weight. Besides conscience was pricking me on P's account.

I talked it over with D and walked into town with W, through Mesopotamia after breakfast, when I told him I would do as he wished. I also said that he must be quite clear that I had not given way because of his fit of temper and that that line would not work again. He affected not to understand . . .

I lunched with Beckett in All Souls. He advised me to try for a fellowship there. We fed in the buttery with a man called Lawrence (formerly of Jesus)[3] and an older one whose name I did not catch. Both were most interesting and agreeable. We drank beer bottled in the 19th century: it is clear red, tastes and smells like toffee, and is very strong . . .

On Sunday we played a good deal of croquet. I amused Andrée

---

[3] Thomas Edward Lawrence (1888–1935) – Lawrence of Arabia. He took a BA from Jesus College in 1910 and was made a Fellow of All Souls College in 1919.

with my attempt to translate the opening of *Aeneid* II into French alexandrines. In the evening we tried to go to the Cowley Fathers to hear plainsong,[4] but got landed instead in the Catholic Church where we were royally bored and where the priest (possibly the Father Burdett S.J. whose name appeared on the door of the confessional) was about the nastiest little man I have ever seen. However, I was glad on the whole, for I have never been to a Mass before, and some of the singing was good.

On Monday we went on the river – Smudge, Andrée, Maureen, W and I in a punt. A good day on the whole, tho' Maureen was rather a nuisance. No doubt it is good for W to be teased by her, but it is very bad for her to learn this sort of licensed buffoonery. A great rag in the garden after supper. W got from the Union a book on *Social France in the XVII Century* by Cécile Hugon, who appears to be the woman I met on July 17th.

All these days D has been in good form whenever I have had a moment with her, and everything goes well. Smudge is much better. Andrée in great form, W seems to get on well . . .

Tuesday 15 August: A fine day. W went into town in the morning and I settled to work on my dissertation, continuing till lunch time and making fair head way . . .

During the afternoon I went to D's room to find a box of matches and ran into her sitting with Maisie Hawes who was in tears. D told me the whole story afterwards and it is just what one would have expected from that foul hag Mrs Hawes. Maisie had always been badly treated – usual Cinderella story – did all the work – cursed and struck in the face – taken away from school – forbidden dancing at which she has real talent and told she must take up nursing which she loathes. Last year they told her she was not their child, but the illegitimate child of her sister. Characteristically they told the other children too. Since then things have become worse. Even the children throw their boots at her, she is constantly hit and is not allowed a single penny of her own. What she dreads most of all is the return next month of Commander Hawes, that gallant officer: when he is at home she is literally imprisoned in the house.

The thing is so bad that other people have noticed it and occasionally ticked the children off for their behaviour to Maisie. On

[4] A colloquial name for the priests of St. John the Evangelist, an Anglican monastic order founded in the parish of Cowley, Oxford. They have since moved to London, but after he became a Christian this was where Lewis went for confession.

these occasions the little dears go to their mother and say that Maisie has been "making mischief": then she gets hell from the old woman and physical violence. She also said that both Mrs H. and the Commander "gushed over" her in public. A sickening story.

D and I racked our brains to think of anything we could do. Unfortunately it seems not quite bad enough for effective police interference and anything short of that only makes matters worse. As the Hawes know nobody there is no possibility of influencing them by public opinion, and the wretched Maisie has sworn us to secrecy . . .

Wednesday 16 August: In the morning I accompanied W into town in order to return some books to the Union, walking in through Mesopotamia. We spent a pleasant morning, chancing on an unusual number of celebrated curiosities in the bookshop windows and finishing up with beer in the courtyard of the Mitre.

Home to a very late lunch. While we were still at the table the Pasleys appeared and delayed us for some time before the whole lot set out to tennis. W and I of course remained, and played pingpong till tea time . . . Thence to the nameless pub in Old Headington to drink beer in the back room.

On returning we found the others ministering to Smudge, who had collapsed during tennis. She proved a most intractable patient and insisted on walking upstairs: D thinks it was no real faint, but hysteria and I am afraid the analytic explanation is sufficiently obvious.

At supper D told the story of Frank and our brush with the Ludgershall doctor in 1918, which amused W hugely. I went with him after supper to buy rum and D made Smudge an egg flip. It now became necessary for someone to take her home, and W very decently offered to bear me company. We accordingly bussed to Summertown, a pleasant enough drive through the twilight. We had to run to catch the return bus after seeing Smudge to her house and thus avoided a terrible route march home . . .

I forgot to say that Maisie was here to tea, escaped under pretence of going somewhere else. Plain of face, she has an admirable figure: seems honest, cheerful, intelligent and has so small a touch of vulgar accent that one wonders how that witches cave of a home has not affected her more. We all liked her: she played tennis with the others after tea. As soon as I can have a talk with her I am to write to Barfield about any opening in dancing, as she has been trained by some famous woman whose name I cannot catch.

Thursday 17 August: . . . As soon as our late lunch was over I took the bus, having been asked to tea with the Carritts. A beautiful afternoon. Bussed to Carfax and thence to Abingdon Turn, arriving at Heath Barrows at 4.15. Tennis was in progress. I was introduced to Basil Murray of New College, who seems a clever fellow. Carritt promised to criticise my dissertation if I sent it to him. Murray teased him with questions about symbolic logic and the relations of mathematics and philosophy. Carritt frankly had no opinion of their supposed connection. He mentioned a lecture which he had heard in which the point was that because you had no really accurate measuring rod, therefore things equal to the same thing were not equal to one another, which was childish. After tea tennis set in again, so I departed, making W my excuse and walked to Carfax through S. Hinksey with great enjoyment.

Arrived home to find the others fresh from bridge with Mrs Stevenson. Andrée, Maureen, W and I played croquet till supper time: afterwards Andrée and I had very poor luck at bridge against D and W. Earlyish to bed. D in good form – my own neuralgia nearly gone.

Friday 18 August: W and I bussed into Oxford after a late breakfast and he went to have his hair cut. After our usual beer drinking at the Mitre we went to All Souls. Beckett was not in his rooms – or rather in those of Sir John Simon, which he uses – but by good luck we met a porter who led us to the Codrington Library. We were both much impressed with the room, where we'd never been before. Beckett was dug out of one of the smaller rooms. I introduced him to W and he promised to come out to lunch.

After a drink at the Roebuck we two came home and Beckett arrived shortly afterwards. Everyone seemed favourably impressed by him. I found to my surprise that he is twenty six years old. During lunch we talked of the legal status of men and women: Beckett said there were actually more injustices in the woman's favour than in the man's. I find that that cheery old boy I met on the 12th of August was Zulueta, the Professor of Roman Law and the son of the ex-Spanish Ambassador.[5] D remarked afterwards that a close friendship between Baker and Beckett was not what one would have expected.

After lunch I worked on my dissertation and started recopying it.

[5] Francis de Zulueta (1878–1958), an academic lawyer, was All Souls reader in Roman Law 1912–17, and Regius Professor of Civil Law 1919–48.

I find that the second draft will be very different from the first and I am not sure that I have even broken the back of the job.

Both the Pasleys were here for tea. They, Smudge and I (afterwards joined by W) played pingpong and I was badly beaten by everyone. After supper D, Andrée, W and I played bridge – in which I was equally unsuccessful. Smudge started home on her bicycle at about 10, but returned in a few minutes, very much rattled as she had been followed by a Headington rough. W and I accordingly turned out (it was now raining) and walked with her to the White Horse . . .

Forgot to mention our argument during supper in which D and W maintained that education was a cause of unhappiness and that the labourers of the early 19th century, with all their miseries, were happier than those of the present day. I of course took the opposite view.

Saturday 19 August: A fine morning. Into town with W through Mesopotamia, as has become customary, after breakfast. Found an extraordinarily cheap pipe for 2/6d which I got – it seems to be a success.

As we were returning by bus, we fell to talk of our father. W said that in spite of the old rows, despotisms and absurdities of our childhood, P could have made a friend of him in the last five years if he had had any serious will to do so, and had not consistently sneered at his profession. I thought the same was true of me: quite recently it was still possible for a slight effort on P's part to remove the barriers, but that effort had not been made and the cleavage – moral, intellectual and of habit – is permanently fixed . . .

Supper late: everyone in great spirits. Afterwards Maisie danced to us. In so small a room one cannot get a picture of the whole body, and of course the effort is much too visible. She seemed good to me but I know nothing of dancing.

It was now a lovely pitchblack night, and I suggested hide and seek in the garden: this looked like developing into a good rag, but Smudge had to go and she was in such a state of nerves that I accompanied her to the top of Headington Hill. She was in poor form – shell shock I call it. Her father died heavily in debt and as the others were too young, she has had everything to do for six years. I am afraid something is going to snap if the strain goes on much longer.

I came back to find that W had seen Maisie home and he had

returned in semi-comic dudgeon after having blundered over all the ditches of Highfield in the dark . . .

Sunday 20 August: I spent the morning at work on my dissertation and made some progress. Shortly before lunch I walked out with W. to our usual pub, where we sat in an unusual room – same where I sat with Pasley discussing marriage two years ago – and drank cider. W said it had not the tang of the Worcester cider, and I think he was right. After lunch I played croquet with him - absolutely off my game, could hit nothing.

I then changed and cycled to Warneford Rd. Mrs P told me that Pasley had just left and I overtook him (on foot) this side of college. We then went together to call on the Mugger. We found his wife in the garden and were soon joined by himself. We talked of Hutchinson's novels. The Mugger said the style suggested an effort to out-herod Carlyle.

The maid then appeared from the house, trying to keep ahead of a couple of visitors: the woman however outstripped (her) and arrived a short head in time to announce herself. "I'm Dr Meade and this is my husband." They were Americans. Pasley says the man had gold links in his right cuff and silver in his left, but I did not notice it myself. He opened the conversation by saying "Our town is just the other side of Connecticut" and described it at some length. He then asked the Mugger "Can you tell me what are the functions of a Master of a College in this University?" The Mugger replied "Hm – hm – rather hard to explain – hm – hm – looks after the administration and the – er – administration of finance – tho' to be sure the Bursar looks after that.– hm." He also told the Mugger that many of the MS in the Bodleian were irreplaceable! Dr Meade enquired of Pasley and me "What are you two young men doing here at this time of year?"

When we left, the Mugger affectionately armed me to the door and asked me about my plans. He said they wd. be very pleased to see me again if I wanted to stay up another year. Pasley accompanied me along the Iffley Rd. talking about his chances of an All Souls Fellowship.

We met Andrée, Smudge, and W outside Cowley St John: Pasley departed and the rest of us went in. Quite an interesting show: plainsong seemed to me curious rather than beautiful, but in parts it had a faint charm.

From here I went to Warneford Rd. to have supper with the

Pasleys. In spite of all prepossessions in her favour, I have not succeeded in liking "Johnnie". She seems empty, plain, and a little bit common: but it is true that I found my evening less unpleasant than I had feared.

Pasley seems still happy and that is the great thing. He talked about history – also about immortality – usual negatively hopeful attitude that you couldn't *dis*prove. He told me the idea of a play he hoped to write, turning on the progress of toleration which was reaching such a point that since every opinion "had much to be said for it" no single opinion could be held at all. I said he was the extreme example himself: for his play would preach toleration of intolerance . . .

Monday 21 August: Despite all my efforts we have slipped into late hours again and, finding the Headington air sleepy on its own account, come always to breakfast in a kind of coma . . .

Andrée, W. and I went into town after breakfast, only to find the library already shut and no order about return of books . . . We then went to [University College] chapel where I showed them the Dutch windows and held a crowd at bay while W took a photo. We then went to Merton and saw the library and chapel where I have never been before: afterwards to the House to see the pictures. We went to the courtyard of the Mitre where W and I drank beer while Andrée put away a cocktail in the manner born.

. . . Supper in fairly good time after which Andrée and W went to the Stevensons to play bridge. Left alone, we fell to talking of W. D said he was nice and "just missed being very nice indeed" but one couldn't tell how. I said probably because you felt that he had no need for you. She admired his slow, whimsical way of talking, which was attractive and which one found oneself unconsciously imitating . . . Later in the evening I had a conversation with D, memorable both for its exceedingly tortuous course, and for its content which certainly was an eye opener.

Tuesday 22 August: When I woke up I felt that the events of the previous night had happened in a dream. Smudge was here at breakfast time: we were all relieved to hear that she had an invitation to spend a few days at Brill. I eagerly advised her to accept this . . .

After lunch I worked on my dissertation till tea time, having first washed up whatever of the lunch things were left by Dorothy and Ivy, and laid as much of the tea things as I could.

After tea Maureen, W and I bussed in to the station to meet Daisy

Perrott – silly woman – and to look for the cake which is supposed to be on its way from Little Lea. After Daisy's arrival W and I dawdled behind, looked for the cake in both stations, and finally came on to the Mitre. W asked me about Daisy: I restrained a desire to pour out the vials of my dislike and described her merely as a dud. "The Dud" she has accordingly become in our conversation.[6]

Home and to supper, after which Maisie danced to us. This poor girl wins golden opinions on all sides. Tomorrow there is talk of her being taken to London by the bitch she calls mother, I don't know with what devil's purpose of forcing her into nursing or worse, against her will. Perhaps we shall not see her again.

Smudge behaved very strangely. W and I played bridge against Andrée and D. Daisy's meaningless face overhung the game and D had to keep up an intermittent conversation with her wh. led to a mistake and lost them the rubber. I had a few minutes alone with D. She thinks I have gone to the other extreme today and been almost rude to Smudge. She is doubtless right, but I hardly know whether I am on my head or my heels and heartily wish Smudge out of the house, tho' to be sure I am still heartily sorry for her.

Wednesday 23 August: . . . After tea, as Andrée looked restive, I suggested a walk. She and Smudge accompanied me up the fieldpath through what used to be "The Red Land". Rather a rum conversation on Paramnesia (Andrée, who introduced the subject, calls it "fausse reminiscence"), were-wolves, damnation and decapitation.

I had just gone up to my room after our return when Smudge knocked at the door. She had come to apologise for going for a walk: she had thought we were all coming and wouldn't have come if she had known it was Andrée and me – we could have had a much better walk without her – etc., etc. Little ass! On the spur of the moment I said "Oh rot! – it's so much easier to keep up a conversation between three people than between two": realised afterwards what an admirable and pregnant reply I had made . . .

Thursday 24 August: A tolerable morning. Daisy and Andrée decided to go into town and W. and I went also, but independently . . .

On coming home we found Smudge starting an early lunch in order to be ready for her departure for Brill. It was at this juncture that an adventure happened: D – the only witness – described its first reel. She saw a figure at the door whom she took for an unusually

---

[6] Daisy Perrott was Maureen's godmother.

ugly errand boy. Just as she was going to ask him his business, Andrée appeared at the head of the stairs, paused a minute, then rushed forwards crying "A-A-Aah! Gerges. C'est tu!"

It was her cousin – Georges Sée – and D asked him to lunch . . . A more repulsive looking dago I have never set eyes on. He and Andrée left us immediately after lunch and Maisie appeared. The plot now began to unfold. Andrée it appeared had spoken to D about "rooms" and later, by imperceptible change, about "a room" for the . . . boy, and it had gradually become apparent that she was proposing to feed her curio at our table. Of payment, there had of course been no suggestion. I can hardly describe the state of horror into which this threw every single member of the household: but as the thing had been assumed by Andrée and not requested, as the monster had been slipped into our midst with admirable coolness – we had no notion how to proceed . . . .

We were then joined by D and W and another feverish council of war took place. D was for sticking it till Monday when Mrs Raymond's return would make a natural excuse to eject him. The rest of us were agreed in urging early and forcible action, but no one could decide on a feasible plan . . .

We now concluded that D must speak plainly to Andrée when she returned. W. and I then went to our pub to drink large whiskies. W had a headache. We came back and continued our croquet until Maureen rushed out to tell me that Andrée was come.

Going in, I found her with D in the kitchen. D asked her if she had found rooms for her cousin. Andrée said she had heard of something in Windmill Rd. "But can they do for him there?" "Do for him? What do you mean?" "I mean can they feed him?" "Aah! But can you not do that?" D explained as politely as possible that this was out of the question. Andrée gave way at once. Her face was rather an odd colour and rather an odd shape. To be frank, she did not strike me as one who had made an embarrassing blunder by accident. I thought she knew – and knew that we knew – and that *we* knew that she knew – that she had attempted a monstrous imposition and failed . . .

Pasley had returned "Dymer" with some interesting criticisms. He likes Canto II the best: disapproves of "C.C.S." as "inexcusable modernism": objects to "the intrusion of allegory" in III (what *is* the allegory?) and concludes "Go on and prosper but use the knife freely." In bed about 12.

Friday 25 August: ... W and I then went into town to make our arrangements about tomorrow's travelling, paid a farewell visit to the Mitre and returned home. Andrée returned soon afterwards without Mr Sée, which relieved us from any fear her morning's conversation had caused. Maisie Hawes came after lunch. She and I played croquet against W and Andrée, leading for the first half of the game: then my aim went to pieces and we were beaten. D and Maureen went out after tea ...

Both the Pasleys came to supper. He showed me a cartoon which he had drawn to represent the adventure of yesterday. The drawing may not be academic, but it is an amusing relic. After supper we had a great rag playing "French and English" on the lawn: the clothes line was used to divide the grounds. D tells me we could be heard all over Headington. W and I had not taken such violent exercise since Lord-knows-when.

Saturday 26 August: ... W. and I did most of our packing before breakfast. We were delayed for a few minutes to have a photo taken by Maureen, and then departed, carrying his tin trunk between us. His visit here has been a great pleasure to me – a great advance too towards connecting up my real life with all that is pleasantest in my Irish life. Fortunately everyone liked him and I think he liked them. We found that we were running it very close for my 10.50 so I had to jump for the station bus and leave him to manipulate his box alone.

I arrived just as the train was ready to go and got put in a 1st Class compt. alone in which I travelled to London in great comfort. Baker met me at Paddington and took me (via tube to Baker St.) to lunch at Karraways where, he said, "The Baker millions are made". Here we met another of his aunts: the one I met at Aclands has conjunctivitis. Baker was pale and not very well, but I was delighted to see him.

From here we went to the Haymarket to see A.A. Milne's *The Dover Road*. Tho' it collapses in the third act, this is one of the most amusing things I have ever seen. Henry Ainley (as Latimer) was not very good, except in his brief authoritative speeches. In the long ones he adopted a strange parsonical monotone which (Baker said) must be "for a purpose" but was very bad. John Deverill (as "Nicholas") pleased me best.

Back to Karraway's for tea and thence out to 9 Staverton Rd. Here we met Baker's third Aunt, the most interesting of the three, tho' all are kindly and sensible women. After supper they sang old English carols – a new kind of music to me, and very unlike what is usually called a carol. At the time I thought I would give all the great composers for a budget like these. A most enjoyable day. Early to bed after some chat with Baker in his room.

Sunday 27 August: I walked with Baker in the morning through suburban avenues and parks, finally through mean streets. As I remarked "London is very like Belfast", he replied "Of course it is." As we went on I told him about Maisie Hawes. I said something must be done quickly as the Commander was coming next week and then it appeared they would try to rush her into a nursing home. On the other hand everything hinged on the legal position. If her "parents" really had power to bring her back, it would be no good finding her a job . . .

Back for lunch. Afterwards he and I were left alone with his sensible aunt and the question of Maisie was raised again. She was positive that at 19 a girl could not be forced to live with her parents if she could support herself. I then retired to my own room to write up arrears of diary.

After tea they sang carols again, to my great delight: in the evening he gave us what he called an "orgy" on his gramophone. I heard the Kreutzer Sonata for the first time: also the death scene from Mussorgsky's *Boris Godunov* sung by Chaliapin. I am beginning to get a solid impression of this household. The aunt whom we saw at Oxford is an unbearable woman. It is she who usually manages Karraway's: during her illness this is being done by Aunt No. 2 – a plain, sensible, but dull creature. Both are religious. The third is very different: more common in face and voice than her sisters, she has humour and humanity. She runs a club for young girls on the stage and works on the medical board of a district. She alone approves of Baker's going on the stage.

Baker – the mightly Baker – is lamb-like in his own house and bears the nagging of his eldest Aunt with a patience which I cannot too much admire. He even goes to church with her, tho' he has now quite passed the religious phase. Yet he tells me he had an altar in his bedroom two years ago!

I laughingly reminded him of the part he had played in our arguments in 1919 and of his prophecy that my chimney stack would turn into a spire . . .

Monday 28 August: A muggy, thunderous day. Shortly after breakfast

I went with Baker to the Old Vic where he begins his job today. When we emerged from Waterloo I remembered for the first time that I had been to hear *Carmen* (very bad) at the Old Vic years before on my way to Bookham. He was naturally rather rattled: as he said "In any profession the first day is hell." Saw him disappear through the door and walked back over Waterloo Bridge . . .

I took the desperate resolve of entering the National Gallery, where I finally came to the conclusion that I have no taste for painting. I could make nothing of the Titians. The only things (besides portraits) that I cared for much were Botticelli's Mars and Venus with satyrs, and Veronese's (?) "Unfaithfulness" in which I liked the *design*, tho' I confess the actual figures always seem dull to me. However, the Italian rooms are nothing like so boring as the English.

From Trafalgar Square I tubed to Waterloo and waited for Baker at the stage door of the Old Vic. He came out at half past four after I had spent half an hour admiring Waterloo Rd. and been scowled at by a very villainous stage carpenter. We tubed to Karraways and he talked about his day. He seems to have been well treated, all things considered. He is to play Westmorland in *Henry IV* and to be a basket bearer in the *Merry Wives*. They went all through *Henry IV* today – over and over some parts again – in a small room with a shut window. We then went to Paddington where I caught the 6.5.

I have enjoyed my stay with these people very well, except of course the eldest aunt. After a very pleasant journey I arrived at Hillsboro about 8.30. D was in poor form after a very hard day, interrupted by many visitors, including Cranny, who really seems to be going off his head. Earlyish to bed.

Tuesday 29 August: Dreamed that Andrée made a series of attempts to stab me. I behaved like the prig hero of an adventure story, each time gently forcing the dagger away and appealing to her better nature. Finally I gave her a long and paternal lecture and kissed her hand: she gave it up in despair and departed – presumably to a convent!

In the morning I worked on my dissertation. Maisie came before lunch and we held a consultation over her. She has had another offer of a job and the Bitch won't allow her to go to London for an interview. And the Commander is returning on Saturday. We decided we must get clear about the legalities. After lunch I therefore bussed into town and made an appointment for 3 o'clock tomorrow with Walsh, the solicitor. Back again and helped D with the plum jam which she has to make for Mrs Raymond. Andrée and Maisie went to the theatre in the evening.

Mr Raymond turned up . . . Lord, I never knew he was such a bore! A little dapper man with a grey moustache, his conversation consists in a steady outpour of absolutely trivial information about everything he has done for the last week. If you start any other subject he just waits till you've done and then begins again. He occupies my room and I am sleeping at Mrs Wards.

Wednesday 30 August: Since the arrival of Father Raymond our life has run on Leeborough lines: we look forward with joy to the end of breakfast and dread the approach of evening. This morning he mooted the proposal that D should bottle his plums for him. Of course we couldn't directly refuse, as we are under an obligation to him for the house, and for this, as for most "kindnesses", he apparently proposes to get his return in one way or another. Fortunately it was a wet day, so further picking and jam making were impossible.

However, it was range day and joint day so D was pretty busy and I spent most of the morning helping. Dorothy's sister Ivy is now with us – a very pleasant girl. After lunch Maisie appeared and went into town with D.

I tried to get on with my dissertation, having finished my attack on Hedonism and arrived at Kant. I was dissatisfied with my former argument, but could not get on without a text, so I fell, idly enough, to turning over the pages of Ian Hay's *A Man's Man.* Technically he knows how to string a novel together, but his ideas and ideals are fourth rate Kipling and water and his crude wish-fulfilments only fit for the Christinas of a school girl. The only redeeming feature is the humour . . .

As soon as I could get D alone I heard the result of her visit to the solicitor. The interview had been rather funny at first, because he took D for Maisie's mother, and when she asked what power a parent or a guardian had over a daughter of 19, replied severely "None whatever, Madam, none whatever!" This was eminently satisfactory. Walsh was very kind and promised free advice to Maisie if she needed it again. He advised her to take out a summons against the Commander or his wife if they struck her again. He said that they had no power at all, except to turn her adrift.

We were all jubilant. I wrote at once to Baker asking if his aunt cd. meet Maisie in town and take her to her interview some day soon: also a "board and lodging letter" to the other aunt . . .

Smudge . . . got into a terrible state of nerves before going to bed: I had to go upstairs and show her that there was really nothing in any of the cupboards and also kill two spiders . . . Maureen is sleeping at Lady Gonner's and Smudge is in D's room.

Thursday 31 August: Harris the plumber arrived before breakfast to see to the waste pipe in the scullery sink which was blocked. He put it right very promptly for 2/- and we were hoping to keep a discreet silence about the affair: but it had not escaped old Raymond who observed at breakfast "I saw Harris going away Mrs Moore. Anything wrong?" So we told him and he replied "Hmh" after his fashion . . . After lunch we all picked plums and Andrée (who is becoming highly domesticated) very kindly offered to stone them for D while I went to my dissertation.

I found I was utterly useless and could think of no new arguments: then an infernal Salvation Army band established itself in Windmill Rd. and began singing hymns punctuated with five minute sermons. Religion proved more than a match for philosophy and I had to give it up . . . and then went to help D with the jam.

Old Raymond returned and went out to mess with his new ferns in the garden. We went on hard with the jam. Every now and then he came in out of the rain and fidgeted about and talked about the jam: never a word of thanks or any reference to the trouble we were having. Of course he is quite right: he lent the house and we've got to do his jam. Once he observed pleasantly "You look very busy." . . .

Friday 1 September: All morning I sat in the dining room and worked on my dissertation, trying to prove that no pleasure could be considered bad, considered in itself. I found it necessary to descend into pathology and rather doubt if I have done wisely . . .

Poor D had been making jam again, but I think it is done with now: may it be as molten lead in their mouths and as dragonets in their stomachs! She tells me that old Raymond is in very good form over it. Like most egotistical bores, he is just a child after all, easily pleased and easily put out.

After supper I took Maureen to the Gonners. On the way we met Smudge who had been home, and I had to walk back with her. She told me she had passed her exam, but made me promise not to tell the others till tomorrow as "she couldn't stand any remarks tonight". She asked if there was anything she could do in return for my coaching. I said I'd tell her if there ever was, and laughingly suggested that I might ask her to murder someone. She replied gravely "I would if you told me." Then she remarked how "utterly miserable she was tonight". Altogether an infernally uncomfortable tête-à-tête.

Then, of course when we got back there was a spider in the drawing room and she rushed out into the garden. After a lot of calling, Andrée and I found her lying on the lawn under the apple tree: as usual, not a real faint . . .

Saturday 2 September: . . . I spent the morning at my work in the dining room, writing about the concept of desert with great interest and enjoyment.

Mr R. was in for lunch: Maisie also turned up just as we were finishing. We are all glad to hear that The Bitch has a painful attack of lumbago. She had been grousing in bed and Maisie said "For goodness sake put a better face on things." The little woman growled at her "Ach-h – if I could get up I'd take a stick to ye." 'No you wouldn't," said Maisie. "You wouldn't dare. If you ever try that again I'll take out a summons against you." The Bitch simply gaped at her and said nothing.

I had a letter from Baker which I gave Maisie to read. His aunt has found out about Iris de Villiers of New Bond St. with whom Maisie was to have an interview. She appears to be rather a fraud: her plan is to see the candidate dance, say that she needs a little more training and offer to give it at a nominal price, pending a final engagement. The whole thing is just a dodge for getting pupils . . .

Sunday 3 September: . . . The Commander returned yesterday. The Bitch told [Maisie] she might go out today as it would be the last time she would ever go out anywhere. She also made a variety of complaints about her to the Commander, mostly untrue. The Commander said Maisie didn't work, and therefore he wouldn't start her in a dancing career: they both settled down to write long letters – presumably making some arrangements about her.

During the afternoon Smudge's brother came out: he is a very quiet youth whom I think I rather like. We play croquet, Andrée and I against Maisie and Mr Wiblin.

After tea I went out to do some message or other – I forget what: as I came back into Western Road I passed one of the Hawes children leaving "Hillsboro" on a bike. "That means trouble," thought I. I cut her, more through preoccupation than anything else. As soon as I got back I found that the child had been sent with a peremptory message for Maisie's return. Maisie had sent back asking for a few moments' grace as she was in the middle of a game, and the child had come again with the message "Maisie is to come home at once." She was now preparing to obey: she was quite unnerved for once, and everyone felt that there was going to be an outburst.

At her request I accompanied her home, after D and I had both advised her to escape to us if things became unbearable. She led me round to the back of her house where we found the whole family "joined in synod unbenign". I said we had promised all our guests that Maisie shd. dance for them and I hoped very much that it would be possible for her to stay to supper. Whereupon a figure that sat with its back to me, turned half round and said that we could promise what we liked but "She cannot, she CAN NOT: and that's why I sent for her, for I'm not going to have her going out and leavin' the place like a pig stye, so there, and she can understand that." (All this seemed to be delivered in a strong Belfast accent, tho' I suppose it must really be Scotch.)

The Bitch at this point showed a desire to keep up the fiction of friendliness and interrupted "My dear, this is Mr Lewis." The figure

– a very fat blue figure with a red face – then turned fully round and extended a right hand from which two or three fingers were missing. I took it – it seemed better so. He then poured out a good deal more of the same sort with a lot of abuse of Maisie. Finally I said "Good bye," glancing in her direction, and came away.

Came home in a sort of drunk state of agitation and had supper: old Raymond was fortunately out. Afterwards I helped to wash up and then read two tales of Tolstoi, *Where God is, There is Love* and *The Godson*: the latter is the better, but neither impressed me much.

Old Raymond came in and began talking about Peru. Then, at about 11.30 came a tap at the door: I went, and there was Maisie saying "I've come." She had crept out after all the devils were in bed and carried all her clothes away with her.

As soon as Raymond went to bed, D, Andrée, Smudge and I met in conclave in the drawing room. As soon as I had left, the Bitch and her husband had started a row with Maisie. The pretext was the untidiness of her room . . . The Bitch supplied an obbligato to this row by throwing knives and forks about. The Commander was going to strike her but she cowed him by the mere mention of a summons. They said he would take her back to Belfast when he went there and make her a nurse. As a parting shot the Commander told her to "do out" the whole ground floor of the house before she went to bed. The others (including the kids) then retired to have some champagne in the parent's bedroom, and so to bed. Maisie also went to bed (in her clothes): then got up again and came to us.

We now thought out our plans – arguing a good deal in circles: Andrée showed very clear insight. Our chief object was to guard against the possibility of a visit from the Commander on the morrow, as we could not have a scene in Mr R's house while Mr W. was there. It was decided that Maisie should sleep the night at Mrs Wards and go up to London in the morning to see Miss de Villiers: not that we doubted Baker's advice about that lady, but so that we could truthfully declare that she was not in Oxford. She then wrote a note to the Commander explaining that she was gone, and gone to London, and adding that further communications should be addressed to Walsh the solicitor.

It was arranged that I should take this note. Maisie then went to Mrs W's to sleep in the room which I have been using: I wrapped D's scarf round me (my coat being at Mrs W's) and set off with my note: it obviously had to be delivered at once (if the red herring was to work) and delivered without waking anyone. I felt as if I were on a veritable patrol. A cold cloudy morning with diffused moonlight.

At the end of the Hawes road I met a bike: crept down to the Hawes: found lights still on in the house opposite. I went to the hall door with considerable caution and managed to get the note through the letter box without making much row. This done, I came down to Warneford Rd. and let myself in: very much of an empty house with all the windows bolted and a disused smell. I looked through some 14 stout bottles left by the Pasleys but found never a drop. The bed was still made in my own room and I retired at 1.35 to sleep in my shirt and be wakened by the crying child next door.

Monday 4 September: . . . As we were all in momentary expectation of a visit from the Commander we could not prevent a rather windy and comfortless atmosphere from pervading the group mind. Maisie had gone off to town by the earliest train with letters to introduce herself to Baker's aunt. We breakfasted. As soon as old Raymond was out of the house, Andrée, following a pleasant idea of her own, biked to the Hawes': during her absence I shaved in D's room. Andrée then came back and told us her adventure.

She had seen the Bitch: said she came round to say good bye: was the Commander there? No – in Oxford. Well wd. Mrs Hawes say goodbye to him for her? and could she see Maisie? "Maisie's out," said the Bitch: "I'm not quite sure where. She isn't round with you is she?" "No," said Andrée, "I haven't seen her today."

As soon as I had heard this story I bussed into town and called on Walsh the solicitor, after hanging about for some time to make sure that I shd. not meet the Commander in the waiting room. Walsh proved to be the jolliest old gentleman I ever met: he has a big nosed, big toothed face like a rabbit, and very bright eyes. Over his mantelpiece a notice catches your eye: – "When in doubt tell the truth."

I explained who I was and told him the situation up to date. He said that D had not mentioned me, and that I, simply because of the sex, made a difference. He was horrified to hear that Maisie had slept in what was my room and asked if I wanted them to bring me before the city court for abduction. This was quite a new idea to me, and rather alarming. However, he presently decided that a girl of 19 couldn't be abducted anyway "though they change the age so often these days that you'll soon be able to abduct a woman of eighty."

I spoke of our efforts to avoid a scene between the Commander and Mr R. "You surely don't mean," said he "that this Commander is going to commit an assault on an innocent old gentleman pulling up dandelions in front of a hall door!" He advised us to tell no lies, to refuse to see the Commander, and to answer no questions. There appears to be no legal bother at all. I showed him Beckett's alarmist letter and he simply handed it back with a smile and a shrug. So much for a first in jurisprudence! I parted from him in great good humour.

Came back to find that no visit had taken place . . . A wire came from Maisie "Return Paddington 7": we could find no such train in the guide book.

Then came a ring at the door. I answered it, bracing myself for another encounter with the Commander, and found instead a Nun, who said "I'm Sister Hilary – a friend of Maisie Hawes. May I see Mrs Moore?" Had a hurried consultation with D over this development and decided that no information must be given, whatever the Nun seemed like. Then D went to see her in the dining room. Went out to take chaircovers to the wash etc. After a long wait D emerged from the dining room and told me her story. Sister H. is a friend whom Maisie has mentioned as trustworthy. She came to D from the Hawes. The latter are not much worried about Maisie's disappearance and think she is still in Headington, probably with us.

The Sister is naturally worried about her. She had noticed "things" when Maisie was a child and wondered about her treatment: she said it was a case of "misunderstanding" between her and her parents. She said that the Commander had admitted that he lost his temper last night and said things he hadn't meant – both to Maisie and me.[1] He said that they were proposing to take Maisie to London on Wednesday and get her a dancing job: that the nursing yarn and the Belfast yarn were only threats. He had also complained that Maisie did no work in the house. D replied by a few facts about Maisie's real life in that house: and the Nun certainly opened her eyes. She agreed that the Commander's story about "having arranged to settle about Maisie's dancing on Wednesday" was probably a lie – and a very clever lie too, if it is designed to make us believe we've been on a fool's errand.

The Nun then asked D directly if she knew anything about Maisie. D refused to say: but promised to tell her *if Maisie wrote to her*, and

---

[1] A similar apology for his behaviour to me was made by the Bitch when Andrée called in the morning. – C.S.L.

said that she knew Maisie had friends in London who would look after her. The Nun did not press any of her questions. She said she would tell the devils only that D said she was not in the least surprised at Maisie's flight. They parted on excellent terms although the interview had been difficult, each naturally regarding the other with suspicion.

From the Ry. Guide we now perceived that one of the trains which Maisie *might* mean by "the 7" would be in any moment and some one must go down and let Maisie into Warneford Rd. where she was to sleep tonight. Rushed down to the tennis court and sent Smudge to do so . . . Smudge turned up towards the end of the meal – Maisie not having arrived.

As she insisted – God knows why – that her brother must not know of the matter – it naturally became necessary for me to go down in time for the next train: which was imprudent. Then D had to go and smuggle the key of Warneford Rd. out of Smudge's pocket – Smudge being still at supper and on the duty list, listening to old Raymond. As soon as this had been successfully done I took a basket of food for Maisie's supper and breakfast and hurried down to Warneford Rd. Came in and lit the gas so that it could be seen thro' the fanlight. Maisie soon turned up, having had an excellent day with Baker's aunt, and mindful of Walsh's advice I left her at once and came up.

At the end of Gipsy Lane I met Smudge, walking down to sleep with Maisie at Warneford Rd. Saw her back as far as the lamp posts – the last thing on God's earth that I wanted to do.

Home at last, very footsore and tired: positively giddy with one of the worst colds I've ever had – now developing into a cough . . .
Tuesday 5 September: Rose feeling more tired than I have been since we left the Jeffreys – whom God reject![2] We set to work as soon as we could and slaved . . . all day, packing against time. We all kept up wonderful spirits considering everything.

Andrée went off by the 10.50, Mr Sée calling for her and carrying her case. She is a remarkable character. This last week she has shown herself at her best, taking a hand in everything and helping us . . . Perhaps there has been a real change in her – D has a great knack of getting the best out of people . . .

---

[2] Of the many places that Lewis and the Moores had lived since 1919 the most horrible was a flat over a butcher's shop in 58 Windmill Road. Mrs John Jeffrey was both butcher and landlady.

We got down to Warneford Rd. at about five. D and Maisie did most of the work upstairs while I worked in great haste below, settling in. Ivy gave us a fright by getting a bad heart attack. She had not told us that she was subject to them, but apparently she is – and if so, it is small wonder that the frightful pressure we've been going at has brought on one. Went twice to the pub to get brandy.

In the midst of all this confusion Smudge flitted from room to room saying she thought she'd better go home tonight. A thousand times I felt tempted to reply "Well then GO!", but of course she always yielded to D's pressure. Indeed she has been very good and has not spared herself in helping: but I must confess I find her presence an intolerable addition to the strain of these days . . .

Found that D, with a momentary lapse from common sense, perhaps in pride at being alive after such a day, was making Smudge play. So we had to sit and listen and I felt I didn't care if the roof fell in. When that was over there was endless delay in getting to bed and of course, as the last straw to a perfect day, I was left alone with Smudge. To bed at last, and I had a few moments alone with D, who stands this bad time wonderfully. Cold seems rather worse.

Wednesday 6 September: Still feeling pretty rotten. By the morning post Ivy got a letter from her fiancé saying he would arrive at Carfax by car at 9.30 and would she meet him. She of course was for going, but D thought this very dangerous as she had had another bad turn this same morning. Ivy proved obdurate and the only thing was for me to rush into town and try and forestall her by bringing the youth out.

Ivy, by the by, is rather wonderful: the daughter of a shepherd, herself a trained nurse and yet content to do domestic work for us so as to give Dorothy a holiday . . .

In the afternoon I sat in my own room and wrote up arrears of diary. Very tired and full of cold. D is still busy settling in and Maisie works like a brick.

Thursday 7 September: A bad, feverish night – all full of confused dreams and no good from my sleep . . . In the afternoon I tried to work but felt too fuddled and ended by lying on my bed. A letter from Walsh saying the Commander had been to him and asked for Maisie's address, which he had truthfully replied he did not know. He now has a letter from her. Early to bed.

Friday 8 September: Stayed in bed till tea time. Called for the *Odyssey* and beginning at Bk. V read to the middle of Bk. VIII with great pleasure. Cold still pretty bad.

Saturday-Saturday 9-23 September: Between my Friday's entry and my departure for Ireland the only event of importance has been an interview between D, Ivy and myself. The origin of this was some trouble between Ivy's people and herself . . .

On Monday (11th) I travelled to Belfast, by Liverpool. On Thursday morning my first vision was of the town in its familiar squalor under heavy rain . . .

My Father made some considerable opposition to my returning in ten days time, but I showed a firm front and after this preliminary unpleasantness he was really, with a few exceptions, at his best during my stay.

W was in good form and he and I did a lot of motorbiking. Besides short rides over the hills to Holywood – the objective usually being a drink in the "Central Hotel" – he took me to Island Magee, to Newcastle, and to Browns Bay where we lunched with Kelsie and Gundred at K's hut.[3] The country is very beautiful and if only I could deport the Ulstermen and fill their land with a populace of my own choosing, I should ask no better place to live in. By the by it is quite a mistake to think that Ulster is inhabited by loyalists: the mountains beyond Newcastle and the Antrim "hinterlands" are all Green.

At this time I read Galsworthy's *Forsyte Saga*: one of the finest novels I have ever read, and mercilessly true. I spoke of it to Mrs Greeves, herself a Forsyte, wife of a Forsyte, mother and daughter of Forsytes: she had read, and enjoyed it apparently, but without the least comprehension of the author's purpose.[4] She could not understand what I meant when I said the Forsytes were terrible people and thought "it was a great pity of Soames". The sinister figure of Soames is the great creation of the book – and Irene, one of the very few heroines whose beauty is made convincing, though it is never described.

I also read the greater part of James Stephens' *Irish Fairy Tales*: his curious humour and profundity of course peep out in places – but the author of *The Crock of Gold* is simply wasted on other people's tales. Beyond these two I read nothing.

---

[3] See **Isabella Kelso Ewart** and **Mary Gundred Ewart** under **The Ewart Family** in the Biographical Appendix.

[4] Mrs Mary Gribbon Greeves (1861–1949), originally from Brooklyn, New York, was Arthur Greeves's mother.

W had rigged up the croquet lawn, after some ten years lying idle. During this time the hoops have got lost or been stolen, and he had erected pairs of sticks to serve in their place – which presented a very curious appearance to me on my arrival. We played a certain amount, and until the very end, I was incredibly bad. We also persuaded our father to play, which he did in the funniest way imaginable, sometimes regarding the whole thing with lordly tolerance, and at others becoming intensely serious. After a while he developed powers by no means contemptible.

Croquet and rain brought it about that we had very little of the after dinner strolling which is *de rigeur* there in the summer. I had a curious feeling that my father has "given me up": I feel that he has ceased to ask questions about me, regards me as a hopeless enigma. The strain of conversing with him, the hopelessness of trying to make him understand a position, are of course old news: but this time one felt – rather pathetically – that the effort was over for good on his side. I can truly say I am sorry I have contributed so little to his happiness: whether he deserves it or not is another matter. Almost the only pleasure he can derive from me is that which may come from academic or literary successes in my career.

In the evening W and I often played chess with varying fortune, but I think he usually won. Arthur was at home when I arrived, intending to sail for England the next day. This, however, was prevented by a chill which brought him to bed and after that he put off his departure from day to day so that I could not let D know many days ahead: consequently she was able to send me only one letter during my stay. I saw Arthur frequently. Whether it was his health or my absorption in other things I don't know, but we found practically nothing to say to each other. I worked on my dissertation nearly every day and finished it.

On Thursday 21st W and I left and crossed to England by Heysham. This route was new to both of us. If you can face the early start – 5.45 boat train from Heysham – it has every advantage. The boats are more comfortable than either the Liverpool or the Fleetwood and – what is unique – they give you really good coffee. We travelled first class all the way and had a most comfortable journey: a breakfast-car came on at Leeds in which we had a capital meal, and, later, a morning drink. We had a compt. to ourselves. I was reading H.G.Well's *Modern Utopia* – a poor, hazy, affected book. On reaching St Pancras we went at once to Karraway's where

Baker, according to a letter from me, had left tickets for the St Martin's. I got these and spoke to his aunts – they tell me he has got the part of Page in the *Merry Wives* – and then rejoined W. After lunching at the Euston Hotel we drove to the theatre – one of the nicest small houses I have been in and very quietly decorated. We saw Galsworthy's *Loyalties* and Barrie's *Shall We Join the Ladies?* The latter was rather poorly acted, but an amusing conception. *Loyalties* was as well done as anything I could have imagined: every part a little masterpiece in itself and yet subordinate. A capital play, though, to my mind, it errs in concentrating the interest of the last act on Dancy and thus leading to a rather obvious ending, while the real issue – the issue suggested in the title – is dropt out of sight. But perhaps I have not quite understood it.

From the St Martin's we returned to have a whiskey at Euston, and thence to Paddington where [Warnie] saw me off. He is under orders for Colchester – not the best place in the world, but good enough, provided they don't send him to this infernal Turkish war.

I travelled down to Oxford comfortably enough, nearly asleep, and arrived home at 9. D in good form. Maisie still here, but in touch with a good job at Cardiff.

Saturday 23 September: After breakfast I went into town and gave my dissertation to the typist who promised to have it ready by Thursday. I then went to College and got from Frank the notice about the Magdalen Fellowship. I there found to my horror that the dissertation and testimonials were to be handed in on Monday and not on the 30th as I had supposed.

I therefore went to Magdalen and spoke to the porter who told me that I had better see the President. I accordingly called at his residence – opposite the great gate – and was admitted to a blue panelled ante room which I shared for 20 minutes with a female secretary who did not ask me to sit down.

Sir Herbert Warren proved to be a stout man with a short grey beard, thick lips, and an affable manner. He has the reputation of being a great snob but is supposed to be a good champion to all who have a College claim in him.[5] He said I might certainly send in my dissertation in MS if I liked. I then went to the Union and wrote to the Master, to Carritt, and to Stevenson asking for testimonials. I found in College that the Mugger was not in

---

[5] See **Sir Thomas Herbert Warren** in the Biographical Appendix.

College, so I shall hardly have his reply by Monday . . .

Sunday 24 September: It was a glorious morning and we decided that Moppie (Maisie Hawes), Maureen and I should go out. I washed up after breakfast and laid lunch while Moppie "did" the rooms: but we had been so late in getting up that we were not on the road till 12 . . .

After lunch I helped D to compose a letter to Moppie's prospective employer Miss Quinlan of Cardiff. She had sent a form of agreement involving the father's signature and we had to explain why this was impossible.

Later on I started Maureen on an English essay and tried to give her some ideas about structure. I am to teach her Latin and English for the "School Certificate" and the task — especially the English — appalls me. After supper Smudge arrived, looking much better for her holiday. Sat up with D alone after the others had dispersed and talked for some time . . .

Monday 25 September: . . . I bussed into Oxford and called at the typists: she had not yet finished my dissertation and asked me to return at a quarter to six. I spent the interval in the Union reading Chesterton's *Browning*. At quarter to six the typescript was indeed finished but not collected so I had to take the MS after all.

I called in Univ. where kind testimonials from Carritt and Stevenson had been left for me and, armed with these, proceeded to Magdalen. Here I met Ewing back from Geneva and competing: later on Dodds turned up (from Reading) also competing. There are about eleven candidates – one rumour made it 60 – one of whom is Freeman of the House. Our interviews with Warren were very short and we filled up forms.

Home by about 7.30 to find Smudge here. This evening I was bitterly tired and I can't think why: D says that possibly I miss the drinks that I have got into the habit of with W. I am accordingly finishing in small tots the brandy which was bought for Ivy.

Tuesday 26 September: I was woken this morning by Moppie putting her head round the door and shouting "I'm going to Cardiff." This turned out to mean that there was an answer from Miss Quinlan saying that she would take her without the form of contract. She is to go on Thursday and they "will discuss matters when she arrives". It will be pleasant to be by our selves again, but we will miss Moppie's odd presence. She is terribly, childishly naive and retains many obstinate vulgarities from her upbringing: but there isn't a spark of bad in her. In fact she is rather like a large and intelligent dog about the house. I have hopes that, in this case at least, D's kindness has not been misplaced.

After breakfast I walked to Magdalen and from 10 to 1 we did an English essay on "The use and abuse of satire". I should be sorry to have my production survive as a specimen of my work - but I think there was enough guts in it to attract attention . . .

At 3 I returned to Magdalen: meeting D on the bus. From 3 to 6 we did "literary unseens": Hesiod, Dionysius of Halicarnassus and Ausonius. I found the Hesiod rather difficult. Tea was brought to us in hall at 4.30 – an admirable innovation in exam methods . . .

To bed at about 11. I was much less tired and am beginning to slough my Little Lea skin.

Wednesday 27 September: . . . After breakfast to Magdalen by 10 o'clock and did a Philosophy paper. I think I put in some good work on the importance of Time to ethics and on generalisation: but my answer to the Kant question was uneven and I foolishly wrote a lot of poor pudding about Pragmatism.

Walked home to lunch . . . Back again to Magdalen at 3 to write a Latin Prose. This afternoon one courageous candidate set the precedent of lighting a cigarette and we all followed. I sit beneath the portrait of Lord Selbourne and wonder what he thinks of it.

Home by bus to find D very busy mending clothes for Moppie and teaching her how to pack. I sat and wrote "M.Blake" on tapes with marking ink, as Moppie has decided to use Moira Blake (my invention) as a professional name . . . I wrote out some notes for Maureen as an introduction to the *Aeneid* – a few picturesque details about Vergil's life and an explanation of what an *epic* is. Late to bed at quarter to one.

Thursday 28 September: In to Magdalen as usual after breakfast – a bright, autumnal morning. We did a paper on Ancient History and Political Philosophy with which I was fairly satisfied. I answered at great length a question as to whether the Greeks recognised the difference between East and West: also one on the mixture of obligation and violence in sovereignty.

I walked home rather late to find that the others had already lunched and Moppie was on the point of departure. She went off firmly but D tells me that she had cried at saying good bye to her before I came back.

I hastened over my lunch so as to be able to wash up before I went and was just starting to do so when D asked me to get out some old rolls of carpet which Miss Featherstone wanted and for which she might call any day . . . I finally unearthed them with some difficulty from the cupboard beneath the stairs, hurriedly completed my washing up and bussed back to Magdalen.

Here we did Philosophical Unseens – a piece of Plato, one of Aristotle, and one of Tertullian. I could make very little of the latter and had to leave it unfinished . . .

I bussed home to find D tired and in rather poor form. As soon as I had written my diary for the previous day I laid supper. Without disrepect to Moppie it is delightful to be by ourselves again, almost for the first time this summer which seems, as I look back, to be time lost, full of vanity and vexation of spirit. We were finished and washed up by half past eight.

In the evening at D's request I read to her my diary for June from the beginning of this volume. We were early to bed.

Friday 29 September: Walked into Magdalen after breakfast. Meeting some of my rivals in the cloister, I discovered that it was Greek prose this morning and decided that I would do myself no good by going in and spoiling paper. I therefore came away to the Union.

I now decided to act as though I had not got the fellowship and make such beginnings as I could for the English School by making up Milton, whom I shall take for my special subject. After looking through some old papers – which seemed pretty easy – I took out Mark Pattison's *Milton* and the second volume of Masson's edition, which looks possibly out of date, but contains a chronological table of the early works . . .

In the afternoon I returned to do French Unseens. The first was a criticism by Rostand on Borrier "Fille de Roland". This is the first prose of Rostand I have seen, and it impressed me very favourably. The second was a passage in Alexandrines by Victor Hugo about the boyhood of Palestrina (who was Palestrina?) rather influenced by the *Prelude* and quite good. Both contained several words I did not know but I made hardly guesses and, from the purely literary point of view, I was rather pleased with my rendering of the Rostand.

I came out soon after tea and bussed home. Supper early. Before lunch I had finished an analysis of the *Aeneid* up to the point where we begin, for Maureen.

I now applied myself to "Dymer" and worked hard. I began to feel with Rasselas that "it is impossible to be a poet": not so much a dissatisfaction with my own powers in particular as a conviction in general that good poetry is beyond the reach of human endeavour altogether. I know that it *has* been written but that doesn't alter the feeling somehow. Sometimes I fancy that the English language has completed its cycle.

After Maureen had gone to bed I read to D my diary for July. She was less tired tonight . . .

Saturday 30 September: I forgot to record in its place a singularly beautiful dream which I had yesterday morning. I seemed to be reading an Irish fairy tale, but passed gradually from the position of reader to that of actor. I and another – who was at first labelled Warnie but became a nonentity – were visiting a brother and sister: their house looked rather like Leeborough, but I understood that it was a house in faery and that our hosts were Danaan people. I was floating to and fro in the air in and out through the branches of a tree with very feathery leaves which I kept shredding off and throwing at the girl who lay on her back in the long grass. She was very fair and dressed in blue I think – or possibly yellow. The whole thing was extraordinarily luminous and airy and a delight to remember.

This morning, as there was only Greek and Latin verse to do, I did not go in to Magdalen. After breakfast I washed up and did the dining room. I then went to my room and started to work again on the VIth Canto of "Dymer". I got on splendidly – the first good work I have done since a long time . . .

After supper I worked on "Dymer", bringing it to the end of the storm. I was so transported with what I considered my success that I became insolent and said to myself that it was the voice of a god.

After Maureen had gone up I continued reading my diary to D up to date. Then read some Pattison and late to bed.

I forgot to mention an absurd episode during lunch. Maureen had started saying she didn't mind which of two alternative sweets she had: and D, who is always worried by these indecisions, had begun to beg her to make up her mind in rather a weary voice. Thus developed one of those little mild wrangles about nothing which a wise man accepts as in the nature of things. I, however, being in a sublime mood, and unprepared for jams, allowed a silent irritation to rise and sought relief in jabbing violently at a piece of pastry. As a result I covered myself in a fine shower of custard and juice: my melodramatic gesture was thus deservedly exposed and everyone roared with laughter.

Sunday 1 October: . . . After washing up I went to sit by an open window and work on "Dymer". What I wrote was not as good as yesterday but I thought that resulted from the difference of subject and since there must be ups and downs in a narrative poem, I was not dissatisfied . . . D was pretty busy all day with sewing, but in pretty good form . . .

Monday 2 October: . . . I . . . looked into a book on Mozart and read the story of the *Magic Flute* which I found very suggestive. The opposition of Sarastro and the Queen and the meeting ground in the girl makes a good myth – as already used by Lowes Dickinson, but he left most of his opportunities untouched.[1] I thought curiously of how this might be used for a big poem some day. I believe a modern poem about Ultimate must not be, like *Paradise Lost*, about good and evil but must exhibit what Hegel calls dialectic: and a poem on Sarastro gives the opportunity for this . . .

Smudge came for lunch and afterwards, till four o'clock, I did Unseens with her. Miss Featherstone came but did not stay for tea. Ivy, tho' unasked, is staying till tomorrow – an arrangement which D and I – hungry for peace and quiet after all these months – do not much care for . . .

When the others were in bed we had a long talk together, D and I, about Moppie. Baker's letter in wh. he asked me "for the nicest motives and in the strictest confidence" for Moppie's own account of her day in London, together with the fact that she had spent an unaccountable lot of money, suggested that she told us at least a silent lie . . .

Tuesday 3 October: Worked all morning in the drawing room at Milton making notes on the earlier poems and writing down quotations to remember . . .

D was in very poor form in the afternoon. During my absence she had made an unwilling third to a quarrel between Ivy (who went

---

[1] Goldsworthy Lowes Dickinson, *The Magic Flute: A Fantasia* (1920).

today) and Dorothy who came back this morning. The details are hardly worth recording but it seems to have been a silly business. After tea I went repeatedly over some Virgil which Maureen is to prepare for tomorrow: then, alone, I wrote out a vocabulary containing almost every word in it and a few explanatory notes. This took me till supper time . . .

Wednesday 4 October: To my room immediately after breakfast and continued my notes on Milton. Coming as far as *Il Penseroso*, I got up the *Anatomy of Melancholy*[2] from the dining room to look at the prefatory poem. I was snared in Burton and wasted some time reading his passage about scholars: but finally recovered myself and finished *L'Allegro* and *Il Penseroso* – greatly struck by the nonsensical discussions in Masson, trying to locate all the scenery. Critics are past praying for. After lunch I walked to the Union to get out some book which would give me a historical background for the times.

I looked into Clarendon's *History of the Great Rebellion*[3] – a most attractive work which I hope I shall some day find time to read. I took out the 3rd volume of Green's *Short History*[4] and Vol. II of Hamilton's *Gallipoli Diary* in a hope of being (at last) able to finish reading it to D. I then walked home again.

A wet afternoon. After tea I read a good deal of Green, of whose profundity and style I do not somehow think very much. Later I read to D till supper time. For supper came Smudge and afterwards I worked with her on Tacitus's *Agricola* which she is reading for Pass Mods. We got on well. After she had gone I read to D again. Lateish to bed. Every night this week I have enjoyed wonderful moonlight in my room.

Thursday 5 October: . . . I called on Walsh in St Aldate's and showed him the new agreement which Miss Quinlan has sent us, in which D instead of the Commander appears as guarantor of the £50 payable in the case of Moppie's breaking the contract. I explained that she could not possibly raise £50 and he replied – as he had before replied to D – that this was all the more reason for signing. He said that the document was only there to impress us and that the clause in wh. Moppie is forbidden to teach in Cardiff within three years of the

---

[2] By Robert Burton (1621).

[3] Edward Hyde Clarendon, *The True Historical Narrative of the Rebellion and Civil Wars in England* (1702–4).

[4] John Richard Green, *Short History of the English People* (1874).

expiration of her contract is illegal according to the latest decisions . . .

I found D and Dorothy busy getting the back room ready. A P.G. [paying guest] is expected tomorrow. Lady Gonner asked us to take this woman for a few days, and we could not well refuse. We now find that the few days is to be two or three weeks. I need not write down my feelings at thus having our long deferred privacy taken away from us before we have had time to taste it – I shall remember them well enough.

I put in some good work in my own room before lunch. In the afternoon I sat with D in the dining room and continued Milton, finishing *Comus* and *Lycidas*. *Comus* I think I have never enjoyed more . . .

Friday 6 October: . . . I . . . worked pretty well and got half way through the 2nd Book of *Paradise Lost*. I find it rather hard to spot possible gobbets as hardly any line raises conscious difficulties. I enjoyed the reading of it immensely – I have lost some of the old thrills but there are other new ones . . .

At six o'clock came Mrs Hankin, our compulsory P.G. She is best described by recording that when D and I came in the evening to ask each other what we thought about her we found that neither of us had thought anything.

I went to my room till supper time and read part of the *Doctrine and Discipline of Divorce* and the whole of the *Tractate on Education*, both of which are interesting. Poor D had a good deal of extra fixing up for supper – and I, of course, some extra washing up afterwards – as both Smudge and Mrs Hankin were here. This was our first real winter night and we had a fire in the drawing room. Mrs Hankin went early to bed - a very laudable practice which we devoutly hope she will continue. I read Keat's letters in the evening.

This whole day is overshadowed by the news in the evening papers. Our negotiations with the Turks have broken down and I cannot for the life of me see how a war can be avoided. Miss Featherstone has heard from some big wig that such a war wd. involve taking on all Islam and that conscription would be applied at once – not that that matters much, for I suppose one would have to go anyway. Late to bed, with a headache.

Sunday 8 October: . . . After tea I walked to College and found Carlyle out again. The town looked so fine in the wintry evening light that I decided to walk down Holywell, where by good luck I saw a light in the windows of the Carlyle house. I rang and his daughter came to the door – the family having returned unexpectedly without maids. I was with Carlyle for about three quarters of an hour.[5] He said he was glad to hear that I had managed the Magdalen exam comfortably. I said I thought that I had done pretty badly, but he told me that, to his knowledge, the Magdalen dons were "favourably impressed".

We then discussed my idea of taking English if I do not get the Fellowship. He said I should get private tuition for the Anglo-Saxon . . . He said he didn't know who my regular tutor would be, but that most of them were "good literary men you know, but a bit foolish" . . .

Speaking more generally he said that, with due respect to other poets, Wordsworth *was* the Romantic Movement, and the great odes were Wordsworth's. He thought no one in his century was worth reading except Malory. He also drew my attention to the continental influence of Goldsmith, Sterne and the other sentimentalists. Came away and walked after a very pleasant and useful time . . .

Mrs H. has by this time shown herself a talker very much of old Raymond's type. She spent all supper time telling us of some woman who founded a church in Zanzibar on six pence half-penny and prayer. She is a little, sweet, upright, prim old lady – very much of an officer's widow – very patriotic – very unemotional – high church – highly correct – a regular pattern of a "nice" old woman. A greater bore I have never met: passions and sympathies I fancy she has never known. Worst of all, she has given up her habit of going to bed immediately after supper.

Monday 9 October: Another cold morning. I went to my room and finished fair copying Canto IV of "Dymer". I read the whole thing through and felt fairly satisfied with the general movement of the story, the faults being, thank goodness, mainly in matters of detail. Some of it seemed too concise.

At 10.30 Smudge came and I went with her to the drawing room to do the *Agricola* until shortly before lunch. She seems to make progress. D brought us tea and biscuits in the middle of the morning . . .

I also looked again into the book on Mozart where I read that Goethe had written a continuation to the story of the *Magic Flute*.

---

[5] See **Alexander James Carlyle** in the Biographical Appendix.

It is really extraordinary how much this subject has been in my mind lately.

Walked home to find D engaged with a woman who wants her to make a jumper out of two most hideous shades of red silk. In the drawing room I found the Doc and Mary, who returned yesterday. The Doc seemed pretty cheerful. When D's client had gone we came into the dining room and had tea. The Doc told us some amusing stories of Cranny's cowardice. Once they had been walking together and met a dog with a loud bark: at which Cranny thrust his stick into the Doc's hands, saying "Do you think you can hold him Johnnie?" and then took to his heels . . .

Then followed the usual muddled, but enthusiastic talk about psychoanalysis, suggestion and so forth. I made one or two temporary retirements to my room where I started a poetical epistle to Harwood in a super-Augustan style. The Askins did not go till late: a lot of talk about Rob and Grace King, their flirtations together and their joint selfishness towards Edie. Maureen says Grace was detestable at Bristol.[6] . . .

Tuesday 10 October: . . . I settled down to Milton. I read Books II and III of P.L. and went through Masson's notes to them, finding many new points. D gave me some tea during the morning – very grateful and comforting in this bitter spell of cold.

After lunch I went for a walk. It was by now a beautiful afternoon, cool, but absolutely still: the colouring grows better every day. I walked up Shotover and on to the far end: thence by the bridlepath to meet the main road beyond the railway, then home through Horsepath and along the road turning into the woody lane before Cowley and finishing up through the golf links. Whether my eyes were unusually open I don't know, but the country was full of good bits . . .

I . . . went to the drawing room myself to do the IV Book of *Paradise Lost*. Coming to the first entry of Adam and Eve, I was struck by the absolute necessity in poems of the largest sort, of having a subject already familiar and very simple, so that there may be room for a fine obviousness. This rather dashed my recent dream of a Sarastro poem.

D remained with Mrs H. in the other room for a very long time.

---

[6] See Robert "Rob" Askins in the Biographical Appendix. Edith "Edie" Askins (1873–1936) was Mrs Moore's sister, and she lived in Bristol near their brother "Rob".

When I at last heard the other go upstairs I came in to console with
D. She however had not been bored. Mrs Hankin had (like everyone
else) been making D the confidante of her troubles and D's sympathy
had conquered ennui. Apparently Mrs H. is very poor and really to
be pitied: like her I cannot . . . Later I sat with D: we talked of Mrs
H's troubles and of the terrible poverty among the people we know.
Wednesday 11 October: The temperature this morning was 42°. To
my work after breakfast and finished the Vth Book of P.L. with much
delight. At about 11.30 I started to do Vergil with Maureen. She was
readier to think and more intelligent than I have found her before –
tho' she would insist on calling Aeneas "Ananias". We continued till
lunch time . . .

I finished my epistle to Harwood and read part of the VIth Book
of P.L. I must be losing some of my old powers of accepting an
author's premises with loyalty, for it wrung several laughs from
me . . .

Thursday 12 October: Immediately after breakfast I started Virgil
with Maureen and continued till 10.30, at which Miss Brayne came
to give her a violin lesson. I then retired to my own room where I
put on my dressing gown and thus continued comfortable enough,
though it was, for the first part of the morning, intensely cold. I
finished Book VI and began Book VII: then, after a cup of tea, not
feeling very Miltonic, I turned to Chaucer. I read the whole of the
Book of the Duchesse, looking out all the words that I didn't know.
I liked it very well – not only the prologue and the dream scenery,
but even the speech which is an example of that very rare thing – a
panegyric on a woman which really conveys some sense of beauty
and freshness.

During lunch D quite unexpectedly found in the *Times* and read
out that the Magdalen fellowship had been given to Price of New
College.[7] I find that this has affected my spirits very little.

I then walked into town. In the Union I met Carlyle. He was sorry
about my news, but spoke encouragingly about the English School.
I then went to College to report, according to Farquharson's
instructions. Term began today and there was a great bustle of cabs
at the gate, and luggage and plenty of people.

In the porch I met Poynton. He had heard of my news and came
up at once to offer his regrets: he said that I had done well and that

---

[7] See **Henry Habberley Price** in the Biographical Appendix.

Warren had expressed himself "greatly impressed" but that "it was hardly my examination". I explained that I would be "up" this term: he said he supposed my scholarship had ceased. I said this had been discussed at the end of last term and that the Master had held out hopes of its being extended . . .

Friday 13 October: . . . Shortly before one I saw Farquharson. He told me to go to Wilson of Exeter for tuition in English.[8] He then gave me a paternal lecture on an academic career which was not (he said) one of leisure as popularly supposed. His own figure however lessened the force of the argument. He advised me, as he has done before, to go to Germany for a time and learn the language. He prophesied that there would soon be a school of modern European literature and that linguistically qualified Greatsmen would be the first to get the new billets thus created. This was attractive, but of course circumstances make migration impossible for me . . .

Home to lunch: thence rushed back and went to Exeter. Wilson was not there but I found him in his house in Manor Place. He is a fat, youngish man: his face impressed me well. He tells me I shall have my work cut out to manage the work in the time.[9]

Having fixed up work and lectures I hurried home, where I found Jenkin. I strolled out with him before tea. He is staying up to write for his B.Litt.

After tea I went in to see Carlyle . . . He was delighted to hear that I had got Wilson. He gave me a letter of introduction to Miss Wardale and I hurried off to Wellington Square to find her: but it appears that she has left that house . . . Altogether a not very pleasant day: late to bed, very footsore. A mile of pavement walking is more than a five mile country walk.

Saturday 14 October: Hurried over breakfast and went as quickly as I could by bus to St Hugh's to inquire for Miss Wardale's address. I found her in a house in Margaret Road. She is an elderly, pallid woman, rendered monstrous by a lower lip hanging loose enough to expose an irregular gum. I am to go to her on Tuesdays at 12.[10]

Having fixed this up I came back, taking a volume of Chaucer from the College library. At home I went to my room where I read

---

[8] See **Frank Percy Wilson** in the Biographical Appendix.
[9] He was referring to the fact that Lewis planned to read English in nine months.
[10] See **Edith Elizabeth Wardale** in the Biographical Appendix.

till lunch, finishing the first and two thirds of the second book of *Troilus*. I enjoyed it very much.

After lunch I bicycled to Merton St. as arranged and called for Jenkin. We set off along Parks Road, then through Wolvercote and Port Meadow. We went by the tow path, between golden trees, crossing many bridges, to Wytham village. Here, in defiance of the notice "strictly private" we entered with bated breath just under a game keeper's house, where my bike made a great noise. We met no one. The wood was glorious. It contains all kinds: in places there are open glades of green trunked oaks and brown bracken, elsewhere the intensest thickets. We got into open country on top of the hill – grassland with a lot of little valleys walled (partly) with some kind of white rock. Below was a huge landscape, behind us the edge of the wood, chiefly silver birches. It was at once so lonely, so wild, so luxurious, that we both thought of Acrasia's bower of bliss. To add to that suggestion, Jenkin saw at no great distance, a very comely couple *in flagrante*.

We went down the other side of the hill, emerging on the road at Swinford Bridge. We turned right and came along the river bank under the side of the wood. At Godstow we had a cup of tea in the Trout Inn, and so back to town. Jenkin remarked that natural beauty always affected him as the suggested background of a happiness that wasn't there: the scene was set, but one couldn't enjoy the scenery for wondering why the play never began.

At Gadney's I bought Sweet's *Anglo Saxon Reader*. I reached home by 6.30 and was sorry to find that D, since I had expected to be back for tea, had worried about me. After supper I started on a piece in the *Reader* which Miss Wardale had directed me to – Alfred's account of "Ohthere, the old sea captain". Late to bed.

Sunday 15 October: . . . Worked all morning in the dining room on my piece in Sweet's *Reader* and made some progress. It is very curious that to read the words of King Alfred gives more sense of antiquity than to read those of Sophocles. Also, to be thus realising a dream of learning Anglo-Saxon which dates from Bookham days.

At 12.45 I changed and bicycled to Chadlington Rd. to lunch with the Stevensons. Besides the family there was a pretty woman and a very tall man whose names I did not catch. We all laughed at Stevenson carving. Nothing of much interest was said, but I like both Stevenson and his wife very well. They are thoroughly unacademic.

Home by about 3.30 and did Anglo-Saxon till tea: afterwards went on with *Troilus*. Smudge came at 6.30 and I did Latin with her till 8, when we had supper. After that and washing up and more *Troilus* up till nearly the end of Book III. It is amazingly fine stuff. How absolutely anti-Chaucerian Wm. Morris was in all save the externals.

Joined D in the front room as soon as Mrs Hankin was gone to bed. D is becoming very dissatisfied with Dorothy and also with Ivy's habit of coming here daily almost, and inviting herself to meals in the kitchen . . .

Monday 16 October: Bicycled to the Schools after breakfast to a 10 o'clock lecture: stopping first to buy a bachelor's gown at the extortionate price of 32/6d. According to a usual practice of the Schools we were allowed to congregate in the room where the lecture was announced, and then suddenly told it would be in the North School: our exodus of course fulfilled the scriptural condition of making the last first and the first last. I had thus plenty of time to feel the atmosphere of the English School which is very different from that of Greats. Women, Indians, and Americans predominate and – I can't say how – one feels a certain amateurishness in the talk and look of the people.

The lecture was by Wyld on the History of the language.[11] He spoke for an hour and told us nothing that I haven't known these five years: remarking that language consisted of sounds, not letters, that its growth did not depend on conscious changes by individuals, that two and two make four, and other deep truths of that kind . . .

After lunch I bicycled again to Schools to seek out the library of the English School. I found it at the top of many stories, inhabited by a strange old gentleman who seems to regard it as his private property, talking about "I" and never "we". I got out W.M.Rossetti's collation of *Troilus* and *Il Filostrato* and came home . . .

I went back to *Troilus* and nearly finished Book V. It is simply amazing. Except *Macbeth* and one or two of the old ballads I don't know that any poetry has affected me more. Unfortunately whenever I look up a particularly fine stanza in Rossetti, hoping it will be Chaucer's own, it always turns out to be pure Boccaccio . . .

Tuesday 17 October: Bicycled to town after breakfast and went to Wyld's second lecture. Today he was clear and interesting, though still telling us what everyone should know already: the mere giving

---

[11] See **Henry Cecil Kennedy Wyld** in the Biographical Appendix. The series of lectures Lewis was attending was called "Outlines of the History of English" and they were given every Monday and Tuesday in Michaelmas Term.

of names to old conceptions is however useful . . .

I then cycled to 12 Margaret Road to Miss Wardale and had an hour's lesson. She gave me a kind of scheme of grammar: I am to read the *Riddles* for next time. She spoke of Classical education and said that for us English, who have no grammar of our own, it was a necessary introduction to the study of language. I thought this perfectly true . . .

From lunch till tea time I worked at an essay on *Troilus*. My prose style is really abominable, and between poetry and work I suppose I shall never learn to improve it.

Another very warm afternoon. D in excellent form. After tea I walked to Iffley churchyard and back. It was now a fine frosty evening. The village was beautiful, and especially the church with the trees all golden. As I walked, my head began to be full of ideas for the VI Canto of "Dymer". Forgot to mention that I wrote a fragment for the Vth last night, but without very much success . . .

Wednesday 18 October: After breakfast I sat in the dining room doing Vergil with Maureen: bicycled to Schools for a 12 o'clock lecture on Chaucer by Simpson, who turns out to be the old man I found in the English School library. Quite a good lecture.[12]

I found a letter from my father awaiting me in College. He has seen the result of the Magdalen show and writes very kindly. I then rode home (against a strong wind, bitter, tho' it was very bright) lunched, and retired to my own room. I began to have a headache and to feel very tired: lost control of my thought and finally gave it up. So left my books and walked to the foot of Shotover, thence by the field path to Cowley Barracks and home on the golf links.

I was just starting to work when Jenkin arrived and I went to him in the drawing room. We talked of *Troilus* and this led us to the question of chivalry. I thought the mere ideal, however unrealised, had been a great advance. He thought the whole thing had been pretty worthless. The various points which I advanced as good results of the Knightly standard he attributed to Christianity. After this Christianity became the main subject. I tried to point out that the mediaeval knight ran his class code and his church code side by side in watertight compartments.

Jenkin said that the typical example of the Christian ideal at work

---

[12] Percy Simpson (1865–1962) was Librarian of the English School 1914–34, Fellow of Oriel College 1921–36, and the editor of Ben Jonson. His lectures this Michaelmas Term 1922 were on "Chaucer".

was Paul, while admitting that one would probably have disliked him in real life. I said that one got very little definite teaching in the Gospels: the writers had apparently seen something overwhelming, but been unable to reproduce it. He agreed, but added that this was so with everything worth having . . .

Thursday 19 October: . . . Sat too long over my last cup of tea at breakfast and had to bus into town, thus arriving late at the Schools for my 10 o'clock lecture. This was by Onions on M[iddle] E[nglish] texts.[13] He is a good lecturer, but unfortunately stammers: tho' I noticed that in quoting verse (which he does well) he got rid of the stammer.

From this I came home and started to read the *Hous of Fame*, a work I do not much care for. I continued it after lunch until Dorothy suddenly announced that Cranny and his daughter were in the drawing room.

I went in, shook hands with him, and was introduced to her. I saw a girl over six feet high, broad in the shoulder as Tolley, with a large, sullen face, and a gruff, vulgar voice. She seemed to fill the whole room when she rose. "She could have ta'en Achilles by the hair." She refused to talk and never smiled. D presently joined me. Conversation was rather difficult.

With the girl it was something like this: "You have had a pony haven't you Miss Macran?" "No, worse luck." "We have had a very poor summer." "I got plenty of tennis thank goodness." "Maureen thought your school at Wantage very nice." "I don't." D remarked that we had a P.G. who was rather stiff: the girl said "Bring her to me. I'll unstiffen her." Her father said that the clergyman with whom he had been trying to exchange, seemed to have told him a lot of lies: upon which the girl said "Just like a parson." I said that Mr Goodacre had been a man with no mind: she shouted "Like me!" After each remark, which she blurted as if some demon were compelling her to break a vow of silence, her face relapsed at once into its settled expression of implacable ferocity and discontent. When I went out to make the tea, D set her to the piano: she vamped some rubbish and then sang a suggestive song in a high soprano – her speaking voice having the timbre of a coalheaver.

At tea Smudge and Maureen turned up from this afternoon's concert where they had heard Vaughan Williams' new symphony.

---

[13] See **Charles Talbut Onions** in the Biographical Appendix.

Shortly after them came Jenkin. He persuaded me to come in to his rooms for a few minutes. He showed me one or two poems of Donne's which I liked: he also read me some ballads recently written by Cornish miners: two of them were the real stuff. I asked him if he ever wrote verse now. He startled me by replying "No, you stopped me doing that." I asked him what he meant. He said I had told him, after seeing some of his work, that he needed a long course of technical discipline. He had thought this true, but decided that since he wouldn't give all his energies to it, he might as well give up . . .

Friday 20 October: In to the Schools for an eleven lecture on the O[ld] E[nglish] poetry by Miss Wardale.[14] We had the usual Schools business of being shifted twice before we were finally settled in the North School . . . Miss W., in her cap and gown, looks a very odd figure: quite a good lecture, but her voice is not strong enough and the strain of listening is tiresome. She drew a distinction between the pessimism of O.E. literature and the comparative cheerfulness of the Icelandic.

From there I bicycled through wind and rain to Wilson at 9 Manor Rd. I think I shall like him. He caught me up very sharply when I mentioned Fairfax in my essay, asking "What did he write?" This shows the sort of people he has to deal with, and I really think he was surprised to find that I had read Fairfax. We agreed over most points. He quoted from Legouis a view that Chaucer's Pandaurus was indistinct and merely a transition between Boccaccio's and Shakespeare's. What nonsense! He lent me Ker's *Mediaeval Essays*.

I came home. Mrs Hankin departed for London immediately after lunch: this was a delightful event, spoiled only by the prospect of her speedy return. I went to my own room, and after messing about with the prologue to the *Legend of Good Women* (pretty, but hopelessly mediaeval) I began the *Canterbury Tales* in great glee. Continued these till supper time, by which [time] I had reached the third part of the Knight's Tale.

Poor D is in very poor form these days. She has taken on too much work in the sewing line and is worried with it: she is also bothered by the laziness and uselessness of Dorothy . . .

Saturday 21 October: Up rather late and started Vergil with Maureen

---

[14] "Literary Introduction to the Poetry of the Anglo-Saxon Reader", which lectures were given every Friday during this term.

after breakfast, going on till eleven o'clock. Then I set to on my O.E. *Riddles*: did not progress very quickly but solved a problem which has been holding me up. Sweet is certainly an infuriating author . . .

D was much more cheerful than she has been for some time and for an hour or so we were quite merry. After tea I went to the drawing room and continued the *Tales*. Then supper: D's work, which has all my maledictions, had her worried again by that time, or perhaps it was depression. A delightfully small wash up, thanks to the absence of Mrs Hankin and other visitors. Afterwards I got as far as the end of the Reeve's Tale, which is pretty poor: but the Miller's capital.

Sunday 22 October: Up late and a fine cold morning. I went out shortly after breakfast taking *Two Gentlemen of Verona* in my hand. I finished it during my walk: it has some lines which are pretty in a faint way, and Launce with his dog is good, but on the whole it is poor stuff. I walked up Shotover and home by the wood path and Morris' works. There was a fine display of colours on the hill, I never saw them better. I remember particularly one tree, golden apple coloured with red bushes underneath.

Home to lunch at one thirty. Afterwards while D worked I sat in the dining room and went on with Chaucer, reading the *Man of Lawes Tale* – pretty work. D was in good form and we were all very merry at tea.

Afterwards I retired to the drawing room and had a go at the *Riddles*. I learned a good deal, but found them much too hard for me at present. I finally left them and learnt the passage on Cynewulf and Cyneheard from the *Chronicle* which I could manage well. Then supper and washing up, after which I started the passage of Aelfred on the state of learning in England.

Last of all D and I settled down by the drawing room fire. She read me from the *Sunday Times* the week's instalment of Mrs Asquith's *Biography*.[15] This week it was on the shell controversy, wrapped up in a lot of allusion and rhetoric, but with no clear defence that we could see. We talked of Mrs Hankin and her apparent indifference to her son's return from Spain. To bed, very jolly, at midnight.

Monday 23 October: Walked into town after breakfast to the Schools: there was a greater confusion than ever about the rooms, Wyld being announced "unable to go upstairs". We were finally shepherded into

---

[15] This was Vol. II of *The Autobiography of Margot Asquith* (1922).

a room that would not hold us, most of the audience standing outside and gradually trickling away. Wyld had a sprained ankle and delivered his lecture sitting: it was pretty interesting. He quoted a passage from *Prometheus Unbound* and said he didn't know where it came from.

I came home and did some more O.E. before lunch. Afterwards I sat in the drawing room and worked on Chaucer. My mind was disturbed somewhat by thinking what a poem could be written on the harrowing of hell: and I saw that most of the ideas which occurred to me in connection with Sarastro would come into this . . .

Tuesday 24 October: . . . After breakfast to the Schools to hear Wyld, who managed to come upstairs today. After his lecture I went to College, thence to the Union and to Taphouses to do a message for Maureen. I then bicycled to Margarets Road and did my tutorial with Miss Wardale. I think this old lady will not be much use: she is too much interested in phonology and theory of language, delightful subjects no doubt, but life is short . . .

Wednesday 25 October: . . . I went into town on foot and returned two books to the Union: taking out . . . a volume of Burns to prepare myself for tonight's Martlets . . .

I . . . went to the J.C.R. where I found Fasnacht, Salveson, Jenkin, Robson-Scott, Davie and others.[16] We had some amusing conversation and then departed to the Martlets meeting in the rooms of one McCissack.[17] These turned out to be the rooms I had when I first came up in 1917. Here I first was brought home drunk: here I wrote some of the poems in *Spirits in Bondage*. D had been in this room. It was all very reminiscent.

Curtis, who is now secretary, came in late and read the minutes between gasps: for some reason we all, including the secretary, dissolved into laughter and every word of the minutes became pregnant with ridiculous meaning. It was a good example of the group mind at work. Carlyle came in after the paper had begun.

It was on Burns, by a Scot called Dawson, a douce lad, whom I liked very much and shall try to get into touch with.[18] He, Salveson, and I had some talk during the interval: he and I arguing that the good emotions were more intense than the bad and that an amorist

---

[16] Keith Maitland Davie matriculated in 1919 and took a BA in 1922.

[17] Audley McKisack matriculated in 1921 and took a BA in Modern History in 1924.

[18] John Hill Mackintosh Dawson matriculated in 1921 and took a First in Classics in 1925.

might write tolerable songs, but it took a man of one affair to write the *Divine Comedy*. Salveson did not see the point and remained convinced to the end that we were defending good emotion *qua* good: whereas we were merely claiming that they happened to be the most interesting. The discussion after the interval was very good.

Carlyle was in great form. Curtis was rather absurd. By the bye, with his large nose, prominent teeth, straight hair and tortoise shell spectacles, he is exactly like the hero of *Tons of Money* in his parsonical scene. Carlyle said "The long poem was a will o' the wisp." I wonder is this a warning.

I walked home part of the way with Jenkin and Robson-Scott: later with a man called Mort. We went very fast along Cowley Road. I couldn't get him to talk. At last I said "You're the only man in Oxford who walks at a reasonable pace." He replied "I was just going to say the same thing."[19]. . .

Thursday 26 October: Woke very tired and with a headache, taking aspirin before breakfast. Walked to the Schools and heard a lecture by Onions.[20] As I came back I realised I had to finish the *Canterbury Tales* and write an essay on them by tomorrow: so to my room and went on at the *Clerke's Tale* (beastly story) reading at a pace which is rather an insult to the author.

When I came down for lunch D reminded me that Smudge was coming for lunch and lesson: this seemed to take away the last hope and it was so unexpected (I had quite forgotten her) that I am afraid I cursed her aloud in rather an inexcusable way. Soon afterwards she arrived and we had lunch. I did Latin with her till four o'clock and then resumed work.

With breaks for tea, supper, and washing up, I continued till 12 o'clock, by which time I had finished to my comparative satisfaction. Then to bed with sore limbs – the paradoxical result of brain work as I usually find it . . .

Friday 27 October: . . . After breakfast I did Vergil with Maureen till it was time to go to Miss Wardale's lecture in the School's. From this I cycled, a very wet ride, to Wilson. I arranged to come to him at 4.45 on Fridays in future instead of at 12, as I was then always necessarily late. He asked me to tea at four next Friday. I read him my essay and we discussed. He very sensibly refused to have any

[19] Arthur Basil Sutcliff Mort matriculated in 1919, read Modern History, and took a BA in 1923.
[20] "Middle English Texts."

theory about Melibeus and the *Monke's Tale*: one could imagine several things . . .

Letter . . . from Carritt. One of the Magdalen examiners has said that I was "probably the ablest man in": but that my fault is timidity and too much caution in letting myself go. He also asks me to come and see him . . .

Saturday 28 October: It grows colder every day. By first post D had a letter from Mrs Hankin saying that her son would not be coming up to Oxford and that she herself was staying in London to look for a job: she might or might not be coming back to us, and would we mind if she should not. Would we mind! . . .

Sunday 29 October: . . . Immediately after breakfast I got out my bicycle and started for Forest Hill. It was one of the coldest days we have had and a strong wind in my face all the way. As a result, tho' it cannot have been much about freezing, I was dripping with heat by the time I arrived.

She [Aunt Lily] is in a cottage which I once went to see for us a long time ago. From the windows you look across fields to the ridge of Shotover – she did not know of its connection with Shelley and was glad to hear of it. There is a very pleasant kitchen sitting room.

She has been here for about three days and has snubbed a bookseller in Oxford, written to the local paper, crossed swords with the Vicar's wife, and started a quarrel with her landlord.

The adventure of the Vicar's wife was good. That lady, meeting her in the Forest Hill bus, asked who she was, and promised to call. Aunt Lily said she might call if she liked, but she wasn't going to church. Being asked why, she said she had vowed never to enter any church until the clergy as a body came out in defence of the Dog's Protection Bill. "Oh!" said the priest's wife in horrified amazement, "So you object to vivisection?" "I object to all infamies," replied Aunt L.

Nevertheless the Vicar and his wife came to her all humble at the journey's end and said "Even if you don't come to church, will you come to our whist drive?" She says all parsons look like scolded dogs when you challenge them on this subject.

I refused an invitation to lunch, but stayed till one o'clock. She talked all the time, with her usual even, interminable fluency, on a variety of subjects. Her conversation is like an old drawer, full both of rubbish and valuable things, but all thrown together in great disorder. She is still engaged on her essay, which, starting three years ago as a tract on the then state of woman suffrage, is still unfinished and now embraces a complete philosophy on the significance of heroism and maternal instinct, the nature of matter, the primal One, the value of Christianity, and the purpose of existence. That purpose by the way is the return of differences to the One through heroism and pain. She thus combines a good deal of Schopenhauer with a good deal of theosophy: besides being indebted to Bergson and Plotinus.

She told me that ectoplasm was done with soap bubbles, that women had no balance and were cruel as doctors, that what I needed for my poetry was a steeping in scientific ideas and terminology, that many prostitutes were extraordinarily purified and Christ like, that Plato was a Bolshevist, that Bateson (?) at Oxford was one of the worst vivisectors in the world,[21] that the importance of Christ could not have lain in what He said, that Pekinese were not dogs at all but dwarfed lions bred from smaller and ever smaller specimens by the Chinese through ages innumerable, that matter was just the stop of motion and that the cardinal error of all religions made by men was the assumption that God existed for, or cared about, us.

I left "Dymer" with her and got away, with some difficulty, at one o'clock. I imagine a morning with Coleridge must have been something like this . . .

Monday 30 October: After breakfast I walked to the Schools and heard Wyld's lecture. Walked home again and settled down to Anglo-Saxon. Maureen back from a not very successful lesson with Mr Allchin. After lunch I went to the drawing room. Got the wretched *Riddles* finished at last – the one about the sun and the moon has got a sort of nursery rhyme charm about it which the poet, I am sure, never suspected. Went on with Aelfred's translation of the *Cura Pastoralis* . . .

At supper we talked of operas and Maureen asked me some questions about the *Ring* in a way that looks as if her imagination were coming to life at last . . . After finishing work I sat with D by the drawing room fire. She had a headache and was very worried about Maureen's slowness and dawdling and consequent inability to manage her work . . .

Tuesday 31 October: To Wyld's lecture after breakfast. I found a formal letter in College from the Mugger informing me that the

---

[21] She probably meant William Bateson (1861–1926) who had been Professor of Biology in Cambridge.

Master and Fellows had decided to continue my scholarship. I replied at once in the J.C.R. Then . . . I cycled to Miss Wardale. She startled me by promising to give me for next week a paper on all the phonetics and laws of mutation wh. she has been talking about and wh. I have not been listening to! . . .

I took out Hassal's *European Tables*, came home and started, with the help of it and Saintsbury, making out a table of English literature from 1500. I worked hard on this for the rest of the day . . .

Wednesday 1 November: . . . It was a wet, windy morning. I decided to skip Simpson's lecture and spent the morning hard at work on my table. After lunch I went to the library of the English Schools and read Wyld's most elementary book (I forget the title) by way of preparing for Miss Wardale's paper[1] . . . I then walked to the Union and took out a volume of Gower, containing the *Vox Clamantis* . . . the Latin poem is pitiable muck so far as I could see. After supper I began my essay, and brought my table down to the end of the 18th Century before going to bed.

Thursday 2 November: . . . I . . . went to the Schools library. Here I puzzled for the best of two hours over phonetics, back voice stops, glides, glottal catches and open Lord-knows-whats. Very good stuff in its way, but why physiology should form part of the English School I really don't know.

From there I went at four o'clock to the Union and took out a volume of Gower. Walked back. D and I were just sitting down to tea when the Doc turned up . . . After tea I came into the drawing room and went on with my essay: the Doc did not stay long. D is busy on her jumper for Miss Brody and again has a bit of a headache: we are afraid it may be her eyes. After supper and washing up I finished my essay.

Friday 3 November: . . . After lunch I went in to the library again and worried away at my phonetics, trying to master the laws of i-mutation. While I was there, a stout youth came in and began to talk to Simpson who was pasting in book plates at my table – the rule of silence apparently does not obtain in this library. He asked Simpson if [Walter] Raleigh had not been preparing a book on Chaucer before his death. Simpson said "No, he funked it, and he was quite right. He'd have been caught out on the scholarship. Now he once suggested to *me* that we might collaborate in a book on

---

[1] *A Short History of English* (1914).

Chaucer. I would have done the scholarship and he would have done the appreciation."

God above! Polonius and Ariel, Wagner and Euphorion would be well mated to this! Simpson droned on just beside me till he drove me nearly mad and I went out and bought pressed beef.

I then walked to Manor Place and had tea with Wilson. Perhaps he had a cold, or had been asleep over his fire: for whatever reason, I found him a little dull. I told him of my shock at finding that Miss Wardale expected me to know something of her phonetics. He said exactly the same thing had happened to him, but added that "Betsy Wardale had a fine mind."

He had been lunching with Gordon,[2] and Gordon had been talking about the difference between an Oxford and a Scotch audience at a lecture: here we sat looking as if we were bored, whether we were or not. There, they stamped with their feet when they were displeased and loudly applauded every good point. We agreed that the Scotch was the best practice. It would certainly do Simpson, Joachim and Joseph a lot of good.

Afterwards I read him my essay on Gower: he approved, I think, on the whole, but thought I should have read more. I like this man, tho' he is a bit sleepy . . .

Saturday 4 November: . . . I . . . got out my bike and started for Forest Hill – a delightful ride, tho' I have seen many an autumn with better colours. I met Aunt Lily coming down the hill to get milk and bread, in which duty I joined her after putting my bike in.

When we got back to the cottage she gave me some pages of her essay to read. I really had a great surprise. It is not in my line and I hope it is not true, but I must say I thought it great literature. It seemed to me – with all the obvious faults that some people will find in it – to have just "*that*" about it. I really believe it's going to last: not for its matter but for its enthusiasm.

You can see at any rate that she's a real, convinced prophet and not a bit of a quack. Her absolute inability to take in anything that cannot be used as fuel for her own particular fire is also a prophet's characteristic fault.

We talked on several subjects. Speaking of a wife who had left a bad husband she said "Her consolation is that she has stopped a bad heredity from perpetuating itself: her strain and her bringing up has

---

[2] See **George Stuart Gordon** in the Biographical Appendix.

made good the children, so that particular man is done with – biologically."

She said the part of Hamlet could never be done properly on the stage because Hamlet wd. have to be fat: his particular trouble – inability to feel the emotions which the intellect clearly recognises as right – was dementia praecox which goes with obesity. She surprised me by liking *The Taming of the Shrew*: she said that Petruchio was the only one of all Shakespeare's heroes whom she herself would have married. She also declared that Richardson was, next to Shakespeare, the greatest knower of characters and perhaps Shakespeare's equal. She also put Jane Austen very high in that line. She said that Bergson's chapter on "Rein" was the worst in the book and in it he had relapsed into intellectualism: I thought it the most intuitive and wonderful of the lot.

She strongly disapproved of "Dymer" which I had left with her last week. She called it brutal. She said "Where has all your old simplicity and rightness of language gone?" She said I seemed to be deliberately slipshod and wrong in my words and "positively like Bill Patterson".[3] She also said I "must *not* describe". When she came to a description of a wood in a poem – whether in Keats or me!! – she gave it up. She didn't mind a man writing a poem just about a wood: but to have a wood flung in your way when you were reading about a man – !

She said what I needed was the sort of swing you get in *Don Juan*: I was surprised to find that she knew *Don Juan*. She said it was the only thing of Byron's she could ever read. She ridiculed the view that it was immoral. What she particularly liked was the swing forward. She said I had utterly failed to get this: or, relenting, that I had only a trace of it here and there. I asked her if she disliked Dymer himself: she said, no, it was me: Dymer was just a young animal let loose.

She said that in reading Bacon she had often been struck by Shakespearian echoes: and when the Baconian theory first came out she had taken it up keenly. Later on she noticed that the Baconian bits of Shakespeare usually came in the speeches of Polonius and such characters: so that Shakespeare was not indebted to Bacon's writings but to Bacon the man, much as he was indebted to the original of Dogberry.

---

[3] William Hugh Patterson (1835–1918) was an ironmonger in Belfast and a friend of the Lewis family. A liberal curiosity and love of punning caused him to take up intellectual hobbies, and in 1920 he published a volume of poems.

I left – or started leaving – about 3.30. She kindly insisted on my taking away a bottle of cream and a volume of Emerson. This last she had intended to give me one day at Holywood: but I had said in the course of our talk "Damn Emerson!" and so she refrained even till now . . .

Monday 6 November: In the morning to Wyld's lecture. I was very much impressed by his abuse of the privilege of monologue. He said of a certain word "Some of you superfine young gentlemen may pronounce it so – if you ever deign to mention such a vulgar thing. I don't care if you do. I pronounce it so." This is the only occasion on which I have ever noticed a similar hectoring strain: and all the women laughed obsequiously . . .

Coming home I found Jenkin here. He had called to ask me out for a ride, but this was of course impossible. I spoke of the personnel of the English school. I said that I had expected to find them more liberal and "humane" than the Greats people: but, instead, they seemed pedantic and rather ill bred. He agreed with my feeling about Wyld. Wyld, he said, had been heard to boast that he enjoyed frightening people at vivas: and at some minor university where he had been, female candidates usually left him in floods of tears. He was in fact an ordinary bully: and, while professing a purely scientific attitude towards rival pronunciations, he was in fact morbidly class conscious. A snob, who liked to picture himself a country gentleman of the old school and piqued himself on saying "wescitt" . . .

Tuesday 7 November: My cold still very heavy. I decided to skip the Cad Wyld's lecture and worked hard translating the *Wanderer* till 11.30 when I bicycled to Miss Wardale's. She seemed quite pleased with what I had done, and we had a useful hour.

On getting home I heard from D that Mrs Stevenson wanted me to tutor Sydney in Latin. This at first I refused point blank to do: but afterwards I found that it could be swopped against Mrs Stevenson's tutoring of Maureen and thus save money. We are too poor to waste and I arranged to take her on Sundays.

After lunch I bicycled to Jenkin's rooms . . . We started by the Botley Road and went through Ferry Hinksey . . . When we got to Thessaly we laid our bikes down in the bracken and walked into the wood. We went further than I have ever been, across three ridges. We were as pleased as two children revelling in the beauty, the secrecy, and the thrill of trespassing. Jenkin's undisguised delight in the more elementary pleasures of a ramble always bucks me: one really would not be surprised if he suddenly said, "Let's pretend to be Red Indians." I got the real joy in this wood. We spent a long time there and got back late to his rooms, where we had tea. He read me a new piece of his which I liked: he made me read aloud "Foster" which I had lent him and which he liked very well . . .

Thursday 9 November: . . . I worked hard all morning finishing *Piers Plowman*: I read it all in the C text, except the last passages on Antichrist. It contains some bits which, all said and done, have more of the real thing than poor old Chaucer could ever have managed – and very little of the usual mediaeval cackle about Cato and Boethius. In the few minutes before lunch I started my essay.

Smudge came to lunch and afterwards I did Latin with her till tea time. After tea I continued my essay, and so also after supper. D rather depressed and suffering from a headache. Extraordinarily tired tonight.

Friday 10 November: I had the devil of a night. I was twice sick and spent the rest of the time between sleeping and waking in a sort of feverish muddle of headache and dreams about *Piers Plowman* – the sort of dream which seems to go on for years and years and is so wearisome you'd be glad of a nightmare for a change. Some very heavy rain just as it was getting light . . .

Got home and changed (in preparation for the concert) . . . to which I was to go with Maureen. I read for a few minutes when D saw an advertisement of a house to let in the *Oxford Times*. I at once bussed to Ship St. to Galpin's the house agent, but found it shut. Home again and supper: after which Maureen and I set out.

Tho' not much better I did not greatly want to come and was therefore the more pleased at finding I could enjoy it. The best thing was the Beethoven Sonata – like a Titan's laughter but with all the melancholy just underneath. I find it is no good for me to hear Chopin immediately after Beethoven – seems so luxuriously self pitying. Home in fairly good time and to bed.

Saturday 11 November: Into town to Galpin immediately after breakfast to find that there have been forty applicants and the house was already let. Then home and worked at O.E. Grammar as long as I could stand it. Then turned to the *Wanderer*. For a few minutes before lunch I walked round the circle of the roads taking

The Return with me. I understand very little of the dialogue in this book: worth reading for the one sentence "We are all like children playing knuckle bones in a giant's scullery."[4] After lunch, having got held up in the *Wanderer*, I began *Beowulf*. Worked hard rather than well till tea time: a wet afternoon and very dark.

D was better than yesterday but depressed by the day. At tea time the Doc turned up. He seemed in good form and was very full of Dr Brown's last lecture. I had meant to go out but stayed talking after tea. We discussed Tennyson: the Doc was enthusiastic about *Ulysses*: we also joined in the innocent amusement of raving our common praises of our favourite parts of Keats and Shelley . . . At about 6.30 he left and I walked back with him, talking of everything in and out of earth in such voices that the passers by may have taken us for politicians. We went beyond his lodgings to the end of Iffley village to look at the church and the trees in the starlight. I don't know how, but we fell to talking of death – on the material side – and all the other horrors hanging over one. The Doc said that if you stopped to think, you couldn't endure this world for an hour. I left him and walked home.

Flashes and bangs from Oxford where they were celebrating Armistice night . . .

Sunday 12 November: . . . After an early lunch Maureen and I cycled to the Sheldonian to hear the Bach Choir. We got seats on a window sill just under the painted roof. There was a great press of people. I noticed Curtis, Fasnacht, Emmett, Robson-Scott, Mort and Cyril Bailey:[5] the latter was in the Choir and got apple red and wagged his head over the *Dies Irae* in a way to warm your heart – a good old boy. From the windows opposite I looked out on the roof of the Clarendon Building and other gables beyond, with a wintry sky, so that it was a good way to hear music.

The chief item was Verdi's Requiem Mass, a very enjoyable work, tho' not so fine as the composer meant it to be. The contralto was good. We also had Elgar's Funeral March from *Grania*, Parry's *Jerusalem* and Vaughan Williams' setting of "For all the Saints". The march I liked: the other two were spoiled by the bad, sentimental practice of making the audience join in. V. Williams' tune seemed

---

[4] Walter de la Mare, *The Return* (1910), ch. XVI.
[5] The Rev. Cyril William Emmet (1875–1923) was Chaplain and Fellow of University College 1920–3.

just as dull as any ordinary hymn. Maureen enjoyed the Mass enormously.

We bicycled home and had tea, after which I finished my O.E. for Miss Wardale. In the evening I started a new fair copy of "Foster" and made some corrections which pleased me exceedingly. I then read Mrs Asquith's instalment to D. Afterwards we fell into a gloomy conversation on death and chance and permanent danger . . .

Monday 13 November: . . . At breakfast D had an answer to *her* answer to an advertisement of a house she had seen in the *Oxford Times*. We decided that no time was to be lost, and I set off on my bike. Directed by the G.P.O., I rode down St Aldate's and beyond the river, turning before the railway bridge to my left into a very squalid alleyway. I followed this, thinking I had come to a poor place: but after several cottages, it brought me over a number of wooden bridges and among fields and willow trees to the house itself beside the weir.

The squalor was quite out of sight: to the back of the house lay a complicated arrangement of pools, ratchets, waterfalls and bridges overhung with pollards: and in front of it level fields with two haystacks in view. Just by the railing of the garden was a man with a bicycle who turned out to be a rival tenant. We had both been told in our letters that "Mr Tombs" would be there to show us over it before 10 or after four. No Mr Tombs however appeared: my rival told me that Mr T. lived at No. 7 and so departed.

The sun was coming out nicely now, and the whole place looked enchanted. I had some difficulty in climbing the railing. Once in, I surveyed everything as well as I could without a key. It is an odd cottage with big bow windows of later date put into it. The principal rooms were back to back and windows at opposite ends of the house: they were low but large rooms and very jolly. It appeared however to have outdoor sanitation and of course no gas or bathroom. The large garden was surrounded by a fence and a ditch and inhabited by hens. The sound of the weir was over everything. I went to No. 7 but no Mr Tombs was there . . .

I biked home through Iffley and reported to D. I felt like doing nothing but expiating on the beauty of the place, but pointed out all the practical drawbacks. I promised to try again at 4 and then went to my work.

After lunch I went to the English library, returned two books and read Ascham's *Schoolmaster*, also referring to a *Beowulf* crib for some hard passages. I left the library and walked via Folly Bridge and the towpath to the Weir House . . .

Reaching the house I found another man climbing out over the railings. I crossed the bridges and knocked at No. 7. No answer. I waited for a long time, watching many ducks in the lane, two rabbits scratching each other in a hutch and a fine red sunset over Bagley Woods. I tried to get into talk with my new rival but he would not. Presently Mr Tombs – appropriately a very dark man – turned up. The rival at once engaged him in a whispered conversation. When at last he was free, I asked to see over the house. "It's all settled," replied Tombs and I walked home thro' Iffley with this news.

D and I were very wise now and decided for excellent reasons that the place would never have done . . .

Tuesday 14 November: Many degrees of frost this morning and a thick fog, which, as D read in the paper, is all over England and Europe. I set off after breakfast to the Cad's lecture: Southfield Road with its iced cobwebs was very jolly. I was already on top of the bus when Maureen joined me on her way to Dr Allchin.

I was late at the Schools, but this did not matter, as the Cad was late. He lectured for about half an hour, devoting most of his time to an attack on Bridges and to boasting of his victory in discussion over one unnamed who had lectured somewhere on the pronunciation of English. "I had him in the hollow of my hand," said the Cad. To do him justice, if his own account was fair, his adversary seemed to have been absolutely wrong, and even silly . . .

I bussed to Miss Wardale's where I had an interesting hour. She tells me that the theory of an Asiatic origin for the Aryans has been abandoned and their cradle now placed on the shore of the Baltic . . .

Wednesday 15 November: The fog was still here in the morning but not so heavy. D had a letter from Moppie by the first post. In this she told us that she had written to the Bitch from Swansea for a skirt she wanted, which the Bitch had sent her. Since then the Bitch had written her several letters asking where she is etc., to which Moppie has not replied: and she has now got one asking her about the bicycle. Moppie ended by urging us not to come into contact with her "for fear of her terrible tongue".

This letter worried us both. We were surprised that Moppie should have so little prudence and so little pride as to write any request to the woman: we also thought it unfair of her to do so without telling us, the more so that it had apparently happened long ago and we should never have heard of it but for the trouble about the bike.

It had also been arranged that Moppie should send D what money she cd. manage from week to week in payment of the considerable amount we had to pay for her escape etc. None of this has ever arrived, nor has Moppie ever mentioned the subject. D, who hates a lie of all things, was very disturbed: and indeed has never quite trusted Moppie since the Baker affair. Of course it is natural that the girl shd. be deceitful after such an upbringing, but the thing is a worry . . .

Friday 17 November: After breakfast I worked at *Beowulf* in the dining room until 11.30 when I walked to the Schools to hear a lecture by Gordon, Raleigh's successor . . . Gordon was very good and I am sorry to have missed his earlier lectures.[6]

I walked home and had lunch, at which Smudge turned up. She said she couldn't go to *Samson and Delilah* and it was arranged that I should take Maureen.

Almost immediately after the meal Cranny turned up. I persuaded D to stay alone in the dining room while I went to the drawing room and sustained conversation, which I found very tedious. Cranny, apropos of a boy who had been brought up for the church and found himself thinking too far to believe, said that his own parents had taken it for granted that he wd. be a parson: he had got to the stage of reading Renan before he was confirmed but he hadn't known what else to do – and there he is . . .

I . . . bussed with Maureen to the theatre. It was the Carl Rosa company, but at their worst with none of the best singers and – worst of all – a miserable orchestra: it sounded like two second hand violins and a penny whistle. They were all slack, especially the conductor, and did not even make the best of their wretched resources. Under these conditions we had a poor show: but I think the opera was rubbish, apart from the rendering. It has not simple melody like Sullivan nor pure musical development like Beethoven, nor (of course) passion and pictures like Wagner. It just drivels along, sentimental, bombastic, "operatic" in the worst sense of the word. I was very disappointed as I had always thought St Saëns was a good man from the bits I knew. The audience in our immediate neighbourhood behaved abominably.

---

[6] The lectures, Monday and Friday, were on "Shakespeare".

Came home with a headache and found D still pretty wretched. She had had some talk with Cranny after I left. He was in deep depression: "Life is one tragedy. I haven't had any big troubles like you, but all my life has been a disappointment. And now my boy is – a policeman!" He had said, poor man, that he hoped his son would be like me – a modest request. Then came the tragi-comic remark: "Violet (see 19 October) of course gets on with everybody!"

Lateish to bed. Today was Paddy's birthday: D reminded me that this day five years ago I sailed from Southampton. (Dreamed the night before last that I was with my father and he complained of my letters. His complaint appears in waking memory as if he said "they are just one word after another", but I understood it well enough in the dream.)

Sunday 19 November: I went out for a walk after breakfast, taking *The Cenci* with me. I went up Shotover – a misty morning and cool ... I was reading *The Cenci* industriously and I find that one really sees more of the country with a book than without: for you are always forced to look up every now and then and the scene into which you have blundered without knowing it comes upon you like something in a dream. I went all through the thickest part of this valley with great enjoyment. The mist improved it: the autumn colours, tho' not as splendid as some years, were very pleasant and there was a good smell ...

Monday 20 November: After breakfast went to the Schools to the Cad's lecture. He distinguished himself this morning by doing what I've never seen nor heard of a lecturer doing. He suddenly turned upon a man sitting in the front row and exclaimed "Do you understand that? Could you give an explanation of that?" The man very naturally made no answer. "H'ngh!" grunted the Cad, "You weren't listening, were you? I should advise you to listen if I were you." It is really ridiculous how angry this little incident made me for the rest of the day ... At 12 I returned to the Schools to hear Gordon on Shakespeare's language – a capital lecture.

Walked home and had lunch and spent the afternoon on my Old English. At tea came Jenkin who worked with Maureen. I had to go to town again to return two books to the Union and walked both ways. Afterwards I walked a little of the way back with Jenkin. I told him of the Cad's action this morning. He said this sort of thing was quite common. He had once turned upon a girl in the front row who was turning over the pages of her note book and bellowed

"Haven't you found the place yet, there? I am not going to lecture in this Sunday School way." I begin to understand why the Greats School was called *Literae Humaniores*.

After supper I finished my paper for Miss Wardale. I am becoming reconciled to this phonetic stuff which gives me new lights all the time – and her *Grammar* is very good: a great advance upon Sweet. D seemed very much better this evening: we talked about Moppie more cheerfully than before. Started *Love's Labour Lost* just before going to bed.

Tuesday 21 November: Finished the first act of *Love's Labour Lost* over my morning tea. It is deliciously musical. Maureen had been suffering from pains near the heart yesterday, and as they were still there this morning, D decided that she must see the Doc. D said she would be quite fit to go with her: and as I wanted to make up a lot of my tutorial with Miss Wardale I very foolishly believed that this would be so. They two accordingly set off and I worked at *Beowulf* till 11.30 when I bicycled to St Margaret's Road. I had a good and interesting hour and came home.

Here I found the Doc and was met with the bad news that D, who had walked instead of bussing via the Plain, had had a collapse on the road and nearly fainted – luckily meeting the Doc, just at that moment. He had got her into a neighbouring house where she had been given whiskey and rested, after which he brought her back. I blamed myself very much for having let her go, and her for having walked. The whole thing was a sickening surprise and frightened me . . .

After lunch I biked to Jenkin's rooms: I found him also in poor form, having been depressed and worried by a conversation held last night with a religious person. We discussed where we should go. As it was a gloomy and fogged day I suggested that we should seek out "fountain heads and pathless groves" or any melancholy place which would underline the mood of the day to grandeur. He voted for Binsey and off we went. He led me onto the tow path between pollards which goes to the Trout Inn: then over bridges and a common, along a muddy lane and onto an avenue of trees with gates.

Finally we came to a sad church by a woodside. This is the church of St Fritheswide.[7] The door way has a Norman arch so low that I

---

[7] Lewis was wrong about the name. He was in the little Church of St Margaret, Binsey (built c. 730), confirmed as belonging to St Frideswide Priory in 1122, and which is today held in plurality with St Frideswide Church, Osney.

almost touched it with my head and, inside, the church was very dark. We struck matches to try and read the names on the brasses. Coming out, we investigated the well which sprang up in answer to the prayers of St Frithswide. The water has miraculous powers and used to be sold at a guinea a quart. Here Jenkin found a silver plated pencil. We then shuffled through a lot of dead leaves among the graves to where the churchyard is divided from the wood by an almost quite black stream.

A felled tree, tho' half rotten, made a bridge which took us safely across. It was a good but dreary wood: and very dark. When we had got into a thicket we were driven back by the smell of something dead and had a little difficulty in finding our original track among the marshy places.

I said I had lately been suffering from *timor mortis conturbat me*:[8] Jenkin was in the same state – the suffocating feeling. He also said his great trouble was to know which is the real ideal. Was one to crush the physical desires altogether – to be pagan or puritan? He added however that he had a fear of knowing the real ideal for certain – it might be a startler. I was much interested in this. We crossed back into the graveyard and rode home.

He said this religious person had worried him by laying an exaggerated weight on things which Jenkin considered trivial – such as dancing at the Masonic and kissing grisettes. Jenkin hadn't the least doubt really, he said, but such a conversation stuck in his mind. He confessed to a feeling that possibly even trivial things might be all the while preventing you from getting something else out of life, which, perhaps, people like his friend had.

We had tea in Jenkin's room, consuming much bread and butter. He asked whether one ought to think about Death or put it out of one's mind: since we could never find out what it meant. I said one wanted to go on thinking about it till one reached a point of view from which it didn't matter whether you were immortal or not. One wanted to find a value wh. was quite full in one moment and independent of time. We agreed that there must be such a thing because, as a fact, human beings had found it. I remarked that this was obviously what Christ had been talking about: but either he or his reporters had utterly failed to explain what it was or how you got it. Jenkin said he did not think that there was

---

[8] "The fear of death is troubling me", the refrain from William Dunbar's poem "Lament for the Makaris".

any question of "Getting it": it had to come "from without" . . .

Thursday 23 November: . . . After lunch I went out for a walk up Shotover, thinking how to make a masque or play of Psyche and Caspian. I went to the end of the ridge and then by the footpath to the heath part overlooking the Horsepath lane. It was a very grey day with one bit of break high up in the sky. I went down by the side of the fence on my right, straight down where I have never been before and got into a thick woody part. Beyond the fence was a deep glen – just like the Irish ones – with very big trees and all rich brown. I got a very good touch of the right feeling. There was a great scurry of birds. Some pheasants flew out and gave me rather a start. I went as far down as I could, then to my left, and up again . . .

I don't know if I was in a particularly receptive mood or whether it was the day, but this afternoon the trees and the sky and everything had quite an extraordinary effect on me.

I was struck by the idea that the feeling some chatterboxes get in solitude and wh. they would call "the pip" may be exactly the same as what I had, only I like and they don't.

Found D busy on work for Lady Gonner with the Varmint on her knee. As soon as I had been to Robertsons for some tobacco we had tea, after which I read *Henry IV* part I till supper time. I think this is one of the best things I have ever read – especially Hotspur . . .

Friday 24 November: Another very cold morning. After breakfast I worked in the dining room on my notes for Wilson until 11.30 when I walked to the Schools to hear Gordon's lecture. There I met Robson-Scott who asked me if I would go to Cambridge with the Martlets next week, which of course I refused. He asked me if seven would be too many to send, to which I replied with a very strong affirmative. Jenkin came and sat by us. I asked R-S what was to be done about Wyld: he was not greatly interested and went on to say that Gordon's lectures were "too chatty", which I thought silly. Probably he said it for cleverness. Just then Gordon came in and gave a very charming lecture. Afterwards Jenkin walked with me as far as the bridge end. We talked about Hotspur.

I then came home and had lunch alone with D. Afterwards I finished my notes and read *Henry IV* till time for an early tea, after which I bussed to Carfax . . . and walked to Manor Place. Here I was just preparing to read my notes when I discovered that I had brought the wrong note book – an old one full of philosophical essays and bits of poems. Luckily I remembered what I had written pretty

well and so had a profitable hour. My opinion of Wilson improves:
but he needs to be pricked, he sleeps too much and sits by the fire ...
Saturday 25 November: ... I reached Aunt Lily's cottage at about
2.38. She was still getting lunch ready and asked me to have a second
meal, which I refused, and talked to her while she ate. We threshed
out her mysterious letter. My first complex apparently is the common
or garden wall complex which, she said, shows itself in the IVth
Canto of "Dymer".

My "other complex" is the "Dymer" myth itself. She told me that
I had had at the age of six or seven a "little dog" who hurt his paw
and with whom I sat up all night: and that my father sent the dog
away "because of Mr Patterson". She must be referring to Nero who
did hurt his paw. But he was a collie, not a "little dog": I never sat
up all night with it: he was sent away because he chased sheep: I do
not remember feeling murderous about the subject – altho' just as I
write these words I remember a great deal more emotion than I
thought I did: possibly this is paramnesia.

The coarseness of "Dymer" depended apparently on the word
"wenched" in the first Canto. She took this very seriously: excused
me on the ground of having no mother or sisters and because Oxford
men were notoriously coarse – coarser than those of Cambridge. I
reminded her that it was Cambridge undergraduates who had torn
down the gates of women's colleges and jeered at them. She replied
without hesitation "The young men are quite right to defend
themselves."

She then told me a very disgusting story of two medical students
here in Oxford, who she had seen dragging off a dog into the
laboratories: and they were laughing together as they talked of the
old man who had sold it making them promise to give it a good
home and be kind to it. After that I no longer defended Oxford again
nor ever shall.

Of "Dymer" she took a more favourable view than before,
especially of the first canto. She said Shakespeare's Theseus was the
most perfect gentleman in all literature, and *As You Like It* the best
comedy. She agreed with me that Keats would have been greater than
them all, even perhaps than Shakespeare, if he had lived: for he had
a perfect medium, but died before he found much to say through it.
She praised Tirrell (Conservative member for the county) very highly
for his honesty. She also told me how Asquith had completely broken
down under the Suffragette campaign of 1913 – and had wept before

two women in Edinburgh (armed with parasols) until they had to hold him up. She knew one of these women intimately . . .

Sunday 26 November: A heavy frost, a cold wind. We were rather late in getting up and after breakfast I walked out, taking Ben Jonson with me and began the *Alchemist*. I got far enough to enjoy the fine vigour of the first scene — like Corneille, tho' so unlike, he gets something superhuman into his characters — tho' mere comedy rogues — when it became too windy to read.

I crossed the river at Iffley lock where they are building a pretty, new bridge, roofed like a lych-gate. On the other side it was delightful: a sky like steel with a very pale yellow sun that you could look at as easily as the moon, and the river all whipped up by the wind. There was a good deal of ice among the weeds. I walked as far as the weir just before Sandford lock: stood on the bridge and watched the water for a long time till the bridge seemed to move backwards.

Walked home again and chatted till lunch. D was in very good form. Afterwards I read *Henry V*. Started by hating it because it is about a most inexcusable war lord, but was quite converted before I finished . . .

Monday 27 November: Worked at Anglo-Saxon grammar and the *Battle of Maldon* till lunch time and after lunch till 3 o'clock. *The Battle of M.* is ripping and I am glad to have found the original of a passage I have known for years . . .

On emerging at supper time I found that Mrs Taylor had called. D had wondered why and bided her time and presently out the cat came from its very miserable bag. Mrs Taylor is hoping to get Uncle Bunny's (Kempshead of Magdalen)[9] house. It is to be let and Mrs T. has seen over it. D had pooh-poohed the idea, telling her that we had been to see about it nearly a year ago: when the old man told us he wanted to sell, and if he *did* let he had already forty applicants.

"Oh, are *you* looking for a house?" asked Mrs Taylor, who knows well that we have been looking since 1919 and often talked to us of the matter in the days when we saw more of her. She is now greatly surprised to hear of our desire for a house: and after suggesting that we might go to Iffley and remarking, apropos of Lord knows what,

[9] Chaloner Thomas Taplin Kemshead (1854–1929) was a Lecturer in French and German at Magdalen College 1905–23.

that her sisters could not do without a servant "as they had never been brought up to that sort of thing", she departed. It is an indignity to be angry with Mrs Taylor tho' God knows she lied: she lied like a procuress.

What really worried me was Uncle Bunny. He was a man of our own class with no ground in the world to bear us a grudge: and I began to have a sinister feeling that there is something really queer in us that makes us permanently unfortunate in these matters. Uncle Bunny, by the way, is the Headington mystery. Some say he lives in an incestuous amour with his niece "Peter" Grimbly and pity his wife: others, that his wife is mad, and pity the poor old man. The story however seems to come from Wendy and I doubt if it has any evidence. D said she was quite convinced that she wd. never again live in a house of her own.

All supper time we sat in judgement on Headington and its people (whom God reject) and perhaps felt the better for it. D had rather a bad headache. She had been disgusted to hear that Mary proposes to drag the unfortunate Doc to London next week to buy her a fur collared coat, tho' he wears the cast offs of his friends and does not even buy himself a newspaper . . .

Later on D and I fell to talking of all the people who had failed us as mysteriously as those who had turned enemy. As we turned over the list I could not help exclaiming that with few exceptions I loathed the female sex . . .

Wednesday 29 November: D got an answer about a house in Woodstock Road and we decided to see about it at once. D said she was quite well enough to go. We all three set out after breakfast and bussed to Carfax, thence to 204 Woodstock Road. It was a beautiful frosty day with a blue sky: D was naturally delighted at being out again and we were all in good spirits.

The house stood on the right side of the road and opposite it were open fields looking across to Wytham Woods – a delightful view, not spoiled to my mind by two tall chimneys and a sheet of water. The house, except for the smallness of the garden, was everything that could be desired, but of course we hardly dare to have hopes of getting it: and as the rent is £100 I consider it a very dangerous experiment.

We had just come out from seeing it – we were shown over by a maid, the mistress being out – and were waiting for a bus, when a woman who had seen us came out and spoke to D. This turned out to be the owner, and D returned with her to the house, while Maureen and I walked up and down.

As we passed a house with very large bow windows I happened to look up: and in the window I saw an old lady whom I thought I recognised as Cousin Mary.[10] I could not be sure and did not risk a second glance. I returned alone on the far side of the road and kept out of sight until D came out again. This little episode was quite enough to spoil the blue sky for me, and I was rather poor company (I'm afraid) for the rest of the morning. D had been nicely received by the owner (Mrs Waters I think) and we have been promised first chance if the house is let: but of course they are thinking of selling it . . .

This was my birthday and I am now twenty four: whether it was that, or the face at the window this morning, I don't know, but I was depressed and remember this as rather a nasty day. On the other hand it was a great comfort that D was none the worse for being out and I think really the better. We had a horrible episode this evening (Tibbie being sick in the drawing room after a gorge of stolen fish wh. Dorothy had foolishly left within her reach.) Late to bed.[11]

Thursday 30 November: Poor D had a miserable night, first being kept awake by toothache and then woken again by an unusually bad nightmare. We were all late in getting up. I spent the morning starting my essay on Bacon and made very satisfactory progress . . .

I showed Jenkin the end of Canto II of "Dymer" which he had never seen since I put in what Barfield used to call the "PASH". He pronounced it "simply splendid". I then walked back with him to his rooms: listening to a diatribe against women. He said no woman under forty was to be trusted. We became very merry later on . . .

---

[10] Lewis's "Cousin Mary" was his mother's first cousin, Lady Ewart (1849–1929) who lived in Belfast. While it seems most unlikely that Lady Ewart would be in Oxford, Lewis was worried about his family discovering that he shared a house with Mrs Moore.

[11] This day 1917 I arrived first in the front line at Monch le Preux. – C.S.L.

Friday 1 December: . . . I . . . finished my work: thence to Gordon's lecture at Schools where I met Jenkin. The lecture was excellent, tho' the best part was a long quotation from Lessing on the question of historical truth in drama. He also told us that this would be his last lecture for the term and referred humorously to the usual practice of lecturers who pretend to be very annoyed if anything prevented their lecturing. I like everything about this man . . .

I walked in to Wilson and read him my essay on Bacon. He seemed pleased with it, and we had some good discussion: afterwards on Spenser, in whom he could find no foreshadowing of Milton tho' afterwards he admitted some of my examples and even advanced others of his own . . .

Maureen gave us an amazing account of lunch with the Raymonds today. Mr R. was drinking sherry and his wife asked for some. "This sherry is nearly finished," replied he "why not have some port?" "That's just like you," retorted mother Raymond, "you're always getting wine for yourself and you'll never let anyone else have any." This quarrel continued throughout the meal, while by a species of domestic counterpoint, the children kept up a separate one between themselves . . .

Saturday 2 December: By the first post came a letter from Harwood, couched in the kindest terms imaginable – tho' the saying that both he and Barfield thought my mock epistle one of my best things was rather a shaky compliment. He included two new poems of his own, "The soldier's coat" and a poem about an empty room and pocket Horace.[1] These both seemed to me extraordinarily original. He has got hold of a queer little haunting province of his own. I was more pleased with them than with anything that my friends (including myself) have written for a long time . . .

Ivy had called and presently D came in to tell me the shocking

---

[1] "The Soldier's Coat" and "The Empty Room" are found in *The Voice of Cecil Harwood: A Miscellany*, ed. Owen Barfield (1979).

story of how Ivy had mentioned the death of her fiancé – sandwiched in between an account of some private theatricals and a description of hospital politics – apparently with no feeling. He died the day before yesterday. Ivy went still lower: she said it was hard luck, "I never even thought of any other man: I never flirted with anyone." She seemed to think she deserved the praise of a heroine because she had gone to see him at 4.30 a.m. when he was ill: I am very surprised and disappointed in Ivy: I had quite believed in her. Dorothy seems to have felt as D did.

After lunch I biked to Forest Hill at top speed. Aunt Lily had not got my letter saying I would not come to lunch: so I forced myself to have some soup . . . She propounded a theory that genius resulted from a process the opposite of that which produced identical twins – from the coalescing of two ova: and remarked that this was supported by the fact that genius seldom reproduced itself – having already exchanged differences in its own person . . .

We ended by discussing her philosophy. I said she urged us to co-operate with Life: I asked whether, remembering what Life might be really aiming at, there was any reason to help? Was the game worth the candle? She said there was the choice. It wasn't her business to choose for anyone else. I showed her Harwood's two pieces, which she pronounced with conviction to be real poetry . . .

Sunday 3 December: . . . After lunch Maureen and I biked to the Sheldonian where we again got window seats in the upper gallery. We had a very complicated bill of fare and unfortunately could not get programmes. Sir Hugh [Allen] conducted: the orchestra being rather smaller than before. They gave Bach's "Sleeper awake" which I didn't make much of, Besley's "Dominus Illuminatio" which I liked, and Vaughan Williams' "Fantasia on Christmas Carols". This was interesting, especially his device of making the chorus *hum* in places which produces a very fine effect.

Best of all, they did some fragments of the *Messiah*, in which I got quite unexpected pleasure – for at one time it was quite staled to me on the gramophone and in my Wagner craze I despised Handel. The afternoon closed with some carols in which the audience lugubriously joined. In the whole, I enjoyed this show less than most – and what I really remember was the excellent view from the window we sat in – a kind of stage scene with Hertford Bridge for the backcloth and Clarendon Building and Old Schools for the wings . . .

Monday 4 December: Found to my relief that D had had an unexpectedly good night so far as the face was concerned, tho' she was and continued all day very poorly with indigestion. I spent the morning doing a paper for Miss Wardale . . .

Jenkin came rather late to tea. He complained of the bad feeding in College. He said the kitchen committee was always composed of hearty people who dined out every night of their lives. Years ago it had been suggested that they might occasionally have baked potatoes. Since then they had had them baked for two years without a change! He then retired to work with Maureen. Afterwards I walked with him up the hill to the Asylum gate. He told me he was going to Italy this vac: oh the luck that men have!

I then returned, had supper, and washed up. After this I wrote to my father and then continued the *Judith* which despite its bombast is really admirable – especially the march of the Hebrews. D was very poorly and depressed in the evening and we were afraid the tooth was going to start again. Luckily it did not and we were in bed fairly early . . .

Tuesday 5 December: . . . I forgot to say that yesterday I met Fasnacht in town, when he again asked me to tea: I had to refuse, and as he looked rather vexed, I asked him to come here this afternoon . . . I thought little of Fasnacht: there is too much Oxford about him. I was not surprised to find that he admired Earp and Rowland Childe: I said pretty plainly that I did not.[2] He said apropos of eugenics, that he would extend Pasley's principle (i.e. "the same disgrace which now attaches to an illegitimate child shd. attach to a child too many") to all children, on grounds taken from Schopenhauer and Von Hartmann. Fasnacht is therefore a pessimist.

We discussed the ideal of extinction for the planet: he admitted that it was hopeless, as you couldn't destroy all life before you retired yourself, and even if you did, nature might still have something up her sleeve. He then went on to expound what he called Idealistic Nihilism – the theory [that] nothing at all exists . . . I attempted to give a serious answer to Fasnacht's theory and this led to an argument on Nothing. I used the same line as in my essay to prove that there were no alternatives to the actual whole.

He is a very close reasoner and I have seldom had the satisfaction

---

[2] The poems of Thomas Wade Earp (1892–1958) and Wilfred Rowland Childe (1890–1952) were well known in Oxford, and both men contributed to the various volumes of *Oxford Poetry*.

of driving a sound adversary so consistently from position to position until he acknowledged that "there could be no *pure* nothing". He took refuge in what he called an *impure* or imperfect nothing: I objected to this conception but he beat me by bringing in mathematics.

Fasnacht was once more proof how little purely intellectual powers avail to make a big man. I thought that he had not *lived* a single one of his theories: he had worked them with his brain but not with his blood. I think I rather surprised him by remarking that he was a remarkable guest, for he had made me talk more solemn nonsense than I had done for two years.

When he went I walked with him to the corner of the road. I said I believed the things I had said but he had been playing with counters. He admitted he could only clinch his view by committing suicide. He then left me. I forgot to mention that he referred to everything he liked – including Idealistic Nihilism – as "very sweet". Faugh! He also professed to find my view of a Reality with no margins intolerable, expiating on the *pressure*: I said I loved it[3]. . .

Wednesday 6 December: . . . I went . . . to College [for the Martlets Society meeting] . . . Here I met Jenkin who led me to King's rooms where the meeting was to be held. Present were King, Dawson, Curtis, Robson-Scott, Currie, Fasnacht, Ziman, Simpson, some freshmen whose names I have not yet got on to, a new don called Keir, and Carritt.[4]

Carlyle was speaking on the relation of history to literature. It is a beautiful, dark panelled room. Carlyle's lecture was rather in the nature of a polemic against the English school. He was very convincing, humorous, and full of knowledge as usual: but drove his case too far . . .

The discussion afterwards was very lively. Ziman, Simpson and I led off by pleading in our several ways that Carlyle had gone too far, but we really made nothing of it till Carritt came in with the only good thing of the evening. He said that history, as such, was quite irrelevant to literature: but you had to know a writer's language, and that had implications. For instance did "wine" to that writer

---

[3] George Eugène Fasnacht (1898–1956) took a First in Modern History and received his BA in 1922. After leaving Oxford he was a Tutor in Social History and Economics at the University of Sheffield 1925–8, head of the Department of History at the University of Leicester 1928–37, and in 1937 he returned to Oxford as a Lecturer in History at Nuffield College.

[4] See David Lindsay Keir in the Biographical Appendix.

mean an occasional luxury to the rich or the daily drink of the people? Did breakfast mean a cup of tea at eight or a roast of beef at eleven? Carlyle never really answered this: indeed as the discussion went on he became very sophisticated, tho' exceedingly entertaining . . .

Thursday 7 December: . . . At 6.30 I went to the Schools where Wilson had told me to go to the preparatory meeting of Gordon's Discussion Class. Gordon saw twelve of us in the English Staff Room. Robson-Scott was there: so also was a perfectly enormous man whom I have often noticed – I saw him first in the Corn Exchange at the Ballet. He has a most striking face, and is, I should think, a man to reckon with: but he has a devilish supercilious look and I doubt if he is an aesthete. His name is Daroll or Darlow.[5] I had settled that if asked to read a paper I should offer either Spenser or allegory but someone else said he hoped to hear on these very two subjects.[6]

Everyone except Robson-Scott was marked down for a paper. I offered allegory but was deprecated by Darlow (rather agressively I thought) before Gordon had time to reply. He said he was afraid "it would end in the Byzantine church". Gordon said he thought symbols should be private. I hadn't the least notion what they meant: but fixed on Spenser. I was very pleased to find an Indian in the class who was to read on Tagore . . .

Tuesday 12 December: This morning I decided that the job of seeing the Bursars of John's, Hertford, and Merton about houses must be tackled at last. I was very nervous about tackling these great men, and set off after breakfast as cheerfully as if I were going to a dentist. It was a mild grey morning. I walked first to St John's where the clerk of the Estates Bursar was able to tell me off hand that they had nothing. From there I went to Merton – beautiful place – where a clerk again saw me. He said they had nothing, and if they had, it would go to people connected with the College. He had no objection however to writing D's name on a bit of paper: it looked a convenient size to make a spill of. If was the same tale at Hertford . . .

D was still stiff with lumbago and this was one of the worst days yet for her toothache, tho' fortunately it is always cured by going into a cold room . . . Before going to bed I had a talk with D about ways and means: we are not on our beam ends at the moment, but

---

[5] For a note on T.S. Darlow see 26 January 1923.
[6] The sense of this is obscure. Perhaps we should read "hoped to be heard". – W.H.L.

too near to be comfortable. I also read aloud a good part of the last volume of my diary.

Wednesday 13 December: . . . I set out taking Lyly in my pocket. I walked first to Cowley village, then past the barracks to Horsepath, up the bridle path and so home over Shotover. The loathsome depression which we have all been living in these last few days now first thoroughly lifted and I had a most enjoyable afternoon. During the duller parts of my walk I read the greater part of *Endymion*,[7] with which I was agreeably surprised. It's got an air about it, I don't know what, that seems to make the absurd style rather brave . . .

While D and I were having tea a letter arrived from Warnie. This brought the good news that he is having a week's leave and that I am to meet him at Euston on the 23rd. He very decently offers to put up the difference between the fare via London and the fare via Birkenhead . . .

Thursday 14 December: . . . The three of us proceeded to the House to see the ceremony.[8] I don't know why I found it very uncomfortable – gave me a sort of suffocating feeling and nervous. The Bishop in his address spoke like a man: tho' of course he couldn't help bringing in the absurd statement that this day would be the one of all their school days which they would remember most vividly. However it was over at last, and someone played a fine fugue on the organ.

Immediately after the service we met Mary and the Doc. The Doc agreed with me that the thing was a pretty arrant farce. I said I felt as if I'd been forced to come and see a pig killed. There's some good glass in this cathedral. D asked the others home to tea and they all went back by taxi, including Smudge, whom we found under Tom Tower. I walked home.

After tea I had a good deal of talk alone with the Doc, chiefly on philosophy. He explained to me (from the scientist's point of view) the difference between epiphenomenalism and parallelism which I hadn't quite clear before. We argued about the source of things: I said his "awareness" was too qualified, there must be a bare "is" beyond it. We drifted into psychology and I mentioned my trouble of becoming "self conscious in solitude". After premising that I must not be alarmed he said it was a mild form of dissociation and certainly ought to be avoided . . .

---

[7] John Lyly, *Endimion* (1591).

[8] They went to Christ Church Cathedral to see Maureen and other girls from Headington School confirmed.

Friday 15 December: . . . After breakfast I bussed to the Union where I finished and noted *The Broken Heart* and read nearly all of Beaumont and Fletcher's *Philaster*, a very jolly romantic play – the only Elizabethan one I have yet found which avoids rant and has a sense of restraint. B & F could certainly have taught Shakespeare a lesson in this line . . .

I finished *Philaster* and after writing a note on it, began *The Maid's Tragedy*. This was an absolute revelation to me. It is a great pity that Shakespeare's plays both good and bad have been made into such an institution that a man might never open Beaumont and Fletcher if he didn't happen to read the English School . . .

Saturday 16 December: A raw, wet day. I spent the morning doing Vergil with Maureen. She was extraordinarily stupid and seemed to be making no effort – which I suppose is always the teacher's fault in some way, tho' I can't quite see where I fail.

At 12 o'clock I set out for Forest Hill . . . Aunt Lily combined cooking and philosophy and we did not lunch till 3.30 – off chops and a capital plum pudding wh. she had bought at Buols. I found her very tedious today: tho' I like enthusiasm one gets desperately tired of a fixed circle of ideas. She pays for her depth by narrowness. It was all the old business today: Shakespeare (praised, not as a great poet, but as a kind of monstrosity of intuition), the inevitable Emerson, the *élan vital*, the "exchange of differences", heroism and the forward plunge.

There was one inexplicable anecdote. She had been held up by a crush of prams at Carfax and had asked one obstructive woman to take her pram off the pavement. The woman replied that she had a right to be there. Aunt Lily retorted that she had *no* right to bring these children into the world for other people to look after and still less to block up the pavement. The woman said she was shopping. Aunt Lily said it was bad for the child to be taken shopping and the only good thing was that it killed some of them off.

I asked her why on earth she said such a thing. "I was angry," she answered. I replied, quoting Plato, that anger was an aggravation, not an excuse. She added that she had a lot of leaflets issued by the C.B.C. (Constructive Birth Control): and she was going to drop one into every pram the next time she went into Oxford, wh. would indeed be a good joke: but I don't think she saw it that way.

Lunch was a slow business and after-lunch tea a slower, so that it was after five before I knew. I then left her and walked home. It was almost quite dark, with wind in the trees and a little grey light over Shotover Hill: it was like plunging into a cool bath after all this afternoon's jargon. What I can't stand about her is that she knows everything: the Holy Ghost discusses all his plans with her and she was on the committee that arranged creation . . .

Reached home shortly before seven to find the Doc, Mary and the Brat here and D rather worried as she had expected me earlier. The Doc is to vaccinate us all tomorrow.

Maureen came in with the news that Mr Raymond – who is leaving for a job at Watford – is proposing to let his house (Hillsboro) unless he gets a good offer of purchase, and was surprised that we hadn't made an offer. I am to go and see him about it in the morning: I suppose it is a wild goose chase like all the rest . . .

Sunday 17 December: I dreamed in the night that the Doc was "vaccinating" Baker. I came into a room and found the patient lying nude on a hearthrug: the Doc was using an instrument like a spanner – which was not screwed together but sprang together at the pressure of a trigger. The operation in my mind was understood to be vaccination, tho' at the same time castration. I fled from the room and woke.

It was a miraculously bright morning. After breakfast I walked up to Hillsboro where I found father Raymond engaged in "dogging". I stood by the kennel and listened to him for a few minutes, until Mrs Raymond appeared and we retired to the drawing room. I then broached the subject of the house. The answer was a series of uncertainties. Mr Raymond does not know when he will leave nor where his new job will be. If his new place offers a good house they will move thither, if not, they will keep Hillsboro and he will live in rooms. Or again, they may let it furnished – and so on. The only fact that I could get was that he would sell for £1200 and let for £75 and that he would rather sell than let. After a little talk on politics I came away.

Having reached home again and given my report, I wrote a little until stopped by Maureen's practising in the next room. After lunch time the Doc arrived and we all prepared for execution – Maureen keeping up a torrent of comic relief. The Doc used a sterilised nail file and the scullery for a theatre: we were all done, including Dorothy. Maureen apparently has the thickest skin and the Doc was a long time scraping her, which she bore with admirable stoicism. When my turn came I found it less painful than it looked . . .

Monday 18 December: Very tired again this morning. I dreamed in the night that my father had taken one of the paper shops at the bottom of Divinity Road, and Baker had taken the other. The dream turned mainly on my efforts to avoid being seen by my father when I went into Baker's shop for a chat across the counter.

After breakfast I went in to the Union and started Chapman's *Bussy D'Ambois*: of which I couldn't make head or tail, partly because it is such execrable drivel, partly because I was feeling so poorly. In the end I gave it up and came home with a volume of Middleton and a headache. D and Maureen had gone into town independently and were still out. After lunch I read the *Changeling* in the drawing room[9] – next to *Bussy D'Ambois* the worst Elizabethan play I have read, but it has one good scene. I am wondering if any Elizabethan except Shakespeare ever thought of writing except on adultery. Afterwards I began *Women beware Women* which is very good and made ample amends.[10] Every now and then it actually has a line that scans.

At tea D told me that Dorothy's family are all furious with her for having been vaccinated. After tea I was just going to go out when D remembered that Smudge was coming for a lesson. I continued reading until she came and then did Tacitus with her till 8 o'clock when we had supper. D pretty well today.

Thursday 21 December: . . . I then came to the Union and wrote to Baker and to my father. This done, I went round to the bookshops to choose a present for the latter, and after some difficulty, fixed on *What the Judge Thought*[11] – a rather bad book for a present as it cost a guinea and looks worth twelve shillings. But it is the sort of thing I think he might read. My arm worried me rather more this morning.

I then came home: after lunch I went into the drawing room and started my table for the nineteenth century. D worked very hard in the dining room putting up parcels for all her poor pensioners: we had tea at 5.45, alone, Maureen having gone to play progressive bridge at the Taylors. We were both in as good form as could be expected, with this wretched Irish visit hanging over us. In the evening came Smudge: all very merry at supper. Afterwards I did Latin with her. Not in bed till nearly one.

---

[9] Thomas Middleton and William Rowley, *The Changeling* (1653).
[10] By Thomas Middleton (1657).
[11] By Edward Abbott Parry (1922).

Friday 22 December: My arm has thoroughly taken by now and is pretty sore – tho' nothing to Maureen's. After breakfast (which was very late) I went on with my table for a little while: then, finding that Saintsbury ceased to give dates as he got near the present day, I bussed in to the Union and did some research on the eighty-ish crowd.

The Doc was here for lunch . . . He gave us an account of the awful clothes his father had made him wear as a boy: he had had a fad for "government flannel" and fitted all his sons out with thick grey shirts of that prickly material. D said their father had been a very good man really, and disagreeable nowhere except at home. The Doc agreed.

I got him to talk travellers talk: he described a sail in the iceberg regions, bergs, one after the other like tents in a camp, stretching as far as you could see, and tremendous sunshine. He said one of the best places he'd ever seen was the straits of Magellan: he said it really gave you the feeling of the world's end.

We talked of the wreck of the Titanic. He said when the Captain saw the berg ahead, he should have kept straight on: in that case he would have smashed his bows, but as the impact lessened he would have come up against the first watertight bulkhead and the rest of the ship would have been safe. As it was, he put his helm hard down in a hopeless effort to get round the berg, and so got his whole side ripped up . . .

D and I were alone for tea: afterward I walked down Cowley Road and bought a razor blade. Sat up pretty late in the evening talking over this last year and what bad times we had had – especially its beginning and the cursed visit of the Askins and their patient efforts to ruin my Schools and, what was more important, D's health.

Saturday 23 December: Up betimes, having packed the night before and left home immediately after breakfast. I caught the 10.5 – a beautiful sunny morning. I was met at Paddington by Baker, who seemed well and cheerful. For some reason we found that we had very little to say to each other, tho' not for lack of will on each side.

He told me that Barfield was engaged to be married to a Miss Dewey[12] who was at least thirty seven. We both agreed that the possibilities of success in such unequal marriage depended entirely

---

[12] Miss Douie.

on the individuals, and that it might turn out very well. He said the pity was that there could be no children and Barfield was obviously made to be a father. I saw no reason why a woman under forty shd. not have a child.

He took me to the flat which he shares with Beckett, a very tiny place in a large block of similar ones, which are mostly inhabited by the mistresses of great men. Baker is getting on excellently at the Old Vic and has had encouraging messages from "in front". He is now doing Herod's chancellor in their Nativity play.

I tried to get his views of Moppie. He said his aunt had seen at once that truthfulness was not one of Moppie's virtues and was afraid we might be deceived over the main issue. He could give no explanation how she had spent so much money in London, as he had paid everything.

At 12.30 we went out and lunched at the Good Intent: we then tubed to Charing Cross where he had to leave me, after a most disappointing meeting . . . I then wrote a card to D, got my ticket and strolled about Endsleigh Square, where I had been in Hospital in 1918.

Shortly before 4 I returned to the Central Hall at Euston and there was met by W, when we immediately went and had tea in the refreshment room. He gave a most favourable account of Colchester which, he said, was a very old world town in an Arthur Rackham country. We caught the 5.30 for Liverpool: what between dinner, drinks, and conversation the journey passed very quickly: we succeeded in sitting in the dining car the whole way. We had two single berth rooms in the boat, with a communicating door. I was greatly worried all day by the pain in my armpit. A rough night, but we both slept well.

Sunday 24 December: We got out to Leeborough in the grey of the morning, not in the best of spirits. My father was not up yet. When he finally appeared, he was in poor form and rather shaky – for whatever reason. He approved of my new suit. Then followed breakfast and the usual artificial conversation. We vetoed church-going and went out for a walk at twelve o'clock.

My father chose his favourite route "round the river bank": that is, crossing the railway at Sydenham, we walked in the black and leafless park which lies between the slums and the shipyards, separated from the latter by an impure channel in which they are at work building an island of garbage. The path was so narrow that the other two walked ahead and I was left, not to my own thoughts, for in Ireland I have none, but to the undisturbed possession of my own lethargy.

We came back and had some sherry: W and I have often remarked on the extraordinary effect of this sherry. Last night I drank four whiskies without any undue result: today, in the study, my one glass of sherry led to a dull and cheerless shadow of intoxication. We had a heavy midday dinner at 2.45. The rest of the day was spent entirely in the study: our three chairs in a row, all the windows shut. I remember little of it. I read a certain amount of Inge's 1st Series of *Outspoken Essays*. I talked with W for some time after we were in bed.

Monday 25 December: We were awakened early by my father to go to the Communion Service.[13] It was a dark morning with a gale blowing and some very cold rain. We tumbled out and got under weigh. As we walked down to church we started discussing the time of sunrise; my father saying rather absurdly that it must have risen already, or else it wouldn't be light.

In church it was intensely cold. W offered to keep his coat on. My father expostulated and said "Well at least you won't keep it on when you go up to the Table." W asked why not and was told it was "most disrespectful". I couldn't help wondering why. But W took it off to save trouble. I then remembered that D was probably turning out this morning for Maureen's first communion, and this somehow emphasised the dreariness of this most UNcomfortable sacrament. We saw Gundrede, Kelsie and Lily.[14] W also says he saw our cousin Joey.[15] . . .

We got back and had breakfast. Another day set in exactly similar to yesterday. My father amused us by saying in a tone, almost of alarm, "Hello, it's stopped raining. We ought to go out," and then adding with undisguised relief "Ah, no. It's still raining: we needn't." Christmas dinner, a rather deplorable ceremony, at quarter to four.

Afterwards it had definitely cleared up: my father said he was too tired to go out, not having slept the night before, but encouraged W and me to do so — which we did with great eagerness and set out to

---

[13] The Lewises were communicants of St Mark's Church, Dundela. Jack and Warnie's maternal grandfather, the Revd Thomas Hamilton, had been the Rector there.

[14] See **The Ewart Family** in the Biographical Appendix.

[15] Joseph "Joey" Lewis (1898–1969) was the son of Albert's brother, Joseph. His family lived near Little Lea.

reach Holywood by the high road and there have a drink. It was delightful to be in the open air after so many hours confinement in one room.

Fate however denied our drink: for we were met just outside Holywood by the Hamilton's car and of course had to travel back with them.[16] Uncle Gussie drove back along the narrow winding road in a reckless and bullying way that alarmed W and me. We soon arrived back at Leeborough and listened to Uncle Gussie smoking my father in his usual crude but effective way, telling him that he should get legal advice on some point. The Hamiltons did not stay very long.

Afterwards I read *Empedocles on Etna* wh. I read long ago and did not understand. I now recognised Empedocles' first lyric speech to Pausanias as a very full expression of what I almost begin to call my own philosophy.[17] In the evening W played the gramophone. Early to bed, dead tired with talk and lack of ventilation. I found my mind was cumbling into the state which this place always produces: I have gone back six years to be flabby, sensual and unambitious. Headache again.

Tuesday 26 December: The same sort of morning in the study. W is reading Dill's *Roman Society* and he started discussing it with me. We wondered whether the pay for the legions was carried in gold from Rome or whether they possibly had some credit system. At this moment my father suddenly cut in, observing derisively "No, it was taken in specie." Not even an "I think" or a "Probably": and he has never to my knowledge read a word about the Roman Empire!

We were invited by telephone to lunch at Glenmachan and while we were changing Kelsie called and we walked up with her. Gundred was out hunting: we met Bob[18] and Cousin Mary. The latter, despite my real respect for her, made me indignant by supporting the Ulster

---

[16] Augustus Warren Hamilton "Uncle Gussie" (1866–1945), a life long friend of Albert's, was the brother of Jack and Warnie's mother. After leaving school he had gone to sea, but he returned to Belfast and founded the firm of Hamilton & McMaster, marine boilermakers and engineers. In 1897 he married a Canadian lady, Anne Sargent Harley Hamilton (1866–1930).

[17] Lewis probably had in mind these lines from Matthew Arnold's poem:

> The Gods laugh in their sleeve
> To watch man doubt and fear,
> Who knows not what to believe
> Since he sees nothing clear,
> And dares stamp nothing false where he finds nothing sure.

[18] See **Sir Robert Heard Ewart** under **The Ewart Family** in the Biographical Appendix.

government's prohibition of Midnight Mass and describing Cardinal Logue's very moderate letter as an incitement to rebellion.[19] But one can't argue with old ladies and I said "Yea, yea and nay, nay".

Kelsie bored me to death: and made one horribly revealing remark. She said it was a pity that the Rolls Royce people had started making small cars: for in the old days "to have a Rolls Royce meant that you were Someone, but now anyone would ask, which sort?" After this we left.

A rather grey afternoon. We walked down to Tillysburn and went to town by rail motor: at the station we had drinks and I sent off a post card to D. One of the bright spots of a holiday like this is the schoolboyish sense of escape and delight wh. W. and I feel in our otherwise prosaic little jaunts. We then rail motored back to Sydenham and arrived at Leeborough to find our father out: after tea – at wh. we now get plum cake alone – I began *Jude the Obscure*[20] and read this most of the evening: having read and hated Burke's *Present Discontent* in the morning. *Jude* is splendid. I heard today or yesterday that Arthur is away in Surrey – a piece of news which for more than one reason did not increase my cheerfulness. Early to bed.

Wednesday 27 December: Up late again. W spent most of the morning in the little end room making out a "programme" of gramophone records for the evening. I sat in the study and read *Jude*. My father took short strolls in the garden, fidgeted, and read a little before lunch. W and I played croquet after lunch (which my father ordered for "2.30 sharp"). W and I went into town. Back lateish and gramophone in the evening.

Thursday 28 December: My father went back to town today. He came into our room to say good morning fully dressed and we were not up till he was out of the house. After breakfast we repaired at once to the little end room where we have had no chance to be yet. It is the only part of the house where we have any sense of possession or of being at our ease. I spent a busy and laborious morning making up my diary from the time when I left home. During the morning Janie McNeill rang up and invited us to lunch.

---

[19] Michael Cardinal Logue (1840–1924) was the Roman Catholic Archbishop of Armagh and Primate of All Ireland. The following statement appeared in *The Times* of 27 December 1922 (p. 10): "No Midnight Mass: Cardinal Logue announced on Sunday morning that he had decided to abandon holding the midnight Mass which had been arranged. The authorities had declined to relax the curfew regulations to enable congregations to attend."

[20] By Thomas Hardy (1896).

W suggested a walk and in the afternoon we set out. We went up to the hills by the usual route and along to the turn before Craigagantlet. Thence down by the waterworks into Holywood. It was most enjoyable: there was white frost on the road and a cold sky, grey with yellow patches deepening into mauve near the horizon. The country with its bare trees, tumble down cottages and glimpses of the Mournes was very fine: but sad. In the hotel at Holywood we drank and sat for a long time by a fine fire in the smoking room, talking pleasantly on indifferent subjects.

We then caught the rail motor and, getting out at Sydenham, reaching Leeborough just at the same time as my father whom we met at the gate. He was depressed and fidgety. He talked of the possible invasion of Ulster by the southerners in a cowardly strain that annoyed us.

When we had sat down to dinner news was brought that a lady was outside with a message for me. Going out, I found Mrs Greeves who greeted me with surprising affection, pressing my hand between hers. She then handed me a letter from D. She said I was not to worry about it at all and not to protest, and would I come over and see her. I was a little worried at finding her as my confidante, for I had never thought her very discreet, but I was very pleased and grateful on the whole. Her husband (the notorious Thistle Bird) is in hospital in London for anaemia and she is alone with John.[21] When I returned to the table I was surprised to find that no pressing enquiries were made.

Afterwards I finished *Jude* which is certainly a great tragedy. I looked into Yeat's later poems: they are too obscure. In *Two Kings* he interested me by using a story I had wanted to write on myself. I then took up De la Mare's *Veil*: unwisely, for I was already lonely and depressed and they made a very vivid impression on me. W and I were late to bed. In D's letter I read that the tooth had begun bothering again. Hardly any headache tonight.

Friday 29 December: After breakfast we repaired to the little end room where I wrote to D, giving an account of Mrs Greeves' visit and directing that letters should be sent to Bernagh, but not too frequently. I then wrote up my diary: and we had got up so late that

---

[21] Joseph Malcomson Greeves (1858–1925) – the "Thistle Bird" – was Arthur's father. He was Director of J. & T.M. Greeves Ltd, Flax Spinners.

John Greeves (1892–1969), one of Arthur's brothers, lived with his parents across the road from the Lewises in the house named "Bernagh".

this, together with some reading of an old MS from the playbox ("The Sailor") and some chat over our morning beer, took us till 12.30 when it was time to change to go to lunch at the McNeills.

Here we had the usual lively and outrageous conversation and some *very* excellent coffee after lunch. Janie told us a scandalous story about Bob [Ewart]: his mother had been considering the purchase of a new car, but said that she was so old now that it would be hardly worth while. Bob replied "Oh well a Ford lasts about four years," and had suggested that they should use the doctor's advice in buying it. W and I both disbelieved the tale. We had a great deal more of chaff and scandal and some mildly literary conversation.

Janie told us that Cousin Mary thinks I am "greatly improved" – whatever that means: perhaps it is her way of saying (what everyone else has said) that I have got fatter. Janie pulled my leg and said I was "getting to look fearfully *adequate*" . . . As W and I walked back we laughed at Janie for pretending to have read Rabelais. W said it was a pity she was so proud of her little bit of literature and her little bit of emancipation.

On the way back we met Mrs Calwell and her sister, fat Miss Robertson, whom I should not have known. They delayed us for a long time but told us one good bit of news, that Miss Harper is now living with Hanie Hewson and her husband near the Curragh and looking after the children: so we may hope the poor old thing is in an atmosphere of comfort and cheerfulness.[22]

Having got back to Leeborough we changed and had some tea: after which we walked down to Tillysburn and there took the rail motor for Holywood. When we came out from Holywood station on the "front" there was a faint mist of level blue grey with a few lights here and there and a break in the clouds out to sea. It was beginning to rain. W remarked on the insensibility of nearly everyone to beauty: "How many would notice *that*?" he asked. I said nobody (almost) looked at the sky.

We then went to our usual hotel where we found the smoking room inhabited by a very old man and two fine dogs. We had our drink. He talked of immortality: he said all he wanted was this world improved. I argued that whatever else happened, *that* part of you couldn't be immortal. He complained that reality never came up to our dreams. I propounded my condemnation of dreams, and he

---

[22] Miss Annie Harper was Warnie's and Jack's governess from 1989 to 1908.

understood me better than most – for I have never been able to explain this decently, except to Baker and to him only because he had thought it himself. I don't think W agreed with me at all. We then came back by rail motor, getting out at Sydenham.

After dinner I began to read grandfather Hamilton's diary of his voyage to Calcutta in 1852.[23] My recent interest in eugenics and some vague smatterings of the Mendelian Law etc, made me feel a new interest in community of blood. It was strange to feel that I had really been there on the old East Indiaman. An interesting book, this diary, despite the awful picture of my grandfather as a pompous and conceited evangelical boy.

After I had read for some time, John Greeves came in. He said almost nothing: but my father became very interesting and agreeable and we had some fairly good talk. I felt I could get on with him splendidly if he would always be as he was that evening. This showed me that it is a change in him and not the mere process of my growing older which makes things so increasingly difficult – for I seem to remember him once being usually as he was, exceptionally, tonight. Fairly early to bed, much less depressed than last night.

Saturday 30 December: A fine morning: after breakfast to the little end room. Yesterday Mollie Boyd had rung up on the telephone and invited us both to play bridge for some evening a fair way ahead. W had answered that he was going to England tonight and that I was going on the 7th. At first I was delighted at this escape, but soon realised that they would be almost sure to see me here later than the 7th. After some hesitation I wrote this morning a letter to Molly Boyd explaining that W had made a mistake: adding, however, that they must not change their tables again on that account and deprecating my powers as a bridge player. After this I wrote up my diary and was preparing to write a letter to D when W pressed me to come out. As it was late and his last day, I wrote a card to D and came.

We walked to Tillysburn by the High Holywood road and the "sandy loaning", thence by rail motor to Holywood. Here we sat a good while in the smoking room: I forget what we talked of. We came back by rail motor to Sydenham and arrived at Leeborough to

---

[23] This diary of the Revd Thomas Robert Hamilton (1826–1905) is reproduced in the unpublished *Lewis Papers: Memoirs of the Lewis Family*, vol. I.

find my father already there. During the afternoon I went on with my grandfather's diary.

By afternoon post there came a letter to me addressed in Arthur's hand and containing one from D. Arthur had included a small note of his own – so ridiculously small in comparison with the whole that I could not read it in the presence and had to leave the study abruptly. Arthur writes that the people with whom he was staying in Sussex have got ill and he is now back at 4, Cleveland Terrace, Hyde Park, London, W.2. I was of course unable to read D's letter and for some absurd reason I felt a conviction that it wd. contain bad news: this kept me very anxious all evening.

Just before dinner an unpleasant episode occurred. W was complaining of the expense of a small mess such as they have in Colchester and my father began, as usual, to make fun of the army and of army troubles. W, who is morbidly sensitive on this score, was stung into retorting "It's all very well for you, living in the study and spending £1400 a year on yourself."

Tho' just, this was really rather rude after W has been drinking his whiskey for a week and especially since my father told him yesterday that he need not repay the £20 lent him at the time of Mc-Grigors failure.[24] My father took it very well, all things considered.

After an excellent cold supper (the only meal I like in this house) my father and I went in to the Liverpool boat to see W. off and returned in the same taxi. I felt thoroughly miserable. My father remarked that it "made him sick" to think of a man of W's ability wasting his time in the army.

After he had gone to bed I opened D's letter and found to my great relief a most cheerful, homely and comforting letter wh. bucked me up a good deal. One more example of the vainness of premonitions. I then read Boswell till fairly late and, after I was in bed, a little of Morris's *Jason* wh. is an old friend. My eye was caught by his poem "In Prison" in the same volume, which exactly expressed my own feelings at present. I was a long time getting to sleep.

Sunday 31 December: Up late as usual. A desperately long day. After breakfast we went to church which, on these occasions, is a refuge to me: for at all other times, shut up alone with my father, I am on the *qui vive* for something or other to turn up, and the end of the day finds me quite demoralised as if I had been walking over a

---

[24] The failure of McGrigor's Bank earlier that year.

precipice or smelled the wrong end of a machine gun. Lily walked back with us from church.

I decided that this would be a good opportunity of tackling Meredith and accordingly began *Beauchamp's Career* in which I made considerable progress before nightfall. I got little pleasure from it: it is obviously written for a person of quicker, subtler and maturer mind than I – perhaps for a person of finer technical breeding too.

"Dinner" at 2.30. I also read *The Faerie Queene* in my big edition by Dent, beginning at the VIth Book. After that I announced that I would go out: my father, tho' I know he didn't want to, accompanied me. We met the McNeills on the road and I was asked to lunch again on Tuesday. I didn't want to go, but I had no excuse ready and so accepted.

We then walked nearly to Holywood along the high road and back the same way. It was frosty, with a thick white mist and a moon over the hills and a continual sound of boats horning from the Lough. If I had been alone it would have been sheer ecstasy: as it was, it was a relief from all day confinement in the study.

After he had gone to bed I sat up for a long time reading Spenser, till it almost carried me away from Leeborough. I find I am fit for phantasy these days, but hardly for real imagination. After I was in bed I heard the horns and sirens at the docks blowing and the bells ringing for the old year. Found it very hard to sleep, being all uneasy in my mind and feeling isolated: I was also threatened with toothache but when I lay on my back so as to keep my cheek cool, it went away. A frosty, moonlight night and I left my curtains open.

1923

Lewis remained with his father in Belfast until 12 January when he crossed to England by cross-channel boat, arriving in Oxford on 13 January. Because he had decided to read English in one academic year, instead of the usual three, he had only two terms to prepare for his final examinations in June. He was primed to get the most out of this, with the welcome addition of Professor George Gordon's "Discussion Class", when Dr John Askins came to "Hillsboro" and went mad. Thus began a very miserable period for Lewis and Mrs Moore. They were so poor that they continued to take in Paying Guests, and Lewis began correcting School Certificate essays. By midsummer a college fellowship was still eluding him, and his father offered to extend his allowance so that he could begin a research degree while waiting for something to turn up.

Monday 1 January: Early awake and began wondering whether New Year's Day was a business holiday in Belfast: however, my father came in fully dressed and was out before I came down. A very frosty morning. Breakfasted alone, reading *Beauchamp's Career*, and went afterwards to the little end room. Here I wrote up my diary and also wrote a letter to D. I was rung up, first by Molly Boyd, who made me promise to go to progressive bridge on Friday next, and then, a few minutes later, by Mrs Greeves. She asked me to come out for a walk with her and lunch at Bernagh afterwards. I did not much enjoy the prospect but felt it absolutely necessary to go, in common decency, and went over as soon as I had finished my writing.

We walked to Knocknagoney by the High Holywood Rd., then down and back by the low road. Mrs Greeves annoyed me very much by bewailing the hard times wh. had fallen on the linen business since the war. I was not in a position to tell her (as I wished) that only shame ought to prevent her from giving thanks for the success with which her family had shirked the war. When once this subject was over, we got on very well. She is very simple (up to a point) and humble. We discussed the possibility of Arthur's coming home and

I promised to write and urge him, drawing his attention to the reduced fares which she had forgotten to mention in her letter.

She referred openly to "this lady whom Arthur calls Minto" and asked how she was: she told me she would not bring any letters over, but I was to come to Bernagh for them – which relieved me, for I have been very nervous of her doing something foolish. She also went up 100% in my opinion by speaking sensibly about the enormous families among the lower classes.

In answer to their plea that "God never sends a mouth but he sends the means to fill it," she said roundly that "God isn't such a fool." I could hardly believe my ears: of course she tried to take the sting out of it afterwards and "Hoped it wasn't irreverent", but still – the words must remain to her credit. We met Gundrede and talked to her for a few minutes before we went into Bernagh.

After lunch Mrs Greeves asked me with delightful naivety what philosophy was: Arthur had told her I did philosophy. I declined to answer, as nice as I could. She said she wished she could talk like my father and me – a truly dreadful ambition! I tried to enlighten her and make her believe how very different really good talkers (Yeats for instance) are. I then came away and wrote a short letter to Arthur: urging the reduced fares, his mother's solitude, his father's absence, my presence . . .

After having posted this I read W's W. African diary for a few minutes until tea was ready: and after tea walked down to Strandtown to buy some cigarettes. Coming back, I settled down to Sweet's *Anglo-Saxon Reader* and continued with a break for dinner, until my father went to bed at 10.30.

My father brought home tonight the two volumes of Donne wh. I asked for as a Christmas present. I think I shall love Donne: surely the only old poet who understands love in the modern sense? After my father had gone to bed I read two more cantos of the *Faerie Queene* and was in bed by 11.30. I find that when I think of D in the evenings there is nearly always some anxiety mixed with it – wh. doesn't increase the pleasures of Little Lea. A very wet night: went to sleep sooner than usual.

Tuesday 2 January: Up rather late and after breakfast to the little end room where I wrote to D and made up my diary. Janie rang me up to remind me that I was lunching with her today and to ask me to come out for a walk with her and Gundrede: which I refused to do, on the pretext of work. By the time I had finished my writing and had my morning beer it seemed hardly worth while to begin. I rummaged about the books and things in the little end room rather aimlessly for half an hour and then changed and went to the McNeills.

A very aged great aunt of Janie's was there when I arrived, but soon departed. Mother and daughter both talked to me about the Glenmachan atmosphere, wh. they said was the cause of Bob, and about the Irish atmosphere in general. They seemed to feel it as I do: tho' I doubt if they have ever been out of it long enough to see it objectively. The rest of the talk was mainly about books.

I mentioned I was going to the Boyds and wished that I could have a little practice first. Janie suggested that we should both go to Schomberg and make Lily and Gordon play with us in the afternoon. She then remembered that Lily would be out: and very decently asked me to come round after dinner tomorrow and she would find two others.

I left soon after lunch, came back, and started Anglo-Saxon. After tea I went out for one of the finest walks I have ever had. As I left the house the full moon was just rising behind the hills, the "shepherd's hut" and its neighbouring trees standing out in black against it. The rest of the sky was almost entirely covered with dark grey clouds and only one break, to the west. A terrific wind was blowing, however, and this soon began to tear huge gaps in the cloud, leaving cold looking bits of sky and sending the clouds packing in such odd, hostile looking shapes.

As I got further up the hill the wind became so tremendous that I thought it might bring a tree down. My special luck was that I saw two moonrises: the horizon having risen so, as I approached the hills, that the moon was out of sight again for a time. I walked as far as Sandy Loaning on the high road, then turned up to the right, up again at the corner of Glenmachan Glen, down by the side of the Robber's Glen, so and back.

I then started Anglo-Saxon once more and continued until dinner and after dinner till 10 o'clock. My father was reading Inge's essays: he said "If you were living at home I believe I should start serious reading again: the thing's infectious." After he was in bed I read *Beauchamp's Career* for a while. I was a very long time getting to sleep.

Wednesday 3 January: After writing to D and making up my diary I went out for a walk. A fairly calm morning. I walked up the hills to the third glen and then turned off to my left, intending to come back by the Shepherd's Hut: but I found the path, which I have used these ten years, blocked by a fence and so had to come back the way I went. I was meaning to go to Bernagh on the return journey, but I met Mrs Greeves at the bottom of the hill. She had no letter for me, as indeed I expected. She had not heard from Arthur. She arranged that I should go with her next Monday or Tuesday to see a Mr Osborne who has been at all the Universities of the world.

I then came back and lunched off chops, cabbage and mashed potatoes, all tepid. I was unable to open the bottle of beer wh. my father had left out for me. This uninspiring meal was enlivened by a welcome letter from Harwood, enclosing a poem which I do not think quite a success. Harwood is very depressed and is getting a job on the North Euston Railway. After lunch I did Anglo-Saxon grammar. After tea I read some more of *Beauchamp's Career* and began Webster's *White Divel* but did not make much of it. Very spiritless and stupid this afternoon.

After dinner I changed and walked to the McNeills: another beautiful evening of wind and moonlight. Janie explained to me that Gladys Leslie had failed her and that we should have to play cutthroat. The third was a Miss Ethel Rogers – a Scotch girl with a round nose. We got on quite nicely. Later on Florrie Greeves (who had not been asked) came in on her way home from a concert and made a fourth. The Rogers girl and I won. Janie and Florrie wrangled all the time, Janie boisterously and outrageously, Florrie in a resigned peevish manner. She is reputed to be very clever (Janie says she is a doctor of philosophy) but is intensely vulgar and prim in her voice and manner.

As I walked home I felt very strongly the difference between coming back to Little Lea and coming back to my real home of an evening. My father went to bed as soon as I came in. I sat up and tried to write a new poem on my old theme of "Alone in the House". I soon found that I was creating rather too well in myself the creepy atmosphere wh. I was trying to create in the poem, and gave it up. I then read Meredith's letters, to get rid of the atmosphere, and went to bed.

Thursday 4 January: After breakfast I tried go on with my poem without much success. I then wrote to D and made up my diary: then down to the study and worked at Anglo-Saxon grammar until just before lunch time when I went over to Bernagh to see if anything had come. Mrs Greeves was out: but as she had ordered letters to be given to me and nothing *was* given, I suppose nothing had come.

After lunch I began work again and continued till tea time. Over my tea I read Frazer's *Golden Bough* in the new abridged edition. Afterwards I went out and walked as far as Sloan's Seat and back the same way. A cloudy evening and no moon: as I was coming back the lights in the valley and especially at the docks were rather fine.

My father had just got in when I came back. After dinner I did the piece about Caedmon in Sweet's *Reader*, which kept me busy until ten o'clock when my father went to bed. I then read a little more of Frazer and went to bed, rather pleased at having done a fair day's work. A night of pouring rain: I was full of gloomy forebodings about the future – and nervy during the day.

Friday 5 January: Did my usual letter and diary writing after breakfast in the little end room. I then came down to the study and worked at Anglo-Saxon till lunch time. Immediately after lunch I went over to Bernagh. Mrs Greeves was out but the servant handed me a letter, which I came home and devoured eagerly, having first posted my own. Poor D has been having a terrible time with the tooth. I then shaved, not having done so this morning, had tea, and walked down to Strandtown to buy some cigarettes.

I changed before dinner and went off at 7.30 in a strange elongated taxi which (I couldn't help thinking) looked exactly like a hearse. I was among the first to arrive at the Boyds, who have a very beautiful house. "The Boyds" consisted on this occasion of Mrs B. and two daughters, Molly and Dot, neither of them pretty but both very nice. Mr Boyd was in England on business and the duties of host were performed by Colonel Yatman of the Somersets, a very cheery old boy. Except for the Heyns I didn't know a soul: the men were mostly officers of the Somersets.

I enjoyed my evening very much from the mere sense of being among ordinary commonplace English people and in a clear atmosphere. During the stand up supper I foregathered with Maurice Heyn and felt strangely tempted to ask him if he knew my friend Commander Hawes. I decided however that it would be risky. Left at about eleven, after a very enjoyable evening: I think I behaved creditably over the Bridge, or at least did nothing outrageous.

My father went to bed as soon as I got in. He had announced that he wouldn't go into town tomorrow. I sat up for a little and then went to bed, feeling not too cheerful.

Saturday 6 January: My father called me very late – just then preparing to go to the bathroom himself – and I spun out my dressing as long as I could, to shorten the long day. When I came down I was told by the servant that Mrs Greeves had already been trying to get me on the telephone. As I thought she might have something private to say and as our telephone stands in the hall so that a conversation on it can be heard all over the house, I went over to Bernagh as soon as we had had breakfast. I found that she had merely wanted to arrange for me to go with her on Wednesday to see a man called Osborne.

While I was sitting with her, Lily turned up with two dogs. She had been asked to the Boyds' party but Gordon (who hates going out himself) had frightened her into refusing by drawing pictures of the good bridge players she would meet. I enlarged on the delights of the party, and her childish regrets were quite funny. I thought her very pretty today, and much nicer than she usually is. It was a splendid sunshiny morning. I walked with Mrs Greeves and Lily half way up the Glenfarlough Road and then very reluctantly and dutifully turned back: for tho' they were neither of them real friends I could at any rate be easy with them and the morning was jolly.

Coming back, I found my father debating whether we should go out or not. I helped to make up his mind for him and we set out for our usual walk through the slum park. Even here the morning was not without something brisk. We talked a lot of solemn nonsense which I have forgotten. Back again, sherry, and Anglo-Saxon till 2.30 dinner of boiled mutton – a dish I loathe. I continued Anglo-Saxon for the rest of the day.

After tea my father began asking me if I wanted to go out again. I was ready to do anything to escape from the study. He stated roundly that he didn't want to go, but nevertheless insisted on accompanying me, adding "Unless I'm forbidden" in the jocular pathetic tone I so hate. Out we trudged again – like a prisoner and warder handcuffed together.

By a funny coincidence we met the McNeills just as we had done last week. Janie said she was bored. Mrs McNeill was just starting to explain to my father "what was wrong with Janie" when Janie very properly shut her up. I think I quite understood Janie – mentally she can just see beyond Strandtown and of course there must be sexual despair as well. "Lord, send them somer sometime."

We came back and had supper. Afterwards, being on the *qui vive* as usual, I heard the servant going to the front door. By great good fortune I was able to slip out in time and meet John who gave me a letter. Knowing that I was lost if he just went away and left me to explain to my father who had come, and why, and why he did not come in, I persuaded him in desperation to come in and have a chat. He stayed for a long time and we had a lot of silly conversation.

After my father had gone to bed I read and burned the letter. I was very glad to get it and thank goodness, the tooth seems to be better. The evening's adventure however left me in terrible discomfort. I felt now, that however late in the evening it was, I could never be safe. I became shamefully ungrateful to poor Mrs Greeves and cursed myself for trusting to such a fool. I reflected that there might be a letter from D tomorrow and wondered how I could possibly warn Mrs Greeves not to send things over. I went to bed very late and lay awake for a long time.

Sunday 7 January: Woke up very tired with a headache and a sense of panic. Spent the whole time till we went to church watching for John or Mrs G. in the hope that as a last resource I might meet them on the avenue. Nobody, however, appeared. While I was in church my terror was that one of the fools would leave something for me at Little Lea while I was out. Barton preached a capital sermon.[1]

Came back and was relieved to find nothing. I then took my chance and said I would go over to Bernagh to see if Mrs Greeves had had any news from Arthur. My father made no comment beyond saying that in that case I had better not have my usual glass of sherry for fear Mrs Greeves might smell it. Even in my intense desire to be off and put things safe I had time to feel what an awful social atmosphere this revealed: all the worse because my father was probably quite right. I went over and saw Mrs G., impressing upon her the peculiar conditions of life at Little Lea and telling her never to send anything over. She read me a letter from Arthur, who is not coming home. I already knew this, as he had written to D. I came back from Bernagh greatly relieved, but feeling rather exhausted: there is nothing I hate worse than anxiety coupled with the knowledge that I must continue to talk and never for a moment appear to be anxious.

During the afternoon I read a good deal of *The Faithful Shepherdess* with much pleasure.[2] I also finished *Beauchamp's Career* – a fine

---

[1] The Revd Arthur William Barton (1881–1962) was Rector of St Marks, Dundela, 1914-25. All three of the Lewises liked him, and he was a frequent and welcome visitor at Little Lea.

[2] By John Fletcher (1610).

book, tho' there is a good deal I do not understand. Everard Romfrey, Cecilia, Rosamund Culling and Nevil himself are however characters whom I hope I shall remember for a long time. After tea I went out for a walk, and for once my father did not come with me. In the evening I began the *Autobiography* of Trollope. So, at last, to bed hoping that I shall not have another Little Lea weekend for many a long day.

Monday 8 January: As the weekend involved two *dies non* I had this morning to make up my diary since Thursday. After doing that and writing to D, there was just time to walk to the post and call at Bernagh before lunch. There was no letter for me. After lunch I returned to the little end room and worked very well at Sweet till tea time. After tea I went out for a short stroll round the back of Glenmachan: it was a clear and beautiful evening. I then came back, spoke to my father for a few minutes and changed. He told me that old Graham was dead, for which I was very sorry.

I then walked over to Schomberg.[3] At the corner a lady passed me whom I thought to be Mrs Greeves: I was however going to pass her, as it was quite dark and I wasn't sure. Mrs Greeves recognised me and gave me a letter. At Schomberg there was only one other guest, Miss Wharton, who is at present a student at a university settlement (whatever that may be) in Birmingham. She has been a matron at several schools in England, including one that was run on the principle of no compulsion. If a girl didn't want to go into form one morning, she just didn't. Miss W said it worked very well.

She is rather pretty: when I was left alone with Gordon after dinner he went out of his way to tell me that she was much older than she looked, forty three in fact. I wondered why. Afterwards she told us many amusing stories – one specially good one about her unsuccessful efforts to get rid of a packet of sandwiches which someone had pressed upon her for a journey.

Lily annoyed me by her blasé account of her travels to Italy and elsewhere: she hates them all, it seems, because trains are sometimes crowded, journeys sometimes tiring, and Italy was full of horrible Italians. She much preferred Donaghadee – because there she could have such a rest. To my knowledge she has never done a day's work in her life. I left at about 10.30.

After my father had gone to bed I read D's letter: a most unhappy

---

[3] The home of Gordon and Lily Ewart.

one, what between toothache and the final loss of the house in Woodstock Rd. Before going to bed I finished Trollope's *Autobiography*. He is a very self-satisfied, self-made man, quite unconscious of his strain of genius, hopelessly bad in criticism of his own work, proud of the moral tone of his books, and still prouder of his punctuality, industry and ability to get on. One forgives him for a certain disarming honesty. Late to bed.

Tuesday 9 January: I was rung up by Janie after breakfast and accepted yet another invitation to lunch. I then went up to the little end room, despatched my writing, and worked at Wulfstan's address to the English till lunch time when I changed and walked to the McNeills. It was a very cold and blowing day and had snowed during the morning.

Today, I think for the first time on record, I had some real and serious conversation with Janie: she talked about her longing to get away from Strandtown and the impossibility of doing so, as she could neither leave nor transplant her mother. Her idea of going to Oxford or Cambridge had been knocked on the head years ago by her father's death. She talked about the abominable vulgarity of the set in which Ruth Hamilton lives.[4] There was one dreadful story of Ruth and her friends shutting up a drunk boy in the bedroom of Kelsie's hut while Kelsie was out: such are the jokes of the gilded youth at Holywood!

She also told me some funny stories about Warnie and Mona Peacocke when they were both staying with Kelsie at the hut.[5] Mona used to escape with W every day to the mainland to drink cocktails and W used to "do" her hair every night. The evidence for these adventures is Mona herself. I thought Mrs McNeill particularly nice today and shrewd.

At about three o'clock I got up to go, hoping to get a letter from Bernagh and then settle to work. Janie however volunteered to come with me, refused to come in to tea, and made me instead go for a walk with her. On the way back she came into Little Lea to borrow a book. I foolishly gave her a cigarette and then, though I had told her I wanted to go and see Mrs Greeves before my father turned up, she sat on for an interminable time. She found out that I was sailing

---

[4] Ruth Hamilton (1900–), now Mrs Desmond Parker, is the daughter of Mr and Mrs Augustus Hamilton.
[5] Kelsie had a hut on what is called Island Magee, which is a peninsula some eight miles long that joins Co. Antrim at the entrance to Belfast Lough. Mona Peacocke was the daughter of the Revd. Gerald Peacocke, Rector of St Mark's 1900–14.

on Friday and expressed her regrets with a vehemence that I didn't care much about.

When at last she rose to go I accompanied her, and we met my father on the avenue. I parted from her at the gate and hurried across to Bernagh, to find that Mrs Greeves had just gone out. She has given up the practice of leaving letters for the servants to hand to me, which I think is very wise, tho' in this case it was annoying.

My father was very fidgety and depressed this evening. He read from the paper a proposal for further heavy reductions in the army and enquired "What on earth that fellow Warren would do if he were kicked out." I said it was unlikely as W was a fairly senior Captain and had been out from the beginning of the war and seemed to be now in a position of some importance. My father observed with a sort of desperate cheerfulness "Ah well, he'd just have to go to the Colonies," adding that "the thing had been ridiculous from the start".

Later on he unexpectedly opened the question of my allowance. He asked me if it was sufficient. As I had already said so in my letters, I felt I had to reply that "I could manage," which indeed is true. To my remark that anyone would naturally like a little more if it was possible, he remarked that he was a poor man but that he could raise a little more if it was "necessary". I could not say that it was.

The whole thing happened very suddenly and did not take the lines I was expecting: so that I really spoke first and reflected afterwards. My only regrets were on D's account: but I reflected that the arrangement was nearly over now anyway and that I could hardly have said an increase was necessary: tho' I am afraid that D will hardly take that view.

Worked hard till 11.30 and then to bed, feeling far from cheerful. A very stormy, magnificent night. Forgot to say that I had a long argument with Janie today, defending myself against the charge of inhumanity which she brought against me. By inhumanity she meant not unkindness, but I think, a kind of detachment, an untouched centre: the attitude of Puck's "What fools these mortals be", wh. she quoted. She attributed the same quality to herself and seemed to consider it a thing to be proud of. I was not flattered.

Wednesday 10 January: Immediately after breakfast I crossed over to Bernagh and excused myself from lunching there on the ground of work: I also got a letter – yesterday's – from D, chiefly concerned with Dorothy's latest delinquency. After answering this and making up my diary, I started on Anglo-Saxon and continued till lunch time. After lunch I wasted some time reading Arnold Bennett's *Human Machine* till it was time to change and call for Mrs Greeves who was taking me to see Dr Osborne, a don from some Australian University.

She gave me a second letter which I had time to read before we started: D seemed a little better. On the walk over to Knock I could have believed that Mrs Greeves was parodying herself. She spent some twenty minutes telling me that she had sent two new hair brushes to Arthur and why and how. She went to endless trouble to point out to me the house of Mrs Purden in the distance: I had never heard of Mrs Purden, whose celebrity seems to rest on the fact that she has been recently killed by a motor lorry. Mrs Greeves had forgotten the name of Mrs Gilmore's house at which we were to meet the great man, but we found it at last.

Here I was plunged into a stagnant pool of such vulgarity as I have seldom met. In England I am not a snob: I can talk with those who drop their h's and like them: Belfast vulgarity I have not yet mastered. In a stifling room, small and with shut windows and a fire like a furnace, we met Mrs Gilmore and her ugly daughter and Dr Osborne, the latter a good looking man. In spite of a rather lecture like manner (he does not bear his learning as easily as our own dons) he seemed a good fellow. We were presently joined by a very small and very ugly woman who had been so upset by the execution of Mrs Thompson that she had passed a very bad night.[6] We sat there a long time and I found it very dull.

On the return journey Mrs Greeves (decent soul) was inclined to be disappointed for my sake because the great man had not talked about the universities of the world. I assured her in the most convincing language of which I was capable that I had enjoyed myself immensely and been very interested in hearing about the rabbits in Australia, the supremacy of American poetry, the poisonous effects of tobacco and the true history of Buffalo Bill.

After seeing her into Bernagh I came back here, finding my father already in, changed, and had dinner. I worked well afterwards and finished the *Beowulf* section in Sweet. Before going to bed I read a chapter or two in Strachey's *Adventure of Living* which seems a

---

[6] Mrs Edith Thompson and her lover murdered Mrs Thompson's husband in Ilford, Essex in October 1922. They were executed on 9 January 1923.

curious and delightful book. I was much excited by his account of what he (from Berlioz) calls *isolement*. I found great difficulty in deciding whether it is like my "sense of the is-ness of things" or my "Joy", but concluded that it was really different. Had a good letter from Arthur today, but containing nothing new. To bed and slept well.

Thursday 11 January: After letter and diary writing I turned to Anglo-Saxon and read till lunch time, a good part of the *Fall of the Angels*, which is very fine indeed: in Satan's feeling about his own powers of creation (if that is what the author means) it gets a point which even Milton missed.

Noticing just before lunch that the post had come, I went over to Bernagh, but was surprised and rather worried to find nothing for me. After lunch I walked out to the post, and, coming back went to the little end room where I fully intended to continue the Anglo-Saxon.

As I came into the room, however, I was suddenly flooded with the conviction that now at last I should be able to write some more "Dymer". I sat down at once and went at it with a run, securing eight stanzas with which I was well pleased.

After this I read Macdonald's *Phantastes* over my tea, which I have read many times and which I really believe fills for me the place of a devotional book. It tuned me up to a higher pitch and delighted me.

I then went out and walked to Holywood: descended through the town to the low road and rejoined the high road by the lane which skirts the barracks. By going out a little before five and returning at 6.15 I managed during this comparatively short walk to get a great variety of light and colours. It was a clear, quiet evening: as I came back there were very brilliant stars. I was quite unusually happy.

My father was already here when I came back. In the evening I finished the *Fall of the Angels* and read some of the *Gnomic Verses* which seem great rubbish. Then, after finishing *Phantastes*, to bed at half past eleven.

Friday 12 January: Immediately after breakfast I went over to Bernagh and found again that there was no letter. Mrs Greeves told me that she was setting out for town at 2 o'clock and if anything came by the second post she would then give it to me. I then came back and went up to the little end room where I made up my diary and wrote to D – a postcard.

After this I trammed into town, got a new Homberg hat at Laird's, or rather the shop that used to be Laird's, and came back, getting off the tram at Mopsi Todd's. Here I got a sponge and some shaving soap and walked to Leeborough. As soon as I had finished lunch I went out and paced up and down the front path until I saw Mrs Greeves passing. She gave me a letter and I said good bye to her, thanking her warmly for her services.

I was not best pleased to read in this letter that D was giving a party for Maureen tonight – but I suppose it is necessary. I next made all preparations for packing and then wrote three more stanzas of "Dymer", which seemed fairly satisfactory. The vein however soon ran dry and I came down to the study and read Bernard Shaw's *Candida* (an amusing trifle) till tea and finished it. After tea I went for a short stroll round by the fenced tree: a cold misty evening.

Coming back I went upstairs and had hardly started packing when the cook, "The Witch of Endor" as my father calls her, came to my door and announced in her breathless manner that she had made me a cake and it wasn't very big and could I fit it in my case.[7] As I have had nothing but cake for three weeks at tea time this kindness was a little disconcerting. I thanked her profusely: but when she produced a cake of some five pounds burthen, which almost completely filled my suitcase, I had to ask her to send it after by post.

I then went down to greet my father who had just come in, and returned to finish packing. For some reason I had a horror of this last tail end of my long penance, and, I am afraid, spun out packing as long as I could. After dinner I changed.

The taxi came at 8.15 and my father accompanied me into town. Up to the moment of leaving Little Lea I was still feeling that I was not yet out of the wood and half expecting something to turn up.

Once alone and on the boat I experienced a great sense of relief and security, tempered by sympathy for my father. I had Mrs McNaughton's *Lame Dog's Diary* with me, which has some charm: but I fear it is a toy book. After reading this in the smoking room till ten o'clock and drinking a bottle of stout I retired to my single berth room where I was very comfortable and above all, at last, easy in my mind. Slept excellently.

Saturday 13 January: I was called by my steward at 7.30 and shaved

---

7 "The Witch of Endor" – Mary Cullen – combined the work of cook and housekeeper at Little Lea from 1917 until the brothers left it in 1930.

and dressed while the boat was moving from the landing stage to the dock. After a very good breakfast on board, which I ate with extraordinary appetite, I crossed by ferry and arrived at Woodside Station shortly after nine o'clock. It was a typical Liverpool morning, grey and foggy, but with a certain cheerfulness on the river.

I came down by the 9.35, an excellent through train with a luncheon car, reaching Oxford at 2.18. I travelled with an interesting man, a civil servant of some sort. He was not a man of breeding but had travelled a good deal in Germany and Italy. He contrasted the civility and refinement of continental life – the music, the gardens, the bowing managers of hotels etc. – with our English barbarism. During the morning I finished the *Lame Dog's Diary*. A good deal of the country was flooded, with ice here and there. I had lunch at 12.30.

I arrived home about [3] and was glad to find that D, tho' tired, was much better – the tooth being painless for the time. After I had changed and had a bath we spent most of the rest of the day talking. D described to me the curious affair with the Askins. The Doc had been, according to Mary, "much hurt" by some chaff of Maureen's. If this is true it shows only how ill the poor man must be. The party last night seems to have been a great success. Maureen went out shortly after my arrival.

I was so delighted at being home again that even the news that we must all support Maureen tomorrow morning at her first experience of the uncomfortable sacrament did not damp me. After supper it was delightful to write up my diary – describing a Leeborough day while sitting here. D, rather extravagantly, has presented me with a desk, which will be a great comfort. We were in bed by 11.30.

Sunday 14 January: All of us were up by 7.30 and, after tea and biscuits, up to Headington on our bicycles. On the outward journey it seemed a mild morning. Mr Clarke and a curate who came in late, officiated.[8]

On the return journey we found it had turned much colder. After breakfast I spent most of the morning putting my things into my new desk and destroying a lot of old MS books. D was slightly threatened with the tooth off and on today, but was otherwise in excellent form. After lunch I made a new start on the Vth Canto of "Dymer". What

[8] Now that she was confirmed, Maureen was receiving the Holy Communion for the first time.

between my stanzas written at Leeborough and selections from those written before I went to Ireland and some new ones today, I have now a continuous opening of sixteen stanzas with which I am fairly pleased.

After tea I read through my Magdalen dissertation preparatory to sending my father a copy and chatted with D: then, at about six, I walked up to Headington, down the Green Lane and home by the old London Rd. where there was a fine display of stars through the bare trees.

We had supper at 7.30 and after it I assisted D in the composition of a letter to Moppie. Moppie had written to D saying that she had saved 30/- a week and given it to Miss Quinlan to keep: and proposing, so far as we could gather, to spend this on further lessons for which she would go three times a week to London while living here for the six months which she is out of work. It had been understood that she was to try and find temporary work for this period: or, at the worst, that the saving would go to help the common stock while she was with us. We felt her letter rather cool: she seems to have no compunction about being a deadweight and we cannot entirely trust what she tells us.

In the end we produced a letter which laid the facts before her, I hope without being unkind. We explained that she had run away to a poor family and that we could not afford the arrangements she suggested. The business is a worry to us and D has quite lost confidence in Moppie: I still try to hope for the best.

After posting this letter I came back to a belated wash up and then sat in the drawing room where D and I talked of a lot of things – death, second marriages, and whether one would feel horror at the ghost of a friend. In bed about twelve o'clock.

Monday 15 January: . . . After lunch I went over my notes on the Elizabethan plays, which I find that I remember very well. I finished them after tea and began Lodge's *Rosalynde* which is almost quite worthless. I continued it till supper time and afterwards went on for a page or two with my fair copy of "Forster", making a few corrections.

Later I had a long and interesting conversation with D in which she answered several questions greatly to my enlightenment. To bed about 12. I forgot to say that I met the Doc as I was returning through Iffley. We had some talk, but nothing of interest.

Tuesday 16 January: . . . After lunch I did some work on Anglo-

Saxon grammar and later on began to write my paper on Spenser for Gordon's discussion class. Just before tea the Doc appeared and I joined him and D in the dining room. D and I both remarked afterwards that he was very much worse: we also heard him swearing to himself in a very odd way in the bathroom, which is a bad sign in a man of his sort. He seems less interested in life than he used to be and can hardly be got to talk outside theosophical philosophy.

After tea he and I had our usual kind of talk. I told him what Fasnacht had said – that as, by perspective, you could represent a three dimensional object in two dimensions, so you must be able to make in three a model of a four dimensional object. He agreed with my objection that one would have no means of recognising it when made . . .

Thursday 18 January: . . . After breakfast I worked all morning on my paper on Spenser. D had a letter from Moppie in which she says she has been advised by Miss Quinlan to take more lessons during the summer and apparently intends to do so and believes that she can on her savings. It was a beautiful bright day and I tried to persuade D to come out for a ride: as she had been busy all morning she wisely refused . . .

I . . . hastened to get tea, intending to go into town afterwards and have a look into College – today being the beginning of term. During tea however a card came from Wilson telling me to call on him at 9.45 tomorrow and I decided that I would make one journey do. After tea I went on with Donne and read the *Second Anniversary* which is "a new planet": I never imagined or hoped for anything like it: also the *Soul's Progress* which is mostly bosh and won't scan.

Just as we were getting supper Smudge arrived unexpectedly, looking much thinner than when I last saw her, but in very good form and greatly improved in appearance. She has been making good progress with her exercise. Maureen has a curious instrument, a cylinder of cardboard which turns on a handle and when made to revolve executes an arpeggio: it sounds like a cross between a violin and a concertina. We had arranged to try this on Smudge and during supper I twirled it outside the dining room door. To our surprise, the first strain of the music, which has rather a weird way of swelling up from nowhere, reduced her to abject terror. And even afterwards she refused to look at it or have it brought near her, saying it was a device of the devil. She has a bad term before her, working for Smalls. After supper we had a lot of talk and chaff in the drawing room. She left about ten.

Friday 19 January: . . . I . . . rode to Manor Road: on the way I met Robson-Scott and one unknown who were also going to Wilson. There were others with him already and we three sat in his dining room downstairs to wait. When I went up he dictated a collections paper to me and advised me to see Miss Wardale at once.

As soon as I left him I rode to Margaret Rd. and caught her just before she went out. She also promised to send me a paper (which arrived this afternoon), said, in answer to my enquiries, that I owed her five pounds, and hoped I had had a pleasant vacation. I said that I had and hoped that she had had the same: whereupon she dropped her lower lip, shot out her eyes, looked as if I had insulted her, "roseate and pained as any ravished nymph" and said nothing.

I picked up my gloves and stole away to the Union where I read Santayana's *Reason in Art* for an hour: very pugnacious and bracing and mostly true. I then came home and read a little Homer – *Iliad* 16 – before lunch. D and I were alone, Maureen being at lunch in Headington . . .

Saturday 20 January: I spent the first part of the morning doing the O.E. translation paper with moderate success: and then, till lunch time, looked up O.E. grammar . . . After tea I began my O.E. grammar paper. I realised as soon as I had opened it that it contained a lot of unexpected questions and almost thought of putting it away and reading up some more. I decided however that this would be unfair and proceeded to do a shockingly bad paper. When I had finished it I put it in an envelope, enclosing £5 as a peace offering, and posted it.

In the evening Smudge came to supper, bringing her sister: she had threatened to do so because we had been condemning the sister for going to London in the Vac and compelling Smudge to look after her mother: and in general for her selfishness towards Smudge. Smudge thought she would cure this by showing how nice her sister really was. She turned out to be very plain, with an old maid's manner, as self confident as Smudge is shy.

I was left alone with her for a few minutes before supper. She said she always made her pupils promise never to touch the piano during the holidays. She said that children should be sent to boarding school as early as possible – say at the age of two: because no mother could have "the sympathy and wisdom" that the ideal school marm would have.

During supper she explained that she had given up meat for vegetables and then vegetables for fruit: she hoped to give up milk and eggs soon and finally to live without food at all: tho' she admitted that she hardly expected that in this life. She said (under examination) that animal food was gross. Asked why a pig was grosser than an apple – the pig being more highly organised matter – she said you should eat the lower kingdom rather than the higher. Asked why again, she said something which I do not remember. The legitimacy of pork eating, I gathered, depended on the age of one's soul: a young soul might eat it, but not an advanced one. During this dialogue she executed a great many curious gestures with her arms above her head. After supper I did Tacitus with Smudge. D and I both thought S's sister a perfect fool . . .

Monday 22 January: . . . At twelve o'clock again I went to Schools and heard Gordon give a capital lecture by way of introduction to Shakespeare's tragedy.[9] As I was getting my bike from College afterwards, I met Stevenson, who tells me that Wyllie has still got no permanent job – anxious news for me. Forgot to say that I had a card from Jenkin yesterday, from some place South of Naples: he is not coming back till February, so I have now no friend in the University at all . . .

After a little opposition from D I succeeded in being allowed to wash up: after which I came to the drawing room and had hardly sat down to my desk when I saw Cranny opening the gate. Much against my will, I ushered him into the room. He was in great form, enormously improved since his last visit. D turned up presently and we listened to him till tea time . . . At tea we talked of music. He said that the Americans had used a gun for the accompaniment of Handel's "Wonderful conqueror" passage in the *Messiah*. I said it was a cheap passage: he said it was the finest in all music. He asked whether Christ, apart from the question of his divinity, was a great teacher or a fanatic? He also doubted whether Christian ethics were practicable.

After tea I escaped to the drawing room and attacked my essay on the influence of Donne on 17th century lyric. I decided an essay (for tomorrow) was out of the question and did notes instead.

At supper the subject of personality arose – I said that it made one

[9] Beginning 22 January, Gordon gave a series of eight lectures, Mondays and Fridays, on Shakespeare's Tragedies.

giddy to think that oneself might not have been. Maureen said "Yes
– I was wishing the other day that you had married someone else (to
D) and then I thought, Oh it wouldn't make any difference to me, I
shouldn't have been there." This shows she thinks more than I hoped
for.

After supper went on with my notes and read a little O.E. Poor
D very miserable and depressed today . . .

Tuesday 23 January: A busy day. Cycled into town after breakfast
and worked in the Union at my notes on the Metaphysicals: I read
Johnson's passage in the life of Cowley, and found that I had been
rather off the track. Worked hard to pull it straight and went to
Wilson at 12, where I had a good hour.

So home. D insisted on doing the washing up after lunch. For the
rest of the day I did Middle English, reading the reign of Stephen
from the *Chronicle*[10] and a passage from *Havelock*, which is great
stuff. Then I started a paper on the *Chronicle* passage for Miss
Wardale and continued very busy till 11 o'clock.

Thursday 25 January: . . . Biked to College where I got a note from
Carritt inviting me to dine in Hall some day next week. I answered
at once, accepting for Tuesday . . .

I went to Schools at 10 o'c. to hear Onions on Middle English.
Here I met Robson-Scott who told me there would be a meeting of
the Martlets on Wednesday next, though there were no cards printed
yet. Onions gave a delightful lecture: the best part being the
quotations, which he does inimitably. Once he repeated nearly a
whole poem with much relish and then observed "That wasn't what
I meant to say." A man after my own heart.

Friday 26 January: . . . After lunch and washing up I changed and
went in to Schools to "assist at" the first meeting of Gordon's
Discussion Class.[11] It was held in an upper room, on the High, to
the right of the entrance hall: a bare, over-heated room with a round
table. I was there early and watched it gradually fill up with a crowd
of people who were certainly not there when the show was arranged
and the papers alloted. Robson-Scott was there, but with a friend,

---

[10] *The Anglo-Saxon Chronicle.*

[11] This very popular "Discussion Class" had been inaugurated earlier by Sir Walter Raleigh, and was
continued under George Gordon. Each college tutor was allowed to send one or two of his pupils to the class,
and in order that they be small enough for discussion, there was one for men and another for women.
Beginning in the Hilary Term 1923 the minutes of the men's class were written in Chaucerian verse, and those
for 1923–24 have survived. Lewis's reminiscences of the Discussion Class are found in *The Life of George S.
Gordon 1881–1942* by M.C.G[ordon] (1945), p. 77.

and I did not speak to him. Darlow (see Dec. 7. 22.) who was to read, came and sat close to me and talked to another man, tho' eyeing me from time to time with what seemed a glazed insolence but may have been unintentional. Gordon arrived rather late.

Darlow's paper on the 18th century was really very good: above all it was spoken from notes and not read, for which I admired him. At the same time – such was my dislike – I was ashamed to find myself pleased that he had a vulgar accent, saying "taime" for "time". His paper was almost entirely historical. The discussion which followed was disappointing, as we were too large a party for informal conversation and tended to break up into groups.

Gordon was sensible rather than brilliant. Some of the best things were said by a Scotsman (I think), a middle aged man whose name I didn't hear. I had one or two passages with Darlow – opposing his view that Hume showed the extreme of reliance on reason and his stranger view that Johnson's kicking a stone to refute Berkeley showed the same thing. He proved quite civil and even agreeable in argument. Sometimes I thought him a little bit stupid.[12]

Got home in time for tea and read Donne and Ralegh till just before supper when I heard a knock and going out, found Barfield. The unexpected delight gave me one of the best moments I have had since the even better ones of leaving Ireland and arriving home. He had come up, he said, to give a dancing lesson, and was leaving next day. We went at our talk like a dogfight: of Baker, of Harwood, of our mutual news, of the *Beacon* which is now all but dead. He is working with Pearsall Smith who is genuinely *trivisus* and an utter materialist.[13] He (Smith) and De la Mare are fast friends and imaginative philologists of a type which they have christened "milvers" – partly because it is a good word, partly because it "supplies a long felt want" in rhyming with silver. Barfield hopes soon to meet De la Mare.

He sees Squire fairly often. He says Squire is a man who promises more than he can perform, not through flattery but because he really believes his own influence to be greater than it is. I asked him if he

---

[12] This colourful undergraduate was Thomas Sherrock Darlow. He was born on 5 December 1901 and was the son of the Rev. Thomas Herbert Darlow who published a number of theological works. He was educated at Gresham's School in Holt and matriculated at Magdalen College in 1920, where he read Natural Science before changing to English in 1922.

[13] Logan Pearsall Smith (1865–1946) taught on the English Faculty at Oxford. His many books include three volumes of *Trivia* (1918, 1921, 1933).

knew Darlow. He did, and thought he was probably a homosexualist and was only eighteen: if so, he is certainly brilliant and may grow into a good fellow yet.

Barfield showed me – or wrote out for me from memory – his new poem "Lama Sabacthani" beginning "It is impossible to keep awake". I pronounced it perfect and thought it one of the finest contemporary poems I have seen, perhaps the finest. His rhythm is remarkable.

I showed him my "Requiem Mass" and "What? Has the night" etc. He approved very much of the "one spirit" part in the Mass and liked the lyric fairly: he went on however to a very serious and honest review of my work in general. He said it always surprised him that my things were as good as they were, for I seemed to work simply on inspiration and did no chipping. I thus wrote plenty of good poetry but never one perfect poem. He said that the "inspired" percentage was increasing all the time and that might save me in the end: the fact that I so often get there for a line or a stanza even, was, he thought, "promising".

I thought his insight was almost uncanny and agreed with every word, wishing that I could "chip" more perseveringly and had time to do it. This led to a long talk about poetry and ended in his reading to me out of *The Veil*.

D came in and pressed him to stay the night, but he had arranged to sleep at Wadham and we had to be contented with his promise to come to breakfast. I walked back to Wadham with him in the moonlight. He said that when one had accepted the materialist's universe one went on and on to a point and suddenly exclaimed "Why should *my* facts be the only facts that don't count?": then came the revulsion and you took a more spiritual view till that too worked itself to its reaction and flung you back to materialism: and so to and fro all the days of your life . . .

Saturday 27 January: D woke me this morning with the news "It's half past eight and Dorothy hasn't turned up and Barfield's coming to breakfast at half past nine." All hands on deck forthwith: D naturally very angry, but soon restored to cheerfulness and wouldn't allow me to do the grates. We got everything shipshape in time, and I was ready to meet Barfield when he came and fed him on bananas till breakfast was ready.

After breakfast – at which he talked a great deal about music with Maureen – he asked to be shown "Dymer". His verdict on the fourth canto was most enthusiastic: he called it "great" wh. is a lot from

him and pointed out how I had done things there which I had failed
to do in the lyrics.

He told us he was being married in April. I walked to Wadham
with him, where he packed his case, and we then took a turn in the
gardens – beautiful they are all the year. He said his first year at
Oxford had been extraordinarily happy. We talked of Yeats, whom
he considers ruined artistically by self love, tho' his later poems were
rather better. Finally I saw him off at the station and came home . . .

Tuesday 30 January: . . . I reached the Senior Common Room just as
the dons were preparing to move in to dinner. There were a
good many present – an American pianist called Antony, Carlyle,
Stevenson, Keir, a man unknown, Allen, Emmet, and Carritt.
Farquharson, who was in the chair for the night, came in late and
said he had been delayed by a lady who wanted him to explain
Aristotle's dictum about poetry being more philosophical than
history. Carlyle talked about realism to Antony during dinner but
from where I sat I could not hear all of it. I think he was being
paradoxical and perhaps gently smoking his guest.

When we retired to the Common Room Antony soon departed to
Carlyle's house and his hosts proceeded to talk about him. Farquharson had told him that Carritt was an eminent philosopher, wh. he
said was exciting to a stranger who didn't know that we had dozens
in Oxford: and he boasted that he had added the finishing touch by
whispering "ascetic" in the poor man's ear when introducing him to
Carritt. Allen (who I think, but not for this reason, I dislike) observed
that people were always rather shocked at a philosopher who was
not a beaver.

Carritt, Emmet and I fell into a conversation on the expressionist
theory of art. I contended that two persons might be equally
expressive, but in practice one preferred the one who had the better
content. Emmett agreed with me. Allen was brought in on the
question of whether any emotions were unfit for art and a lot of
jokes wh. I did not understand passed between him and Carritt.

The party broke up very soon, and I got up to go. Carritt followed
me out and asked me to come up to his room. We talked about
books chiefly. He explained to me his mysterious conversation
with Allen. Nearly a year ago there had been an argument on the
same subject and Allen had said, as an example, that the emotions
of a man going to the ————— could not be matter for art: Carritt
had taken up the challenge and written a poem on that subject.

He said it was not very good, but he thought it had proved his point.

He happened to get on the subject of Matthew Arnold, and was surprised to find that I shared his flair for Arnold's poetry. We became almost intimate over this, for he is the most reserved of men. He said he always felt in reading it that "this was a man I'd have got on with": on my demurring he said what he really meant was "this is the kind of poetry I should like to have written myself". Now I have often thought that Carritt must at one time have wanted and tried to write poetry. We talked also of Pearsall Smith and why there was no English sculpture . . .

Wednesday 31 January: . . . After an early supper I bussed into College and went to the Martlets held in Dawson's rooms. Present were Terry, Ziman, Curtis, Robson-Scott, MacCissack [McKisack], Rink, and another.[14] MacCissack read a paper on Galsworthy, which I thought distinctly poor. As soon as it was over I approached him and said I believed he came from Belfast, and told him that I did so too. He said he never went there if he could avoid it and agreed (I think he said it "ultro" before I had said it) with my own view that it was full of Forsytes. A fairly good discussion followed.

In the pressure of conversation I discovered a new idea of my own which I think true: what we call the "philosophy" of these modern novelists is a habit they have of attaching their characters to what they assume to be big movements of the Zeitgeist – as for example the revolt of youth in Walpole's novels. But this is really a literary device: parallel to the King and Queen setting of tragedies or the supernatural – a means to avoid the purely private and individual, wh. we don't really like. I am surprised that they all with one accord condemned Galsworthy's plays . . .

---

[14] Philip John Terry read Law and took his BA from University College in 1923.

Thursday 1 February: Up rather late and had a rush to get in to Onions' lecture.[1] After hearing this and buying some margarine I biked home again in wind and some rain. Maureen was having a violin lesson when I arrived so I went upstairs and worked at Milton's prose, in a singularly uninspired mood . . .

After lunch – we are having all meals in the kitchen these days – I went on with my work till 3.30 when I walked into town to have tea with Fasnacht. I met him in the Union alley talking to Robson-Scott and he took me to the Cadena. Rather a dull afternoon. We talked a little philosophy and a little about books. The most interesting thing that he told me was that the Mugger is definitely retiring in April: also how Rink had got leave off chapel by going to the Mugger and saying he had ceased to believe in a personal God. The Mugger had said "I hope if we fully discussed the matter I should show you that your opinion is not well grounded, but perhaps we had better not go into that." . . .

Friday 2 February: . . . We were a very much smaller gathering [George Gordon's Discussion Class]: the crowd last week having apparently turned up unbidden because they had seen the class on the lecture list and had assumed it was open to everyone.

This afternoon a good looking fellow called Coghill from Exeter read a very good paper on "Realism" – as defined in his own special sense – "from *Gorboduc* to *Lear*".[2] He seems an enthusiastic sensible man, without nonsense, and a gentleman, much more attractive than the majority.

The discussion afterwards was better than last week's. Coghill's definition of realism was attacked: he claimed Hobbes' immunity of definitions and I supported him: but Lloyd-Jones and I opposed his view that realism, in his sense, was not to be found in Corneille.[3] Mr Singh, the Indian, made a lot of remarks which seemed to me

[1] On "Middle English Texts".
[2] See **Nevill Coghill** in the Biographical Appendix.
[3] Harry Vincent Lloyd-Jones of Jesus College, who took a BA in 1923.

foolish.[4] Gordon said, apropos of something else, that one remembered the choruses in Aeschylus chiefly by their difficulty: of
which remark the most charitable explanation is that he was trying
to raise a cheap laugh.

Oh for a sitting in full force in Bee Cottage or Wadham and how
we could have blown away all these blindworms and got down to
something! The best man in the class is the Scotsman (Strick, I think)
from Wadham.[5] Darlow was not there today, wh. was a pity as the
secretary pulled his leg in the minutes . . .

Sunday 4 February: . . . I . . . went off by bike to have tea with Miss
Wardale. The sun was now going down very frostily and the town
looked splendid. I found Miss W. alone. After we had talked for a
few minutes I was pleasantly surprised by the arrival of Coghill. He
was followed in a short while by a girl whose name I didn't catch:
she struck me as being quite nice but she was too shy and breathless
to contribute much to the conversation. Miss W., apart from a few
sensible remarks on Wagner, was content to sit back in a kind of
maternal attitude with her hands on her knees.

Coghill did most of the talking, except when contradicted by me.
He said that Mozart had remained like a boy of six all his life. I said
nothing could be more delightful: he replied (and quite right) that he
could imagine many things more delightful. He entirely disagreed
with my love of Langland and of Morris: the girl agreed with both.

He said that Blake was really inspired: I was beginning to say
"In a sense – " when he said "In the same sense as Joan of Arc."
I said "I agree. In exactly the same sense. – But we may mean
different things." He: "If you are a materialist." I apologised for
the appearance of quibbling but said that "materialist" was too
ambiguous. He gave a description of a ballet which he spun out much
too long.

When I rose to go he came with me and we walked together as
far as Carfax. It was very misty. I found out that he had served in
Salonika: that he was Irish and came from near Cork. He had had
the appalling experience of being caught by an Irish mob, threatened
with lynching, let go, called back again, stood up and pointed at with
revolvers, and finally released. He said it was much more terrifying
than any war experience. Apropos of my condemnation of Ulster he

---

[4] Fateh Singh of St John's College, who took his BA in 1923.
[5] This was Richard Boase Kelynack Strick of Wadham College who took his BA in 1923.

asked me if I were a Catholic which made me suspect he might be one himself.

He said (just like Barfield) that he felt it his duty to be a "conchy" if there was another war, but admitted that he had not the courage. I said yes – unless there was something really worth fighting for. He said the only thing he would fight for was the Monarchy, adding "I don't mean the Windsor family." I said I didn't care twopence about monarchy – the only real issue was civilisation against barbarism. He agreed, but thought with Hobbes that civilisation and monarchy went together. He returned abruptly to the duty of being a conchy: at all costs we must get rid of the bloodthirst and have more Christianity.

He had read Stoddart and accepted his views. He agreed with me that Darlow was an egregious ass. Before parting I asked him to tea: he said he had just been going to ask me, and we finally arranged that I should go to him on Friday. I then biked home. I thought Coghill a good man, quite free from our usual Oxford flippancy and fear of being crude: much inferior to Barfield and Beckett in intellect and still a little undeveloped . . .

Monday 5 February: . . . Biked into town after breakfast and duly attended the Cad's lecture at 10 o'clock.[6] All the usual old tricks – including the tirade against people who didn't know the history of the language. How long has he lived and got no further than this?

Afterwards I saw Robson-Scott and asked him if he could possibly get anyone to read to the Martlets instead of me. He said he couldn't at such short notice. I felt that my paper on Spenser was quite unsuitable: and besides I had read once before on Morris and once on Narrative Poetry (or twice rather, for I read it again at Cambridge: its first reading here was on the night when Farquharson brought M. Goblet who chanted Breton epic songs to us): and to read again on Spenser would be to finally label myself as having only one taste.

I biked home and found Mary in the kitchen. After I had been working for some time the Doc appeared and we had some talk. Starting from dissociation he went on to speak of the awful depths that one sometimes caught sight of underneath ones own mind. I agreed with him that most of us could find positive Satanic badness down there somewhere, the desire for evil not because it was pleasant but because it was evil.

---

[6] On "Middle English Dialects" every Monday and Tuesday at 10 o'clock.

He expiated on the freedom of the Yogis, but confessed that Yoga was too hard for him. I read Barfield's poem to him: he said it might have been written under the influence of a drug, wh. is ridiculous. He was much more cheerful today, but looking wretched, his eyes all sunken . . .

After lunch I went out. I had decided to try and patch up some notes on *Prometheus Bound* for the Martlets: I took the book with me. The great point which struck me was the way Shelley sets out with the quite commonplace idea of a world ruled by a supreme devil and redeemed by love: then he runs up against reality, finds the whole thing much bigger, and so the inscrutable Demorgorgon (the IT-IS) becomes the real character: and the redemption is affected by inexplicable inspiration: i.e. Panthea doesn't know what her own dream was. In other words Shelley throws the whole thing over to the untried forces of a logical situation welling up from the *élan vital* – and neither he nor we ever find out what really happens. It is much deeper than he meant it to be . . .

Friday 9 February: . . . By the second post came back my "Waking" from *The Challenge*, with the usual printed notice of rejection . . . I shall try *The Spectator* . . .

Soon after lunch I set out on foot and went into town . . . I repaired to the Schools . . . The others gradually arrived and we began our meeting [of the Discussion Class]. The minutes, in verse, were really quite clever.

I then read my paper on Spenser. Thank goodness my cough behaved decently. Gordon was pleased with the passage about *yávos* [inner brightness] and made me read it again.[7]

The discussion was entirely dominated by Darlow, who talked great nonsense. He described Spenser as coming "at the end of a period": that was why he had nothing strong and positive: nor had Catullus, who also came at the end of a period. I think he was gambling on the chance of no one having read Catullus – which he obviously has not done himself. Of course he was contradicted at once by everyone. We asked him what about the passion and the

---

[7] The minutes of this meeting were written in Chaucerian verse by Nevill Coghill, and most of them can be found in the Preface to Lewis's *Selected Literary Essays* (1969). Nevill Coghill gave this description of Lewis:

> Sir Lewis was ther; a good philosópher
> He hadde a noblé paper for to offer.
> Well couthe he speken in the Greeké tongue;
> And yet, his countenance was swythé yong.

friendship in Catullus. He took up the desperate position that passion and friendship were negative things: then suddenly asked me if one could afford to neglect the allegory in Spenser. I reminded him that the prohibition to discuss allegory came from himself.[8]

He replied to this by proceeding, after a short sketch of Arisoto, to say that the great beauty in Spenser was that, despite the allegory, one could be quite interested in his characters: one could always go on working out what little was given. Several of us demurred to this preposterous view of Spenser. I forget how but it soon developed into a tirade from Darlow on the necessity of facing facts, the flippancy of the Victorians and the "moral earnestness" of our own generation.

The sight of Darlow with horned spectacles, aesthetic tie and white lily in buttonhole, looking eightyish to the last degree and putting himself up as representative of an earnest generation was too much, and we all roared.[9] He went on however. I turned and whispered to Strick "Can't you put an end to this nuisance?" He came suddenly out of a brown study and hissed in my ear with quite surprising virulence "Yes! I will." His own contribution however was quite futile and only supplied a few moments obligato to the steady trombone of Darlow. All attempts to answer or interrupt him failed.

At last I succeeded in getting a pause in which I made everyone agree that his way of reading Spenser was a peculiarity of his own, not a manifestation of the moral tendencies of our generation. I then had a smart bit of fence with him and actually succeeded in shutting him up for a while. This was not really a dialectical feat, for he was talking nonsense that would go over at a touch. My only merit was

[8] Nevill Coghill's minutes:
> *Daun Darlow* answerde "What of allegory,
> What meneth swevnés in Daun Spenser's story
> Why useth he swich women's artifice
> Al vigourless, effeminate, and nice
> As Daun Catallus doth in al his wirche?"
> "I wold not end in the Byzantine Chirche" (Kirk)
> Quod Lewis, "And Catallus, I dar seyn
> Hath nought to do with Spenser, to be plain."

[9] Nevill Coghill's minutes:
> *Daun Darlow* was there of a high corage
> Whan he to speken wyslye wolde beginne
> There was noon auditour conde on him wynne.
> Ful byg he was, of brawn and eke of bones
> Ful oft he spak in high and noblé tones
> Of historye: he hadde a purplé tye
> And in his button-hole a dayës eye.

that by saying "Wait a moment!" in a loud voice I succeeded in making him hear my answer. I did not hear a single enlightening remark from anyone all afternoon.

I left with Coghill and Martley, both of whom complimented me on my paper.[10] At tea in his rooms, besides us three, were Coghill's younger brother (a subaltern, his guest) and a fool called Cuthbert.[11] We talked about spiritualism, dreams and futurism: pretty silly, but I should have liked Coghill if I had got him alone.

So home on foot and to supper. Worked afterwards. On getting into bed I was attacked by a series of gloomy thoughts about professional and literary failure – what Barfield calls "one of those moments when one is afraid that one may not be a great man after all".

Saturday 10 February: . . . After lunch I had to go into town again to return books to the English Library. While I was there looking in vain for more information about *Prometheus* Strick came in and began to talk to me. We began of course by a few criticisms of Darlow. Strick doesn't think much of Gordon or of any of the English dons except Simpson. He said Raleigh had been dead sick of the English School before he died, "It was life that interested him." This agrees with what Jenkin has often said.

He talked to me for a long time. I can only describe what he was like by saying that without returning to any one subject too often or doing anything to suggest a fixed idea, he gave me the impression of a man with a fixed idea . . .

Sunday 11 February: . . . A beautiful springlike morning with great sunshine. I called at Exeter and found that Coghill and his brother were there – the soldier brother being still in his dressing gown. Coghill however was ready and we walked out at once. We went via Lake Street and S. Hinksey up to Thessaly and down by Ferry Hinksey. We talked on a great many subjects.

He apparently has been great friends with the Earp, Childe, Crowe and Harris set. I said I had been rather taken up by them in 1919 but not quite taken in. He defended them, but agreed with most of my criticisms . . .

I found to my relief that he has still an open mind on ultimate questions: he spoke contemptuously of the cheap happiness obtain-

---

[10] Averell Robert Martley of Hertford College, who took his BA in 1923.
[11] Sir Jocelyn Ambrose Cramer Coghill, 1st Lieut., South Wales Borderers 1922–25.

able by people who shut themselves up in a system of belief. When in doubt he is still quite content with the Promethean attitude: if God doesn't aim at what we call good, so much the worse for God. He is quite confident in the sanctions of one's own impulse and says you must take it for final. He seems very ignorant of literature and thinks music the greater art, because it can do two things at once. He is quite right there. He agreed with me that women were bores until they were forty.

We went into the pub at Ferry Hinksey where an old customer informed us in whispers that it was before time. When the beer was brought we had a lot of talk from this old fellow – about prospects for the boat race, his early days as a boxer, and other pleasant themes. We parted at the Turl.

Home and had lunch. Afterwards came Sidney and I had an hour and a half with her. I find it impossible to make her do any serious preparation for me. After tea, having first written to my father, I began to work on my "Requiem". Worked as hard as I have ever done on a poem, trying to resist all my clichés, shortcuts and other original sins . . .

Monday 12 February: A thick fog this morning. Dorothy came back today after her long absence. D gave her a great telling off about all the things which have come to light while she has been doing the work herself and told her that she must do things in our way or clear out. Dorothy seems to have taken it very well.

After breakfast I walked to Schools and heard the Cad's lecture. Wynn came and sat next to me:[12] according to my invariable custom with new acquaintances I gave him a full list of all the Cad's enormities and he seemed duly impressed. He says he thinks we shall have no sound laws etc. this year and seems to think that Miss Wardale is going too deeply into it with me.

Walked home again. After lunch I walked over to Iffley and got back my Wordsworth from the Doc's rooms: I then crossed the river – there is a fine rush of water at the new weir – intending to go down by Sandford, but it was such a marsh in the meadows that I turned back. I then walked up the field path opposite the church, reading the opening of the last book of the *Excursion*. I tried the experiment of treating it as real philosophy, taking it as prose and trying to follow the thought conscientiously. The result was rather

[12] George William Nevill Wynn of Worcester College, who was also in the Discussion Class.

discreditable either to me or to Wordsworth, I am not sure which. What has the "active principle" in all things got to do with the passage (a fine passage) about old age? . . .

Coming home again I sat down to work a little more on my "Requiem" when Cranny arrived. He seemed in much better form, tho' his exchange is still hanging fire . . . Cranny was somehow funnier than usual today. He talked so hard at tea that at first we couldn't get him to help himself at all: at last, under pressure, he stretched out his hand absent-mindedly and took the whole half of a cake.

Today, for the first time, I found out something that Cranny really believes: that is, the moral order of the world as manifested in history. He gives various examples. He said the fall of all empires based on force was the central fact. The Hebrew prophets did not of course foretell particular historical facts but they were prophetic in the sense of seeing this moral order. This is the nearest approach to a religion I have ever heard from him and I was impressed at the time: though I decided afterwards that it would be better to believe in pardons than to see moral order in the change from Rome to the Middle Ages.

After tea he left and I worked on the Vth Canto of "Dymer", not without a little success: feeling as confident today as I was depressed yesterday, wh. shows how much worth either mood is.

D has a tiresome cough tonight, and has had a sore back (of which she had said nothing) for the last few days – doubtless the result of the unusual work. She struck out a most excellent phrase tonight, saying of Dalkey, where houses of all kinds are mixed together, that it looked as they had been rained from heaven. I at once hailed this as literature and announced my intention of stealing it . . .

Tuesday 13 February: Worked on *Beowulf*, revising, most of the morning and then bicycled to Manor Place where I read my essay on Milton to Wilson. Quite an interesting hour tho' I don't know that I learnt anything new . . .

Afterwards I began Dryden. Started him with great good will and managed to raise some feeble appreciation of the Cromwell stanzas: but the *Astraea Redux* seemed to me such unutterable sawdust that I relapsed into my usual view of the Augustans . . .

D was very miserable all today: I discovered finally that her finger joints were bothering her and also forebodings as to how bad they might become. If only we could move to drier ground! Began this evening to read *Tess of the d'Urbervilles* aloud.

Wednesday 14 February: ... After lunch I walked into Schools and worked all afternoon supplementing my Spenser paper with a short review of Wyatt, Surrey and Sackville. On reaching home for tea I was greeted with the cheering news that Jenkin had been here and would come to the Martlets tonight. From tea to supper time I worked on and completed my paper.

Then after supper I bussed to College. Going into the J.C.R. I found Jenkin sitting with Terry, Robson-Scott and Fasnacht. I seated myself on the floor and we talked until it was time to repair to Anderson's rooms in Durham buildings – new rooms where I have never been before. They are divided into two by an arch and are quite pretty. Present were Anderson,[13] R-Scott, Curtis, Terry, Jenkin, McKissack, Rink, and Keir. Arrangements were made about the dinner next week when the Cambridge Martlets were coming.

My paper was very kindly received. In the discussion the conception of γάνος raised a lot of talk of a rather aimless kind – was there γάνος in *Lear*? Was there in *Tamburlaine* etc.? I had, in my paper, applied Murray's view of Pindar to Spenser, i.e. he failed to be a great poet because he was only a poet. This presently led to an argument of which the skeleton was something like this.

RINK: "Do you say that a work of art cannot be the greatest in kind if it is only art?"

SELF: "Certainly."

RINK: "But can't it be judged and oughtn't it to be judged just as art?"

SELF: "Well taking art as an expression it must be the expression of something: and one can't abstract the 'something' from the expression."

RINK: Stated Croce's position.

SELF: "You can't judge it simply as expression, in practice. A lyric which perfectly expressed the pleasure of scratching wd. not really be judged equal to *Lear*."

RINK: "But it would be, *quâ* art."

SELF: "But not *quâ* thing."

RINK: "Perhaps not: but it could be criticised just as art without reference to its further nature as thing and that is what Croce means."

SELF: "I suggest that the object of a work of art is not to be criticised

[13] John Edward Anderson of University College took his BA in 1925.

but to be experienced and enjoyed. And that which appeals to the whole man must be greater than that which appeals to part of the man."

RINK: "I don't think so, provided the emotion of the artist is perfectly expressed."

SELF: "That's all right, if you consider the artist alone. But you forget that art is a social thing."

ROBSON-SCOTT and RINK (together): "Oh no, certainly not, you can't mean that."

SELF: "Why not? Isn't the object of the artist to communicate his emotion?"

RINK: "Oh! Then you make art not expression but communication?"

SELF: "Yes. I'm sorry I said expression before. I mean communication."

RINK: "But is it not disinterested? Does the artist, while at work, think about an audience or about anything but perfect expression?"

SELF: "No artist has ever taken that view. Why are all artists so eager to be understood? Why do they bother to alter their first drafts?"

RINK: "To express more perfectly."

TERRY: "Mere jottings might be the most expressive of all – to the artist."

SELF: "The artist goes on altering phrases which are merely expressive to himself and hunting for those which will reproduce the right emotion in the audience."

JENKIN: "Yes, I agree with that."

KEIR: "Keat's first draft of the *Nightingale* was found scattered all over the garden: so he had no idea of communication."

JENKIN: "That was mere accident – carelessness."

RINK: "But how can the essence of art depend upon its being communicative? If an Athenian had written Wagnerian music it would have communicated nothing to his contemporaries but it would have been art."

SELF: "I don't mean what 'happens to communicate' in fact: but what is 'such as to be communicative', tho' of course mere accidents – e.g. a MS getting lost – may prevent it ever actually arousing the right emotion."

FASNACHT: "Potentially communicative?"

SELF: "Yes, I suppose so."

TERRY: "But almost anything would be that. A mere sign would be communicative to a person who happened to have the same associations as the artist."

RINK: "No, communication won't do: it will have to be expression."

SELF: "What do you mean by expression, if you don't mean what is potentially communicative?"

RINK: "I mean that which embodies the form of the artist's experience."

SELF: "Form in the Platonic sense?"

RINK: "Not exactly – I mean like the form of a penny."

SELF: "That comes to the Platonic form. That which corresponds to the round form of the penny, in a pain say, is Painfulness. You don't mean that the expression of the particular pain is the concept of painfulness?"

RINK: "There's a difference. There are many pennies but every emotion is unique."

SELF: "Well can you talk about form and content in a unique thing?"

RINK: "Why not?"

SELF: "Well take the *whole*. Is its form inside it or out and what happens in either case?"

FASNACHT: "It is neither, it is diffused."

SELF: "Can you distinguish it in this case from the particular?"

FASNACHT: "The difficulty comes not from the uniqueness of the Whole but from its Wholeness."

RINK: "In any case, I take back Form in that sense. I really think I mean the form you impose on the experience. As perception is the forming of sensation."

SELF: "But do you impose that? Isn't it given?"

RINK: "Oh no – for instance I impose form on that lamp. If it was on the edge of vision it would have none."

FASNACHT: "But that isn't a mental operation, it's the turning of your head."

SELF: "Yes, the form depends on your body: but to you, as Mind, it's part of the given."

(This led to a longish argument on "sensations when not attended to" – were they sensations? – and so on to a discussion of the Ego. Did it exist when not filled by an object? Rink thought it did potentially. I trotted out my favourite argument about the potential being always resident in the lower actual, greatly to Fasnacht's amusement. Rink said the actual in which potential subjectivity resided was the spirit unknown in its essence. We then returned to our muttons.)

RINK (Having abandoned the word Form as hopeless): "The work of art is the crystallised emotion – the emotion made permanent."

FASNACHT: "Made permanent in whose mind?"

RINK: "I mean potentially permanent."

SELF: "Doesn't that mean, capable of rearousing the original experience?"

RINK: "Well yes."

SELF: "Then the issue is that I think art is communication, you make it auto-communication."

RINK: "The work of art is capable of recreating the original experience but that is an accident of it."

SELF: "Well what is its essence?"

RINK: "I don't think I can put it into words. What I object to is making its essence depend on the future and on its contingent success in reproducing the experience. I want to make it retrospectively what this makes it in the future."

We all now agreed that we had a certain inkling of what he meant. I said this was certainly not what I meant by art: in fact it stood to art as ———. Rink walked part of the way back with me and invited me to lunch tomorrow . . .

Thursday 15 February: . . . Again today – it is happening much too often now – I am haunted by fears for the future, as to whether I will ever get a job and whether I shall ever be able to write good poetry.

This spring term seems always rather nasty: last year it was Mary and the Brat, to whom may Malebolge be hospitable, the year before that it was the Jeffries.

Friday 16 February: D stayed in bed today, very bad indeed with her violent cold and neuralgia. After breakfast I made another attempt to get something out of Wyld: but after despairing I finished the *Ancrene Riwle* and went on with *Sir Gawain* . . .

I then went to Schools for the Discussion Class. I was for some time alone with Payne who seems a pleasant fellow.[14] The others gradually arrived and Macdonald read a short and very bad paper on the adapters of Shakespeare in a monstrous high pitched voice with a Scotch accent.[15] The discussion which followed was pretty

---

[14] Frederick Lewis Payne of Queen's College took his BA in 1923.

poor, but better than usual. Darlow was fairly silent.[16] The only really amusing thing was Coghill's minutes in Chaucerian verse, which, excluding some lapses, were good . . .

Wednesday 21 February: . . . I proceeded to 14 Longwall Street to lunch with Rink. He provided a very pleasing lunch of salad, cheese, jam, tangerines, dates, walnuts and coffee . . .

Shortly before three we went out for a walk. It was only after this that we began to progress. I started a new attack on expressionism on the ground that it didn't (by his definition) cover the phenomena of failure. He had defined expression as the pure disinterested and intelligent consequences of experience. I said this described a bad poem as well as a good one. He failed to defend by an examination of "intelligent" but finally cut me off by inserting "complete" in his definition. Having thus come to a temporary standstill we reversed positions and he attacked my theory. In spite of many well contested points I was gravelled in the end by the simple question of communicative to how many . . . He had distinctly the honours today . . .

Coming in, I found the two Raymonds here. He is moving soon and will let his house for three years if he can't sell it. As D said afterwards, this means he will get high rent, get the house done up by the tenant and retire thither with all to the good. After tea I was left with him in the dining room and endured wonderful boredom.

I was the more annoyed by hearing the Doc come in. At last Father Raymond made a move. The Doc had just gone as we two came out of the dining room. I found D in great distress about him and at her suggestion ran after him to see if I could have a chat. I did not overtake him till the end of Magdalen Road. He was walking very stiffly, but that is not uncommon. He was rather abstracted: talked about immortality. At Iffley Turn I left him and came home by bus.

D said he had seemed in great worry and ready to break down: in the very few minutes which she had had alone with him on the doorstep he had said that he was going down to Bristol to see a specialist. D is afraid it is cancer. I tried to take the view that doctors often imagine things in their own case: but indeed the poor old Doc

[15] Robert Macdonald of Lincoln College who took his BA in 1925.

[16] This was the last thing Lewis was to record about T.S. Darlow. This may have been because he left the Discussion Class. In any event, he left Oxford fairly soon after this, without a degree, and settled in London. Sometime later he began working for the *Daily Herald* and at the outbreak of World War II he became a very successful war correspondent for the *Daily Herald* in France. He was sent on an assignment to the R.A.F. headquarters in France, became ill, and died shortly afterwards on 10 November 1939.

is the last man to do so. D cried out against the old enemy – fate and all. As we said, he is the most unoffending, the gentlest, the most unselfish man imaginable . . .

Friday 23 February: . . . Mary and the Doc came before lunch. D told me the Doc was very bad and must stay here. After lunch he began raving. Quieted later and explained that he was haunted by horrible blasphemous and obscene thoughts. Talked quietly a long time with me alone. Had two more bad attacks before tea – very violent. The third was the worse. Thinks (while in the fit) that he is going to Hell. Dr Hichens came in the evening. After his visit Doc told Mary and D that he was doomed – lunacy and death. Traced it to V.D. in his College days. D said he was quite lucid but exaggerated repentance and misery something incredible . . .

Rob came. Completely reversed the earlier view: said the whole thing was neurasthenia and bunkum. He tried to hearten up the Doc who seemed at first to listen to him. When we started trying to get him to bed on a mattress in the drawing room there was another frightful fit – rolling on the floor and shrieking that he was damned for ever and ever. Screams and grimaces unforgettable. The fits began to get more frequent and worse. I noticed how exactly he reproduces what Faustus says in Marlowe. We spent most of the time holding him quiet – very hard work . . . While we were struggling with the Doc, Rob nodded at me and muttered "mad", so I knew he's given up the neurasthenic theory.

Dr Hichens came. They chloroformed the Doc. I had to hold his legs – dript with sweat, he's got as strong as a horse. He was ages going over: and kept on imploring us not to shorten his last moments and send him to Hell sooner than need be. When he was finally over Dr Hichens said "Now is the time to decide what to do with him." As D and I said afterwards this was the worst moment of all: it seemed so treacherous.

They agreed that there was nothing for it but the asylum in the morning: or rather Rob pretended to agree, but it was only tactics as we afterwards discovered. They injected some strong narcotic, not morphia, I forget what, and Dr Hichens went away, promising to come back at 8.30. The Doc was now quite quiet but soon began to mutter. I was with him alone for a long time.

Saturday 24 February: The Doc continued fairly quiet under the drug, but gabbling. After it had got light Rob watched him and I went out and took a few turns in front of the house. It was raining. Maureen of course had been awake all the night owing to the horrible noise and very much rattled.[17] Mary had slept a good deal. I found the worst thing I had to contend with was a sort of horrible sympathy with the Doc's yellings and grovellings – a cursed feeling that I could quite easily do it myself.

Dorothy came. I was watching the Doc again for some time. Had some tea and a little bread and butter: but went upstairs and was sick as soon as I had swallowed it. The Doc seemed to become quite sane again and kept on saying irrelevant things: was threatened with several further attacks but they didn't come on. Mary and I had to hold his hands a good deal. Sometimes he talked quite sensibly for several minutes: expressed gratitude to us in a way that would break your heart. We got him to take a little warm milk with great difficulty.

Hichens, despite his promise, did not come till 11.30. The Doc seemed quite glad to see him. Afterwards Rob and Hichens retired to consult while I stayed to watch the Doc. In their consultation (D told me) Hichens took a much more cheerful view. Rob told him how many of the Doc's symptoms were normal in his case. They concluded that it might possibly be mere hysteria, partly constitutional, partly from the war: but chiefly because the poor man thought that his syphilis had come awake and was going to drive him mad.

During the day there were many encouraging signs. Tho' often threatened with the attacks the Doc himself recognised them as a nervous ailment and didn't talk about Hell. At about one o'clock Rob sent me into town to engage an ex-policeman for tonight in case of emergencies, since next time, instead of the Hell idea, the Doc might decide to murder someone. I did so and came back after lunch.

Things seeming fairly quiet, I went up and lay down on my bed. Found I was now getting frightfully nervy: never having seen madness before, I was afraid of every odd thought that came into my own head. I kept thinking I heard the Doc start to rave again downstairs but it was only imagination.

Came down for tea. D – looking wonderfully fresh and cheerful – told me there was nothing to do, and after some tea (not v. much, still feeling sick in the stomach) I went back to bed. Couldn't stick

[17] After this Maureen was sent to stay with Lady Gonner for the rest of the time her uncle was at "Hillsboro".

it and came down at once to potter about with D for company. She was amazingly good. Everything really much more cheerful this evening, but somehow I found it much harder to stand.

The Doc came in to supper and was coaxed to eat a little. Soon however the beastly preliminary signs came on and we had to lead him into the drawing room (Rob and I). The poor fellow had got his will back and was making an effort. He begged us to help him: accepted our "suggestions" that he was alright and was now mastering it. My "perfectly safe" turned out a most efficient catchword. Rob spoke to him sternly when he got wild and I spoke to him soothingly when he got scared. We managed to keep the fit in hand. Just before we got him to bed he started a bad one again, but asserted himself, using the phrase which I had suggested the day before about being a man and not afraid of bogeys. We had got him to take his sleeping draught a little earlier. He held my hand for a long time after he was in bed.

The others lowered the gas and went away, Rob to bed and D to the next room. The Doc most pathetically thanked me for staying with him: he began to get a little extravagant, calling me an angel etc, but soon checked himself and said "Yes, I know that's all sentimental nonsense". At last to my delight I heard him go to sleep – not a gabbling drug sleep, but steady snoring. At first he woke up a little startled whenever the clock struck: but after a word or two with me in which he invariably thanked me and apologised for keeping me up, he turned over and fell asleep. Once he started up and started the old contortions: but after I had spoken to him he lay down.

I felt much better than in the afternoon – quite fresh and not at all nervy. Sat and smoked in the firelight till 4 o'clock. It wd. have been quite safe if I had slept: but whenever I began to doze, horrible faces came up, and I daren't risk a nightmare, so I had to keep awake. At 4 o'c D went and called Rob to relieve me. She and I had just gone upstairs when the Doc – where Rob was I'm not sure – awoke and came up to the lavatory of his own accord. He seemed absolutely himself when he came out. Rob and I got him back to bed and he then said that he must see . . . Got to bed a little before five and slept like a log.

Sunday 25 February: Woke up about eleven o'clock or later. Found that the Doc had slept well after I left him. I shaved for the first time since the trouble began, washed and had a large breakfast. I heard that Jenkin had been round to see me and asked me to go in. Rob said it would be quite safe for me to go out and D encouraged me to go, promising that she would rest that afternoon. I looked in to see the Doc, who was quite normal, tho' naturally very much exhausted, and apologised for having been "such a fool".

With inexpressible relief I came out of this house of nightmare and walked in to Merton Street. Jenkin was just finishing lunch. Afterwards we rode on the top of a bus to the Banbury Road terminus, then crossed and returned' by the Woodstock Road bus. It was a lovely springlike afternoon and all the almond trees were out. After our ride I had tea with Jenkin and walked home.

Began to get a little nervy as I neared the house. Everything however was alright. The Doc was moved upstairs tonight, he and Mary taking my room. We discussed plans for the future. Rob promised to see early tomorrow morning about arranging for the Doc to be boarded and taken into a Pensions Hospital for war neurasthenia. We were left with the uncomfortable prospect of the Doc and Mary here and Rob gone, indefinitely, should this fail.

Mary throughout this time has behaved with her usual relentless selfishness, rudeness, ingratitude, and sullen gluttony. She slept and cried upstairs while we were saving her husband from an asylum: she called us out of Hell on Saturday morning to get her a hot bath: come rain come fine, her cups of cocoa had to be ready when she wanted them. Tonight she called D upstairs to bring her biscuits when she was in bed. To be short, we must endure her for his sake: but there's no two and sixpenny whore from a garrison town and no oily old gipsy woman who wouldn't be a more welcome guest. She is not a woman at all – she is a stomach with a voice to ask for food without a please.

I slept on the dining room sofa: lay very hard, so that I awoke feeling sore all over.

Monday 26 February: The Doc and Mary – thank God – slept very late. I tried in vain to work. Rob went into town to make arrangements about the Doc being boarded preparatory to his being admitted to a Pensions Hospital. He returned with the good news that the people he had seen were ready to further the matter and hoped that it would be easily managed. It was not till afterwards that I gathered from D that at the very best there would be a delay of ten days – jolly news for us. Rob then went upstairs and told the Doc what he had done. The latter seemed to approve and to be quite ready to go to hospital. Rob then departed – lucky man! The Doc came down for lunch – quite normal and looking very much better than he did before the attack.

In the afternoon came Jenkin on his bike: D thought it safe for me to go out. I rode with him to Horsepath and back over Shotover. I don't think much of importance was said.

Coming back, I had tea and afterwards went out for a walk along Cowley Road with Mary and the Doc. The latter was really wonderfully improved: hummed tunes: made a few attempts at conversation: said he would never forget what I had done for him etc. After we came back I had to go out to the post and took him with me. He said he felt one of the hysterical attacks coming on again but it did not materialise. Later at supper he started the same thing, and again at bed time. Later still, after I had gone to bed, I heard him starting again and had to go to him. D holds out wonderfully. Myself still worried with the feeling of sickness.

Tuesday 27 February: D told me the Doc was very much better this morning than he has yet been. He stayed in bed till lunch time. At 12 o'clock I went to Wilson and explained to him that I had not done any work and why. He was very sympathetic. He agreed with me about the absurd slowness of getting things through the Ministry of Pensions and cited examples from his own experience. We employed the hour talking about Elizabethan criticism on which I should normally have done my essay today.

I then biked home. Was just going upstairs to change my clothes when Mary said "Johnnie says he's got the horrid feeling again and you can stop them." I went to the drawing room and did so. In the afternoon I tried to work on *The Owl and the Nightingale*: but was much too tired and rattled to make any headway. At suppertime we had the usual performance of the threatened attack . . . and in a few seconds [the Doc] had himself worked up into a very good beginning of a fit. We succeeded in staving it off and gave him Horlick's with a sleeping powder in it. He and Mary were soon snoring.

D said she must have a few minutes peace to read the papers to herself but urged me to go to bed. I did – to lie awake for an hour or so, thoroughly nervy and miserable. Got up and found D just going to bed, and already in her room. I asked her if there was any milk to spare. I was sorry, for she came downstairs again to find some for me. I had a cup of hot milk and retired to bed, still to lie awake. A very windy night. Kept on thinking that I heard the Doc and at last I really did. I decided to try D's advice of letting him alone. I heard Mary get up and she came into my room. I pretended to be asleep. She glided out again. I must have really fallen asleep soon after this, for I heard no more.

Wednesday 28 February: Woke up deciding that the bed in Maureen's room (where I lay) was a very much poorer affair than my own. The Doc unfortunately woke early. I went in to Miss Wardale and explained why I had nothing done. She taught me for a solid hour and I found it very tough to sit it out.

Came home after leaving a note asking Jenkin to come out this afternoon. During the morning D had a very straight talk with the Doc, telling him that he knew and we knew that he was perfectly alright and that the continued hysteria was mere selfishness and nonsense. He remained quiet during the morning. We had another scene during lunch but succeeded in keeping him in hand.

Afterwards I waited for a long time for Jenkin and finally rode in to Merton St. but he was out. I then turned and began to ride to Cowley but was driven back by rain. Coming home, I found all well, except that there had been a blowdown of soot in the drawing room. When it cleared up I went out on foot: walked up to Headington and along the private road in beautiful sunshine. I tried hard to detach myself from the atmosphere in which we have now lived for what seems eternity – with some little success, but not much.

Came back to find Mary sitting alone by the drawing room fire. I passed on hastily to the dining room where I found D engaged in battling down another of the Doctor's fits. As I heard afterwards, he had started on the damnation stunt again and had confessed new sins. He says that what is really on his mind is that he once betrayed a girl in Philadelphia: she wrote in despair telling him that a child was coming, and he never answered. Of course one can't believe what he says: but if this is true, then the hell the cur is now going through serves him jolly well right[18] – but it seems rather rough that we should have to share it.

Before we started tea, Jenkin came in: he and I sat with the Doc for some time and all went well. Tea was a nervous meal for everyone. Afterwards Jenkin and I walked with the Doc as far as Claytons,

---

[18] Later: I am convinced that the whole story, like that of the syphilis and the hell complex, were all equally delusions. – C.S.L. This note, judged from internal evidence, appears to have been made some years after the text on which it comments. – W.H.L.

where I got some more of the powders: Jenkin came back with me and then left. During the walk the Doc was absolutely silent. He remained alright till supper and made some little response to my efforts at conversation. Towards the end of supper he began again. After much wear and tear we got him round again. I took him upstairs, helped him with . . . and got him into his bath. When he came out I brought him Horlicks with a powder in it, wh. though now perfectly compos mentis he refused to drink. Mary then went to bed.

D and I then sat in the drawing room till 11.30 and then went to bed ourselves. I went to sleep at once. Presently in the middle of a complicated and interesting dream which I have forgotten – I was woken up by Mary. Went into the Doc's room. Poor D was with him and had been for some time: as she said afterwards she had only called me because she was afraid of him getting absolutely out of hand again. He was nearer the complete breakdown this time than he has been since Rob left. Contortions horrible and screaming always just about to begin. At an enormous cost of will and muscle we kept him in control. They had succeeded in giving him the drug before I was called and he fought off its effects perversely for a solid hour. Then at last he went to sleep and we returned to bed, rattled and shivering with cold – *forsan et haec.*[19]

---

[19] *"Forsan et haec olim meminisse iuvabit"'*— "Perhaps even these things it will be a delight one day to remember." Virgil, *Aeneid*, I, 203.

Thursday 1 March: ... I got up and had breakfast alone with D in blissful quiet. Our two charming guests remained fast asleep. D then despatched me into the town to buy pressed beef and pork pie.

On returning home I found the Doc, who had now woken, was very well this morning. I looked in to see him. The poor devil naturally looked tired, but peaceful and easy and apologetic for last night. There was also a wire from Rob (to whom both D and Mary had written yesterday) to say that he was coming up by the 11.35. This was a great relief. I resolved, if human entreaty could compass it, to make him stay: for after all, as even Mary admits, the Doc is *his* ruddy brother and not mine . . . .

Jenkin came and I told him I could not go out with him. While D and I were talking to him at the gate, Rob appeared. The Doc had another attack soon after his arrival: Rob – who had lunched in town – faced the music while D, Mary, and I escaped to have some food in the kitchen. Rob afterwards went off to interview the pensions people in St Aldates. He came back with the news that the Doc could go before one Dr Goode next Tuesday. If necessary Goode (who lives at Littlemore) could come out here instead, but it would need some pressure to manage that. In the meantime Mary and the Doc had been out for a walk: they returned about tea time, the Doc again on the point of starting "The Horrors".

After tea I went up to the Gonners for another mattress. Rob accompanied me the greater part of the way. He had just been looking at Maureen. He suggested that she had been overworking. I explained the necessity of the situation: in order to be fully qualified for a musical career she would have to pass the Oxford Senior. He said "Are they betting on a sound horse? Miss Whitty said that she had very little talent, certainly nothing above the average." I was very surprised to hear this: Rob thought that Miss W. had already said as much to D. He went on to enlarge on the disadvantages of a musical career and the delights of teaching domestic science. I asked him whether D ought to be told, but he wd. not commit himself.

He left me at the corner of Gipsy Lane and I went on to borrow the mattress. After a little chat with Lady Gonner I came away with it. I strapped it up in a roll and by bringing the loose end of the strap over my shoulder and bending down at an angle of 45 degress I was able to carry it home on my back. It was one of the heaviest loads I have had. At our gate I found Rob setting out for the Gonners with Maureen.

During his absence the Doc had another attack wh. I managed to fight down. To supper came Smudge and afterwards I did Anglo Greek with her. How far it was any good I don't know, for I was very sleepy and nervy and the noise of scenes going on upstairs was worse than if I had been in them.

After she had gone D, Rob and I met in the drawing room. Rob was debating whether to communicate with Goode or not and try to get him to hurry up. During this conversation he remarked that he wd. be leaving us again tomorrow. I laid before him as strongly as I possibly could the dreadful position in which he was leaving us. He refused absolutely to stay and then went to bed. D and I sat up for a little time – poor D is naturally beginning to be very tired. I slept on the dining room sofa, Rob having my bed.

Friday 2 March: At breakfast D, Rob, and I had a council of war. After many arguments we concluded that it would be better not to bother Goode. Any hint of urgency, anything in the nature of an S.O.S. wd. only arouse Goode's suspicions. Of course the fact of the syphilis would be pretty sure to emerge anyway: our only hope was that Goode would decide "This man has had syphilis and is therefore liable to insanity: but his present trouble is neurasthenia induced by worrying about that possibility, and by the war." Of course if they ruled that the present trouble was syphilitic they would not only not take him, but would cut his pension. And this was more likely to happen if they saw we were panicking to get him out of the house. Rob announced that he had changed his mind and wd. stay on to see the thing through. I have seldom been so grateful for any words . . .

Lunch was very late and immediately afterwards I bussed into town to the Discussion Class. Gordon was ill, but seven of us carried on alone. My minutes were well received.[1] Burns read a capital paper on Schools of Poetry: he quoted from the "Imagists" one or two poems which I liked immensely – tho' I was prepared to dislike them in theory.[2] The discussion was quite jolly – and infinitely comfortable – a glimpse of the clean, sane, outer world again . . .

Afterwards D and I went out to do some shopping – even in Cowley Rd. it was delightful to be together and away for a few minutes. Coming back – a big moon – we met Rob walking outside: he said "Johnnie is quite happy, confessing his sins to Mary." Rob told us that the girl whom the Doc had "betrayed' was a common prostitute. Thank the Lord! We all remarked how the poor man would regret his many confessions if he ever recovered. At supper the Doc was nearly asleep and Rob got him up to bed soon afterwards.

I soon came up with a hot water bottle and stayed to help in restraining an attack. Pretty near the edge this time and he said "I'm in Hell" for the first time since Friday night . . .

Saturday 3 March: Woke up after a very good night but too sore to lie on the dining room sofa any longer. After my tea I went upstairs and lay on the bed which D had just vacated, where I fell asleep again. Had breakfast alone in the dining room and afterwards did messages in Cowley Road: a most glorious fresh morning of blue sky and puff'd clouds. The Doc and Mary slept late: he had had a fairly good night but she had been forced to give him the second dope.

Rob wrote a letter to Goode asking him to interview the Doc here instead of holding a board in town and I cycled with it over to Littlemore. Maureen was down here all morning from the Gonners with whom she has been staying ever since the trouble began. I found her and Rob playing catch in the road when I came back, which was really rather comforting.

The Doc had rather a bad attack at lunch. Even between the attacks he never rallies now: a frightful expression of misery and lethargy has settled on his face, he replies if spoken to, only in monosyllables

---

[1] Lewis's minutes pick up from Coghill's reading of his, and begin with Gordon's choice of another speaker:

> But whan that Coghille had his tale ytold
> Our Professour gan round about bihold
> And lough and seyde "Unbokeled is the male!
> Let see now who shal tell another tale;
> And namély Sir Burns as thou art able
> Telleth anon som matere profitable."

[2] This was Gilbert Talbot Burns of Christ Church who took his BA in 1924.

and in a whisper. Nothing can wring the ghost of a smile from him. For painfulness I think this beats anything I've seen in my life . . .

D pretty tired today and had to cook a joint in addition to everything else. We got to bed about 12.30, I on the dining room sofa where I at once fell heavily asleep. At about three I was aroused by noises above: went up and found D (who had not slept at all) trying to quiet the Doc. The same old hopeless business and we got him over at last . . .

The sight of these attacks has almost changed my deep rooted conviction that no mental pain can equal bad physical pain. Down again and noticed that it was 5.30. Soon asleep again.

Sunday 4 March: Up about 9.45. As no one dare wash in the bathroom these mornings for fear of waking the Doc, and the scullery is always in use, I seldom get a chance of a morning wash. Just after I had shaved in Rob's room Jenkin turned up. I went out with him: we rode to Garsington, then to our left and home by the windmill and Horsepath. Jenkin and I seldom say anything of importance on our jaunts these days, but it is like cool water to be out with him . . .

After lunch I looked over an atrociously bad Latin prose by Sidney Stevenson: then Rob and I walked out on the golf links with the Doc. He had rather a bad attack soon after we had reached it: then pulled himself together and made some horribly pathetic attempts to join in the conversation. On the whole he was very bad this afternoon and (what was perhaps the most terrible thing of all) asked us what we were going to do with him. When we got home we found D on the doorstep who told Rob he was wanted in the drawing room.

I knew at once that Dr Goode had come. (Goode, it appears, had been here for half an hour and D was on the verge of collapse, having been left to make nerve racking conversation with him.) Shortly after the three Doctors had been closeted together, D, who listened in the hall, announced that they had got on to the dreaded subject of the syphilis. Mary seemed to feel the suspense least: Maureen, tho' of course not understanding the real issue, was trembling all over. D very nearly on the edge but holding on. I couldn't stick the dining room any longer and went and smoked cigarettes in the lobby upstairs for the windiest hour and a half I have spent except under fire. It was freezingly cold.

D came up now and then with news of what she cd. overhear: the prospect gradually improved. Goode had been heard to say "You have none of the symptoms of G.P.I."[3] Then he was heard talking to him about neurasthenia, particularly about the Hell idea, wh. results apparently from being frightened by one's father in youth. The first fearful question was thus settled – Goode did not think that the poor old Doc was going mad. Of the next questions – whether he would be admitted to hospital and how soon – we cd. only hear the most tantalising murmurs.

I was now given a little early supper so as I could set off to the Gonners with Maureen. Before I set off Goode left and Rob followed him out into the road. The Doc, who had been heard during the interview talking in a strong and ordinary voice, was now collapsed again. He was nevertheless more like himself and, poor fellow, very penitent for the trouble we had had. He said Goode was getting him into hospital but "it won't be for a few days, and how can I go on staying here?" Before Maureen left she kissed him and he smiled naturally for the first time this many a day. When I came back from seeing Maureen up to Red Gables the others were at supper and I went up to sit with the Doc, who was in bed. He said he was "afraid he'd upset my applecart", meaning my work: I reassured him on this point . . .

All the others early in bed. As I was taking up the jars[4] for D I heard the Doc making noises as if he were going to be sick. Anon out came Mary and said she was going to get him his second go of dope. D and I were very doubtful about the wisdom of this, and after some hesitation I woke Rob to ask him, and he said sleepily, "Give it to him." I went into their room. The Doc showed no signs of hysteria but was complaining of flatulency wh. kept him awake. Mary kept on grumblingly urging him to take his dope. He became naturally angry in a way which was rather comforting to see, and shouted out, "I'm not going to take it Maimie." And Mary got angry too, and I held up my finger and recited "Birds in their little nests agree" which didn't amuse anyone – except me . . .

Monday 5 March: Rob came into the dining room while I was having my morning tea and asked Dorothy to get him his breakfast at once as he had to ring up Goode between nine and ten. Later I went up and lay on D's bed, she having looked into the dining room to tell me that it was empty. She presently came to me with the news that

---

[3] General paralysis of the insane.
[4] Earthenware hot water bottles.

Rob was going back to Bristol today: which of course pleased us very little . . .

When I went up to shave in Rob's room he followed and made some tentative remarks about this being a nasty business for me. In fact he wanted, in addition to the pleasure of his own escape, the pleasure of being told by me that he was quite right to leave us and had been very good to stay so long and of course we couldn't expect any more etc. He did not get it. He left the house at about ten.

I began to work on Sidney's Latin prose: the post-prandial demands of nature became so urgent, however, that I had to bus into College – our own lavatory being now inaccessible in the morning for fear of waking the Doc. In College I had a good wash in the bath rooms. Bussed back and finished my job. D and I were just going to have our own lunch when the Askins were heard stirring overhead. The Doc just as depressed and lethargic as ever today . . .

Tuesday 6 March: Up lateish, bussed into town and washed at the Union: thence to Wilson to tell him again that I had done nothing. He quite understood the position of course, but said that all this waste of time was a very serious thing for me.

I then came home and worked on *Sir Gawaine*. The others got up for lunch: Mary said he had had a tolerable night without any dope. This was (at first) one of the best days he had had. He seemed perfectly normal and made some effort to join in the conversation . . .

After tea I began work on my paper for Miss Wardale. The Doc soon began to get restless and an attack was staved off. Mary got him to bed after supper and D had to go up and sit with him while I worked. I just managed to finish my paper when Smudge turned up – by appointment of course, but we had all forgotten her. I did Anglo Greek with her till twelve thirty, with a long interruption to soothe the Doc.

After she had gone D and I sat down for a while: when I went up for the jars I heard the Doc making noises as if he was going to be sick. We knew this was the prelude to trouble and didn't think it worth while to go to bed. Presently Mary came down and got him hot milk, but without powder, contrary to the advice of D and me who saw that powder would be necessary tonight. At about half past one we ventured to go up. I had just got into bed when I heard the Doc beginning: I waited a few minutes, then, seeing that it shaped badly, I hopped up. I succeeded in quieting him and Mary got him to take the dope. Before going back to bed I looked into D's room and saw that she was sleep, for wh. I was very glad, tho' it is a sad proof of how exhausted she is.

Wednesday 7 March: Was called by D at 9.30 with the horrible news that there was no letter from the Pensions people: we had foolishly been hoping that the end of this hell might be announced today. Dorothy was poorly this morning: she had (D said) been wanting to get up all night, but, with the exaggerated niceness of her class, she had been afraid to do so.

I went to see Miss Wardale and did my hour. Afterwards I did some shopping and came home. New trouble was afoot: Dorothy was suffering from acute pains and a dose of D's salts had had no result. Before lunch I had to go up and talk to the Doc while he dressed. I hope I sympathise with the poor wretch, but, by God, never do I want him again to be within twenty miles of me – never.

At lunch D discussed Dorothy's condition. With unpardonable folly we all asked the Doc's advice. D explained that she had already given her salts and cascara. The Doc advised further a strong dose of Epsom salts. After lunch I biked to Claytons to get this and when I came back it was administered under the Doc's supervision. A few minutes later he began announcing, "Oh, I'd forgotten she'd had cascara as well. Oh dear, oh dear, I've killed her! The girl will die! Get her an emetic at once!"

After the first shock I saw that this was probably another of his hysterical scares: but of course there was the possibility that it might be true. D, inclining to the latter view, was naturally nearly frantic. Mary was despatched to Dr Hichens. The unfortunate Dorothy was made to swallow a cup of mustard and water. I had to take the Doc into the drawing room and keep him quiet. It was tough work and by the time Mary returned I had passed a truly awful half hour, trying hard to hope for the best. Poor D broke down for once when Mary brought back the blessed news that it was alright and the Doc had been talking through his hat . . .

D and I both feel pretty bitter against Rob for sneaking home and leaving us to hold the front line: we cannot believe that it is really inevitable. Mary and D both wrote him their accounts of the situation tonight. D and I sat up till about 12.15 . . .

Some time afterwards we went to bed. After an hour or so of sleep I was awakened by the usual noise: went in and found D already there. He was very bad this time . . . We got to bed again at about four. About an hour later we were hauled up again. Mary said the dope had apparently had no effect. After another ghastly struggle . . . we got him to take a second dose. In bed again about six. The light was coming into my window and a lot of birds were singing – sane, clean, comfortable things.

Thursday 8 March: . . . There was nothing from Rob – I had been hoping, like a fool, that last night's letters would have fetched Rob. D was rather hurt when I described him as a cur: but I really find it hard to take any other view of his behaviour . . . Dorothy was of course pretty poorly after yesterday's dietary of salts, mustard and cascara. D had done most of the work in the morning (so far as Dorothy wd. let her, for she is most anxious to spare D, to whom I think she is really attached) and I now washed up.

Afterwards I did the *Bruce* passage in Sisam – good honest stuff. Mary went over to Iffley to get some clothes. She came back at about four thirty and went up to their room from which, a moment later, one of the patient's best screams was heard. I went up and succeeded in pulling him together again. As soon as he came downstairs he started the paralysis stunt until Mary took him out for a walk . . .

The Doc had an attack after tea, followed by several others (I think). D wrote a letter to Rob wh. was practically an S.O.S. Plenty of trouble with the Patient both at supper and afterwards. He and Mary had hot baths (I wish to heaven D and I ever had a chance of a bath these days) and we gave him his dope afterwards. As soon as he saw me bringing it into the room he started, or tried to start, "the horrors" but I succeeded in hushing him up and Mary gave him the stuff by spoonfuls . . . Tho' expecting to be called up again at any minute, D and I now went to bed, about 2 o'clock I think, and actually had a whole night.

Friday 9 March: Nothing from the Pensions this morning, nothing from Rob all morning in answer to D's S.O.S. of last night. I went into College for necessary reasons after breakfast. Coming home I found that Miss Featherstone had been to see D and promised, in her capacity of nurse, to come up and help with the patient today.

D had been bucked up no end by Miss Featherstone's visit and insisted on my going to the [discussion] class this afternoon, which I did, after an early lunch. It was held this afternoon in Gordon's house in Chadlington Rd. Singh read us a paper on Tagore: really very courageous and praiseworthy but frightfully funny, full of the most impossible Babu rhetoric, through no fault of his own but just because some things won't work in English.

I came away before tea and walked back to Carfax with Burns, who was inclined to be friendly in his cold way and asked me to have tea with him, which of course I refused. Came home. Miss Featherstone and the Patient were in the dining room. D told me that she had been simply splendid with him: but she had been hard put to it, and but for her this would have been the hardest day of all. There had been a wire from Rob asking "could we hold on till tomorrow." I should like to know what alternative we have. I went in and spoke to Miss F – very cheering to see that queer, homely, common, sensible old face again . . .

Saturday 10 March: Awoke after a quiet night to find that a communication had at last come from the Pensions people. It was a masterpiece. The case had been put to them as urgent on Monday: they now asked to know when Dr Askins could be ready to go to hospital at Henley. As Rob was expected up today and we did not know when he was leaving Bristol, it was useless to wire for his advice. All morning we were expecting a wire from Rob, but none came. I managed to do a little work for Smudge . . .

I soon had to come in to attend to the Patient. He was very bad in his horrors today, flinging himself on the floor and restrained with difficulty from screaming. I was alone in charge for some time. He got a little better before tea: but at tea the effort to make him eat anything had the usual result in screams and contortions . . .

He finally lay down on the sofa and I sat on the table and talked to him: all the old wearisome assurances that he was quite alright, that it was nothing but nerves, that he was getting better, that there was no such place as Hell, that he was not dying, that he was not going mad . . . that he was not paralysed, that he could master himself. It is a sort of devil's litany that he must be as sick of hearing as I am of saying . . .

Sunday 11 March: Up late and very sore from the sofa, to which I don't seem to get any more accustomed – as one rapidly did to much harder beds, in France, say. After breakfast I walked into College and there had a hot bath – a delicious treat in these days . . . Afterwards I went in to the Union and worked patching up some sort of an essay for Wilson on Elizabethan criticism – a subject that I shall always hate for its association with this time.

I had tea in the Union and went to Chapel to hear the Mugger's farewell sermon, which was quite moderate, and not the "heavy sob stuff" which Jenkin had anticipated. It was followed, comically enough, by "Now thank we all our God".

Came home, had supper, worked for Smudge, and so to bed on the sofa. The Doc had several fits (indeed, tho' milder, they have become almost continuous) but Rob attended to them. Rob is very impatient with him and bullying rather than masterful, wh. only excites the poor fellow more.

Monday 12 March: Into town by 10 o'clock for my hour with Wilson. Came back to hear that Rob had fixed everything up by a trunk call to Pensions and the Doc was to go to Henley this afternoon. One of the most delicious moments I have had this long time: I could have gone on my knees to thank any deity who cared to claim the credit for this release. Pottered about revelling in the end of term feeling till lunch time.

The Doc was very violent at lunch time and when the taxi (wh. Rob had ordered) came, I was afraid we would never get him into it. All through the meal he had been hooting and kicking and spitting out mouthfuls of food: he now began his "paralysis" in a very acute form and fell on the floor. He bade "a last farewell" to Mary. It was all very painful. I hoped it was mainly an hysteric's instinct for melodrama, but I am afraid there was a certain amount of real pain in it too.

Rob and I at last got him on board and the three of us drove to Henley. The country for the last half of the journey was very pretty, but it was a cold day. When we got to the hospital Rob went in alone, leaving the Doc and me in the taxi. He was away for a long time. I was in agonies lest there should be some hitch at the last moment. The poor Doc described his symptoms to me once again and very nearly began the screaming. At long last Rob appeared with a very fat man and they took the patient in.

Thank God! Rob was going back to Bristol direct from Henley, so I drove home alone. Found D dreadfully tired, and no wonder. Worked after tea and went out just before supper to have a large whiskey and soda. Mary goes tomorrow. I hear she is buying me a present: I had thought it was not in her power to annoy me more, but this is the last straw. However, may the intention be accounted to her for her righteousness – for by God she needs it, the gaunt she wolf of Washington.

Tuesday 13 March: Awake once or twice in the night and had the delightful experience of imagining that I heard the Doc and then realising that all that was over: then turning luxuriously to sleep, with the sound of heavy rain.

Mary, of course, had breakfast in bed: D and I had ours alone downstairs. It was delightful to be able to make a noise. Worked on M.E. in the drawing room all morning till Smudge came at 12, and I did Anglo Greek with her. Tho' horribly overworked, she seemed in excellent form at lunch . . . Sidney came at three with a much better prose. I worked with her till after five . . .

After tea Jenkin appeared on his bike and I gladly went out with him. We rode round by Elsfield. I talked nonsense all the time and he commented on the outrageous joy which I emanated. I said what we had been through was almost worth it for the relief I now felt: to wh. he replied that one could and did get just as much relief out of the smaller troubles which one imagines to be bad at the time. We were extraordinarily merry. I said I should like to motor to London and there dine. We expiated on this theme for some time – our mental age, for the nonce, being about twelve.

A grey cold evening. Home and had an enormous supper alone with D in delightful privacy, peace and jollity. Finished my paper for Miss Wardale afterwards.

Wednesday 14 March: Woke lateish after an excellent night and read a few pages of Hazlitt's essay on "Going a Journey" over my tea with extraordinary gusto.

After breakfast biked to Margaret Rd. and had my last tutorial with Miss W. A cold morning. Home again and was presented with a woolly waistcoat left for me by Mary: really very good of her and I must in fairness say that, tho' American and tho' poor, she is not mean. But I cannot help remembering some other facts . . .

After a fish lunch I went in by bike to Merton St., where I found Jenkin reading De la Mare's *Return*. He said it produced exactly the atmosphere of flu. I thought this a sound criticism. He had heard De la Mare read a paper on "Atmosphere" the day before yesterday to the Plantagenet Club in Oriel, which was really good. They had had a good evening otherwise, for Jenkin had retired afterwards to hear ghost stories in a select company, of which the leading light was an army officer aged about fifty and recently become an undergraduate, who had learned some very primitive kind of magic from the blacks in Jamaica. This man also indulges in the Oriental habit of obtaining ecstasies by the contemplation of his own navel.

In pursuance of my light headed mood I proposed we should go to the pictures as Jenkin had suggested yesterday. This however was vetoed, and we rode out instead: Jenkin remarking maliciously "You'll be very cold without a coat" as he put on his own and turned up the collar. We rode through Kennington, up the Bagley Woods road and so to the pretty village of Sunningwell which he has quite recently discovered . . .

We separated in Iffley Road and I came home. Mrs Hume-Rothery and Betty were with D when I got in, but soon left. Before supper I read *The Battle of the Books* – very good in its way, but not much in my line.[5] Maureen back tonight: three of us (and no more) at supper so that we are now really back to the normal again . . .

Friday 16 March: D had a long letter from Mary with nothing new about the Doc, except the opinion given by Rob that he would be kept in hospital for a long time and we must hope for the best. He went, by the by, to Richmond in the end, and not to Henley.

Maureen had a temperature of 101 this morning and was kept in bed: presumably flu, which she may have caught from Lady Gonner . . .

After lunch I bussed into town and went to Merton where Gordon was reading to a joint meeting of the male and female discussion classes. It was held in the Senior Common Room – a comfortable place, but without the dignity of our own . . .

Gordon talked about the writing of literary papers. He complimented us on those which had been written, as everyone expected him to do, and then went on to attack several critical heresies, introducing them artfully as "things which he was glad to see we had not done". He was particularly down on the sentimental, esoteric school, as represented by Mackail. What was most interesting, he claimed that Couch's chapter on jargon has been largely taken without acknowledgement from Chapman and himself.

Best of all was his discussion of the large audience of the semi-educated people who "never would know" to whom critics and "bribed poets" were now always talking.[6] Such people wanted to be told about beauty, sensibility etc: in fact about all that side of literature which men of letters took for granted and never mentioned. I was delighted with this. Afterwards there was some discussion on

---

[5] By Jonathan Swift (1704).
[6] 1933. He has since become one of the chief caterers for this public. – C.S.L.

the method of conducting the classes, and Coghill (backed by several others including myself) suggested that they shd. be more formal . . .

Saturday 17 March: D had a letter from Mrs Stevenson announcing that Sidney had complained of feeling ill and might not come this morning – news which I received with great equanimity. The same letter contained a lot of Job's comfort about the Doc: she said that his ego was now eclipsed, but we must hope that it would soon assert itself. Even if it did not do so in this life, we must look forwards to the happy time when he would have an etheric body. Then followed a long rhapsody on the delights of spiritualism.

This was rather unfortunate as spiritualism, together with Yoga and undigested psychoanalysis seem to have hastened and emphasised the Doc's collapse. On the very first Friday he said himself that Baker had told him long ago he was a fool to have any thing to do with them. I at any rate am scared off anything mystical and abnormal and hysterical for a long time to come.

Maureen still in bed today, but her temperature only 99. After breakfast I finished *Gulliver*. It does not give me the horrors which the critics say it ought to – I fancy because it overshoots the mark. We know things aren't so bad as all that. Just before lunch I tried my hand at some fourteeners – the idea of a Gulliver like poem having developed in that way. They were not a great success. If you make them regular, they deafen you: if not, the possible variations are so rich that it would take a better man than I to make order out of the chaos.

After lunch I bussed into town (a most beautiful afternoon) and went to the Union where I read most of the first book of Chapman's *Iliads*. I had no idea what splendid stuff it was – tho' it didn't help me much in my metrical problem . . .

Saturday 18 March: . . . After lunch I sat down to work on "Dymer". I had just started in high hopes, when I was called upstairs to help in fixing up the curtains in D's rooms: which, having been fixed with rawlplugs, come down in an avalanche about once a week.

While I was doing this Dorothy announced that Sidney had come for a lesson. Heartily wishing her in Hong Kong I came down and did Latin with her for two hours. While we were working, Sheila Gonner called to see Maureen. After tea I heard that she had brought news that I need not take the Gonners' mattress up this evening: of which I was very glad, as I was afraid the whole day would be lost . . .

Monday 19 March: Maureen still in bed . . . After supper I had to work very hard to get my essay done. Before going to bed D and I fell into a conversation about my position – not knowing whether I should stay in Oxford, whether we could get the Walters' house, or whether we shd. take the Raymonds'. As the latter is in urgent need of repairs and as Raymond proposes to leave all repairs to us for three years and then return to the house, which we should almost have rebuilt, I regarded that as a trap. We agreed that I should go into town tomorrow to try and get information about the house in Woodstock Rd. from Brooks; and also see Carlyle and Stevenson about my prospects. D has a headache again – from darning stockings in the bad light in her room where she is now sitting with Maureen all afternoon and evening . . .

Wednesday 21 March: Pouring with rain this morning. I forgot to say that a copy of James Stephens' *Insurrections* came for me yesterday, sent by Rob who has two and promised me one. They are very odd and in one sense not poems at all, but some of them have a good, tho' eccentric flavour of their own: in matter they are chiefly easy pessimism of the sort I did in *Spirits in Bondage*, only I really think I did it better!

During this morning I went on with the *Prelude*. The drop after the fourth book is appalling . . .

In the Union I met Robson-Scott. He is up till Saturday and has moved into College, which he says is almost as full as in term time, with school boys up for Entrance, Responsions and Scholarships. He said that the rumour went that the new Mugger would certainly not be one of the fellows, as they all hated one another too much: nor would it be Carlyle, who was very unpopular, and, for that reason, had not been re-elected to his own fellowship. I suddenly conceived a violent loathing for all these creepy old charlatans – Allen with his sneer, Carlyle a mere sink of facts, the Farq. with his rather cruel looking face, flattering us all and a bit mad, the sentimental Mugger and all the rest: except Carritt and Steve whom I still think to be good fellows in their different ways . . .

Got home very tired and depressed: D made me have some tea. I told her (what had been on my mind all afternoon) that I didn't feel very happy about the plan of staying here as a more or less unattached tutor. I do not want to join the rank of advertisements in the Union – it sounds so like the prelude to being a mere grinder all my days. If it wasn't for Maureen I think I should plump for a minor university if possible. We had rather a dismal conversation about our various doubts and difficulties . . .

Thursday 22 March: After breakfast I walked into town. I went to Carritt's room and returned his Aristotle. I then went and saw Stevenson, whom I found sitting in his rooms by a hot fire, very miserable with a bad throat and not able to talk much. I asked him what prospects there were of my being able to exist as a free lance tutor until something turned up. He said there was practically no such work to be had in my subject. Pupils were now so well looked after by their colleges that the thing was dying out . . .

He said he thought I was pretty sure to get a fellowship soon and went on to remark that Bourdillon was resigning his, and that it was quite possible that I might get it.[7] In the mean time he advised me to get a job at a minor university: this would not put me out of the running for a fellowship, and if I were elected in September after being established elsewhere, I could still accept it and either defer my residence or put in a modicum at week ends etc. as he had done while holding a lectureship at Edinburgh. He thought it likely that College, after Bourdillon's resignation, might decide to have an English don now that the English School was getting so popular. I remarked that I might very easily fail to get a first in English: he thought that would not matter with my previous record.

I left him and went to the Appointments Committee, now in Broad St., and asked about the Nottingham job . . . I then came home . . . and discussed the situation with D. We were both greatly depressed. If one cd. be sure of my coming back to a fellowship after a term or two at some minor University we could take the Woodstock Rd. house – but if not? And then again, if we all moved to some unearthly place and had to come back again after a short time, we should have lost the chance of a house here, interrupted Maureen's work and had many expenses for nothing. It was certainly a damnably difficult situation.

Thence we drifted into the perennial difficulty of money, which would be far more acute if we had to separate for a time. When I began to work after lunch I was thoroughly bothered and found it hard at first to concentrate . . .

D and I had another very miserable conversation. She was afraid

[7] Robert Benedict Bourdillon (1889–1971) was Fellow and Praelector in Chemistry at University College 1913–23.

it might be her duty to stay at Oxford for Maureen's music, wherever I went: I did not know how to answer this . . .

Sunday 25 March: A most delightful day – very mild – blue sky with moving clouds and a faint south wind . . . After lunch I rode out again. I went back to Prattle Wood by way of Marston and Water Eaton . . . I explored the wood much more fully today, and it is splendid. If I hadn't been bothered with the short lived headache which comes on so often when I am out, I should have been in the seventh heaven. As it was I enjoyed it very much. I picked and brought home as many primroses as I could, but they are very few . . .

I found to my delight that D had been out on the golf links with Maureen and was in very good form. After tea I wrote to my father. As it was impossible to tell him what had really been happening during the Askins trouble, I had to account for my silence by a lie. I said I had had flu – which I consider justifiable because I have been going through something very much worse . . .

Monday 26 March: Another beautiful day. In the morning I read in Sweet and finished three acts of *Othello*. After lunch I biked into the Union where I read the whole of Santayana's article on Lucretius . . . In my present mood, still remembering the Doc, Santayana's almost aggressive sanity is very attractive, but I suspect it is but one more cul de sac . . .

In the evening there was an announcement in *The Times* inviting applications for a Research Fellowship at Exeter. Touch wood, but this looks a less wispy will-of-the-wisp than the others.

Tuesday 27 March: Worked on O.E. in the morning. After lunch I went up to Stile Rd. in Headington where Aunt Lily is now living and saw her . . . She is full of a recent "discovery" which has carried her further, she says, than Bergson and Plotinus ever went. The discovery is that time consists in sacrifice: the continual annihilation of A to create B, the continual "making room". But the essence of the world is also sacrifice: *ergo* time is the very essence of the world. She seemed to use God, Time and Being as synonymous . . .

When I was going she spoke very strongly about the brute Carr in Univ., who had been fined for setting dogs on cats and watching them worried. She said that if it hadn't been for her relationship to me she would have sought him out and beaten him, adding "I once broke a man's wrist with a horse whip." On the subject of pit ponies I mentioned the days when young children had crawled about pulling trolleys in the mines. She said she much preferred that: she had no sympathy with the children because they all grew up, and would grow up to be brutes themselves. I asked her if she did not mind cruelty to human beings. She said it did not affect her as cruelty to animals did: humans were less helpless and also they were so vile that they deserved less sympathy. I was very disgusted with her abominable confession . . .

Smudge was here for tea and told us that Walter's house had been sold. This, coupled with last night's will-of-the-wisp, inclined us again to the Raymonds' house. I biked off at once into town and enquired at all the agents whether it was still easy to sublet houses in Headington. All the replies were favourable and after coming home again I went up and told Mrs Raymond that we wd. take it after all. Worked after supper and all merry.

Thursday 29 March: . . . I had tea in the Union. I also met Carlyle . . . I mentioned the Exeter Fellowship. He seemed to remember it as something which had temporarily escaped his notice and said he was very glad to know that I was going in for it. He thought I was just the man, and proceeded to give me some hints.

He said that what they particularly wanted in a candidate for a Research Fellowship was a definite programme. I told him the line I wanted to follow in Ethics: he seemed to approve . . . In the meantime he promised to see Marett of Exeter and get what he could out of him.[8] . . .

I now repaired to the station in heavy rain and met W[arnie]: – who had brought a Leeborough suitcase. We left this in the Union and went and had some beer in the Mitre . . . We came out by taxi. After supper W and I gossiped for a while, but he was so sleepy that he soon went to bed. I went too, reluctantly leaving D downstairs, and Lord knows when she went to bed.

Friday 30 March: . . . After lunch I began Sidney Colvin's *Life of Keats* and W also read a book. D sat alone in the dining room without a fire. This worried me and I came in to remonstrate with her. Unfortunately I asked her "not to make herself miserable" and she misunderstood the words in a way that is easily understood but impossible to explain on paper. We came as near a quarrel as we ever do over this, which, coupled with the fact that she was thoroughly tired, made me very miserable.

---

[8] Robert Ranulph Marett (1866–1943) was Tutor in Philosophy at Exeter College 1891–1928, after which he became Rector of the College.

As well, for no assignable reason, certainly through no fault of his, I found W's society, which I had looked forward to with some pleasure, quite unbearable this time. His contented cynicism, his rejection of everything warm and generous and ideal, above all his constant and self conscious assumption of this Gryll's attitude[9] as if it were something to be kept up every moment at all costs – well for some reason I couldn't stick it.

Saturday 31 March: This morning W and I walked into town. He had hoped for a ramble in the bookshops, but of course they were all shut. I got *Typhoon* (Conrad) and Havelock Ellis's *Kanga Creek* out of the Union for him. He took me to have a drink at the Roebuck which they have completely altered since the old days when we used to frequent it.

Sitting there and drinking, as usual at his expense, I was quite worried at the change of my feelings towards him, as I remembered so many jolly sittings in the same place. Perhaps it is only the recent upset I have been through and may pass . . .

---

[9] After Gryll, the hog in *The Faerie Queene* (II. xii. 86) who was unhappy at being changed back into a man.

Sunday 1 April: . . . W took took me to the Mitre and fed me with beer – for which, as it was now a very hot day, I was duly grateful. It is certainly a good trait in him that he puts up with our domestic life and he is always "generous" in the narrower sense of the word: but I have been wretchedly strained and tired and depressed this time and can't help feeling that I don't want to see him soon again.

We bussed home to lunch. Afterwards we sat in the garden and I wrote three stanzas of the VIth Canto of "Dymer" – who is a year old today.

It was a delightful afternoon. D and Maureen went up to tea with the Raymonds. Later on W and I had ours alone in the garden. Afterwards I asked him whether he had any ready money and if he could lend us anything for the move. I heard to my amazement that (besides income) he had, or had had only £60 invested. The £500 which he had saved in the war had gone in the first year of peace when he had spent £1200: and had been paying off debts ever since . . . He said he was afraid the £60 was gone and all he could offer was a fiver in reply to an S.O.S. now and then. So closed one of the beastliest of the many beastly scenes I have been forced into by poverty.

Later on we went out for a stroll on the golf links. Coming back we found D and Maureen already at home, with the unexpected news that there are three purchasers after the Raymond's house and that Father Raymond has come down in his price and is probably going to settle it. I was very disappointed and realised that D wd. be very much more so – tho' of course, from the money point of view, it is a momentary relief . . .

Monday 2 April: W departed by the 10.50 to attend a football match at Aldershot between the A.S.C. and some Scotch regiment. I bussed in with him and saw him off. Before leaving he told me to write to him in a few days and tell him whether the Raymond's house was definitely "off": if not, he would set about trying to realise his elusive £60 . . .

I came home and sat in the back room with D, reading Colvin's *Keats* till lunchtime. I must admit that the sense of being to ourselves again was very pleasant. Afterwards the sun came out and we both sat in the alley way. I finished Colvin and read *Isabella*, *St Agnes*, and the Odes. I am a bit scared of Keats for he could resume complete dominion over me with very little trouble . . .

Wednesday 4 April: Another warm day. By the first post came a letter from Harwood enclosing a proposed Epithalamion for Barfield and asking my opinion of it by return. I thought it quite tolerable tho' far below his best, and replied telling him so.[1]

There was also a card from Aunt Lily changing our engagement for today . . . I rode to Headington and saw Aunt Lily and explained that I couldn't go today. We arranged for tomorrow instead and she kept me a considerable time. She talked about mutation. In her typical Hamilton way she thinks she has the secret of it – just as uncle Gussie thinks he anticipated Einstein. She says Bateson will never find it out by vivisection.[2] As far as I understood her she thinks that a species gets into a low state through lack of differences, and then mutates producing variations whose wide diversity gives good crosses for healthy reproduction: it is best studied in corn . . .

Thursday 5 April: A very much colder day. Worked on O.E. all morning and succeeded in concentrating, but without interest . . . D had spent the morning boiling marmalade and was very tired and had a headache . . .

I went on to Stile Rd. and had supper with Aunt Lily. We talked of a great many subjects – I forget most of it – I am tired of her inhumanity.

Got home after ten and found D in the depths of despair, having had a particularly tantalising disappointment over the house. If we had gone yesterday we might have had it! – and for the amazingly low rent of £45 a year. It was every way delightful and we should have saved £60 a year. To add to our troubles Dorothy had come in with news that Miss Featherstone had spoken to her mother expressing a hope that we would let her have the house for three

---

[1] Owen Barfield and Cecil Harwood had been members of the English Folk Dancing Society, and it was through this Society that they became part of a song and dance company organised by the Radford Sisters to tour the villages of Devon and Cornwall. It was while Owen Barfield was with this company in St Anthony in Roseland, Cornwall, in the summer of 1920 that he met his wife, Matilda "Maud" Douie (1885–1982), a professional dancer who had worked with Gordon Craig. They were married on the 11th April 1923.

[2] The biologist, William Bateson (1861–1926).

months in the summer. To bed late, after lamenting our luck.

Friday-Wednesday 6-11 April:[3] On Friday I worked getting into shape a prospectus of my ethical work to show to Carritt. On Saturday morning there came by the second post a letter from Rob announcing the death of the Doc the day before from heart failure. I forget most of that day. Rob had said that the funeral would be at Richmond on Tuesday, but we heard later that it would be at Clevedon on Wednesday. Rob said that he had been unconscious at the end . . .

Tuesday was a bitterly cold day: I had an ear ache. Had great difficulty in getting together black things: I borrowed a black overcoat from Mr Taylor and had to get a new bowler from Walters. D and Maureen went at about six and I saw them off. Had a pretty miserable evening here: read Byron's *Beppo* and *Vision of Judgement* (both good).

As I was to go by the 9.30 in the morning I told Dorothy to call me at 7.15 which turned out to be much too early. I had finished breakfast before eight and had to fill up the time by walking to the station . . .

Arriving at Bristol station I met Cranny who was coming to the funeral. His daughter was with him . . . I sat with them until D, Edie, Maureen and Grace turned up with wreaths and other grisly things – it is a natural idea of course, but why should lilies be spoilt for ever by these associations?

With them came a most distinguished man in a tall hat and clerical frock coat, with a white moustache: D's brother Willie from Cavan where he has a parish.[4] He is rather a hero in his own way, and his name has been twice on the death list of the irregulars.

Ourselves and the flowers took up so much room that we had to divide on getting into the train. I was with Willie and Cranny who talked clerical shop. It was half sleeting, half raining. We seemed to be a long time getting to Clevedon . . .

We had another long wait at the church – it is up on a hill and Arthur Hallam is buried there. At last the hearse arrived, and shortly after, the others. Cranny and Willie read the service. While we were waiting Cranny had been talking with me about immortality – neither of us very optimistic. Rob had remarked "a ditch at the back of Ypres is better than this" – I think he was right. Mary behaved very

---

[3] During this time Lewis and Mrs Moore discovered that it was possible to rent Mr Raymond's house, "Hillsboro", after all.

[4] See **William James Askins** in the Biographical Appendix.

bravely. When it was over Rob and Willie stayed, the others went back to the flat by taxi: Cranny and I found our way back to the station and had tea in a stuffy little cake shop beside it . . .

Here followed a period of laziness, depression, irritation and constant anxiety about the future during which I gave up my diary together with most other things. D was very tired and depressed and had several sick turns. I had an interesting talk with Carritt, who preferred to my ethical scheme my other idea of a metaphysical critique of modern psychology. After several days of very hard work I made out a scheme from this which I submitted to J.A. Smith.[5] He has not yet answered me – which adds to the fidgety atmosphere I have got into.

Preparations for moving to Hillsboro have meanwhile been going on. The furniture removers' tender, under pressure from Rob, has come down to £28 and Willie has lent D £30. We are therefore able to do without W's loan, for which, with great generosity, he raised, or prepared to raise, a mortgage on his life insurance. Wall papers have been selected – the other evening I turned over 2000 odd patterns for D in a huge book.

I have been working at O.E. and have also read *Richard III*, *Twelfth Night*, *Timon of Athens*, and *The Phoenix and the Turtle*. At the beginning of this time I finished my fair copy of "Foster" to my satisfaction. Since then poetry has been below the horizon.

I have disgracefully accumulated arrears of correspondence - wh. is a fool's game and leaves a permanent background of small worry in one's mind. Maureen and I are taking phospherine. All this time the weather has been colder than during the winter, dust and wind alternating with foggy frosts. The spring blossom on the trees has disappeared.

Everything now depends on my getting the Exeter Fellowship.

Lewis kept no diary during 12-19 April

Friday 20 April: A very cold day. I finished *Beowulf* and worked on the *Battle of Maldon* all morning . . .

I had meant to go into town: but I realised that I should have to go after tea anyway and as it was now a little sunny and pretending to be like spring again I walked to Iffley instead. My hope thus to

---

[5] See **John Alexander Smith** in the Biographical Appendix.

cast off some of this idiotic stupid mood was disappointed and I did not much enjoy my walk . . .

Came back and found poor D busy darning – she also in pretty poor form. Maureen seems cheerful – but I think the giggly mood she is in is also another kind of collapse: for I get into it now and then myself and it is really very different from optimism . . .

I got into Hillsboro: the garden with the grass grown long and the general desertion was rather attractive. I found Tolley – a protégé of the fish mongers who is doing the paper – and plied him with innumerable questions from D. I then walked home by the barracks and the golf links. I had a Wordsworthian adventure – being asked for a penny in a woeful voice by two gypsy children who had been playing happily the minute before. Home again and after supper I finished *The Battle of Maldon* (good stuff) and began *The Fall of the Angels*.

In the evening I happened to tell D that I had dropped my diary pro tem. She was very opposed to it and urged me to begin again.

Saturday 21 April: Another cold morning. After breakfast D, Maureen and I went into Oxford taking with us Baker's book of patterns from the shop. We went first to Elliston and Cavell's and ordered paper for the hall, then to Baker's and ordered paper for the bathroom. We then proceeded to the gas office in St Aldate's to see about hiring a stove. Here they had nothing but elaborate new stoves with very small ovens, all of which could be had only on the hire purchase system. Apparently they are trying gradually to kill the established practise of hiring stoves. D tackled the man with her customary vigour and he admitted in the end that they had some older models for hire, which could be seen at the works in Speedwell St.

Thither accordingly we went through dreadful slums in clouds of driving dust. We came first into a yard full of the most appalling smell: then waited endlessly before a little window until D took the bull by the horns and opened a door marked private. We were thus finally taken some notice of and led into a place of sheds, steam, leaking pipes, and smells and scrap iron, where Maureen and I sat on a bench while D negotiated with the attendant spirits . . .

Sunday 22 April: . . . Immediately after breakfast Maureen and I set out for Hillsboro to paint . . . Tolley was painting the bathroom when I arrived and he abandoned it to me . . . The small quantity and bad quality of the work and the curious way in which he has done – nibbling now at one room and now at another has very much worried us: his behavior is so queer that we hardly know whether to call him dishonest or half witted. D decided that she must come up in the afternoon and investigate. After lunch I returned at once to the bathroom at Hillsboro and continued my painting, where I was presently joined by Maureen and later by D who had come up by bus.

After looking at the state of the house D felt pretty hopeless and we went to Windsor Terrace where Tolley emerged grinning and blinking from his Sunday afternoon's sleep. D told him that at the present rate he would never get the place done in time. He said he was getting a man in tomorrow who would finish the ceilings in two days . . .

Tuesday 24 April: A glorious spring morning – very bright but cold – with a glass blue sky. Walked up to Hillsboro after breakfast and immediately began painting. They say everything will need two coats. I worked solidly till 1.15, by which time I had finished to the skirting, door, window sill and mantel piece of the drawing room. Tolley appeared at about noon, put in a stepladder through the cellar window and then disappeared. I came home to lunch and found that Dorothy had just cleared out the cupboard at the back of the stairs which D calls the "back of beyond" . . .

Smudge, who had been playing duets with Maureen in the morning, was here for lunch. She has found out that tho' she failed in Mods. she has passed in Anglo Greek. After lunch I bicycled up to Hillsboro and began work on the drawing room . . .

Wednesday 25 April: In the morning came a letter for D from Moppie. She is taking lessons in London and is apparently making no effort to get a summer job. Doubtless she intends to spend all her money and hang on us as a deadweight till September. I had a card from Jenkin acknowledging my apologies in the kindest possible terms – a contrast to the glum silence of the Bakers. It was a wet morning, but the greenery looked and smelled delightful in the rain.

After breakfast I walked up to Hillsboro. I painted the hall door and most of my own room . . . Before leaving I again asked Tolley what he proposed to do about the holes in the ceiling of D's room and of Andrée's. He assured me that they would be done with "mortar and adamantine" – with which truly Aeschylean phrase I departed . . .

Friday 27 April: I dreamed first that I was sitting in the dusk on

Magdalen Bridge and there met Jenkin: then I went up a hill with a party of people. On the top of the hill stood a window – no house, a window standing alone, and in the sashes of the window a sheep and a wolf were caught together and the wolf was eating the sheep. The wolf then disappeared from my dream and one of my friends began to cut up the sheep which screamed like a human being but did not bleed. Afterwards we proceeded to eat it . . .

This morning I worked on O.E. After lunch at about three o'clock, all three of us proceeded to go into town. I had to carry in the wringer, a miniature mangle which we have never used and which we are trying to sell to Eaglestons or give in part exchange for a lawn mower. It was a very heavy load and I had to carry it under my arm with its long crank projecting behind, rather like a bagpipe – greatly to Maureen's delight. We got rid of the monstrosity at Eaglestons and went on to the gas office where we ordered the stove . . .

I left the others and went to College where I found that Sadler had that day been made Master.[6] I met Ewing in the porch – emerged from his burrow for the Exeter Fellowship no doubt.[7] Thence I went to Manor Place, where I found Wilson and Robson-Scott finishing tea. Robson had been at Stratford to see the festival performance of *Measure for Measure* and *Midsummer Night's Dream*, of which he spoke very highly indeed. We discussed the Birmingham performance of *Cymbeline* in modern clothes. Wilson thought it a mere freak. We decided that the *Merry Wives* would have worked best and had an amusing discussion of the proper costume of Falstaff – we fixed on a very old blazer and plus fours in the end. After Robson had withdrawn Wilson dictated a collections paper to me and arranged for a tutorial hour . . .

Lewis kept no diary during 29 April-21 May.

---

[6] Sir Michael Sadler (1861–1943) was an educational pioneer and a patron of the arts. He was Master of University College, 1923–34.

[7] Alfred Cecil Ewing (1899–1973) took a First in Greats from Oxford in 1920 and a D.Phil. in 1923. He was a Lecturer in Moral Science in the University of Cambridge 1931–54 and Reader in Philosophy at Cambridge 1954–66.

Tuesday 22 May: After my last entry there followed a period so busy and on the whole so miserable that I had neither time nor heart to continue my diary, nor poetry, nor pleasant effort of any sort.

Our move to "Hillsboro" was carried out according to plan: but our friend Tolley (whom we had to turn off) had left so much undone and so much to undo that we had to put off the arrival of the furniture for a fortnight. The interval of "camping" – helped by a spell of delightful weather – was not so uncomfortable as I expected and we sat down so seldom that the scarcity of furniture, borrowed from Miss Featherstone, was hardly noticed. The garden was a great joy and there were some pleasant moments when we saw our chosen wall papers going up and the Raymond atmosphere gradually defeated.

We naturally hoped more and more intensely every day that we should get the Exeter Fellowship: but Carritt told me just before I sent my papers in that Joseph of New College said it was a dud election – they had a candidate of their own already picked out for it. This disappointment threw me into a very childish rage against the old men and I believe I really understood how the Queen Anne satirists used to feel. I have now got over it . . .

So far I have not been caught by Aunt Lily. Warnie was here for the Whitsun week end and departed yesterday: this time I thoroughly enjoyed his visit, although it has unsettled me with acute envy of the comfortable, care free, pleasant life by which he has solved the problem of existence: *vobis parta quies.*[1] I think I have the curse of something of my father's luck and temperament and shall be in a fidget as long as I am above ground.

On Sunday last I dined at the High Table at Magdalen. I have had a charming letter from Harwood. He and Beckett and Baker are going for a walking tour on the Sussex downs – which sounds to me

---

[1] Virgil, *Aeneid* III, 495. "You [Andromache and Helenas, survivors from the sack of Troy] have won your rest [unlike me, Aeneas, who has to sail to Italy]."

like a rumour of heaven heard this side of the great gulf.

The weather has been mostly cold and wet all this time. Today I worked all morning on a paper for Miss Wardale and on O.E . . . I came home thinking of the possibility of a modern Ariosto: at first I thought of adventures in far lands but soon realised that London is really the modern equivalent of the forest of romances. I thought a story of impossible and complex adventures in London in the spirit of old romance, as modern as *Don Juan* but not so satiric, might be made very good. In the evening I read *The Testament of Cresseid*[2] and part of *The Flower and the Leaf*[3] with much enjoyment.

D is naturally rather tired and worried these days.

Wednesday 23 May: Biked to Miss W at 11.45 and had my usual tutorial . . . I then came home, having taken three volumes of Johnson's *Lives* [*of the Poets*] from the English Library. I changed and sat down in the drawing room to read the life of Savage and wait for Ewing whom I have had to ask to tea.

He was with me at Univ. in 1917, when he was known as the Rabbit and was, I'm afraid, everyone's butt. He is a First in Mods. and Greats, a John Locke scholar, a senior demi of Magdalen, and a Doctor of Philosophy. He is standing for the Exeter fellowship. He is a very small man, usually dressed in a neat, old fashioned style with a stiff collar and a watch chain, and a strange, quick, jerky action suggestive of a Robot, which results I believe from some nervous weakness and saved him from the war. He has a smooth pinkish face, prominent teeth and a little moustache and speaks in a shrill falsetto. He is a non smoker. No one has ever been able, to my knowledge, to establish a personal contact with him: he is the standing example of intellect in the narrowest sense and industry, but without wisdom, imagination, or humour. Perhaps I am misjudging him. We talked mainly about philosophy. He said he had met Pilly of Exeter who is supposed to be the pet candidate for the fellowship . . .

Thursday 24 May: I spent the morning working on Johnson's *Lives* and on Hurd in the drawing room, which I begin to like very much. After lunch I biked in to town, took Warton's life of Pope from the English Library and went to the Union where I worked on Addison. I had tea there.

---

[2] By Robert Henryson (1593).
[3] Formerly attributed to Chaucer.

Coming home I found Jenkin and allowed myself to be persuaded to accompany him up Shotover with bikes. Just before lunch I had thought of a new stanza (aabccbcb) which pleased me very much: this set me talking to him about the Ariosto idea. He disapproved of it saying that the only romance anyone would expect or tolerate in such a poem would be a sexual one, and anyway why not do it in prose.

A very funny conversation followed. We rested at a gate on the Horsepath lane looking east. It was a sunny evening, the Chilterns very blue and transparent in the distance. Jenkin said he always perceived rather than felt this kind of scenery to be beautiful. He hinted at the danger he was now in of becoming a scholar, a mere potterer: I thought the danger rather real specially as he is a Celt and therefore chosen by nature to effect nothing. As it was now too late for him to get supper in Hall I asked Jenkin to sup with us. It is very strange that a man who is in every way so well bred should eat so noisily . . .

Friday 25 May: . . . I worked all morning on my essay for Wilson very busily, *curarum oblitus*.[4] After lunch I biked in to him, for he had changed my time till 2.30. We had a capital hour, more literary chat than tutorial. I made him give me a correct list of the papers I am really taking in Schools, with which I hastened to the Assistant Registrar's office . . . .

After an early supper I bussed in to the Discussion Class . . . At Exeter when I arrived in Coghill's rooms I found Martley alone and asked him "what had happened on the river" – in order to appear normal and interested.[5] He however after some reply asked me what had happened to Univ. the day before – which completely nonplussed me. Coghill himself had left a note for Gordon and was not there.

Lloyd Jones, a fool who spoke in the Farnell debate, read very badly a bad paper on Swift.

The discussion afterwards was pretty interesting. My remark that literature which simply gave vent to passions, literature born of conation not of imagination and tending to vicarious satisfaction rather than truth was all to be treated as pornography whatever passion I dealt with, raised strong opposition from Bateson, and

---

[4] "forgetting my anxieties."

[5] Averell Robert Martley of Hertford College, who took his BA in 1923, was Secretary of the Discussion Class.

Robson-Scott.[6] Martley, backed by Gordon, held the balance and said that there must be a little of both in most literature. I saw afterwards that they were right. Martley told me that Bateson was the editor of *Oxford Poetry* this year, and for a moment I thought of sending something in: but soon decided that it was a puerile wish . . .

When we were leaving Gordon called me to him in the street. He said he had heard that I was standing for the Exeter Fellowship and could he give me a recommendation or help me in any way. I thanked him profusely and explained that I already had the only ones I was allowed.

He said he had dined at Magdalen lately where they had talked about me and "thought very highly of me. Price had been elected because he was a little more mature, and even so they had been very doubtful." I thanked him again and said with a silly giggle "I have got my two official references and I suppose informal references are hardly fair" – an odious remark as I realised a moment later . . .

Monday 28 May: A rather better night, though I was awake with my cough for some time when it was just getting light – with the result that when I did get to sleep I overslept and woke up with a headache and feeling rather stupid. At supper last night I had felt my weak gland in the throat beginning to swell: but thank the Lord it was no worse today, though it had got enormous when I was coughing during the night . . . D got hold of me and took my pulse and temperature. The latter was alright but the pulse was "very fast" and I agreed to stay in by the fire as it was a bitterly cold day of wind and rain.

I decided to give up work and have a real day off in the hope that this would rid me of my long lethargy. I read Ovid's *Metamorphoses* most of the day, beginning at the beginning and reaching the Pyramus story in Book IV. I used no dictionary but with the aid of the very full and very quaint Latin notes by five Germans in my edition I was hardly ever stumped . . . The style is a little affected but what really matters is the genuine narrative power and the scenery – the latter, *quâ* scenery, hardly to be bettered in any ancient poet. The speeches are not so rhetorical, in the bad sense, as I have been led to believe:

---

[6] Fredrick Wilse Bateson (1901–78) was an undergraduate at Trinity College, Oxford, and Fellow of English Literature at Corpus Christi College, Oxford, 1946–69. He was founder and editor of *Essays in Criticism*.

in fact they give just so much sense of reality and passion as is needed for this kind of holiday poem – far better than most of the speeches in *The Faerie Queene* . . .

Tuesday 29 May: . . . As we were at supper Jenkin came in and afterwards he and I sat in the drawing room. He began by showing me an article of his which had been rejected by the *Daily Mail*: a description of a night in a mine, much too good for his market and not highly coloured enough.

From that we passed on to a discussion of the horror play in which we are thinking almost seriously of collaborating. It is to turn on the idea of a scientist who discovers a means of keeping the brain and motor nerves alive in a corpse by means of injections. The victim is kept in cold storage but occasionally allowed a turn round the house, wearing a mask: the scientist tells people he is a poor fellow whose face was badly smashed in the war. He is always sitting over fires and complaining of being cold and always being chased away by the scientist for obvious reasons.

The hero and heroine find the corpse lying in a box room in its coffin packed in ice: but there will be a long leading up to the moment at which they realise that the corpse upstairs and the figure they have seen wandering about the house are one and the same. The heroine of course has been designed as the scientist's next victim: the play turns on her escape.

Jenkin had seen in the Bodleian this morning the man whom we shall take for our model of the scientist. He had a bright red beard, Mephistophelian in shape but reaching to his waist, very thick lips and one leg shorter than the other. We were half tempted by the idea of a much better and clearer play about Helen as Thaïs redeemed by Simon Magus, but realised that that would have to be real literature and returned to our shocker.

We discussed all this, appropriately, till near eleven in a dark room beside a moribund fire. Later we drifted into a different vein talking of the futility of most things: the outgrowing of half gods without the courage to face real ones . . .

Thursday 31 May: After breakfast I started work on my essay on Cowper and Crabbe but soon found that I could not go much further without more fuel. I biked into town in a cold wind and took two volumes of Crabbe's and Cowper's moral satires from the Union.

Before leaving town I looked (according to my invariable custom) into the Exeter porch to see if the result of the election had yet been announced. Though I have no grounds for any hope I have enough childish clinging to the hundredth chance to make this daily visit, in the long run, very trying to the nerves . . .

Friday 1 June: ... Rink ... asked me if I should like a free seat for the Folk Dancing tomorrow. I replied that I really did not understand that sort of thing: I could be said to like dancing only as a girl who picnicked in a ruin could be said to like architecture.

. . . Coming back to College I heard with interest what is I suppose my nickname. Several Univ. people whom I don't know passed me. One of them, noticing my blazer, must have asked another who I was, for I heard him answer "Heavy Lewis".

At 4.30 I went to Wilson where we had a most interesting hour. I forget how we drifted away from Crabbe and Cowper, but we ended by agreeing that Wordsworth and Shakespeare had this curious point in common – that in their great passages neither had any style that you could call their own.

I biked home, had supper, and bussed in to Exeter. A small gathering [at the Discussion Class] – Gordon, Strick, Martley, Coghill, Wynn, Bateson and Payne.

Strick read us his paper on Tragedy. Tho' I recant no former opinion of the absurdities in Strict, I was amazed at the excellence of his paper. It was more on life than on letters. He defined Tragedy as the irreparable and inquired if it were real, rejecting the views of Bradley and Bosanquet. He also enquired if indignation against the Demiurge were an essential or an accident of tragedy. The essence seemed to him to be the frustration of an act of faith: every tragic hero was a person who gave of himself lavishly, who chose (this choice was always unfree) to trust the dynasts and got evil or nothing in return. There was some good discussion on the points which he had deliberately left open. Later we drifted to talking of Masefield and then to war reminiscences between Gordon, Strick, Coghill and me.

Coghill then produced some port to celebrate our last meeting, and we drank Gordon's health. I for one drank with great sincerity, for he is an honest, wise, kind man, more like a man and less like a don than any I have known. My opinion of him was rather low at first and has gone up steadily ever since . . .

Saturday 2 June: I decided to take today and tomorrow off, preparatory to a severe week of revision. After breakfast I went out for a walk – a thing I have not done for a long time. I had thought it an ordinary day but I discovered that tho' cool and grey and full of damp, it was an "alive" coolness with a sort of heat underneath – in fact that it was summer after all . . .

Coghill did not come till five – he had been doing papers for some College prize which he is taking in his stride. We both praised Strick's paper, but Coghill pointed out that Strick's talk yesterday was as silly as any other day – in fact "he writ like an angel and talked like poor Poll".

We talked of co-education, of which he is a very violent opponent: then of the education of boys in the earlier stages. I reminded him that looking back in one's own life one found so many things exercising influence or failing to influence in a way which no other person could anticipate or believe, that one was reduced to despair: one could calculate nothing.

This led to discussion of psychoanalysis – did not that also discourage one from "influencing" young boys? He was rather silly about psychoanalysis, adopting really the position that it couldn't be true because "how unpleasant if it were". He laughed at himself when this was pointed out, and took the much firmer ground that sympathy and commonsense would carry you through most difficulties if you were made to be a teacher.

He is an admirer of Meredith's and thinks *Modern Love* a great poem. I said I had never read it. He also writes poetry himself – of rather a subtle and social kind I gathered, chiefly sonnets. We compared notes over methods of work. He is going to try a longer piece in the next vac. and proposes to show it to Wilson. I agreed that Wilson's criticism would be valuable but admitted that I had not the face to do it.

I said my own line was chiefly narrative: he stated that he didn't care for narrative and then made exceptions in favour of *Paradise Lost, The Earthly Paradise, Don Juan, Troilus and Cresseide, The Ancient Mariner.*

I discovered that he is a nephew of the "Somerville" in Somerville and Ross. He was at Haileybury. He left at 7.30 after a (to me) very interesting time.

I like and admire this man so far as I can judge: but the funny thing is that in recording this conversation I have had to control a tendency to misrepresent him all through. Which is what never happened to me before since I kept a diary, and I do not know the explanation . . .

Sunday 3 June: A real summer day at last and quite hot. I played a game of croquet with Maureen in the morning and she won. Afterwards I read Ovid in the garden till lunch time. After lunch I began the *New Arabian Nights*, reading the "Suicide Club" and the "Rajah's Diamond". I thought them very good in their style: the humorous part in the diamond story especially. After tea I played another game of croquet with Maureen and beat her.

I then went over to see Aunt Lily, shamefully taking my bicycle that I might seem to come from away.[1] She is very full of a new book she has discovered – *Space and Individuality*, by a Scotch minister called Allan. She says he is greater than Bergson. I was of course sceptical about this, but it looks really interesting . . .

Monday 4 June: Hard at revision all day except between lunch and tea when I walked into town.

Tuesday 5 June: The same. Worked in the Union in the afternoon. The drawing room has (to my mind) been spoiled and Victorianised today by lace curtains.

Thursday 7 June: The same. Into town in the afternoon where I met Robson-Scott and we stood nearly half an hour in the High comparing notes and anyone wd. have laughed to see us stumping one another with strange bits of knowledge: not in the least from malice, but to acquire a kind of Dutch courage.

Saturday 9 June: In town in the morning and called on Coghill to find out our times. Found him closeted with Strick doing O.E. Strick seems to know very little but talked well. To my remark that there was no evidence of Chaucer's having read Langland he retorted "There's no evidence of your having read Chaucer," wh. was good.

Memorised all afternoon. D gardening. High wind still blowing.

After supper I read *Antony and Cleopatra* – the most intelligible play in the world – clear through like a theorem – and lovely.

Wednesday 13 June: Dined in the Senior Common Room with Carritt, Stevenson, and the Greats men of this year, who seemed

---

[1] His Aunt Lily lived in Stile Road, which runs parallel to Holyoake Road and, so, is only a very short distance away.

rather a dull lot. Carritt and Steve very jolly and agreeable . . . Stevenson had a good story from Wilson about an American pupil who had brought him an essay on Falstaff beginning "I've no use for Falstaff. He isn't a white man and the way he talks to Mrs Quickly gets my goat. No gentleman would do it."

I left very early. I took white wine instead of red at dinner for the first time and liked it very much but I have forgotten its name.

It was during 14-19 June that Lewis took examinations in the Final Honour School of English. Candidates were required to show competent knowledge of the English language at all periods, including Old and Middle English, and of English literature.

Thursday 14 June: Began Schools today. Old English in the morning. The translation and literary questions were alright but I could make no serious attempt at the grammar despite all my painful memorising and did the worst paper I have ever done since I came up.

I saw Payne, Martley and Coghill afterwards and they were all equally dejected. Lunched in College on tongue and beef with salad.

In the afternoon we had history of the language which was even worse: and even when I got a question on Milton wh. I knew, my memory deserted me and I could do nothing. I realised what Schools must be like to the unhappy dunces and felt like *Lear* – "I have not thought of this enough."

Biked home and mowed the lawn in the evening.

Friday 15 June: Middle English in the morning. To my great surprise this was quite a good paper with the exception of the one compulsory language question and I think I did really well. In the afternoon we did Chaucer and again I was very satisfied. I did rather badly in the gobbets but everyone I spoke to seemed to have done even worse. Biked home and gardened in the evening.

Saturday 16 June: No paper in the morning. I spent most of the time clipping and cutting straight the border of the lawn.

After lunch I biked in to Schools and did a paper on the age of Shakespeare which I thought most perverse and unfairly set. The Spenser question was tied up by asking you to compare Spenser with any other non dramatic poet of the period. I took the non dramatic Shakespeare and Marlowe, tho' I doubt if they will allow it: tho' I think they will have to give me some credit for the tons of Spenserian quotation and appreciation which I flung at them. I did a good answer on Bacon and also on Sydney's *Daniel*.

Afterwards I met Coghill who bade me and Strick to tea . . . We all condemned what Coghill called this bloodstained paper. Coghill read us the *Decameron* version of the *Reeves Tale* which is very good. Strick is very despondent and silent and pleaded guilty when I rallied him for a victim of wanhope.

Sunday 17 June: Spent most of the day reading *Waverley* which I shall always like because I first read it at Old Cleve in that one glorious month which is worth all the hard years we have had since – almost since Bookham days.[2]

Monday 18 June: Paper on Shakespeare and Milton in the morning. I was bad, as I expected to be, on Shakespeare. The Milton questions were set with cruel malice and I revenged myself by doing them, I think, very well indeed – this being the one question on which even Simpson's ingenuity cannot beat me.

In the afternoon we had a paper on the Seventeenth Century. Like the Age of Shakespeare it was well tied up – Bunyan coupled with Shadwell so that one's knowledge of Bunyan might have no credit. It is of a piece with the whole school: neither for Mods nor Greats did I ever meet cads for lecturers and malicious papers as I have done in this. I hope more than ever for a first, if only to defeat the old men.

Afterwards I had tea with Jenkin in Merton St. He showed me the diary of Dr Dee who was a noted astrologer and occultist. It was very funny, tho' very natural, that his diary should consist almost entirely of the most hum drum and ordinary events.

Tuesday 19 June: Paper on the Eighteenth Century in the morning, the first really catholic and comprehensive one we have had – tho' even this left out Johnson: no disappointment to me, but bad examining all the same.

At lunch a little dark man whose name I don't know but whom I met at the Greats dinner sat opposite me. He talked to me about ordinary things till the end of the meal and then asked "What is this Fellowship at Exeter which has just been awarded?" "Oh, has it?" said I. I then heard that Mr Studdert Clarke of Balliol had got it. I rather disliked the way in which my informant had broached it:

---

[2] Following his examination for Honour Mods, Lewis had a holiday in Old Cleve with Mrs Moore and Maureen during March-April 1920.

perhaps after all it was only his way of "breaking" the news and I am beginning to suffer from a conspiracy complex.

After I had left hall and was in the porch, up comes Ewing pattering along like a little dog under the shade of his large homburg hat, swinging his watch chain: shows his teeth, titters, looks as if he were going to trot away again and suddenly blurts out in a high falsetto "I suppose we shall have to condole with each other now."

On my way back to School I met Coghill who told me that Strict had had a nervous breakdown. In the afternoon an easy paper on the nineteenth century which I did pretty badly because it was easy and tempted you to impossible undertakings ...

Wednesday 20 June: ... I biked down Cowley Road to Strick's address at 390, which is one of the new white council houses beyond Magdalen Rd. I found him in bed. He is not allowed to read, stammers a good deal, is pale and drained dry of all good. Luckily the trouble seems to have gone to his stomach and produced no "horrors". He was obviously not fit to talk and I soon came away.

Rode home and read Wycherley's *Country Wife* before lunch. The Country Wife herself is really funny: but I must admit the sulphurous brutality of all the characters is about as much as I can stomach. Clever stuff.

After lunch I rode out to Stanton St John and tried to find my way into the woods where I once went with Baker. The fields were very beautiful with the yellow weed. I could not find the wood. I was depressed: full of worries and near the kingdom of Wanhope – or Dulcarnon.[3] I went into a church in the village and in quite a whimsical mood tried Sortes Virgilianae out of a Prayer Book.[4] The answer well repaid me for my tomfoolery, for the first thing I saw was an injunction to administer the sacraments in the sense etc. etc. I came out: surveyed with interest the tomb of Mary Annie Lewis, whoever she was, and rode home.

Found D and Dorothy polishing in D's room. Had hardly left them when I heard an awful crash and rushed back thoroughly frightened and half believing that the wardrobe had fallen on D. I found however that it was only she herself who had fallen and hurt her elbow: she

---

[3] "I am, til God me bettere mynde sende,
At dulcarnon, right at my wittes ende."
(Chaucer, *Troylus and Cryseyde*, III, 881.)

[4] "Sortes Virgilianae" is the attempt to foretell the future by opening a volume of Virgil at hazard and reading the first passage lit on.

was badly shaken. All attempts to get her to stop polishing and rest on her laurels were treated in the usual way. After tea she went on again and said I could not help: finally she came down quite breathless and exhausted.

This put me into such a rage against poverty and fear and all the infernal net I seemed to be in that I went out and mowed the lawn and cursed all the gods for half an hour. After that (and it was about as far down as I have got yet) I had to help with rolling linoleums and by the time we got to supper a little before ten, I was tired and sane again.

Decided at whatever cost of labour to start my diary rigorously again, wh. has been dropped during Schools, as I think the day to day continuity helps one to see the larger movement and pay less attention to each damned day in itself . . .

Thursday 21 June: After breakfast I wrote up arrears of diary since the 9th. When I had finished that I went upstairs and laid linoleums in the odd corners of D's room which were still bare. This took me till lunch.

Immediately after lunch I went round to Stile Road and saw Aunt Lily. She is not going to Stratford after all but has taken an unfurnished house beyond Gt. Milton for £25 a year: the curious thing being that her landlord will turn her out in three months if his beloved agrees to marry him, but he has proposed so often before that he thinks Aunt Lily will have every chance of staying.

I remarked, in answer to some question, how rushed I had been by the shortened time in wh. I had taken this School. She said "Why did you?" and that it wasn't fair either to my father or myself, who had nothing to do with his money and only wanted to keep me there. I said that, on the contrary, he wanted to retire: she said that W and I had been provided for and my father had been in a position to retire long ago before my mother's death but she (my mother) had persuaded him to continue his police court work and make more. Who knows? She then told me some very funny yarns about the Suffern family . . . .

After tea I walked through old Headington, down the cemetery lane and joining Elsfield Rd. near the bridge and cross road: then up to Elsfield and home across the fields with great pleasure. When I emerged into Western Rd. again it was beginning to rain and I almost ran into Aunt Lily who stood looking into the shop window at the corner. I passed straight on and trusted to luck that she would either not look round or would not recognise my back. I "fetched a compass" thro' Windmill Rd. and round again and this time succeeded in getting home . . .

Friday 22 June: In the morning I read *Venice Preserved*[5] which contains more loathsome sentimentality, flat language, and bad verse than I should have imagined possible.

Later I scraped and began to stain the exposed passages of floor in the hall, which was work both hot and hard. After lunch I finished the hall and did the same for the drawing room and helped D with some changes of furniture in the dining room. Sheila Gonner and Helen Munro were here for tea and I made a fourth at croquet with them afterwards. It was a warmish day with a pleasant wind.

At six I walked out to find a new field path that I had heard of . . . This brought me up hill beside a very fine hedge with wild roses in it. This, in the cool of the evening, together with some curious illusion of being on the slope of a much bigger hill than I really was, and the wind in the hedge, gave me intense pleasure with a lot of vague reminiscences . . .

Saturday 23 June: A glorious summer day at last. After breakfast I biked to Margaret Rd. and saw Miss Wardale and went over my language papers. She thought them "unexpected" and had been making representations to Craigie.[6] His question, "Give the definite forms of the adjective" was unintelligible to her. She said I ought to come through alright on my translation and thought I should probably be viva'd on my literary papers, while advising me to look up the grammar as a precaution . . .

At quarter to five Jenkin arrived for tea, bringing his mother as had been arranged. She is a very cheery old soul and was soon going off in fits of "inextinguishable laughter". After tea we sat in the garden and I tried to teach Jenkin croquet. Time passed on and after a very complicated discussion they agreed to stay to supper – I mean there was some difficulty which induced them to stay on as they wd. not probably otherwise have done, but what it was all about I couldn't gather. Supper was an uproarious meal, recalling Arthur's visits . . .

Monday 25 June: After making up my diary I had a look at the fourth canto of "Dymer" and got some ideas for a better ending. As I had

---

[5] Thomas Otway, *Venice Preserv'd* (1682).

[6] William Alexander Craigie (1867–1957), lexicographer and philologist, was Rawlinson and Bosworth Professor of Anglo-Saxon 1916–25 and one of those who set the examination Lewis had just taken. The other examiners were Percy Simpson, H.F.B. Brett-Smith, and A. Mawer.

promised to paint this morning, I then had to leave it. It took me till lunch time painting the two hall doors and some things in the bathroom.

After lunch I set out to bike to Aunt Lily's new abode at Lower Farm, Thame Road. It was a case of "heaven uphalt but ugly thereunder" when I started and had developed into a Scotch mist before I arrived. Her new cottage is in rather dull and flat country, but being absolutely surrounded by meadow, is rather attractive. The railway is in sight, and Aunt Lily agrees with me about the romance of a train in a lonely place.

She had provided strawberries and cream. We talked chiefly about Archibald Allan and she showed me the letter he had written her – a letter very like the book except that it was much more dogmatic and appeared to be the work either of a fool or of a confident genius.

I biked home in torrents of rain. Later I played croquet with Maureen. She got an enormous lead but threw most of it away and I nearly won in the end. After supper I wrote two new stanzas for "Dymer" – I think they will do. D in good form.

Tuesday 26 June: This morning I biked into town and called on Wilson whom I found newly returned from a long week end. We discussed Schools. Apparently the Spenser question in the Age of Shakespeare was marked compulsory by a printer's error and the examiners have their tails very much between their legs over it. He agreed that this was a rotten question. He promised to try and get me some work examining for the Oxford Local, but warned me that it was probably too late. He is to come to tea on Thursday . . .

Wednesday 27 June: Went to my own room after breakfast and re-copied the whole of Canto V with the alterations and additions. It is I hope very much improved: at any rate it was delightful to have a whole morning's self pleasing work on poetry after so long . . .

After lunch I went out. It was now very warm after a misty morning and the flies were troublesome. I walked nearly to Forest Hill by the field path and then turned into the road and left it again at the stile on my right beyond the turn to Forest Hill. From here the path led up through a field where the mowers were at work and there was a first rate smell: then up by the side of a spinney through a field alive with rabbits, most of them mere babies who let me get quite close to them. Of the full grown ones I was amused to notice how some would always sit out and face me a good minute after the commonalty had galloped into the spinney . . .

I came home after a very enjoyable walk, but disappointingly tired and with a headache – wh. I thought a poor reward for my recent drastic reductions in smoking . . .

Thursday 28 June: To my own room after breakfast where I began an opening for a new Canto introducing the semi-Kirkian character who has been in my mind lately.[7] Some stanzas of colloquial dialogue wrote themselves with extraordinary ease and for the times I was pleased with them . . .

Wilson came shortly before five and he and I had tea in the garden. We talked of wounds, pensions, income tax, and Farquharson: Wilson agreed with the usual view of the latter's insincerity, but doubted if he were quite sane. I asked him if he cared for Doughty. He had read only *The Cliffs* and thought poorly of it. Of *Childe Harold* he said he had enjoyed it very much as a kind of verse guide book after visiting some of the scenes. He is a great admirer of Bridges. He asked me if I wrote poetry and I said that I did. I wondered if this was an opening made for me at Coghill's mediation but I hardly felt justified in taking it that way . . .

Friday 29 June: A glorious day and the best we have had yet. After breakfast I sat in the garden and tried to go on with "Dymer": I was soon displeased with the colloquial dialogue and judged the Kirkian figure both beyond me and unnecessary – I must beware of too much philosophy . . .

I turned along Cowley Road and went on beyond Garsington to a turn to Cuddesdon. By the roadside I met a man hedging who had a white beard and a scarlet face. He shouted out to me "It's a waarm day sir!" and burst into roars of laughter. I said yes, but we wanted rain. He said "That we do sir!" and went off into huge guffaws again. It did one good to look at him . . .

Saturday 30 June: I dreamed several people in the English School, of whom Martley was the most conspicuous, including myself, had done very badly in the exam and been imprisoned in a kind of barracks as a punishment. The dream was chiefly occupied by my adventures in a strange town into which I got leave to go for a few hours.

After breakfast I cleared out all the furniture from the dining room and sand papered the varnish off the floor preparatory to staining . . . Just as I was finishing D's room I was brought down in a great

---

[7] "Kirkian" means like his old friend and tutor William T. Kirkpatrick (1848–1921). He is described in Chapter IX of *Surprised by Joy*.

fright by a noise in the garden and found that D had had a bad fall in the garden: having tripped over some bundles of pea stakes. Providentially she had not hurt her ankle. She was badly shaken and I begged her to stop gardening – uselessly of course. I then went back and finished my staining. After that I had the garden to water. Supper about 10.45. I was very tired and had a bad headache.

Today came a very decent letter from my father discussing the future and offering to keep me here some years longer if I thought it advisable.

The post-war "bulge" of men reading for degrees and looking for jobs was at its worst, and Lewis had already failed to secure a Fellowship in Philosophy at two colleges. He was now facing the prospect that even with a Double First in Classics and a possible First in English it might be some time before a Fellowship fell vacant. Because of this, his tutor, F.P. Wilson, suggested that he work towards a post-graduate degree. Albert offered to extend his son's allowance for some time longer, and Jack wrote to him on 1 July explaining his position:

"The number of other hungry suitors with qualifications equal to mine, tho' not very large, is large enough to put up a well filled 'field' for every event: and the number of vacancies depends, as in other spheres, on all sorts of accidents.

"What it comes to is that there is a pretty healthy chance here which would, on the whole, be increased by a few years more residence in which I should have time to make myself more known and to take some research degree such as B.Litt. or Doc. Phil. and which would be, perhaps, indefinitely or permanently lost if I now left. On the other hand, even apart from the financial point of view, I very keenly realise the dangers of hanging on too long for what might not come in the end. Speaking, for the moment, purely for myself, I should be inclined to put three years as a suitable term for waiting before beating a retreat," Letters of C.S. Lewis (Revised Edition), p. 185.

Tuesday 3 July: Woke very tired this morning and with some headache: a cool grey day. There was no job to be found for me after breakfast so I sat in the garden hoping to get over my tiredness. This of course was the worst thing I could do, and I tried to write "Dymer" and read Wordsworth equally in vain. I managed however to read the next story in *Rubezahl*. I find German, particularly in fairy tales, a language saturated with romance – it smells good . . .

Read a little more Ovid in the evening and am now in the middle of Orpheus' song. I feel that Ovid's powers are much greater than he shows: if only he had bucked up and kept clear of dirt and rhetoric and stuck to the pure fabling at which he is unsurpassed: he is a literary waster.

Wednesday 4 July: I spent most of the morning with D seeing to the stair carpet. We were chiefly concerned with the mathematical problem of making a right angled corner in a straight strip of carpet. D managed it in the end by the help of a model in folded paper – very cunningly I thought. Later on I gave first coatings to the worst parts of the stairs.

After lunch I biked to town via Divinity Road and Cowley Road in order to change a cheque at Robertson's. As I came down past Warneford Road I thought how quickly those parts had changed . . . I wondered that they had not been more unpleasant to live in than they were – for indeed they looked very squalid today.

(This set me thinking of all our different homes, and most of them vile, since 1919. They were, (1) Miss Featherstone's at 28 Warneford Rd. when I first came up and was living in College. That was during the very cold winter when Miss Drew was coming to teach Maureen.

(2) Mrs Adam's, Invermore, a very jolly little house, but very small and with no bathroom. We did a lot of gardening there that summer. There Rob came to stay with us in a very bad state of nerves, contemplating suicide, and used to keep D up nearly all night talking. Arthur also came and got ill and that was the first time he and D met. There I wrote and destroyed over seven hundred lines of a poem on Medea.

(3) Mrs Morris's in [76] Windmill Road where we had two rooms and I slept on a sofa. The Morris's had been in India – he was an engine driver. She was mad I think, and gave us an account of the centaur (she didn't call it centaur of course) "with the most beautiful face you ever saw" that came begging round her bungalow in India.

(4) Rooms (called a flat) at Mrs Jeffrey's in [58] Windmill Road, where we were bullied and slandered and abused and so haunted by that butcher woman with her stone coloured funny face that D and I dreamed of her for months afterwards. Here Cranny came to see us first and here I first read *The Prelude.* Just before I left this I took Mods.

(5) Then came one month at Old Cleeve in a cottage smothered in flowers, where I walked every day on the big moors and this was

the happiest four weeks of my life. There I wrote the blank verse version of "Nimue".

(6) Courtfield Cottage where we had rooms with that filthy whore Mrs Marshall and her daughter got diphtheria.[1]

(7) Lindon Cottage on the other side of Headington where we were very happy for a time.

(8) Old Cleeve were we had rooms with the Hobbs. It was a cold summer and D had a very miserable time there while I was "doing time" in Ireland.

(9) Miss Featherstone's again where we remained until the beginning of this diary.) . . .

Thursday 5 July: A glorious summer day. In the morning I read *Rubezahl* in the garden. A Miss Bone, a possible P.G., had written to say she would come and see D this evening so our afternoon was spent in clearing out the yellow room and putting it to rights – hanging pictures and curtains, airing blankets and the like. We had tea late, after I had had a cold bath and changed.

Later on Jenkin appeared. He has been up again since Saturday but protested that he had not had a moment to come to Headington. Our talk was not very exciting. He said that the authorities here loved nothing better than to keep young men who were promising hanging on for research degrees and so forth all their life, if possible, with vague promises of work in the future, as this secured a supply of theses which kept up an appearance of activity in the outer world . . .

Afterwards D and I started hanging photos over Paddy's desk . . .
Saturday 7 July: Another exquisite day: best of all there had been a little rain very early in the morning, when I was awake for a few minutes and there was a delicious cool and freshness reminding one of the appropriate passage in *The Ancient Mariner* . . .

I went in by bus . . . to the Station where I met Harwood. He is working on a temporary job connected with the British Empire Exhibition and says that he is becoming the complete business man. He was in excellent form. Our easy wandering conversation and our perfect satisfaction in it was a glorious contrast to the disappointment of my recent meetings with Baker. We walked to Parson's Pleasure to bathe. It was the first time I have been there this year. They had finished mowing in the meadows beyond the water: all was cool and

---

[1] "Courtfield Cottage" is in 131 Osler Road, Headington.

green and lovely beyond anything. We had a glorious bathe and then lay on the grass talking of a hundred things till we got hot and had to bathe again.

After a long time we came away and back to the Union where he had left his suitcase and thence bussed up to Headington. D and Maureen had of course got home before us and we all had tea on the lawn.

Afterwards Harwood and I lay under the trees and talked. He told me of his new philosopher, Rudolf Steiner, who has "made the burden roll from his back". Steiner seems to be a sort of panpsychist, with a vein of posing superstition, and I was very much disappointed to hear that both Harwood and Barfield were impressed by him. The comfort they got from him (apart from the sugar plum of promised immortality, which is really the bait with which he has caught Harwood) seemed something I could get much better without him.

I argued that the "spiritual forces" which Steiner found everywhere were either shamelessly mythological *people* or else no-one-knows-what. Harwood said this was nonsense and that he understood perfectly what he meant by a spiritual force. I also protested that Pagan animism was an anthropomorphic failure of imagination and that we should prefer a knowledge of the real unhuman life which is in the trees etc. He accused me of a materialistic way of thinking when I said that the similarity of all languages probably depended on the similarity of all throats.

The best thing about Steiner seems to be the Goetheanum which he has built up in the Alps: Harwood described to me its use of the qualities of concrete which everyone else has treated in imitation of stone till Steiner has realised its plasticity and made it flow. Unfortunately the building (which must have been very wonderful) has been burned by the Catholics . . .

Sunday 8 July: . . . After lunch I lay on the lawn reading Boswell while Harwood and Maureen played duets to their great satisfaction. Just before tea I had gone into the house when I saw someone at the hall door and opening it found Stead. I talked to him in the drawing room for a few minutes and then brought him out and introduced him to Harwood and disappeared to get tea. He talked philosophy to Harwood and I threw in impertinent interruptions whenever I came out to put a cup or a cake on the table. Presently D came and we had tea.

Stead, fresh back from Venice and Rome, gave as his verdict that

"Italy was a pleasant surprise to him. He had always imagined the Italians a degenerate people but found that they were really quite go ahead and up to date." They were also more patriotic than the English, for they were always waving flags and went mad over the name of Italy whereas "he had never found that Englishmen showed any great enthusiasm over the mention of England". They and their landscape were, he said, hardy and vigorous whereas one always felt the softness of England. Stead is an American and has not been to the war.

We also talked of Fascismo. We were all inclined to favour it except Harwood who said it was only a more successful version of the Ku Klux Klan and that Mussolini had the face of a villain. Asked if he believed in Fascist atrocities, Stead said that they committed atrocities only when they were *deserved*.

Harwood and I then bussed in to Long Wall and went for another delightful bathe at Parson's Pleasure: thence to the Cathedral to hear the organ recital. The organ is a thing I cannot learn to like.

After supper we played croquet – all four of us. Later Harwood read "Dymer" up to date and covered me with enough praise to satisfy the vainest of men.

Monday 9 July: Harwood went off immediately after breakfast: I think we all enjoyed his visit. In the morning I sat in the garden and made an attempt at looking up odd points for my viva – but it was a gloriously hot day, I was very sleepy and the net result was pretty small. After lunch I continued the experiment. In the morning I had been idle because I was half asleep, in the afternoon I was equally idle for the opposite reason, because my brain teemed with new and fascinating projects for the next canto of "Dymer" . . .

After tea I rode in to the Union where I read nearly all of Turner's *Journey to Cytherea*, a very second rate production in the erotic-metaphysical manner tho' some of the imitations of Yeats were pleasant and there was occasionally a bright thought – but give me the *Lays of Ancient Rome* for choice.[2] Afterwards I took out Raleigh's excellent *Six Essays on Johnson* and read them in the Union Garden . . .

Tuesday 10 July: Up betimes and dressed in sub fusc and white tie. Arrived at the Schools at 9.30 and met Martley and Lloyd Jones who were also vivaed today: Smudge, who was up today too, was not to

[2] By Thomas Babington Macaulay (1842).

be seen. At 9.30 we entered the viva room and after the names had been called, six of us were told to stay, of whom I was one.

I then sat in the fearful heat, in my gown and rabbit skin, on a hard chair, unable to smoke, talk, read, or write, until 11.50. I had plenty of leisure to examine my examiners. Brett-Smith seemed a pleasant man:[3] so, in his grim surgical manner, was Craigie, the Scotchman.

Most of the vivas were long and discouraging. My own – by Brett-Smith – lasted about two minutes. I was asked my authority, if any, for the word "little-est". I gave it – the Coleridge-Poole correspondence in *Thomas Poole and His Friends*.[4] I was then asked if I had not been rather severe on Dryden and after we had discussed this for a little Simpson said they need not bother me any more.

I came away much encouraged, and delighted to escape the language people – one of whom, not a don, was a foul creature yawning insolently at his victims and rubbing his small puffy eyes. He had the face of a pork butcher and the manners of a village boy on a Sunday afternoon, when he has grown bored but not yet quite arrived at the quarrelsome stage.

From Schools I went to the Union and took out *The Egoist*:[5] thence home and read a good deal of it in the garden before lunch. It is worth twenty of *Beauchamp's Career* and I think I shall like it immensely . . .

Wednesday 11 July: Hotter than ever. D was in very bad form today. She and I spent most of the morning working putting up blinds – a very troublesome job. Just after lunch I finished what I think is the last picture for her room.

I then bussed in to the station where I met Arthur. We took, or rather he took, a taxi out, stopping for some shopping of mine at Eaglestone's. I was delighted to see him: we renewed our earlier youths and laughed together like two schoolgirls. We arrived out here and both had cold baths – I am keeping off bathes since 4d a day would soon counterbalance any saving effected by my big reductions in smoking. Afterwards we all had tea in the drawing room – the garden being much too hot to sit in.

---

[3] Herbert Francis Brett-Smith (1884–1951) took his BA from Corpus Christi College in 1907, and was lecturer in English Literature in several of the colleges of Oxford. He was Goldsmith's Reader in English, and editor of Thomas Love Peacock.

[4] By M.E. Sandford (1888).

[5] By George Meredith (1879).

Arthur and I were alone for a long time and he told me his various adventures since we last met, particularly round about last Christmas. It was a depressing story and in many ways not easy to sympathise with but, I suppose *"Homo sum etc."*[6] We had supper outside and after watering, Arthur, Maureen and I had an uproarious game of croquet.

Thursday 12 July: Arthur said he was faint and called for brandy in the morning. Today was the hottest for twelve years. Bathed this evening with Arthur after tea and met Wilson on the way back. He said that he had been told that Coghill and I were the best men in Schools this year. Earlyish to bed.

On the 16th July the examiners' awards for the English School were published – the only two Firsts going to Lewis and Nevill Coghill.

Sometime later, when compiling the Lewis Papers *Warren Lewis had this to say about his brother's achievement: "When we reflect on the circumstances of Clive's life during the time he was reading this School – the shortness of the period at his disposal, his ill health, the constant anxiety inseparable from supporting a family out of an undergraduate's allowance, his fears for the future, the unceasing domestic drudgery, the hideous episode of Dr John Askins' final illness, and the move to Hillsboro – we are astounded at the extent of an achievement which must rank as easily the most brilliant of his academic career" (vol. VIII, p. 140).*

Friday-Wednesday 13-25 July: Arthur was with us for a fortnight. He is greatly changed ... Someone has put into his head the ideal of "being himself" and "following nature". I tried on one occasion to point out to him the ambiguity of that kind of maxim: but he seems to attach a very clear meaning to it – namely that the whole duty of man is to swim with the tide and obey his desires ... He has taken over from psychoanalysis the doctrine that repression is bad and cannot be brought to see that repression in the technical sense is something quite different from self control. I tried to put him on to Baker's distinction between will-men and desire-men but he took no interest in it.

I argued that immortality – which he believes in – was not likely

---

[6] *"Homo sum: humani nihil a me alienum puto"*—"I am a human being: I think nothing to do with humans irrelevant to me." Terence, *Heauton Timorumenos*, line 79.

to fall to the lot of everyone, since "gift is contrary to the nature of the universe". He on the other hand is confident that we should all be immortal anyway: he gave me the impression of believing in Heaven but not in Hell, nor in any conditions attaching to Heaven. On morals he thought that our whole duty consisted in being kind to others. I pointed out that a man who was "natural" could not be kind except by accident.

I soon introduced him to Parson's Pleasure and after that he spent a good deal of his time there bathing and sketching. He showed a remarkable facility for picking up new acquaintances. One day when we were lying on the grass, Thring of Univ., whom I had quite forgotten, came up and spoke to me. I had to ask him his name before I introduced him to Arthur. When he left us I saw that Arthur had something on his mind. It came out gradually. "I say Jack, that man had a tennis racquet. Pity we didn't . . . Och well I may meet him tomorrow. I might get talking to him about tennis and he might give me an invitation." I devoutly hoped he would not meet Thring again, as I hardly knew the man myself and did not want him exposed to such naked cadging . . .

His old besetting sin of greed came out several times at our table. Like other poor families, we usually eat margerine with jam – except Dorothy of course, who "CAN'T" eat margerine. Arthur soon made his position plain, stretching across to the butter and remarking that he much preferred it.

Another good example of "nature" occurred in the first two days of his visit when we had tropical weather. D, being the most free and easy of mortals, had made no objection to Arthur wearing pyjamas till lunch time. It was left to Arthur to take the one step further from freedom to beastly familiarity by taking off his slippers in the dining room and laying his bare feet on the table. His feet are very long and he perspires freely. After that I did not repeat the pyjama stunt.

It was during the first week of his stay that I discovered that I had got a First in English. Shortly after this I went to tea with Wilson. He asked me if I had a book in my head. I said at first "No – unless you mean an epic poem," but afterwards trotted out various schemes which have been more or less in my mind. He thought my idea of a study of the Romantic Epic from its beginning down to Spenser with a side glance at Ovid, a good one: but too long for a research degree. For that, he liked rather my idea of a study of the German element in the Romantic movement – tho' that depends of course on the speed with which I can learn German.

All this time D has been very overworked, worried and miserable. Dorothy it appears has turned out very badly since we moved up here. Poor D complains that she has to keep a dog and bark herself: and indeed Dorothy has been the exclusive subject of conversation when we are alone together. I do not blame D for this in the least, but of course it makes things very miserable. D has also done a lot more painting: and I, tho' very seldom allowed to help, have had a day sandpapering the stairs.

I continued some work on "Dymer", but coming across my old poem on "Sigrid", I began to turn it into a new version in couplets with great and wholly unexpected success. Next morning Arthur and I walked up Shotover . . . He talked about the *Ring* and said how, with all its huge attraction, it left you discontented and ragged – not satisfied and tuned up as by Beethoven. We agreed that this was because the *Ring* was pure nature, the alogical, without the human and rational control of Beethoven. I am almost sure this is what he was trying to say, though of course he expressed it quite differently. The only good talk I had with Arthur was this one and some discussions for the design of his summer picture. But he was quite obviously discontented from the first day of his visit till the last, and often (unintentionally) very rude and objectionable – miserably changed since last year.

On Saturday last after bathing I walked through the Park – the first time I think since 1917 – and happened to meet Poynton in the Parks Road. He had a long talk with me: he is far honester than the other dons. He told me he was very doubtful how the vacancy at Univ. would be filled up . . . He promised to try and get me some tutoring among the women and seemed confident of doing so.

When I left him and come up I was pleasantly surprised to find Harwood here – he, D, Arthur and Maureen being all on the lawn. Harwood had been at Long Crendon seeing the Barfields: but B had been called unexpectedly up to town and Harwood had biked hither. Arthur and he were alone together for some time while I was getting up the supper and they didn't much take to each other.

Afterwards Harwood and I walked up and down the lawn and talked – or rather he did most of it. He said he had recently met the most beautiful woman he had ever seen in his life.

He said "I was asked by some people whom I hardly knew to

come and sing glees and told to 'come just as I was'. When I got there I found everyone else dressed. They were quite beyond me in music and I made rather a fool of myself. This was where the lady was so sympathetic. She was about forty – very beautiful and with an extraordinary graciousness – you know how they sometimes are at that age. About a week later I was asked quite unexpectedly to go somewhere where I should have seen her. Do you know, I refused, tho' my wishes were quite opposite the minute before I spoke. Do you understand that?"

SELF: "I suppose something subconscious takes you in hand . . . ?"

HARW.: "No, no. It is when something you have longed for intensely but considered impossible is suddenly put into your hands – you can't believe it."

SELF: "Speaking purely for myself, I can't quite imagine a case in which that language would not be hyperbolical – for me, mind you."

HARW.: "Are you like Dymer – do you always know what you want and go for it?"

SELF: "No, I am not like Dymer."

HARW.: "I admit my story is rather mediaeval. I don't suppose that anyone who has not had such an experience can even begin to understand the *Divine Comedy*."

This was said without the least element of a snub, tho' it looks rather like one, written down. The whole episode was a revelation to me. Harwood stayed till Monday afternoon and was a real sunbeam – perpetually cheerful, interesting and companionable. D likes him immensely and he and Maureen are great friends.

Monday-Tuesday 30-31 July: The whole of this week end I was working all day correcting English essays – about 150 – for the Higher Certificate.[7] As I had never done the work before I could get my

---

[7] School Certificates have disappeared, but they were a kind of miniature "Schools" which had been introduced by the Board of Education in 1905. Every boy or girl who had reached the age of sixteen, and who had not left school at the age of fourteen, was allowed to sit for these examinations. The universites of Oxford and Cambridge had a large say in the matter of the certificates. To obtain a Certificate one was required to pass a minimum of five subjects of which English, Maths and Latin were mandatory. Upon completing the Certificate to the satisfaction of The Oxford and Cambridge Schools Examination Board one could, if one wished to enter Oxford or Cambridge, take either the Board of Education's Higher School Certificate or Responsions – the "entrance examination" administered by the two universities. Lewis was earning some money by marking English Essays from the Higher School Certificate.

standard only by going through the whole lot and dividing them into three classes, and then going through each class and so sorting them into a final order. The work was of course interesting in a way but very tiring when done against time. There were very few really good essays and much ridiculous blundering, with ignorance and vulgarity beyond what I would have expected: I was particularly ill impressed with the almost illiterate Upper VIth of Lancing.

On Monday 30th I was still hard at it and D had to go into town to meet Maurice Delanges of Valenciennes who was coming to us as a paying guest. After she had been gone about half an hour, Dorothy came to my room where I was working and told me that the French gentleman had arrived – alone. I came down and found a very dark skinned, shockheaded youth in knickerbockers and Norfolk jacket. He spoke quite intelligible English – though nothing like so good as Andrée. He explained that he had come by an earlier train.

I sat with him for a few minutes in the dining room and we made conversation with fair success. Finding the work on which I was engaged, he asked me not to let him interrupt me, and after showing him to his room I left him to unpack and returned to my job fairly well satisfied with what I had seen of him. That afternoon I walked with him into town – we talked mainly of educational matters.

Next day I was still at my exams and he and Maureen went out otter hunting with the Rowells. They returned very tired after a boring day and poor Maureen had had a very uncomfortable time as Maurice showed his boredom very plainly. It was that evening that we began to wonder whether we could endure for five weeks the amazing noises he made over his food – chewing with his mouth open, smacking his lips, and sucking like a pig – but we still tried to put it down to the difference of foreign manners and hoped all was well.

Wednesday-Monday 1-6 August: This was a wasted and comfortless period. I finished my exam. work: I also finished *Middlemarch* (by far the best of G. Eliot's books) and began Carlyle's *French Revolution*. These three items, and these only, can be put down to the credit side. On the other there is a good deal.

In the first place Dorothy, after being sulky and idle for months, has given notice. How or when this state of affairs began it is impossible to say. She was out every evening and often till near eleven: she was treated as one of ourselves and I do not think it is our fault. D has been generous with her and all her family. Dorothy has however visibly been getting discontented for a long time and complained that D had "never been the same to her since Ivy was here" – whatever that may mean. Now she has revenged herself (I don't know for what) by leaving us in this time of stress when we are saddled with Maurice. She is to go on Friday next – and may now be included with the Dud, Frank, and Moppie in the list of people who have never forgiven kindness from D.

Maurice, who behaved tolerably for the first few days, has now thoroughly settled down and shown his true colours . . . His bestial way of feeding was bad enough, but his habit of stretching across everyone to grasp everything on the table was worse. Then his familiarities began. He started pulling Maureen's hair and digging her in the ribs and jeering at her during meals. We put a stop to this by setting them at different ends of the table: but he continues to be very offensive to her when they go out to tennis.

Then there was the evening of the sunset when we all went out to see a most beautiful crimson cloud effect from the lawn. The little blackguard presently came sidling out after us and finding me looking at the sky, prodded me in the stomach. I pretended to think that he was nudging me for the matches, and handed them to him with a look which said as plainly as words how dearly I should love to smack his face. As I continued to look at the sky he enquired "Have you never seen it before?" This question really beat me: for I almost think it was asked in good faith.

Next day I took him out in the morning in Smudge's sister's punt from St Clement's. I punted with fair success. He told me that English girls were very different from French. I said nothing.

BLACKGUARD: "Those girls at the otter hunting yesterday, they jump over streams, they lift their skirts up so – so high. In France now they would rather have stayed where they were than show their legs so."

SELF: "A possible explanation is that in France the young men would have been looking at their legs more attentively."

BLACKGUARD: (after a grin that made me retch) "Ahh . . . They are not girls in England, they are boys. In France at that age they always thinks of love."

We punted on . . .

On Friday Warnie arrived by the 5.58. I went in to meet him and we repaired as usual to the courtyard of the Mitre for a drink and a talk. We were there some time: the beer was good, we were both in fine humour and it was a cool evening – the whole scene a delightful moment's relief from dancing attendance on the Blackguard. We bussed out to Headington and had time to turn round before Maureen came back from tennis with the Blackguard.

I think it was this evening that the latter began kicking the footstool away from D under the table – also urging his chair up against that of Smudge who sits next him and making the strangest grimaces at her. Whether he is trying to conduct a very primitive kind of flirtation or whether he is mad I don't know. On the whole he was a little quieter this evening.

On Saturday morning W and I escaped for a book hunt and drink in Oxford, on condition of meeting the Blackguard at Longwall corner at 11.45 and bathing with him. We were a few minutes late at our rendezvous and apologised to the Blackguard, asking, in the usual way, if he had been waiting long. He replied emphatically that he had, adding as a rider that English people were always late. We went on to Parson's Pleasure. Maurice of course wore a bathing suit, and apropos of the rest's nudity, remarked to W that "in France no man could undress himself in that way". This of course is merely a difference of custom and no one could blame him for it. The water was rather cold. The Blackguard complained that it was very shallow and that he had touched the bottom when he dived.

On the way home he told us about his school days in Paris: they used to drink champagne and play poker all night: when he smoked in form he was told to do so on the other side of the room so that it would be invisible from the street. These schools are all run and inspected by the state . . .

Lewis did not keep a diary during 7 August-7 September.

Saturday 8 September: Last night D expostulated with me for having let so many weeks pass without my diary, specially as the record of Maurice's insolence and vulgarity would some day make good reading. He is still with us and goes, thank God, next Monday.

Most of this time we have suffered intolerable slavery. He rowed every morning as long as we had the boat and every morning I had to go and steer for him: sometimes I had some pleasure from the sunshine and the wind on the water, but everything was spoiled by his hideous face in front of me. I honestly believe that I am not carried away by my hatred and contempt when I say that it is one of the most unredeemed animal and vicious faces I ever saw . . .

Yet sometimes I feel I could endure his grossness and filthiness if only he were not, in addition, such a fool. Though he loves to pose as a man of the world he has the intellect of a child. When, on one or two dreadful occasions I have walked with him, he has told me the make and merits of every car that passed – a thing I have never had to endure since I left Cherbourg.

He is forever telling me pointless stories about himself, designed to show either how much money his father has or what a fine, dashing, reckless young fellow he is himself. Conversation he has none in the proper sense of the word.

The joke of the thing is that I half believe he thinks I like him. I ply him with irony and veiled insult but he is such a fool that I lose my pains. Lately he has taken to playing croquet. When he was still learning and I of course could still beat him, I discovered that I could not with comfort allow myself to get too much ahead as he at once began to get ill tempered: and once or twice he really sounded as if he were going to burst into tears.

Now he can beat me two times out of three: but he still asks seriously, nay pathetically, for sympathy whenever he misses a shot and attributes all his failures to the unevenness of the ground or to the fact that the balls are not spheres. The other day I was stung into pointing out that if his bad shots were accidents resulting from the imperfection of the balls, then, by a parity of reasoning, his good shots must be similar accidents. This however was too subtle for the little Blackg. and I daresay he was quite honest in his failure to follow me . . .

Early during this period a postcard came to D from the Beast[1] asking for the name of Maureen's school which he wanted for an income tax return. This had been forwarded from Bristol, but next day another came addressed direct to Hillsboro. This was naturally worrying. D and I had a conversation on the various troubles that have pursued us: losses for the past, fears for the future, and for the present, all the humiliations, the hardships, and the waste of time that come from poverty.

Poor D feels keenly (what is always on my mind) how the creative years are slipping past me without a chance to get to my real work, so that I was sorry I had ever mentioned this to her. I told her not to take too seriously what might be after all only the excuses I make to myself. What is far more serious is the continual overwork and worry to which she is exposed. Everyone, friends and enemies alike, seem to conspire against her. This was a bad time.

I began again to think of the pleasures of death, as I used to: not melodramatically, as of suicide, but with the longing for the state of an old, successful man of genius, sitting with all his work behind him, waiting to drop off.

This of course was nonsense, as D with her usual sanity told me: we had so little life and plenty of the other thing anyway. So far, thank God, (and touch wood) the Beast's card has been followed by no evil results.

We have also been been very lucky in getting another girl to replace Dorothy: an enormous girl of fifteen, called Ada, who never speaks but beams all over her large face and works very well and intelligently.

Since we stopped having the boat I have had a good many mornings to myself: and, as if to refute my fears, have had a burst of good form which has carried me through two very difficult cantos of "Dymer" – the sixth and seventh. I have written about twenty stanzas

[1] Mr Moore.

(good I hope) for the eighth and am now stopped by structural difficulties – how to work my "peripety": so I am afraid the push is over . . .

Sunday 9 September: . . . My head was very full of my old idea of a poem on my own version of the Cupid and Psyche story in which Psyche's sister would not be jealous, but unable to see anything but moors when Psyche showed her the Palace. I have tried it twice before, once in couplet and once in ballad form.[2]

Monday 10 September: A very beautiful morning with thick dew and a grey sky with the sun breaking through – it might, at eight o'clock, have been mistaken for five on a midsummer morning. We had breakfast a little early to let the Blackguard catch the char-a-banc to London. He parted with D very civilly. I carried one of his bags to the bus stopping place, bade him a very short goodbye, and went down to the fields beyond Mrs Seymours to look for mushrooms . . .

It was delightful to be by ourselves and to feel free. The spare room was thoroughly done out this morning and has been left with doors and windows wide open ever since, but it still has an atmosphere – moral and material – hanging about it. After tea I read two more tales in Crabbe with much enjoyment and started the second volume of *Richard Feverel*.

At about six o'clock D and I walked down to the fields to look for mushrooms. On the way we passed several children returning with loaded baskets, and naturally we found no mushrooms. It was dusk when we reached home and Ada had been nervous. I remarked how common this seemed to be among people of the servant class. D at once gave what is the obvious and true explanation, tho' I had never thought of it before: namely that in their ordinary life in small houses with large families, they are never alone either by day or by night . . .

Wednesday 12 September: I had a most horrible dream. By a certain poetic justice it turned on the idea which Jenkin and I were going to use in our shocker play: namely that of a scientist discovering how to keep consciousness and some motor nerves alive in a corpse, at the same time arresting decay, so that you really had an immortal dead man. I dreamed that the horrible thing was sent to us – in a coffin of course – to take care of.

[2] Readers will discern here the germ of Lewis's novel *Till We Have Faces* (1956). The only thing which survives of these early attempts at writing the story is a fragment of 78 couplets. They are in the *Lewis Papers*, vol. VIII, pp. 163-4.

D and Maureen both came into the dream and it was perfectly ordinary and as vivid as life. Finally the thing escaped and I fancy ran amuck. It pursued me into a lift in the Tube in London. I got away all right but the liftman had seen it and was terribly frightened and, when I saw how he was behaving, I said to myself, "There's going to be an accident in this lift." Just at that moment I noticed the window by my bed and found myself awake.

I had a moment of intense relief but found myself hopelessly rattled and as nervous as a child. I found I had no matches. Groped my way to those on the landing, lit my candle, went downstairs and returned with a pipe and a book. My head was very bad. I got restored to sanity pretty soon and slept, tho' with several breaks before morning. I thought at first that this was a good example of the falsity of the rule given by L.P. Jacks that authors never dream about their own inventions: but on second thoughts I am not sure that the idea of the play did not originate in another dream I had some years ago – unless the whole thing comes from Edgar Allan Poe . . .

Thursday 13 September: Thank goodness I had a dreamless sleep all night through . . . I decided to go for a walk in the hope that this was the best cure for my recent feebleness. I went through Mesopotamia and then to Marston where I had some beer and a packet of cigarettes – an extravagance of which I have not been guilty this many a day . . .

Coming home, I found D hanging up washing – much to my annoyance as I had hoped (it is these hopes that are the pest) she would do very little now the Blackguard is gone . . . I found that D had been making jam and had not yet sat down though when I left she promised me she would be done in a minute or two. Even the kindly fruits of the earth become one more enemy in this hopeless business of trying to save D from overwork.

After tea I went on with Fairfax's Tasso.[3] As a story it beats all the other poems of this sort. It manages somehow to combine the important and serious unity of a real epic with the mazey charm of a romance. It is always just not losing itself in the episodic adventures and one is never allowed to forget the central thread. His whole heroic world is firmly imagined – not a mere kaleidescope like Spenser . . . I am delighted with everything. It is very interesting to see how

[3] One of the books Lewis chose as a College prize was Tasso's *Jerusalem Delivered*.

Tasso was before Milton with the epic management of Christian mythology . . .

D and I went out for our usual little stroll before supper. Afterwards I read some more Repington aloud. No headache this evening, tho' I had it earlier in the day. I was slightly threatened with the bogey mood this evening, but I think I now have the situation in hand.

Friday 14 September: A pouring wet morning. Mr Allchin came to see D shortly after ten and later on I was called into the conclave. He asked me if I agreed with D that it would be a good thing for Maureen to drop the Oxford Local if she could do so without damaging her musical career. I asked whether, apart from the possibility of her earning her living at music, she was good enough to find it a sufficient intellectual resource – whether, in short, after giving up a general education, she might find herself a fifth rate musician with no interest in life. He thought she could be "first rate" as a teacher – which I suppose he regarded as an answer by implication to my question: whether she could be a pianist was always impossible to predict.

With regard to the question of earning a living the difficulty was that registration was now demanded in all music teachers. Of course one could not say how long this would last: but he was afraid the tendency would increase rather than diminish. This year there are still other paths to registration than the Oxford Local – such as a Teacher's Course for adults. He promised to ask Sir Hugh Allen if there were any such alternatives offered for the future.[4] We all agreed that Maureen should drop the Oxford Local if there were any loophole.

After this the conversation drifted on to more general subjects – chiefly the modern practice of teaching "musical appreciation" to those who don't do music. I asked if he thought it a good thing. He said it depended entirely on the individual – and mentioned Peppin of Rugby (formerly of Clifton) as a very successful teacher in this kind. I said that one was always afraid "teaching appreciation" would end in sentimentalism. He agreed that this was a danger, that is he said so, but I had the impression that he did not really agree or else was not interested and wanted to change the subject . . . I feel that

---

[4] Sir Hugh Allen (1869–1946) was the director of the Royal College of Music 1918–37, director of music, University College, Reading 1908–18. In Oxford, where he was Professor of Music 1918–46, he obtained creation of the music faculty in 1944.

Mr Allchin is inclined to talk down to one and at the same time to be a little subservient in expressions of opinion: at the same time (which is funny) I like him . . .

Monday 17 September: Great excitement today over the arrival of the puppy who is to be called Pat. He is quite ready to be friendly to the cats who maintain an armed neutrality.

In the morning I began re-reading Bergson's *L'Évolution Créatrice* more thoroughly than I had done yet. I spent most of the afternoon gardening. Before supper we all went for a stroll through Old Headington and Barton End. This evening we had a fire and sat in the drawing room for the first time. D in rather poor form. My coming journey to Ireland cast its familiar shadow over us both.

Lewis did not keep a diary during 19 September-10 October. On 22 September he arrived at "Little Lea" for a visit with his father, and he remained in Belfast until 10 October. In his own diary Mr Lewis recorded on 11 October: "While Jacks was at home I repeated my promise to provide for him at Oxford if I possibly could, for a maximum of three years from this summer. I again pointed out to him the difficulty of getting anything to do at 28 if he had ultimately to leave Oxford."

Thursday 11 October: I crossed last night from Ireland after nearly three weeks at Little Lea. In two respects my compulsory holiday was a great improvement on most that I have had, for I got on very well with my father and held the usual mental inertia at arm's length by working steadily at my Italian.

Before I left I had just time to finish Tasso's *Gerusalemme*, reading the twentieth canto on my last day. This was in the edition which I bought at Charing Cross in 1917. On the whole I was pleased with Tasso. As a narrative poet he stands high, the *Jerusalem* being really a very good historical novel. He quite fails to reach sublimity or even grandeur but there is a fine noble simple spirit. He believes in chivalry with a boyish faith which I don't find in Spenser. His third great merit is that he knows something about fighting: his single combats read like the real thing, not like what I find in Spenser and Malory. He loves a good scientific swordsman.

This is the good side of my story in Ireland: in revenge, I was never really well, suffering from headaches and indigestion. In the loneliness of that house I became hypochondriacal and for a time imagined that I was getting appendicitis or something worse. This worried me terribly, not only chiefly for its own sake but because I didn't see how I could manage to get back here in time. I had one or two dreadful nights of panic.

I did many long walks hoping to make myself sleep. I was twice up the Cave Hill where I intend to go often in future. The view down the chasm between Napoleon's Head and the main body of the cliffs is almost the best I have seen. I had one other delightful walk over the Castlereigh hills where I got the real joy – the only time for many years that I have had it in Ireland.

This morning I was called at 7. I had a single berth room on the boat deck. It had been so rough that, tho' I am never sea sick, I was woken up by the rolling and kept awake most of the night. I had breakfast on board and crossed by ferry to catch the 9.35 from Woodside, an excellent train which brought me without change to Oxford at 2.18. I had lunch on the train. I travelled most of the way with a very pleasant boy who was coming up to Queen's, having left Shrewsbury last term.

On getting out at Oxford I found myself in a crisp wintry air and as I bussed up to Headington I felt the horrors of the last week or so going off like a dream. At home I found Maureen with her leg in splints, having broken a cartilage at hockey. D and she had had very little sleep last night. Poor old Tibbie [the cat] after a long illness, had had to be chloroformed. We shall miss her. Miss Pearce came to tea. Afterwards D and I went out for a stroll with Pat: then after an early supper we bussed into town to see Allchin about putting off Maureen's lessons. He was out. The evening was very mild now and we both took a childish delight in our little outing. On the way back we met Jenkin, whom I was glad to see. So home, full of happiness, and early to bed, both being very tired and sleepy.

Friday 12 October: ... D and I went into town before lunch ... she going to Allchin and I to College. There I met Curtis and Allen, the don from whom I heard that Salveson had been elected to a Fellowship at New College. I had no sooner come out of the Porch than I ran into "Doctor" Ewing who is up for this term. Even the pouring rain did not induce him to hurry past me and I was walking brisky along, followed as briskly by him, when I saw Carritt. The latter stopped to speak to us and when the group thus formed had broken up, from it I shot away up the High hoping I had left Ewing behind. He followed me, however, pestering me to go for a walk with him. When I had finally escaped I went to Parkers and ordered Boiardo in two volumes ...

I went into town again and visited Poynton in the Bursary ... He then led me into his rooms beyond the bridge and told me he was writing to two women to see if they cd. get me any pupils. I asked him if the "stinks party" were winning the day over the Fellowship. He said nothing further had been done. He said he was not without hopes for me and if they decided to elect a member of their own body they would prefer no one to me. On the other hand they might find that they had to elect by examination for a non-teaching fellowship. He said I had many friends in college. On the whole his remarks were fairly encouraging . . .

Saturday 13 October: This morning came a note from Stevenson offering to mention me to the new Master in the hope that the latter might get me some journalistic work for the time being. After breakfast I went in to College and returned some books to the library. I called at Stevenson's rooms but he was out.

I then walked to Manor Place to see Wilson and waited downstairs so long that I had time to read several chapters of a translation of *Candide* with which I was rather disappointed.

Wilson welcomed me very kindly. I gave him back Archibald Marshall's *The Eldest Son* wh. he had lent me with strong recommendations. I explained that I had thought it very bad and we both laughed over this impasse. He thought my idea of "Translation of the VIIIth Century" as a subject for a B.Litt very promising. After a little chat I came away, did some shopping, looking again for Stevenson and bussed home.

We had a bread and cheese lunch as we shall always do now on Saturday. Poor D still worried with indigestion but less than yesterday. Jenkin arrived and he and I went for a walk to the copse this side of Stowe Woods. Taking example from the autumn sky we fell into a conversation on the difficulty of describing all save the most blatant and obvious sky effects. We also talked of "homeliness" in landscape, which he hardly appreciates.

Home to tea and afterwards D went out alone: not before an accident in the kitchen – the clothes horse falling into the soup pot. Jenkin helped me to clean the stove while D mopped up the floor. D came back rather late after Jenkin had gone, having had a nasty fall in the dark. She was covered with mud and a little hurt, but there seems no harm done. She said (and I agreed with her) that Jenkin had been rather dull today.

This evening we sat in the dining room. I continued reading *The Ring and the Book* wh. I began in Ireland – I am now at Pompilia's monologue. The whole poem is strangely above Browning's other work and contains, I am certain, some of the very greatest poetry I

Little Lea, 1905

C.S.Lewis (Jack) with his father, October 1917

C.S.Lewis after returning from the war, 1919

C.S.Lewis and his friend Paddy Moore punting
on the Cherwell, Summer 1917

Arthur Greeves

Warnie Lewis at Glenmachen House,
24 May 1916

University College from the High

University College Freshman of January 1919
Back row, left to right: A.C.Brashaw, C.L.Barwell, J. de F.Thompson, R.E.Owen,
A.K.Hamilton-Jenkin, G.O.Vinter, K.S.Sandford, H.L.Addleshaw, T.E.Lindop, H.L.Hopper
Middle row: N.S.Millican, P.C.Raiment, G.M.Morton, P.W.Rucker, C.A.Minoprio,
K.M.Davie, L.Chalk, O.D.Ballinger, H.P.Mitchell
Front row: M.M.Hallett, D.R.Gawler, H.P.Blunt, B.P.Wyllie, G.D.Kirwan, G.Chilton,
C.S.Lewis, R.M.S.Pasley, A.R.L.Gaussen, H.W.Turner

28 Warneford Road, where C.S.Lewis and the
Moores lived, at times, between 1919 and 1922

"Hillsboro," 14 Holyoake Road, Headington, where Lewis and the
Moores lived from 1922 to 1930

Jack, Maureen and Mrs Moore at Perranporth, Cornwall, September 1927

C.S.Lewis at Stonehenge, 8 April 1925

The Fellows of Magdalen College in 1928
Standing, left to right: G.R.S.Snow, Professor E.C.Titchmarsh, H.C.Stewart (organist), R.Segar, K.B.McFarlane, E.Hope, unidentified, S.G.Lee, H.M.D.Parker
Sitting: Professor C.C.Foligno, J.M.Thompson, Sir Charles Sherrington, Professor W.H.Perkin, Reverend A.W.Chute, Reverend C.R.Carter, E.S.Craig

Standing, left to right: R.P.Longden, unidentified, C.S.Lewis, C.E.Brownrigg (Headmaster of Magdalen College School), C.T.Onions, J.T.Christie, unidentified, M.H.Mackeith, G.R.Driver, J.J.Manley, Reverend H.E.Salter
Sitting: Sir Herbert Warren (President of Magdalen), Professor C.H.Turner, P.V.M.Benecke, Reverend F.E.Brightman, Professor J.A.Smith, Professor H.L.Bowman, Professor A.L.Dixon, Professor A.G.Tansley

Magdalen College and Magdalen Bridge

have ever read. The Prologue and "Caponsacchi" are the best books so far . . .

Sunday 14 October: . . . Before lunch I started gilding an old frame for a reproduction of Leyden's portrait of a young man, which we have cut out of the *Queen*. From the same source we have already cut out and framed a "Gentleman" by Vandyke and a "Head of a Poet" by Palma Vecchio.

After lunch I went on with the job for half an hour or so and then helped D to give Pat a bath – my first experience of dog bathing, and a very memorable one. Miss Baker came for tea and Maureen came downstairs for the first time and lay on the drawing room sofa. After tea, when I had removed the things (Ada being out) I went back to my picture framing and finished the job . . .

Tuesday 16 October: A note from Stevenson this morning saying that the Master would see me at 9.30. I bussed in after a very hasty breakfast. I found that the new Master, Sadler, is living in poor Emmet's old rooms in the Radcliffe Tower. Allen was with him when I arrived and I was shown on to his dining room where I waited for a few moments. When I came back he greeted me very kindly indeed, congratulating me on my past career and adding "We will do whatever we can for you." He is a short, clean shaven, white headed man, honest looking I think, and very easy in his manners: also very direct and economical in his speech. I was very well impressed with him.

He asked me if I wanted journalism as a career. I said that I did not: [he] said he thought I was wise: but that reviewing etc was a good thing as it put one in touch with many important people. He said that at my age "he had got a great deal out of it". He asked me what paper I would prefer: this rather nonplussed me and I said that I had been wishing rather than willing in the matter and made no plans. He gave me Garrod's *Wordsworth* (which I have been wanting to read for some time) and asked me to bring him a trial review of it. He would then talk it over with me and see which paper I was nearest the "tang" of.

After leaving him I went to see Stevenson and thank him for opening the thing. We had about ten minutes' talk. He exclaimed "I don't mind telling you that it will be a scandal if this College or some College doesn't give you a fellowship soon." We compared notes over examining for the Higher Oxford [Certificate]. He ended up by saying that he was now going to give a Pass Mods. lecture and hadn't thought a word about it yet. I felt like adding, from my recollections of his style, "I can quite believe it." . . .

In the drawing room I began Garrod's book and read it for most of the afternoon and evening. It seems pretty good . . .

Wednesday 17 October: Rather warmer today. After breakfast I went to my own room and got to work on a first draft of Garrod's book. I continued the same after lunch and by four o'clock had produced what I think will have to do . . . I took up Herodotus and read a good deal of the first book with much enjoyment. I find that the words whose English I wrote in the margin in 1920 (when first reading Herodotus) are still those I don't know! . . .

Thursday 18 October: After breakfast I looked over my review again and wrote up my diary and so into town where I went to see the Master. He read the review and pronounced it "much to the point" and really suitable for any of the papers he had mentioned. He advised me to see Gordon about the *Times Literary Supplement*: in the meantime I was to get my review typed and he would send it, with a personal letter, to five editors. He agreed with my main view over Garrod. He asked me about my previous education and when I told him of Kirk exclaimed "Oh, then you are the Lockian private pupil! Now that's very interesting." He advised me to read Locke's *On Education* (I had already done so at Grendon in 1921) and Rousseau's *Emile* in the light of my own experience. I left him, took Locke from the College library, did some shopping and came home after leaving the review to be typed in Cornmarket . . .

Friday 19 October: Soon after breakfast I went into town and taxed the typists office with not having sent my MS to Univ. as was promised but they insisted that they had. I went round to College and there found to my relief that it had, after all, come yesterday and the Master had already taken it to his own room . . .

I had an early tea and caught the 4.30 to Paddington, Harwood having invited me up for the week end. The country about the Chilterns where it is most wooded was far gone in autumn colours and was very delightful. Reaching Paddington I came by Metro to Victoria and there waited in a downpour of rain, until, in despair of the bus, I took a taxi and so came to 2 Lupus St., Pimlico, S.W.l.

It was very good to see Harwood again. The flat which he shares with Beckett is very nice and furnished, tho' sparsely, with great taste and comfort. Harwood was cooking potatoes when I arrived and told me there would be a guest for dinner – Miss Olivier, one of his folk dancing friends whose father was formerly Governor of Jamaica.

The lady when she arrived proved very pleasant. About 40 I should imagine, good looking, and well able to talk.[1] After dinner (which was eaten in the white kitchen) we had coffee in the study and read *Comus* together – each taking a part. Miss Olivier (Harwood addresses her as Ariel) reads well: Harwood himself not so well. They made me Comus. When this was done we had some tea and talked – mainly about Steiner, both the others being disciples.

He and I then accompanied her home: our route lay mostly along the Embankment. The rain had stopped: on the far side of the river we saw the tree tops of Battersea Park. We became very merry. On the return journey I told Harwood how much I liked his friend: he said "I am very fond of her." We got back at 12.45 and so to bed. Beckett's bed in which I slept was very luxurious, but I was wakeful for some time.

Saturday 20 October: Was called by Harwood and we breakfasted at 8.45. A beautiful morning and as we are above the surrounding houses it has the effect of being on a mountain top – I never before realised the beauty of garret landscapes. After breakfast Harwood went out to his "breadwinning".

I went by bus to Hyde Park corner and walked through Hyde Park and Kensington Gardens to Arthur's studio at 119 Westbourne Terrace. Arthur was away for the week end. Having walked and bussed back, I began to read Barfield's faery tale "The Silver Trumpet" in which with prodigality he squirts out the most suggestive ideas, the loveliest pictures, and the raciest new coined words in wonderful succession. Nothing in its kind can be imagined better.[2]

Harwood returned and after lunch and a smoke we went for a walk. He took me along the embankment to Westminster, our main objective being Rodin's group of the Burghers of Calais. The individual figures are very strong but we agreed that it is not much

---

[1] Daphne Olivier (1889–1950) was one of the four daughters of Sydney Haldane Olivier (Lord Olivier), who was Governor of Jamaica 1907–13. She was a member of Newnham College, Cambridge, where she read Medieval and Modern Languages, taking a BA in 1913. During the summer of 1923 Cecil Harwood and Owen Barfield attended an Anthroposophical conference at which Rudolf Steiner spoke, and it was there they met Miss Olivier, who was already a convinced Anthroposophist. Cecil Harwood married Daphne Olivier on 14 August 1925, both having taken a leading part in setting up the first Rudolf Steiner school in this country at Streatham.

[2] Owen Barfield's *The Silver Trumpet* was published by Faber and Gwyer (now Faber and Faber) of London in 1925. It was reprinted by Wm. B. Eerdmans Publishing Co. of Grand Rapids, Michigan in 1968, and by Bookmakers Guild of Longmont, Colorado in 1986.

of a group. We were forced to walk through the Houses of Parliament in order to reach Westminster Hall – as Harwood said "we had sugar cake shoved down our throats before we were allowed to eat our honest bread and butter". The Hall was very like my recollection of it and as "cool, sweet, sudden" as you could ask for.

We walked on and leaned over Westminster Bridge a long while looking at the County Hall – by a new architect in almost a new style. We crossed and investigated it closer. It is the finest modern building I have seen and, as I said, almost realises one's Babylonian dream. We also attached ourselves to a party that was being guided through it: the interior is very nearly as good – specially the courtyard. On the front to the river there is a monster of a new kind – all arms wh. gave me an idea for Dymer's son.

We had tea and so home to the flat. After an early supper we set out to wait in the pit queue for *Hassan*: but we found that there was no possibility of getting in and went instead to Munro's *At Mrs Bean's* which had been recommended to him by Barfield. It turned out to be the worst play we had ever seen and we were amazed at Barfield. We had beer after the first act. Harwood said "We have tried it sober and we have tried it drunk but it's no use." I said "like the Persians in Herodotus". We walked home, probably deriving as much pleasure from damning it as we would have had from the recollection of a good play. Then a glass of whiskey and a chat and to bed.

Sunday 21 October: Began reading Butler's *Erewhon* in bed this morning. After breakfast wh. we had v. late, we set out for a walk. We took the Metropolitan to Richmond, in the streets of which we were held up by rain for ten minutes. How delightful all expeditions are with people who don't mind rain! We then went into Richmond Park. I was quite unprepared for it. There was hardly anyone to be seen. In a few minutes we were in an absolutely deserted open rolling country full of bracken, standing pools and all kinds of woods and groves under a splendid grey autumn sky. We had as good a walk as ever I have had, coming down at about 2 o'clock into Kingston on Thames. Here we were overtaken by sharp rain and finding all the hotels shut were reduced to a very hasty lunch for ten pence each in "a low eating house" – a phrase I never really understood before.

After lunch we walked into Hampton Court Park. This was at first less beautiful than the other: then gradually we came to the end of a very long sheet of water with huge trees in autumn colouring on each side and Wren's "back" of Hampton Court just visible at the end. At the same moment the sun broke out: the grass (*very* level) and the dead leaves on it, the trees, the swans, and one little stag that did not run away, took on glorious colours. We were alone: the silence was intense. It was all just like one of those luminous dreams I have so seldom dreamed. We walked up the whole length of the water to the fine old ironwork gates – still not a soul about and into the Palace gardens. This approach will be a great memory to me

The diary breaks off here, the last sentence uncompleted. Lewis supplied the following "Note", but did not resume his diary until 1 January 1924.

NOTE

My last diary, after fluttering for some time on a broken wing, came to an end on 21 October 1923 when I was with Harwood at his flat in Pimlico. On that Sunday evening he read and condemned in no measured terms the two new cantos of "Dymer" (VI and VII) which I had brought to show him. After discussion I largely agreed with him and decided to cut them out: in spite of the work I had put into them I felt surprisingly little disappointment at giving them up. I suppose that in the expulsion of anything bad from the mental system there is always pleasure.

Sometime after my visit to Harwood I cycled to Long Crendon to spend a night at Barfield's cottage there, thus meeting his wife and mother in law for the first time. His wife is plain, and undistinguished in manner – which I take for a good sign in a marriage so unequal in age. She is very quiet, a little shy, I think: "homely" both in the good and the bad sense of the word. I like her, and I think I should like her more, the more I saw of her. His mother in law, Mrs Dewey [Douie], is a "character part": a very caustic old Scotch lady.

Barfield has, if anything, improved by marriage. I enjoyed my little stay greatly. We talked a great deal, about Steiner, the Douglas Scheme, and the changes we had gone through even in the short time we had known each other.

He made one excellent remark. "I am not bored," he said. "I still have always a waiting list of things to do, even if it's only walking to the bottom of the garden to see how a bud is coming on." He saw me as far as Stanton St John on the way back. While I was with him I saw several of his new poems, some of which are very fine. He approved of "Dymer" V and tolerated my new version of VI.

I saw little of Jenkin this term. D began to be very poorly about this time and started a course of medicines for indigestion at the advice of Dr McCay. The latter was often here doctoring Maureen's mysteriously damaged ankle: he soon proved himself a fool, promising her that it would be all right next week and changing his promises often.

Harwood came down for a very jolly week end, during which we played Boy's Names, walked, talked and laughed, keeping entirely free from shop. D and Maureen both like him very much, and indeed, in many ways, he is an ideal companion. It was during this stay that he met Jenkin again and they became friends – Jenkin having been rather repelled by his manner when they met before.

Later on Barfield came to stay for one night. He and I talked till three o'clock: one of the most satisfying conversations I have ever had. Although the subject of his marriage was naturally never mentioned, a lot was understood and we each saw that the other felt the same way about women and the home life and the unimportance of all the things that are advertised in common literature. He agreed that, as I said, "either women or men are mad": he said we could see the woman's point of view absolutely at times – as if we had never had any other – and this was a sort of relief.

He has completely lost his materialism and "the night sky is no longer horrible". I read to him in my diary the description of the talk I had with him in Wadham gardens when he was still in pessimism, and we enjoyed it. Although he agreed with several Bergsonianisms of mine (specially that "the materiality is the intelligibility") he has not read Bergson. He was surprised that I shared most of his views on the nature of thought.

It was shortly before this that I read Flecker's *Hassan*. It made a great impression on me and I believe it is really a great work. Carritt (whom I met at the Martlets shortly after) thinks that its dwelling on physical pain puts it as much outside literature as is pornography in another: that it works on the nervous system rather than the imagination. I find this hard to answer: but I am almost sure he is wrong. At that same meeting of the Martlets Sadler read an excellent paper on Day, the author of *Sandford and Merton*.

Soon after this I had to leave – at an unusually early date in order to conform with W's time of leave.[3] The usual wretchedness of going away was increased by D's state of health: and to crown all, Maureen had to be sent to Bristol during my absence to have her foot properly seen to by Rob. Poor D, who was thus left alone had a dreadful time, and admits now that she was at times afraid it was going to be a gastric ulcer. Thank heavens she seems better now. My three weeks in Ireland, tho' improved by W's presence, were as usual three weeks too long. I had a good deal of toothache.

On the return journey W and I stopped for a night in town. For the first time since we were children we visited the Zoo with great gusto: but the cages are too small, and it is cruel – specially for animals like foxes, wolves, dingoes and jackals. We also went to see a musical comedy called *Katherine*, wh. was very bad. We had meant to go to *Hassan*, but after reading it W decided that it would be too harrowing for his feelings.

While I was in Ireland I read Tolstoy's *Anna Karenina*, Masefield's *Daffodil Fields*, J. Stephen's new book *Deirdre* and Henry James' *Roderick Hudson*.

---

[3] Warnie was still stationed at Colchester. He and Jack arrived at Little Lea together on 9th December and were with their father until 28th December 1923.

Jack Lewis was reading the works of Henry More (1614–87), the Cambridge Platonist, with the thought of writing about him for a D.Phil. degree. Despite the fact that Lewis was not a Christian, he had chosen Henry More because of his own interest in ethics. His belief in the importance of morals and ethics was very strong and in March he read a paper to the Philosophical Society called "The Promethean Fallacy in Ethics". The scholarship from University College had run out, but his father promised to keep him in Oxford while he looked for a fellowship. He failed to get either of those he applied for at St John's College and Trinity College, and he continued to try and make ends meet by correcting essays for the School Certificate. In the spring University College offered Jack the chance to take over the tutorials and lectures of E.F. Carritt while he was spending a year at the University of Michigan. For this he was offered a salary of £200 a year, and in October he began tutorials and a series of lectures entitled "The Good, its position among the values". Jack visited Warnie at the army base in Colchester during July, and they travelled to Belfast together in Warnie's motorcycle to spend Christmas with their father.

Tuesday 1 January: . . . After breakfast I bought a new MS book at Hewitt's and settled down to read through the philosophical works of Henry More and to make an abstract of them. I spent the morning on the preface general and also wrote into my book the detail of the title page . . .

Wednesday 2 January: I worked all morning on More's *Antidote to Atheism*,[1] reading and abstracting the first two books, which are very curious . . . After tea I went on with the third book of the *Antidote*.

Shortly before supper time I went out to pay our Income Tax and house dues (the former is fortunately deducted from our rent by Raymond) to the local "publican", old Mattock, who lives in a little

---

[1] *An Antidote against Atheism* (1652; 1655).

cottage opposite the "Brittania" – a cheerful, respectful old body . . .

Friday 4 January: . . . After breakfast I sat down to my work and finished *Enthusiasmus* and began More's Latin correspondence with Descartes . . . I did various jobs and went to the Union where I looked at Campagnac's *Cambridge Platonists* and decided it wd. be no use to me. I brought away Seth's *English Philosophers* and came home by bus. It was a typical Oxford evening of frost and fog. After tea I went on with the Cartesian letters. The muddiness of poor old More's mind becomes very striking when you see him at close quarters with a real thinker like Descartes. After supper I went on working. My throat was so sore that I did not read out to D . . .

Saturday 5 January: We were rather late getting up and almost immediately after breakfast set off all three for town where Maureen was to have a tooth drawn. It was colder than ever – frost and wind without sun. A present of three woodcock arrived today from Willie, which I left at the poulterer's to be plucked and trussed before we went into town.

I . . . went to the Union. Here I read the opening of Bertrand Russell's *A.B.C. of Atoms* and after finding that the notion of atoms which I have from general reading is sufficiently correct, decided that there was no need to go further and took up his *Philosophical Essays*.

In his "Worship of a Free Man" I found a very clear and noble statement of what I myself believed a few years ago. But he does not face the real difficulty – that our ideals are after all a natural product, facts with a relation to all other facts, and cannot survive the condemnation of the fact as a whole. The Promethean attitude would be tenable only if we were really members of some other whole outside the real whole: wh. we're not. His essay on ethics I found very interesting. I came away bringing out Santayana's *Winds of Doctrine* . . .

Sunday 6 January: . . . After making up my diary I got a fright through not being able to find the first volume of "Dymer", but soon ran it to ground. Although I disagree with all Santayana's definite conclusions, the atmosphere of sanity and coolness which pervades his book has influenced me in the direction of discontent with the whole plan of "Dymer": it seems "full of sound and fury, signifying nothing". I spent the morning rewriting the opening of the "Wild Hunt" and, I think, greatly improving it . . .

I . . . helped to get ready for the Thurstons – thanks to whose impertinence poor D had been busily making cakes all morning. They arrived presently. Mrs Thurston, on a fuller view, turns out to be very ugly. The children are too delicate to eat cakes, and elected to have boiled eggs instead. After tea Maureen and I played animal grab with them: the little girl climbed on the sofa and stood on the chair and tried to break the metronome and stuck my favourite pipe in her mouth . . .

We had woodcock for supper and they were a supper fit for the gods. Afterwards I worked a little more on the "Wild Hunt" and then read to D. Poor Maureen was very ill after having her tooth out and had a temperature of 101. D is afraid she may get a septic mouth.

Tuesday 8 January: This morning I decided to see what I could do about writing a thesis for St John's, D having pointed out to me a possible fellowship there. I looked over my old "Hegemony of Moral Values" thinking that I might use an improved version of it: at any rate it will be useful as a fallback if I cannot get anything else ready in time. On the whole however I decided to try and write instead an answer to Bertrand Russell's "Worship of a Free Man", in fact a prose version of "Foster" . . .

After lunch I walked into town and got my typescript and, in the Union, wrote to Squire telling him that I had a poem 480 lines long and asking whether, if he liked it on other grounds, its length would exclude it from the *Mercury*.

I then took out Huxley's Romanes Lecture,[2] Russell's *Philosophical Essays* and Ward's *Realm of Ends*. I came home and had tea. I then read Huxley's lecture which is a very noble and tonic piece of work. After it I went on to Ward's book. I had taken it out because I foolishly misread the title "Reality of ends" and therefore supposed that it would be on my problem. I found it to be a silly, soft kind of book . . . .After supper I sat down with paper in front of me and began to follow the argument where it would lead me, conscientiously avoiding the conclusions I desired to reach. It led me almost into impossible antimonies: but I got a lot of interesting stuff.

I then read out to D for a little and we went to bed. When I took Pat out (as I always do before going to bed) I found that it was snowing and the ground covered with snow.

Wednesday 9 January: The snow was piled very deep on all the windows this morning and had covered the arm chair in my room

---

[2] Thomas Henry Huxley, "Ethics and Evolution" (1893).

near the window. It was unusually dry snow – firm and powdery like sand.

I spent the morning working on my new paper which I intend to call "The Promethean Fallacy in Ethics" and wrote the first draft of a section which will come near the end, in which I reject the kind of solution offered in Balfour's *Theism and Humanism* . . .

I then changed my clothes and walked through Headington Quarry to the Hinckleys . . . We played various very simple games and it was really quite good fun.

I came away at 6.45 and got home to find old Taylor here who stayed to supper. Although it was an interruption for everyone's business we were all very glad to have him. I discovered that he was a reader of Trollope and we had a good deal of talk about that. After supper he and Maureen amused themselves on their fiddles. My throat was rather bad again tonight. In bed about one o'clock.

Thursday 10 January: . . . I . . . went to the Union and took out the second volume of Martineau's *Types* [*of Ethical Theory*] and Sorley's *Moral Values and the Idea of God*: and so home . . . After lunch I settled down to work and worked for the whole of the rest of the day till 10.30 with breaks of course for meals, trying hard to curb my infernal rapidity and to write the sentences instead of letting them write themselves.

Poor D had a headache and a sick feeling most of the day and was very miserable. As soon as I stopped work at ten thirty I got a very sharp headache which however soon grew milder. I read out to D till bedtime . . .

Saturday 12 January: . . . At the Union I returned Sorley and Martineau and took out Balfour's *Theism and Humanism* and *Theism and Thought*. It rained and blew furiously all day. After lunch I worked hard and satisfactorily till supper at 8 o'clock. In the evening I read *Theism and Thought*.

About 10 o'clock Maureen discovered a rash and a temperature which D pronounced to be chicken-pox. My first thought was that this would save D all the extra work connected with the party: but I am afraid it will only give her more trouble in the long run. It is infernally hard luck on Maureen after all her other troubles and will dish her chances of getting into the team this term. She was put to bed and I got coal from the cellar and carried it up and laid the fire in her room. Very late to bed, very tired.

Sunday-Wednesday, 13-16 January: Three unpleasant days. I divided

my time between doing housemaid's work for D (Ada having been
sent away lest she should catch the chicken-pox) and finishing my
essay as best I could. I suffered from a very bad sore throat, headache
and earache, and was very tired from morning till night.

Thursday-Sunday 17-20 January: Much the same except that, praise
God, I got rid of my various disorders. I decided that any effort to
continue my regular work at present could only lead to exasperation
and, lest the time should be wholly wasted, I began to continue the
Phaedrus from the point where I left it off some years ago.

Pat however soon put an end to that project by pulling the volume
of Plato off the table one day when I had left him alone for five
minutes and eating most of it. Afterwards I began to have ideas and
am now re-writing Canto III of "Dymer" and re-reading *The Life
and Death of Jason.*[3]

Monday 21 January: Pouring with rain. After late breakfast, washing
up, and cleaning vegetables, I corrected the typescript of my "Promethean Fallacy in Ethics" and bussed into town. There I had
Carritt's and Wilson's testimonials typed out and, enclosing them
with an application and the essay, took the whole packet by hand
and left it at St John's.

Home by about two where I had a cold lunch, washed up, "did"
the kitchen, and the scullery and worked on "Dymer" till tea, which
we had in the kitchen at five and afterwards (with a few minutes of
Jason) till supper time.

Maureen was bothered with her throat again tonight. D much
better these days: she attributes this to the extra "bustling about"
and talks of getting rid of Ada, in whom many heinous sins have
been discovered during the last week.

Tuesday 22 January: Up rather earlier than usual, tho' still late:
breakfast, washed up, cleaned vegetables, and was finished by eleven.
I worked on my new Canto III and, finishing it, went to Hewitt's
for a MS book and began to fair copy it. Lunch about 1.30: washed
up, brushed the kitchen and mopped the scullery and came back to
my fair copy . . .

Thursday 24 January: After finishing my morning chores I began my
work on More again, feeling that I could not remain idle for ever.
After I had worked for a few minutes I had occasion to leave the
drawing room for a moment: whereupon Lady Gonner was shown

---

[3] By William Morris (1867).

in and D had to go and talk to her, thus shutting me off from my books. Lady G., though charming in a way, is one of those idle and talkative women who imagine that time is as free for everyone else as it is for themselves. D and I were both annoyed at being held up in our several businesses for twenty minutes. As soon as she was gone and I was fairly started again, Mrs Wilbraham arrived. After this I went up and worked in my own room.

A very cold day. I worked again in the afternoon and read Carr's translation of Bergson's *Energie Spirituelle* in the evening, which I did not find interesting. Bergson always seems almost incoherent in English.

Friday 25 January: A cold bright morning. I walked with Pat to Stowe Woods and strolled there for some time: it was very springlike, tho' there are no primroses yet – there is *one* in the garden. D found in *The Times* yesterday that Coghill has got a Fellowship at Exeter. Worked all afternoon . . .

Saturday 26 January: A fine day. D had to go into town in the morning and I worked on Henry More. After lunch, which was very late, I was just about to start my chores when a ring brought me to the door and there I found Ewing. Thank heavens the blessed name of chicken-pox prevented him from coming in. He wanted me to read a paper to the postgraduate philosophical group next "Thirsty" as he pronounced it, which I agreed to do. While he was talking to me Jenkin arrived on his bike . . . I had to leave the washing up to D and go for a walk with Jenkin.

We went up Shotover by the Quarry path, where he had never been before, talking of architecture, parents and children, his leaving Oxford, Havelock Ellis on dreams and other things. A wonderful lurid sunset on the way back . . .

Monday 28 January ad fin: After two days during which my jobs seemed inexplicably laborious and I was always cold, D found on Wednesday afternoon that I had a temperature of 102. It turned out to be this wretched chicken-pox and I lived for the next week in the yellow room. Towards the end I took walks in the garden. If you cross the lawn seventeen times you have walked a mile. As I could not shave for fear of cutting the spots on my face, I grew a considerable beard and have – provisionally – retained the moustache.

During my illness and solitary confinement I read the first three volumes of Gibbon with great enjoyment. I also read *Vanity Fair* for the first time and it has largely removed my old blindness to Thackery's merit, tho' I still detest his horrible "knowingness" and winks to the reader. He is almost wholly negative. He finds meanness in all things but he does not show us any "light by which he has seen that darkness": hence his pessimism, being based not on any original vision of the ideal, but simply on ready made morality as he found it in his class and age, is of a very low order. I admire his art, but I have no affection for him.

I also read *Don Juan* all through. The Cantos of the shipwreck, the island, and Constantinople are not worth reading twice – the rest not worth reading once: an indefensible swimming with the tide – a mere flinging out of everything that came into Byron's rather ordinary head. The violences in metre soon cease to be amusing.

I re-read the first book of *The Faerie Queene*, except the fight with the dragon, and enjoyed it as much as ever. I think I never before saw how much real beauty there is in the religious parts. I read Maurice Hewlett's *Fool Errant* – over-sexed like nearly all his work, but rather *distinguished*: also Mrs Humphrey Ward's *Lady Rose's Daughter* which is "as good as the first novel you will pick up".

I re-wrote "Dymer" VI – or rather wrote an entirely new canto with which I am pleased. "Foster" was sent to Squire and refused. Appleton of the *Beacon* wrote to me saying that he had found "Joy" again and asking if I still wanted it to appear. An unknown publisher called Stockwell wrote saying that "a mutual friend" had told him I would soon have enough poems for a book and telling me he would be pleased to see them.

D kept wonderfully well.

*Up until now Lewis's Scholarship at University College had paid
his College fees and left him with £11 per term. To make up what
was needed Mr Lewis had been giving him £67 per term as
well as paying incidental expenses. This would have been enough
for an undergraduate living in college, but it was not nearly enough
for a householder with two dependents. Now that the Scholarship
was at an end Lewis wrote to his father on 4 February asking for
help:*

*"You know that my Scholarship is at an end. It was nominally a
scholarship of £80 a year. What I actually got out of it was about
£11 a term. Sometimes it would be a little more or a little less, but
it generally averaged out to £33 a year. I had hopes of being able to
make up that in other ways – pupils and the like – but they have not
been realised and I am afraid I must ask for help."* Letters of C.S.
Lewis, *p. 191.*

Lewis did not keep a diary during 1-19 February.

Wednesday 20 Febuary: I walked into town after breakfast and called
on Farquharson. There was a pupil with him and he himself was
sitting by the fire looking very sleepy. I told him I wished to go for
a D.Litt. He asked me if "I had it ready". I replied, with some
surprise, that I had not – I understood that one had to send in one's
application before, not after the work was done. He said yes, that I
must make out a scheme showing the authorities and MSS I was
using etc. – all in fact that I can only know when the work is done.

I thanked him and went to the Union where I began to read
Haldane's *Daedalus* – a diabolical little book, bloodless tho' stained
with blood.[1] This must be read and digested – or vomited.

I met Robson-Scott and we retired into the upper room to talk.
He told me that he had had the same trouble with the Farq. and that

---

[1] J.B.S. Haldane, *Daedalus or Science and the Future* (1924).

it didn't matter. He thought poorly of the O.U.D.S. *Hamlet.*[2] This led to a discussion of the whole value of presentation as a test of plays, in wh. I forgot where we were and suddenly found myself lecturing in a voice which cd. be heard all over the library. We were both reduced to laughter. I am to go to tea with him next Tuesday. He told me that once, on being asked his name suddenly in strange company, he had actually been unable to give it for one terrible moment.

I got back the typescript of a new version of "Joy" for Appleton and bussed home after some shopping for D. I washed up after lunch and read Oliver Elton's *Sheaf of Papers.* Miss Featherstone came for tea. In the evening I sent "Joy" to the *Beacon,* wrote to Stockwell explaining that I was under contract to Heinemann, and to Harwood refusing an invitation to London which we cannot afford at present. Later on I started reading out *The Crock of Gold* to D, but I don't think she cared greatly for it.[3]

Thursday 21 February: . . . Immediately after breakfast I took Biddy Anne in to Gillard to be vetted. Biddy Anne is a yellow cat that has recently adopted us. I walked in from the Plain, called at College and went to the Union, coming home again by bus.

I then made up my diary since my illness. After lunch the weather changed. A startling mildness came over the air and it was like spring though there were heavy black clouds to the east. After D and I had strolled in the garden to enjoy this, I came in and read over my diary for this time last year. It is dully written – I recover the horrors from memory and not from the words.

A letter from Aunt Lily came by the afternoon post in answer to one I had written her recently protesting against her assertion that the last words of Pompilia in *The Ring and the Book* were the last words of his wife. I read her letter and began to answer it . . .

Friday 22 February: I had an unusually nasty dream connected with my father in the night – a dream of the clinging sort.

After breakfast I took down all the gas globes for D to clean. I spent the morning working on Henry More's *Defence of the Cabbala,* a fantastic, tedious work. After lunch I crumbled a ham and swept the kitchen and scullery and then went out for a walk with Pat . . .

Saturday 23 February: A dreamful night. Up and into town to get

---

[2] *Hamlet* performed by the Oxford University Dramatic Society.

[3] By James Stephens (1912).

a washer for one of the hot water bottles, and other things.

We were all of us very little pleased at the prospect of the Pasleys' arrival today for a week end. They invited themselves and I strongly advised D not to have them, for they gave us plenty of room for escape, but she insisted. I washed up after lunch while D got their room ready: everything was in a pandemonium.

They arrived at tea time. Mrs P. seems to have got rid of a great many of her affectations. The deafness is not worse. I liked her better this time. After tea, which we had in the kitchen, we talked in the drawing room. I think he still likes his married life but he is overworked and takes little interest in his work.[4] They have few friends, and, tho' they are within reach of the country, they seldom take a walk for more than half an hour. He is a little fatter and a little paler. He has learned to sleep after dinner and grown sensitive to draughts. He gave me an interesting account of the diary which his great-grandfather Admiral Pasley kept while serving in the war against America. I wish he would publish it.[5]

After supper D insisted on washing up – as indeed she insisted on doing everything during the whole week end, so that she and they hardly ever met. We played Boy's Names in the evening – quite good fun. D and I of course were late to bed – D very tired and bothered. **Sunday 24 February:** The Pasleys take a prodigious time to dress. After breakfast they and I went for a walk up Shotover, taking Pat. I would willingly have spun it out, as Maureen wanted the drawing room to practise in, but Pasley is not much of a walker, tho' his wife is. He is quite insensible to nature – I think he always was.

Home shortly after twelve and read the papers. Then flurry and scurry in the kitchen and lunch and more washing up for D despite all that I could say or do, while Mrs P. read and Pasley tried hard not to sleep over the drawing room fire. After tea D came and sat in the drawing room for the only time during their visit – except a little in the evening. They showed us several photos taken on a delightful trip they had this summer in some birdless country of lakes and sand dunes near Bordeaux and Arcachon ...

They also showed us others taken at Valentia last Easter and told us about their visit to a bull fight, which they enjoyed. I denounced the immorality of this cruel and cowardly business. Pasley trotted

---

[4] Rodney Pasley was Assistant Master at Alleyn's School, Dulwich, 1921–5.
[5] It was published as *Private Sea Journals, 1778–1782, kept by Admiral Sir Thomas Pasley*, ed. R.M.S. Pasley (1931).

out the usual irrelevant answer that some English sports were quite as bad, and then they both actually pleaded as a *justification* the fact that they had enjoyed it. I said "What a debauch!" and pointed out that that made no difference.

Pasley denounced me as an *a priori* philosopher who made human institutions subservient to my internal notions of right and wrong: but of course it took only a familiar bit of argument to show him that he did the same. I was forced to admit that the pleasure we took in action was a justification in the sense that, other things being equal, the less the temptation the greater the crime. It is fortunate that I didn't overhear (what I was told later) Mrs P. telling D about the Spaniards sticking their darts into the bull to rouse him – "but it doesn't hurt him". If I had I might have said regrettable things. It was all disgusting.

After supper I begged D to let me wash up, but she asked rather savagely, "Do you want me to die?" and explained that she had been frozen in the drawing room as Mrs P. blocked up the whole fire. So I returned to the drawing room . . .

Pasley . . . complained of living in a state of tension: he always feels he must be "getting on". If he sits down to read he must hurry on to get to something else: if he walks out he must hurry back. Mrs P. said to him "You are not so bad as you were a year ago," and he agreed. He knows himself that this is one of the roads to a nervous breakdown. I hardly knew what to say to him. It is hard to see where salvation can lie for a man who never loved nature and no longer loves art and for whom religion is out of the question . . .

Monday 25 February: . . . D was more affected by this week end than I had ever seen her by all Mary's tiresomeness, and said she was getting too old to bustle about slaving for two young slips who thought such a lot of themselves . . . Pasley explained to me at great length that when he came up again to dine at All Souls he would not be able to stay with us, as he would have little enough time for dressing and going in and out. The Pasleys left me at the Plain to bus home and I walked . . .

A little wet snow was falling. Then came the cream of the day: to sit by our own fire, to chat and read, to have our own easily prepared and quickly despatched supper – all peaceful and delightful after the effort of these two days . . .

Tuesday 26 February: A bright morning that soon darkened and settled into a heavy fall of snow. I worked all morning on More, finishing his "Appendix to the Defence of the Philosophic Cabbala" (a tedious work) and beginning the *Defence of the Moral Cabbala*. We had lunch in the kitchen. Afterwards I wrote a short letter to Aunt Lily and walked in to the Schools where I visited the English Library and found Ward's *Life of Henry More*. I read it there for some time and then, taking it out, went to Robson-Scott in St John's St.

I found him alone. We talked of W. de la Mare, the only great Georgian. He agreed with me that the common view of de la Mare as the poet of faery and fantasy leaves out all one side and that the most important one. I was sorry to find that Robson had invited Bateson (whom I used to meet at the Discussion Class) and Ziman, both of whom soon joined us. A poor conversation. Bateson told us that Gadney the bookseller had gone mad – a fact which he and Ziman seemed to regard purely as a joke. We also condemned Saintsbury. I discovered that More – the lout whom I saw yawning in candidates faces at my English viva – is a friend of Wyld's: so that the latter's "*saeva rusticitas*" is apparently the badge of a school. Robson has two pupils whom he got through Carlyle.

I came away early and walked home. After supper I began trying to pick out a chronological framework from Ward, but it is nearly impossible. Last of all D and I fell into a talk about the bad year that is gone and all the bad years before it: but consoled outselves somehow and ended up fairly cheerfully . . .

Wednesday 27 February: A letter from my father this morning, answering my last, in which I had pointed out that my scholarship had now ceased and that I should need a little supplement to carry on. This question had been raised before. He replied with a long and pleasant letter with a sting in its tail: offering what was necessary, but saying that I had £30 extra expenses last year (which I cannot account for at all) and remarking that I can always put money in my pocket by spending more time at home. There comes the rub – this cannot be answered: yet to follow his suggestion would be nerves, loneliness and mental stagnation.[6]

I finished More's *Philosophical Works* this morning and made out

[6] Mr Lewis's letter to his son of 24th February has not survived, but in his diary for that day he said: "Wrote Jacks a long letter in reply to one from him asking for an increased allowance: 'What I shd. like is to have an annual sum fixed for the remainder of your stay at Oxford so that I shd. know where I am and what I must provide for. If instead of lodging £67 a term to your account I lodged £85 a term to cover everything, would that be sufficient? *You must be quite frank with me* etc. etc.'" *Lewis Papers*, vol. VIII, p. 186.

a table of chronology from Ward's *Life* and my old table done
for the English school. After lunch I went first to the Union where
I extracted several facts from the *Dictionary of National Biography*
subvoce More and then went to Wilson to borrow his *Theo-*
logical Works . . . In the evening I began *The Mythology of God-*
liness[7]. . .

Thursday 28 February: Worked all morning. As it was blowing with
"sharp scimitar" and getting ready to snow, I decided to skip my
provisional arrangement with Aunt Lily: I went out with Pat and
walked through Barton End and down the lane: then over fields to
Elsfield paths and up the edge of the big field and past the copse
where the stream comes out of it. The sky was very dark ahead of
me but I had some sunlight at my back which made a strange cold
brassy light on the bare fields. The thick mass of bullrushes etc. on
the edge of this copse made a great crackling. As I rounded it the
snow came, very light and slow but gliding almost horizontally. When
I turned round I saw Oxford in the sunlight. Came home past Mrs
Seymour's and through Old Headington. Worked for the rest of the
day on the *Mystery of Godliness*.

Friday 29 February: Worked on the *Mystery of Godliness* in
the morning. Did all that D would let me (which is to polish the
stove and sweep the kitchen and scullery) after lunch and then
went to Napier House to fetch Helen Rowell who is to spend
her half term week end with us. She is a nice child and very little
trouble, but for D's sake I wish it had not come so soon after the
Pasleys.

Shortly after tea, which was very late, I went up to dress,
preparatory to dining with Carritt . . . Those at dinner were Farquharson, Carritt, an American Dr Blake, the junior fellow (Bowen
I think) and an old member whose name I didn't catch. Before we
went in Farquharson approached me with some solemnity and asked
if I would enter my name in a list of people who would serve in the
next war. I replied at once "That depends Sir on who it is against
and what it is about."

At dinner Carritt put into my hand the notice of the vacancy at
Trinity – an official fellowship in Philosophy, worth £500 a year.
After dinner in the Common Room Farquharson became very
amusing indeed, telling us anecdotes of his boyhood.

[7] Henry More, *An Explanation of the Grand Mystery of Godliness* (1660).

As Carritt said when he and I were walking to Allen's digs in Holywell for the Philosophical Society, "F's talk has a peculiar flavour about it. It is very good – often better than it was tonight – and yet is always within an inch of being mere silliness." I suggested that the face had a lot to do with it. So it has: the great bird-like nose and forehead and the eyebrows and wrinkles arched up *"quasi enitentis"* like Vespasian.[8] At Allen's we found Ewing, Rink, Curtis, Ziman, Fasnacht, King and others.

Ziman read a poor paper on "Some Heresies". The discussion however was very good. Ziman had said that pleasure was always adjectival to the satisfaction of desire – desire being the instinct reflected upon. We challenged him on Plato's flower smells from the *Philebus*. He fell back upon unconscious or potential desire. This led to my usual move re potentiality. Then Carritt wanted to know what instinct really was. This led to Rink telling us about the wasp in Bergson, and Fasnacht caused great amusement by waiting till the whole story was over and then saying, "I'm very sorry but all those facts have been contradicted." Carritt said this was hardly fair in a philosophical society. We kept it up till about 11.15. I walked back to College with a nice man whose name I do not know.

Having got back my shoes from College I walked home, looking at the details of the Trinity fellowship as I passed the lamps. For some reason the possibility of getting it and all that would follow if I did came before my mind with unusual vividness. I saw it would involve living in and what a break up of our present life that would mean, and also how the extra money would lift terrible loads off us all. I saw that it would mean pretty full work and that I might become submerged and poetry crushed out.

With deep conviction I suddenly had an image of myself, God knows when or where, in the future looking back on these years since the war as the happiest or the only really valuable part of my life, in spite of all their disappointments and fears. Yet the longing for an income that wd. free us from anxiety was stronger than all these feelings. I was in a strange state of excitement – and all on the mere hundredth chance of getting it.

A dark night with a few stars, freezing, with a wind that would

---

[8] From memory of Suetonius, *Life of Emperor Vespasian*, xx: *"vulta veluti nitentis"* – "with an expression as if of one straining."

skin the bones. Before going to bed D and I had some talk about the Trinity job. She again urged me to try for an All Soul's Fellowship and thought that the D.Phil. was a mere waste of time. If only I could get an All Soul's Fellowship it certainly would save a great deal.[9]

---

[9] All Souls College was founded by Henry VI in 1438. It is unique in that it consists of a Warden and Fellows (originally 40), and no undergraduates. Lewis was thinking of the advantages of being able to enjoy a life of scholarship without having to teach.

Saturday 1 March: I spent most of the morning in the kitchen cutting turnips and peeling onions for D, and then went for an hour's walk in the fields. After lunch and jobs I took Euripides from his shelf for the first time this many a day, with some idea of reading a Greek play every week end (when I am not writing) so as to keep up my Greek. I began the *Heracleidae.* Coming back to Greek tragedy after so long an absence I was greatly impressed with its stiffness and rumness and also thought the choruses strangely prosaic. The effort to represent a scuffle between Iolaus and the Herald is intolerably languid. After the first shock, however, I enjoyed it.

Its noble matter of factness is really the great thing. Macaria, unless I read more into her than the poet meant, is a really well conceived character. She sees at once the *real* position which everyone else has hushed up, and even that her party will be ridiculous if no one steps into the lead: she knows that someone has got to make the offer and does it with very little fuss. There is no attempt to sentimentalise her: there is a sort of cold impatience in most of her speeches − as there probably is about martyrs in real life. But I wonder if Euripides meant it so, or is he merely trying to find motives for an altruism wh. he has seen in life but has no theory to account for . . . ?

Tuesday 4 March: After breakfast I walked into town. I went to the library in College and looked up in Paley three passages in the *Heracleidae* that had baffled me. Paley emended one of them and "supplied" words and sentences to the other two. How easy it is to translate anything on these terms!

I then walked to New Inn Hall Street. Raymond alias Herr Steinshen (whom may the prophets utterly reject) has coolly sent us there to see about some rates which have been sent in to him for the second time. Loose, the tax gatherer, said it was simply a mistake and promised to write to Raymond . . .

By great ill chance, I met Aunt Lily. I followed her into Buols where she was lunching and talked to her till her food came. She has just (for the seventh or eighth time) discovered the secret of creation.

It has something to do with wave lengths. She has also discovered that there is no such thing as matter but only energy: and since mind and matter are both unknown energies therefore they must be the same thing. In about ten minutes she poured forth as many misleading metaphors, paralogisms, and downright contradictions as would have made Socrates happy for a twelvemonth. Is she mad – or is this only what every active mind must come to if left without dialectical discipline? . . .

After lunch I went for a walk with Pat. It was a bright day with a blue sky full of large slow moving clouds . . . I walked along to the Horsepath lane and met Ewing with Price, who got the Fellowship I tried for at Magdalen. I had always thought that Price was the little beetle faced Jew whom I constantly see about and was glad to find my mistake, for the real Price seems a pleasant fellow . . .

Afterwards I went on with the *Hippolytus* – splendid stuff. I wish I knew how Euripides meant the Nurse to be taken. Some of the things she says are sublime: others appear comic to us – I fancy only because we are not simple and matter of fact enough . . .

Wednesday 5 March: I returned to Henry More this morning with considerable reluctance and went on for a little with the *Mystery of Godliness*. It had no flavour about it.

Every since my conversation with D about the wisdom of a D.Phil. I have been in an unsettled state. I reflected that the degree itself would be no passport to a living and that while I worked at my old mooncalf [the thesis on Henry More], tho' I might learn a great deal about the 17th century, I should be letting my Greek and my philosophy slip, and be losing, in part, my qualifications for any work that might come along. On the other hand if I read hard in history, philosophy, English and Greek, I should be keeping myself in readiness for anything and increasing my chance of an All Souls fellowship. However small that chance might be, *non temptasse nocet.*[1] So at last I made my decision and shut up my wormy folio of mooncalf. For the rest of the morning I read through again my "Promethean Fallacy". It is more intelligible and, on the whole, more cogent than I thought: but not so well written (in the literary sense) as I had hoped.

After lunch I walked into town and to the English library to return Ward's *Life of More*. Simpson, with another man, was sitting at the

---

[1] "Not to have tried does harm."

desk and told me I would have a notice fining me half a crown for the book. I said "And if the notice does not arrive Sir, I presume the half crown – ." SIMPS: "The half crown remains." He very nearly gave me 10/- short in my change, but I watched him carefully for he is a great scholar.

Hence to the Union where I studied the Ordnance Survey map of the Bookham district – having been lately haunted (as I am every now and then) by an acute memory of my excellent walks "in that delightful land". I would give a good deal for a fortnight's stay there . . .

I also looked into the *Girdle of Aphrodite* – a new book of translations from the *Anthology*, very good: and then into G.K. Chesterton's *Life of St Francis* – the chapter about naturalism and what it led to among the pagans, wh. I thought pretty true: tho' whether Christianity made any immediate difference on the masses is not so clear . . .

Thursday 6 March: I spent the whole morning composing a long and difficult letter to my father.[2] . . .

I walked into town and went to the library in College. I looked into G.K. Chesterton's *Browning* – a thoroughly bad book, full of silly generalisations. There is nothing in his chapter on *The Ring and the Book* to show that he has read it. I then looked into Noyes' *William Morris* – the chapter on *Jason*. I should not have thought it possible that in half an hour I could have read so much new truth about a poet I know so well. It gave me the very feel of Morris – more than Morris himself.

When I came out of the dark library (at about 4) the air was wonderfully bright and soft in colour. It was like a summer evening at six o'clock. The stone seemed softer everywhere, the birds were singing, the air was deliciously cold and rare. I got a sort of eerie

---

[2] Lewis was replying to his father's letter of the 24th February, which reply is found in the *Lewis Papers*, vol. VIII, pp. 193-5. After going into detail about his many small expenses he said: "You ask me whether £85 a term to 'cover everything' would be sufficient. If by 'covering everything' you mean covering my books, shoes, shirts, socks and other items that I have hitherto sent you, I am afraid it would not. As I said, if you wish it, I will try to undertake my own books in the future, and, at any rate to cut them down . . . If on the other hand you see fit to lodge £85 a term and to pay for such extras in the way of clothing etc. as may occur, I will try to make them as little as I can . . .

"I have made a change in my work. I started work experimentally on Dr Henry More – a 17th Century theologian – with the idea of 'doing' him for a D.Phil . . . I had not however gone very far in this naïf wonderland without deciding that I was on a fool's errand. The D.Phil. would add very little to my Firsts in the way of qualification: and in the mean time I should be letting my knowledge of philosophy and above all my Greek rust. I have determined instead to go on vigorously improving my philosophy and classics and also to learn some history – history being the gate to an All Souls fellowship."

unrest and dropped into the real joy. Never have I seen Oxford look better. It looked as it used to when I saw it in my cadet days and used to long for it to be a University town again. I took two or three turns up and down the Broad. Although it is only a few hours old I see that this is already becoming transfigured by memory into something that never was anywhere and never could have been.

I then went to Manchester (after going into Mansfield by mistake) and with some difficulty found my way to the room where the Postgraduates' Philosophical Group were meeting. There were only three there when I arrived: a nonentity, a chinless parson who talked in a kind of gobble and a very beefy man with a face black from shaving and very moist lips who crooned in his voice and was inclined to shut his eyes when he talked. They talked about Troeltsch.[3]

Presently Price came in and then a man in gold rimmed spectacles who had negroid hair and skin but the features of a sheep. His trousers were very well creased and he was called "Mr Jones". He never spoke but to say "Good afternoon". Then Stout came in – a funny looking little man with a whimsical way of talking that was very attractive.[4] Tea and bread and butter were brought: and Stout produced some cakes unexpectedly from a paper bag. He told us a good story of a female solipsist who had written to Bertrand Russell – "Dear Mr Russell, I am so glad you have become a solipsist. I have always wondered that there were not more of us." Ross of Oriel came in and I was introduced to him.[5] As there had been some hitch about tea we were very late in starting.

I read my "Hegemony [of Moral Values]" paper. At one point Stout, not having heard, interrupted me to ask "What was the subject of that sentence?" I imagined for a wild moment that he was going to ask what was the subject of this paper.

During the adjournment the beefy man came and crooned Browning at me. Then Stout said "Order, Order" and we all sat down. Ross opened the discussion. He was very complimentary about my paper. Part of what he said may be discounted as the usual courtesy bow, but what really pleased me was that he said "Mr Lewis explains

[3] Ernst Troeltsch (1865–1923), theologian and philosopher, was Professor of the History of Philosophy and Civilisation at Berlin from 1915 to 1923.

[4] Alan Ker Stout (1900–83) took his BA from Oriel College in 1922 after which he became a Research Scholar. He was Lecturer in Philosophy at University College of North Wales 1924–34, and Professor of Philosophy at the University of Sydney 1939–65.

[5] William David Ross (1877–1971) was Fellow in Philosophy at Oriel College 1902–29, and White's Professor of Moral Philosophy 1923–8.

the precedence of moral good in a very ingenious way which I really think is quite new – and, at first sight at any way [rate?], I find it attractive."

What was even better, when we were breaking up I overheard him saying to someone else "That was *new*." We had not much time for discussion and what there was was poor. The Beefy Man shut his eyes more tightly than ever and talked absolutely off the point. Stout made some good remarks. As we left, Ross asked me if I was going to publish it. I said that I certainly would if I had any chance. He advised me to send it to *Mind* or *The Hibbert*: *The Hibbert* would pay more, but *Mind* was the better thing . . .

Friday 7 March: Worked on the *Hippolytus* in the morning and just before lunch looked into Gilbert Murray's *Greek Epic* – a great piece of imaginative work which I like as much as ever in spite of its detractors.

After lunch Ewing called for me and we walked over Shotover and thence by Horsepath and Cowley to his digs in Iffley Road where we had tea. It was a beautiful sunny day with a blue mist on the valley and I would have enjoyed it had I been alone or in congenial company. We spoke of Ziman's paper. I said I didn't think much of it. Ewing replied, "One mustn't expect too much of an undergraduate paper." We spoke of Kant. I said I had not read him since Greats. Ewing tittered and said, "I look back with horror on the ideas I had of Kant when I took Greats."

I found that Ewing (who was unfit for active service) had also been approached about the next war, but I was flattered to find that Farquharson had dealt with him and me rather differently, asking me simply if I would serve and pointing out to Ewing that if he would put his name down for civil service he would be safe from being put into work "unsuitable for him" if conscription came in . . .

Saturday 8 March: D waked me suddenly this morning saying "You'll have to get up at once." It turned out to be a card from Carritt asking me whether I could dine on Monday to meet Prichard and needing an immediate answer.[6] I jumped up, flung some clothes on, wrote an acceptance, and ran to the post . . . There was also a card from Barfield asking me to meet him outside the Cadena at 11.0 today . . .

[6] Mr Carritt was anxious for Lewis to meet Harold Arthur Prichard (1871–1947) who was the Philosophy Fellow of Trinity College 1898–1924. Prichard was later White's Professor of Moral Philosophy 1928–37, and he was already well known for his *Kant's Theory of Knowledge* (1909) and an influential paper, "Does Moral Philosophy Rest on a Mistake?" (*Mind*, 1912).

I went to the Cadena and waited. Just there, and at that time of a sunny morning, one sees the worst of Oxford – the splendid children with "plus fours" and long cigarette holders, walking insolently and talking loudly with the intention of being overheard, and the corresponding girls.

After I had waited for half an hour I found Fasnacht at my elbow. We began to talk philosophy. He was very sceptical and almost an "instantaneous solipsist" tho' he denied it. After a little Rink came past with a bicycle and joined us. He told us about the paper he had written for the Jowett. He had tried to combine a sort of Bergsonian view of reality wh. was "not harmonious nor rational" with a separate "knowable" such as we find in mathematics. I said this left out the fact that mathematics did conform to experience wherever the nature of the case allowed them to touch it and that this was in fact the reason why we called them true.

A policeman came past and told Rink to take his bicycle off the pavement. We, as good Heracliteans, told Rink not to worry since it was impossible to step twice into the same policeman and the bicycle was already off the pavement. He preferred to act in the vulgar sense. Our argument continued and was at its height when an enormous man with a white moustache appeared behind Rink. Rink told us in a whisper, "This is the greatest bore in Oxford and I know he is going to catch my eye" and continued edging his nose into the middle of us and keeping his back to the big man, explaining the while that tho' the sense datum of two marbles plus the sense datum of two more marbles gave the datum of four marbles, none of them were really marbles in the conceptual sense.

The big man however edged round and round and finally plucked him by the sleeve saying in a hearty voice "I have three tickets for *Katinka* and I don't know how to get rid of them so I'm going about like a fairy godmother" – at this moment I saw Barfield's face in the distance and fled.

He had missed his train from Long Crendon and biked, calling at "Hillsboro". We put his bike into the Union and walked into St John's garden. We talked of the function of the Greek chorus, of Squire (in spite of all, Barfield advises me to send up "Dymer" when it is done), of Henry More and of the difference between Dionysiac and Apolline art.

He had got from some book the idea of Dionysiac as mere wish fulfilment. I tried to formulate my own very different view, but was defeated on particulars, since whenever he asked me in which class I put a particular work I had to say "Oh, Dionysiac of course – well no, perhaps it is really Apolline" or the like. This led to some talk about Steiner's "polarity". Barfield has given up the chance of a permanent £500 a year on the staff of *Truth* in order to have leisure for his own work. We lunched at the Cadena where his wife, who had been giving a music lesson, joined us. After lunch we did some shopping all together and then separated to meet again in Wadham gardens.

I took Alexander's *Space, Time and Deity* out of the Union and went to Wadham where I sat and walked in the garden reading the introduction, enjoying the beauty of the place, and greatly interested by my author's truthful antithesis of enjoyment and contemplation.

When the others turned up we had some talk about memories of childhood and then went to tea at Yeats' tea rooms. I promised to come over for the night on Thursday week, and so left them after a thoroughly enjoyable day . . .

Monday 10 March: In the morning I read some more of Alexander, who grows more and more difficult as I proceed. I also started tentatively an essay on the "Whole" which I thought might be a more systematic exposition of my theory of potentiality.

After lunch came a letter from Pasley to say that he had dined with Baker at Beckett's and the former had tackled him about me. Pasley had replied as vaguely as possible and tells me that I must expect a letter from Baker.

Ever since the Doc's death, when we heard nothing of him, our friendship has been suspended. Unfortunately, tho' his silence on occasion was the efficient cause of the present break, my coolness, thus occasioned, was retrospective. For a long time I had been troubled by his egoism and his hardly hidden contempt of D and everyone else he met in our house. Irrespective of D's wishes I really do not want to in any way renew my intimacy with him: but how to answer his letter when it comes, I cannot imagine. D and I had a good deal of talk about it. She urged me, and of course sincerely, not to consider her feeling about him, but that is only one chapter in the story . . .

I went to Senior Common Room where I met Carlyle who promised to write to the Trinity people about me. Carritt soon came in, "undressed" because Prichard (who soon followed him) was also so. Prichard is a little weak-looking man with a straw coloured moustache. It was a very dull evening. Carlyle talked all the time about India and South Africa: and even in the pauses I failed to get into any sort of conversational touch with Prichard. Poor Carritt!

Wednesday 12 March: ... As my old flannel trousers have worn beyond shabbiness to indecency, I have to wear my ex-best brown suit whenever I go out now and it chafes me ...

After lunch I went to Headington cross roads and waited for the Aylesbury bus to take me out to Aunt Lily's. As soon as I was on board I asked the conductor where I should get down for Lower Farm. He didn't know where it was. I explained that "Lower Farm, Thame Road" was the full postal address: whereupon a very respectable white whiskered man of the small farmer class exclaimed to the conductor, "Why, Jarge, don't you know - it is that old girl who lives all alone." "*That* old girl!" said the conductor. "Yes, that'll be the place," said I. The white whiskered man said "You'll have a job to get in there when you do get down": and explained to the passengers in general that I was going to see "The old girl who lives all alone with them cats".

The bus was very hot and very unsteady. After a while the conductor came and sat down beside me, producing a cigarette from behind his ear and remarking "There's one thing about that old girl, she's a very good sort."

SELF: "Oh yes. She has her little peculiarities but she's very decent."
COND.: "That's right. I know her very well. There's a cat of hers I was taking in and out to the vet every day for a while. But I don't know how she sticks it, living there all alone."
SELF: "She's very busy. She spends all her time writing."
COND.: "I suppose she'd be very clever then?"
SELF: "Oh yes, very."

We then had some further talk about his job and about the strike they had some time ago. When I left the bus I was struck by the "sweet sudden silence" on the lonely strip of road, the clear blue sunshine and the pale, almost white beauty of the fields.

Aunt Lily came out to meet me – looking, in spite of differences, strangely like what I remember of my mother. Her cottage is now furnished and very pleasant inside. The walls of her sitting room are entirely covered with prints – mostly of the early Italians. She talked of the "incredible folly" of the Socialists' last proposal of giving full

unemployment pay to every child that left school – as if this were
not simply to encourage all the worst to breed like rabbits. I heartily
agreed with her. We had a very rambling talk – touching hardly at
all on the subjects of our recent rather fierce controversies by letter.
She said that she found *Lear* too painful to read. We talked of
Meredith, of inspiration, and of Mr Allen. She mentioned as
something that had often been in her mind, the fact that we cannot
be sure that consciousness really ceases in what we call a dead body.

She showed me the three prints which she had long since destined
for me. The two smaller ones are a head unknown and a head of
Vergil: the larger is Giotto's Francis before Honorius. She is giving
me this one because she says Honorius is a portrait of me. I could
easily see what she meant, and to look at my pre-natal portrait was
a very strange experience.[7] As I could not take all three, it was
arranged that I should take this one today and come back for the
other two.

It is certainly a magnificent . . . present. I am only partially able
to appreciate such things – I can get the satisfying, unwearying
decorative effect and the sentimental pleasure and a little of the naïf
pleasure in the mere seeing things wh. the people for whom they
were painted had in them. Perhaps a fuller appreciation will come
when I have lived with them. Just before I left we fell into a close
argument on the Self, wh. she considers capable of actual coalescing
with other selves or with Spirit.

I came home holding my picture on my knees: it was so high that
I cd. not see over it . . . Poor D had a bad head again tonight. Early
to bed, dog tired.

Thursday 13 March: . . . I . . . bussed into College to the Philosophical Society. In Ware's beautifully panelled room I found Ware
(who turns out to be the man I walked home with from Allen's the
other night) and King.[8] The latter has just started reading *The Crock
of Gold* and is pleased tho' puzzled with it. Carritt, Ewing, Price of
Magdalen, Rink, Ziman, Fasnacht, Curtis and several others came
in. Carritt read a paper on the "Moral Faculty": it was rather
disconnected and hard to follow. He seemed tired and abstracted.

In the interval I had some good talk with Price, mainly about the

---

[7] The picture now [1933] hangs in Clive's rooms in Magdalen College; the Honorius is remarkably like
Clive as he was in 1924. – W.H.L.

[8] Robert Remington Ware and Richard Henry King read Greats at University College and took their BAs
in 1925.

distinction of essence and existence, with a digression on Croce's aesthetics. We look at things from rather similiar standpoints. I should like to see more of this man. He opened the discussion in a style that amused me – it was so characteristically Oxfordish and donnish. Perhaps he will outgrow it. He took up (I think only for dialectical purposes) the line that the distinction between willing, judging etc., was only "sophistication": that when one said one was hungry one simply contemplated attractive food without "enjoying" in Alexander's sense, the act of wanting it. This led to some good discussion.

Later on I trotted out my "antinomy of the practical reason" which also gave good sport between Allen, Ziman, Rink, and myself. Came away at 11.20 and walked home by moonlight in half an hour . . .

Friday 14 March: I spent most of the morning at my essay on the Whole, trying to tackle the question of *essentia* and *exisentia*. After lunch I washed up while D washed Maureen's hair.

Later on I played croquet with Maureen for the first time this year, greatly to the excitement of Pat who regards the slow rolling and resonant balls with a religious feeling . . .

Sunday 16 March: Poor D had a very uneasy night and was still suffering from sickness and headache this morning.

After breakfast I set off at once and, finding no bus, walked to All Souls. It was a delicious morning with the road sparkling between the long shadows and no mist visible *per se* but a faint blueness and haziness over the more distant trees. The High in all its early emptiness, cleanness, light and space was a thing to make a man shout.

I went up to Sir John Simon's rooms (very good oak panelling) wh. Beckett uses and waited there reading Russell's *Icarus* till Beckett turned up from breakfasting elsewhere, followed shortly afterwards by Harwood. We were all, I hope, delighted to meet, and soon set out on our walk.

We went under the railway bridge and thence to Ferry Hinksey. I discovered that Beckett had been a brass hat in the war, first in Macedon and later in the Caucasus where he had a military government and was really a satrap and even condemned a man to death – who escaped. From Hinksey we struck into fields and went up the hill dropping down to where the three factory chimneys are, into Cumnor and so by the Long Leas down to Bablock Hythe. There was no good *talk*, but excellent chat all the way. At Bablock Hythe we sat down on the grass this side of the river and talked more at large of *Hassan* and whether the cinema could ever become an art: but the "clop-clop" of the choppy water and the sunlight are more memorable.

After some time we went on to Stanton Harcourt where we were to lunch. Before we reached it the sun suddenly disappeared and the sky got white and a cold wind sprang up. In the inn parlour we consumed large quantities of bread and cheese and draft cider. Harwood found a delightful book here – a *History of Rome* "related in conversations by a father to his children with instructive comments". The children made such comments as "How pleasing is filial piety, Papa!" and "My dear Sir, surely you have been too indulgent in describing the vices of Honorius as weakness."

Afterwards we went into the bar (delightfully warm after the tomb-like parlour) where Beckett talked to a discontented farmer about co-operation in a masterly manner which showed the budding man of affairs.

After investigating the church we walked back, pretty fast, and arrived for tea in Beckett's rooms after about 15 miles of walking. I was rather footsore.

During tea Beckett talked of his mysterious colleague Lawrence. He started the Hejaz business and got a job in the Foreign Office, which he held for a time, refusing to take any salary, but soon dropped it. He then took his Fellowship, but again refused the money and hung about All Souls, never dining in Hall, and haunting the Common Room of evening in ordinary clothes, talking very well when he did talk, but far more often silent. Now he has gone back to the army as an infantry private soldier under an assumed name. He is believed to have no private means to speak of: no man is intimate with him.[9]

I then asked Beckett for advice and information about an All Souls Fellowship. I find that it is only £200 a year and that you can never sleep anywhere else in Oxford while you hold it. This pretty well spoils it for me. He said I would have been "almost certain" to get it after Greats, but that my age was now rather against me. On the whole however he spoke optimistically. He thought that Pasley had v. little chance of it. I said that Pasley was "dead": Beckett

---

[9] This is T.E. Lawrence, whom Lewis met in All Souls on 11 August 1922. In September 1922 Lawrence joined the RAF, changing his name to T.E. Shaw.

said that he thought him "still struggling – struggling very hard".

I left them and bussed home. D still feeling pretty rotten but not so bad as in the morning. It was unfortunate that old Taylor should select this evening to visit us, tho' otherwise we should have been glad to see him. He stayed to supper and the conversation ranged over all things.

Monday-Tuesday 17-25 March: During this time it was unfortunate that my first spring flood of "Dymer" should coincide with a burst of marmalade making and spring cleaning on D's part which led without intermission into packing. I managed to get in a good deal of writing in the intervals of jobbing in the kitchen and doing messages in Headington. I wrote the whole of a last canto with considerable success, tho' the ending will not do. I also kept my temper nearly all the time. Domestic drudgery is excellent as an alternative to idleness or to hateful thoughts – which is perhaps poor D's reason for piling it on at this time: as an alternative to the work one is longing to do and able to do (*at that time* and heaven knows when again) it is maddening. No one's fault: the curse of Adam.

Wednesday 26 March: Up early and finished packing. We set off by taxi at 11.30 with our two cats and Pat and all the rest. We had a very good journey. A "jolly" person of the usual professional buffoon type travelled with us to Wantage Road. He knows Cranny and told us a delightful yarn of Cranny saying to him in his queer brogue gobble "You know I've been over here so long now that no one would think I was Irish."

We got to Clevedon[10] much earlier than we had hoped for and found Edie at the flat, who had been working like a slave or a saint to get all snug for us and had brought us edible presents enough to feed a garrison. I was delighted with the flat. As you walk into the sitting room you are faced with a window which gives you an oblong of pure sea and sky with nothing else at all. As you come nearer to it, it is spoiled by the usual pier below: yet the pier is not so vulgar as might be feared, and the little Japanese pavilion on the end is almost pretty at times. During tea Edie told us a lot about Willie and Carrie. Poor Edie, she is very run down and her rapid conversation is quite incoherent and rather reminiscent of Miss Bates's "That would be so very – " in *Emma*.

---

[10] This is a seaside town west of Bristol in Somerset. Lewis and the Moores were spending a holiday in Mary Askins' flat in "Osborne House", Elton Road, Clevedon while she was in the United States.

Lateish to bed, v. well pleased with everything. D and I both suffering from colds and coughs.

Thursday 27 March: . . . I went eastward and had almost begun to despair of ever escaping the residential streets beyond Dial Hill when suddenly as in a vision the whole thing, so to speak, fell to pieces before me. Ahead was a smooth grassed down with a ruined castle on top – Walton Castle they call it. To my right was a long level bank of wooded hill with a sudden sheer gorge through whose V shape I could see the inland country, flat as a table and blue with distance. I scrambled up the green hill to my left, which is occupied by a golf links and open to all men: that is the one good thing I know of golfers, that they keep stretches of fine country from being spoiled.

After a stiff climb over spongy, rabbitty grass with grey stone showing through here and there, I reached the castle. Its appearance and position are more like a boy's dream of a mediaeval castle than anything I have ever seen. After I had walked all over the shaved turf of the courtyard and been into the roofless keep and watched the clouds hurrying across the circle of open sky at the top, I came out into the wind again and continued my walk on a path which runs along the very top of this long hill, so that I had a good view of the valleys on each side . . .

Thence by road to my left till I struck the coast and began coming homewards across fields that sloped down through gorse to the water's edge. In a field inhabited by two horses and a donkey (they all moved together at intervals, carefully synchronising movements) I ran down nearly to the rocks and sat down for a moment amid the gorse. I was out of the wind. The sun grew hot. A big tramp was anchored just below me. I have seldom had a better moment . . .

Friday 28 March: My cough was so bad this morning and my temperature so far below normal that I took a day in bed. I ate enormous meals, read a good deal in an English translation of Goethe's *Dichtung und Wahrheit* – wh. I began to read in the original with Kirk a long time ago. It was rather charming. I also read Thoreau's essay on Walking and his really noble speeches on John Brown: but I can't quite say what it is that is wrong with all that Bostonese set. I tried the *White Doe of Rylstone* and found the first canto really delightful, the second tolerable and the next unreadable.

In the evening I collapsed into George Moore's *Confessions of a Young Man*. It may have merits of style to which I am insensible. In *matter* it is just the idea which any eightyish, Frenchified prig of an undergraduate would like to have of himself. In fact one cannot read it impersonally. I have met so many people exactly like George Moore and they bore and irritate me in life or in "confessions" equally. In other words the book produced just that effect wh. the author wanted it to have on people like me. But it doesn't follow that the laugh is on his side.

Saturday 29 March: . . . In the morning I did odd jobs and then, at D's suggestion, that it would please Edie, I walked along to the church to look at the Doc's grave. It is of course a kind of office to the dead which I would never pay to anyone of my own free will – "wherefore all this wormy circumstance?" It was a morning of bright sunlight and wind. The church between its two cliff hills is certainly beautiful: though the glaring ugliness of the grave stones – the crosses, the scrolls, and the female angels – rather spoils it.

Home and to lunch. Afterwards Maureen and I walked up past the post office and along a really delightful road to Strawberry Hill . . . In the little village at the bottom Maureen and Pat left me and I went on alone up the wooded side of the next hill. After a delightful ascent through thick and steep woods I came out on to a level and rabbitty place dotted with gorse and clusters of trees, with a long green path on the ridge of the hill. I followed this. On my left lay the long valley which divided me from Walton Castle and its beautiful roll of Downs: on my right a flat plain stretching out to low, but peaked, blue hills a long way off. I passed a horse that whinnied at me and rolled on its back . . .

Sunday 30 March: . . . I . . . walked out along Highdale Road past Strawberry Hill and from East Clevedon up the Court Hill. Here I spent a long time wandering in and out of the woods all round this end of the hill. The sun came out when I was at the top: the sun broke out and suddenly changed the whole landscape – the pointed tree tops of the further woods jutting out like needles where they had been flat a moment before. I became every minute more enamoured of this country. The steepness of the slopes on which I scrambled, the trees hiding the ground below me, and the suddenness of my changing views of the valleys all produced, in little space, a real mountain feeling. *Sed omnia nisi vigilaveris in venerem abitura.*[11]

Home for a late tea and afterwards all three of us to call on Miss Rimington whom Mary calls "Dogs" – a pleasant old lady with seven

---

[11] "But everything, unless you are vigilant, will go off into sex."

cats who all have biblical names as Peter, Moses and the like. We found her in a room overlooking the sea from which we watched a fine, tho' frosty sunset. We came home by a delightful path above the sea, all enjoying it, and had a kingly supper of sausages, fried tomatoes and chips. In the evening I worked on "Dymer".

Tuesday 1 April: . . . After my jobs I finished fair copying the canto which will stand last in "Dymer" when he is finished and pleased myself greatly over it.

I then began *David Copperfield*. I read part of it at Wynyard about 1910 and I find I remember a good deal. I can remember too how much grimmer the Salem House parts were when I myself was at a school not at all unlike it . . .

Afterwards I went out alone. I walked up towards the Castle and down between the quarries and across the valley. I climbed the Court Hill range at the place beyond the lodge where I came down the other day and continued along the top by the telegraph posts. Huge clouds kept rolling up from the Bristol direction and I was alternately met by sleety rain and by bursts of brilliant sunshine – during which the grass and moss on the downs assumed a more jewel like glittering green than I ever saw in my life. Once I had to take refuge in a small wood. I reached Cadbury camp wh., as a camp, is not to be compared to the Malvern one. But the landscape from there is wonderful: the Welsh hills (now much closer), the channel, Avonmouth and more hills, and a valley flat as a pancake reaching to the Mendips on my right. The blues and the pale, pale almost yellow greens and the reds were almost unimaginable – and changing every minute with the movement of the clouds.

I came home along the hills all the way in great delight and, arriving at 10 to 6, found the flat empty and had tea alone. Read *David Copperfield* till suppertime and after. At suppertime D was called down to speak to a Mrs Clarke who lives in the flat below. We call her and her little daughter the Gollywogs on account of their quite unprecedented coiffure . . .

Saturday 5 April: By this morning's post came a letter from Wilkinson giving me some examining work in July – God be praised:[1] also the

---

[1] Cyril Hackett Wilkinson (1888–1960), Vice-Provost of Worcester College 1920–47, was the Oxford Secretary of the Oxford and Cambridge Schools Examination Board and the one to whom Lewis was answerable regarding the School Certificates.

proofs of "Joy" from *The Beacon*.[2] After breakfast I returned the proofs, replied to Wilkinson and wrote to Carritt for a testimonial, and also did my ordinary jobs.

In the afternoon I walked with Maureen up to Walton Castle and into the wood beyond it where I dawdled about (very little bored considering) while she picked primroses and white violets. There are so few in the woods this year that it seems wanton to take them. We then went down into Walton-in-Gordano and came home by the shore path. It was sunny and very warm out of the wind and we sat down for some time in my lately discovered alcove. After tea the others went to the churchyard: I was glad I did not know in the wood for what purpose these flowers were being picked.

I walked down into the squalid streets beyond the station to interview the gas people, and to explain that Mary was in America and would pay her bill when she came back in May. D had been afraid that they might suddenly cut off our gas for her sins. Much warmer tonight.

Sunday 6 April: For the first time since we came there was no wind blowing this morning. The channel was glassy smooth, tapering away into mist with no horizon line: and there was sunlight everywhere tho' slightly blunted by mist, and promising a warm day.

After usual jobs (i.e. "run" with Pat before breakfast, fetching earth for the cats, cleaning the bath and cleaning potatoes) I sat in the front room. I did a few minutes' work on a new Canto VII of "Dymer" and looked into Mrs Browning's *Sonnets from the Portuguese*. They looked very good and I felt not the slightest inclination to read one of them to the end. Spent the rest of the morning over *The Sunday Times* and *David Copperfield*. The Dora parts are odious . . .

D had said at lunchtime "Do let's have tea in good time today" and as I wished particularly, and have wished all along, to get her out earlier before the sunlight is gone, I cut my walk short and was home soon after four. D however was writing letters when I arrived and we did not have tea for over an hour. Afterwards we all went out and D dropped in to say a few words to Miss Rimington. Maureen, Pat and I sat on the wooded bank opposite for about half an hour until the sun had set and it had grown chilly. When D at

---

[2] "Joy" was published in *The Beacon*, vol. III (May 1924), pp. 444-51. This was probably the first work Lewis published about "Joy" as intense longing, the experience that was to become the subject of *Surprised by Joy*.

last reappeared I discovered that she and "Dogs" had been talking on that perennial subject, the selfishness of Grace and Rob and the sufferings of Edie . . .

Tuesday 8 April: A windy morning. After fetching clay for the cats and fetching a pail of salt water for Maureen's foot from the shore – there are forty steps to this flat – I went to Rowles the coal merchant and finding that they cd. not send today, carried home the third part of a hundred-weight on my back. D had decided to go into Bristol today, so we had lunch almost as soon as I had finished coal heaving. Maureen says I remind her of Christian with his burden in Bunyan. She and D departed after lunch and I washed up . . .

I had some tea and set to work on "Dymer" and pleased myself fairly well, tho' I now think I was writing rubbish. I had finished *David Copperfield* earlier in the day. I am rather glad to be quit of it. I think the bad parts outweigh the good. The set funniness of Micawber etc. is very mechanical and really I think fit only for children. The really good parts are the semi-funny little trivialities and the town scenery – but the storm is good. What a pity that it is but the overture to such claptrap!

I read some of Alice Meynell's essays – v. good indeed – and then started to put up curtains in the kitchen. The others came back before I had finished. A flat is the worst place to be alone in and our cheerful supper and evening was a pleasant contrast.

Wednesday 9 April: . . . It was a day of bright sunshine alternating with sleety showers. I walked by road to Walton-in-Gordano and up the hill beyond it. I was then at once in unknown country and owing to the curve of the hill could not see far ahead. I was under as bright a sky of blue and white as I have ever seen. On my right hand I saw a succession of ridges like waves – their intervening valleys being invisible – getting bluer as they receded to the horizon and giving a feeling of enormous space.

Once again I was impressed with the almost dreamlike brightness of the landscape – the transparent arsenic green of the grass, the bright red of the clay. My little circle of hilltop horizon advanced as I moved and the scattered beginning of a wood began to come up above it. I passed through the outskirts into a little red path with the trees very close on each side – winding every minute so that I could never tell what I was coming to. The intense silence (once broken by a jay) increased my excitement. The path gradually led me to my left and out of the wood across a field on to the Portishead Road.

Here I saw a splendid sight. The nearer half of the channel was in brilliant sunshine and in it lay a big tramp steamer with all its shadows very sharply picked out. About a mile beyond it was a huge dust coloured cloud with very ragged edges, in the very act of stumbling face forward into the water: and behind it the Welsh coast, miraculously near, with woods and the divisions of fields visible as never before. The wind was already tearing round me and the sand banks in mid channel had a white cud of foam round them.

I walked along the Portishead Rd. till I found another running inland to my right, up which I turned. As I got over the crest of the hill I had a sudden view of the hills and valleys ahead, all chaotic from this new angle – and suggesting much bigger valleys between them than there actually are.

By now the first scudding rain was going past me. Presently I came to a notice "To the White Harte Inn" and just here I found a ruined cottage where I took shelter. There was no roof left. One gable was thickly overgrown with ivy and there were brambles in the opposite corner. I got a very comfortable seat in the fireplace. The rain turned to snow. The whole thing – the rushing wind, the view of an old orchard framed in one of the empty windows, the ducks at the bottom of the orchard, and the big flakes of snow drifting over my feet while I sat in the greatest comfort – all might have been arranged to suit my taste down to the smallest detail. The snow melted as soon as it fell. After about a quarter of an hour the sun came out as bright as ever.

The various delights of my walk home – through Weston-in-Gordano, up hill to the same wood I started in and home by the sea path, are too long to describe. All was as good as can be anywhere or any time: and for the whole afternoon I was soaked in mere seeing and free from all thought and wish . . .

Thursday 10 April: Jobs and diary writing in the morning. I read through "Dymer" VIII[3] and was more satisfied than when I wrote it . . .

Edie was down today and went with D and Maureen to the churchyard. She had not time to come in for tea – tho' I saw them all talking at the door for a space that would have done me for tea. D and Maureen went out again after tea.

I sat in the front room working at "Dymer" VII – rather more

---

[3] i.e. IX. – C.S.L.

successfully than before but not really well. I have always assumed that I could go back to my romantic Avalon-Hesperides-Western business whenever I wanted. Now that I need it I find it difficult . . .

Friday 11 April: . . . Had a walk on the hill beyond Walton. In the wood full of sorrel, where I met a cock pheasant, I had a wonderful moment of indefinable memories. I began Nietzsche's *Beyond Good and Evil.*

Saturday 12 April: Jobs in the morning. After lunch I set in and made a fresh start on "Dymer" VII – this time much more hopefully. There was rain and a wonderful stormy sky all day . . .

More Nietzsche. So far there is nothing new about it - just what the ordinary egoist has always believed and acted on. I had a dream last night. I went out with W and saw a moon about the size of a cathedral rolling rapidly along the sky. Tho' shining intensely, it cast no light on the landscape which remained a perfect black blank, except for the silhouettes that came up in succession against the moving moon. There were ruins, spars of rock and crosses. We were climbing among pits and broken things. I was given to understand that it was the end of the world and there was a great sense of sublimity and awe about it all.

Sunday 13 April: Today the house was turned upside down in the morning to prepare for the arrival of Ruth and Willie. After lunch I went out with Pat and got soaked with rain, tho' sheltering for a long time in a delightful cave on the shore. Home and found the guests already here. The rest of the day is a nightmare of greasy washing up, never ceasing voices, wet clothes, headache, housemaid's jobs, and intense heat. Got "down to it" on the sofa at about quarter past two – cold and tired. Poor D, this is her "holiday"! Willie has many sterling qualities. His talk is of bullocks and bishops.

Monday 14 April: Woke up feeling as if I had been on a debauch for a week. Washed up after breakfast and went down to the coal merchant expecting to have to carry coal home. Luckily they agreed to send today. Home and made up my diary. Lunch very late, and I washed up after it and after tea wh. followed immediately. The guests departed after it. V. tired all evening.

Wednesday 16 April: The others went up to Bristol by an early bus. I filled my claybox, took Pat for a run, carried the blankets back to Miss Rimington, did shopping, cleaned the bath, washed up the breakfast things and got to my writing at about quarter past twelve. I got on rather better, but as soon as I reach the dialogue part the old difficulty crops up – a little hard irreducible pellet of connecting narrative that must somehow be made into an end in itself.

Lunched about two, fed the animals, wrote a little more and walked out at 3.30 along the shore with Pat, finding many soaking machines and dawdling so that I did not reach home till 6.15. I began *Erewhon* which is very good fun.

Friday 18 April: On this day W arrived from Colchester by motor bike, having lain the night at Oxford. I had proposed to go and meet him at Bristol, but as it was Good Friday there was no means of going there. This I discovered on the Thursday and sent him a card telling him to pick me up between two and four o'clock at Clapton-in-Gordano.

I set out shortly after breakfast to walk to this rendezvous. It was a glorious glittering day and I never felt better in my life. I walked to East Clevedon and up through the woods on Court Hill, thence along the top to Cadbury Camp where I ate an apple and lay for a smoke on the dyke of the camp. The walk down into Clapton was lovely beyond expectation: through very young fir plantations into a landscape even more shining than all the others I have seen here.

At the solitary pub of Clapton I ate my sandwiches and had a pint of beer, and tho' I was not very long there the conversation of the villagers included one infanticide and one indecent assault.

I waited for W. in the village for two hours – very little bored, for it was quite a satisfying place. It consists of one deep cut lane with primros'd banks and a stream at the side, a few cottages, a walled rectory with a castellated gate house, and a church up on a little hill. It was here that I found W at last, seated under a tree. He had gone as far as East Clevedon before thinking to look for Clapton and then come back: thus entering the village from the home end, not the Bristol end where I naturally looked for him. He is fatter than ever before. We had tea in the village and I came home in the sidecar.

Saturday-Saturday 19-26 April: W's visit was on the whole a pleasant time: tho' there are always little discomforts when anyone but ourselves is in the house. Maureen left on Saturday to stay with Valerie Evans at Chipping Norton. The manner of our life was this. In the morning I did my usual jobs and shopping if necessary, and then walked out with W and Pat, usually along the coast, stopping to soak in a cove and stopping for beer at the Pier Hotel on the return journey. They keep there one of the best beers I have ever drunk.

In the afternoon W generally read: I often went out to get something, or else read and wrote. After tea all three of us went for a most excellent ride in divine weather. We rode through Yatton and Wrington into the Mendips, passing within sight of D's well beloved Winscombe – a steeple on a hillside seen for a moment in the heart of a beautiful long ridged wooded *crooked* country. After that we ran through a small gorge out on to the barer southern slope of the Mendips and down into the narrow little streets and beetling houses of Axbridge – glory! what a town and how placed!

Thence on to Cheddar by a road that skirts the hills. Here I saw many fields and trees quite white with blossom and daisies. At Cheddar we caught sight of the gorge up to our left quite unexpectedly: and then while I was still in a confused impression – the speed of a motor cycle is sometimes a great aesthetic advantage – W suddenly turned and ran up it. I lay back in the side car and watched the huge coloured cliffs pushing up further round us and closer till it seemed like going into a tunnel. I was quite unprepared for anything of the sort. It was a great moment.

We turned on our tracks and went on to Wells. Just before reaching it we turned off left at a signpost "To Wookey Hole" to find some quiet pub where we cd. eat our lunch. The lane wound on so long that we began to fear that Wookey Hole was a natural feature, a devil's punch bowl or the like, and not a village. A village however it turned out to be, with a pub where we sat on a curiously comfortless bench and ate our sandwiches and drank cider. We then went back and into Wells where W was charged 6d. for leaving the bike in Wells Square by the town authorities, who however "took no responsibility of any sort" for it.

W was delighted with the outside of the Cathedral but less pleased with the interior. I think I agreed with him. I also agreed with his view that King's Chapel, Cambridge, is the perfect building. We then strolled all round the Palace talking of all things that arose therefrom – Barchester, abbots, mediaeval siege tactics. Our ease and freedom and pleasant chat made this visit to Wells far better than my first when I came here on the motor tour with my father and the Hamiltons.[4] In many ways W is the ideal person to go for a jaunt with . . .

---

[4] This motor tour is described in Lewis's letter to Warnie of 7 August 1921, and is found in the *Letters of C.S. Lewis*, pp. 142-156.

It was shortly before W's arrival that I had a long letter from Baker, giving me his news, and saying that it was apparent there had been some considerable misunderstanding between us – wh. he had also gathered from his conversation with Pasley. He said he had written to D at the time of the Doc's death and then, later, to me, and had had no answer to either of them. I was in considerable doubt how to answer this. My only alternatives seemed to be silence, insincere acceptance of his account with mental reservations on my part, or the whole truth.

In the end I wrote accepting his explanation (i.e. that he had sent letters tho' I had never got them) but adding that this was only the occasion of my coolness: the real reasons were certain qualities in him with wh. I was growing more and more discontented. I explained quite bluntly what those were, adding, at the same time, that I hoped we shd. find it possible to take up our old friendship again.

On Saturday 26th we all came back to Oxford. It had been arranged that I shd. travel in the sidecar. It was obvious that one of us shd. do so to save fares and D, of course, refused to be that one. I therefore *trained* with her to Yatton and saw her into a through train to Bristol with the luggage, and W, Pat and I got aboard the bike. As we were making all snug outside Yatton station, a hamper, wh. had just been taken out of the train, was suddenly opened just beside us to release a cloud of pigeons that filled the air with an amazing noise before we knew what was forward. It was a curious experience for I had not suspected the hamper of containing anything live. It was raining when we started but soon cleared up. We got into the main road shortly before Wrington and entered Bristol by Bedminster . . .

From Faringdon we came along at a very good speed thro' Bickland, Kingston Bagpuize, Fyfield, Bessels, Leigh, Cumnor and Botley to Oxford. It is a tame, well combed, cheerful country of tidy well growing woods, white gates, dark tarred roads, comfortable cottages, sometimes exeedingly beautiful, green hedges and flat blue distances. The speed, the sunlight, and the sense of coming home put me into an unusually prolonged fit of "joy". Home by about five to find D quite well, tho' after a rather uncomfortable journey. Maureen turned up at eight o'clock. In the evening I introduced W to the poems of W. de la Mare and made him, I think, a convert.

Sunday-Wednesday 27-30 April: W left by bike for Colchester soon after breakfast, in pouring rain. His departure left me disquieted and unsettled for an hour or so – it is bad for me to get into the way of living with anyone who has leisure and money and ease of mind – until I came to my senses and was glad enough to be settled down to our own ordinary life again. There is always a pleasure in being to ourselves after anyone has been here for a while.

In the course of the next few days I had an invitation to dine at Trinity, and also a mysterious wire from the Master asking me to come to his lodgings at 9.30 on Monday evening "to meet Farquharson and Carritt".

Pat became very ill and Gillard came out one day and pronounced it to be valvular disease of the heart and ordered him whiskey. At this time I took to using the attic (where Ada used to sleep) as a study. I finished and fair copied Canto VII of "Dymer", and so, for the first time there was actually a text of the whole thing in existence. Domestic interruptions (nobody's fault) made it impossible for me to get a chance of reading it all through at one sitting: but even without that I soon found that there was something wrong. It lacks unity. I came to the conclusion that Canto VI wd. have to be altered, and started a new one.

Sunday 4 May: Dined at Trinity this evening. I went first to the President's house and he brought me along to Hall.[1] His manner was rather repellent at first, but I think unintentionally so and he became better later on. I found that he knew my old form master at Malvern, H.W. Smith, "Smugy" of blessed memory: but I couldn't get him to talk much about him.[2]

We were a very full table. I talked to my neighbour who was a scientist newly imported from Cambridge and seemingly a pleasant fellow: also to my opposite number who is their law tutor – a very dark, smooth skinned, clever looking, laughing, serpentine man whom I took a dislike to.[3] He was however very agreeable.

At dessert I was beside Pritchard who condemned Jane Austen, or rather the life presented by Jane Austen, for its narrowness and triviality. I, and a very nice man with one arm, tried to defend her and pleaded that one had to use historical imagination to get over this, as one did to get over the vices in Plato. But we did not make much of it.

We then went to have coffee and smokes in an upper room, for the President will allow no smoking in the Common Room proper. Here I had some talk with their Mods Tutor about Mods, Poynton, Bailey, and Myres, whom this man had known in the Aegean. An elderly man in holy orders and in liquor came and sat by me (Patterson, senior Tutor)[4] and, after taking me for someone else, discovered I was from Univ. and said "Ah . . . ! then you'll know my dear friend Farki". He proceeded to tell me how Farki's daughter had just got the sack from a London hospital for feeding a child who had diabetes on plum cake in the article of death. He also told us some stories from Jeremy Bentham's letters.

[1] The Rev. Herbert Edward Douglas Blakiston (1862–1942) was President of Trinity College, Oxford, 1907–38.

[2] Lewis pays a handsome tribute to Harry Wakelyn Smith (1861–1918) in ch. VII of *Surprised by Joy*.

[3] Philip Aislabie Landon (1886–1961).

[4] Melville Watson Patterson (1873-1944) became a Fellow of Trinity in 1897 and was Vice President and Senior Tutor until his retirement in 1938.

After him came Kirk, their chaplain.[5] Conversation became general. We talked of Dickens and of the grace *Benedictus benedicatur* wh. no one cd. translate. Came away after a very enjoyable evening and discovered when I got into the open air that I was not quite sober.

Monday 5 May: Spent the morning working at a new version of my "Hegemony of Moral Values" for *Mind*. D and I took Pat out for a gentle walk in Cuckoo Lane after tea.

After supper I bussed in to College and found Carritt and Farquharson with the Master. The latter laid before me the proposal that I shd. take over part of Carritt's work during the next year, wh. Carritt is to spend in America. He said he recognised that there must be two things in my mind: the Trinity job and the ultimate possibility of a Fellowship at Univ: but perhaps for the moment we had best leave these in the air and without prejudice. I said that for me it came down to one question "Does my undertaking this work involve my withdrawing my candidature for Trinity?" The Master said that no one had contemplated making any such demand of me. If Trinity elected me it was quite possible that Trinity wd. not object to my doing the Univ. work as well: if they did object Univ. wd. release me. "Or," added Carritt, "if you, although Trinity allows it, find the double work too much."

I thanked them for taking such a liberal attitude and said that this removed the only objection I cd. have. We then proceeded to finance and what I made out after many convolutions of Farquharson's tongue was that I cd. be sure of £200 for the year, as a minimum. Needless to say I agreed to everything and came away at about ten. It was arranged that I should lecture twice a week next term.

Tuesday 6 May: Worked on my paper again in the morning. After lunch and my usual jobs I went in to have tea with Robson-Scott in his rooms in Beaumont St. It was just what happened last time: we were just getting into a really interesting talk when in came his friend Bateson. I cannot imagine why Robson always insists on asking this young prodigy to meet me. We talked of Yates, W. de la Mare, Walter Scott, and Marlowe: I was glad to find this much good in Bateson, that he really does feel the speed and spring of Marlowe's blank verse.

---

[5] The Rev. Kenneth Escott Kirk (1886–1954) was Chaplain and Lecturer in Theology at Trinity College 1922–33, Professor of Moral and Pastoral Theology and Canon of Christ Church 1933–7, and Bishop of Oxford 1937–54.

Sometime after this he observed that as he progressed he found his interest in a poem centred more and more round the author. I said this seemed to me inconsistent with real aesthetic experience. In a few minutes, by some circumbendibus I can't remember, he was saying that his enjoyment of a poem consisted in understanding and watching and analysing the effect it had on himself. He said that on my basis of mere direct alogical enjoyment one cd. never prove that a thing was good – one cd. only say "I like it."

I asked him if it was possible to prove goodness on his basis: to wh. he made the egregious reply "It may not be *possible*, but it's *easier* than on yours." I asked him whether this pleasure (of analysis etc.) cd. not be derived just as well from bad poetry as from good: to wh. at first he assented, but afterwards said that the effects to be analysed were more complex and intense in the case of good poetry. Asked how his enjoyment could be called enjoyment of the poetry, he said "Because the poetry is necessary to it." I asked him if oxygen and digestion and other things were not just as necessary. He ended up by saying that at any rate other people felt as he did, people like W. Pater and J.A. Symonds: so I suppose these are his gods. Needless to say he is a follower, or believes himself to be a follower, of Croce, and cares almost nothing for nature.

Home by about eight after calling in the Union to take out Leibnitz.[6]

Wednesday 7 May: I spent the morning in my attic reading the *Monadologie*, the first book of *Sur L'Entendement Humain* and the *Systeme Nouveau* of Leibnitz. There is more subtlety in him than I expected.

After lunch I had time to sweep out the kitchen and shake out the mats and do my other jobs before Ziman, who had really forced the engagement on me, appeared to take me for a walk. We went by field path to Stowe Woods road and home by Elsfield etc. It was a beautiful day and a fine bit of country – blue and white sky, cuckoos everywhere and innumerable colours in the hedges. I don't think Ziman cared twopence for it, tho' he was able to *talk* well enough about a cloud effect that I mentioned. After all, they teach them that here.

By dint of taking everything steadily *au pied de la lettre* I fairly soon induced him to stop being clever and some conversation

---

[6] Lewis was beginning to get in his Greats reading before he started teaching in October 1924.

resulted. Came home and [had] tea: afterwards he sat with me till 7.30, talking of what he called "happiness" by wh. he apparently means my "real joy", and of many other things. Not a bad fellow, but what a waste of an afternoon!

Thursday 8 May: This evening to the Univ. Philosophical Society after dinner to hear McMurray of Balliol read a paper.[7] He is Lindsay's successor, a Scotsman, with a mind that seems to me curiously perverse.

The moral judgement for him is primarily the judgement "This is evil", wh., since he is a Bradleyan, means "the whole is such that this is evil" and he finds a difficulty about the universe being logically coherent and morally incoherent. A good discussion afterwards.

Sunday 11 May: A short walk to Stowe Woods with Pat in the morning. Washed up after lunch and read Malory for the first time since I was about sixteen. I read the book about Balin and Balan, and tho' I have often called Malory "dreamy" in a loose sense I now saw for the first time how strictly like a dream the whole scene in King Pellam's castle is, and indeed the whole story of Balin's inexplicable superhuman guilt and bad luck. I enjoyed it greatly.

Monday 12 May: . . . I washed up etc after lunch and then locked up the house and went down to Ewing's digs in Iffley Road – he having invited me, for my sins, to walk with him. We went to Iffley and back. I asked him if he suffered as I did periodically from a sense of the vanity of learning: he had no notion of what I meant. He said that Price (of Magdalen) was a dangerous man for the Trinity hope, as he had been asked to dinner there. I said "Won't all the candidates be asked?" He replied "Oh dear no, only those in the running." Back for tea in his digs and a long talk on Theism. I don't know how it is that Ewing can talk quite well and yet he never interests one.

On the way back I called to see Miss Featherstone because D had had a bad dream about her last night. Miss F said the dream was postdated, for she had been very ill about five weeks ago but was now better. She is a great heart . . .

Tuesday 13 May: I spent the morning in the attic reading through the new version of my "Hegemony" paper which I am sending to *Mind* and altering the ending. I also wrote a few stanzas of "Dymer" VI.

---

[7] John Macmurray (1891–1976) was Tutor in Philosophy at Balliol College 1922–8, and Professor of Philosophy of Mind and Logic, University of London 1928–44.

After lunch I went out with Pat and walked over the allotments to Quarry, thence up Shotover and down into Pullen's Gap wh. is now a sea of green and white. It was a bright warm day with an endless succession of clouds crossing the sky. The ground covered with blue bells and some gorse, tho' much less brilliant in colour than down at Clevedon . . .

Thursday 15 May: Went into town shopping in the morning and sat for a long time in the Union reading Bosanquet's *Suggestions in Ethics* wh. I brought out for the sake of the beautiful passage about the Absolute eating out of your hand. Bosanquet has apparently the right point of view about most things . . . but a little bit woolly.

Home again, lunch and chores, and then to the attic where I worked on Locke (with a break for tea) till supper.

In the evening I read Masefield's *Right Royal* with intense enjoyment and excitement – but of course one can't really tell what it is worth till it has been re-read without the excitement.

Sunday 18 May: A lovely summer day. After breakfast D had the sudden idea that we ought ourselves to lay down linoleum in the kitchen instead of waiting for Knight to come and do it – why, I don't know. All that hot day which ended in a thunderstorm we worked on our knees in the kitchen with short intervals for rather squalid meals in the scullery till half past ten in the evening. Then we went to bed.

Monday 19 May: D very tired and cross today. Went into town after breakfast and did shopping for her. Hurried home and was immediately sent out into Headington on another message: when I came back from this D turned on me rather savagely for having forgotten to take Pat out with me. I made no reply, knowing that it was in my power to speak or not to speak but fearing that if I once began I might say regrettable things. In practice however I think my silence had an unkind and sulky appearance and was not really the right line to take. Poor D – I was probably as bad or worse for the rest of the day, though I honestly tried not to be disagreeable. I am afraid I have a good deal of my father's unhappy nature in me.

After lunch the nervous irritation bottled up inside me reached such a pitch and my thoughts became so irresponsible and foolish and so out of control that for a moment I was really afraid that I was going into hysteria.

I spent the afternoon finishing the linoleum job in the kitchen: another hot day. Poor D was busy making cakes for the sake of her cousin Norah Murray who is coming to stay tomorrow. This was Edie's suggestion: she thought it would be "so nice" for us to get to know her.

This night I began again to have the same pains that frightened me so in Ireland last summer: the imperfectly localised pain which makes its headquarters near the appendix and which I hope is indigestion.

Tuesday 20 May: Norah Murray arrived today – tall, plain, very Scotch, uneducated, an earnest bridge player and golfer. A storm came on at tea time and she was so afraid of the thunder that D put her to bed in the yellow room and went to sit with her. She is about thirty five and as a child was one of Rob's "girls".

Friday 23 May: The Holmes children arrived after breakfast and D soon took me aside and told me that Mrs Holmes was dying and that the children would stay with us for the night and until further notice. She and I went upstairs in haste to arrange beds and so forth. Afterwards I washed up. I suggested sending a wire to put off Harwood (who was to come for the week end) lest his arrival should only mean fresh trouble for her and his visit moreover be wasted in these conditions. But D would not let me . . .

We had supper in good time and were finishing (D and I) when Harwood arrived. Tho' I wished exceedingly that his visit could have come at a better time, I was delighted to see him – such a breath from the comfortable, easy outside would. While I washed up he talked to me of his walking tour with Beckett in the Tyrol. I got so much vicarious enjoyment that it was only afterwards that I felt the pains of envy. Later on all three of us sat in the dining room. Harwood and I had a good talk of books and of friends and every sentence brought me back to sanity. He is setting up a publishing business with one Lewis May, a great Vergilian who had resource to the Sortes Vergilianae before committing himself and fell upon the words *Una salus ambobus erit.*[8]

Tonight I slept in my garret. My pains were pretty bad and of course the case of Mrs Holmes so near to hand brings certain thoughts rather prominently into my mind: but it makes an enormous difference being at home and not exiled in Ireland. I was also very cold until I went downstairs to get my overcoat.

---

[8] Virgil, *Aeneid*, II, 710. Aeneas to his father, whom, with his young son Iulus, he is leading away from the sacking of Troy – "There will be one [way of] deliverance for us both."

Saturday 24 May: I washed up after breakfast while Harwood did Trojan service in amusing the children and tho' he admitted it was a strain in the end, you could see he had a natural aptitude for it. I did various jobs till about twelve when he and I set off to carry Norah's luggage by bus to the station – a welcome task – and thence went to All Souls to lunch with Beckett.

We had lunch (as before) in the "round house" and afterwards sat in a small walled garden surrounded by fig trees, outside the smoking room. We were all rather sleepy and the talk did not go well: indeed I always find it hard to establish much contact with Beckett, tho' I both like and admire him.

At about 3 we left and Harwood looked to see if Bodley had a copy of Traherne's *Christian Ethics* wh. he thinks of reprinting. We walked home by Mesopotamia and Cuckoo Lane, stopping at every bridge to watch the water. It bore down infinite hordes of drowned and drowning insects. We talked of the horrors that occurred in one square mile of the insect world every month. Harwood thought that their consciousness might be so rudimentary that their death struggles might mean no more than a confused malaise. At the rollers the Cherwell was very flooded and turbid.

Reaching home we found not only the boys but Joy Holmes here for tea. D told me that Mrs H. had died this morning: after the last few days it was a great relief to know that she was safely out of the reach of pain. From what was said at tea I gathered that the two boys were leaving us this evening: but I soon discovered that they were taking the elder one and leaving the younger – wh. seemed an extraordinary arrangement. After I had washed up the tea things I came out to the lawn where Harwood was still gallantly amusing the children: at their age how I would have rejected grown up interference as an interruption of my own endless drawing and soliloquies. Presently however the Holmes' car appeared and I found that they had changed their minds and were going to take both the children away. I was very relieved, chiefly for D's sake, and then for Harwood's and my own. When they were gone Harwood told me a wonderful example of childish obtuseness: Bobbie (aged seven) had come up and asked him "Guess who died today?" But I think this argues a defect in mental age.

D and I then went out shopping and later Harwood and I took Pat for a stroll. In the evening we enjoyed blessed peace and leisure free from the boys and Norah.

After supper Harwood read most of "Dymer" and gave me a budget of his new poems to read – "Epitaph on Sudden Death" in which he really touches sublimity and classical perfection . . . a little poem about a lark which is almost perfect too, tho' in a much slighter style: octosyllabics to "R.M." a most interesting poem containing real titbits ("The table spread/Lacked all things lacking common bread" – "A triple fate designed/Jump with the chord our eyes aligned") but still in need of revision: "At ille labitur" wh. fails at the end: "A modern journey" wh. is good: and two other pieces of less interest.[9]

He has advanced splendidly. I still think my poetry better than his, but I envy his grace, his courtliness, and a certain choiceness and nicety. It is all so clean, so dapper, so humorous, so exquisitely "right" in his good things.

He approved strongly of "Dymer" VI. Of VIII he said that the whole thing was overshadowed by the "natural history" difficulties of the brute as Dymer's son: he wd. prefer a Caliban sort of person.

Late to bed in the attic. Pains a good deal better.

Sunday 25 May: A cool, grey skied summer day. Harwood and I with Pat had a delightful walk – to Stanton St John where we lunched off bread and cheese and shandy, thence through the woods and by field path to Beckley, passing one of the loveliest country "places" I ever saw (at Woodferry I think) – a Georgian house with great gates, smothered in lilic, and far retired from a lane that was far retired itself: surrounded by deep meadows overhung with chestnut trees and full of black pigs that were as clean and strokeable as young horses. Home by Stowe Woods and Barton End. Harwood left us after supper.

[9] "An Epitaph on a Sudden Death", "A Meeting with R.M.", "At Ille Labitur" and "A Modern Journey" are found in *The Voice of Cecil Harwood* (*loc. cit.*).

326

Sunday 1 June: Up betimes and did the hall and dining room before breakfast. It had rained all night but was now a bright morning. After breakfast I went out with Pat and crossed the fields to Stowe Woods and thence by road down the hill towards Islip. At the bottom of the hill I struck in to my left across the field I had reached on Wednesday and got to the corner of the wood after great difficulty and floundering in the mud. I then came home by Elsfield and Old Headington after a very unenjoyable walk – or rather "unenjoyed" for there was plenty of beauty if I had been in the right mood.

After lunch I did my usual jobs and washed up and then took down all the pictures from the drawing room preparatory to the sweep's coming tomorrow. D spent most of the afternoon making further preparations and would not let me help.

After tea I wrote to my father and finished the first part of the *Pilgrim's Progress*. The end is poor: indeed nothing shows the lowness (in one respect) of the original Christians so much as their idea of Heaven wh. they have handed down. Compare this glummery of golden streets and hymn singing with Vergil's *"largior hic campos"*[1] or the isle of the Hesperides or Isaiah or even Nirvanah . . .

Wednesday 4 June: Raining all day, as usual now. Worked in the attic after breakfast at my essay on Locke. In the afternoon, it being too wet for walking, I bussed in to the Union where I read with great delight in Oddenowski's *Man and Mystery in Asia*. It is extraordinary to read the mixture of Rider Haggard and Algernon Blackwood and know that it is true. The story of the Black Monk at first struck me as a capital theme for a poem – but really there is nothing left for the poet to do.

Home again and up to the attic after tea where I worked on my paper for *Mind*, turning, as I thought, a very difficult corner where I have stuck this long time.

---

[1] "Here a more abundant ether clothes the plains with brilliant light" – Virgil, *Aeneid*, VI, 640 – talking of the abode of the blessed in the underworld.

Then, after an early supper, we all went: D and Maureen to the staff play at the school and I to the Martlets. Arriving early in King's rooms I found only Ware and King present and had a little talk with the latter about the *Crock of Gold*. Presently others turned up, Carritt, Fasnacht, Dawson, Ewing, Allen, Carlyle, Stevenson. Carritt read a delightful paper on Arnold, of which he announced that I was "the begetter". The discussion afterwards was not very good.

I walked home with Ewing. He asked me if I knew what was happening about Carritt's pupils. I said, "They have asked me to take some of them." *Ewing*: "How many?" *Self*: "About thirteen." *Ewing*: "How many does that leave?" *Self*: "I'm not sure but I'm afraid the Farq is taking them." *Ewing*: "Oh, I had hoped to get some of them." *Self*: Yes. I always feel this position is degrading for all of us, but we can't help it. I'm very sorry." *Ewing*: "Congratulations." A horribly uncomfortable dialogue . . .

Thursday 5 June: Worked on my essay on Locke in the morning. D woke up today with a shocking headache but it got better during the morning.

After lunch I walked out with Pat along the lane that turns off to your right and so over the fields nearly to Horsepath. When I was in sight of it I turned up to my left and so through the bracken to my favourite fir grove where I sat down for a long time and had the "joy" – or rather came just within sight of it but didn't arrive.

In the evening to Touche's and King's rooms in Beaumont Street where the Phil. Soc. met and Fasnacht read a paper on the General Will.[2] In the interval I asked how the habit of applauding at these societies had arisen – for it was unknown when I first came up. King said it had started with Curtis who had gone to sleep one night, and, waking up suddenly as the paper stopped, applauded through mere force of habit. Carritt agreed with me that it was a bad habit.

Saturday 7 June: Letter from the Pres. of Trinity saying that they had made their decision.[3] . . .

Monday 9 June: . . . I dined with Carritt in hall. While I was waiting about in the Lodge, having arrived rather too early, I had a conversation with Rink. We were joined by the Master who first of all asked if I were in for Schools – thus showing how little he

[2] George Lawrence Capel Touche matriculated at University College in 1921. He took a first in Greats and received his BA in 1925.

[3] Lewis must have found it painfully ironic that the man who won the Fellowship at Magdalen which Lewis had applied for in 1922 – H.H. Price – had now been given the Fellowship at Trinity.

remembers me: which is very natural and by no means culpable. Then came Raymond the doctor, who was up here in old days.

With him I went into Common Room. It was a big night. Poynton was in the chair: with him was Miles of Merton, Leys, Bowen,[4] two unknowns, Allen, Farquharson, Raymond, a third unknown, Carritt and myself made up the party. But there must have been one more whom I can't remember.

Poynton was in great form. He told us that the only people who really pronounced the Latin AE as AI came from Praeneste and spoke through the nose. Farquharson told us some stories about the late Master at golf. I had some talk with Leys and also with Allen about *Antic Hay*.[5]

In the Common Room afterwards Poynton rose to hand the wine and then observed, "I am for the outward passage. We are thirteen and I got up first. It was just how it happened with poor Emmet. The only thing to do is to drink as much port as possible." After that he became very good and gave us an imitation of his idea of a Greek chorus. Leys, Carritt and I had a really good little talk about Wordsworth. Later on I went up to Carritt's rooms and he gave me a lot of wrinkles for my forthcoming duties . . .

Thursday 12 June: Started Berkeley this morning. After an early lunch Maureen and I bussed in to Oxford and joined the queue outside the Sheldonian for the Bach choir. We had a very hot wait, the sun being for that moment out and strong, and I was rather worried by catching sight of Aunt Lily: but I think she did not see us.

We got seats in one of the windows – the best place to be, but still very uncomfortable. They gave us first of all the Kyrie, Credo and Agnus from Beethoven's *Mass in D*. I was bored with the Credo but enjoyed the rest pretty well: they then proceeded to the *Choral Symphony*. The first three movements I enjoyed greatly – the second "even to rapture": the fourth with its choir I didn't care for. The finale – such is my ignorance – sounded to me like something from a Revue.

Maureen then bussed out and I wrote a note for Coghill in the Union, saying that I would come in *after* dinner on Sunday: I left this in Exeter and bussed home to find Jenkin at tea with the others

---

[4] Sir John Charles Miles (1870–1963) was the Tutor of Law in Merton College 1899–1930, Domestic Bursar 1904–23, and Warden of Merton College 1936–47.

Kenneth King Munsie Leys (1876–1950) was Fellow of Modern History at University College 1911–42.

[5] By Aldous Huxley (1923).

in the kitchen. I was delighted to see him. He is just home from Switzerland and the Italian lakes – *terque quaterque beatum!*[6] He has also been to Wembley and denounces my lack of interest in exhibitions as a fashionable affectation . . .

We had supper in good time and I bussed into town and went to W.H. Sutton's rooms in Christ Church to attend a meeting of the Postgraduates. I was the first there. Presently Stout and some others arrived. Stout was the only person I knew and as he neither spoke to me himself nor introduced me to anyone else (not even to our host) I was reduced to the entertainment of my own thoughts. This did not matter at first, but by the time the others had stood talking in semi whispers about jobs and the famous men they had met for half an hour, and my head had begun to ache and my tobacco had run out, I began to think I might have meditated more comfortably elsewhere.

I was seriously thinking of getting up and saying "Good night. Thank you for a pleasant evening" when at last they showed signs of starting the meeting proper. The reader turned out to be Mr Catlin whom I met at the Encaenia in 1921 when we were both prizemen. The man before him on that occasion had read rather too long an extract from *his* composition, and Catlin had whispered to me with a shake of his head, "*Much* too long". He had then risen and read twice as long himself in a very parsonical voice with strong rhetorical rhythm.

He is pale and slight with a long yet bulbous nose and very thick pale lips: his hands, which are large, he holds before him and washes "in invisible soap". His smile is the most fascinating thing about him: when he is spoken to he suddenly twitches his head over to one side till his nose is nearly horizontal. Then there is a rapid extension of his mouth as far as possible in each direction: this grin begins and ends quite suddenly and does not affect any other part of his face. He varies the *intensity* of the smile by maintaining the contortion for a longer or shorter time: thus when someone asked him to tea it lasted for about forty seconds. He stands sometimes on one leg, sometimes on the other: never on both. The continued contortions of face, hands and body reminded me of Uriah Heep.

He read a paper called "Prometheus", modelled on Haldane's *Daedalus.* Just as he was starting a man (the most gentlemanly one

---

[6] "O three times, four times blessed!" (are those who died in battle at Troy). Virgil, *Aeneid*, I, 94.

there I am sorry to say) came and squashed himself in between me and my neighbour on a Chesterfield, so that I was in great discomfort. It was at this point that I really got angry: I can stand mental isolation but not physical proximity.

Catlin's paper however gave me intense enjoyment – tho' not of the sort he had intended. I don't know what his thesis was: only that we must avoid the prejudices of the "vulga – a – a", and that "there is no permanent social evil" (not evil but iv-il – pronouncing all your letters) "for that would mean a normal abnormality", that we should distinguish between "the adultery of the heart and the passing peccancy of the body" and "that the future of religion lay between Christianity, and some religion yet unknown". I was hard put to it to keep a straight face at times – tho' there was sense in the paper and plenty of it amid the affectation.[7]

A man near me – a great coarse blackish thing, negroid or Jewish, I don't know which – gave up the attempt and lay face downwards with his face in a cushion. My neighbour put his feet up on the sofa on which I was sitting.

As soon as the paper was over I went over to Sutton and said "Thank you. I have a bus to catch. I'm afraid I must go." Sutton looked up and made no answer at all: so I went out and home by bus from Carfax. The only other people there I can remember were Mr Dickie (one feels that all of them should always have the "Mr" somehow) and the "crooning" man whom I met there before.

Friday 13 June: This morning was a good deal colder and the sky full of clouds: but a strong damp wind from the North West had chased away this horrible heaviness that has hung over us so long. This exhilarated me so much that I went out after breakfast with Pat and walked on Shotover.

From eating indiscreetly on a rather tough bit of bacon at breakfast I had set my left jaw and the whole of that side of my face aching: and tho' the pain was slight in itself, the fear that it would localise into a definite toothache and the effort of will to prevent this kept me from enjoying my walk. On reaching home I took some aspirin and wrote up my diary: by lunch time I was alright. After lunch D

---

[7] (Sir) George Catlin (1896–1979) took his BA from New College in 1924. Upon leaving Oxford he was Professor of Politics at Cornell University 1924–35, after which he became concerned with Atlantic Community policy and was the founder of the Movement for Atlantic Union (UK). Besides lecturing all over the world, he wrote numerous books on philosophy and politics and he published an autobiography, *For God's Sake, Go* (1972).

went into town and I, after washing up and usual jobs, went to my attic and worked on Berkeley.

Maureen, Aideen and I had tea alone in the kitchen at 4.45. Shortly afterwards D came back in very good form and loaded us as usual with presents for everyone. The dining room table was soon covered up with foodstuffs, new dressing slippers, notebooks and paper fasteners for me, shoes and umbrella for D, pads, toilet paper and what not.

I did a little more Berkeley before supper: after wh. I washed up and took Pat down Cuckoo Lane. In the evening I read a little in Th. Browne's *Urn Burial*. All very merry and earli-ish to bed.

Saturday 14 June: A great drop in the temperature this morning. After breakfast I finished Berkeley's *Principles*[8] and wrote a little critique on it. I then began Hume: and greatly enjoyed the perfect clarity, ease, humanity and quietness of his manner. This is the proper way to write philosophy.

After lunch I half expected Jenkin to turn up, but when I had finished my jobs and still he had not appeared, I set off alone with Pat. The sun had now come out with a sudden autumn like intensity and it was hotter than it has been for many days. The heat quivered on the grass: I went through Quarry and up Shotover. There was a sort of whiteness over the landscape. I strolled along "the plain" and down the little alley that leads to the railway bridge – enjoying everything very much. On my return journey I went down into the bottom of Pullen's Gap and rested for a long time under a clump of young silver birches wh. made around me a curiously crisp rustling.

Reaching home I found tea set on the lawn and Jenkin there with D. He showed us many photos collected in his travels – Lemone, Benacus, Venice, and places in the mountains. He had just been reading Masefield's *Philip the King*. He said that the part in which rumour of victory arrives is a failure, because, knowing the history, one feels all the time that this is only being done to heighten the climax. I said I didn't feel that myself. He told me of a new letter of Sir Thomas Browne's recently discovered and quoted a fine passage – "every hour so addeth to that dark society".

He also talked of Oxford – how quickly he had got out of touch with it. "When I lunched with Ziman and Curtis the other day," he said, "I felt firstly that everything they said was silly: and secondly

---

[8] George Berkeley, *Principles of Human Knowledge* (1710).

that there was an intellectual gloss which I had absolutely lost in a few months." He was afraid that he was really "rusticating" but I told him (wh. was the truth) that I found no change and that to talk with him was like slipping into a well worn shoe.

When he left I found that Maureen and D had disappeared somewhere, so I brought Wordsworth out to the garden and there in the delicious coolness I read Book I of *The Prelude*. This poem is really beginning to replace *Paradise Lost* as my literary metropolis. D and Maureen turned up from shopping in Headington with loads much too heavy for them. D of course made light of it: but I was rather sickened to find that my hour or so's talk and read, enjoyed all innocently, had led unawares to this. So exacting is ordinary life: one cannot turn aside for a moment . . .

Sunday 15 June: . . . After supper I bussed into Exeter and went to Coghill's rooms where, after a short wait, I was joined by Coghill and Morrah.[9] The latter is very dark, slight, and vivacious: such a man as might be begotten by the marriage of a firefly with a rat. He is a Fellow of All Souls. He told me of some Canadian university who wants a young man as Professor of English and offers £1000 a year: they need not elect anyone and are in no hurry. He gave me an address to write to about it.

The talk fell on Catlin, whom Morrah had examined when he tried for an All Souls Fellowship. Catlin had filled his papers with quotations from the Vulgate. "It was his misfortune," said Morrah, "to fall into my hands, who am the only Papist in the society. I saw at once what he was doing – taking the Authorised Version and translating it into Latin: but the trouble was that he did it in Ciceronian Latin." I then remembered how Catlin had quoted a Papal Bull in his paper the other night: and felt "sudden glory".

I happened to remark jokingly that All Souls was an indefensible institution. Morrah said its function was to keep the University in touch with the *grande monde*: and in developing this thesis became just a little too like an after dinner speaker (of the serious kind).

He told us a good story of how H.G. Wells had dined at All Souls and said that Oxford wasted too much time over Latin and Greek. Why should these two literatures have it all to themselves? Now Russian and Persian literature were far superior to the Classics.

---

[9] Dermot Macgreggor Morrah (1896–1974) was a Fellow of All Souls College 1921–28. He was a leader writer for a number of newspapers, and he published a number of books on the Royal Family.

Someone (I forget the name) asked a few questions. It soon became apparent that Wells knew neither Greek, Latin, Persian, or Russian. "I think," said someone, "I am the only person present here tonight who knows these four languages: and I can assure you, Mr Wells, that you are mistaken: neither Russian nor Persian literature are as great as the literatures of Greece or Rome."

I asked Morrah if he believed in the usual cant about dons being so much in need of humanizing and the *grande monde*: he gave an answer so carefully balanced that the result was nil. After a little talk about Gilbert Murray, Lindsay and other things, he left us: a man distinguished in manner, ready with the tongue, but somehow lacking something that wd. make him a really agreeable fellow.

Coghill and I then had a long and pleasant tête-à-tête until interrupted by the arrival of Dawson, a Professor in Exeter and a great friend of Coghill. We had very good talk triangular, chiefly on books, till I left at 11.30 and came home in great haste through milk white moonlight . . .

Monday 16 June: . . . Lunch was very late and by the time I had finished my jobs it was after three. I then bussed into town to do some shopping. I also went to the Union where I read the whole of De la Mare's *Ding Dong Bell*, a beautiful little book in prose.

Bussed home and had tea alone in the garden with D: after which I set out to take Pat for a run and was unexpectedly pleased to meet Jenkin just turning into our road. We walked together down Cuckoo Lane – which is also called "The back of the hill" and "Joe Pullen's lane". I spoke of the Pasleys' action in going to a bull fight. Jenkin strongly disapproved of it and said that the fact of their being foreigners and English made their behaviour more important for, strange as it may seem, disapproval of strangers, specially of Englishmen, had altered the feeling about animals in some places before now. He instanced the Italian marble quarries and said also that the presence of the English armies in France had done something to improve the French treatment of animals since the war. I shd. be glad to believe this . . .

Tuesday 17 June: I dreamed in the night that I had a painful and (I understood) final parting from D and shortly afterwards found myself in a large swimming bath whose sides and bottom were of green turf. Here I discovered that a group of particularly unpleasant under-graduates – aesthetes of Satanic sneer – became very rude and violent. One of them however I converted and he came with me to an hotel where, being wakened in the night, we looked out and saw the streets all lit up with red fire. I knew it was the aesthetes who had done it and woke up remarking "I suppose this is the second fire of London." . . .

Wednesday 18 June: . . . In the evening I bussed into College to read my paper on J. Stephens in Donald's rooms – Edwards' old rooms.[10] Here I met King who told me that Carritt had been run into by a motor bicycle and had seemed all right for two days except for a black eye: but that now he had retired to bed.

We were a small meeting – King, Donald, Fasnacht, Dawson and two young strangers.[11] My quotations from Stephens produced much mirth and I think I made some converts.

During the interval Fasnacht told me about Sutton – my host of the other evening at Christ Church. He was given a Studentship there before Schools and afterwards got only a Second. Fasnacht said he was the worst bore and the worst reasoner of all people whom one met at philosophical societies . . .

Saturday-Tuesday 21-24 June: I left Oxford by the 10.50 for my week end with Harwood and travelled to London in a train crowded with undergraduates going down. There was one in my compartment who added the words "I mean" at the end of his every sentence, and, what was more inexcusable, kept the window shut.

From Paddington I Metro'ed to Victoria and thence, after some difficulty, caught a 24 bus to Lupus St. I had been in the flat for some time before Harwood arrived. He discovered that I had never seen the Elgin marbles, so after lunch he "carried" me to the British Museum.

Our attention was caught and held for a long time by the bull gates of the Assyrian Palace. I said "What cruelty – Hassan – one can imagine it all inside those gates." "No," said Harwood, "It's more the cruelty of nature."

By contrast the Greek things were all the more effective. We sat down for a long time opposite the pediment from Aegina, wondering what on earth it looked like to a company of streetboys who were wandering there. The best of all were the busts just outside the Elgin room: specially those of Pericles, Homer and Chrysippus.

---

[10] An account of Lewis's paper from the Martlets' minutebook is reproduced in "To the Martlets" in *C.S. Lewis: Speaker and Teacher*, ed. Carolyn Keefe (Grand Rapids, 1971; London, 1974).

[11] Douglas Alexander Donald matriculated in 1922 and received his BA in 1927.

The things from the Parthenon I appreciated more than I had hoped. If only the whole sweep of the pediment which has the horses rising at one end and diving at the other had survived. Besides that what impressed me most was the Artemis among the reliefs of the other gods – the only one that I have ever seen that is virginal but *not* in the way that appeals to a man's base love of virginity – and without being girlish or insignificant. It is just thoughtful, unconscious of itself, serious, inhuman and (so to speak) irrelevant – out of our world.

The other gods, so far as I could see, had nothing divine about them. After this the Assyrian things, as we passed them on our way out, were simply savage and stupid.

We had tea in the garden of a little teashop near the Museum. I forgot to mention that Harwood had taken me into the reading room at the Museum. He is a reader, but I am not: he managed it admirably, saying, "Now walk on as if you came here every day." Then an official shouted something at us and Harwood cried "That's all right" over his shoulder and so we were in – a most depressing place it is. We sat over our tea in the garden a long time and had some good talk.

Then home to supper and afterwards to the pit of the New Oxford to see the Old Vic people perform *As You Like It*. They were dreadfully bad and it is a bad play. We remarked (the word "came into existence" somehow between us and I do not know who is the author) adapting Boswell, "We'll go no more *before* your scenes Baker: the white bosoms of your actresses *fail* to excite our amorous propensities."

After the show we went round to the stage door to see Baker. I consented because I thought it easiest to get my first meeting over in the presence of a third party. We were admitted after a long wait and led down many stairs to a long narrow stone passage in the bowels of the earth wh. reminded me of nothing so much as an underground lavatory: then finally into a little greenwashed cell where we found Baker unmaking his face.

He greeted us both warmly and asked our opinion of the play. We hedged rather, saying we hadn't been able to hear well – wh. was true. Baker, very typically, took charge of the whole play in a seigneural manner and apologised for it – like a host apologising for some hitch in one's dinner. One other amusing and characteristic thing occurred. "These are fine boots," said Harwood picking up a pair of strange gambadoes. "No, they're not," said Baker with much seriousness, "but these," (producing another pair from his cupboard) "these are the real boots."

We then emerged from our den. A crowd of people were waiting outside the stage door and as I came past someone asked me "Do you know when Cyril is coming out?" I might have been thrilled at this my identification with the theatrical world if Baker had not assured me that I had been mistaken for an electrician.

These stage electricians he told us have no efficient trades union and are horribly sweated: some of the men in this theatre had not had their boots off for eight days. Their driver is the same Cochran who is responsible for the notorious Rodeo. He seems one of the worst nibelungs in London.[12] Harwood said it was wonderful that the crowd had spontaneously objected to the cruelties of steer roping. It showed that we were not yet decadent, that even if gladiators and bull fights were introduced, the people themselves would reject them.

The three of us went for some coffee to a place near by and then parted, arranging to meet Baker in Kew Gardens next day. That night I was again bothered with indigestion.

On Sunday morning we were late in rising and did nothing till lunch time. After feeding we trained to Kew and found Baker under the Pagoda – an ugly erection. It was a day almost intolerably bright and the light and shade on the cedars was wonderful. After walking about for some time we found a shady place and sat down. We talked of savage religion, the Russian stage with its mad, one dimensional business on ladders and of Shakespeare – how far he really believed in people like Romeo and Coriolanus – how often he had his tongue in his cheek.

We had tea in the gardens and then walked thro' the rockeries – Baker has become a gardener. We then came back by train and had supper at a restaurant "Espagnole" in Soho, where Baker stood us a bottle of Chianti. It was here that he announced his engagement in a very amusing manner.

Harwood and I left him soon after this as he had persuaded me

12 Sir Charles Blake Cochran (1872–1951), the showman who promoted boxing and wrestling matches, and music-hall acts such as Houdini, as well as introducing onto the popular stage such people as Sarah Bernhardt and Diaghilev's ballet.

to go with him to the Anthroposophical Society – chiefly I think to pull my leg. We had to take a taxi. Arriving at a quite innocent looking house we climbed many stairs into a small and insufferably hot room where some twelve people of various sexes and ages sat together.[13]

I was introduced to a plain and rather crushed looking woman, Mrs Kauffman. Harwood told her I was quite new to the game. She said it would be rather difficult for me, having my first lecture at this stage in the course, but added "perhaps I shouldn't say that. I don't know how much you have done." *Self*: "I am an absolute neophyte at this sort of business." *Mrs K.*: "Oh. That means that you have condemned it beforehand." *Self*: "I don't think you can really take that meaning out of my words." Shortly after this Barfield came in and sat between him and Miss Olivier.

Kauffman himself now appeared, a very dark, smooth shaven, broad browed man with a sort of unction about him. He sat down at a desk with his wife just beside him and read us his lecture in a very impressive manner, letting his dark eyes rest on everyone in turn with a sort of sugar sweet, spiritual familiarity. A priestly type beyond doubt.

But he came out best in question time after the lecture, when a number of very shy, rather silly and quite good hearted, ordinary girls put questions to him beginning with stammers and hesitations and ending with little bursts of gush – and then they would dart back into their holes, frightened at the sound of their own voices. At this time he would lean forward with an indescribable expression of encouragement, helping them out and saying by every gesture, "Yes – yes – I at least understand you my dear – what a lovely soul you have." It disgusted me.

Harwood said afterwards that my objection was not to spiritual conquests in general but to spiritual conquests made by anyone but me: that I disliked Kauffman because I was a rival Kauffman. "Thought horrid if true!"

We arranged to meet Barfield at the *Truth* offices on Tuesday and lunch with him. We then "carried" Miss Olivier home to the flat by

[13] Cecil Harwood had taken Lewis there to hear George Adams von Kaufmann (1894–1963). Kaufmann was born in Poland and for some years he had been one of the leading lights of the Anthroposophical Movement in England.

bus and she had coffee with us, and after some good talk Harwood saw her home.[14]

On Monday we decided suddenly after breakfast to go to *The Valkyrie* at His Majesty's tonight. This proposal raised me to the heavens and I was surprised to find how warm my old Wagnerian enthusiasm came back to me – it was like revisiting one's native town. When Harwood had gone to his work I went out and was so afraid we might not get into the gallery tonight that I went to His Majesty's and got two tickets for the upper circle. On my way home I went into the Tate and saw a lot of things which interested me, but I have forgotten what they were.

What happened in the afternoon I don't remember clearly. I think it was then that Harwood showed me some of his new poems including the excellent one on Donne's saying that "it is no where recorded that our Lord Jesus laughed." It has a very fine and specially Harwoodian flavour about it. In the refrain he accepted my emendation of "*Fac tecum nos maerere*" for his "*Fac nos tecum*".[15] It was also this afternoon I think that we passed through Charing Cross Rd on our return from somewhere forgotten[16] and looked into many bookshops.

Despite great heat the hours at His Majesty's were as glorious as any I have passed. It is not art – it is an irresistible sin or a religious expression. It is wonderful how in all the long scenes between Wotan and Brynhild or Wotan and Fricka (wh. some people find dull) he really gives us the feeling of assisting at the debates of the gods, of seeing the very most ultimate things hammering it out between them. "Thou great Argument heardest and the large design that brings the world out of the ill to good." Edna Thornton as Fricka was immense: the only one that really gave you the feeling of divinity.

In answer to a question of Harwood's about the plot I explained

---

[14] Plans were being made at this time for the setting up of a school in Streatham, London, "to educate boys and girls in the light of the educational teaching of Dr Rudolf Steiner". Miss Olivier was expected to be one of its teachers, and she and Cecil Harwood went down to Torquay during 9-23 August 1924 to hear Rudolf Steiner lecture on "True and False Paths of Spiritual Investigation". It was at this conference that Cecil Harwood met Steiner, and so bowled over was he by Steiner that he at once became totally committed to Anthroposophy, and remained so for the rest of his life. Michael Hall School, the first Steiner school in the country, was founded in January 1925 with Cecil Harwood and Daphne Olivier, who married on 14 August 1925, as two of its original five teachers. See Owen Barfield's "Cecil Harwood", *Anthroposophical Quarterly*, vol. 21, No. 2 (Summer 1976), pp. 36-9.

[15] "Make us grieve with thee." The poem is called "The Repentant City" in *The Voice of Cecil Harwood* (*loc. cit.*)

[16] From a walk in Kensington Gardens. – C.S.L.

that Fricka was my "old, old matriarchal dreadfulness"[17] wh. he repeated to Barfield next day at lunch, and everyone roared with laughter.

We walked home through Pall Mall striking the stars with our sublime heads. Beckett had returned so I slept on the camp bed (a v. comfortable one).

On Monday we lunched with Barfield in a little underground restaurant near the offices of *Truth*. They both attacked me about my scepticism about anthroposophy and I defended myself vigorously. Barfield and I turned out to be pretty much in agreement in the end. I was glad, for (as I said) it was always a shock to come up against something irreducibly different from oneself in any human being: that one *had* to believe that every *thou* was only a diguised *me*. Harwood said that I wanted to do away with all human personality, but Barfield agreed with me.

Barfield had to go to a theatrical garden party of all things, and Harwood to his work. I dawdled about for a bit, got my suitcase from *Truth* office and then, driven by thirst and curiosity, went for the first time in my life to a soda fountain – and the last. A more disgusting drink I never tasted. I then Metroed to Paddington and so home after a capital holiday: and yet glad, as usual, to be back.

Wednesday-Monday 25-30 June: A quiet time. I took Pat to bathe in Parson's Pleasure wh. they have rather spoiled by clipping the tops of the trees.

D and I had some delightful evening walks after supper down by the cemetery. Maureen goes regularly every evening to walk with Joy Holmes. Mrs Phipps, our charlady, has been ill and D took her her meals (whatever we have been having) daily.

---

[17] In Lewis's *Dymer*, Canto VI, 18.

Thursday 3 July: Today I went to Colchester in order to travel back in W's sidecar. I left by the 10.50 and metroed from Paddington to that desolating place Liverpool St., where I had a rather poor lunch for 4/6d in the G.E.R. Hotel. I travelled down to Colchester in the same compartment with some soldiers and a man of the poorer classes who was apparently an invalid (neurasthenia I think) and had a horribly pathetic parting with his wife – "Lord send them summer sometime."

A brisk shower of rain came down as I reached Colchester where I was met at the station by W and driven to the Red Lion where I had tea. This is one of the oldest hotels in England, curiously and beautifully beamed. W tells me that the American who insulted Kipling at the Rhodes dinner in Oxford has made a great name for himself (of a sort) in the army. W had just been reading *Puck of Pook's Hill* for the first time: he praised it highly and I agreed with him.

While we were sitting under the roof of a kind of courtyard after tea waiting for the rain to stop, a Major came up, to whom W introduced me, telling me afterwards that he was a very well preserved specimen of the real old type of army bore.

When it cleared a little we walked out to see the town, which is a very pleasant sprawling old world place, not unlike Guildford. The Roman castle is very fine in a kind quite new to me, as also the remains of the old gate of Camolodunum. There is also a pleasant old house (now an office but it ought to be a pub) bullet-marked from the civil wars.

After all this we motored up out of the town to a higher, windy land, full of camps. W's camp consists of a small old country house ("a Jorrocks house" he called it) and its park, now filled with huts. The C.O. lives in the Jorrocks house. I was taken into the mess (Lord, how strange to be in such a place again!) and of course given a drink. The "Orficers" were really very nice to me. It was odd to me to see a mess full of people in mufti.

We then motored back to town to a civilian club of which W is a member, where he had provided a royal feast of the sort we both liked: no nonsense about soup and pudding, but a sole each, cutlets with green peas, a *large* portion of strawberries and cream, and a tankard of the local beer which is very good. So we gorged like Roman Emperors in a room to ourselves and had good talk. W told me he had given *Dauber*[1] to a Major Falle (a friend of his) who, tho' a hater of poetry, had enjoyed it, but made one criticism: viz. that the sailors wd. not have despised Dauber's paintings: even if they had ragged him they would have been inwardly impressed.

We drove back to camp. W. had turned out into another hut and I had his bedroom. He has two rooms for his quarters. The sitting room with stove, easy chair, pictures, and all his French books, is very snug. I notice that a study in a hut, or a cave, or the cabin of a ship can be snug in a way that is impossible for a mere room in a house, the snugness there being a *victory*, a sort of defiant comfortableness – whereas in a house of course, one demands comfort and is simply annoyed at its absence. He "put into my hands" Anatole France's *Revolt of the Angels* in a translation, which seems an amusing squib.

Friday 4 July: We started on our Oxford journey after breakfast in the mess. The day looked threatening at first, but we had fair weather. I do not remember the names of the villages we passed, except Braintree and Dunmow (where the flitch lives).

At St Alban's we stopped to see the Cathedral: I had been there once before in my Wynyard days about 1909 or 1910 to sit and kneel for three hours watching Wyn Capron (whom God reject!) ordained a deacon or priest, I forget which.[2] Yet, in those days, that day without work, the journey to St Albans, the three hour's service and a lunch of cold beef and rice in an hotel was a treat for which we counted the days beforehand and felt *"nessun maggio dolore"*[3] when the following day brought us back to routine. I was rather glad to find the Cathedral quite definitely the poorest English cathedral I have yet seen.

---

[1] By John Masefield (1913).

[2] Eight miles from St Albans, in Watford, the brothers had suffered for several years in Wynyard School. Before its demise in 1910 it had been run by Robert "Oldy" Capron and his son Wynyard, and it is the school referred to as "Belsen" in chapter II of Lewis's *Surprised by Joy*.

[3] "There is no greater pain" (than to remember times of happiness when in wretchedness). Dante, *Inferno*, V, 121.

In the town we bought two pork pies to supplement what W considered the Spartan allowance of sandwiches given us by the mess, and drank some beer. I think it was here that W formed the project of going far out of the way to eat our lunch at Hunton Bridge on the L.N.W.R. where we used to sit and watch the trains when out on our walks from Wynyard. I assented eagerly. I love to exult in my happiness at being forever safe from at least one of the major ills of life – that of being a boy at school.

We bowled along very merrily in brilliant sunshine, while the country grew uglier and meaner at every turn, and therefore all the better for our purpose. We arrived at the bridge and devoured the scene – the two tunnels, wh. I hardly recognised at first, but memory came back. Of course things were changed. The spinney of little saplings had grown quite high. The countryside was no longer the howling waste it once looked to us. We ate our egg sandwiches and pork pies and drank our bottled beer. In spite of W's fears it was as much as we could do to get through them all. But then, as he pointed out, this was appropriate to the scene. We were behaving just as we would have done fifteen years earlier. "Having eaten every thing in sight, we are now finished." We had a lot of glorious reminiscent talk. We developed our own version of *"si jeunesse savait"*: if we could only have seen as far as this out of the hell of Wynyard. I felt a half comic, half savage pleasure (Hobbe's "sudden glory") to think how by the mere laws of life we had completely won and Oldy had completely lost. For here were we with our stomachs full of sandwiches sitting in the sun and wind, while he had been in hell these ten years.

We drove on and had tea at Aylesbury – dizzy by now and stupid with fresh air – and got to Oxford before seven.

Saturday-Monday 5-7 July: On Saturday . . . W and I (after I had done the lunch wash up) biked to Wantage Road where he wanted to take a photo of the fastest train in England. We did this successfully and looked out for a suitable place for tea on the return journey.

A countryman told us that there was no pub near, but that we could get tea at the – it sounded like Dog House. We both felt sure there could be no place called the Dog House, yet presently found it. Here we had strange adventures. I rang at the closed door – it is a little red house under a woodside – and waited for ten minutes: then rang again. At last a very ancient beldame appeared. I asked if we could have some tea. She looked hard at me and asked "Are you golfers?": on my answering "no" she shut the door softly and I could hear her hobbling away into the bowels of the house. I felt like Arthur at Orgolio's Castle.

Anon the ancient dame appeared again and, looking even harder at me, asked me a second time what I wanted. I repeated that we wanted some tea. She brought her face closer to mine and then with the air of one who comes at last to the real point asked *"How long do you want it for?"* I was quite unable to answer this question but by God's grace the witch left me *multa parantem dicere*[4] and hobbled away once more.

This time she left the door open and we walked in and found our way to a comfortable dining room where a plentiful and quite unmagical tea was presently brought us. We sat here for a very long time. A storm of wind got up (raised, I make no doubt, by our hostess, who, by the by, may have been the matriarchal dreadfulness) and the ivy lashed the windows.

On the next day, Sunday, we went to bathe at Parson's Pleasure with Pat who swam twice across the Cherwell. W. left us on Monday. While he was here I read and finished France's *Revolt of the Angels*. A good book – but I can *not* get over real Frenchness. When a young man, on being rebuked by his father for an amour, first feels an impulse to burst into tears, secondly an inclination to fall on his knees, and finally draws a red herring across the trail by drawing the parental attention to the immoralities of his sister – one cannot remain in the aesthetic sphere. A bad smell is beyond the reach of art.

Wednesday-Wednesday 9-16 July: I spent most of this time looking up the books I was to examine in: and the books which I wrongly believed I was to examine in: Lamb, Wordsworth, *Macbeth, Hamlet, Richard II, Lear, Twelfth Night, Eōthen, David Copperfield* and Macaulay's *Chatham and Clive*.

This is the first time I had looked into Macaulay for many years: I hope it will be many years before I read him again. It's not the style (in the narrower sense) that's the trouble – it's a very good style within its own limits. But the man is a humbug – a vulgar, shallow, self satisfied mind, absolutely inaccessible to the complexities and delicacies of the real world. He has the journalist's air of being a

---

[4] "preparing to say many things" - Aeneas trying (and failing) to answer Dido's reproaches on his leaving her. Virgil, *Aeneid*, IV, 390.

specialist in everything, of taking in all points of view and being always on the side of the angels: he merely annoys a reader who has had the least experience of *knowing* things, of what knowing is like. There is not two pence worth of real thought or real nobility in him. But he isn't dull.

These were days of lovely sunshine and I bathed nearly every day and lay out naked in the sun.

On Wednesday I got my first batch of papers to correct – Higher Certificate Shakespeare – and began work.

Thursday-Tuesday 17-29 July: All these days I worked hard on my examining. At first I had to interrupt myself several times to go in and "collaborate" with my fellow examiners for the *Locals* at the rooms of the Senior Examiner, one Simpson, a parson, in Museum Road. This collaboration was not such a nuisance as I expected: Simpson was v. pleasant and a help, not a hindrance. Here I met Rice-Oxley whom I knew at Keble: also an interesting Major Grey.

When this was over I settled into the following routine. I had breakfast at quarter to eight. For the first few mornings I was so sick that I had only a piece of toast, and even then I was sick a few moments later. I started work at eight and continued till lunch. While drinking my after lunch tea I walked for five minutes or so in the garden. I then began work again and continued till 6.45 or seven, taking my afternoon tea while I worked. At seven I walked over into Old Headington and had a whiskey and soda and came back for supper. Immediately after supper I began again and went on till twelve o'clock when I went to bed.

At first this routine told upon me very severely in the form of sickness, headache, and above all, nerves. I had a terrible reaction each night when I went to bed, feeling quite cowed and shaky. After a few days however I got my second wind and it became a normal and tolerable mode of life.

Poor D suffered as much, if not more than I did. For the first few days Valerie Evans was here as Maureen's guest and of course neither she nor Maureen gave the least help. What mortal dare interrupt *their* pleasures. D thus had a household of four humans and five v. troublesome animals to look after single handed. In addition she was suffering from sickness, like myself, and from corns: she could get no shoes which did not hurt her.

Valerie is prettier than ever: but the knowledge of this fact is rapidly spoiling her. Her main interest is now dress and she has adopted – perhaps innocently and unconsciously (*et mentem Venus ipsa dedit*)[5] – all those provocative little mannerisms which underline the fact that blind nature made her for one purpose. If only pretty women would realise with how many and with *what* people they share the power of attracting in this way!

Wednesday 30 July: I had now got through the worst of my papers and as there was no hurry over the rest, I took a day's holiday. The previous routine work had however left me in no way visibly the worse: indeed I have much more horror of it in retrospect than I had at the time. Today I bought a copy of *Tom Jones* and began to read it . . .

---

[5] "mind also Venus herself gave." Virgil, *Georgics*, III, 267 – changing the meaning from Virgil's, which is about sexual passion seizing mares.

Friday-Sunday 1-3 August: I continued now my old routine for morning and afternoon, but instead of continuing till midnight I usually finished at 6.30: then had my drink, washed up after supper and read *Tom Jones* in the evening. As I came near the end I found it harder to keep my mind on the work and instead of doing the papers I wanted to reflect how few there were still to do.

Tom Jones is a good book. I don't know how it got the reputation of being libidinous. The real point about it is the pure narrative power: it has such a momentum. When novels switch off from one group of characters to another one is usually irritated: Fielding always makes you feel that it is just what you want. The mock Homeric parts are capital – far better than those in *The Battle of the Books*.[1] What surprised me most was the real romantic feeling in the scene wh. introduces the Man of the Hill: though of course his story is rubbish.

Dorothea (or Dotty or Toddy or Totty, for D has not yet settled her name) seems to have many good qualities. She seems plain at first, but her face improves on acquaintance and becomes really rather comely at times. She is the very antithesis of Valerie. She believes herself to be plain, always has holes in her stockings and seldom has clean hands, has girlishly violent views on powder and over interest in clothes: all of wh. is to the good. She is absolutely unaffected – a loud, floundering, untidy, excitable person, all over a room at once: in shape, to quote Stephens "a lank anatomy all leg and hair and stare like a young colt". Intellectually, on the other hand, she is far older than any girls I have met from this school: has read fairly widely and is full of extreme views on all imaginable subjects – just as one ought to be at her age. She is the only one of Maureen's friends who has ever shown the least consideration for D, for whom she has bought oranges – these being now v. hard to get.

[1] By Jonathan Swift (1704).

┌─────────────┐

1925

After the entry for 1-3 August 1924 Lewis gave up his diary until 6 February 1925. He was very busy during this period correcting Local Examination Papers and preparing to take over Mr Carritt's teaching. On 14 October 1924 he began his course of twice-weekly lectures for the University entitled "The Good, its position among the values" as well as tutorials for University College.

Jack and Warnie were with their father in Belfast from 23 December 1924 to 10 January 1925, after which Warnie stopped at "Hillsboro" for a week.

Hilary Term began on 11 January 1925 and on 23 January Lewis began a twice-weekly course of lectures entitled "Moral Good, its position among values". When the diary is resumed on 6 February we find Lewis giving tutorials at University College and correcting School Certificate Essays in his spare time.

Friday 6 February: Into town as usual after breakfast. Buckley brought me an essay on deduction – better than last time.[1] I find it hard to make myself understood with him – we are always at cross purposes. Next came Hogg with whom I read the first and second analogies.[2] Swanwick came in to join us, but as he works with Watson's selections we found it impossible to harmonise and sent him away.[3]

At 12 I went to the Payne for my lecture. Today my audience had dwindled to two – Hawker and the old parson. As they professed a wish to continue the course, I had them to my room. I said we could now be informal and I hoped they would interrupt whenever they wanted. The old parson availed himself of this so liberally that I could hardly get a word in. He seems to be a mono maniac – he has

---

[1] Charles Douglas Buckley took his BA in 1925.

[2] Robert Heuzé Hogg who took his BA in 1926.

[3] Michael Robert Swanwick took his BA in 1926. These pupils were reading Kant, and Swanwick was using *The Philosophy of Kant as Contained in Extracts from his Own Writings*, selected and translated by John Watson (1888).

some grudge against the Archbishop of York – who came in *twice* – I forget how. He also has some psychological hobby horse about "the hedonic tone of psychosis" wh. came in more than once. The funniest thing was when he said that an object *qua* cognition could not *attract*: he held out a very ugly hand with hair on the back and stubbed nails and said "Now suppose I have an object here – a quite unattractive object."[4] Hawker promised to back me up.[5]

Home by 1.30 and an excellent lunch. After usual jobs I went for a walk up Shotover. Am just beginning to be conscious of the face of nature again after a long strange imprisonment in myself. Steel coloured sky, and a cold rain came on. Pat and I hid among trees on the top of Pullen's Gap. On the way home one half of the sky was grey cloud but there was a huge blue gap over Wytham and glittering piles of white beyond it.

Home for tea. Afterwards I set papers on the *Merchant of Venice* and started looking up a suitable "English Story" for L[ocal] C[ertificate]. At 6.30 in to Hall.

A man called Ingles was there as Keir's guest who was apparently up with me, but I had forgotten him – now at Cuddesdon – rather a prig I think. Sat between Allen and Lawson.[6] Quite good talk.

Home by 9 o'clock. Read *Matière et Mémoire* in the evening.[7]

Saturday 7 February: Beattie came this morning with a rather muddled but vigorous essay on the plurality of goods.[8] We had an excellent discussion. Then came Donald on Kant's causation.[9] Interesting and paradoxical as usual, but not very solid. Finally came Swanwick without an essay, and I tried to hammer some interpretation of deduction into him. It is impossible to tell how much he understands . . .

Walked out after lunch and bought *Travels with a Donkey*[10] (which I need for L.C.) at Mowbray's: then bussed home and walked up Shotover with Pat. Went to the grove at the far end by the path wh. has just been re-opened since the foot and mouth disease scare.

---

[4] The Rev. Frank Nightingale had gone to the University of London after being a priest in the Church of England since 1894, and he had now retired to Oxford.

[5] Gerald Wynne Hawker of University College took a BA in 1925.

[6] Frederick Henry Lawson (1897–1983) was Lecturer in Law at University College 1924–25. From there he went to Merton College as Fellow of Law 1925–30, after which he became Professor of Comparative Law and a Fellow of Brasenose College in 1948.

[7] By Henri Bergson (1896).

[8] George Liddell Caruthers Beattie matriculated at University College in 1923.

[9] Douglas Alexander Donald who took his BA in 1927.

[10] By Robert Louis Stevenson (1879).

Home with a headache after a beautiful walk. Maureen had Celia Waterhouse to tea – a dull girl. Read *Travels with a Donkey* in the evening: a glorious book if you could omit the Modestine parts. Lateish to bed.

Monday 9 February: In after breakfast. Little Buchanan came with an essay on Utilitarianism, the first he's done for me: really very good and already far beyond Swanwick.[11] Next came Nash who thought two sides of a foolscap a sufficient essay on the *Refutation of Idealism* and appeared in discussion to have read hardly any of it. I made myself as unpleasant as I could about it, but I am not much good at this sort of thing.[12]

I then went out and got an envelope to post my long delayed letter for Carritt and ordered Gadney's to send over in the afternoon Sidgwick's *Historical Ballad* for L.C . . .

After tea into College and worked over my Berkeley and Hume notes for tomorrow. Dined in. Haig, of my year (now in Nigeria) was there as Ley's guest. A dull evening except for a few quips of Poynton's. Bussed home – a windy moonlight night – and was collared for unseens by Dotty. Poor D still marmalading.

Tuesday 10 February: Rather late up. Into town and worked on my Sidgwick paper for L.C. At 12 came Campbell – rather sleepy I thought, and not so good as usual.[13] Keir and Lawson came for lunch: the usual brisk but not really interesting conversation. We are rather like the three curates in *Shirley*.

Came home and took Pat for a walk in Cuckoo Lane. In at 5.30. Bradley and Gordon-Clark came: the former does nearly all the talking – he is a nephew of *Appearance and Reality*.[14] They had brought me several questions on Berkeley and Hume, all of which I was able to answer, by good fortune.[15]

Dined in hall and left at once to hurry to the theatre for the O.U.D.S. [production of] *Peer Gynt*. D, Maureen and Dotty were already there. I was v. disappointed in the play. The general idea of a history of the soul is all right, but Peer's soul hasn't enough in it to last for four hours: most of him is mere Nordic windbagism. No good making a story of Peer: you only want to kick his bottom and

---

[11] Edward Handasyde Buchanan took his BA in 1928.
[12] Eric Francis Nash took his BA in 1926.
[13] Ralph Abercrombie Campbell matriculated in 1924.
[14] By F.H. Bradley (1893).
[15] Kenneth Grenville Bradley and John Stanley Gordon-Clark took their BAs in 1925.

get on. The Troll parts from the visual point of view were the best
stage devilment I've ever seen . . .

Wednesday 11 February: Up at 7.30 and so to breakfast. Stevenson
had been to the O.U.D.S. too and thought it excellent. Cox didn't
turn up. Henderson and, after him Ross the American.[16]

Keir and Lawson for lunch. I quoted a line from the *Prelude* and
Lawson thought it came from Rowbottom.

Home and for a walk with Pat by the cemetery. Worked on
Leibnitz in the evening in my new edition. He had wonderful insight
in some ways: he has the sense for biology wh. none of his
contemporaries get anywhere near.

Early to bed, all rather tired. D *still* at the infernal marmalade.

Thursday 12 February: In as usual in the morning and a walk in the
afternoon. Back to town by 5.30 and took Firth – a fairly good hour.[17]
I dined in hall: several undergraduates from other colleges there as
guests.

Immediately afterwards I went to Ware's rooms in Worcester St.
for a meeting of the Phil. Soc. – I should have had some difficulty
in finding them if I had not met Ewing. Ziman read his paper on
causality. I, having heard it all from him in the morning, was rather
bored. The discussion afterwards soon drifted off on to Touche's
and Dawson's favourite position and I had an enjoyable argument.
Home late – a wet night.

Saturday 14 February: Beattie came this morning. I like this man
really very well. Then came Donald who read a most pretentious
essay, full of silly epigrams, nominally on the plurality of goods, but
as usual all Gentile[18] and water. I applied the Socratic method, I
think with some good results. What a lot of good a term with Kirk
would do him! Finally came poor Swanwick.

Lawson came to lunch: talked about Iceland which we both want
to visit. Bought a copy of *Peer Gynt* (Everyman) and took Joachim's
Spinoza out of the Union.

Bussed home. Took Pat down by the cemetery and got some rain:
also a wonderful livid light over Otmoor. After tea I worked on
Spinoza – I find the psychology (if one can call it that) very puzzling.
Phippy was here. Thank heavens D has finished the marmalade. She
had a touch of neuritis last night. Long conversation with Dotty and

[16] Kenneth David Druitt Henderson took his BA in 1926, and James Alexander Ross took his in 1925.
[17] Edward Michael Tyndell Firth took his BA in 1926.
[18] The philosophy of Giovanni Gentile (1875–1944).

Maureen at supper time about the difference between men's and women's friendships.

Sunday 15 February: ... Got home about noon and sat in my old room where the fire had been lit to dry the damp out of the wall. I read thro' "Dymer" I-VI. I, II, IV, and V are better than I thought – if only I could have kept it up!

After lunch I washed up and did the usual jobs, then worked on Leibnitz till tea time. D came and sat with me and we were very snug. After tea I took a spell off and read *Mary Rose* – a beautiful and suggestive play.[19]

Then supper and while doing jars etc. afterwards I read most of the *Master Builder* and understood it much better than when I had seen it with Harwood at the Playhouse. Earlyish to bed – a most enjoyable day.

Monday 16 February: I went in in some trepidation lest a staff meeting might have been sprung upon us since Saturday, but fortunately a notice of warning for Friday next came round and set my mind at rest.

Buchanan brought an essay on Thrasymachus. While he was with me Dawson came in and asked me to the Martlets dinner. I asked to be allowed to come en Martlet (i.e. not as a parasite) but he would not have it. I booked him for walk and tea next Saturday. Nash came at 11 and read a much better essay than last week.

The morning was really glorious – Dionysiac. I enjoyed my walk with Pat before breakfast greatly – round by the Croft. Now it was even better, looking from my window down on the crocuses in the garden and over to Merton tower.

Went to the Union and returned Hoffding, taking out Pollock's *Spinoza*: then home by bus. Read a good bit in Pollock before lunch. Afterwards I took Pat down by the cemetery. Home and worked again on Spinoza ...

Tuesday 17 February: ... Went to College, having bought a second hand copy of B. Russell's *Problems* [*of Philosophy*] for 1/-. I worked for some time on Spinoza and finished *Ethics* Part II: then read *Problems* wh. I had not read before since 1917. What an excellent clear book for anyone to begin on ...

Home and read a little Bridges, then, after tea, into town and took Bradley and Gordon-Clark on Spinoza and Leibnitz.

---

[19] By Sir James Barrie (1920).

Dined in. Farquharson in the chair. Heard a splendid yarn about Campbell of Hertford getting drunk on dentist's ether – must remember to tell Tchanie [Jane McNeill]. Farquharson discussed the madness of Mary Lamb – quite interesting conversation. I mentioned my qualms about Swanwick to him just before leaving.

Home in good time. D in excellent spirits.

Wednesday 18 February: Called by D at 7.30 and (after tea and bread and butter) walked to the top of the hill and then bussed in to breakfast in Common Room. Poached eggs cold – why can't they get things hot?

Up to my room where Cox soon arrived. I began to twit him about skipping his last tutorial when I discovered to my horror that he had been absent because his father was dying. Of course I had known nothing about it, tho' they have sent me round slips with the names of every other fellow who has been absent. I apologised of course, and did the best I could, but it was very unpleasant for everyone.[20]

Next came Henderson with an excellent essay: then Ross who was quite unexpectedly good. After him Nightingale and Hawker for lecture. I unhappily mentioned Heathcliff and of course discovered that Nightingale was an ardent Bronte-ite which gives him another conversational opening.

When these had gone I went down to Keir's rooms and lunched with him and Lawson. They also complained of never having their own pupils on the Aeger list. Keir suggested that they put a representative selection of names in to show you: "This is the kind of man who is sick at present."

I took Moore's *Philosophical Studies*[21] out of the library and bussed home. Phippy was here. Started for a walk with Pat before tea but was driven back by rain. Went down Cuckoo Lane with him later on – a beautiful sunset. Read Moore on "External Relations" in the evening. Supper at home and all very jolly.

Thursday 19 February: A very cold day. Low came at 10 and read quite a good essay on Spinoza.[22] Next was Johnson on Kant's *Ethics*: a good discussion and not a bad essay – there's no doubt he's improving.[23] A welcome telephone message came to say that Ziman had a bad cold and could not come for his tutorial.

---

[20] This was Harold Henry Cox, who was able to stay up and take his BA in 1927.
[21] By George Edward Moore (1922).
[22] Marcus Warren Low took his BA in 1926.
[23] Harold Cottam Johnson matriculated in 1922.

Bussed home. After lunch I started for a walk with Pat and was just crossing the allotments to Shotover when I was driven back by rain. Went to my room and looked through "Dymer" VIII: was pleased with it and thank the Lord it's not very *old*. I managed to get a little stroll down Cuckoo's Lane: home for tea and in to College to take Firth on Kant's Causality. An interesting essay. Dined in hall. Poynton and Farquharson both in and very amusing.

Friday 20 February: Up early. Poor D had had a very bad go of neuritis in the night – much worse than before . . .

Buckley came with an essay on Spinoza. I got on with him better than last time. Next was Hogg – a little better but far from good. After him was lecture. Hawker arrived a little earlier than Nightingale and I had a few words with him. He said mine was the most intelligible scheme of ethics he had yet heard. Nightingale was specially interruptive today and remarked "I hope I am not taking up your time – but I find I learn more by talking than by listening." I was tempted to reply "So do I."

Lunched with Keir and Lawson in Keir's room. Keir tracked down Kant's Scottish ancestry – apparently Kant is a good Scotch name. Quite a good rag conversation.

Then bussed home. Feeling very fit. I had a divine walk up Shotover by the main road and down by the path through Quarry. It was frosty with a veiled blue sky and big cloud pinnacles and the most wonderfully fresh and sweet air. Then worked on Moore's "External Relations" after tea and in to dinner. We had wine in the summer common room afterwards, which I always like better. Farquharson in the chair. He and Allen very amusing.

Saturday 21 February: A fine bright morning. Beattie came and then Donald who read an essay full of squibs, quite clever, but off the point. Then poor Swanwick – worse than ever. I have spoken to Farquharson about him but no one takes any notice.

Then home to lunch. Dawson, Touche and Ewing came at 2.30 and we all walked to Stowe Woods, Dawson preaching Gentile at me hard. Of course neither of us moved the other but it was quite good talk. They came back for tea and stayed till 6.45. I liked them all, even that queer little troll of a Ewing. Dawson has a touch of conceit in him and is a little bit edgy but he has it in hand. Touche I take for *anima candida*.

Tuesday 24 Februrary: In to College by 10 o'c. and worked till 12 on Hobhouse – a man after my own heart. Then came Campbell with an essay on Plurality of Goods. Rather an interesting discussion.

A terrible day of cold and driving rain. Bussed home and had lunch: then took Pat for a short walk in Cuckoo Lane, getting wet again. D seemed rather tired and depressed today . . .

I then jotted down a few ideas that had occurred to me on the theory of knowledge. In to College by 5.30 and took Bradley and Gordon-Clark on Kant. The latter talked a fair amount, for the first time: I like him much better than Bradley . . .

Wednesday 25 February: In for breakfast by 8.15. Quite a good morning. One very funny episode occurred when the door was opened for a moment and a snatch of Carlyle's voice croaking away outside drifted suddenly in and threw us all into laughter. Leys gave an excellent sketch of Carlyle in the next world.

Took Cox at 9, Henderson at 10, and Ross at 11 – all good in their degrees . . . Then had Hawker and Nightingale: the latter very talkative but rather more relevant than usual . . .

At 7 I bussed in for the Martlets dinner. Managed to dress while Hayden (the Cambridge Martlet whom they have billeted in my bedroom) was in his bath. He turned up presently and we went together to Cox's rooms. The Master, Allen, and Keir were there. At dinner in the J.C.R. I sat next to Hayden – a most aggressive pup who told me I was "terribly Oxford" and "academic" because I said I disappoved of English as a final honour school.

He read us a paper afterwards on Atlantis in the Senior Common Room, bringing some anthropological and geological evidence which was quite interesting, and then giving us a sketch of Atlantean civilisation: when, by a chain of initiates first planted in the "Atlantean colony" of Egypt and afterwards removing to Tibet, we derive all our ethics and religion to this day. Christ, Moses and a few others were all such initiates or their disciples. The odd thing was that when challenged by Dawson (who is now President) he denied any knowledge of anthropology. Carlyle was very good and roasted Hayden, within the bounds of civility, but exquisitely . . .

Thursday 26 February: Low was absent. Johnson read an essay on the moral faculty which was really quite good in style as well as in thought – a change from his first efforts. I like this man, despite his odd manners and appearance. Ziman, who should have followed him, was aeger . . . Firth at 5.30 – a good and agreeable hour.

Dined in hall and went afterwards to the Phil. Soc. in Firth's rooms where Paton of Queens read a paper on "Duty or Duties". A charming creature: a picture philosopher's face and a soothing voice on whose modulations he has taken pains and not in vain.[24] He is strong on the analogy between ethics and aesthetics and distinguished sharply the legal morality of the vulgar from the creative morality of the saint. He thinks the highest moral good may well be something literally impossible for most men – that the *ought* does not imply the *can*. I thanked my God when a drunk man burst into the room by accident with a genial cry, but he left us all too soon, and we went on. Quite a heated discussion afterwards. Dawson and I for once were on one side. We cldn't make Paton admit any essential difference between art and virtue . . .

Friday 27 February: Buckley, Hogg (much improved) and lecture. At the end of the latter old Nightingale broke forth into a panegyric on my lectures. What between comic despair that my only admirer was such an old ass, and a sort of shame that I shd. return an old honest man's good will by *thinking* him an ass, I was in a confused state . . .

Sunday 1 March: Up late. A grey, raw day, bringing horizons near. Up Shotover with Pat after breakfast. Too many people about, but I enjoyed my walk. The fire was in the yellow room. Sat there when I got home and began re-reading Tasso's *Jerusalem* with considerable enjoyment: but I was disappointed in my Italian. Lunch and jobs and a nice quiet afternoon reading in the yellow room with D: the girls being all at the Taylors, D and I had a pleasant little stroll round Barton after tea.

---

[24] Herbert James Paton (1887–1969) was Fellow and Praelector in Classics and Philosophy at Queen's College, Oxford, 1911–27, and White's Professor of Moral Philosophy, Oxford, 1937–52.

Once again Lewis abandoned his dairy, this time from 2 March until 16 August 1925. While it is a pity that this happened when there was so much of interest going on, the events which he was too busy to record are pretty amply covered in letters to his father. Writing to him in April 1925 he said "This is my last term 'in the bond' at Univ. and there is still no word of the Fellowship. I begin to be afraid that it is not coming at all. A Fellowship in English is announced at Magdalen and of course I am applying for it, but without any serious hopes as I believe much senior people including my own old English tutor are in for it. If he gets it I may get some of the 'good will of the business': I mean some of the pupils at Univ., Exeter and elsewhere whom he will have to abandon. These continued hopes deferred are trying, and I'm afraid trying for you too. About money, if you will put in £40 – if you think this is reasonable – I shall be on the pig's back."

The next few weeks were to be some of the most nerve racking of Lewis's life. Writing to his father about them on 25 May he described what happened about the Fellowship in English at Magdalen: "First of all, as I told you, I thought that I had my own tutor Wilson as a rival, which would have made the thing hopeless. But that I found to be a false rumour. Then I wrote to Wilson and Gordon ... for testimonials, relying on them as my strongest support. Within twenty-four hours I had the same answer from both. They were very sorry. If only they had known I was going in for it ... they thought I had definitely abandoned English for philosophy. As it was, they had already given their support to my friend Coghill of Exeter ... That was enough to make anyone despair: but mark how the stars sometimes fight for us. Two days later came news that Coghill had been offered a fellowship by his own College and had withdrawn from the field. Wilson's testimonial – a very good one – came by the next post. Gordon said he wouldn't write anything as he was going to be consulted personally by the Magdalen people, but he would back *me* ...

"*Then came an invitation to dine at Magdalen on Sunday a fortnight ago [3 May]. This showed only that I was one of the possibles . . . Then came a spell of thundery weather of the sort that makes a man nervous and irritable even if he has nothing on his mind: and the news that Bryson and I were the two real candidates . . . One afternoon, in that week, I saw the said Bryson emerging from Magdalen and ('so full of shapes is fancy') felt an unanswerable inner conviction that he had won and made up my mind on it . . . On Monday [18 May] I had a very abrupt note from [Sir Herbert Warren – President of Magdalen College] asking me to see him on Tuesday morning . . . I got to Magdalen, and . . . when he did see me it turned out to be all formalities. They were electing tomorrow and thought me the 'strongest and most acceptable candidate'. Now, if I were elected would I agree to do this, and would I be prepared to do that . . . The only thing of the slightest importance was 'would I be prepared in addition to the English pupils, to help with the philosophy'. (This, I imagine, stood me in good stead: probably no other candidate had done English as well as philosophy.) I need hardly say that I would have agreed to coach a troupe of performing bagbirds in the quadrangle . . . And then next day – about 2.30 – they telephoned for me and I went down. Warren saw me, told me I had been elected and shook hands . . . It is a fine job as our standards go: starting at £500 a year with 'provisions made for rooms, a pension, and dining allowance.' *"

Sunday 16 August: The day was spent in preparations for our departure tomorrow for Cloud Farm at Oare on Exmoor. How the putting up of three people's clothes for three weeks can take so much labour is a mystery. D spent most of the day making a canvas cover for the new trunk so that the packing proper could not begin till about five and did not end till 2 a.m . . .

In the afternoon I went to order a taxi for tomorrow at Griffins, and finding him engaged, walked down to Nicholls on Cowley Road. A sweltering afternoon. Sometime between eleven and one we drifted into a discussion on packing in which Maureen and I foolishly ventured on some criticisms. I hope it was not my fault, but D was so angry and nettled that we had to drop the subject. To bed with a fairly bad headache but slept sound.

Monday 17 August: Up in good time. Pretty bad time till we got off at 10.45. D called on Herbert to have some small point set right in her new teeth which are, on the whole, a real piece of artistry: not too regular – a life-like if idealistic version of her old ones and comfortable as well. I am glad that business has been so well got over.

In the train to Reading D had lunch with a remarkably unpleasant old woman who told brazen lies about a seat. It was another gorgeous day. I think I never stopped sweating from the time I got up till after supper. We managed the rest of the journey to Minehead quite comfortably, tho' we were crowded till Taunton. We had lunch and tea from our own stores in the train. It was interesting to go through the Old Cleeve country. I was at the window from Watchet to Minehead picking out every detail of that wonderful three weeks in 1920. From Minehead we came to the County Gate (above Glenthorne by char-a-banc: the first time any of us had travelled in one. We didn't like it – either for comfort or safety – specially on the nightmare hill from Porlock).

Once on top of the moor, despite the heat and discomfort of our crowded seats, we all revived: tho' poor D was feeling a little sick. It was heather all round us and a grand smell . . . the sea far down below on our right: and every now and then a glimpse to the left of flattish grey and brown ridges, one behind the other to the horizon – a gloriously large horizon.

At the County Gate we were met by a civil but densely stupid raw boned youth with a two wheeled vehicle on which D and Maureen and the luggage went off. There was a woman by the Gate whom I shall always remember: a cross between the Duchess in *Alice in Wonderland* and the first Mrs Rochester.

Then Pat and I turned in ecstasy to our walk. Pat bolted after the others but I recovered him. I went through a wicket on to the moor and proceeded down hill. In front of me I saw a deep winding valley stretching as far as I could see to left and right and deeply wooded: at right angles to it on the far side, another and narrower combe (which I rightly took for Badgworthy) piercing well into the moor. After a few more steps I could see a broad flat brown river in the bottom before me. On my way down I had a glimpse of a fat fast snake in the bracken. I reached the river and forded it: shoes and socks in my left hand, a stick and Pat's lead in the right.

Here, at the bottom, I was as if between walls: purple walls of heather behind me and green ones ahead: both unexpectedly steep when seen from that angle. I shall remember while I live the feel of that cold yet not biting water and the deliciously cool stones. It made amends for all the troubles of packing and journey.

I then followed a red lane into Malmsmead which proved to be no more than three or four cottages with black pigs at doors and a house of entertainment where stone ginger was the best they could give me. I had some difficulty in finding the path to Cloud Farm: but was finally led to it by a man on a pony whom I met at Oare: a respectful horsy person – a huntsman perhaps, who read me a lecture on the merits of Exmoor ponies. I followed up a path through a wood on to a flat field by the riverside: it was still cultivated land about me but I saw the real moor ahead – the almost black combe opening out beyond Cloud Farm in its windings.

Here I met D and Maureen. The whole thing realised my best dreams. The farm house stands under a wood of fir with one field between it and the river. The rooms were comfortable and the supper good.

After the meal Pat and I went out and having crossed Badgworthy began to follow the valley up. It was an almost colourless evening with one star very much blunted by mist hanging in the V shaped cleft of the hills before me. The river is very broken with rocks and there is plenty of white foam. I went as far as a little wood and here the path went a bit higher, and thence down to a flat platform of turf between the wood and the water. I was quite out of sight of cultivated land here: I looked back and I looked forward and either way saw nothing but high hills.

It was not until I struck a match for my pipe that I realised how dark it had grown. When I got back into the wood it was almost pitch black except for the odd light cast upwards from the stream through the tree trunks. There were many strange appearances of white stones that could have passed for ghosts.

Home and to bed by eleven in that glorious thing – a *good* feather bed. Through my window I saw a side of moorland and a few stars. The sky seemed to have cleared.

Tuesday 18 August: We breakfasted about nine, after a good night's rest, on eggs and home cured bacon: both excellent. D was still rather tired from the journey and said she would take "a lazy day". Maureen and I started for a walk at ten.

We went up the valley in the tracks of my evening stroll. The wood grew even better beyond my last night's farthest south. The trees were very old and mossy, the turf of a jewel like greenness and studded with white boulders. The path rose considerably as we went through the wood. We stopped for our first halt at a stream where Maureen cooled her feet. After we left the wood the path was high above the river and very heathery. The view back down the receding reaches of the valley, deepening as it receded and backed by the great ridge at the County Gate, was one of the finest I have ever seen: and with every step forward increased the sense of penetrating into "the bowels of the land".

Presently we turned up the Doone Valley. Here we were rather disappointed to find a party on ponies in front of us. Just at the shepherd's hut a cow ran at us, but I waved my stick and it considered that honour was satisfied. We put on speed after this until we had passed the ponies and then struck right over open moor. It was very hot. Presently we began to descend and saw a big lump of hill opposite us which I take to be Great Black Hill. To our right we had a lovely new glimpse of Badgworthy Combe and the woods beyond it. About here we got into very dense heather and saw it suddenly quiver in front of us . . . We . . . struck left till we reached a green gully about four feet deep and running quite straight down the hillside. After a few yards descent it developed, as I had expected, into a stream, where we picked our way from stone to stone laboriously. We found plenty of frog spawn and some red mosses.

It was a relief to find another stream running east at the bottom and to stretch our legs on flat gravel. This was Lank Combe . . . We then went on again and a little to our left till we saw the woods of Cloud Farm below us. We intentionally overshot our mark and went on, beyond a little combe, to the green part of the hill. Here we had a long rest.

Maureen, apropos of something, asked me if the evolutionary theory meant that we had come from monkeys. I explained what it really meant. She asked where Adam and Eve came in. I explained that the Biblical and scientific accounts were alternatives. She asked me which I believed. I said the scientific. She said "I suppose if one believes in it then, one doesn't believe in God." I said one could believe in God without believing in all the things said about him in the Old Testament. Here the matter ended. I don't see how I could have answered differently at any point.

. . . We waded the river for our feet's sake and so arrived home at 1.15. D had been unpacking and was very sleepy. Indeed we all felt a drowsiness in the air which increased after a very ample and

excellent lunch of boiled chicken. Maureen and I made some play
with doing German while D very nearly sank into real sleep.

. . . After tea we found more comfortable seats at the top of a kind
of miniature cliff near the farm. I went on with Cowper's *Task* which
I began to read for the second time just before we left home. I was
at Book II, "The Timepiece", one of the poorest parts. At his worst
he is bad enough, but somehow he never irritates me . . .

After supper all three of us went up to the wood as I had done
last night. The difference between society and solitude, together with
a little more delight, altered everything. Last night it had been all
desolation and awe: tonight it was peaceful and drowsy. To bed by
eleven.

Wednesday 19 August: We had some thunder and lightning in the
night and continual rain. When I woke in the morning the view from
my window was a solid wall of fog. Then gradually the dark surface
of the moor would show through and reach a certain point of
clearness: after which it would fade again. The fog went on thinning
and thickening like this for an hour. When I had shaved I went down
to the river. From a few yards away the outline was invisible: only
the swirls of foam showed up rather whiter than the smoky mist. I
took a dip in the deep pool under the fall. It was quite deep enough
to swim in and very cold, so that I did no more than reach the further
bank and come back.

D was more rested this morning and I think she is going to like
the place – a point about which I have had some fears. After breakfast
Maureen and I set out with Pat. We went down the valley on this
side by the path over three fields and through a wood which is the
normal entrance of this farm. The grass was soaking and the fog
very thick. On reaching the road we turned right and went to Oare
where we had a look at the church: a pleasant crowded little building
but neither very old nor beautiful . . .

Just before lunch I yielded to a long treasured desire and wrote
for Geo. MacDonald's *Lilith*: he and Wordsworth being the only
people it seems possible to read here. We had chicken for lunch again:
very good and better than yesterday by the addition of green peas.
We sat in till tea time. I did some German with Maureen and
continued *The Task*.

After tea all three of us went out for a delightful walk. We turned
up the valley, keeping to our own side of the river. It is much rougher
here and, happily, not open to the public. The view both up and

down was beyond anything I have yet seen. It reminded D of Norway . . .

Thursday 20 August: A grey morning. I bathed as before. After breakfast Maureen said she would stay at home and I sallied forth by myself. I crossed the river and turned to my right as if for Malmsmead: then to my left by a lane which brought me up quickly to a high and richly heathered part of the moor. I followed this for some little way and turned to my right by a track which would lead me past the tumuli. Even frequent references to the map did not keep me in the true way. I bore too much to my right and crossed two westward flowing streams instead of one. At the first I had a pleasant halt and a smoke in a little green valley full of boulders overhung with miniature cliffs of heather.

I reached my objective – the upper end of Lank Combe – earlier than I expected, but I was not sorry. On the level tops of these hills with no valleys in view I find it a little oppressive. Indeed on my walks and in my mental pictures these last two days I can trace a little hyperaesthesia. Perhaps it is just as well I have never seen real mountains. The descent of Lank Combe was very laborious, but beautiful.

As I reached the bottom it began to rain. The rest of my walk was unpleasant, not so much because of the rain as of a small boy – *ceteris paribus*[1] the least pleasant type of human being – who tacked himself on to me and followed me with relentless conversation however fast or slow I walked. One touch of nature deserves a record. He asked me (in the wood) if I'd been up here in the dark. I said "Yes" and began to like him better. I asked him if he had been in the river. He replied "No" and, poor creature, looked mortified as if he had relinquished all claims to manhood. Then suddenly a bright idea struck him. "Me and my brother was nearly killed the other day." His brother's head had been cut by a collapse of stone "and he made ten shillings showing it to the visitors".

Got home and changed. After lunch I began St John Ervine's *Alice and a Family* which I found in a cupboard: in many ways a good book, but it plays too much on the mere language of Cockneys. Now this is only a repetition of the child's idea that all foreign languages are mumbled English. Every dialect ought to be got over and taken for granted. Then we can get at what is really going on.

---

[1] "other things being equal".

After tea we had an excellent walk up the far side of the valley nearly to the "Doone Valley". By the way when I see the crowds of lost townspeople who trail up that far side of the river of a fine morning, blind to heather, sky and rock, and deaf to birds and water, to look at one of the least attractive combes because it has been labelled "Doone" and then ask fretfully, "But what is there to *see*?" – I cd. wish Blackmore had never written . . .

Friday 21 August: Another grey day. Bathed. Set out to find the way to the sea at Glenthorne. I walked down our own side of the valley, crossed the Lyn at Parsonage Farm, and up to County Gate. Couldn't find any way down so turned west and went to Brendon. Home by road with a delicious halt in the wood by Malmsmead.

Out after tea with D and Maureen. A card to say that *Lilith* is out of print and an insane letter from Aunt Lily. I am sorry about *Lilith*. I asked for it about two years ago and it was in print then, but in those day 6/- for an unnecessary book was not to be thought of.

Saturday 22 August: A blue sky at last, which held up all day, though full of floating white clouds. After a bathe and an excellent breakfast of fresh whiting I set out for Brendon to see about Mrs Hume-Rotheray's mirror. Just as I had crossed the bridge Maureen ran after me, asking me on Mrs Lock's behalf to buy a lb. of candles. Moral – don't tell where you're going!

The walk over the moor was delightful. I overshot my mark a bit and came down by a long and beautiful glen with an easy path which brought me into the Lyn valley about a mile to the west of Brendon. I turned left to an inn further down where a bridge enabled me to cross into the woods on the other side: and through them I came back to Brendon . . .

After lunch (roast mutton and *such* good peas) we all sat out in the sun under the fir wood. I read *Esmond*. I have never got so far in it before. It is good. After tea we all walked up to the beginning of Lank Combe. D, who had been complaining of lumbago and had not meant to go far, was enticed into turning up and after a short glen we emerged unexpectedly into a lovely open place full of sunlight with the whole combe before us. We spent a long time childishly throwing sticks into the stream and watching their various fortunes and peripeties in the rapids. Maureen gave Ada a music lesson in the evening.

Sunday 23 August: D's pain was much worse this morning. She thought it was a chill on the kidneys. She was very miserable with it all day and I am horribly anxious. I was out in the morning up the glen that D discovered, over Oare Common, down the valley of Chalk River to Oareford (or rather beyond it) and home by road. A changing sky that brightened at first but turned to rain about 12.

Sat in all the afternoon and so did D. Wrote a few lines on Jesseran. Ada gave Maureen a riding lesson. After supper D went to get a warm at the kitchen fire and I went out for a pitiful attempt at a stroll which Pat almost refused to accompany. A grim, ominous looking place this is when one has something hanging over one.

D went to bed at 10.30 with two hot water bottles. Maureen privately suggested to me that we should divide the night and each watch a part. I chose the first as D had great ease from the jars and seemed sleepy. I hoped she would have a good night and that after a few hours I might go to bed without waking Maureen. When I went up at 12 D was awake and had only been dozing. The good effect of the jars seemed to have worn off. Went up again at 1 and found that she had not slept at all since. The pain is pretty bad: but it seems to get much worse from any movement after she has been in one position for some time, which gives me hope that it *is* a chill. I sat with her for about half an hour, interrupting it to go and investigate kettles in the kitchen against refilling the jars. We talked quite cheerfully.

I have suppressed even mental Dymerisms so far. I have been reading *Esmond* which I shall always hate for this, and am writing this at two minutes to two. It gets cold down here. 2.50 down from D again: she is much the same. I have found some peat in the scullery and mended the kitchen fire but I am afraid it will be long before there is any really hot water. I got nice and warm in there. 4 o'clock: I have filled the two jars and the water was really hot. I had almost despaired of my peat fire: it is heartbreaking stuff to boil a kettle by. When I brought the second jar up D seemed to be asleep — I hardly dare to write it down for the superstition. Touch wood: I gave the jar noiselessly to Maureen and crept down. I have found some milk in the kitchen, about half a tumblerfull, on which I shall now feast. Poor Maureen has had hardly any sleep. Tired of *Esmond* and am reading Hilaire Belloc's *Mr Emanuel Burden*. I don't know enough to appreciate it fully, but I fancy it is good.

Monday 24 August: Got to bed about 4.30 and up at 9 this morning. D still pretty bad. As soon as I had had breakfast I set off for the nearest doctor who lives at Rockford: this is the pub with the bridge beyond Brendon and it is some ten miles there and back. I found the walk tedious, though it runs through a glorious valley all the way, and was footsore. I had forgotten to bring money and could get no drink. The doctor lives in a cottage full of trophies: a sad, weather-beaten old man: not quite a gentleman and not very pleasant to speak to. He promised to come in the afternoon. When he came he gave all his directions to Mrs Lock. He left a medicine and ordered a mustard plaster. D quite liked him.

I spent most of the day in the kitchen stoking the fires for the repeated jars which we needed. My powers of perspiration were a source of amusement to the family who apparently feel like Chaucer about it. I must admit that the necessity of being always in and out with them became rather irksome before it was done. D was a good deal better in the evening. I gave her two jars last thing at 10.30 and went to bed. I replaced them at five, being then woken for the purpose.

Tuesday 25 August: D was very much better this morning. I started out in mist and rain to walk over moor to Brendon for the tobacco I had been unable to get yesterday. When I got on top of the moor it began to clear. There was brilliant sunshine with big white sailing clouds. I had a glimpse of the sea. My spirits rose and in a few minutes I was singing my small stock of Wagner and getting what seemed at the moment to be a splendid idea of Jesseram. I came home the same way after an enjoyable walk and a pint of beer in Brendon.

We both sat in D's room in the afternoon. I went on with *The Task*: I am now at "The Winter morning walk". D was much better and very cheerful. After tea Maureen and I had an interview with the two black pigs who were asleep in the field. They hardly looked like animals: more like big leather bottles with curiously shaped stoppers. They lie on their sides and grunt to each other alternately as fast as the ticking of a grandfather clock. Each grunt shakes the whole body. I tickled one with my foot and it made to roll over on its back like a cat. They are perfectly clean. I have never seen pigs at close quarters before. Later on I walked up as far as the Doone Valley.

Wednesday 26 August: D had had a poor night. Walked over to Rockford in the rain after breakfast and reported to the doctor as he had told me to do. He seemed satisfied and gave me another bottle. D was up in the afternoon and more comfortable. Read on with *The Task* and did some work on Jesseram.

Thursday 27 August: D pretty well today but still upstairs. It was a wet morning and there was a hunt on, which two reasons determined me to stay in. I read a good deal more of *Esmond*. After a very late lunch it cleared and the rest of the day had a cool white sky with a few patches of blue and more of pigeon colour.

I went out at 3.30. I walked by road to Oareford in a delightful wooded valley where the river is deeper than ours and very rocky. Tho' a small stream, it sometimes has a rock gorge about fifteen feet deep. I left the road just after it had crossed the stream and began on a path that climbed left, i.e. northward, to the main road. This brought me up the side of a magnificent combe which was chiefly felled wood with that odd grey look about it (how the ground aghast was of the light). The landscape in every direction was beyond hope. Behind was the moor with deep alluring valleys winding up into it: westward the green and stony valley of the Lyn with its path and clumps of fir trees. In front of me this big grey ravine closing up towards the thicker woods that made the horizon.

I reached the main road at a gate lodge where I took some ginger beer. I then crossed into an estate north of the road and skirted along in it for about half a mile. It was partly wood and partly heather. I saw the sea, the Foreland point and the hills beyond Porlock. I then crossed the main road again and found a bridle path in a scrubby wood running south west by a mossy ditch with a hedge of young beeches above it. This brought me out to open heather above Deddy Combe.

I never saw anything better. The whole of the Oare and Malmsmead valley suddenly appeared as a green island in the middle of blue black moor with the first sun of that day shining upon it. Everything was tumbled and crooked, running this way and that, so that one hardly knew where the horizontal was. The distances looked far larger than they really were.

Home by 6 and did French with Maureen. Finished *Esmond* later in the day.

Friday 28 August: D had a poor night and was very stiff and sore in the morning. It wore off during the day. I stayed in after breakfast and finished *The Task*. There are some fine passages in the last book which I had quite forgotten – I may have skipped them before – on the good, old, and inexhaustible theme of the good time coming. It is interesting to read them shortly after *Prometheus Unbound*: wh. I read in London with Barfield lately. After a very late lunch I went out.

There had been rain in the morning but now it was a clear warm afternoon with a very soft air. All the hills were alive with sunshine and the moving shadows of clouds. I went by Parsonage Farm and up to County Gate: thence westward along the main road in hopes of finding a way down to the sea. I was in sight of it all the time: very blue today, with the Welsh mountains showing on the far side. The country between me and it was very attractive with heather and deep gorges but it was all enclosed and I could not leave the main road until the path leading to a farm which my map names "Desolate" . . .

I found a more definite track. This soon brought me on to the road running to the Lighthouse at the Foreland. It was so late that I did not go down. I sat for a long time looking down on Caddow Combe, a very fine grim ravine between two steep hills of grass and shale. A little schooner worming its way round the point gave a more comfortable feeling to the place.

I came back to Brendon by the road that passes Combe Farm where I have not been yet. The Brendon valley and moors beyond, seen from this new angle, astonished me. Indeed the whole walk was quite bewildering with the amount and variations of its beauty. I have never spent a better three or four hours. In Brendon pub I met old Lock who stood me a glass of beer: drinking it and returning it kept me there some time. He was engaged in a game of quoits with some other farmers and all very merry. Home for a late tea.

In the evening we were all in the kitchen where a couple of new visitors – a young man and his wife – were sitting. The young man said of something that it couldn't be because it wasn't useful. "Ha," said I, half joking, "that might lead to an interesting discussion." Greatly to my surprise it did. He is a designer of furniture, well primed with Morris and Ruskin and a worthy person. I don't know which of us was more surprised to find that the other knew of such writers. We had a long and lively discussion which soon cleared the room. After we'd been at it for an hour and a half and were just settling down to the conflict between the artist and the nature of industrial society (or some dear old stager of the same sort) old Lock suddenly turned up.

His family, by the by, had been looking for him all day and when I left him at Brendon he had come out after me to say "You can say you'm an't seen me" – a direction I scrupulously obeyed. Finding his own kitchen empty save for two young men in earnest conversation, one each side of the great open peat fire, Lock surprised me (for he is a most retiring man) by drawing up a small chair for himself between us and saying "Ah . . . you're talking politics. I like a bit of politics now."

We were a little nonplussed at this totally unexpected demand on our conversational powers, but we managed to rally and bring the talk into the channels that were expected of us. Lock summed up the state of the nation by saying "Things were a bit too much one way in the old days and now they're a bit too much t'other." Ada came and said "What ever have you been to all day, Dad?" to which Lock replied with great deliberation "One thing and another, you know, one thing and another." The whole scene reminded me strongly of *Tristram Shandy*.

Saturday 29 August: Poor D had a bad night again with rheumatism; I hope it is not going to become chronic.

It was a grey morning with a light damp wind but Lock said it would probably clear up and I decided to realise today my old project of walking to Simonsbath. Starting at 10.30 I walked due south up the Badgworthy by the ordinary path. The woods and hills all look different when one passes them in a good stride with a day's new country before one. Everything was soaking with dew. Once past the Doone Valley I was in unknown waters. The gorge of the Badgworthy became narrower and the hills on either side lower. Heather soon gave place to rough grass and bracken. There was still a tolerable path. The gorge wound about so much that I was almost at once out of sight of all I knew. There was not even a sheep to be seen and an absolute silence until little by little in the narrowing valley the wind began to make itself heard – a curious muffled blustering round the corners.

In the solitude, the sound of Pat scampering after me sometimes sounded like a whole bunch of sheep or ponies and made me turn round. After I had passed Hoccombe Water (coming in from my right) I was bothered with a dry stone wall a few feet from the water's edge. The ground seemed better on the river side but every now and then there would be hardly any space between the wall and the water. The path had quite disappeared. When the next tributary came in from the right I left the Badgworthy: after a halt at the meeting of the streams in a flat stony valley, I felt already as if I had been all day in this wilderness. A heron rose quite close to me.

I continued my journey up this new stream till the ground became so marshy that I was driven up to walk on the hills to my right. I was now on Trout Hill. I presently rejoined the stream and followed it pretty close as my only guide to the point at which I should cross the next ridge. The water soon became red and curdled and stank abominably: dead sheep I think. I now got into a bad bog, right on top of the ridge. It was the usual business: three steps forward and then my stick would sink up to the handle in front of me: then what looked like an obvious path to the right or left which I followed joyfully, only to be stopped in the same way after a few paces. This went on for about half an hour. The bog was covered with beautiful white flowers and red mosses and inhabited with the most enormous slugs I have ever seen. I was dripping with heat. The view behind sticks in my memory more than anything this day: the absolutely bare grey land sloping away from me as far as I could see without any variation except the little creases which were really deep valleys.

At last I managed to get on to firmer, tho' still soaking, ground, and began to go downward. I saw two deer about three hundred yards off on my right. A long greyish green valley across my path came into sight, and a road eastward which I rightly took to be the way from Warren Farm to the main road. I was so tired of bogs and turning my ankle on hummocks that I gave up my plan of coming out at Cloven Rocks and made for the road. It was a relief to hear one's feet on the metal. The remainder of the walk into Simonsbath was rather tedious: tho' the country – white roads here, not red, and very like northern Ireland – was very pleasant.

At Simonsbath I lunched in Exmoor Forest Hotel: a miserable house where they keep "only wines" or stone ginger. There were three residents at lunch: one a very well bred looking old man with a dry, peevish voice, whom I took to be mentally deranged. He had a grown-up daughter with him (or a nurse) and the talk ran something like this.

He: "Look at this ham. It's all cut in chunks."
She: "Oh do be quiet."
He: "Anyone would think they were cutting it for coal heavers

(pause) or stonebreakers. It's . . . it's . . . wasteful you know, so wasteful."

She: "Well *you* needn't worry about that, need you?"

He (savagely): "Look at that. It's abominable."

She: "Oh *do* be quiet. Get on with your lunch. I want to get out."

He: "What's it like out?"

She: "It's lovely."

He: "Oh yes, I know it's lovely. What I want to know is, is it cold or hot?"

She: "It was cold when I first went out, but – "

He (interrupting): "There you are. Cold. I knew it was cold."

She: "I was going to say, if you'd let me, that it was very hot before I got back."

He (after a pause): "Look at that. It's really disgraceful to cut ham like that. It was a nice ham too. Well smoked, well cured and a good fibre. And they go and spoil it all by cutting it in chunks. Chunks. Just look at that!" (stabbing a piece and holding it up in mid air).

She: "Oh do get on."

He: (something inaudible)

She: "Well they've as much right here as we have. Why can't you get on and eat your lunch?"

He: "I'm not going to be hustled over my lunch. Hustled. I won't let you hustle me in this way." (a pause) "Why don't you ask Mrs Ellworthy to let you make some of that nice porridge of yours?"

She: "How could I in a hotel?" (They had a long argument over this.) Then *He* (almost pathetically): "Why don't you eat some of this salad? It's beautifully flavoured" (here his voice broke and he added almost in a whisper) " – with *cucumber*. If it wasn't for the ham . . ."

And so they went on. I had a cup of coffee and a rest in the garden and left about 2.30. I came home by the main road across the moors. For the first hour or so the broad white road with its high hedges and glimpses of big fields on interminable but gentle slopes, and a white cottage here and there, supported the illusion of being in Ireland. The roaring of the wind in the crisp beech hedge on my left had a homely feeling.

After crossing the "stripling Exe" I came on to open moor and everything changed. The sun came out and shone for the rest of the day. The road, unfenced, wound across the heather to the horizon. To left and right the ground dropped into long and many coloured valleys and then rolled away to the sky, ridge after ridge, blue, purple, grey and green. Instinctively I walked faster: and so, after a long halt at Brendon Two Gates and another on Tippacott Ridge, I came home in a dream and only discovered at tea how footsore I was.

I admit I was annoyed when later on I had to turn out with Maureen and her pony. A day's walking should never be undertaken unless the evening lounge – the crown of the day – is safe. In other words family life is incompatible with real walking. I began Joseph Conrad's *Chance* – one of the very best novels I have read. D seemed much better in the evening.

Sunday 30 August: Poor D had a worse night again and had to wake me for fresh jars – after hours of miserable wakefulness for her – at five o'clock. After breakfast I walked by road to Rockford and saw the doctor. He gave me a new bottle. There seems very little to be done for a rheumatic attack. Very footsore. D much better during the day. Went on with *Chance*.

Monday 31 August: Thank goodness D had a very much better night, probably owing to yesterday's fine sunshine.

It was arranged that I should go to Lynton to do some necessary shopping and Maureen decided to accompany me. We set out at 10.30 or so and went by the road over the moor. The first ascent from the Malmsmead lane, between high hedges, was very muggy and hot and I was afraid we were in for a close thundery day, unpropitious for walking.

As soon as we were on top of the moor we got into fresh breezes and heat and cold kept on alternating with the ups and downs of the country for the rest of the way ... Through a gate we had a glimpse of fields piled upon hills up to some peak in the distance, and sprinkled with cottages. We then went on and down a hill so steep that it was equally comfortless whether you stood, sat or walked, and into Lynton.

We lunched at the Cottage Hotel. The view from the balcony was beyond everything I have seen – not for sublimity or "sober certainty of waking bliss" but for mere luxuriousness and sensual beauty. Straight ahead and across the gorge, the hillside rose hundreds of feet above us into a big cap of well shaped rock. Behind that the Lyn valley opened out in long perspective of winding water and many coloured woods, heather and grass. To the left was the bay, not deeply blue but of a strangely pure clear colour and beyond it a line of surf between the water and the cliffs which fell away East and North, sometimes reddish, sometimes almost purple, and topped with a great perfectly white cloud that covered the whole foreland and sent a few smoky shreds down the hillsides . . .

Tuesday 1 September: D had a good night until six o'clock: which I suppose is better than none at all. It poured with rain all day and I was not out except for five minutes before supper. We had our peat fire (I got the peat) and were quite comfortable.

I finished *Chance*. It is a good book: even great. Whether the denouement has any justification I don't know. He seems to kill Anthony for no reason except the whimsical one of avoiding a happy ending, and then to marry Flora to Powell in a moment of sentimental repentance. Perhaps I have misunderstood it.

Wednesday 2 September: I sat in in the morning and read *The Bride of Lammermoor*[1] which I bought in Lynton. The early parts are a little mechanical, I thought, but it becomes great as it goes on. It has done what it intended and the hags are excellent of their kind: so is the scene of Ravenswood's return.

In the afternoon I walked by the shortest route to the light house at Foreland. I had a headache when I set out but it left me after a while. It was a bitterly cold day with a strong wind, the sea steel coloured, the sky white and dark grey and the further hills black. I usually enjoy such weather and the bleakness of the point when I reached it ought to have pleased me, but somehow I found the whole walk tedious.

I had tea at Combe Farm on my way back – a fine stone house built round three sides of a square and well back from the roads. The spacious beamed kitchen with a bright hearth and much bread and butter largely cured me of my dull humour.

D had had a good night and was much better today.

Thursday 3 September: Another wet day. I had only a short walk after tea when I explored Southern Wood for the first time; the evening sunlight, bright but very cold, was breaking out by now after a day of cloud. I left the ordinary path as soon as I had reached the top of the hill above Malmsmead.

[1] By Sir Walter Scott (1819).

In a moment I was out of sight of everything in a wood of nothing but oak, very low and tangled like a grove of sea weed. There was not a blade of grass to be seen, but the undisturbed moss grew deep on the ground and over the highest branches. The sunlight came slantwise through the trees and the wind roared. Then there were clearings where the path seemed to run straight up into the sky, and others from which I caught glimpses of the surrounding hills, new and hard to recognise from this position. In spite of all my glorious walks round here, it was in this little saunter only (so far) that I got the real joy . . .

Friday 4 September: Read some of the *Kingis Quair* in the morning – a very second rate poem: not to be compared with poor old Lydgate's *Story of Thebes* which everyone mocks. I read it shortly before we left home and thought it a very pleasant romance. All we read about these authors in modern critics usually boils down to this: that the critics are too sophisticated to enjoy romance unless it is helped out by some extraneous interest. They feel no curiosity as to what will happen to the knight when he gets into the garden: this is not a virtue in them but "their necessity in being old".

In the afternoon I went to Rockford to pay the Doctor. I went by road to Brendon and then struck up on the road past Combe Farm. It was a changeable day with occasional sunshine. When I reached the open heather near Countisbury I had a halt to look my last (I suppose) on the most beautiful landscape I know. The Brendon valley was on my left and in front the lower Lyn gorge with its complicated woods winding on to Lynmouth.

I then went westward across the moor, with the telegraph posts on my right and began to descend from such a point that the long straight reach on whose upper end Rockford stands, was straight in front of me. After a steep scramble down bracken and heather I got into thick and silent woods. Every kind of tree grows here, all at an acute angle on the steep hillside. There is plenty of moss and ivy and biggish rocks and boulders, some covered with green, some sticking through like bones of the hill. I sat there and again came very near the real joy, but did not quite arrive.

After this I went down to the water's edge. The stream was smooth here and the valley bottom quite flat (on this side) with big forest trees dotted at wide intervals . . . There was one quite awesome place where I looked down through dead fir trees into a black hole lighted with foam at the bottom: and suddenly a swallow flew out just above the water.

I saw the Doctor and had tea at Rockford. I came home by Southern Woods. Here I struck up to my right and after a beautiful walk through the wood came out on the moor. A dazzling yellow sunshine was coming from the west. I crossed the upper road to Brendon and went straight across the moor for home – with an enormous shadow in front of me. The oddest thing happened here. A swallow came and for ten minutes or so flew to and fro in front of me, so low that it was almost in Pat's mouth, so fast that you could hardly follow its flickering black and white.

In the strange bright evening the view just before I came down into Badgworthy valley was indescribable: the hills were full of colour and shadows away towards Porlock and the little bit of sea which showed above County Gate was burning. It all died out before I reached Cloud and became one uniform grey ... Read Hans Anderson in the evening.

Saturday 5 September: As we had not heard from the garage at Porlock to whom we wrote for a taxi on Monday, it was arranged that I should go there today ...

I walked up the valley past Oare, then through the wilder and narrower valley past Oareford, then up the wooded hill to Oare Post. It had been misty all day and was now raining pretty hard. I continued on the main road with a blurred view of Porlock valley and the strangely yellow, bald looking hills beyond Porlock. Just beyond Whit Stones I went down over the moor into Shillett Wood: as lovely as all the glens in this country and lonelier than most. My face had been lashed with the rain so long that it was a relief to be in shelter. The rest of the walk, constantly crossing and re-crossing the river down Hawk Combe was delightful.

After arranging for a taxi to come to Cloud at 8.45 I had an excellent lunch at the Castle Hotel (where, alas, I lost my stick). I began the homeward journey. At a point mid way between West Porlock and Porlock Weir I found a path going up into the wood. This was the wildest one I have been in: the road was really a sort of trench about three feet deep, full of red stones, and tunnelled through the trees. I saw a weasel quite close. It is not a good place to sit in, being given over to that race of super-ants whom I met before at Old Cleeve.

As I went on I had one or two nice glimpses at the highly coloured valley behind me: but it soon began to rain and blow. It did both, more and more violently, for the rest of the afternoon. I have seldom been in such a storm. As long as I was in the deep dark wood path (so dark in places that the opening of the next tree-tunnel, as you caught sight of it, sometimes looked like, not an opening, but a big solid black object) it was tolerable. Going up Small Combe however, it became impossible to see ahead of me: my feet were soaked through and to look at the map was out of the question. I got up to the Lodge and came home down Deddy Combe – rather enjoying it all in a way I luckily have.

I was lazy for the rest of the day after a change and tea by a good fire. Slept in another bed room tonight to let three stranded women have my room.

The diary breaks off here, and is not resumed until 27 April 1926.

1926

After the holiday at Oare, Lewis went to Belfast on 13 September to visit his father. This time they were easy together, and when Jack left on 1 October Mr Lewis wrote in his diary: "Jacks returned. A fortnight and a few days with me. Very pleasant, not a cloud. Went to the boat with him. The first time I did not pay his passage money. I offered, but he did not want it."

By the time Michaelmas Term began in October 1925 Lewis had moved into Magdalen College, and into one of the most beautiful parts of one of the most beautiful colleges of Oxford. He was given three rooms in New Buildings – No. 3, Staircase 3. "My external surroundings are beautiful beyond expectation and beyond hope," he wrote to his father on 21 October. "To live in the Bishop's Palace at Wells would be good but could hardly be better than this. My big sitting room looks north and from it I see nothing, not even a gable or spire, to remind me that I am in a town. I look down on a stretch of level grass which passes into a grove of immemorial forest trees, at present coloured with autumn red. Over this stray the deer . . . Some mornings when I look out there will be half a dozen chewing the cud just undernearth me, and on others there will be none in sight . . . My smaller sitting room and bedroom look out southward across a broad lawn to the main buildings of Magdalen with the Tower across it."

Beginning in October, Lewis divided his time between Magdalen and "Hillsboro". During term he slept in College and visited the "family" during the afternoons, and when term ended he spent the nights at "Hillsboro" and came into College during the day. One sees why the President of Magdalen spoke of Lewis as the "strongest and most acceptable" candidate for the post he now held. Lewis was giving tutorials to those reading English as well as Greats and the course in Philosophy, Politics and Economics. Most of the pupils who began coming to him in October 1925 were the ones he had when the diary picks up again in April 1926.

Tuesday 27 April: One of the new people, Waddington, appeared on my list this morning, but never turned up. I don't know whether it is his mistake or mine. I went on with Seebohm's *Oxford Reformers* in the morning. It is very bad in style, mean without being simple, and silly in sentiment: the *arrangement* on the other hand is almost the best I have ever seen.

I also drafted a letter to Miss Perham of St Hugh's on a rather ticklish business.[2] She wrote the other day asking me to take one pupil for her this term. I replied refusing and suggesting Ewing, with Hardie as a possible fallback if Ewing was full up. She answered saying "If I were unscrupulous I should ask Mr H. at once, but as I have not yet seen Dr Ewing I suppose I can't. Next term I will approach Mr H. early – " I wanted, if I could without blundering, to say that I would be very sorry if any word of mine had induced her to prefer Hardie to Ewing. But I didn't succeed, and left it.[3]

After 12 it became almost too dark to see: a dead black sky came down behind the trees in the grove. Went out to return books to the Union and met Rowse of All Souls in Chaundy's. I met him first last term when dining with Coghill to meet De la Mare and have been intending to follow him up ever since; I asked him to dine next Wednesday.[4]

From the Union I went out home and found all well there. So far D seems to be very satisfied with Winifred. I went for a walk with Pat up Shotover through Quarry and along the Plain: then down nearly to Wheatley, crossing the railway by the footpath. It was still the same dark, strangely coloured, suspended, end of the world kind of day: but I am very insensible to the country and sky just at present.

After tea back to College and went on with Seebohm till hall. In the evening looked up language and was just settling down to Skeat's introduction when Weldon came in.[5] This meant whiskey and talk till 12.30, greatly to my disappointment. We somehow got on the historical truth of the Gospels, and agreed that there was a lot that could not be explained away. He believes in the Hegelian doctrine of the Trinity and said the whole thing fitted in: in fact he is a Christian "of a sort". I should never have suspected it. Then we

---

[2] Miss Margery Freda Perham was Tutor in Modern History at St Hugh's College.

[3] See **William Francis Ross Hardie** in the Biographical Appendix.

[4] Alfred Leslie Rowse (1903–), a Fellow of All Souls 1925–74, devoted a chapter to Lewis in his *Memories and Glimpses* (1986).

[5] See Thomas Dewar Weldon in the Magdalen College Appendix.

turned to the self. Got to bed v. late at last with a headache, regretting a wasted, tho' interesting evening.[6]

Wednesday 28 April: Another very dark, clouded day – less apocalyptic, but more depressing. Pupils in the morning. Yorke for language.[7] Then Betjeman and Valentin to stumble through the *Voyage of Ohthere*: last of all Hamilton and Hetherington who look as if they would be very good indeed.[8] Hamilton read the Simon Perrott oration in hall the other night.

I then bussed out home, had lunch, and took a walk in Cuckoo Lane and the Private Rd., getting home for an early tea.

I then went to Lady Margaret Hall for my class. Seven girls turned up. Colborne (dignified and fairly sensible), Scoones (lanky, dark), Grant (a very massive, lumpy person who never opened her mouth), Thring (the most talkative), House (nervy, a trifle soulful, and worried), Johnston (who is perhaps the best) and Carter who came very late because she had been looking for her tame tortoise. She is the prettiest and perhaps rather a b****. As hardly any of them had read the *Dialogues* [of Plato] it was a bit difficult to get discussion started, but once they began it went fairly well. Miss Scoones and Miss Thring joined in snubbing Miss House, very acrimoniously I thought: so I did the best I could for her, but she had become sulky and frightened by them.[9]

On my way I looked into Keble Hall for the first time since I was a cadet: it was not v. like what I remembered.

In the evening I finished Seebohm and began *Friar Bacon and Friar*

---

[6] It is impossible to be sure, but there is a chance that Lewis had this conversation with Weldon in mind when he said in *Surprised by Joy*, ch.XIV: "Early in 1926 the hardest boiled of all the atheists I ever knew sat in my room on the other side of the fire and remarked that the evidence for the historicity of the Gospels was really surprisingly good. 'Rum thing', he went on. 'All that stuff of Frazer's about the Dying God. Rum thing. It almost looks as if it had really happened once.' "

[7] Henry Vincent Yorke (1905–73) matriculated in 1924 and was reading English Literature. He was to write a good many novels under the pseudonym "Henry Green" and an autobiography called *Pack My Bag* (1940).

[8] John Betjeman (1906–85), the poet, was one of Lewis's most difficult pupils. He matriculated in 1924 and read English, but went down from Oxford without a degree. The story of John Betjeman's relationship with Lewis is told in Bevis Hillier's *Young Betjeman* (1988).

Deric William Valentin (1907–) matriculated in 1924. He also read English, and also left without a degree.

Robert William Hamilton (1905–) read Classics at Magdalen and took his BA in 1928. He was Senior Lecturer in Near Eastern Archaeology at Oxford 1949–56, and Keeper of Antiquities, Ashmolean Museum, 1962–72.

William Dixon Hetherington (1905–) was a Commoner 1924-28 and read Classical Moderations and Greats. He took a BA in 1931 and went to work in Kingston, Jamaica.

[9] These ladies matriculated at Lady Margaret Hall in 1924 and read English. Lewis's weekly classes were not in English, but Philosophy. His students' names are: Joan Elizabeth Colborne, Diana Dalton Scoones, Violet Augusta Grant, Monica Rose Thring, Bridget Johnston, Nancy Carter and Elizabeth House.

Bungay. It is pleasant enough – "drinking down milk and ale in country cans" and "transporting the whole *ninniversity* by boat to Southwark". I must remember "ninniversity".

Thursday 29 April: Percival and Waterfield came this morning.[10] Waterfield was here first and I had a little conversation with him. He is an attractive, sturdy, humorous personage – a dark Celt I think – and read an essay on Mill: too poetical and I objected to some blank verse lines which he was unaware of – I hope it will act as an inoffensive check on rhapsodising in future. In discussion he was good. Percival was bored and boring. Also he won't open his mouth when he speaks and I have to say "What?" each time, which doesn't help matters.

Worked on Skeat's Introduction (open and close "e" and such dainties) for the rest of the morning. Home to lunch and then out for a walk over the fields in the direction of Forest Hill. It was a very warm day, and misty, the prevailing colour being greyish blue. The fields are in full trim with dandelions and one-o-clocks, and a row of catkins struck me particularly. Home again and had a knock up at badminton with Maureen and Dotty. Poor old Trapp came and asked me not to make a noise: his wife appears to be worse. After that we played in perfect silence, scoring by signs.

For tea came Mrs Wilbraham (who has been very kind during D's illness), her daughter, her nephew Wittall of Oriel – whom I don't much care for – and Diz. After tea D and I got Diz's advice about my income tax returns and life insurance: it was half an hour's horror to me, as such discussions are: moving about in worlds unrealised among "covers" and "policies" and what not.[11] I suppose it is wholesome to know by acquaintance the miseries of not being able to understand.

When I got back to College I went and had a talk with Hardie, who is near enough to my helplessness to be able to give me some vague lights. Finally we both went to Thompson and at last I have some points definitely fixed in my mind.[12] The notice from him

---

[10] David Athelstane Percival (1906–87) read Classics 1924–8 and took his BA in 1928. He afterwards went to Nigeria where he worked in College Administrative Service.

Thomas Edward Waterfield (1905–) read Classical Moderations 1924-7, and later made a special study of the birds of Oxford.

[11] "Diz" was Sydney Cecil William Disney (1892–) who read Law at Magdalen and was with the Inland Revenue Service 1921-8.

[12] The Rev. James Matthew Thompson (1878–1956) was a Fellow of Magdalen 1904–38. He was Dean of Divinity 1906–15 and Home Bursar 1920–7.

the other day is of moneys paid me since my election up to the end of this taxable year: it is on that year I pay tax during the coming year: I pay a premium of a 5th of my fellowship towards the insurance.

Dined in and didn't go to Common Room. When I came back to New Building [I] found battells for £38 odd and am not sure whether they are for the term before last or for last term. If for last, my economies don't seem to have been much use. A worrying day – which seems nothing to worry about now; but that is because I have been reading *The Spectator* since 9 o'clock with great delight. It has been raining. A nice soft rain, just audible through drawn curtains, and a pleasant sound to read to. Twinges of tooth all day.

Friday 30 April: No pupils this morning. Wasted an hour or so on my "Outline of History" poem to very little purpose: then walked to the Turl and bought Trevelyan's *England Under the Stuarts* in order to make up Queen Anne politics with a view to doing Swift with Yorke this term. I also looked in at the Clarendon Press to see if de Selincourt's *Prelude* was there, but could not find it.[13] I read an exciting review of it in Common Room at breakfast this morning. Back to College and read Trevelyan till one with great interest. I wonder is he true?

Bussed out home. D tells me that Dotty was rather offensive yesterday, talking big for the benefit of Diz and then staying up late to work as a result of the time she had wasted. Maureen too has a grouse about Dotty "bossing" her in her punt, for which I don't give a fig. Being in her own house Maureen has far more opportunities of doing that sort of thing than Dotty, and does it. On the whole, if they both must domineer, I prefer Dotty's loud, hoydenish, slapdash method to Maureen's patient, endlessly repeated prim nagging.[14]

It was quite hot today, but with the same dull sky – working up for a thunderstorm I suppose. D in good form. Walked with Pat over the fields to Stowe Woods: extraordinarily beautiful and full of fresh summerlike smells. We had tea in the garden and enjoyed "our thrush" who sings there every day . . .

[13] Ernest de Selincourt's edition of Wordsworth's *Prelude*.

[14] Dorothea "Dotty" Vaughan, a day pupil at Headington School, was boarding at "Hillsboro".

Saturday 1 May: Called at 5 a.m. to do "my observances to the May". A cold, dark morning. I drank what was left of last night's milk, shaved, dressed and went over to the Tower in surplice and hood. There were crowds going up and it was a slow business.[1] The Latin hymn was beautiful: the Vaughan Williams that followed it, inappropriate. In spite of bad weather I was impressed with the landscape towards Marston, the low slopes and the gleam of the river. It began to rain before I left the top of the tower, but I did not get really wet. There was a crowd of visitors, Maureen and Dotty among them.

Came back to New Building at about 7, had a long hot bath, drank a cup of tea, and read Trevelyan. At 8 I had breakfast alone with Benecke and then the ordinary day began.[2]

I had De Peyer and Clark (a desperately stupid pair), Yorke on Steele and Addison, and then Glasgow on Lydgate.[3] . . .

In the afternoon I walked over the fields with Pat to Stowe Woods. Was led somehow into a train of thought in which I made the unpleasant discovery that I am becoming a prig — righteous indignation against certain modern affectations has its dangers, yet I don't know how to avoid it either.

After tea worked on Aristotle. Supper at home and then back to College to spend the evening with Hardie on Aristotle. To bed about 11.30, very tired, and had a terrifying dream in the night which I can't remember.

---

[1] Magdalen Tower is one of the jewels of Oxford. It was completed in 1504 and it is customary on May Day to greet the sunrise with a concert on the roof of the Tower.

[2] See **Paul Victor Mendelssohn Benecke** in the Magdalen College Appendix.

[3] Eric Clarence Evelyn De Peyer (1906–) read Classical Moderations 1925–7 and English 1927–9. He took his BA in 1931.

Leonard Ernle Clark (1906–64), of New Zealand, read Classical Moderations 1925–8. He became an aeriel surveyor, and made a solo flight from the U.K. to N.Z. in 1936. He served in the RAF 1939–46.

Paul John Weade Glasgow (1902–), a Canadian, read English and took his BA in 1926. He took a B.C.L. from McGill University in 1930 and was admitted to the Quebec Bar.

On the bus this evening I heard that the miners had gone out.[4]

Sunday 2 May: Everyone talking about the strike at breakfast. Craig says that the V[ice] C[hancellor] is anxious to prevent the under-graduates volunteering in the town by forming some separate University framework. This has already got abroad in a garbled version. Craig had prevented Boddington from putting up a notice on the subject, because he did not want people to get the idea that Oxford was a "strike breaking" gang. He was very strong on the necessity of the undergraduates keeping their heads and not becoming provocative.[5] Chute's idea was that some of the miners' leaders ought to be cut up into small bits.[6] Hardie and I hoped we might now realise a boyish dream and drive railway engines.

A very fresh day, grey-skied and windy. I walked out home after breakfast. Spent a good deal of the morning reading the papers. The right seems to be mainly on the miner's side if it is true that the Commission prescribed "reorganisation and reduction" and that the miners were then asked to submit to reduction without any guarantee of reorganisation . . .

After tea I had a delightful walk to Stowe Woods by road to Elsfield and home by the fieldpath. I haven't done that round for a long time. After a few more reflections on priggery I pretty well stopped thinking. The wind, specially in the deep beds of heather, with their white flower, was very fine.

Home again and had supper. Worked on Aristotle afterwards, tracking a passage down. D was listening in: the others at the Cathedral. News came through that the Fascists and the Communists had had a row in Hyde Park. These Fascists will spoil the whole thing. As long as it was rowdies on the one side only, we cd. weather a lot without coming to real trouble: once we have moneyed rowdies (without a grievance) acting as agents provocateurs on the other rowdies (who have a grievance) there is bound to be a good deal of trouble . . .

---

[4] This was the beginning of the General Strike. The Samuel Committee had recommended cuts in miners' wages. The mine owners, however, while accepting a cut in wages, insisted on longer hours, and at the end of April they locked the miners out of the pits. The General Council of the Trades Union Congress called a meeting and agreed a "national strike". It was their hope that the threat would force the Government to settle, but Stanley Baldwin called off the talks because printers refused to print an anti-union article in the *Daily Mail*. Beginning on 3 May workers in transport, iron and steel, electricity, gas, building and newspaper printing all stopped work. In every town there was a local strike committee which tried to keep essential supplies moving. Although the miners refused to give in, after nine days the TUC called off the strike.

[5] See **Edwin Stewart Craig** in the Magdalen College Appendix

[6] The Rev. Anthony William Chute (1884–1958) was Fellow and Dean of Divinity 1925–9.

Monday 3 May: A beautiful bright windy day. Worked on Aristotle all morning for Boddington who came at 12.[7]

At one o'c. I went to Merton and lunched with Lawson and Keir. The news in *The Times* this morning had been that negotiations had broken down. Lawson had seen a midday paper which told that the printers of the *Daily Mail*, offended at its leading article, had already gone out and it had not appeared today. Merton had a notice up giving leave to all who wished to go down and volunteer for service in their home areas – rather premature of Merton. Keir disapproved of the V.C.'s idea of a special University organisation as promoting class warfare. Lawson defended the Merton notice on the ground that the undergraduates would be dangerous and troublesome as a body, but easily dealt with if dispersed in their own districts.

We left Merton together. The street was full of cars and motor bicycles. Undergraduates in great excitement and glee were blowing up tyres, pouring in petrol, and strapping on suitcases. Oxford very crowded. We were amused at everyone's idea that the way to help was to keep everyone in movement – from anywhere to anywhere. After looking into the Union (where there was no news) I left them and went home.

D sat up last night till one o'c. and heard the later news. Apparently other people besides the *Daily Mail's* printers had gone out prematurely and the situation was that the Government refused to continue negotiations unless the T.U.C. repudiated this. I had a delightful walk up Shotover and came back to tea in the garden with D.

Back to College about 5.30 and found in the Porch the V.C.'s notice saying that he did not want undergraduates to volunteer in the town and that opportunities would be given them of doing so through their colleges.

In my rooms I found the new de Selincourt *Prelude* and at once began to read it. Many of the fragments rescued from note books are interesting and important: specially the one distinguishing between the images and things recognised as thoughts wh. are "the littleness of life" and our real selves: leading on to the passage about the cloudless east and the cloudless west. This is almost the distinction between . . . contemplation and enjoyment.

Masonic dinner on tonight so we non-Masons made a small party

---

[7] Hubert Cecil Boddington (1903–74) matriculated in 1922 and read Classics, taking Schools in 1926. He took his BA in 1934 and was a Member of the London Stock Exchange.

in Hall. In common room Craig gave us an outline of policy. The undergraduates are to be divided into four classes: (a) those who are free to leave and are volunteering at once for service in their home areas, (b) Those who "for one reason or another" are not free, at the moment. Their papers will be sent in to the Oxford centre, but they will not be called upon until the town has exhausted its own resources. This is to avoid the provocation of "imported labour" as long as possible. (c) Those with cars etc. who will volunteer for messenger service in this distict, wh. (on Craig's view) will not come under the head of "imported labour". (d) Those taking Schools this term. They may fill up forms for service with the town but the forms will be withheld by College until the situation is desperate.

Some very amusing talk in the smoking room, chiefly by Dixon and Benecke, on their war experiences.[8] After that Hardie and I went out for a walk in the Grove, which is most beautiful in twilight. We found a deep pit that we could not account for and also wandered in among the stores in the temporary stonecutting shop. They were very impressive, these pale bulky creatures among the dark trees. How Jenkin would have appreciated the feeling on the scene! Hardie knows very little about that kind of thing, tho' in other spheres he is more than clever and really wise. Back to my rooms by about 9.30 and read the new Wordsworth till bedtime, except for a few minutes on my Outline of History. I was a long time in going to sleep.

Wednesday 5 May: Up at 7.45, very dizzy and wretched. Waddington and Sykes came at 9.[9] They are quite a good pair ... At 11 I took Valentin and Betjeman on O.E.. Valentin translated "twentig hryðera" "twenty hydras".[10]

They told me that Fascists had broken into the Labour Club last night where speeches were being made about strikers' wives and children: and tho' they heckled, before they left they contributed a good sum to the relief of the said wives and children. How gloriously English!

At 12 came Hamilton and Hetherington. The former read an essay: to my surprise, not nearly so good as Hetherington's last week.

[8] See Arthur Lee Dixon in the Magdalen College Appendix.
[9] Thomas Elliot Waddington (1907–77) was a Commoner of Magdalen 1925–8 and read Philosophy, Politics and Economics. He was a Director of Investments and other companies, and served with the K.R.R.C. 1939–45.
  Richard Laurence Sykes (1906–77) was a Commoner 1925–9, and took his BA in 1930. He worked as an advertising agent.
[10] *The Voyages of Ohthere and Wulfstan*, 49; "twenty cows."

Lunched in Common Room: then to Balliol at 2. Meeting in the old Common Room with the V.C. in the chair. Discussion chiefly turned on efforts to shorten the notice: I wonder that they should hold paper so much more precious than time. I was finished by about 2.30 and I went to the English Library and took out Dunbar. Back to College: wrote up my diary, worked at my Outline, and wrote a note to Driver.[11]

Tea in Common Room and then to L.M.H. to take my class. Miss Scoones read a paper: really astonishingly good for an amateur. She and Miss Colborne were very good in discussion. Left them at 6.15 and bussed home.

After a dreamlike morning I had begun to feel better about tea time and was now almost myself. I was worried to hear that D had had a return of the pain she felt at Oare: otherwise all well and a pleasant, idle evening . . .

Thursday 6 May: Began correcting Spencer's English paper – history of language.[12] He raised points I was uncertain about and I went out to buy Wyld's *Mother Tongue*, but I couldn't find out what I wanted.

A bright cold day with a blue and white sky. Home to lunch as usual. D seemed well. I read the papers – *Times* 2 sheets and the *Govt. Gazette*. I had been surprised myself at the party tone of its first number, it certainly ought to have aimed at a colourless and official tone. This has come in for severe and just criticism in the House . . .

At dinner time I heard that the Govt. had raided the *Daily Herald* office. Weldon said that if they continued as they had begun they would probably succeed in making trouble where no trouble would have been. They had done three very provocative things: declared a state of emergency before negotiations had broken down: used the *Gazette* for propaganda, and raided an opposition paper. About the *Gazette* anyway I thoroughly agreed. In the smoking room Brightman was in great form, proposing to go with any one who wd. volunteer and make hay of Carter's new building.[13]

Reports of rioting in Scotland. I came back to my rooms and

---

[11] (Sir) Godfrey Driver (1892-1975) was a Fellow of Magdalen 1919–62, and Professor of Semitic Philology at Oxford 1938–62.

[12] Charles Richard Spencer (1903–41) read Classical Moderations and then English 1922–6 and took his BA in 1926. He became the Assistant Master at Stowe.

[13] Frank Edward Brightman (1856–1932), liturgiologist, was an original librarian of Pusey House 1884–1903, Fellow of Magdalen 1902–32, and author of *The English Rite* (1915).

Cyril Robert Carter (1863–1930) was Dean of Divinity 1896–1902 and Bursar of Magdalen College 1910–30 – thus having much to do with the new buildings being erected at Magdalen.

worked on Dunbar. Hardie came in about 10.30 and we made hot toddy. Bitterly cold.

Friday 7 May: Went on correcting Spencer's paper. Waterfield and Percival came at 12. The latter read an essay of a very vague, aimless kind.

Out home by about 1.30. After lunch I walked over the fields towards Forest Hill: it was a beautiful mild afternoon with a blue sky and I sat down for some time: when I turned to come home I saw wonderful effects. Above and behind me was still bright: ahead of me was a huge bank of clouds with almost black under-side and enormous white pinnacles above, driving fast towards me and making the plain bright blue underneath it. It squirted a hailshower at me just before I reached Barton: big firm hailstones, very painful to the nose and ear.

Changed and had tea. Baldwin's speech in the House (today's *Times*) says that a message demanding repudiation of the *Daily Mail* strike and withdrawal of strike notices in general was sent to the T.U.C. on Sunday evening and not answered and this was the breakdown. They seem to have been nearly in agreement before that.

Back to College by 5.30 and worked on Hoccleve. In the smoking room after dinner Wrong circulated the Petition expressing the hope "that nothing should be allowed to stand in the way of resumption of the negotiations".[14] It had been signed by Sadler, Gilbert Murray, Lindsay, Wrong, Weldon, Lee and others. Segar said it was like sending a petition to Haig asking him to sign an armistice at a moment when his whole business was to frighten the Germans.

I protested against the idea that the Premier during a strike was in the same position as a general at war, or that his business was to frighten. In the end I didn't sign myself because it seemed to me that, if taken loosely, the Petition only meant "Aim at peace," which was not helpful: if taken strictly, it meant "Re-open negotiations on any terms whatever happens tomorrow," which I didn't agree with.

Craig said it was equivalent to a vote of censure on the Govt. That seems untrue. What has really annoyed him and many others is that the Bishop announced a religious meeting in the Town Hall and used it for passing this resolution. The general feeling is that this was dishonest.

---

[14] Edward Murray Wrong (1889–1928) became a Fellow of Magdalen in 1914. He was Vice-Principal of Manchester College of Technology 1916–19 after which he returned to Magdalen.

Back to my rooms and worked on the Chaucerians (making notes on "aureation") till about 11. Then to bed, but not for a long time to sleep, after tidying my room. Raining hard.

Saturday 8 May: News of rioting from many places today.

De Peyer and Clark at 12. Home for lunch at 1.30 or so. Read the papers: the big item today is Sir John Simon's speech on the illegality of the present strike. I am not sure that anything is gained by telling the workmen that they are all "liable to be sued" (that was the headline).

Knight was here mending the lock on the scullery door. He told us the *Worker's Gazette* version of the break off. They had nearly come to agreement on a basis for further discussion when the news of the *Daily Mail* strike reached Baldwin. He then wrote to the T.U.C., practically assuming that the General Strike had begun and asking for some statement. They knew as little of the *Daily Mail* strike as he and wrote back to say so: to which he answered that the door was now closed. The *Worker's Gazette* pertinently asks if he would have behaved in the same way if the premature strike had been in the *Daily Herald* printers. Baldwin's account was (in today's papers) that he wrote asking for a repudiation of the printer's strike and none was given.

It is impossible to discover of what fact these two stories are the colouring. There may be something in Craig's idea that Baldwin was being hustled by Birkenhead and Churchill . . .

We were rather early for the bus, and it was cold, which didn't improve matters, as D is apparently still bothered with the pain in her back. She seemed a little better in the Playhouse. The Vaughan Williams *Shepherds of the Delectable Mountains* was above praise: words, music, acting and lighting all really unified and the result quite unearthly. In the interval I found Benecke, Chute, and Hardie waiting on the off chance of getting in. I also met C.K. Allen and got from him a whiff of solid Univ. Toryism – sarcastic, frightened, worldly-wisdom. The Bach *Coffee Cantata* and the Purcell ballet of the *Gentleman Dancing Master* were both delightful and one didn't really mind the descent from the heights. Altogether a splendid show. All home by taxi, the others dropping me at Magdalen gate.

Sunday 9 May: A bright and beautiful morning. The walks by the Cher as I went out home after breakfast are now "tunnels of green" and hawthorn, full of singing, or, rather, shouting birds, and bluebells.

D seemed none the worse for last night. I spent a very idle day: unconsciously one makes the strike a pretext for dropping all regular habits. Played badminton in the afternoon: beaten by Maureen and beat Dotty. I re-read some of the best stories in H.G. Wells' *Country of the Blind*. One never re-reads an old favourite without finding that it has contributed more than one suspected to one's habitual stock in trade.

Back to College about 5.30. Met Valentin in the cloisters who told me he is going down tomorrow and therefore wd. not come to me. Attended Chapel and read a very relevant lesson, Deuteronomy VIII.

Sat beside Weldon in Hall. He thinks we shall be free of all pupils by the end of this week and shall have to begin thinking of strike jobs for ourselves. He proposes to join with others of our mind and try to get into stevedore's work or something comparatively neutral: we would co-opt Hardie into our company as he is innocent and doesn't know how to look after himself: e.g. on hearing of the new C.C.R., to be issued with tin hats, he said he would refuse to wear a tin hat! . . .

In the Smoking Room there was much interesting talk. Jellicoe says the police and the poor ordinary people (typists and the like) in London are really great.[15] The police and army will break if it really comes to fighting: which he thinks it will.

What he would like (Chute and I eagerly endorsed this) is that the Govt. should win the strike, in the sense of producing a return to work without disorder, and lose the peace, in the sense that the country would, in the Govt's teeth if need be, confirm Trades Unions in their legitimate powers and protect the miners.

Weldon said this was utterly impossible. Birkenhead and Joynson Hicks had deliberately provoked a hostile situation in order to crush Trades Unionism once and for all: if the general strike failed (and it was bound to) Trades Unions would be dead in England, and as there would be no general election, it would be impossible to prevent Birkenhead and Co. from mutilating the corpse. The result would be that moderate Labour wd. be forced to go red. Jellicoe says that Euston parish was enraged by the use of undergraduate labour at Euston. Wrong and I maintained the right to feed oneself and others

---

[15] The Rev. John Basil Lee Jellicoe (1886–1935) was Head of the Magdalen College Mission 1922–7, and Chairman of St Pancras House Improvement Co.

regardless of the industrial issue: Weldon wd. not hear of it. One had no choice but to be a T.U.C. partisan or to be a blackleg as such.

Went to Craig's room with Wrong and Weldon (Chute came in later) to drink whiskey and talk. An obstinate argument by Weldon and me against Craig and Wrong who maintained that one had a duty to support one's country or "the state" even when it is wrong. Craig kept on saying he agreed with me, which he doesn't. Largely because I held that Govt. has a right (by the rules of all negotiation – *ius gentium*)[16] to demand a repudiation of the *Daily Mail* strke. Wrong said "Craig & Lewis think God was a moderate Whig." I only demanded "is" instead of "was" . . .

Monday 10 May: . . . Went to lunch at Univ. with Keir and Lawson. They came in late, both having been listening-in in Univ. Common Room. They had heard that all had been quiet at Hull for the last 48 hours: on the other hand Keir heard from a pupil just back from Hull that martial law is being proclaimed. But as he heard that in the sergeants' mess and late at night, perhaps it ought not to weigh very much.

I then bussed home. There were half a dozen Lancashire miners in the bus, very drunk. They said they had all been soldiers and knew how to shoot: if they couldn't break our pockets they would break our hearts etc. etc. Someone began arguing with them and they answered him (quite sensibly) by saying "Are you a miner?" – " 'Oo the 'ell are you?" – "You're a bloody shop assistant." Not a pleasant journey, tho' I think they were probably quite decent drunks and not so bad as they sounded.

Told D we should all have to go by the end of the week if the strike was still on, which naturally worried her. Miss Baker to tea. Raining. All very depressing.

Back to College for dinner and afterwards with Hardie to "the pictures" where I saw Felix (excellent) and Harold Lloyd for the first time in my life.

We decided to go and see Weldon and have further discussion about our plans. Finding his rooms empty we went to Chute's where we found Craig, Chute, Weldon, Jellicoe and some undergraduates. We found that Weldon had fixed up a party of his own to go docking, and given us the slip. I said I had always

[16] "The right of nations", i.e. Natural Law.

cherished a belief that under his cynical demeanour he concealed a good heart. He replied "Now you know."

Jellicoe's statement that he wanted men for a canteen, however, opened a new door: and the more I thought of it the more I liked it. I am quite muddled about the rights and wrongs of the thing now, but it seems that one can't be doing *harm* by distributing food in a canteen. It also seems fairly safe and one is not being tied up by Govt. London also attracts because of Barfield and Harwood.

Hardie and I went to Weldon's rooms to drink toddy and try Sortes Virgilianae. We got *"At regina pyra penetrali in sede sub auras"*.[17] That didn't seem very explicit, so we tried the Bible and got a line, not of text but of editorial matter, about "the fall of great empires". That was much too explicit so we tried Milton. He gave the passage about "all Hell broke loose" and "anger infinite provoked". Worse and worse! We gave Virgil two more tries: one was about the return of Saturnian kingdoms in Latium, but like fools we didn't stop there, and trying again got *"Miscuerunt herbas et non innoxia verba."*[18] No more oracles for me! . . .

Tuesday 11 May: . . . I meant to get out home early this morning but Hetherington came to see me and we were presently joined by Hardie. Hetherington is for the Archbishop's Appeal and the Balliol Independant whose object is the entirely worthy one of finding as soon as possible some means of rapprochement which will save both parties' faces. That is the only way in which the thing can be ended without great evil . . .

In to Merton for the "English tea" at 4. Here there was hardly any talk of the strike. Discussion turned on Fletcher's proposal to co-ordinate the lecture list with the ordinary course of tutorial work.[19] Everyone agreed, tho' Gordon spoke of the danger of making the thing too much of "an easily running engine that can give no pleasure to anyone except the engineer". Miss Lee talked a lot of nonsense about the need for lessons in pronunciation and beginners' "outlines of literature".[20]

Tolkien managed to get the discussion round to the proposed

[17] Virgil, *Aeneid*, IV, 504 – "But the Queen [Dido], having erected a pyre in the inmost heart of her home, in the open air."

[18] Virgil, *Georgics*, III, 283 – (of stepmothers) "they have mixed together herbs and harmful spells."

[19] The Rev. Ronald Frank William Fletcher was Chaplain and Tutor in English Language and Literature at St Edmund Hall.

[20] Margaret Lucy Lee was Tutor in English at the Society of Oxford Home-Students (later St Anne's College).

English Prelim.[21] I had a talk with him afterwards. He is a smooth, pale, fluent little chap – can't read Spenser because of the forms – thinks the language is the real thing in the school – thinks all literature is written for the amusement of *men* between thirty and forty – we ought to vote ourselves out of existence if we were honest – still the sound-changes and the gobbets are great fun for the dons. No harm in him: only needs a smack or so. His pet abomination is the idea of "liberal" studies. Technical hobbies are more in his line.

Home again. Debate in *Times* today very interesting. There seems to be no adequate answer to the question why the Archbishop's appeal was excluded from the *Gazette*. Churchill is the editor. The Labour report of a collapse of the O.M.S. at Newcastle was repeated with circumstance. Had a quiet evening with D after supper: pleasant home-life again – there is so little of it now.

Back to College by 10.15. Had a talk with Hardie and to bed before eleven. News today reports fewer riots and tonight's broadcasting sees some hope of re-opened negotiations. But thanks to the Govt's behaviour I share with everyone I meet (of any class or party) a profound distrust of the official news.

Wednesday 12 May: Wrote a few more lines of my Outline, and was interrupted by Hardie. We discussed our going to London: he wanted to go tomorrow, I, on Friday. We wrote to Jellicoe and I then went home at 11.30.

I dropped into the bank and got the figures for my last year's income, filled in my forms and posted them. Thank heavens that is off my chest . . .

I decided to go with Hardie tomorrow. At one o'clock I listened to the unexpected news that the T.U.C. had called on Baldwin and said they were terminating the General Strike today. I am at a loss to understand this sudden, unconditional surrender. It was a great relief: ordinary life flowed back into one's mind delightfully as after a dream.

Lunch of cold chicken and tongue. I took Pat out for a walk in Cuckoo Lane and got drenched in a sudden shower.

Back into College about 3.30, and changed. Met Hardie and Mabbott of St Johns. We commented on the fact that J.A. had kept silence all through the strike and enunciated no moral doctrine: we

---

[21] See **John Ronald Reuel Tolkien** in the Biographical Appendix.

thought the portent "J.A. *tacuit*"[22] (cf. *bos locutus est*)[23] ought to be sent in to the augurs.[24]

Tea in the Smoking Room with Benecke, and thence to L.M.H. for my class, thro' the Parks in a sudden burst of wet heat, heavy sunshine, and bright colours on the dripping trees . . . My class was completely unruffled by the strike and still very interested in Berkeley. Miss Thring read a paper. The discussion turned on the self. I told them about Alexander's distinction of contemplation and enjoyment[25] and they all (I think) got it quite clear. Miss Colborne was specially good, saying to Miss Grant (who wanted to "know" the self) "It is as if, not content with seeing with your eyes, you wanted to take them out and look at them – and then they wouldn't be eyes.". . .

Thursday 13 May: . . . The news in this morning's *Times* and by the wireless is bad. Most of the companies are refusing to take back their staffs as a whole, and most of the men are refusing to go back until they are promised that all will go back together. I fear this may still wreck the whole show. In so far as it is not necessary, but a mere reprisal, I blame the masters very much.

D seemed a little better today. After lunch I walked up Shotover: very hot and bright between the showers. The deep colours and threateningly clear outlines of the plain seen from Shotover almost woke me for a moment from the inattentive lethargy in which I usually walk now . . .

To the Union where I took out Gavin Douglas and Robert Graves' *Poetic Unreason* . . . Read Graves' book in the evening. He explains poetry on psychoanalytic principles and does not explain where its poetry lies: i.e. it resolves a conflict, so may a dream. But a dream is not poetry and where is the differentia? A stupid fellow who has been knocked off his feet by psychoanalysis because he hadn't thought enough before he met it. I suppose that is the prig in me again! . . .

Friday 14 May: Read Gavin Douglas' Prologues to Vergil. Poor stuff. I was quite surprised and rather shocked by the arrival of a pupil this morning – Betjeman. He has been in Oxford all the time, "driving

---

[22] "kept silent."

[23] "an ox uttered words" – a familiar Roman portent recorded by historians such as augurs were given to interpret.

[24] See **James Alexander Smith** in the Biographical Appendix.

[25] In *Space, Time, and Deity* (1920).

people round to villages to speak, in his car" – I suppose that means people like my miners in the bus.

Home by 1.15. D seems better today. Read the papers: hardly anyone seems to have gone back yet. Baldwin made rather a great speech in the House yesterday, disclaiming all intention of reprisals and pointing out that he had himself induced some employers to meet the men and hold discussions about reinstatement. Thomas made a good speech too, drawing attention to the action of some Govt. departments and also to the difference between Baldwin's tone and that of the "surrender" number of the *Gazette* . . .

After tea I read (at home) *The Palice of Honour* which, in spite of the barbarous diction, is rather good. The horror of the waste is well done and I got a real thrill out of the music that "distant on far was carryit by the deip". It is nice too to have Venus and her court knocked out for once.

Back to College at seven, feeling fit for nothing. Took Chesterton's *Club of Queer Trades* from the smoking room library after dinner: read in it, made tea, and to bed by eleven or before . . .

Saturday 15 May: De Peyer alone this morning (Clark is still away) for a sticky hour on Butler. Then came Yorke for O.E. He has had amazing adventures. He travelled by a lorry to Bristol, found the docks shut up (it was a Saturday evening) and went to a hotel. Here he met a man who for some reason decided he was running away from home and talked to him on that hypothesis till midnight. On Sunday (he was dressed like a tramp) he went out for a walk and was accosted by a girl of about 12 with the question " 'Ave you got a Sunday?" "A Sunday", apparently, means some one to walk out with on Sundays. Next day he went to a Labour exchange – why on earth he didn't go to one of the ordinary organisations, I don't know, – and could get no work: which is odd. Whereupon he was clapped on the back by another tramp and told " 'Ard luck old man."

I told him about the death of Dent – wh. I am hoping does not affect the publication of "Dymer". Pocock has an agreement signed by me, but I have yet none signed by them.[26]

Home by one. So far I had been been feeling the better for my quiet and early evening last night but no sooner had I set out for my walk after lunch than the old headache and feeling of unreality

[26] "Dymer" had been finished during the Summer of 1925, and it was accepted for publication by J.M. Dent Ltd on 1 April 1926. However, with the death of Mr Dent, Lewis was worried that the contract might not be honoured. He was given assurance by Guy Pocock.

descended on me. Had only a short stroll in the fields below Shotover.

Spent the rest of the day at home lazily, reading the life of Hannah More by William Roberts Esq. (1838).[27] He is a deliciously pompous and peppery evangelical, but the letters (which make the most part of it) are v. interesting. One is glad to see Johnson with Sir Joshua's macaw on his wrist . . .

Sunday 16 May: . . . I continued to read about Hannah More. The account of her work in the Clevedon, Blagdon and Wrington neighbourhood recalls a pleasant jaunt with W and throws a lot of interesting light on the Jacobin and anti-Jacobin period.

It is grim to see the humanist gradually withering in her, and funny to hear the author describing the society of such men as Johnson as the snares of "the world" – "leagued against her" – from wh. she escaped. The diaries are like those of Frances Havergall: one sees the self examination taking a form in which it is bound to become worse and worse: the more you scratch you more you itch. The problem raised is this: how to be seriously concerned with goodness without letting the "empirical ego" become the absorbing object. Perhaps it is insoluble.

Winifred went home to see her people today and I washed up after lunch: went for a short walk after tea and escaped headache etc. So far it had been a pleasant day: the rest was unpleasant. Maureen offered to wash up after supper. Like a fool (or a knave) I acquiesced and she began, not according to D's fundamental principles. D rushed into the scullery and took the implements out of her hands and a violent altercation followed, Maureen claiming to be judged by results, and D saying that if every servant had to learn her ways she didn't see why her daughter shouldn't etc. etc. I kept out of it.

We then got into the dining room and had only a few minutes quiet before another row began. I forget how it started. Maureen said she hadn't forgiven Dotty and me for Friday night. I discovered this meant that D had gone to meet Maureen on her return from the Ladies' Musical and waited for three buses. I can't really see that this was my fault. At any rate Maureen went on to protest against D's imprudence in her usual tactless way, and of course, all in a flash, D was in a raging temper, and became so unjust that I ventured to say something on Maureen's side.

This only made matters worse: and poor D made it a moral issue

---

[27] William Roberts, *Memoirs of the Life and Correspondence of Mrs Hannah More* (1834).

and said she would always do her duty no matter what all of us said, and she had a splitting headache and if we bothered her any more she'd leave the room. I suppose the headache was at the bottom of the whole thing: I am afraid she is still very poorly. In these cases one can be sure only that any line one takes will be wrong.

Back to College at 9, feeling miserable. Spencer met me and came up to my room. He has been a special in London and has had a very good time: only four hours' duty a day, no rows, and much fun. People were driving along the embankment at 70 miles an hour. He confirms the story about the T.U.C. asking for police protection. We were joined by Hardie. Spencer didn't go till 11.45 and I then went to Hardie's room to warm my feet at his fire having got cold in my own room without one. To bed 12.30 with a headache – but possibly slept better than if I had gone there straight on the top of the home troubles.

Monday 17 May: Valentin seems to be still away. Boddington called and arranged to come tomorrow. I worked a little on Aristotle in the morning and read Marlowe's *Edward II*: nothing so good or so bad.

Lunched in my own rooms with Keir and Lawson: the latter as usual stayed for some time and was very boring.

Got home by 2.30 and found a car standing outside "Hillsboro". It turned out to be the Blacks come to take D for a drive. I saw D herself only for a moment, she was suffering from a headache again. Read for half an hour in a new library book I found on the hall table – Rose Macaulay's *Potterism*. I wd. probably have enjoyed it more a few years ago, but it is very good still.

I then took Pat for a saunter down Cuckoo Lane and the Private Road and, not expecting or intending anything more than a dutiful half hour of exercise, became very happy and more myself (that is, less myself) than I have been this long time.

Reached home just as D was returning from her drive: I saw her for only a few minutes alone (as the Blacks were staying for tea). She had enjoyed the run and seemed v. much better.

Back to College soon after five: finished *Edward II* and read some *Tamburlaine*. After hall I looked at Boddington's Aristotle gobbets. Then Hardie came and read me Dr Brown's paper on Personality to which he has to reply at the Jowett on Wednesday night. Parts of it very vague and mythological, but it improved at the end. I agree with what he means to say, tho' not with most of his attempts to say it.

Tuesday 18 May: Boddington at 10 on Aristotle, then Spencer on Lydgate and Hoccleve: the latter a good hour I hope.

I then went home (at 12) chatted and had lunch. They had had a restless night owing to Maureen's being ill & D was rather poorly in consequence, tho cheerful.

I bussed back to College at two to meet Ewing and go for a walk with him, my termly penance. We went through the walks to Marston Road and up by the cemetery to Headington. He has just won the Green prize. The poor fellow was as dull as ever. He sails for New York on June 19th to give summer lectures at Ann Arbor.

Forgot to mention yesterday Keir's account of Ewing turning up at Univ. to dine with Carritt, wearing full evening dress with a made-up bow tie of which a great tail stuck up perpendicularly behind his neck – and brown boots. We had tea at "Hillsboro" and by the grace of God he had to go almost at once.

D and I walked round to Phippy's. This was the first walk D has taken since her illness and great was the excitement of Pat. On the way back we were called in by old Knight to see his pigs which we duly admired: and indeed they are very personable pigs . . .

Wednesday 19 May: Worked on Ascham's *Toxophilus* . . . Hetherington and Hamilton came at 12, and Hetherington read on the Moral Faculty. He was quite good, Hamilton not very. I was very bad.

Home for lunch. Read a little more of *Potterism* – it is not really *very* good – walked in Cuckoo Lane and came in after an early tea to my class at L.M.H. Our usual room was occupied and they led me to Sir Charles' Library. Here again I was very bad and muddling: so they were, or seemed to be.

Back to College, propounded a few questions for the Fellowship general paper & then dressed and went to the Martlets dinner at Univ. I sat next to Fell who is one of the black sheep of the College, but a pleasant fellow enough.[28] Farquharson and Carlyle were pulling each others' legs and both were very great. I had forgotten how good Univ. conversation was.

After dinner John Freeman read us some of his poems. I knew nothing of him but the name and two of the poems in *Poems of Today* which I had looked up this afternoon. He is a man past middle age with spectacles and a lisp: a rather weak chin: not much of a

<hr />

[28] Bryan Greg Fell matriculated at University College in 1924 and took his BA in 1933.

face altogether. Poets ought not to read their work aloud as an after
dinner entertainment: it is extremely uncomfortable . . .

Thursday 20 May: Yorke came for O.E. and we did the *Fall of the
Angels* together. He tells me he met Siegfried Sassoon and other
literary men during the strike. Siegfried spoke of the civil war wh.
(he said) wd. begin, and then, sitting down on a tub in which a tree
grew, laid his head against the tree, shut his eyes, and agonised in
silence.

Are all our modern poets like this? Were the old ones so? It is
almost enough to prove R. Graves' contention that an artist is like
a medium: a neurotic with an inferiority complex who gets his own
back by attributing to himself abnormal powers. And indeed I have
noticed in myself a ridiculous tendency to indulge in poetical
complacency as a consolation when I am ill at ease thro' managing
ordinary life worse than usual . . .

After Yorke had gone I went to Alfred Street – of hated memory,
for there I enlisted in 1917 – to see a man about my income tax. It
appears the College return does not tally with mine. No doubt mine
is wrong.

Bought a Berner's Froissart and bussed home. D in good form.
Short walk and back again to find Mrs Wilbraham there for tea. She
and her undergraduate nephew and friends appear to be coming again
on Sunday. There is one who doesn't play badminton and D very
obligingly said I would like to talk to him. This thing threatens to
become a nuisance. I resolved that whatever happened I wd. not let
it be a custom for me to amuse strange undergraduates (for whom
I am not paid) on the one day in the week when I look to be at home
and at ease . . .

Friday 21 May: A really fine day at last. Waterfield and Percival in
the morning. I shall have to separate these two: W. is quite good and
that grinning nonentity Percival only acts as a drag on him.

Home and had a delightful walk in the fields by Marston. The
hawthorn smells strongest in these low lying sun traps and the path
in a field is a long green line ahead dividing an almost solid yellow
of buttercups. Back to tea . . .

Saturday 22 May: Betjeman, Clark and De Peyer, Yorke (v. good,
on Swift) and Glasgow this morning: home for the rest of the day.

D in good form. Another lovely day. I walked to Elsfield by the
fields, my first good walk for many days. "Mountings of the
mind . . . came fast upon me." Came home and read Descartes'

Meditations with much interest. Played a game of badminton with Dotty: after supper with her and Maureen. The latter then gave Winifred a lesson in the game. She takes it quite well, tho' her guffaws and gestures are very odd. We all sat in the dining room very idly and talked in the twilight till ten when I came back to College.

Wrote a short note on "A paralogism in Berkeley". Hardie came in and pronounced my argument valid.

Sunday 23 May: Out home immediately after breakfast. The walk thro' Mesopotamia gets more beautiful every week. All well and cheerful at home . . .

Came into College, attended chapel and read the first lesson. J.A., Hardie and I left the smoking room together and stayed for a long time in the cloister of New Building talking about books. This is almost the first time I have ever *conversed* with J.A. – tho' I have often propounded theses to him and listened to his answering (but never quite answering) expositions. As Cox said at Univ. the other night, it is a mark of the Italian school – and J.A. is wholly Italianate in philosophy – never to argue.

To bed at 11.30 and read *The Lunatic at Large* in bed for half and hour.

Monday 24 May: Not having made up my diary for two days, I forget what happened this morning. I presume it was spent in profound thought. Just this moment I remember. It was: I was writing a note on what is meant by "present to the mind".

Lunched in Merton with Lawson and Keir, and separated early. Went home. It was very hot and I had only a short walk. Later on I had a strenuous game of badminton with Dotty. Had supper at home: back to College late and to bed.

Tuesday 25 May: Boddington came this morning and we discussed his collections paper on Logic. A note from Spencer to apologise for not coming . . .

Left home after tea and worked on Descartes with much interest. In the Smoking room Segar presented me with a free ticket (but I must pay for it) for tonight's *Ruddigore*, some arrangement of his own having fallen through.[29] I went off at once and arrived about ten minutes after the rise of the curtain. It is years now since I have seen a Gilbert and Sullivan, and this, which I never saw before, was delightful. Sheffield as Despard was particularly good, and also the

---

[29] See **Robert Segar** in the Magdalen College Appendix.

ghost song. Home with moonlight down Holywell, thinking how jolly it all was (touch wood) and to bed by twelve.

Wednesday 26 May: Sykes and Waddington this morning, later Hetherington and Hamilton: very interesting discussion with both.

Home for lunch. Afterwards I took my walk over the fields to the row of firs on the way to Forest Hill, and sat down at the foot of one where there was a pleasant breeze. The place is smothered in daisies and buttercups and hedged with hawthorn. I thought a little – all my ideas are in a crumbling state at present – but, thank goodness, stared more. I suspect that the mystical contemplation of a particular external object, if carried out formally, is a spoof and leads to an inferior mode of consciousness, but just a whiff of it – moment's concentration on a tree or something – usually gives you something you hadn't got before. I enjoyed myself.

Home for early tea and then in to L.M.H. A good hour on Hume's theory of causation. Miss Colbourne has shut up.

Back to College and worked on Descartes. Dined and went into Common Room afterwards. J.A. had an American guest who sat on my left. I said, as I passed the decanter, "This is port." "Tell him what it is," said Cowley, "It's '96. Before you were born." I passed on this important information. "What, 1906?" said the American, "Wall, really."

At about 10.30 Weldon who had been tutoring Elliston, came in and "carried" me for a stroll round the walks: very cool and dark, with the pleasant sound of the weir and a yellow moon. He talked about the absurd financial position here. A third of our net revenue goes to the University and it is thus to our interest to spend as much of the gross as we can: hence this continual succession of walls and ugly and unnecessary buildings with which we are gradually surrounding ourselves. Came back and drank whiskey in my rooms, talking of the ideal state, eugenics, Raymond and astral tobacco, and why the witch hunts came in the 17th century . . .

Thursday 27 May: A cooler day with a fresh wind. Betjeman and Valentin came with O.E. Betjeman appeared in a pair of eccentric bedroom slippers and said he hoped I didn't mind them as he had a blister. He seemed so pleased with himself that I couldn't help replying that I should mind them very much myself but that I had no objection to *his* wearing them – a view which, I believe, surprised him. Both had been very idle over the O.E. and I told them it wouldn't do.

Home for lunch, after working for the rest of the morning on *The Dunciad*. Went for a walk towards Stowe Woods: with the wind and changing sky it wd. have been pleasant, but for the number of children everywhere. Back to tea and all three of us went shopping in Headington afterwards.

I then returned to College and attended a meeting of the Fellowship examiners in the smoking room. I was much struck by the hangdog look of Weldon who keeps up a look of ostentatious boredom on these occasions that must really be more tiring than a show of interest. He's an odd fish. The President amused everyone by suddenly saying "Oh but, Hardie, you're a philosopher, too, aren't you?"

Dined and came away almost at once to work on Courthope, but failed miserably to concentrate. Going down into the cloister I met Hardie and Brightman returning from *The Pirates of Penzance*. The reverend and aged gentleman was in great spirits, striking the attitudes of a pirate king and proclaiming his wish to embrace both the leading ladies. I then went up to Hardie's rooms and talked for a while. Late to bed.

Friday 28 May: Percival and Waterfield this morning. I am getting rather tired of the latter's domestic similes in his essays: long and pointless examples beginning "Once there was a little boy".

Home to lunch where we had a telegram from W hoping that we could put him up for the week end. I walked as usual and came back to College after tea. Tutorial meeting in the Chaplain's room after hall, where I attended and made reports.

Saturday 29 May: Betjeman came at 9 and surprised me with a very creditable essay. Then Clark and de Peyer on Descartes, both stupid, but we hammered out a good discussion all the same. Then Yorke on Pope, really good work: he is coming on in the most encouraging way. Finally Glasgow – a tough morning.

W came at 1 o'clock and "carried" me to the Mitre to drink beer. He had a good deal to say about the strike and had had some unpleasant experiences: as he took a convoy through London the crowd shouted to the Tommies "Why don't you bayonet the b——r?" He says the troops are very solid and the recent events have done much to restore their old contempt for civilians: we must be in a desperate state when one feels grateful for this useful insolence, as I am afraid I did. The men call Saklatvala "Mr Sack-lavatory" . . .[30]

[30] Shapurji Saklatvala (1874–1936) was M.P. (Communist) for North Battersea 1922–3 and 1924–9, and a member of the General Workers' Union.

Here is a good story of a Guardee Colonel, who, when some superior opened an interview by saying that the situation was much more serious than they had thought at first, replied fervently "Yes sir, it is – they tell me at my Turkish bath club that the supply of coal may be cut down!"

We went to Leighton's in Holywell where we had left the byke for a small repair, but they had done nothing to it and the men would not be back till two. We were amused by a man who, being asked if he were in charge, asked what we wanted, and when he had heard the grievance, said "No, I am not in charge."

Went and had lunch at the Town & Gown, then retrieved the byke and went home. Played two sets of badminton with W before tea, and afterwards walked down to Mesopotamia with him and gave Pat a bath. After supper, the girls being in, all four had some amusing badminton. W biked me back to College, came in for a drink, and left me for Headington at eleven.

D tells me that Dotty is rather inclined to "practise" on W: with all her other faults I thought she was free from this. This was the starting point of an idea and I wrote the first sonnet and a half of a sequence which was to be put into the mouth of a man who is gradually falling in love with a bitch, tho' quite conscious of what she is. I don't care for sonnet sequences and it is not the sort of thing I ever imagined myself writing: but it would be jolly if it shd. come off.[31] . . .

Sunday 30 May: After breakfast re-cast what I wrote last night into a stanza I have long had in my mind (a a b c c b blank b). It is still not very satisfactory.

W came at about 10 and took me home in his side car. We spent the morning walking down to Mesopotamia and gave Pat another dip: had some beer in Headington when we came back. Winifred went home after lunch and I washed up . . .

Had an early supper and came back to College whence Hardie took me to Hertford to hear Alexander at the Philosophical Society.[32] We met Price in Hertford quad and remained there chatting till presently the great man, bearded and deaf and very venerable, appeared supported by Pritchard, Carritt and others. Cox was there as Carritt's guest. It was a great evening.

[31] The first version of this sonnet sequence survives in the same notebook as the last portion of the Diary. A revised version of it, entitled "Infatuation", is found in Lewis's *Poems* (1964).

[32] Samuel Alexander, author of *Space, Time, and Deity.*

The first part of A's paper, on artistic creation, was an admirable and, to me, a satisfying attack on all Croce's nonsense: the second part, "cosmic creation", was largely beyond me. He has great humour, as when he remarked, after a dark saying, "I have not time to add the qualifications wh. make this statement true." In discussion a chair was placed beside him to which the disputants came one by one, because of his deafness. Carritt who opened the discussion, was very good: not so the various lawyers and divines who followed, till J.A. took the matter in hand. Back to College with Hardie about 11.

Monday 31 May: Valentin came this morning: pretty poor. I spent the rest of the time before lunch on my new poem and made eight stanzas, doing far better than I hoped. I really begin to think that something will come of it.

To Univ. for lunch with Keir alone, Lawson being away at Stow-in-the-Wold by his doctor's orders.

Bussed home. D had been into town shopping and had a headache. Walked between lunch and tea time, then settled down to Elyot's *Boke of the Governour* for the rest of the day. A good book: the brief description of football is worth remembering.

Had supper at home and came into college at 10: went on with Elyot till 11.30: then read January, February & March in Spenser's *Calendar* and went to bed. I had quite forgotten the pleasant earthy flavour of the Briar and the Oak and was delighted with it. A good day, but shaky and headachy at the end of it.

Tuesday 1 June: . . . Forgot to mention yesterday a letter from Pasley in India, fairly cheerful, but complaining of Anglo-Indian society and with a Pasleyish undercurrent of schemes for the future, implying that he has not yet quite found himself. He has two children now.[1]

Went home and lunched (after spending the rest of the morning on Elyot: *Titus & Gisippus* is a good novella).

D was better today. Walked up Shotover in the afternoon thro' Headington Quarry, where I have not been for a long time. Back to tea at which arrived a letter from Harwood announcing the birth of a son.[2] We were both glad, tho' it is rather dreadful to think of a child born into a house full of educational theories!

D is more and more discontented with Dotty who gives her an hour's work every morning making up meals for her and her friends to take on the river. I am afraid she is one of our many mistakes.

Back to College where I wrote to Harwood (enclosing a note from D) and read Elyot again till hall. Went into Common Room afterwards and sat next to J.A. who was in great form, tho' one of his stories was a familiar chestnut.

I then walked to the Union to return Gavin Douglas – a beautiful clear evening with a cold look about the stone. In Market Street I met Hardie and foolishly allowed myself to be persuaded to go to the Cinema. I was rewarded by a very bad Harold Lloyd. Back to his room to discuss whether one knew of one's own selfhood by knowing other selves (my theory) or vice-versa, till 12.30. He had the best of the argument. A mis-spent evening.

Wednesday 2 June: Waddington & Sykes at 9 o'clock. I felt very tired and dull at the beginning but a lively discussion developed . . . Hetherington and Hamilton came at twelve. Hetherington is an extraordinary man and seems to see the whole of modern idealism

---

[1] Rodney Pasley was Vice-Principal of Rajkumar College at Rajkot 1926–8.

[2] John Oliver Harwood, the first of Cecil and Daphne Harwood's five children, was born on 31 May 1926. After service in the Royal Navy during World War II he came up to Oxford and read English at Magdalen College 1947–50.

by nature. He began on the subjective level but accepted the distinction of the I and the me and thence mounted on his own wings to the back of beyond. What is one to do with him for the rest of his career? . . .

To hall, during which Segar told me of his experiences when torpedoed in the Mediterranean. It was a story of panic and bad conduct worse than any I have heard in the war. The Captain shot himself. Segar, in the water, approached a boat with three men in it: one a man with his jaw shot away, the other a padré temporarily mad, the third unhurt. This one said "Go away, you're making me sea sick" and taking off his boots hammered Segar's hands till he let go of the ropes. He was afterwards picked up by a tug . . .

Thursday 3 June: . . . Yorke on O.E. this morning followed by Betjeman and Valentin who did better. I tried to do something on my new poem but made nothing of it. I am afraid nothing more *can* be made of it.

Home for lunch. D was rather *affairé* making up sandwiches for all three girls (drat 'em) to take on the river for Eights. Went for a short walk down by the cemetery and home for tea.

. . . After tea I came back to College and worked on Spenser, after finishing Elyot's *Governour*. Stayed for some time in the smoking room after dinner doing an impossibly difficult crossword puzzle with J.A. and Wrong. Back to my rooms and spent the whole evening on Spenser with great satisfaction. To bed about 11.30 and heard many sounds of revelry.

Friday 4 June: . . . A beautiful misty warm morning, the mist all transparent and luminous with concealed sunshine, wood pigeons making a noise in the grove, and a heavy dew. It suggested autumn and gave me a shudden whiff of what I used to call "the real joy".

Tried to write after breakfast and copied out four new stanzas, including the swallow one. This poem must wind itself up or else take an unexpected development. Betjeman came this morning, followed by Percival and Waterfield, both very silly.

Home for lunch, walk and back to College after tea, where I began to read Hooker's *Ecclesiastical Polity* (in the library copy) with great enjoyment, having conceived the idea of giving a lecture next term on Elyot, Ascham, Hooker and Bacon.[3]

---

[3] This idea expanded into a twice-weekly course of lectures during Michaelmas Term 1926 entitled "Some English Thinkers of the Renaissance (Elyot, Ascham, Hooker, Bacon)".

After dinner, at which very few were present, I got into an interesting conversation with J.A. on the Norse mythology in which he is well informed.

Saturday 5 June: Another beautiful day. Went out after breakfast and bought the Everyman Hooker in two volumes. Clark & de Peyer, Yorke and Glasgow all came this morning.

Home for lunch. D suffering badly from stiffness after clipping and brushing Pat. I stayed in all afternoon reading Hooker, who is certainly a great man. After tea went for a pleasant walk with Pat, up the crab-apple road as far as the stile and home by the fields: soft afternoon sunshine, improved by a mild wind . . . D and I had a quiet evening to ourselves and I finished the first book of Hooker, coming back to College about 10.30.

There I found a long letter from P[apy]. which I answered at once, and went to bed.

Sunday 6 June: A glorious summer morning. Walked home after breakfast and found all well: D much better today. Took my walk in the morning despite the heat, in order to have the afternoon free, when D would be able to sit out and the chairs wd. be unoccupied by girls. I went to the field with the fir trees and sat in the grass and buttercups for a while, then back to drink beer in Headington, and so home for lunch.

After lunch the girls all went off to the river. We had an enlightened conversation in which Valerie and Dotty explained how one can cry on purpose. One begins at the psychological end by a representation of one's wrongs and desolation, and it is soon quite easy. Valerie is specially instructive because she is more naïf than Dotty and says the most appalling things without knowing it. She admits that she feels "respect" or "feels small" in the presence of girls with really good hats: and as for clothes, she feels ready to "tear them off" their possessors. She said it was very complicated: I said I thought it was the *simplest* feeling I had ever heard anyone put into words.

D and I spent the afternoon in the garden under the plum tree, which looks as if it will bear some fruit this year. I read Abercrombie's *Idea of Great Poetry* which I borrowed from J.A. He is not a great mind but he knows more about poetry than most of those now writing – understands what a long *poem* is – and combats the hectic theory of poetry as existing only in momentary lyrical impressions. Let us hope the tide is turning.

Left home about 5.30 and came in to go to chapel but missed it

. . . A big crowd dining in. Onions introduced me to his guest, Fiedler, and plunging himself into conversation with Brightman, left me to entertain the Bosche.[4] The best thing I got out of him was his statement that before the war he used to delight Farquharson by telling him he looked rather like Moltke.[5] Dawnay was in and Weldon tells me he is going to get a Guards battalion and that he is "far too nice for a soldier".[6] (A good early blank verse line, as we observed.)

As Hardie and I were coming across to New Building we were overtaken by J.A. who proposed a stroll in the walks. We went and sat in the garden till it was quite dark. He was very great, telling us about his travels in the Balkans. The best things were (a) the masterful ladies (English of course) on a small Greek steamer who made such a nuisance of themselves that the Captain said "Have you no brothers? Why have they not got someone to marry you?", and went on muttering at intervals for the rest of the evening "It ought to have been possible to get *someone*." (b) The Austrian minister at some unearthly town who took J.A. and his party out for a walk on the railway line, which was the only place level enough to walk on, and beginning to balance himself on the rails, remarked sadly "C'est mon seul sport." (c) The Greek clergyman who asked J.A. and his sister to tea and, when they departed, accompanied them back to their hotel, repeating "You will remember me?" "Yes, certainly," said J.A. The clergyman repeated his touching request about fifteen times and each time J.A. (tho' somewhat surprised) assured him with increasing warmth that he would never forget him. It was only afterwards they realised that the reverend gentleman was asking for a tip.

We began to be troubled with midges and as J.A. had used all my matches it was impossible to smoke, so we returned. I read a few of Emily Brontë's poems and went to bed.

Monday 7 June: Valentin and Boddington this morning.

Wrote a few couplets for another part of the poem, describing the settlers' town, as an opening to the story of the wood in which the

---

[4] Hermann George Fiedler (1862–1945) was a Fellow of Queen's College and Professor of German Language and Literature 1907–37.

[5] Count Helmuth Johannes Ludwig von Moltke (1848–1916), a German general, was Chief of Staff in World War I.

[6] Col. Alan Geoffrey Dawnay (1888–1938), an old member of Magdalen, was in the Coldstream Guards. He commanded the Oxford University O.T.C. 1922–6, and had been given command of the 1st Battalion 1928–30.

people parodied human action. The idea is expanding and may find room for many things including my old poems of Foster.

Lawson and Keir came for lunch. We considered the Everyman list with a view to suggesting additions, as Pocock had invited me to do: after lunch we sat in the grove – very beautiful with light and shadow this hot afternoon – and continued the job till about three.

I then bussed home: all well there, except that D seems to be more and more worried by Dotty. I did not go out till after tea and then took only a short walk past Mrs Seymour's to sit among the trees by Bayswater brook. There is almost a spinney of pollards among the flat grass and buttercups beside the stream . . .

Tuesday 8 June: Finished setting a Literature and Criticism paper for the Fellowship examination this morning. Rang up the theatre and got three tickets for the *Coriolanus* tonight. Wrote to Spencer in answer to his apologies, to Margoliouth giving him Yorke's name for the English fund,[7] to Driver telling him I had set my paper, to Fell saying I wd. join the Mermaid Club, and to Joan Colborne changing tomorrow's class to 5.30 as she had requested . . .

I skimmed *Coriolanus* until dinner time and glanced at Stead's *Shadow of Mt Carmel*, just published, which he has sent me. He had already shown it me in proof and I had criticised pretty plainly, but it rolled off like water from a duck's back . . .

The performance was bad beyond description. They had only two ways of speaking, to whisper or to shout, and both inaudible. Coriolanus had every trick of the traditional barn stormer, and one wonders how this kind of acting has survived a hundred years of parody. I met Carter in one of the intervals. He thought it good: but to such a beaming Friar Tuck as Carter all things are good. It was a real relief to get out at the end and to be bellowed and grimaced at no longer . . .

Wednesday 9 June: A busy day. Waddington and Sykes came at 9 and we had a good, tho' exhausting, hour.

I then wrote to Stead thanking him for the book and enclosing for his criticism a parody of T.S. Eliot wh. I had just scribbled off: very nonsensical, but with a flavour of dirt all through. My idea is to send it up to his paper in the hope that he will be taken in and publish it: if he falls into the trap I will then consider how best to use the joke for the advancement of literature and the punishment of

---

[7] Herschel Maurice Margoliouth (1887–1959) was Secretary of Faculties, Oxford University 1925–47.

quackery.[8] If he doesn't I shall have proved that there is something more than I suspected in this kind of stuff . . .

Then came Hamilton and Hetherington, and we had a most vigorous and gruelling hour . . .

I went . . . at 3.45 to the board room in old Clarendon for a meeting of the sub faculty. Met Miss Spens who seems to think my class a great success and agrees with most of my report, tho' she is surprised at my thinking Miss Colborne so good.[9] The meeting was rather ridiculous. The air was electric with "sex antagonisms", Miss Rooke being the eloquent and ironic exponent of women's wrongs ("In that term most of our students are doing the XIXth century, and hardly any men take it, and there are no lectures on it that term, so I suppose that's all right.").[10]

Didn't get away till 4.30. Had tea in the smoking room and went to L.M.H. for my class, where Miss Colbourne read a paper on Scepticism and a lively discussion followed.

Home by bus in torrents of rain. Letters from Pocock (1) Acknowledging my list of proposed Everymans (2) Asking me if I wanted any alterations made in the design of the title page of "Dymer", by one Knowles, which came in a separate cover. It is not a bad thing, but there is too much of Beardsley in the faces. After supper I wrote complimenting it as much as I cd., but begging for something more classical and less ninetyish in the faces . . .

Thursday 10 June: Betjeman came this morning and shifted his tutorial to Monday. Then came Yorke and after doing O.E. I broached to him the idea of my literary dragonnade: a series of mock Eliotic poems to be sent up to the *Dial* and the *Criterion* until, sooner or later, one of these filthy editors falls into the trap. We both looked into T.S. Eliot's poems (which Betjeman had lent me) and Yorke was pleased with the idea. He struck out a good opening line "My soul is a windowless façade": then we hunted for a rime and of course "de Sade" turned up, with the double merit of being irrelevant and offensive. We decided to bring Coghill into the scheme . . .

Home at one in a storm of rain and found the whole house buzzing with deliberations about the badminton tournament on Saturday . . .

---

[8] Eliot's "paper" was *The Criterion*, a literary journal he founded in 1922.

[9] Janet Spens (1876–1963) was Fellow of English at Lady Margaret Hall 1911–36.

[10] Eleanor Willoughby Rooke (1888–1952) took her BA from Lady Margaret Hall in 1908 and was Tutor in English at St Hilda's College 1920–41.

Back to College where I found a letter from Stead. It was encouraging to find that tho' I *told* him my "Cross-Channel Boat" was a parody, it has quite impressed him. Poor fellow, he finds in it "a robust and rollicking flavour"! Yorke turned up with a finished poem, all about de Sade and furniture covered with pink rep and drinking mint-julep. I think it will do ...

Friday 11 June: ... I ... enlisted Hardie in the anti-Eliot group. Betjeman came, having done practically no work, and I had a row with him: he is v. conceited which makes him vulnerable.

Bussed home. Proofs of "Dymer" (I, 1-30) arrived from the Temple Press at Letchworth. Back to College after tea. Corrected my proofs and posted them. Wrote another rag poem – very sad and desperate and disillusioned, cheap as dirt. Hardie came in after hall and read me his "A Portrait": good fun, but too funny for a beginning.

Saturday 12 June: A crowded day. Pupils from 9 till 1. Home, to lunch off sandwiches in a topsy-turvy kitchen. Party from 2.30 till 6 ... For the last half hour the conversation of Dotty and Valerie was maddeningly silly. D stood the day pretty well. I hope it has not done her much harm.

More proofs of "Dymer" and a letter from Pocock agreeing with me about the title page design. Back to College at 10.30 fagged out with the unwholesome weariness of long hours' grimacing and pretence. Got rid of that atmosphere over some whiskey and a detective story and went to bed. I am told the party was a success: at any rate it is *over*.

Sunday 13 June: Woke up feeling very tired and stiff. Got drawn into an argument with J.A. on aesthetics after breakfast and was late getting home.

A beautiful morning which I spent partly in the garden correcting proofs, partly in the kitchen helping D. The girls took Pat out. I washed up after lunch.

Spent a quiet and sleepy afternoon, and re-read some of Hewlett's *Lore of Proserpine*. The simile of the three men on the three floors of the house affected me strangely. I began to think that I had let my "forensic" dominate my "recondite" too long and too severely. Of course that was a necessary reaction against the rule of the "recondite" *out* of his own sphere, which means Christina dreams. Perhaps now that I have learned my lesson I can begin to encourage the recondite a bit more. One needn't be asking questions and giving judgements *all* the time. This very crude psychology put me into a mood I have not enjoyed for years: it was like melting, as if I were a man of snow, or having doors open *in one's back*.

Came back to College about 6.30 and gazed out of my windows on to an extraordinary evening light in the Grove. The old white horse was transfigured in it. In Common Room sat next an aged parson who talked to me of the Great Eastern, the first bicycle, and English feeling during the American civil war . . .

(D tired but I hope none the worse. The chief excitement today was over Henry, Dotty's tortoise, who was discovered about two hundred yards from the gate working his passage towards the London road. He was brought back and tethered by a cord round his body, and supplied with lettuce leaves and snails in which he took no interest. He escaped repeatedly during the day. When I buy a tortoise I shall say I want a quiet one for ladies.)

Began G.K. Chesterton's *Eugenics and Other Evils*.

Monday 14 June: Betjeman and Valentin for O.E.: both had worked (according to their lights) pretty well. I corrected and sent off the second bunch of "Dymer" proofs . . .

Bussed home. D rather tired and the girls working her hard: they kept her up late last night and there were four river lunches to be got for Dotty today. They certainly intend to get "real value" out of anyone who will let them. A letter from Pocock saying he sent me my copy of the contract on the 7th of April. It certainly never reached me. Took Pat for a short walk in Cuckoo Lane.

Back to College at 5 to attend a fellowship meeting in Benecke's rooms, with Weldon and Hardie. It was interesting to see again, as I used to see when I was his pupil, Benecke's mantelpiece full of pigs – stone pigs, china pigs, stuff pigs, and brazen pigs. The meeting lasted till 6.30 when Hardie and I rushed off to dress . . .

We bussed out to the Prichards and found that dinner jackets would have done. It was a most rational dinner. The guests were all men – Mabbott, Harrod (?) of the House, Hardie and myself. The daughters were not there and Mrs Pritchard retired almost at once. We then talked philosophy till 11.30, a very good discussion . . .

Tuesday 15 June: Woke up in the early morning from an abominable dream. It began innocently and absurdly enough with W and me walking on a pier and inquiring whether certain minute points of light which we held in our hands were "merely time signals" or something more. But then we were seated by an old man, whom we dared not offend, listening to his triumphant account of someone he had buried alive or was going to bury alive. At least that is as near as the waking mind can get to it: it was really I think a corpse wh. was buried, and decaying, but somehow also alive – the life in death of the poem in MacDonald's *Lilith*. I was just saying with fiendish approval (real or feigned?) "Yes. Just think what it would feel like by about the third day," when I woke up. I was "half dead with nothing" and took some time to get to sleep again.

Valentin on Spenser this morning, pretty poor. Wrote another Eliot-parody . . .

Coghill came for dinner. He told me what Gertrude Stein's "gift of repartee" (as the Mag. calls it) was really like at the meeting in her honour the other night. Cecil of Wadham rose to ask her what she meant by the same things being "absolutely identical and absolutely different" to which Stein (she is a dowdy American) replied "Wall, you and the man next you are abso-o-lute-ly identical the way you both jump up to ask questions, but abs-o-lute-ly different in character."[11] This nonsense was greeted with rounds of approving laughter by the crowd.

After coffee we came over here and were joined by Yorke and later by Hardie. We all read our Eliotic poems and discussed plans of campaign. Coghill thought that if we succeeded it would always be open to Eliot to say that we had meant the poems seriously and afterwards pretended they were parodies: his answer to this was to make them acrostics and the ones he had composed read downwards "Sham poetry pays the world in its own coin, paper money."

Then came the brilliant idea that we should be a brother and sister, Rollo and Bridget Considine. Bridget is the elder and they are united by an affection so tender as to be almost incestuous. Bridget will presently write a letter to Eliot (if we get a foothold) telling him about her own and her brother's life. She is incredibly dowdy and about thirty five. We rolled in laughter as we pictured a tea party where the Considines meet Eliot: Yorke wd. dress up for Bridget and perhaps bring a baby. We selected as our first shot, my "Nidhogg" (by Rollo) and Hardie's "Conversation" and Yorke's "Sunday" (by Bridget). They are to be sent from Vienna where Hardie has a friend. We think Vienna will decrease suspicion and is also a likely place for the Considines to live in.

---

[11] "Cecil of Wadham" was Lord David Cecil (1902–86) who was a Fellow and Lecturer in Modern History at Wadham College 1924–30, Fellow of New College 1939–48, and Goldsmith Professor of English 1948–69.

Our meeting broke up about 12. Hardie and Coghill are in it for pure fun, I for burning indignation, Yorke chiefly for love of mischief. Went to bed, feeling for some reason very nervy and worn out – perhaps this morning's dream, or perhaps the exhaustion of so much laughter.

Wednesday 16 June: Corrected proofs all morning till 12 o'clock and made (I hope) some good corrections. Feeling very stale and shaky and beginning to develop a cough. At 12 came Hamilton and Hetherington on Berkeley: we had a most lively and obstinate discussion which lasted till 1.30.

Bussed home. Poor D seemed tired and depressed. Dotty is out all day and every day this week wh. means that D has to spend two hours or so every evening making up four picnic meals. It enrages me. Took Pat a short walk down Cuckoo Lane and home for an early tea. More proofs today and a letter (not from Pocock) to warn me that I shall have no opportunity of making second corrections for the American edition.

Back to College, thence through the Grove where I saw the Ouds rehearsing *Midsummer Night's Dream* and out to L.M.H. Miss Colborne was away, Miss Scoones surprisingly dull, and the paper read by the lumpy Miss Grant. The hour was a failure and I am rather ashamed of getting a pound for it.

Back to College where I began correcting the new Proofs. Yorke came in with two new and excellent Bridget poems.

Dressed and went to Univ. at 7.45 for the Greats dinner. Sat next to Campbell who is still a great admirer of T.S. Eliot tho' he has transferred some of his admiration to Gertrude Stein. I asked him if he had heard of the Considines – a brother and sister, I believed, who lived in Vienna and wrote remarkable stuff: but I doubted if any of it appeared in England. He hadn't heard but was quite interested.[12]

After dinner I had talk with Cox[13] and also with Henderson, who is going to the Sudan. He is a splendid fellow, a "sound man" who would delight the "hearty", a very tolerable philosopher, a wide and enthusiastic reader of books old and new, a fine athlete, an authority (almost) on sculpture, and without the slightest taint of brilliance, just wise and normal and fully developed in all directions. He has

[12] Archibald Hunter Compbell (1902–) read Classics at University College. He was a Fellow of All Souls 1928–30 and Fellow of University College 1930–35.

[13] Harold Henry Cox took his BA in 1927.

all the virtues of a regular subaltern, a country gentleman, and an aesthete, with the faults of none of them. This is the best thing Oxford does.[14] . . .

Friday-Tuesday 18-22 June: My cold was heavy and I was thick headed during the week end. On Friday came a selection of covers from Dents for "Dymer", sent for my remarks. So far they are certainly a pleasanter house than Heinemann's to deal with. Dined in and went into Common Room where the talk turned on schooldays and boyhood in general. Nearly all joined in exploding the myth of happy childhood: we are all conscious of being much better off as we are. Read John Buchan's *Path of the King* afterwards and went early to bed feeling very poorly.

Spent an idle and headachy morning on Saturday and sent off the last gallies of "Dymer". At 2 o'clock went to the Schools to invigilate, first with Miss Spens (who wants me to take some of my L.M.H. people for ordinary tuition in 19th Century. I shelved.), and then with Miss Wardale. It was very hot, my cold bad, and a long three hours . . .

Back to College by 5.15 and had some tea in the smoking room. Bussed home – for the Vac – taking Conrad's *Lord Jim*. It wd. have been pleasant thus coming out home after the term and a beastly day, if I had been feeling at all well. Went to bed immediately after supper and stayed there all Sunday. Read *Lord Jim*, a great novel, especially Marlow's conversation with Stein, and the whole picture of Stein, where the incredible is made convincing. But alas, philosophy spoils one for all these literary "reflections on life" except in Wordsworth, Meredith, MacDonald and a few more . . .

Could not get up till midday on Monday as Griffin had not brought out my luggage from College. Corrected revised proofs (which came on Saturday) of "Dymer" I, 1-30. Sat in the garden most of the afternoon reading Wells's *Modern Utopia*: fairly good but – ugh! No dogs, no windows in your bedroom, and practically the whole world full of scattered villas. He also thinks he has "discovered uniqueness" by reading Bosanquet, which is a pity.

Took Pat for a short stroll after tea and drank some stout in Old Headington. Early to bed. It is very pleasant to be at home and D

---

[14] Keith David Druitt Henderson (1903–88), who had been tutored by Lewis in 1925, entered Sudan political service in 1926 and was Governor of the Kassala Province, Sudan, 1945–53. In 1953 he was made Secretary to Spalding Educational Trust and Union for the Study of Great Religions, and in 1966 Vice-President of the World Congress of Faiths.

and I rejoice to have the house rid of the Dotties and the Valeries
. . .

Wednesday 23 June: Up very late feeling more fit than I have done
for some time. Sat in in the morning, finished re-reading Trollope's
Warden (I had forgotten how good it was) and read *The Times*. Also
wrote a longish letter to Pasley. I have practically nothing in common
with him now and it did not come easily, but one must, of pure
charity, write to a poor devil of an educated man isolated in Indian
society.

The prospect of dining with the Warrens tonight and meeting Sir
James Craig (I was afraid I might be let in for home politics & get
entangled in my talk) cast rather a shadow over the day,[15] and when
D discovered that so far I had only £300 odd from College, and
suspected that the whole thing "was a do" and ruled that I must see
Thompson at once and find out everything, I began to look forward
to a really bad afternoon and evening . . .

The dinner, tho nothing brilliant in the food line, was quite
pleasant. I took in Mrs James Murrell who was quite easy to talk to
as we disagreed about everything, specially public schools and the
services. She thinks me a horrid crank. On my left I had Mrs
Pickard-Cambridge, a woman of a fine old fashioned dignity, whom
I liked.

In the port period after the ladies had cleared off, conversation
turned entirely on University politics which was rather dull for Sir
James. I had no conversation with him: he seems a little bit uncouth.
Got away about 10.35 after a few moments conversation with Lady
Craig and quite a long talk with Mrs Webb about animals. She is
nice.

Watched the OUDS from the grass between cloisters and New
Building for a few minutes in company with Benecke and then walked
home in the bright moonlight. The others were in bed when I got
back.

Thursday 24 June: Up rather late and into College . . . I spent the
morning on Raleigh's preface to Hoby. I also left instructions with
the librarian to find me Patrizi, who is wrongly catalogued, and
went up into the Founder's Tower to get Erasmus' *Institutio Regis
Christiani*, both being mentioned by the D.N.B. as sources for Elyot's

---

[15] Sir James Craig (1871–1940), later Viscount Craigavon, was the first Prime Minister of Northern Ireland,
1921–40. During the War, when Craig was M.P. for County Down, Albert Lewis had appealed to him for
help in getting his son transferred from the Infantry to the Artillery.

Governour. From the silent sun-and-dust book rooms in the tower I went up and out upon the leads to enjoy for a moment some jumbled and foreshortened views of the College.

Coming back to the Library I was pleasantly surprised by Jenkin who had come up to take his M.A. We arranged to meet at 7.30 . . . Went to Merton Street and found Jenkin in his old digs. The very pictures on his walls were full of pleasant memories. We had supper together at the George, in great contentment. He is engaged on four or five different small jobs, including an effort to raise money for Exeter University, wh. involves a lot of touring in the West country and expenses paid. He has written a book (on the mining business in Cornwall) which is now in the hands of some agency. He is also going to see a specialist: not, I gather, that his health is any worse than it has always been, but as he says "I had made up my mind to it – to live on that basis – but people have advised me to make one bid for better health and then, if I like, settle down to it." We went to Magdalen where we sat till 10.30 when I caught the last bus. He has not changed, and we had a fine talk. Home by moonlight, ate a saucer of strawberries and cream and went to bed.

Friday 25 June: Up to the back room after breakfast and did a little more work on my paper. At about 11 I went in to College and found a note from Benecke in the lodge saying that the fellowship meeting at 12 was still on.

Went to Hardie's room and read with him Yorke's new Bridget poem. It is about a dentist's waiting room and rather good.

We were joined unexpectedly by Lawson (I didn't know that he knew Hardie) and later by one Fordyce. At 12 we repaired to the New Room and met the President, Benecke, Driver, and Weldon. The meeting was very silly and there was needless revision of most papers leading to an unholy hash wh. is going to be finally set. A particularly bad essay subject of Benecke's on the rights of minorities was approved – bad, because only philosophers can really say anything about it. The great triumph was the philosophy paper by Weldon, Hardie and myself. We three sat tight during five minutes pregnant silence while the others looked very wise and finally passed it without alteration.

Got away at 1.10 and hurried to the Good Luck to lunch with Jenkin: afterwards we sat in the garden of the Union. We had a rambling and effortless conversation of the most profitable sort.

Home by three and went on with my paper, till I got myself tied up. I began to see unexpected difficulties. After tea I walked in the fields towards Forest Hill, neglecting a beautiful coloured evening in favour of idle Christina dreams about refuting Eliot and Stein. Returned in a dissatisfied mood and began to re-read MacDonald's *Lilith*.

After supper I went back to College . . . Went into the smoking room, had a cup of coffee, talked and read in the T.L.S. the review of a new long poem published by Heinemanns. How bitter this wd. be if Dent's had not taken "Dymer"! It is called *Two Lives*, by one Leonard, and sounds almost great in quotation though the reviewer is not very favourable . . .

Sunday 27 June: Up to the back room after breakfast to write. My idea was to begin the new poem with an account of an old landlady sitting in the basement: then to the ground floor where we should have the "swallow" man: then to old Foster on the first floor.

D came up to "do washing" and I found that the quiet of College has nearly robbed me of my old power of working in a bustle. It was impossible to go downstairs as Maureen's piano playing there made poetry out of the question. Poor D had difficulties with the washing and was moving about and in and out of the room till 12 o'clock, by wh. time I was rather fidgeted. As soon as I began to get going, I was called down to lunch. After lunch and washing up I renewed the attempt, but what was intended to be a mere exhortation to the reader to use his imagination turned itself into long reams of philosophical gas, quite irrelevant and very mediocre . . .

Monday 28 June: In to College in the morning. I found Hardie on one of the seats in front of New Building sunning himself. We drifted into conversation and agreed to have a game of bowls – Wrong having presented us with a set. We played on the grass in cloisters, much to the interest of tourists, and were presently joined by Thompson and Weldon. I have seldom been anywhere more beautiful. About a quarter of the quadrangle was in shadow – a deep, sharp shadow, ending in the shapes of battlements: the rest was still faintly grey for the dew was not quite dried: overhead was the Tower, enormous and dazzlingly bright, occasionally striking the quarters and the hours, and beyond it a blazing blue sky with huge white clouds, twisted and swelled into every lavish shape you could ask for. Then there was the pleasant noise of the bowls and now and then cool, echoing sounds in the cloisters themselves.

I saw Segar for a minute or two and he is disposed to consider dividing the house in Merton Street. Home and worked till tea time. Played badminton with Maureen, had a bath and a walk, down beyond the cemetery. The swampy places are actually dry at last. Read *Dauber* in the evening. It's as great as ever but Lord!, how incredibly bad in single lines and stanzas. To bed early and lay awake till 12.30.

Tuesday 29 June: Went in to College after breakfast and to Wrong's beautiful house over the weir. I asked him about the house (belonging to College) in Merton St., and he sent me to Carter. We had thought of trying to share it with Segar if Raymond turns us out of this. Carter was out and I saw Teden who told me that it was inhabited and that I shd. go and ask the tenant to show me over. I bussed home and returned with D to Merton St., where, after a wait of course, we were met by Maureen. A fat, amiable and vulgar woman showed us over the house. The stairs make it impossible for D and it would be hard to divide between two families: also there is no garden to speak of. The view from its back windows, over gardens and cedar trees to Magdalen Tower and beyond to Headington Hill, struck us all . . .

Read *Dauber* again in the evening and got some vivid impressions, giving me a good realistic shock to counterbalance my growing idealism in metaphysics. All the part about the wind from the Pole drives home the sense of "an other" . . .

Wednesday 30 June: Spent the morning working on Hoby's *Courtyer*, besides writing a stanza. After lunch, deciding to get at least one beastly job off my chest, I changed and went in at 3.30 to pay my dinner call on Lady Warren. I found Price and Hardie playing bowls and talked with them for a while. Thanks to heaven Lady W was out. Bought a copy of the *Forsyte Saga* and came home.

After tea I walked over the fields towards Forest Hill – frightfully hot but beautiful colours. Maureen came in at supper in great indignation about Miss Woods having introduced some very vulgar people – the Franklins – at the tennis club. After supper D and she went round to see the Disneys about it. As these fools have started a club without any arrangements about the election of new members, they have only themselves to thank. I wrote to Carter, moved by this, to ask if I could get Maureen one of the College courts during the Vac. There's one more beastly job over . . .

Thursday 1 July: In to College by 9.30 to consult Thompson (at D's instance) and find out what is still coming to me. Everyone was at breakfast when I arrived. After sitting for some minutes in the smoking room I saw Thompson and also Carter. Apparently, after all deductions have been made, I still have only about £55 to come. It was less than I expected and I rather dreaded bringing the news home.

Went to the Union where I read Chesterton's *Bernard Shaw* and came home about 1. D seemed to consider the £55 all right. I hope that business is now over. Spent a lazy afternoon finishing Chesterton and the *Merry Wives* in the garden. Mrs Wilbraham and Miss Blaxland came for tea and we had a four at badminton. Afterwards D, who had never tried the game, decided to begin it and I initiated her. Then bath, walk and beer. After supper another game with D who gets on very well. To bed about twelve.

Friday 2 July: . . . After supper all three of us played badminton, and then D went to see old Knight who is suffering pretty badly from sciatica. I came up to the back room again and wrote a little more, with great difficulty. Listened in to "How beautiful they are" from the Immortal Hour, my first taste of that work. I was not greatly impressed but it turned my mind to the Celtic atmosphere and I read a little of Yeats' *Wanderings of Oisin*. It is ages since I looked at it and I wondered how I could ever have thought it anything more than mildly pleasant: it is far below Morris . . .

Saturday 3 July: Woke up at 4.30 from a nightmare about a formidable person suddenly coming in through the window of the little end room at home and saying "Now then, Guv'nor, what are *you* doing here?" There was more in it which I have forgotten.

News today that Dotty and her father are coming to Oxford next week and she proposes to stay here, wh. doesn't please me much and D still less. Finished Hoby in the morning and worked a little on "Sigrid".

At tea time (in the garden) came a letter from Carter saying that

Maureen could have a court – and that it would cost four pounds for the Vac. This was rather a shock to the others, and poor D was much distressed. I said "If you don't mind making me *ask* for these things, which I hate, why should you bother about the money which doesn't worry me?" – a churlish and useless remark which I afterwards regretted.

I then took Pat down to Parson's Pleasure to bathe, but found a notice "no dogs admitted" – an innovation quite sensible in itself but a knock out for me as it means I shall never be able to bathe except on those rare occasions when I have time both to go to Parson's Pleasure and then to take Pat for a separate walk . . .

Sunday 4 July: Went down to Parson's Pleasure after breakfast alone and sat under a tree reading *Citizen of the World.*[1] It was a cloudy morning with a breeze, not very hot. Diz was there and persuaded the man to keep Juno (the Alsatian, a beauty) in the office. Wished I had known the trick yesterday. I bathed at about 12.15, my first bathe this year, and did little more than swim twice up and down.

Walked home. It settled down to a steady rain which we need badly and which was pleasant both to hear and see as D and I sat in the dining room after lunch with the garden door open. It had its usual effect in bringing out all sorts of bird noises that one hadn't noticed for the last few days. After tea I took Pat for his walk and got the only fine interval. I went up the crab-apple road to the stile and back to Barton over the fields. The streams were muddied, the birds chuckling, and a fine, wet-weather smell everywhere.

I spent the afternoon and evening between spells of working on "Sigrid" (which I did with incredible difficulty, but finally pleased myself) and beginning to re-read *The Well at the World's End.* I was anxious to see whether the old spell still worked. It does – rather too well. This going back to books read at that age is humiliating: one keeps on tracing what are now quite big things in one's mental outfit to curiously small sources. I wondered how much even of my feeling for external nature comes out of the brief, convincing little descriptions of mountains and woods in this book.

Monday 5 July: Still raining this morning. D and Maureen went into town after breakfast to shop. I went up to the back room and wrote about ten more lines of "Sigrid" with unexpected ease: then became disgusted with the whole thing. I had meant to work if I couldn't

---

[1] By Oliver Goldsmith (1762).

write, but gave way to the temptation of continuing *The Well at the World's End*, which I did with intense enjoyment till the others came back at lunchtime, and again after lunch till tea time, when it cleared.

After tea I walked down Cuckoo Lane and into College by the back way. I was a good deal bothered by the ease with which my old romantic world had resumed its sway. I shall know another time not to try to establish my conceit by patronising Wm. Morris!

In College I found letters from Waddington & Sykes asking what they shd. do in the Vac: also from Craig, inviting me to a tea fight in Common Room. Brought out the folios of Erasmus wh. I recently borrowed from the library. Restrained Pat in the garden from the gross impropriety of chasing that very respectable animal, the Common Room Cat, and gave him a clip for his pains. Home and answered Waddington & Sykes before supper.

D had a headache – probably from wearing a hat too long this morning . . .

Tuesday 6 July: Woken up about five by D having a nightmare. She had had a good night and got rid of her headache, but still felt sick.

I spent the morning on Erasmus' *Institutio Principis Christiani* and noting parallels with Elyot. It is not very exciting but wd. be tolerable if the folio were less worm eaten and more clearly printed – it is a beautifully formed type, but blurred.

After lunch I went for a walk, the first real one for many days. I went through Headington Quarry, along Shotover, down the fir tree lane beyond Shotover House, turned right over fields, crossed the railway line, and so back. It was a grey windy day, sometimes raining, with low clouds. I got very wet in the fields: the smell, and earthiness, and various sounds shook me into a pretty receptive state of mind. Home for tea, with a sharp headache at 4.30 and changed socks and shoes. Poor D felt too ill to take even a cup of tea.

Afterwards I went over the revised proofs of "Dymer" wh. arrived today from Canto I, 30, to the end of the whole. I never liked it less. I felt no mortal could get any notion of what the devil it was all about. I am afraid this sort of stuff is very much hit or miss, yet I think it is my only real line . . .

Wednesday 7 July: Up to my own room after breakfast, as Dotty now occupies the back room, and worked on Erasmus, finishing the *Institutio*. It is a very different book from Elyot. It is all fine, free, cosmopolitan irresponsiblity, while he is homely and almost fussy. I spent the last half hour of the morning trying to work on "Sigrid", but to no purpose. I think couplets are beyond me.

After lunch I walked: over the fields to Stowe Woods, resting just this side of the road, where there was a fine misty landscape down the valley: then on to Elsfield, with a glance at Otmoor, across the fields to the big house with pigs in the orchard, and then home, with one more halt, which I cut short because of flies.

D feeling very sick and headachy all day – and the usual infernal jam making has begun . . .

Thursday 8 July: D had a good night and felt much better this morning. It was a beautiful misty summer morning. After breakfast I went into town, bought an Everyman *Quentin Durward* (which I examine on for Lower Certificate) and then went to the Camera to order Patrizi's *De Regno*, but was sent to Bodley. Went on to College to answer Craig's invitation but finding I did not know where I'd be on that date, brought it out with me instead, after wasting a pleasant half hour in the smoking room over Godley's *Unpublished Works* . . .

Friday 9 July: Up very late and allowed myself foolishly to indulge in the hope that one of the girls might have taken Pat for his morning run. It has happened once or twice. Of course they hadn't and, annoyed at this further delay, I became grumpy and offensive – a typical business-man-at-breakfast in fact!

Got in to Bodley about 10.30 and spent the morning on Patrizi's *De Regno*. It is a deplorable work, the subject of Kingship being only a peg on which to hang every story from the Classics which the old blether can remember. Thus a chapter on flatterers begins *"Nullum veri assentatoribus inest, ut dixit Democritus"*[2] – and then you are off for five pages of what Agesilaus did and what Philopernon said. I suppose it would be pleasant enough to read in snippets, but it is heartbreaking if you are trying to trace Elyot in it. There is one rather jolly bit about digging up antiques.

Just before I came away for lunch Onions suddenly came upon me and said "You don't mean to say you're reading something. I thought you never read." Went to College for lunch where I met Onions who expressed equal surprise at my being there. I got it back on him by asking whether, reasoning as he did about my reading, he assumed I never lunched except on the days he saw me lunching . . .

[2] "There is no truth in flatterers, as Democritus said."

Saturday-Wednesday 10-14 July: I abandoned my diary under the influence of the heat wave. Saturday morning and afternoon I spent in Bodley, lunching in College, and bathed after tea.

On Sunday I began to read Rose Macaulay's *Lee Shore*, wh. at first I hated. I now think it almost a great work. It has shaken my mind up a good deal and, so far, done good.

That afternoon Mrs Wilbraham came and played badminton – it was the greatest heat I have yet played in.

On Monday I again spent the day in Bodley. It was hot enough in Duke Humphreys under the roof of copper, but even that seemed cool compared with the streets. The beauties of architecture are for winter. During these days Oxford seemed a sort of desert of burning stone. The water in Parson's Pleasure went up to 73°. That day I bought Fielding's *Amelia* and began to read it. It is odd how such a monotonous succession of misfortunes – in wh. the continual assaults on Amelia's impregnable virture become ludicrous – ballasted with such shoddy rhetoric in the dialogue, can be made palatable by dint of sheer narrative power. The born story teller can really do what he likes in literature . . .

On Wednesday I began to write my first lecture in the garden. The sun was a sort of omnipotent fiend penetrating the whole house and even the shadiest spaces on the lawn. I made poor progress.

D has been overworked all these days, partly because of the uncertainty of the Vaughans who are always sending Dotty back for meals when she is not expected or taking her away when she is, partly – the Lord knows why. Having a maid seems to make strangely little difference and I sometimes doubt if anything will ever make any difference . . .

Thursday-Saturday 15-17 July: I spent most of my time composing a Latin oration which I have to deliver at the Gaudy – a laborious undertaking, not only for the language (I have written none of it since Mods.) but for the researches in *fact* wh. one has to make. I wasted two whole days in College turning the leaves of *Who's Who* and the *Magdalen Register,* or Godley's presentation speeches to find the Latin for things like K.C.B. and K.C.S.I. It is rather a futile and tiring occupation.

I finished *Amelia* and began to read the *Kalevala* which I bought years ago and have never read through. It is rather good – a pleasant atmosphere of salmon, ducks, willows, salt ponds, magic, and copper-smith's work: also, there is what in the original must be real poetry in some of the similes: and real good myth as where Ilmarinen watches the strange things that come up out of his furnace and dislikes them and never knows what will come next, tho [it] is his own magic furnace.

Sunday 18 July: Woke up late, heavy and headachy after a gruelling day and restless night. Spent a fidgety morning reading the *Kalevala*, bathing Pat's paw, and going round to Hewitt's every now and then to see if the papers had come yet. Mr Thomas, a dry little old Egyptologist, whom Maureen has picked up somewhere, came for tea, and after tea the Wilbrahams. We played badminton. Mr T. stayed an unconscionable time, and talked a lot. An agreeable man, but a fool. A very fine thunderstorm in the night accompanied (which I have never met before) with a high wind.

Lewis's diary breaks off here and is not resumed until 9 January 1927. He had been attempting to get his father to travel to Oxford and stay in Magdalen as his guest, but when Mr Lewis failed to come, he went to Belfast for a holiday, 11-20 September. He had been working on his narrative poem, Dymer, *since 1922, and it was published by J.M. Dent & Sons on 18 September. It had many favourable reviews, but few readers.*

Warnie learned in September that he had been selected to attend a six months course in Economics at London University beginning 4 October. He and Jack travelled together to Belfast on 21 December to be with their father for Christmas. This was to be the last Mr Lewis was to spend with both sons, and it is fortunate that at the end of it he could write in his diary of 8 January 1927: "Warnie and Jacks returned tonight by Fleetwood. As the boat did not sail until 11 o'c. they stayed with me to 9.30. So ended a very pleasant holiday. Roses all the way."

1927

Sunday 9 January: Called at quarter to seven on the Fleetwood boat, by which W and I crossed last night from Ireland. We had single berth rooms each on deck, but terribly stuffy because the steward had insisted on screwing up the windows in anticipation of a storm which never happened. I had a poor night and a nightmare – a thing I never had at sea before. If sea water, even, won't protect a man from bogies, it's a hard case.

Boat train left Fleetwood at 8 and was very slow all the way, probably because of bad foreign coal. We had both breakfast and lunch on the train. I read *Erewhon Revisited* and thought it poor.[1] The ideas are sometimes capital, but it suffers (as even *Gulliver* does to my mind) from far too much working out wh. you could do for yourself, once the idea has been given you. Hanky's sermon and the Sunch'ston newspaper are at least as dull as they would be in real life.

Reached Euston 2.45 (timed for 1.30), left my luggage at Paddington and then went by taxi with W. to the R.A.M.C. Mess at Millbank where he left his things. I thought the mess a very sound sort of building. He and I walked back to Paddington across the Park, glad to stretch our legs after the long morning in the train.

Left Paddington at 4.10. I had sent D a wire from Fleetwood saying that I shd. not arrive till about 6, and it now occurred to me that on a Sunday the wire might not be delivered and she would be frightened, as I usually turn up about 1.30. This made me quite miserable and spoiled a journey wh. I shd. otherwise have loved, being almost alone in my carriage and looking out on a wild crimson sunset over low black hills and woods, with an occasional gleam of water amidst them reflecting the red of the sky.

Thank goodness D really had got my wire and I found her well and in good spirits, despite the very hard time she has had while I was away – Maureen being laid up with German measles and

---

[1] By Samuel Butler (1901).

Winifred unable to help because she hadn't had it herself. D was called as a juror some days ago, and tho' not actually included in the jury, retained in court, as a sort of understudy I suppose. She was too interested (she says) to be uncomfortable and passed the time during the only case very characteristically, holding the hand of the prisoner's wife.

To bed about eleven after a very pleasant evening of chat and talk. I woke once in the night and imagined myself still in Ireland – then, oh, the relief! Best of all I find term begins on Friday week, not on Thursday next as I had feared.

Monday 10 January: Slept very well and took Pat out before breakfast as usual. I spent the morning setting exam papers for the L.C. and polished off Story, Dictation, and Sidgwick. I also wrote to J. Betjeman.

After lunch I took my walk through Barton and over the fields, coming back by the Crab Apple Road. It was a most extraordinary afternoon. Most of the sky was very pale creamy blue, and there were clouds about, of the coldest shade of dark blue I have ever seen. The further hills were exactly the same as the clouds in colour and texture. But near the sun the sky simply turned white and the sun itself (its outline was invisible) was a patch of absolutely pure white light that looked as if it had no [more] power of heating than moonlight – tho' it was quite a mild day in fact.

I got into a tremendously happy mood, what with the joy of being home again and certain vague anticipations of good things beginning and a general sense of frosts breaking up – like the beginning of the *Prelude*. Some few birds were making a great noise as if it was spring . . .

In the evening all three of us had a talk about Dotty and the trouble which her late hours and lavish entertaining throws on D. I wanted to decide once and for all what we could rightly demand of her and then insist on it – instead of continuing forever to be alternately enraged and indulgent: but D thought me quite unpractical, and I'm afraid I only worried her . . .

Tuesday 11 January: Read *Guy Mannering* all morning, which I remember only confusedly from my last reading. In spite of the crazy construction and the absurd gushing letters, it is a good yarn.

Walked after lunch, with Pat. On my way up to Shotover I met Mrs Hinckley who tells me she is trying to get *Dymer* from the Times Book Club, but has failed. I promised to send her a copy. I went up

Shotover by the little path on the edge of Pullens Gap and along the "Plain" to the end. A very dark grey day, looking like snow but feeling too warm.

Home again to tea for which the others came in, having been calling on the Schofields. He is a don at Ruskin and knew Fasnacht, whom he described as being "far too polite". Finished *Guy Mannering* after supper and set an L.C. paper on it – an irritating little job at which I made several false starts. During supper Maureen remembered "I'm beginning to get excited about term. Are you?" As she knows very well that D and I both hate the coming of term, and that it means a great deal of overwork for D, it is hard to see why she says these things. I suppose it is intended to be a kind of joke. Letter from Warnie today to tell me that he has got seats for *Hansel and Gretel* on Saturday week: but as that is now going to be collection Saturday I shan't be able to go.

Wednesday 12 January: After breakfast I set a paper on *Macbeth*, wrote to Attenborough about the L.C., and to W about *Hansel and Gretel* . . . I next went to the Davenport to see about a set of Milton's Prose Works and found to my annoyance that there is none on the market, Masson being wholly and Bohn partly, out of print . . .

Home and read Wyld's *Mother Tongue* (a curse be on Wyld) till lunchtime. Had a good long walk in the afternoon, over the fields to Elsfield, along the road and home over the fields through Barton. An absolutely dead grey day but without the grandeur or suspense that grey days sometimes have. I, at any rate, was v. insensible and walked along "thinking" as its called: i.e. – mooning . . .

Thursday 13 January: Into town after breakfast where I got my hair cut, paid for my Milton, and brought home one volume, ordering the rest to be sent to College. Began *Reformation in England* and read a good deal of it before lunch – with great enjoyment. For a certain kind of humour, the prose Milton beats anyone I know. He abuses like an inspired coster – like Falstaff.

Hot roast for lunch. Walked up Shotover through Quarry in the afternoon and along the Plain. A very cold day with a beautiful feel in the air, a pale blue sky and bright sunlight. On my way back I had a look at the digging operations in Quarry . . .

Worked hard on Language for the rest of the day, finding out what Wyld says in spite of all Wyld does to prevent me. I made notes of the "West Germanic to Primitive O.E." and wrote a Mnemonic poem on it – this is going to be great fun. I also got well into "Primitive

O.E. to O.E." But it seems impossible to find out anything about Consonants. It's also v. annoying that, having been given an account of what vowels change to under J-mutation, when you come to U-mutation you are told that they change but not what they change to. Are all philologists mad? . . .

Friday 14 January: D brought me in bed this morning an advertisement from a Press Cutting Agency wh. contained, at last, the *T.L.S.* review of *Dymer*. Fausset wrote to me in September to say that he had reviewed it, but thought it might not appear for a few weeks and was writing to let me know: a very enthusiastic letter, and a very kindly act on the part of a complete stranger.[2] Ever since then I have been on the lookout for it, and I think yesterday was the first Thursday on wh. I forgot all about [it]. The Review was very satisfactory indeed and cheered me greatly.

All of us slept v. late this morning. Worked till lunch on vowel changes in O.E., hitching Fracture and J-mutation into rimed octosyllabics, with equal pleasure and profit. Wrote to Fausset thanking him for the review and repeating my invitation.

It was very dark and raining but I put on my mac. and went out – along Windmill Rd. and its continuation to the turn for the Barracks: thence left across the fields and up Shotover by Pullens Gap, and home through Quarry. A very slippery soggy walk, but I quite enjoyed it. Maureen had a girl to tea. Went on with Language till supper time and read Milton afterwards. Finished *Reformation in England* and nearly all of *Prelaticall Episcopacy*. He is not, at this stage, a great prose writer: the exuberance of some passages is too overwhelming, and the argument not really very powerful. I remembered it as being better. Hooker'd have made mincemeat of him.

Saturday 15 January: . . . Worked all morning on the change from O.E. to M.E., with great difficulty but some enjoyment. Wyld's best (that is, his worst) trick is to say that a certain vowel did this or that except, say, in Kentish: but what it did in Kentish he doesn't tell you, and you may read thro' the whole book to find out. Another pretty quip is the example that doesn't exemplify. "Ā in the North, through āē, reached ē. Example, Bruce rimes schame (short ă in O.E.) with blame." One can usually work it out in the end, but after maddening waste of time.

---

[2] Hugh Fausset's review of *Dymer* appeared in *The Times Literary Supplement* (13 January 1927), p. 27.

After lunch I walked out and put a copy of *Dymer* thro' Mrs Hinckley's letter box: then on and up Shotover. It was an afternoon of absolute silence, a feeling of thinness in the air, and a very pale blue sky with white marestails in it. Walked to the end of the Plain and then down thro the bracken, not in Pullens Gap but in the open place next beyond it, where my grove is. Coming down into the fields I heard the "burr" of some birds suddenly rising quite a distance off. The winter sun on the bracken and woods was indescribably mild and pure. Home by the very muddy way.

D's cold still v. heavy at tea time. Went on with my Language till supper and after and began the next stage of my mnemonic. Each day as I set out for my walk I repeat it as far as it has gone, which I find quite easy: it also prevents me sliding into a day dream in the first half mile, and leaves me (when the repetition is done) really receptive.

Maureen out tonight at the theatre to see the *Ghost Train*. Letter from my father today enclosing a bad review from the *Westminster Gazette* and (what's much worse) saying that the Heynes are visiting Oxford and will "look me up".

Maureen came in about 11 and a rather unfortunate conversation took place (I forget the early stages) in wh. I said that D made a great mistake in always concealing anything that was wrong with her until it was really bad. Maureen chimed in with something about D's eyes wh. I didn't fully understand but wh. means, I suppose, that they were bad while I was away. This infuriated D. I tried to pour oil on the waters, and said laughingly that D didn't approve of criticism. Maureen said "When you criticise me, I don't fly into a flaming temper" – wh. tactless, but by no means untrue, expression, of course made things much worse.

Sunday 16 January: D still v. annoyed this morning. I sat in and worked on the first chunk of the "King of Drum", wh. is to consist, I hope, of three short chunks – about 130 lines each. This chunk is a new version of a piece I began writing about two years ago, wh. itself was a re-writing of the "Wild Hunt" (about 1920), which in its turn was based on something I started at Bristol in 1918.

Washed up after lunch, this being Winifred's Sunday for going home to Appleton: then took Pat for a short stroll in Cuckoo Lane. A very cold, dark, deadly afternoon. After tea I went on writing till supper, finished the first chunk to my satisfaction, and tried unsuccessfully to begin the second. Washed up after supper and re-read

some of Raleigh's letters. D is reading Forster's *Passage to India* . . .
Monday 17 January: A heavy white frost this morning. I worked
from breakfast to lunch on language, mainly constructing a Mnemonic for "O.E. to M.E. (Vowels)". I am beginning to enjoy this stuff
and have certainly got further this time than in any of my innumerable
previous attempts to cosm that chaos. What a brute Wyld is – no
order, no power of exposition, no care for the reader. It is satisfactory
to see that no amount of learning can save a fool.

It began to snow before lunch. In the afternoon Pat and I walked
down Cuckoo Lane and into College by the back way. The snow
was at that stage when it gives the greatest variety of colours – the
paths wet brown, the grass half white (like gooseberry fool with
cream) and an occasional streak of real white on a loaded branch.
The river was a very dark green, all but black. Found the fire lit in
my room and clothes and blankets airing.

Home for tea and went on at the language, doing the consonants:
where I half forgave Wyld for introducing me to the beautiful words
"yeave" and "yeavey".

A letter from Barfield to say that he is at Air Hill and will come
over – always good news. After supper I finished *Prelaticall Episcopacy* and read the whole of the first book of *Reason of Church
Govt*. Full of great things – the passage on Discipline (v. Platonic)
and chaps. VI and VII . . .

Tuesday 18 January: A frost and white fog this morning. Worked
after breakfast on Norman influence in M.E., besides learning my
mnemonics up to date.

A splendid walk in the afternoon, the fog having cleared. I went
up Shotover thro' Quarry and along the top to the Horsepath lane
which I went down. A winding lane going down hill before one thro'
steep banks, with trees, but not too many, so that you can see the
further reaches of the lane below you, is one of the best sights. The
sun was straight ahead of me, a watery looking sun, and below it in
the valley the mist was collecting again – very faint purple. As often,
there was a great silence, emphasised by the occasional springlike
chuckling of a bird quite close, or the very lazy crowing of a cock
further off. Went through Horsepath and up again by the field path
into the bracken.

Was thinking about imagination and intellect and the unholy
muddle I am in about them at present: undigested scraps of
anthroposophy and psychoanalysis jostling with orthodox idealism

over a background of good old Kirkian rationalism. Lord what a mess! And all the time (with me) there's the danger of falling back into most childish superstitions, or of running into dogmatic materialism to escape them. I hoped the "King of Drum" might write itself so as to clear things up – the way "Dymer" cleared up the Christina Dream business.

Home lateish for tea and found to my disgust that D's visitors (Mrs Studer and the Thomas's) hadn't yet turned up. They came about 5 and Mr Thomas stayed till 6.30, thus ruining my evening's work.

Went on with Norse influences before and after supper, finding them unexpectedly difficult. Wyld hates foreign influences and wants to account for everything by sound laws – consequently tells you as little as possible. Wright has plenty to say about Norse vowels etc, but will use no examples (hardly) except dialect words.[3] In the end I had to fall back mainly on the popular books – Bradley and Pearsall Smith. Finished the day by reading a good bit of *Reason of Church Govt*. D's cold seems better.

Wednesday 19 January: I intended to go into town this morning but changed my mind and sat in to my Language – starting the M.E. inflexions and making out a map of dialectal areas, which I think I've got all wrong . . .

I went for my walk across the fields to Stowe Woods and home by road. Still puzzled about imagination etc. As I was crossing the big field into Barton on the way back, I suddenly found myself thinking "What I won't give up is the doctrine that what we get in imagination at its highest is real in some way, tho, at this stage one can't say how": and then my intellectual conscience smote me for having got to that last pitch of sentimentality – asserting what "I won't do" when I ought to be enquiring what I can know.

Decided to work up the whole doctrine of Imagination in Coleridge as soon as I had time – and the thought of Wordsworth was somehow very re-assuring. That's the real imagination, no bogies, no Karmas, no gurus, no damned psychism there. I have been astray among second rate ideas too long . . .

I left soon and bussed into College, to look out Collection papers. Found the papers in great confusion. There is not a complete *Ethics* among them all. What's worse I can't remember how much *Ethics*

---

[3] Joseph and Elizabeth M. Wright, *Old English Grammar* (1908; 1925).

my lambs are to have done! While in College I was rung up on the telephone by Betjeman speaking from Morton in the Marsh, to say that he hasn't been able to read the O.E., as he was suspected for measles and forbidden to look at a book. Probably a lie, but what can one do? . . .

Thursday 20 January: Into town immediately after breakfast. There was a thick frost, a bright sky, and it was biting cold. Went to the printers and left my O.E. paper. They undertook to let me have proofs at 3 tomorrow. Bought some butter for D, paid my bill at the Davenant (£22) and came home. D had been to see Hedges who has been in communication with the income tax people about my 1925–26: the upshot is that I have to tackle the Bursar again. I begin to fear this wretched business will never be settled.

Spent the rest of the morning on Raleigh's *Milton* wh. is full of good things and not a good book. Saurat and even Abercrombie are miles beyond him.[4] Raleigh is always complaining about Milton's God not being kind and loving, and saying that Satan is the real sympathetic character – and all that dear old pap. He has no notion of the real theme of individual will against the structure of things, and no notion that Milton might appreciate and sympathise with the individual and yet think that the Universal must be more right and more real. In fact Raleigh is really in the same position as the people who think that if Milton appreciates Comus he can't appreciate the Lady more: they never can see that the man who really likes toffee best is also the man who understands brown sherry and knows that it's nicer than toffee.[5]

Walked into Old Headington after lunch and met Percy Simpson wheeling his two children in a pram: he looked a rum figure, bustling along at about a mile an hour, with his watery eye and his perfectly circular little hat. Accompanied him as far as the corner of Barton, anathematising phonetic-maniacs.

I then went over the fields, round to the stile, and home by road. I was very unreceptive and devoted myself to repetition of mnemonics. Went on with language after tea. A maddening example of Wyldism: – he suddenly remarks in a parenthesis "The normal development of *feaht* wd. be *faught*." You remember him saying that ea became e. Look it up and find you're quite right, nothing about *au* there. Then

---

[4] The books referred to are Sir Walter Raleigh's *Milton* (1900), Denis Saurat's *Milton: Man and Thinker* (1925), and Lascelles Abercrombie's *Principles of English Prosody* (1923).

[5] Some of these criticisms were to find their way into Lewis's *A Preface to Paradise Lost* (1942).

you try it the other way round and look up "New Diphthongs in M.E. Sources of au." Not a word about ea + ht. After half an hour I ran the real explanation to earth in Wright.

After supper I discussed the tax muddle with D and got together the facts wh. I've got to write to the Bursar about. When that beastly business was done I scouted as absurd an inner suggestion that I might do some more work and solved a crossword puzzle instead . . .

Friday 21 January: Woke up to a very cold morning and found that a good deal of snow had fallen in the night. Decided not to lose my last day's liberty in work and settled down after breakfast to "The King of Drum". Produced about 20 lines for the opening of the next chunk, in a metre I have never struck before (rhythm of O.E. verse, but rhyming), with very little effort and greatly to my satisfaction. I also began to simmer with ideas for the further development of the story.

Took Pat out for a short walk down Cuckoo Lane, where the snow greatly excited him. After lunch I bussed in to College where I found the reliable Baxter's proofs of my O.E. paper waiting. Also a note from Barfield in rhymed Latin and a letter from Fausset, saying he cldn't. come at present but asking to be allowed to come at two days notice later on . . .

Home to tea. I had been looking forward all day to resuming the "Drum" poems, but when I came to it after tea I found myself completely dried up. Hammered out about seven bad lines with great labour and gave it up.

After that, a pleasant slack evening by the fire – crossword puzzle and chat with D – marred by the thought of term beginning tomorrow.

Saturday 22 January: Up rather earlier and bussed into town after breakfast for Collections. I found Weldon lolling in the smoking room and learned from him that I am to keep the Greats men this term (whom I thought I was to hand over) and to take them through Aristotle, which is a nasty surprise. Held my Collections in Hall greatly to the annoyance of the College servants.

Lunched in Common Room and then back to my own room where Valentin and Betjeman came to do an O.E. paper. I sat by the chimney corner and corrected papers while they sat at the table and muttered and worked themselves into contortions intended to be expressive of mental agony. They stopped at about 4, saying they had done all they cd. I said something about the uses of imagination in guessing words to wh. Valentin replied with unusual sense "Oh, I could *write a story* all right."

Bussed home. The snow was beginning to thaw and there was a heavy mist. D was out calling on the Studers when I arrived. Had tea and a chat by the fire, feeling rather languid and head-achey.

Back to College for dinner and sat down to finish Collection papers afterward – the Aristotle one raising points wh. took me a good deal of time. I shd. have finished it, however, if Weldon had not come in shortly after 10: this meant hot toddy and bawdy conversation till 1 o'clock. He tells me that his brother is master in a Borstall institution and from that source (1) that among the boy-criminals the murderers are much the pleasantest fellows and those whom careful treatment can make the most of, because they have some character; (2) that it is quite a common thing for people to make £50 a week in town or at Brighton by laying traps and then blackmailing people for sodomy. Bishops seem to be the best prey . . .

Sunday 23 January: Up late. Put my washing under my arms and Sweet's *Reader* in my pocket and set out after breakfast on my walk home. It was more "yeavey" than ever and one had to pick ones steps carefully to avoid a fall. The "walks" were very fine in a sombre way, with the river looking like green ink and the further bank only a strip of white, clearest at the water's edge and then melting almost immediately into a dark grey fog, with a few ghosts of pollards. I was greatly taken by the antics of a water rat, who sat up (apparently on the water, really, I suppose, on some branch just below the surface) to look at me and then in an access of coyness dipped right upside down like a duck.

Reached home very hot from the struggle of shuffling up hill in the slush: felt so heavy all day and had such a headache that I began to think I was getting one of the many current epidemics – but I suppose it is the sudden change from my regular Headington hours and diet.

Spent the morning re-reading Wulfstan's *Sermon*, with some enjoyment. I am really getting into this language at last. All well at home, D in good form.

Went out for a long heavy tramp after lunch to try and get rid of the oppression that was on me. The weather had at least one advantage – it had cleared the countryside of the usual mob of walkers-in-their-Sunday-best. I went to Stowe Woods by road and home over the fields to Barton. The mist v. thick. Occasionally two bushes and a patch of grass wd. be quite free from snow and these, doubly *framed* both with fog and snow surrounding them, had a curiously aloof appearance.

Home about 4.30 very tired but feeling much better. Read some of the *Fall of the Angels* and then bussed in to College. Sat next to Onions after dinner and told him about Wyld's iniquities over the word *fought*. He agreed that that W had no method – but also mentioned the real difficulty, that you have to treat W[est] S[axon] as the Norm for "business purposes", and yet it is least important for the history of the language . . .

Monday 24 January: Overslept myself this morning: was just aware of Hatton coming in to call me, and then, next moment as it seemed, it was 8.30 and my tea was cold.[6]

A good review from *G.K's Weekly* arrived by the morning post, signed by a man called Crofte-Cooke, where *Dymer* figures as "a great poem" for the first time[7] in print.

This morning came Hetherington, then Valentin whom I hounded through some pages of Wulfstan, translating myself and then getting him to do it over again – as Kirk taught me Greek at Bookham.

A new Greats pupil called Campbell came to interview me, a languid youth with half-shut eyes and a drawl – what Parker calls "La-de-da."[8] I was also rung up on the telephone by Betjeman who invited me to tea this afternoon. A damned nuisance but of course one has to accept.

Bussed out home and heard from D that poor M. Studer is dead. It is the best thing for him, but with no money and a wife who has already been out of her mind, the prospect for his children is dreadful.[9]

Walked up Shotover after lunch. The snow has almost disappeared tho the landscape, seen from the hill, is still decorated with a few streaks and splashes of white – often at the edges of fields. It was a sunless afternoon but very pleasant with a loud warm wind blowing,

---

[6] W.K. Hatton, who joined the staff of Magdalen College in 1923, was Lewis's "scout" or college servant.

[7] And last! – C.S.L.

[8] John Colquhoun Campbell (1907–) read Greats 1926–30 and took a BA in 1930. He worked with Anglo-Iranian Oil Co. Ltd until 1952.

[9] Mrs Moore's friend, Mrs Studer, was the wife of Paul Studer (1879–1927) the Taylorian Professor of the Romance Languages in the University of Oxford who died 23 January. They were both Swiss, and had three children.

and the colours of grass and hedges, after the recent white and dirty grey, were very refreshing and soft.

Bussed back into town and to Betjeman's rooms in St Aldates – a v. beautiful panelled room looking across to the side of the House. I found myself pitchforked into a galaxy of super-undergraduates, including Sparrow of the Nonesuch Press.[10] The only others I remember are Harwood of the House (no relation) and an absolutely silent and astonishingly ugly person called McNeice, of whom Betjeman said afterwards "He doesn't say much but he is a great poet". It reminded me of the man in Boswell "who was always thinking of Locke and Newton". This silent bard comes from Belfast or rather Carrickfergus.[11] The conversation was chiefly about lace curtains, arts-and-crafts (wh. they all dislike), china ornaments, silver versus earthen teapots, architecture, and the strange habits of "Hearties". The best thing was Betjeman's v. curious collection of books.

Came away with him and back to College to pull him along thro' Wulfstan till dinner time. In spite of all his rattle he is really just as ignorant and stupid as Valentin.

Came straight back to my rooms after dinner (where Cowley was dining in and lecturing on the cruelty of women)[12] and got rather a shock at getting my Battels for last term – £47. Worked till 11 finishing the Collections papers and thank heaven they are now off my chest. Read Milton for three quarters of an hour and went to bed, v. tired, and did not go to sleep for a long time.

Tuesday 25 January: Worked on Milton (Minor Poems) in the morning, with considerable interest despite a feeling of tiredness and a headache.

Home to lunch where I found D in v. good form but tremendously busy with cooking: I helped to fry the grill for lunch. Went for a walk afterwards, over the fields to Elsfield and home by Barton. A gale blowing, Oxford and the hills beyond it very blue and occasional gleams of yellow sunlight over the nearer landscape.

My walk took me longer than I intended, and when I got home

---

[10] John Hanbury Angus Sparrow (1906–) of New College was elected a Fellow of All Souls College in 1929, called to the Bar in 1931, and was Warden of All Souls 1952–77.

[11] George Harwood matriculated at Christ Church in 1926, and is mentioned in Bevis Hillier's *Betjeman*, p. 188.

Louis MacNeice (1907–1963), writer and lecturer, was educated at Marlborough and Merton College. He published his first book of poems, *Blind Fireworks* in 1930.

[12] Arthur Ernest Cowley (1861–1931) was Bodley's Librarian 1919–31 and a Fellow of Magdalen.

and ate a hasty tea I was very late for meeting Barfield, whom (I now remembered) I had asked to come to College at 3. He had left a note saying he was gone to tea, but presently came in. It was delightful to see him. After a confused chat of philosophy and jokes, we settled down to read Aeschylus' *Prometheus* together, as we had promised ourselves to do.

After an hour or so we went out and dined at the Town & Gown. Coming back we sat up till half past one to finish our play, sometimes convulsed with laughter at our own literal translation – or those of Paley, wh. are even more exquisitely funny – but equally impressed with the poetry when we read it thro' again in Greek. I understood the play better this time. The wild defiance at the end must definitely (for a Greek) have stamped *Prometheus* as one of Τὰ πρὶν πελώρια[13] – a "primitive" properly superseded by Olympians.

Barfield refused to come to an opinion on Aeschylus's moral view. I think he is a little inclined to apply his mythosophical principles in a rather Procrustean way.

Forgot to say that I had shown him the "King of Drum" before dinner and he approved: also thinks the story, so far as I could outline it, a very promising one. He has been experimenting in the *Kalevala* metre with variations, and read me a passage from a non-existent story. It has some real dewy freshness about it (like the *Kalevala*) and I believe he might make a good metre of it: tho' I am in favour of more variations still. To bed with my headache gone, and had a much better night.

Wednesday 26 January: Slept sound till I was called at 8. After breakfast Barfield and I went for a stroll thro Mesopotamia. He told me of a friend to whom he had sent *Dymer* and who had returned it with the comment "The metrical level is good, the vocabulary is large: but Poetry – not a line."

We talked about night fears and whether the death of a person one really cared for wd. abolish the horror of the supernatural or increase it. He also spoke of the reaction that comes after an evening of laughter among your best friends, when the sort of mental security wh. you had among them goes out of you, and you realise that no one but yourself can give you that security.

After coffee at the Cadena he went off to pick up his wife at "Hillsboro" and drive to London. I was sorry to see him go –

---

[13] *Prometheus Vinctus* 151. (Zeus is now destoying) "the former mighty ones."

these meetings are always beyond expectation.

Just before lunch Parker came into my room to discuss Waterfield: but he had no plan of action and only came for the pleasure of looking grave and wallowing in the sense of responsibility.[14]

Lunched in Common Room and attended a meeting of the T.B.[15] As the President was not there, and Craig in the chair we got through v. quickly. It was decided that Wood (who came to see me the other day) could change from Botany to English without losing his Demyship. I am v. glad: it wd. be delightful to have a real enthusiast as a pupil, and he may turn out to be one.[16]

Got back to my rooms soon after three, and found I had no money, so had to walk home, wh. I did by the back way. The high wind was still blowing, and there was a very intense light, making long and clear shadows. I saw the first snowdrops in the garden as I passed, and oh the comfort of it! My spirits seemed to rise continually all the way home.

Found D rather depressed, just having been to the Studer funeral. Walked out to the garden to see if the new year had begun there: there was nothing up, but I felt quite inexplicably delighted with everything. Mrs B[arfield] has apparently been having a heart-to-hearter with D. She "hates, hates, hates" Barfield's Anthroposophy, and says he ought to have told her before they were married: wh. sounds ominous. She once burnt a "blasphemous" anthroposophical pamphlet of his, wh. seems to me an unpardonable thing to do. But I think (and so does D) that they really get on v. well, better than the majority of married people. Mrs Barfield is always glad when Barfield comes to see me because I have "none of those views".

Talked income tax with D after supper and then general chat till 10.15 when she and Pat walked to the bus with me. A lovely starry night.

Went to bed as soon as I got back (after glancing at Saurat's *Milton* wh. I found waiting for me). Felt better in mind than I have done for ages. Pulled up my blind to see the stars, thought suddenly of Bergson: then of how I have been playing the devil with my nerves by letting things I really don't believe in and vague possibilities haunt my imagination. I had a strong conviction of having turned a

---

[14] See **Henry Michael Denne Parker** in the Magdalen College Appendix.

[15] Tutorial Board.

[16] Arthur Denis Wood (1907–), after taking his BA in 1929, joined the family firm of William Wood & Son Ltd, landscape gardeners in Taplow.

corner and soon getting all the "nurse and grandam from my soul". Soon to sleep and had an excellent night. No headache today.

Thursday 27 January: Started the *Apology for Smectymnuus* today and read it all morning till 12.30 when I went out to the Davenant to order a copy of Aristotle's *Metaphysics*.

From there, home by bus. It was more like a March day, high wind still, and alternate rain and sunshine. Found all well at home.

Walked over the fields to Stowe Woods after lunch, to see if any flowers were up there, but found none. It was all I cd. do on the way back to walk against the wind or keep my eyes open against the sun. How one enjoys nature's violences up to the very moment at wh. they become actually painful or dangerous. Went behind a haystack for a moment to get my breath and had a wonderful sudden change into silence, calm, and strong smell of hay – like stepping into a kind of bath.

Home and had tea and a chat and then into College. The *Metaphysics* hadn't come so I went on with Milton. A lot of people in to dinner tonight, including that old humbug Mallam.[17] J.A. told me in the smoking room afterwards that I wd. find Craigie's *Icelandic Reader* in his room and wd. I care to take it, which I did v. gladly against the re-opening of the Kolbitár.[18]

Came back to New Building and after reading through *Ohthere* went on with *Smectymnuus* and finished it and then read Saurat. I also copied various parallel passages from the Bishop pamphlets into my *Paradise Lost* as Notes. To bed about quarter to twelve and slept well . . .

Friday 28 January: Radice, Betjeman & Wood in morning.[19]

Home for lunch. The greatest gale was blowing ever I remember and I had a lovely walk up Shotover in the roaring of the trees. Went up thro' Quarry, along to the end of the plain, down thro' the bracken, and back up the muddy path. Stopped at the stile before the wooded bit to eat an apple and reflected how much I was enjoying it.

---

[17] Dr Ernest Mallam (1870–1946) had read Physiology at Magdalen 1888–92, and he had been Litchfield Lecturer in Medicine.

[18] The "Kolbitár" was an informal club of dons founded by Professor Tolkien for the purpose of reading Icelandic sagas.

[19] Edward Albert Radice (1907–) received a First in Mathematical Moderations in 1926, and a First in *Literae Humaniores* in 1929. He took a BA in 1929 and a D.Phil. in 1938. After a start as Asst. Professor of Economics at Wesleyan University at Middletown, Conn., 1937–9 he went on to become a very distinguished economic historian.

Back to College after tea and took Waterfield. Did some Icelandic after dinner, hammering my way thro the first chapter of the *Younger Edda*, except the Skaldic trimeters (*Gefjun dró fra Gylfi*) of wh. parts proved untranslatable. Forgot to say that all three pupil hours were good this morning and for once I felt fairly satisfied with myself. Spent the rest of the evening on Bentley and Milton.

Saturday 29 January: Hood, Wood & Valentin in the morning.[20] The latter's essay on Milton's Minor Poems was pure Raleigh: I told him I preferred it neat and gave him a sort of viva from wh. he emerged v. badly. He is a useless lump.

Home for lunch. Poor D compelled to be out afternoon at some show of Maureen's. Walked along the Forest Hill path and up Shotover thro' the Park: beautiful wind and sun and many effects of varying light. I got back for tea about 4.30, wh. I had alone, and then worked on Aristotle. D came back about 6. Dotty (a v. unwelcome arrival) turned up. I stayed out at home for supper, came back to college and did some more collating with Bentley – a good mechanical sedative occupation to round off a day of quite astonishing pleasure.[21] Letter from Harwood today promising a visit and asking me to entertain one Kruger, an anthroposophist.

Sunday 30 January: Called at 8. Out home by the back way after breakfast. The snowdrops and celandines in the walks have made no visible progress, but a lovely morning. Worked on Aristotle all morning, with those unexpected gleams of the real joy wh. sometimes come while one is reading, full of memories you can't identify.

Washed up after lunch and Maureen took Pat out. Continued work and after tea went for a little walk with D. Very pleasant, and looked at the Studers' house wh. she thinks we might possibly buy if Mrs S. goes back to Switzerland. The birds were very noisy all day and even now in the twilight were giving delicious chuckles. Washed up again after supper and stayed at home till about 10, beginning now to feel a little tired.

Back here on top of a bus under the most wonderful sky of stars. Looked over Wulfstan and read half a chapter of the *Edda*.

Monday 31 January: Wrote up arrears of diary after breakfast. Then came Hetherington with an essay on Aristotle's criticism of the Ideas,

---

[20] John Douglas Lloyd Hood (1904–), a Rhodes Scholar from Tasmania, took a First in Philosophy, Politics and Economics in 1929, and a BA in 1930. His career has been that of a diplomat.

[21] Richard Bentley published a revised and augmented edition of *Paradise Lost* in 1732.

not one of his best, but we put in (I hope) a fairly good hour. After him, Valentin for O.E., in which I was glad to see at last some improvement. Campbell, the new Greatsman, came at 12 and read his first essay, on Mill: it was all about Christianity and took the view that you couldn't have any ethics independent of your general *Weltanschauung*. I didn't tell him how true this was in the long run but criticised the cruder connections between the two and I think he saw.

Then to Univ. to lunch with Keir, who volunteered to accompany me on my afternoon walk. A bright afternoon. From my windows all morning I had seen our backwater running at a furious speed and the fields are flooded, giving a v. beautiful sheet of water studded with trees.

I just looked in at home to fetch Pat and then went on with Keir up the hill. I enjoy his slow conversation quite well and he professes (sincerely) to enjoy nature, but he is not one of those few in whose company one can continue to get the feel of the day as if one were alone. He told me about David's reign at Rugby and the various fads he had taken up – including the retaining of a pet psychoanalyst to analyse the boys, wh. ought to be a criminal offence.[22]

Home about four with a smart headache. Had tea and a chat with D, then back to College to take Hamilton at five: a better essay than Hetherington's but I am afraid I was not much good. At 6 came Betjeman on O.E. – very bad. I don't know what to do with him.

At dinner J.A. remarked that our new fellow Tansley (one of these professors who comes to us *ex officio* whether we will or no) "fancied himself as a psychologist" so we may expect good Socratic irony from J.A.[23]

In the evening read the speech of Michael at the end of *Paradise Lost* – i.e. most of XI and all XII. Wonderful stuff – I don't read and think of this end part enough. I also read some of Bridges' *New Poems* wh. Betjeman has lent me: they are full of passages of extreme beauty and pathos, and the metre (I mean the "New-Miltonic syllabics") is very successful. The general upshot of the longer

---

[22] The Rev. Albert Augustus David (1867–1950) was Headmaster of Rugby School 1909–21, and Bishop of St Edmundsbury and Ipswich 1921–3.

[23] (Sir) Arthur George Tansley (1871–1955) was a Fellow of Magdalen and Sherardian Professor of Botany 1927–37.

pieces, specially "Come si Quando" wh. is the best, I couldn't understand.

To bed about 11 and had a good night. Had some rather unpleasant (but not bogeyish) dream in the night wh. I've forgotten.

Tuesday 1 February: A bright frost and bright pale sunshine this morning. I have started keeping the bathroom window open again for the pleasure of looking out on the Grove with the level rays between the trees and an occasional deer.

Letter from Aunt Lily, or rather two letters, the earlier v. enthusiastic about *Dymer*, the latter not. She explained her former cryptic utterance about cancer very candidly and courageously. She seems to be safe for the present, but has caught mange from one of the cats. Her bravery is astonishing – all these things are mentioned by the way, while the main part of the letter is criticism and philosophy.

Read the *Doctrine and Discipline* all morning. Home to lunch and found all well there. Went for my walk afterwards by road to Stowe Woods and home across the fields. The sun had gone and it was a greyish day, very cold, but the incessant chuckling and chattering of the birds kept up the sense of spring. Enjoyed it greatly – I had forgotten to say yesterday that while out with Keir I saw and heard a lark, the first one this season . . .

At 7.5 there was a meeting in Common Room to admit Tansley. As I came into the room, wh. was crowded, Craig said to me "I don't think you know Tansley," then turning towards the hearthrug said "This is Lewis." I thereupon performed the most ludicrous act of my life by walking forward in the direction wh. seemed to be indicated and warmly shaking hands with Manley, who of course has been here for years and whom I have met dozens of times, but in the heat of the moment I didn't realise it.[1] *Soluuntur tabulae risu!*[2]

Hardie dined tonight and I arranged to go to his Thursday show on the *Theaetetus*. Went to Peacock's room at Oriel afterwards to

[1] John Job Manley (1863–1946) had been an undergraduate at Magdalen. He was elected a Fellow in 1917 and was Curator of the Daubenay Laboratory 1888–1929.

[2] "The tablets [containing the legal charge] will be melted with laughter." Adapted from Horace, *Satires*, 2, I, 86.

the Mermaids.[3] I don't know why I am in this society. They are all (except Brett-Smith) rather vulgar and strident young men, who guffawed so at every suggestion of obscenity in the *White Divel* wh. we were reading as to ruin the tragic scene. There's no doubt at all when one passes from the Greats to the English crowd, one leaves the χαριεντες for the τυχουτες, the men of taste and wit and humanity for a mere collection of barbarians. It is a great pity...

Wednesday 2 February: Thick snow and a dull sky this morning. Worked till lunchtime on the *Divorce* pamphlets. By then a brilliant sunshine had come out and every roof was dripping.

Lunched in Common room and went at 2 to the College meeting. Craig was in the chair, as the President is still in bed – an exchange so eminently desirable that we were finished by 3.30. An announcement was made about the boy who accidentally shot another boy at the School (Carter had already told me of it during lunch) – a nasty business.[4] The rest of the meeting was mainly taken up with a question of grants for buying books not worth putting into the library wh. occasioned a sort of duel between Driver and Weldon, the latter surpassing even himself in disagreeableness. It is a sort of hobby with him, as he once confessed to me, to make himself as offensive as possible in debate on points that he cares nothing about, to people he has no quarrel with. I never hear him speak at such times without being converted to the other side: there's something threatening in his logic that rouses one to say "Damn it I will be inconsistent if I want to!"

Bussed home and found a lot of papers sent me by some people calling themselves the Panton Arts Club, asking me to join ... D came in about 4, having been into town to buy a cinder riddler, and seemed in excellent form.

I spent the rest of the day at home in great peace and comfort, going on with my Milton – except for a rather unpleasant discussion with Dotty who came to appeal against D's decision against her giving mixed parties. The point is that we can't really give up one of the sitting rooms whenever she happens to want it, as Maureen's

[3] The Mermaid Club was founded in 1902 "to promote the reading and study of the Elizabethan and post-Elizabethan drama." Quite a lot of dons took an interst in it, or pretended to, and Lewis was President of the Mermaids during Michaelmas Term 1927. Conway John Peacock was an undergraduate member of Oriel College.

[4] A cadet at Magdalen College School was accidentally shot by the captain of the school team while the latter was extracting what he thought was an empty catridge case from his rifle.

practising in the drawing room makes the rooms permanently needed. Of course we kept a firm front and I am all in favour of resisting her continual impositions on D – but I wish our resistance cd. have come over a less seemingly churlish point. That's the devil of it with D's good nature: if one won't resist really outrageous demands (as the daily sandwiches) from the start, one has to take up a less pleasant S.O.S. line later . . .

Thursday 3 February: . . . Home for lunch. A beautiful day of sunshine and all the birds singing. D has got hold of some snow drops for the dining room.

After lunch I walked up Shotover, down the field into Horspath, and home by road. There was a good deal of snow about, and some beautiful sights: specially looking north from the top of the hill across a field of unbroken snow in the foreground, and beyond that the very pale blue of the half-snowed country on the horizon. Enjoyed my walk immensely, even the tramp home, where the current of snow water flowing deep and fast in the ditches, gave a new liveliness to the road.

Home for tea and then back to College on the top of a bus. This ride down the hill towards the sunset is always pleasant: this time it put me in a rare exaltation, recovering huge feelings (it was all mixed up with Plato's Ideas on wh. Waterfield was coming to read me an essay) that I have lost for months.

Finished working out in my Lydgate a "tree of Troy" wh. I'd begun in the morning. Waterfield at 6.15, not very good.

Dined in and sat in Common Room beside J.A. who told me of a lady who had long worried him by coming up at the end of lectures to ask questions, and finally wrote offering him her hand. "She pretended it was a joke afterwards," he said, shaking his white head, "but it wasn't. And she wasn't the only one either. A man who lectures to women takes his life in his hands." . . .

Friday 4 February: Radice, and Wood in the morning, Radice v. good and interesting. Wood was disappointing, tho', poor fellow, he had done a prodigious amount of mere horse work. His idea is to put down every fact he is able to find out and venture on no exercise of his own judgement.

Home to lunch and found the *Panton Magazine* had arrived, containing a very eulogistic and quite silly review of *Dymer*. The rest of the magazine was on the same level, except for the deeper depth reached by a selection from some woman's *Modern Book of Proberbs* wh. is rather like Tupper. I am glad I didn't rush hastily into such a mess.

After lunch walked down by the cemetery and across the field path, with Marston on my left, to meet the road: then up the hill to Elsfield and home across the fields. It was a bright calm afternoon, birds singing, and the stream flowing gloriously full under the bridge by the turn to Water Eaton . . .

Back to College after tea and sat down to the "King of Drum", when I was most annoyingly interrupted by the arrival of Valentin who said I had told him to come at that hour. Wrote again after dinner and made about twenty lines describing the King's "Levee". To bed, rather fidgety and discontented.

Saturday 5 February: Pupils all morning including Betjeman who read an excellent essay wh. I soon discovered to be a pure fake, for he knew nothing about the work when we began to talk. I wish I cd. get rid of this idle prig.

Home for lunch. Started out for a walk afterwards but yielded to rain and came in to waste time doing nothing particular till tea, and after tea made the attempt again. This time I persevered in spite of rain and had a wet but not unpleasant walk in the twilight.

Supper was v. late because both Winifred and Maureen were going to dances: for the same reason I had to wash up afterwards. Had hoped to get on with the "King of Drum," but lost the vein, as one usually does when the general order of the day doesn't pan out as you expect. Wordsworth got it right – the "spirits that refuse to flow when plans are lightly changed."

Sunday 6 February: A beautiful day. Walked home after breakfast, enjoying the mild air and the sunshine, and the birds and the noise of water. Found all well at home, except that D had a headache. I spent the morning writing, got over the King's first interview with the Queen and made a start on the "College meeting".

After lunch walked thro Quarry up Shotover, nearly down to Wheatley, then over the fields to the railway line and up again by the top of the tunnel. In spite of the presence of Sunday walkers, it was v. delightful and every moment almost was full of elusive suggestions. Home to tea.

Came back to College and dined in, having a talk with Webb, whom I rather like despite his oddity.[5] Back to my rooms, fair

---

[5] Clement Charles Julian Webb (1865–1954) was Tutor in Philosophy at Magdalen 1890–1922.

copied what I had written, and read a little Quarles.

Monday 7 February: A very, raw grey day that soon turned to rain. Hetherington came to read on Μεσοτης[6]: his essay was mostly Spengler and not very good or not good from such a good man. Then I had a break as Valentin got leave off for relations.

Went out v. foolishly to buy a copy of the *Theaetetus* (against Hardie's caucus) and only realised when I got to the Davenant that it was already in one of the volumes I have. By good luck, however, I caught sight of a new Everyman (*Trench* on Study of Words) wh. I immediately bought and began to read at once. He is quite a pioneer, very ignorant of course as he couldn't help being then, a little prosy: but he has real enthusiasm and the feeling of life, and occasional eloquence in spite of the over elaborated style.

Campbell came at 12, and for the second time all philosophical discussion was held up by his religious views. I have never had such a case before . . .

Home on top of the bus in pouring rain. D dissuaded me from taking Pat out and I went on with Trench in the dining room. D had to go out to tea.

Back to College to take Hamilton at 5 and then Betjeman on O.E. who was a little, a véry little, better. After dinner began the *Theaetetus* and read about 10 pages, then Trench. To bed at 12 after a very pleasant evening . . .

Tuesday 8 February: . . . Spent the morning partly on the *Edda* . . . Hammered my way thro' a couple of pages in about an hour, but I am making some headway. It is an exciting experience, when I remember my first passion for things Norse under the initiation of Longfellow (Tegner's "Drapa" & "Saga of K. Olaf") at about the age of nine: and its return much stronger when I was about 13, when the high priests were M.Arnold, Wagner's music, and the Arthur Rackham *Ring*. It seemed impossible then that I shd. ever come to read these things in the original. The old authentic thrill came back to me once or twice this morning: the mere names of god and giant catching my eye as I turned the pages of Zoega's dictionary was enough . . .

Had an interesting conversation after dinner in the smoking room with Segar (Weldon & Tansley also there) about the fate of virtuous heathen, whom Segar declares capable of salvation according to the

---

[6] A middle or central position.

doctrine of his Church. If this is true I shall be greatly surprised. The whole point of the Trajan story, in the Middle Ages, surely is that it was an exception.[7]

Back to my rooms and went on with the *Theaetetus* and a little more Trench. Also read the myth from the *Politicus* in Jowett's crib, wh. worried me by being so anthroposophical, till it occurred to me that of course Steiner must have read Plato. A pest on all this nonsense which has half spoiled so much beauty and wonder for me, degraded pure imagination into pretentious lying, and truths of the spirit into mere matters of *fact*, slimed everything over with the trail of its infernal mumbo-jumbo! How I wd. have enjoyed this myth once: now behind Plato's delightful *civilised* imagination I always have the picture of dark old traditions picked up from mumbling medicine-men, professing to be "private information" about facts.

To bed and had a much worse night than I have had for a long time. (N.B. It all comes to this. Once you have got into your head the notion of looking for the wrong sort of truth in imagination (i.e. occult matter-of-fact) you have lost utterly the truth that really is in imagination (i.e. rightness of feeling – the "affective" side of a cognition without the cognition) and made good food into poison. Just to be delighted with the *feel* of the nymph in the tree is to share emotionally that common life of all living things wh. you can't fully comprehend intellectually: to believe that by certain ceremonies you can make a girl come out of the tree, is to put yourself a thousand miles further from any spiritual contact with the real tree-life than you were before – and a good many miles nearer the asylum.)

Wednesday 9 February: ... Bought a copy of the *Volsunga Saga*, having had a card last night to say that the Kolbítar are reading it this term and I am put down for Chapter I and II at the next meeting. Began working on it. Felt v. poorly and depressed all morning. It was one of those days when the cold is an intense positive sensation – wind blowing over black frost and a sky full of snow that won't fall ... Looked at Morris's translation of *Volsunga Saga* in the Union ...

Shortly after 4 turned up at the Driver-MacKeith at home in hall.[8] At first found no one I knew except Manley and his wife who seems

---

[7] Lewis no doubt had in mind the legend that St Gregory, through his prayers, brought the dead Emperor Trajan back from Hell and baptised him into salvation. This was known to Dante who mentions the virtuous Trajan in *Purgatory* X and *Paradise* XX.

[8] See **Malcolm Henry MacKeith** in the Magdalen College Appendix.

a very common old woman, poor soul. Then got onto the Carlyles. He told me a lot more about the murderer of Rasputin,[9] who had been incapable of passing any exam and had suggested to the Fark that "of course, he presumed, there wd. be no difficulty in arranging these things in the case of a person of quality." Being told that the organisation of our exams was inflexibly democratic he exclaimed "But what am I to do? My parents will not let me marry unless I get some sort of certificate or diploma – they will only send me on to some other university." Finally Farquharson & Carlyle made him out on parchment v. solemnly a sort of certificate of their own.

Got away about five, Mrs Driver saying to Craig, Chute and me as we all came up together for handshaking "I have been timing you all. You have all done very well and stuck it for a good long spell.". . .

Thursday 10 February: . . . Home for lunch. D seemed rather tired and depressed today tho' she denied it. Went for a delightful walk after lunch, along the Forest Hill path, up through Shotover House Park and home along the hill. I was not so receptive as sometimes, but quite enjoyed it, specially the peculiar cold, sweetness of the air.

After tea came back to College. Waterfield didn't turn up and I read *Troilus*. Went into Common Room after dinner, an unusually jolly evening. We all taxed J.A. with his proposal (it is to be made at the next meeting) of introducing women into the Philosophical Society. He said he was the greatest anti-feminist in Oxford and had really done it because the Society had had no private business for so long.

I went on to Corpus – Hardie having sent me a note to say that the *Theaetetus* was off, but would I come round and talk. We had an evening of pleasant and desultory tomfoolery, enriched later on by the arrival of Weldon. Someone started the question "Whether God can understand his own necessity": whereupon Hardie got down St Thomas's *Summa* and after ferreting in the index suddenly pronounced, without any intention of being funny, "He doesn't understand anything." This lead to great amusement, the best being an imaginary scene of God trying to explain the theory of vicarious punishment to Socrates . . .

Friday 11 February: . . . Radice, Wood & Betjeman in the morning. Wood a little more interesting, but I am afraid he has much more good will than power and will retain his schoolboy mind. I discovered

---

[9] Prince Youssopoff, of the Imperial House of Russia. – W.H.L.

however that Fiona Macdonald is his favourite author, wh. is a very illuminating and useful thing to know. It will be good to have a romantic after all these scoffers: and it's a good basis. A man can rise from fairies to *Paradise Lost* (I ought to know), but never get from Restoration Comedy to anything of the sublime. Betjeman fairly good.

Bussed home, still feeling poorly. D thought it was probably a touch of the flu' and took my temperature which was about 99°.

Spent the afternoon dozing over the fire with Laurence Housman's *Trimblerigg*, wh. is v. amusing but quite machine-made and one laughs but never for a moment dreams of believing in Trimblerigg and Dividina. Housman knows that the clear headed, perfectly conscious hypocrite of earlier literature is artificial, but he thinks that he uses that knowledge sufficiently by just *telling* us that Trimblerigg believed in himself: he doesn't make us *feel* him doing so. He writes in hate, hate of an external object: he ought to have drawn on the hypocrisy he found in himself. That's the only kind of satire that is literature – the method by wh. Willoughby Patterne & Soames Forsythe were projected.

Back to College and took Percival & Waterfield together . . .

Saturday-Sunday 12-13 February: A good deal better on Saturday morning. After pupils, home for the week end, wh. I spent out there in great ease and comfort, all very jolly. Was quite cured when I returned to College on Monday morning. Had one very nice walk on Saturday in the frost, the heaviest I ever saw. Noticed on many branches up Shotover that the frost does not coat the twig round but lies all on one side of it in a strip edgewise to the branch.

Monday 14 February: Still heavy fog today as it has been all the week end. Hetherington, Valentin, and Campbell in the morning. Gave Valentin a dose of Socratic questions, wh. I seldon do, and found he really didn't know what he meant by most of the things in his essay. He needs this sort of exposé every now and then.

Lunched with Keir. Home for a short walk and tea: then Hamilton & Betjeman. Dined at 7.30 in New Room with Benecke, Driver, Parker, Blockley and the Torpids. Quite a pleasant lot.[10]

Had a conversation with Slade, who gave up Greats a year ago.[11] He tells me I was successful (when I was his tutor) of demolishing

---

[10] The Rev. Thomas Trotter Blockley (1864–1950) was Chaplain of Magdalen 1897–1911.
[11] Humphrey Slade (1905–) went on to read Law and took his BA in 1927. He became an Advocate in Kenya, and in 1963 he became Speaker in the Kenya House of Representatives.

all his original beliefs in morals but not in replacing them. I don't know how seriously he meant this . . .

Tuesday 15 February: Spent the morning on Trevelyan's *England in the Age of Wycliffe* and partly in reading Gower, a poet I always turn to for pure, tho' not intense pleasure. It's a rum thing that Morris shd. have wanted so desperately to be like Chaucer and succeeded in being so exactly like Gower . . .

Walked after lunch up Shotover, down into Horspath, and up again by the field – in my foolishest state of mind at my old game of thinking out great attacks on all sorts of things, such as Steiner and J.C. Squire (really because Squire hasn't reviewed me, but the pretence was on various grounds). Got rid of all this on the way back for a bit and opened my eyes . . .

Back to College and read Gower till dinner time: after dinner to meet D and Maureen at the theatre where the O.U.D.S. were doing *Lear*. We decided that we wd. give up going to them hereafter. It was all that sort of acting wh. fills one at first with embarrassment and pity, finally with an unreasoning personal hatred of the actors. "Why should that damned man keep bellowing at me?" They nearly all shouted hoarsely and inarticulately.

Bussed with the others to Magdalen gate, all v. cheery in spite of our wasted evening. Looked into the smoking room and found Benecke with whom I talked for a while. Then over to New Building, made tea, and to bed. Slept very sound.

Wednesday 16 February: Worked on my "task" (a pleasant one) of the first two chapters of the *Volsunga Saga* and finished them, except for some obstinate phrases. Walked to the Union to consult W. Morris's translation. The day had begun with the usual mist but half way through the morning there was a faint brightening, just the ghost of a shadow here and there in the Grove, and at last an actual ten minutes of sunlight. The birds were chattering and there was a great sense of stirring after so many days of dark.

Bussed home: D seemed none the worse for a very short night owing to being late to bed and up early on account of Dotty. After lunch I walked my familiar round, out through Elsfield and home through Barton. The suggestion of sunlight had disappeared but the air remained deliciously mild and the birds very loud. In the flat fields beyond Mrs Seymour's, the mist still hanging, there was a wonderful mixture of warmth and hush and freshness. Enjoyed my walk v. much . . .

After dinner Waterfield came in to talk to me about universals. He proved a persistent and not unskilful dialectician, but all in defence of outrageous paradox which he doesn't really believe. He stayed till 10 to 12 and I think we both enjoyed our tussle . . .

Thursday 17 February: News that Harwood can't come. To Corpus in the evening to read the *Theaetetus* with Hardie and his three pupils Erskine, Green and Shewring. All very good fellows. Discovered in Liddell and Scott the glorious word "porwizzle".

Friday 18 February: To the Kolbitár at Exeter in the evening. Very pleasant. Followed a good deal better than before.

Sunday 20 February: Home all day and did a good deal of the "King of Drum", not much to my satisfaction.

Back to College afterwards and went to the Philosophical. Hardie read a good paper and got a "moral reproof" from J.A. of exactly the same kind that I got, only worse. J.A.'s motion for admission of female guests defeated but only by one vote.

Monday 21 February: Usual pupils. Betjeman came, but v. ill and I sent him away. Spent evening answering philosophical letter from Prichard & reading Gower.

Tuesday 22 February: Valentin for O.E. this morning. He is greatly improved and seems to be reading a book about myths and taking an interest in primitive poetry which is a very good sign. I think all real interest with boys (as opposed to vanity and cotterie posing and the desire to be up-to-date) must begin from the romantic end. *Introitus sub specie infantis.*[12] . . . Hamilton turned up to talk about the practical syllogism . . .

After dinner read the *Knightes Tale*: then came Weldon to drink whiskey and chat till 12.15. Told me an excellent story of the President's writing to some American (totally unknown to him) about a testimonial for an overseas student and saying "When I heard of your distinguished father's murder I was so moved that I wrote a sonnet wh. I enclose."

Note from Coghill today saying that the "V.O.," whose favourable review of *Dymer* in the *Irish Statesman* had seemed to me not "good" in any sense except that of being favourable, is really A.E. (Russell).

Wednesday 23 February: . . . Lunched in and was able to become an evangelist to all men by telling them that I had met the President in the morning and he was not coming to the T.B. We met at two. The

---

[12] "Entrance under the appearance of a child."

main question was the election of (nominally) a lecturer but (really) an official fellow in Physics: Johnson, who is now up here, to be made a "lecturer" but not to lecture so that there may be a means of financing him for a year's work abroad before he becomes a fellow – a sort of lecturer *in partibus*. Parker led the opposition and I agreed with him, as no one had had the opportunity of considering possible rivals and the account of Johnson's work was not very encouraging. His chief qualification seemed to be that he was a blue and a "very good fellow" wh. as far as I was concerned "cast ominous conjecture on the whole" election. We defeated it, and it is to be postponed.[13] . . .

Bussed home for tea. D was well, but rather tired after a disturbed night owing to the noise of wind. Took Pat for a short stroll after tea. Did a good deal of work on "Drum", including the Chancellor's speech . . .

Thursday 24 February: This morning the German whom Harwood asked me to be civil to, named Kruger, arrived, looking more like a war cartoon of a German than I wd. have believed possible. As he was already engaged to dine at the House and was leaving Oxford early in the morning, I couldn't entertain him. He stayed till about 12.30 and departed, promising to come and see me in the evening. He made one glorious remark, when he described his war experience by saying "I could not connect myself with that life – I could not grasp the reality of that war, that soldier: so I became v. ill."

Bussed home in the steady rain, feeling rather flat and jaded – not so much from Kruger as from having worked at "Drum" before he came. D has got a book of 12 crossword puzzles out of wh. we are all to make our fortunes, and I tried the first after lunch. Took a short, wet and uninteresting walk in Cuckoo Lane.

Back to College after tea. Waterfield came, pretty good hour, I hope. Went into Common Room after dinner and got into an argument with Benecke on the difference between poetry and rhetoric. Then back to my rooms and began to read Waller while waiting for Kruger. He didn't turn up and I read Waller till midnight: the couplets on public events are "stark naught" but all the Amoret and Sacharissa stuff is delicious, sometimes nearly faultless. I am surprised how much I like it.

[13] Patrick Johnson (1904–) took a Second in Mathematical Moderations 1924 and a Second in Natural Science (Physics) in 1927. He took his BA in 1927 and was made a Lecturer at Magdalen that same year. He was a Fellow of Magdalen 1928–47 and University Demonstrator in Physics 1934-47.

Friday 25 February: Radice, Valentin and Wood in the morning: the latter is improving.

Home to lunch in cold and heavy rain. Too wet to go for a walk in the afternoon so I began Rose Macaulay's *Mystery at Geneva* – v. readable.

Back to College after tea and took Percival. After dinner I read some more Waller and Johnson's *Life of Waller*, which is full of good things. I then began Denham and was about half way thro *Cooper's Hill* when J.A., who had been tête-à-tête with himself all day owing to 'flu, looked in and asked me if I wd. come up and "pay him a short visit". So I did, and quite enjoyed [it] tho he is (in the photographic sense) v. positive and one cannot influence the course of the conversation oneself. He told me all about Sweet: how he was the son of a tyrannic father who put him into a bank and tried to prevent him from becoming a philologist (wd. God he had succeeded), and how Sweet made so many enemies that he was put up for the Philological Society simply in order to be blackballed . . .

Saturday 26 February: Pupils in the morning, and home for lunch. Everything pretty beastly at home: D v. tired from being continually kept up late by Dotty and suffering from headache, and everything upside down in preparation for the arrival of the de Forest girl. Raining again after a lovely morning.

Back into town at 7 to meet the Barfields for dinner and theatre. We fed at the Good Luck – he and Mrs B. and his two sisters. They are not beautiful and extremely dowdy in dress but both v. nice and intelligent – I believe I wd. have thought them so even if they had not had the crowning grace of being admirers of *Dymer*!

The play was Munro's *Rumour*, wh. I enjoyed enormously. It is nearly a great work: great in conception, admirable in construction, and failing only because the characters remain too confined to their particular settings – I mean, except in the case of one of the financiers, one hardly felt the universal evil or pathos showing through the individual.

Sunday 27 February: Talked to Thompson at breakfast about the *Rumour*, wh. he thinks one of the worst plays he has seen.

Trudged home thro' a hot, wet, clammy day. D still tired and poorly and things upset. Tried desperately hard to re-write the Queen's speech in the "Drum" poem, all morning, without the slightest success. The old difficulty of smelting down a nasty little bit of factual stuff (the Queen's *conviction* of the others) into poetry: one only succeeds in expanding it into rhetoric.[14] Washed up after lunch. The rain stopped and a great wind began: I got a good blow walking over the fields to Forest Hill, among waving hedges and deep racing brooks – the best period of a not v. nice day.

Read Plato's *Erastae* after supper, wh. contains a v. comic little account of the ideal Gk. gentlman – v. like the renaissance one, in a way.

Back to College and think I was feverish in the night – always half awake and asleep in a skein of muddled dreams, v. thirsty.

Monday 29 [28] February: (the dates have got wrong somehow). Woke with a headache and feeling shaky. Got through the morning pretty well, discovering to my delight that Hetherington is an admirer of *Phantastes*. Home for lunch. Still raining. D was better today tho' still tired. Back after tea to take Hamilton & Betjeman. After dinner decided to nurse myself and shake off this whatever-it-is. Sat over my fire with a detective story and hot toddy till about 10.45 and then went to bed.

Tuesday 1 March: Woke after a good night feeling much better. Spent the morning noting parallels between Donne, Milton and Burton.

Hudson came round from All Souls to give me the recipe for the punch, as I am entertaining the Mermaids tonight, drat 'em. They are nothing but a drinking, guffawing cry of barbarians with hardly any taste among them, and I wish I hadn't joined them: but I don't see my way out now.

Home for lunch. D seemed still v. tired. We all tried talking French at lunch. It was not raining when I set out for my walk, over the fields to Stowe Woods, but came on just as I turned homeward on the Crab Apple Road, and I got pelted.

Back to College, and had to spend most of the time getting things ready for the sons of Belial. The evening passed off all right I think: Tourneur's *Revenger's Tragedy* was read, a rotten piece of work, whose merits, pretty small to begin with, were entirely lost in the continual cackling wh. greeted every bawdy reference (however tragic) and every mistake made by a reader. If one spent much time

---

[14] Beyond what he says here, little is known about the development of this poem. By 1938, when he showed it to John Masefield, it had become *The Queen of Drum*. It was published in Lewis's *Narrative Poems* (1969).

with these swine one wd. blaspheme against humour itself, as being nothing but a kind of shield with which rabble protect themselves from anything that might disturb the muddy puddle inside them.

Put the room straight after they'd gone and sorted out clean from dirty things for the benefit of Hatton. Then to bed and slept well, and oh the beautiful silence and fresh air after all that evening!

Wednesday 2 March: A bright, beautiful morning. Read Courthope's chapters on Wit. There's nothing in them ("She's empty. Hark, she sounds"). Anyone can do this talk in generals about the break-up of scholasticism, and it gets you no further. What you want is something that will make you realise from inside *how* the break up of scholasticism might have made you yourself take to paradox. One can do it for oneself better without Courthope.

I also read some Dryden in the attempt to find out what he meant by wit. But he means something different each time. He's a rum case of a man who was just a poet and nothing else – no magnanimity, no knowledge, no power of thought: just rhythm and gusto.

Went to Bodley and ordered the 1st, 2nd, 3rd, and 4th Edns. of *Paradise Lost* for tomorrow to find out about "crouch" or "couch". Met Cowley there who bowed with his hand on his heart and invited me to make use of his services. Then set off home, in excellent spirits till I suddenly got something in my eye.

D still v. tired and bothered, having been dragged to the cemetery by Mrs Studer again this morning. I do hope Mrs S. leaves the country or quarrels with D before she has made her ill. And Dotty had kept D up, and Winifred had annoyed her, and a visitor came to tea – oh curse it all! Is there never to be any peace or comfort?

Epilogue

There was to be much peace and comfort. In 1930 Mrs Janie Moore and Jack bought such a house as they had always wanted. This is The Kilns in Headington Quarry, with its own pond and woodlands. There Mrs Moore remained, with her many pets, for most of her long life. Besides a large garden, she had a gardener called Paxford in whom she never found a fault. In 1949, when she was very old and forgetful, she went to a nursing home in the nicest part of Oxford. Jack visited her every day until her death on 12 January 1951. Her husband, Courtenay Moore, never left Ireland. When he died, six months after Janie, he left everything to the Dublin Society for the Prevention of Cruelty to Animals. Maureen went to the Royal College of Music and became a music teacher. She married Leonard Blake and they had two children. In 1963 she became quite unexpectedly Lady Dunbar of Hempriggs with a castle in Scotland. Warnie retired from the Army in 1932 and came to live at The Kilns. He pleased everyone by writing six delightful books of French history. And Jack Lewis, as nearly everyone knows by now, was converted to Christianity. You can read about this spiritual journey in his autobiography, Surprised by Joy. The literary career, which he had already begun to combine with his academic one, blossomed unfalteringly and books of all sorts poured from his pen.

Biographical Appendix

ALLCHIN, Basil Charles (1877–1957) was from Oxford. He was a member of Oxford's Society of Non-Collegiate Students and took his BA in 1898, after which he went to the Royal College of Music in London. After returning to Oxford in 1905 he became a member of Hertford College, where for over 20 years he was College Organist. During World War I he was a Captain in the Oxford O.T.C., and Lewis was taught map-reading, platoon-drill and other military subjects by him. Besides taking pupils privately at 15 Beaumont Street, Allchin gave lectures in the University on "Aural Training". In 1920 he was appointed a member of the board of the Royal College of Music and he was Director of Music at the Ladies' College, Cheltenham, 1921–8. He became the Registrar of the Royal College of Music in 1935, and in 1940 he published *Aural Training: Musicianship for Students*. He was considered to have a genius for explaining complex matters in simple language.

ASKINS, Dr John Hawkins (1877–1923) – "the Doc" – was Mrs Moore's brother. He was the son of the Rev. William James Askins and Jane King Askins and he was born in Dunany, Co. Louth, where his father was the Church of Ireland priest. He was educated at Trinity College Dublin, where he obtained a Bachelor of Medicine in 1904. In 1915 he became a Lieutenant in the Royal Army Medical Corps, a Captain in 1916, and he was wounded in January 1917. Following his marriage to Mary Emmet Goldworthy of Washington, D.C., they lived in Osborne House, Elton Road, Clevedon, where their daughter Peony was born. Dr Askin's health seems to have been broken by the war, and after his discharge he devoted much of his time to psychoanalysis. Shortly before 1922 he and his family moved to the village of Iffley, just outside Oxford, so he could be near his sister. C.S. Lewis never forgot having to watch the madness of Dr Askins shortly before his death, which episode is recorded in the Diary. It was of Dr Askins that Lewis

459

was writing in *Surprised by Joy*, ch. XIII, where he says: "It had been my chance to spend fourteen days, and most of the fourteen nights as well, in close contact with a man who was going mad . . . And this man, as I well knew, had not kept the beaten track. He had flirted with Theosophy, Yoga, Spiritualism, Psychoanalysis, what not?"

ASKINS, Dr Robert (1880–1935), another of Mrs Moore's brothers, was the son of the Rev. and Mrs William James Askins. He was brought up in Dunany, Co. Louth, where his father was the Church of Ireland priest. He took his Bachelor of Medicine in 1907 and his M.D. in 1913, both from Trinity College Dublin. He was commissioned a Lieutenant in the Royal Army Medical Corps in 1915, a Captain in 1916, and was mentioned in Despatches in August 1919. He practised medicine in Bristol for many years. Later he moved to Southern Rhodesia, where he was Director of Medical Services. In 1931 he married Mollie Whaddon, and he died at sea on 1 September 1935.

ASKINS, the Rev. William James (1879–1955) was a brother of Mrs Moore. His parents were the Rev. and Mrs William James Askins, and he was brought up in Dunany, Co. Louth, where his father was the Church of Ireland priest. He took a BA from Trinity College Dublin in 1901, and was ordained a priest in the Church of Ireland in 1903. He was a Curate of Kilmore Cathedral, Co. Cavan, 1902–6, Rector of Kilmore 1906–30 and Dean of Kilmore Cathedral 1931–55. He was married to Elizabeth Askins (d. 1941) and they had two children, Charles and Frances.

BAKER, Leo (1898–1987?) matriculated at Wadham College in 1917, but left to serve as a Flight Lieutenant in the RAF. He was awarded the Distinguished Flying Cross in 1918. He returned to Oxford in 1919 to read History. He and Lewis met in 1919 through a mutual interest in poetry, and for a while they worked on an anthology of poems for which they were unable to find a publisher. He took his BA in 1922 and had a brief career on the London stage.

BARFIELD, Owen (1898–   ) was born in North London and educated at Highgate School. He won a Classical Scholarship to Wadham College, Oxford, in 1919. After receiving his BA in 1921 he took a B.Litt and a B.C.L. It was while an undergraduate at Oxford that he met C.S. Lewis through their friend, Leo Baker. Owen Barfield had been at Highgale School with Cecil Harwood, and in 1922, while writing his B.Litt thesis on "Poetic Diction", the two men lived in "Bee Cottage" at Beckley. Barfield and Harwood became interested in the works of Rudolf Steiner during 1922 when he was in England, and both became Anthroposophists. In 1923 he married Matilda Douie (1885–1982). Owen Barfield was a solicitor in London for twenty-eight years. Since his retirement in 1959 he has been a visiting professor at a number of American universities. His books include *Poetic Diction* (1928), *Romanticism Comes of Age* (1944), *Saving the Appearances* (1957), *Worlds Apart (1963), Unancestral Voice (1965), What Coleridge Thought* (1971), and (as G.A.L. Burgeon) *This Ever Diverse Pair (1950)*. Although Barfield and Lewis disagreed about many things, especially Anthroposophy, there is probably no one Lewis admired so much. There is an affectionate portrait of Barfield in chapter XIII of *Surprised by Joy*, and an affectionate one of Lewis in *Owen Barfield on C.S. Lewis* (1990).

BECKETT, (Sir) Eric (1896–1966), was in the Cheshire Regiment 1914–18 and served in France and Salonika. He took a first class degree in Jurisprudence from Wadham College in 1921 and was a Fellow of All Souls College 1921–8. He was called to the Bar in 1922 and he was assistant Legal Adviser to the Foreign Office 1925–45 and Legal Adviser 1955–53. Eric Beckett often went on walks with C.S. Lewis, Owen Barfield and Cecil Harwood.

CARLYLE, the Rev. Alexander James (1861–1943) was a political philosopher, eccesiastical historian, and social reformer. He was ordained in the Church of England in 1888, and became a Fellow and Chaplain of University College in 1893. He had to give up the fellowship when he married in 1895, but he continued to serve the College as a lecturer in Politics and Economics and as Chaplain. He was the mainstay of the Christian Social Union. His works include the influential *History of Mediaeval Political Theory in the West* (6 vols., 1903–36), which he wrote in collaboration with his brother, Sir R.W. Carlyle.

CARRITT, Edgar Frederick (1876–1964), C.S. Lewis's tutor in Philosophy, was a Fellow and Praelector in Philosophy at University College 1898-1941. He was considered an excellent lecturer, combining as he did a very logical procedure with commonsense illustrations. He was not content with the familiar track, and in 1902 was the first in his Faculty to lecture on Aesthetics. From 1933 he gave a regular course on Dialectical Materialism. Some of his lectures were amplified in published works. They include

Theory of Beauty (1914), *Philosophies of Beauty* (1931), and *Ethical and Political Thinking* (1947) in which is summed up the conclusions drawn from what he himself reckoned to be 15,000 hours' discussion of moral, political and aesthetic philosophy with pupils and colleagues. Mr Carritt, a devoted Socialist and steadfast supporter of the left wing, was not a Christian. An argument he and others had with Lewis is referred to in Lewis's "Christianity and Culture" found in *Christian Reflections* (1967).

COGHILL, Nevill (1899–1980). He was born at Castle Townshend, Skibbereen, Co. Cork, of distinguished Anglo-Irish parentage. His father was Sir Egerton Bushe Coghill, and his mother was the daughter of Col. Henry Somerville and sister of E. Oe. Somerville, the authoress. After leaving Haileybury College he was a gunner on the Salonika front in 1918. He matriculated at Exeter College, Oxford, in 1919 and read History and then English. Following a short period of teaching at the Royal Naval College, Dartmouth, he became a Research Fellow of Exeter College in 1924, and he was a Fellow of English at Exeter College 1925–57. In 1957 he was elected Merton Professor of English Literature, which position he held until his retirement in 1966. Coghill was one of the best known and best loved men in Oxford. To get a theatre for Oxford was one of the main aims of his life, and to this end he worked ceaselessly. His own productions were brilliant and seemed to hint at a new art form. Among other things, he is credited with giving Richard Burton his first part. Coghill was an admired scholar of Middle English Literature and his translation into contemporary English of Chaucer's *The Canterbury Tales* (1951) has enjoyed a wide audience. He performed the same service for Chaucer's *Troilus and Criseyde* (1971). This delightful man recalled his friendship with Lewis in "The Approach to English", found in *Light on C.S. Lewis*, ed. Jocelyn Gibb (1965).

EWART FAMILY, THE. The head of this Belfast family was Sir William Quartus Ewart (1844–1919) who obtained a degree from Trinity College Dublin and entered the family firm of Wm. Ewart and Son Ltd, Flax Spinners and Linen Manufacturers. In 1876 he married Mary Heard (1849–1929), who was a niece of Lewis's maternal grandmother, Mrs Mary Warren Hamilton. These are the relatives that Lewis refers to as "Cousin Quartus" and "Cousin Mary" in *Surprised by Joy*. They lived near the Lewises in a house called "Glenmachan". The children of Sir William and Lady Ewart were: (1) Robert Heard Ewart (1879–1939), who succeeded to the baronetcy after his father; (2) Charles Gordon Ewart (1885–1936), who married Lily Greeves (sister of Arthur Greeves); (3) Hope Ewart (1882–1934), who in 1911 married George Harding and moved to Dublin; (4) Kelso "Kelsie" Ewart (1886–1966), who lived near Glenmachan all her life; (5) Gundrede "Gunny" Ewart (1888–1978), who married John Forrest in 1927.

Writing about this family in chapter III of *Surprised by Joy* Lewis said: "Less than a mile from our home stood the largest house I then knew, which I will here call Mountbracken, and there lived Sir W.E. Lady E. was my mother's first cousin and perhaps my mother's dearest friend, and it was no doubt for my mother's sake that she took upon herself the heroic work of civilising my brother and me. We had a standing invitation to lunch at Mountbracken whenever we were at home; to this, almost entirely, we owe it that we did not grow up savages . . . Cousin Mary was the very type of the beautiful old lady, with her silver hair and her sweet Southern Irish voice; foreigners must be warned that this resembles what they call a 'brogue' about as little as the speech of a Highland gentleman resembles the jargon of the Glasgow slums. But it was the three daughters whom we knew best. All three were 'grown-up' but in fact much nearer to us in age than any other grown-ups we knew, and all three were strikingly handsome. H., the eldest and the gravest, was a Juno, a dark queen who at certain moments looked like a Jewess. K. was more like a Valkyrie (though all, I think, were good horsewomen) with her father's profile. There was in her face something of the delicate fierceness of a thoroughbred horse, an indignant fineness of nostril, the possibility of an excellent disdain. She had what the vanity of my own sex calls a 'masculine' honesty; no man ever was a truer friend. As for the youngest, G., I can only say that she was the most beautiful woman I have ever seen, perfect in shape and colour and voice and every movement – but who can describe beauty?"

FARQUHARSON, Arthur Spenser Loat (1871–1942) went to University College in 1890 and took a first class degree in Classics. After a short time as a schoolmaster he returned to University College as a lecturer and was a Fellow of the College 1899–1942. From 1900 until the outbreak of the First World War he held the office of Dean, and this brought him into contact with many generations of undergraduates. During the War, when he was Chief

Postal Censor, he took missions to France, Belgium and Italy and was twice mentioned in Despatches. In 1918 he became a brevet Lieutenant-Colonel in the Territorial Force, and he was made a C.B.E. in 1919. Farquharson taught Philosophy to men reading "Greats", and later to those taking the new school of Philosophy, Politics and Economics. He also had a keen interest in English Literature, which was stimulated by his brother-in-law Sir Walter Raleigh. He was a keen student of military history, and the figure of Marcus Aurelius, the soldier-philosopher, made a special appeal to him.

GORDON, George Stuart (1881–1942) was educated at Glasgow University and Oriel College, Oxford. He was Merton Professor of English Literature 1922–8, after which he was President of Magdalen College 1928–42. Sir Walter Raleigh had inaugurated a Discussion Class for those reading English Literature, and Gordon continued this practice when he became the Merton Professor of English Literature. Lewis contributed a description of Gordon's Discussion Class to *The Life of George S. Gordon 1881–1942* (1945) by M.C.G., p. 77.

GREEVES, Arthur (1895–1966) was one of the five children of Joseph Malcomson Greeves and Mary Margretta Greeves, whose house, "Bernagh", was directly across the road from that of C.S. Lewis's family. Although Arthur and Jack Lewis were in Campbell College at the same time, they did not meet until April 1914 when Lewis was at Malvern College. This important first meeting, which led to a close, life-long friendship, is mentioned in chapter VIII of *Surprised by Joy*. They corresponded fairly regularly and Lewis's letters to Arthur are published under the title *They Stand Together* (1979). The Greeves family were Plymouth Brethren, and there is much in the letters about Arthur's influence as a Christian on Lewis. Arthur had a bad heart, and with an income from his family, he never had to work. Except for the years 1921–3, when he was at the Slade School of Fine Art in London, Arthur spent most of his life in Belfast. In 1949 he moved to Crawfordsburn. Whereas Arthur had been more theologically orthodox than Lewis when they were young men, this was reversed as they grew older. Near the end of his life Arthur became a Quaker.

HAMILTON-JENKIN, Alfred Kenneth (1900–80) matriculated at University College in 1919 and took a BA and a B.Litt degree. He came from a family closely connected with the mines and miners of Cornwall since the eighteenth century. This was to remain a special interest all his life. After leaving Oxford he became a distinguished writer about Cornish mines and other aspects of his beloved Cornwall. His first book, *The Cornish Mines*, was published in 1927 and remains the standard work. His other works include *Cornish Seafarers*, *Cornwall and the Cornish*, *Cornish Homes and Customs*, and *The Story of Cornwall*, all written in the 1930s. These were followed by numerous articles and books, including *Cornwall and its People* (1945) and *News from Cornwall* (1951). Mr Hamilton-Jenkin assisted in the formation of Old Cornwall societies, and he took a large part in setting up the Cornwall County Record Office, which is one of the finest in the country.

HARDIE, William Francis Ross (1902–   ) is one of the sons of W.R. Hardie, Professor of Humanities at the University of Edinburgh. He was educated at Balliol College, and became a Fellow by Examination of Magdalen College in 1925. He was a Fellow and Tutor in Philosophy at Corpus Christi College, Oxford, 1926-50, and President of Corpus Christi College 1950–69. His published works include *A Study in Plato* (1936) and *Aristotle's Ethical Theory* (1968). W.F.R. Hardie is not to be confused with his brother, Colin Hardie, who is not mentioned in the diary. Both were friends of C.S. Lewis, and Colin Hardie was a Fellow and the Classical Tutor at Magdalen College during 1936–73.

HARWOOD, Cecil (1898–1975) had been at Highgate School, London, with Owen Barfield. He came up to Oxford in 1919 and read Classics at Christ Church. He and Owen Barfield attended an Anthroposophical conference in 1923 at which Rudolf Steiner spoke, and it was there that Harwood met his future wife, Daphne Olivier, who was already an Anthroposophist. He met Rudolf Steiner in 1924 and in 1925 he married Daphne Olivier. This same year he and his wife took a leading part in setting up the first Rudolf Steiner school in England, Michael Hall School at Streatham, where he was a teacher. He was Chairman of the Anthroposophical Society in Great Britain 1937-74. His published works include *The Way of a Child, an Introduction to the Work of Rudolf Steiner for Children* (1940), *The Recovery of Man in Childhood* (1958) and *Shakespeare's Prophetic Mind* (1964). There is a pleasing portrait of him in chapter XIII of *Surprised by Joy*.

KEIR, Sir David Lindsay (1895–1973) was born in Scotland, a son of the manse. He was educated at Glasgow University, after which he served with the King's Own Scottish Borderers 1915–9. He went up to New College, Oxford, after demobilisation and took a First in Modern History in 1921. He was Praelector in Modern History at University College, Oxford, 1921–39. Between 1939–49 he was President and Vice-Chancellor of the Queen's University, Belfast. Under him Queen's successfully completed the first major phase of postwar development and he left the University very strong. He was Master of Balliol College, Oxford, 1949–65. He was not in sympathy with some recent trends in Oxford education, such as post-graduate training and the proposals for co-education. He did much to maintain its high reputation, including the revival of the tradition of making the Master's Lodgings a port of call for all old Balliol men and others of distinction. Sir David was an able historian with a special interest in constitutional history and law. He wrote *Constitutional History of Modern Britain* (1938) and (with F.H. Lawson) *Cases in Constitutional Law* (1928).

LAWSON, Frederick Henry (1897–1983) was born in Leeds and educated at Leeds Grammar School. He served in the European War 1916–18, after which he went up to Queen's College, Oxford, and took a First in Modern History. He was a University Lecturer in Law at University College 1924–25. In 1925 he became a Junior Research Fellow at Merton College, and an official Fellow and Tutor in Law 1930–48. After serving as University Lecturer in Byzantine Law 1929–31, Lawson became Professor of Comparative Law and Fellow of Brasenose College 1948–64. Following his retirement he was part-time Professor of Law at the University of Lancaster 1964–77 and he lectured in many American universities. He wrote many books, among which are *Negligence in the Civil Law* (1950), *Constitutional and Administrative Law* (1961) and *The Oxford Law School 1850–1965* (1968)

LEWIS, Albert James (1863–1929), the father of C.S. Lewis, was a police court solicitor in Belfast. He was the son of Richard and Martha Lewis and was born in Cork. The family moved to Belfast in 1868. In 1877 Albert went to Lurgan College in Co. Armagh, where the Headmaster was William T. Kirkpatrick – the "Great Knock" – who years later was to have Jack Lewis as his pupil. Albert qualified as a solicitor in 1885 and he soon began a practice of his own. He was also known for his love of English literature. After courting her for nine years, he married Florence Augusta

"Flora" Hamilton in 1894. She was the daughter of the Rev. Thomas Hamilton, Rector of St Mark's, Dundela. Their first son, Warren Hamilton, "Warnie", was born on 16 June 1895, and their second son, Clive Staples, "Jack", was born on 29 November 1898. In 1905 this happy family moved from Dundela Villas to "Little Lea", on the outskirts of Belfast, which Albert had specially built for Flora. They enjoyed this for only three years as a family, for in 1908 Flora died of cancer. Thereafter nothing was the same for the others, each unhappy in his own way at the breakup of the family. Albert never stopped grieving over his wife. He had never liked going away from home, and thereafter he gave most of his time to work. From an early age Albert had been a very sincere member of the Church of Ireland, and he continued all his life to be a loyal parishioner of St Mark's, Dundela. He became ill with cancer in 1929, and he bore it patiently and bravely to the end.

MCNEILL, Jane "Janie" (1889–1959) was the daughter of James and Margaret McNeill of Belfast. Mr McNeill had had Lewis's mother as a pupil when he was a master at Campbell College, Belfast, and he considered her "the cleverest girl pupil he ever had". Years later when Mr McNeill was Headmaster of Campbell College he was Lewis's favourite teacher. Janie was their only child and she remained in Belfast all her life, looking after her mother when her father died in 1907. Although she was a particular friend to Jack, she was fond of the whole Lewis family and visited Albert Lewis regularly. Janie also taught at Campbell College, and in an obituary written for *The Campbellian* (July 1959) Lewis said of her: "She was a religious woman, a true, sometimes a grim, daughter of the Kirk; no less certainly, the broadest-spoken maiden lady in the Six Counties. She was a born satirist. Every kind of sham and self-righteousness was her butt. She deflated the unco-gude with a single ironic phrase, then a moment's silence, then the great gust of her laughter."

MACRAN, the Rev. Dr Frederick Walker (1866–1947) – "Cranny" – was an old and valued friend of Mrs Moore and Dr John Askins. He was born in Ireland and took a BA from Trinity College Dublin in 1886, after which he became a priest in the Church of Ireland and served in a number of parishes in Co. Down. He moved to England and was Rector of Childrey 1905–23, after which he moved to the diocese of Chelmsford. Lewis described him in *Surprised by Joy*, ch. XIII, as "an old, dirty, gabbling, tragic, Irish

parson who had long since lost his faith but retained his living . . .
All he wanted was the assurance that something he could call
'himself' would, on almost any terms, last longer than his bodily
life."

ONIONS, Charles Talbut (1873–1965), lexicographer and gram-
marian, gained a London BA in 1892. In 1895 J.A.H. Murray
invited him to join the small staff of the English Dictionary at
Oxford. From 1906 to 1913 he was entrusted with the special
preparation of various portions of the Dictionary, and then began
independent editorial work on the section Su-Sz. He was also
responsible for Wh-Worling and the volumes containing X, Y, Z.
In 1922 he began to revise and complete William Little's work on
a *Shorter Oxford English Dictionary* (1933). He was a University
lecturer in English 1920–7, Reader in English Philology 1927-49,
and a Fellow of Magdalen College 1923-65. His most enduring
work is likely to be the *Oxford Dictionary of English Etymology*
(1966).

PASLEY, (Sir) Rodney (1899–1982) was educated at Sherbourne
School and served as a 2nd Lieutenant in the Royal Artillery during
1914-18. He took a BA from University College in 1921, after which
he was Assistant Master at Alleyn's School, Dulwich, 1921–5;
Vice-Principal of Rajkumar College at Rajkot, India 1926–8;
Assistant Master at Alleyn's School 1931-6; Headmaster of Barn-
staple Grammar School 1936–43; and he was Headmaster of
Central Grammar School, Birmingham, from 1943 until his retire-
ment in 1959. In 1922 he married Aldyth Werge Hamber –
"Johnnie".

POYNTON, Arthur Blackburne (1867–1944). He came up to Balliol
College in 1885 and was one of the most distinguished undergraduate scholars of his generation. He took a First in Classics in
1889 and in 1890 was elected to a Fellowship at Hertford College.
In 1894 he went to University College as Fellow and Praelector in
Greek and a tutor in classical scholarship. Poynton was recognised
in Oxford not merely as one of the most brilliant of classical
teachers, but one of the most able and accurate of scholars. Greek
oratory was his own main study, and he probably knew more
about it than any of his contemporaries. The depth of his oratorical
style was demonstrated in a sparkling lecture delivered in Greek
in the manner of Isocrates in November 1927. His teaching ability
can be seen in his admirable edition of *Cicero Pro Milone* (1892),

and the grace and breadth of his teaching in *Flosculi Graeci* (1920) and *Flosculi Latini* (1922). He was Master of University College 1935-7.

PRICE, Henry Habberley (1899–1984). He served in the RAF during 1917–19 and then took a first class degree in Classics from New College, Oxford, in 1921. He was a Fellow of Magdalen 1922-3, a Fellow and Lecturer in Trinity College 1924–35, and a University Lecturer in Philosophy at Oxford 1932–5. In 1935 he became Wykeham Professor of Logic and a Fellow of New College. Price was a founder member of the Oxford University and City Gliding Club. He was also interested in Psychical Research and was the President of the Society for Psychical Research. On more than one occasion he debated with Lewis at the Oxford University Socratic Club, and Lewis's essay "Religion Without Dogma?" (in *Undeceptions*; and in the U.S.A., *God in the Dock*) is an answer to Price's "The Grounds of Modern Agnosticism".

RALEIGH, Sir Walter (1861–1922), critic and essayist, had been an undergraduate at University College. He was Professor of Modern Literature, University College, Liverpool, 1889–1900, and Professor of English Language and Literature, Glasgow University, 1900–4. In 1904 he became the first holder of a new chair of English Literature at Oxford and a Fellow of Magdalen College, and in 1914 he was elected Merton Professor of English Literature and a Fellow of Merton College. He contributed enormously to the development of the School of English Language and Literature at Oxford and his lectures aroused great enthusiasm. His works include *Style* (1897), *Milton* (1900), *Wordsworth* (1903) and *Shakespeare* (1907).

ROBSON-SCOTT, William Douglas (1900-80) matriculated at University College in 1919 and took a First in English Literature in 1923. It is evidence of his remarkable range of gifts that he was appointed assistant lecturer in Dutch at Bedford College, London, in 1929. He took up residence in Berlin in 1932, and moved to Vienna in 1937, where he took a doctorate in English and German. On his return to Britain in 1939 he was appointed lecturer in German at Birkbeck College, University of London. This was interrupted by the War, during which he worked for the War Office. He afterwards returned to Birkbeck College, where he was promoted to Reader in 1961, and in 1966 to Professor of German Language and Literature. He is the author of *German Travellers* in England 1400–1800 (1953) and *Goethe and the Visual Arts* (1970).

SMITH, John Alexander (1863–1939), philosopher and classical scholar, was educated at Edinburgh University and Balliol College, Oxford, where he took a First in Classics in 1887. He became a Fellow of Balliol in 1891 and he was the Waynflete Professor of Moral and Metaphyscial Philosophy and a Fellow of Magdalen College 1910–36. He was a distinguished Aristotelian scholar, his translation of *De Anima* appearing in 1931. Smith maintained the idealist tradition of T.H. Green and Edward Caird. He was much influenced by Benedetto Croce and Giovanni Gentile.

STEAD, William Force (1884–1967) was born in Washington, D.C., and in 1908 he was appointed to the U.S. Consular Service, serving as Vice-Consul in Liverpool and Nottingham. He took a degree from Queen's College, Oxford, in 1916 and became a priest of the Church of England in 1917. He was Chaplain of Worcester College, Oxford, 1927–33 and it was during this period that he baptised his friend T.S. Eliot. Stead published many volumes of poems, and besides having this interest in common with Lewis, his wife was the sister of Mrs John Askins. He returned to the United States before World War II, where he converted to the Catholic Church. His published poems include *Verd Antique* (1920), *The Sweet Miracle* (1922) and *Festival in Tuscany* (1927).

STEVENSON, George Hope (1880–1952), C.S. Lewis's tutor in History, was born in Glasgow and educated at Glasgow University. He went to Balliol College, where he took a First in Classics. In 1906 he was elected to a Fellowship at University College as Praelector in Ancient History at University College. He remained there till his retirement in 1949. Stevenson was at his best when taking private pupils, but he was not considered a good lecturer. He made a number of important contributions to the study of Roman history, and mention should be made of his *Roman History* (1930) and *Roman Provincial Administration* (1939). A man of high integrity, he was a keen Churchman with Anglo-Catholic convictions. For many years he was a church warden at St Margaret's Church, Oxford. In later years he learned to serve at the Altar, an office usually performed by youths and boys.

SUFFERN, Mrs Lily (1860–1934) – "Aunt Lily" – was the eldest daughter of the Rev. and Mrs Thomas Hamilton of Belfast, and thus the sister of Lewis's mother. There is a portrait of her by

Warren Lewis in the *Lewis Papers*, II, 148-9 in which he says: "Lily was a clever, but eccentric woman, handsome in her youth. Her cutting insolence and her extremely quarrelsome disposition made her the stormy petrel of the family, with all or several of whose members she was perpetually at war. Albert [Lewis] never forgave her for the arrow she launched at him in writing to another member of the clan on a legal problem, when she observed of him in an airy parenthesis, 'for poor Allie is *so* ignorant'. The good nature of her nephew Clive Lewis (whom she addressed as 'Cleeve') enabled her for many years in later life to conduct a pseudo-metaphysical correspondence which bears melancholy evidence of a good brain run to seed." She married William Suffern, who by 1886 was in an asylum in Peebles, Scotland. In 1900 he was declared insane, and he died in 1913. After this her chief solace was the poetry of Browning and a numerous collection of cats. She led a wandering life, living successively at Peebles, Edinburgh, Hollywood, Co. Down, Donaghadee, Oxford, Broadway and Perranporth.

TOLKIEN, John Ronald Reuel (1892–1973) was born in Bloemfontein, South Africa, and brought up in Birmingham. He was educated at King Edward's School, Birmingham, where his love of languages was already in flower. He matriculated at Exeter College, Oxford, in 1911, where he read Honour Moderations. For his special subject he chose Comparative Philology and was taught by Joseph Wright. He went on to read English Language and Literature and took a First in 1915. It was also during his undergraduate years that Tolkien developed his interest in painting and drawing. He was a Lieutenant with the Lancashire Fusiliers during 1915–18 and took part in the Battle of the Somme. It was while he was still in the army, convalescing from an illness, that he began writing *The Silmarillion*. After working for a while on the Oxford Dictionary, he became Reader in English Language at the University of Leeds 1920-4 and Professor of English Language at Leeds 1924. In 1925 he returned to Oxford as Professor of Anglo-Saxon. It was during 1926 that he and Lewis became friends, and a few years later he began *The Hobbit*. He was Merton Professor of English Language and Literature at Oxford 1945-59. *The Lord of the Rings* was published 1954–55.

WARDALE, Edith Elizabeth (1863–1943) entered Lady Margaret Hall, Oxford, in 1887, and moved a year later to the recently opened St Hugh's Hall (now College). After obtaining a First in Modern Languages she became Vice-Principal and Tutor of St Hugh's Hall and Tutor to the Association for the High Education of Women. She was intimately connected with women's education during some of the most important years of its history. She was Tutor in English at St Hugh's until 1923. Her publications include *An Old English Grammar* (1922) and *An Introduction to Middle English* (1937).

WARREN, Sir Thomas Herbert (1853–1930) came up to Balliol College in 1872 when Benjamin Jowett had been two years Master and the College was at the height of its reputation. There were other great men there at the time, and Warren held his own in this distinguished society. He took a first class degree in Classics and was chosen to represent the University at Rugby football. Probably the greatest influence upon Warren was Jowett whose ideal of a college was a training ground for public life. In 1877 he was elected to a prize fellowship at Magdalen, and shortly afterwards to a classical tutorship. In 1885, at the age of 32, he was elected President of Magdalen, an office he held until 1928. At times he seemed over-anxious about the social standing of his undergraduates, but this seems to have been his desire to secure the best for Magdalen. It was an unusual tribute to the position of his College that King George V in 1912 chose it for the Prince of Wales. He wrote two volumes of verse, *By Severn Sea* (1897) and *The Death of Virgil* (1907), and was one of the founders of the *Oxford Magazine*.

WIBLIN, Vida Mary (1895–1937) – "Smudge" – was born in Oxford and educated at the Cathedral School and Oxford High School for Girls. She matriculated at the Society of Oxford Home-Students (later St Anne's College) in 1920 and received her Bachelor of Music in 1924. She went on to read for a degree in Latin and Greek. She took her BA in 1926. Miss Wiblin, who never married, was musical director at Magdalen College School 1926–37, where she was a well known and loved figure. She was also pianist to the Bach Choir and the Eglesfield Musical Society at Queen's College, and she worked hard and loyally as co-secretary of the Oxford Orchestral Society.

WILSON, Frank Percy (1889–1963) – Lewis's tutor in English – took a BA in English from the University of Birmingham, and then a B.Litt at Lincoln College, Oxford, on Thomas Dekker. He was in the Royal Warwickshire Regiment during World War I and was badly wounded on the Somme. He returned to Oxford in 1920 as a University lecturer, and was appointed Reader in 1927. He was Professor of English at the University of Leeds 1929–36, and Merton Professor of English Literature at Oxford 1947–57. He was, with Bonamy Dobrée, the general editor of the *Oxford History of English Literature*, and he invited Lewis to write *English Literature in the Sixteenth Century* (1954).

WYLD, Henry Cecil Kennedy (1870–1945), philologist and lexico-grapher, was educated at the universities of Bonn and Heidelberg and then at Corpus Christi, Oxford, where he studied philology, phonetic and linguistics with Henry Sweet. He took a BA from Oxford in 1899 and was appointed a lecturer in the English language at University College, Liverpool. In 1904 the University of Liverpool elected him first Baines Professor of English Language and Literature. He remained at Liverpool until 1920 and by teaching, lecturing and writing he established himself among the foremost philologists of the country. It was then that he wrote his *Historical Study of the Mother Tongue* (1906) and *A Short History of English* (1914). In 1930 he was elected Merton Professor of English Language and Literature in the University of Oxford, with a Fellowship at Merton. At Oxford he completed his *Studies in English Rhymes* (1923) and wrote the *Universal Dictionary of the English Language* (1932).

Magdalen College Appendix

In the same notebook in which Lewis wrote the last portion of his diary he included "portraits" of nine of his colleagues at Magdalen College. All nine are printed here, for they seem to have been intended as illustrations to the diary. Unfortunately, Lewis stopped keeping a diary before he had mentioned Edward Hope and Stephen Lee, but I have retained his descriptions of them.

BENECKE, Paul Victor Mendelssohn (1868–1944) was the great-grandson of the composer Felix Mendelssohn. He was elected a Fellow of Magdalen in 1893 and taught Classics until his retirement in 1925. Lewis gives this portrait of him:

"*Simplicissima Psyche.* He has a face of extraordinary beauty and carries his head a little tilted upwards and his body very straight though he is old. He is a fast and furious walker and strong, but his hands shaky. He takes his bath cold, drinks no wine, fasts on Fridays, rises very early, and misses no services in Chapel. He is regarded by some as a saintly man, by others as an old woman, and both are right.

His holiness he shows clearly, not by his asceticism, but by his wise and curious understanding of beasts. He said at one time that he saw well why the Indians found in the elephant a manifestation of the divine: and at another that the life of every animal appeared sad and empty from the outside, and that the melancholy in a dog's eyes was its pity for men. It is only on this subject that he speaks with confidence.

For the most part he cannot advance a proposition without at once qualifying it, and then again modifying the qualification, so that no one knows at the end the purport of his speech as a whole. This hesitation, which amounts to a kind of mental stammer, makes him ineffectual at meetings and committees, where he speaks often and long, not for the love of his own voice (for it is visibly nervous and unhappy), but because he conceives it to be a duty.

For the same reason it is commonly he who talks to a tedious guest or shy newcomer. If anyone is rude to him he thinks the fault was his own and apologizes. He is ridiculed behind his back, and sometimes insulted to his face, by younger men, and was never seen to be angry. He seldom leaves the College, and if he does, it is to stay with his sister. The College is his wife and children and his mother and father: he knows all its statutes as well as his Prayer Book, and forgets no one who has belonged to it for many generations.

His leisure is consumed in charitable and educational works. If the formation of a school or a society, or the running of a hospital, involves any dull and laborious work of organisation or correspondence, that work is sure to fall to him. He has the air of a man who has never looked for thanks and very seldom got them. His greatest pleasure is in music: and there even those who despise him find it necessary to reverence his judgement."

CRAIG, Edwin Stewart (1865–1939). He was a Demonstrator in the Electrical Laboratory of the University of Oxford 1905–13. He was a Fellow of Magdalen 1918–30, during which time he was Vice-President of the College 1926–8, and Registrar of the University of Oxford 1924-30. Lewis gives this portrait of him:

"The Bureaucrat. He has the face of a colonel or a civil servant rather than that of a scholar: ruddy of complexion, with heavy folds in the cheek, smiling lips, and a neat 'toothbrush moustache'. He is very bronzed: he goes very neatly dressed and well groomed and contrives always to carry about him the air of the great world – as if a little bit of Whitehall or the Foreign Office had come among us.

At his first appearance he shows himself of all men the hardest to overlook, or to use with flippancy: his very face and voice carry the sort of authority that comes from long familiarity with business, faultless breeding, the habit of command, and the consciousness of having a place in the system of things. Alone of the older men he is treated by his juniors with invariable respect. He silences opposition by his perfect knowledge of procedure and knows well how to meet an argument not with a contrary argument but with a point of order: or, not seldom, by a silence at the right moment or a mere raising of his eyebrows. He is aware of his own powers, but by no means vain.

He is always kindly, but his kindness is more distant than the ill-temper of others. To his seniors, or to dignitaries from without, his manners are irresistible and produce at once, without servility, all that servility aims at. With all these resources, he has neither serious nor original designs whereon to use them. What his power enforces has often been suggested to him by others, or by mere precedent: he has been described as the incarnation of an agenda paper. He is by no means proof against flattery: still less against the boyish charm of an undergraduate with a clean face and a good family. Propriety, decency, expediency, he well understands: good and evil would seem to him rather bad form.

He has been engaged in business so long that he has forgotten all intellectual interests. His reading is trash: his pleasures entirely sensual: he is a good judge of cookery, of wine, and of spirits. He is ageing rapidly and bears his infirmities with great courage as to the dangers, and no patience at all as to the discomforts."

DIXON, Arthur Lee (1867–1955). He was a Fellow of Merton College 1891–1922, and Fellow of Magdalen and Waynflete Professor of Pure Mathematics 1922–45. Lewis says of him:

"*Epicuri de grege Porcus.* He is a tousle-headed man with a ragged moustache, now grey, but showing traces of reddish-yellow. Having come here late in life he is junior to most of those who are younger than himself: this, combined with the possession of an invalid wife at Folkestone, gives him an unattached air. He is the cheerful spectator of all that goes on about him, but seldom takes the stage himself. He seems to have slipped into the college as an experienced traveller slips into a crowded railway carriage: giving no trouble to others, yet easily making himself comfortable because he knows how to fit in anywhere. He is happy here, and would be happy at the North Pole or in the last trench: he looks as if he had never met a man whom he could not get on with. He loves a good murder story or a good epic poem, a good conceit or a good game of bowls, a good philosopher or a good charwoman, with the same impartiality.

His knowledge is very great and yet no one would think of him as a learned man. He talks to all of us so readily on our own subjects that one forgets he has a subject of his own: or rather, mathematics seem to lie so easily side by side with Ovid, Tasso, golf, Kant, Gilbert & Sullivan, Trollope, and French inns, that it appears as one of the normal human interests. It is a mere accident whether a man happens to include mathematics among his hobbies – as it is an accident whether he includes draughts.

He is a man who seems to have solved the problem of living, without (what is rare) turning egoist in the process. As far as a man can go on the purely world level – without divine discontents or ultimate misgivings or crying for the moon – so far he has gone. A man to be depended on to the end: he is at peace, like the animals, but with the added charm of reason: a good man, a good (almost a great) gentleman, but no more spiritual than the worst degenerate in whom – for everything else – one would find his opposite. If he had physical beauty he would be the Pagan ideal of the 'good man' perfectly realised."

HOPE, Edward (1886–1953) was educated at Manchester University and Magdalen College. He was a Fellow and Tutor in Chemistry at Magdalen from 1919 until his retirement. Lewis wrote of him:

"*Natura apis*. By his appearance he is a black Celt. A little, dark, fragile man, so quiet and self contained that you would take him for a sneak if he were not obviously honest, and for a mystic if he were not obviously commonplace. He is a son of the people, still carrying strange Northern provincialisms in his speech, and noisy over his food. No one ever disliked him. His life is in his science: he lives isolated among us laymen and in the simplicity of his heart supposes all men to be as expert in their own studies as he is in his. He is no talker. He minds his own business: for working hours, science, and for leisure hours, his own digestion. This is bad, and is the only theme on which he is eloquent.

This is one of those men in whom knowlege and intellect have taken up their abode without making any difference: they are added on to a decent drab nonentity of character, and the character has not been transformed. If you wiped out his technical knowledge there would be nothing left to distinguish him from any respectable shopkeeper in the Tottenham Court Road. Yet he is not vulgar: for conceit, sham-gentility, and greed of money or attention, have never crossed him mind. A modest, able, laborious, charitable, unpretentious little man, whom no one could describe without wishing to be able to speak of him more favourably than truth will allow."

LEE, Stephen Grosvenor (1889–1962) was an undergraduate at

Magdalen 1908–12, where he read History. He was Assistant Master at King's School, Worchester, 1912-13, and a Lecturer at Magdalen 1913–14. During the War he was a Captain in the 6th Rifle Brigade 1914–18. He was a Fellow and Tutor in Modern History at Magdalen 1920–47, and of him Lewis wrote:

"He is a well-looking, clean-limbed, open-air sort of man like the hero of a lady's first novel: his teeth very white, his eye clear, clean-shaven. Though no fool, he is out of his place in a college: if he could take his charming wife and lusty children with him and be set down on a hundred acres of farm in the colonies he would have found his vocation. He has far too much sense of duty to neglect his work – he comes of God-fearing dissenting stock – but the term is a weariness to him, and he is never happy till he has taken his family away to his little Welsh bungalow among the heather and crags of the Gower peninsula, where he can spend the day hewing wood and drawing water. He would sooner handle a spade than all the pens that ever were, and covets a saddle more than any professional chair.

Of all this, that is visible to everyone else, he is only dimly conscious himself. He thinks himself lazy because his heart does not turn to his work: though in reality his energy is unbounded, and what is left over from teaching pupils and bathing the children goes upon boy-scouts and the League of Nations. By a paradox (which is no paradox to those that understand him) he is, on the one hand, a very modest, and even a humble man, who would learn from anyone: on the other, the distance between him and those who really [are] of the scholarly type, is a thing that he has never dreamed of. He would be too good to feel anger if anyone tried to show it to him: but it would be impossible for him to understand."

MACKEITH, Malcolm Henry (1895–1942). He was Fellow and Tutor of Magdalen College 1922–33, Demonstrator in the University Department of Human Anatomy 1921–3, University Demonstrator in Pharmacology 1922–33, and Dean of the Medical School 1930–3. Lewis gave this portrait of him:

"A sprawling, slouching sort of man who sits most often with his chair tilted at an angle of forty five degrees, his hands in his pockets, and his coat unbuttoned, swinging his legs. His face is sleepy-looking and wears usually a sly smile, as of a knowing yokel. It is so natural to imagine him with a straw in his mouth that one hardly knows whether one remembers to have seen it there in fact or no. He speaks in a nasal twang, very slowly.

He has all the appearance of good nature, though he is not known to have done anyone a service. He has never been seen angry, nor sorry. He goes in the company of those who alway have their own way and gets his share, but without violence. It is as if he used them as they use the rest of us. When one of his confederates has cleared the way with a savage exposition of *realpolitik* and the other has paved it with precedents and formalities, he heaves onto his feet, speaks some halting words that tire but half conciliate his opponents and relapses heavily into his chair.

He thinks he knows a thing or two, but has not yet reached the level of cynicism. He lives in a farmer's world where over-reaching and under-mining are taken for granted, and nothing could be more simple minded than his honest pride in deceiving his colleagues. As he has never suspected the existence of any different world, he feels no need to defend himself by a conscious doctrine of cynicism. He thinks that he only does a little better what all men invariably do as well as they can: and while realising that the beaten party in a deal will grumble, he could not understand the kind of animosity that his actions really arouse.

He differs by the whole width of the sky from our first character [Weldon]: as the unconscious from the conscious: as the pagan from the aspostate: as the naïf rogue, at peace with his world of roguery, differs from the defiant apostle of immoralism. You might say that they differed as earth from iron – but only if you remember that earth can eat iron up, slowly, without noticing it. Being entirely happy, he is good company. He will never go to hell – the gallows would be quite enough to settle his purely human, and even touching, account."

PARKER, Michael Denne (1894–1972). He was a Fellow and Tutor in Ancient History at Magdalen 1926–45. Lewis usually referred to him as the "Wounded Buffalo" or "Wounded Bison", and gave this picture of him:

"*The plain man.* He is a picture of rude health. His face is very red and rough, like a beefsteak, the lips thick, the jaw heavy and usually thrust out to support a heavy pipe. He has a slouch in his walk, like an athlete off duty, and goes with his hands (which are hairy and like the hands of a workman) in his pockets.

He thinks of himself as a plain man with no nonsense about him, and hopes that even his enemies regard him as an honest fellow at bottom, and that even cleverer and more subtle men allow him to be a good judge of a practical matter. The desire to be always exercising this shrewd practical common sense leads him to endless discussions on everything that happens: he will draw anyone who listens into a corner and stand there exchanging husky confidences about his pupils and colleagues as long as you will. Whatever his audience may be he always implies that 'we two (or three, or four) are the only people in College who understand this matter and we must hold together'. The very same people against whom he marshalls his confidants on Wednesday will themselves be taken into council on Thursday.

His passion for feeling that he holds the reins and is in the secret thus gives him the appearance (and, in practice, the qualities) of an unscrupulous intriguer: but not the guilt, for he is as innocent as a schoolboy playing at secret societies. He believes all that he says for the moment, but being as weak as water, takes a new colour from every group he falls into. What you say to him carelessly and in public one day, he will bring back to you the next day, in perfect good faith, as an original idea of his own to be communicated in close secret, with a wink and a nod – *verbum sapienti*. The habit is now so settled on him that even when he is only borrowing your matches or passing the time of day, he sidles up to you in such a manner that anyone out of earshot would think he was discussing the destiny of the University.

He is not a man of intellect. He reads (beyond his subject) nothing but detective stories, and has no taste for any of the arts. His pleasures are those of an athlete. His humour is raillery and banter: rough bludgeon work bordering on the clownish. His temper is easily raised and easily appeased. Of morals his highest reach is a blunt hatred of unchastity and a public schoolboy's belief in the value of watching cricket matches. Both are sincere and he would probably boast of being unable to give his reasons for either."

SEGAR, Robert (1879–1961). He was educated at Stonyhurst and Liverpool University. He became a barrister of the Middle Temple in 1903, and during the War served as a Captain in the Worcestershire Regiment in France. At the age of forty he became a Commoner at Magdalen and after taking his BA he was Lecturer in Jurisprudence at Wadham College and Tutor in Law at Magdalen 1919–21. He was a Fellow of Magdalen 1921–35. Lewis gives us this portrait of Robert Segar:

"A squat, ugly, cheerful-looking little man, with a twinkle in his eye. He wears a bowler hat and carries a little brief-bag, which combine with his broad, vulgar face to give him the appearance of a prosperous and benevolent commercial traveller. He often chews the stump of a cigar.

He is a Papist and has settled his accounts with the other world: for the rest of his time he is free to play golf, eat his dinner, and crack his joke. He has been seen to hand a cigar to a beggar in the street with a quizzical expression. He takes the rough with the smooth, and laughs everything away: the humour is all in his face, and he might do well on the music hall stage. He brings about him the air of a bar parlour: to sit with him is to be snug and jolly and knowing and not unkindly, and to forget that there are green fields or art galleries in the world.

All this is the side he shows us day by day: but there is more behind, for he is a war wreck and spends his nights mostly awake. He will die game. His heaven would be a cosy public house with a billiard room and a bet won from a man who could afford to lose it: his hell, a pupil."

WELDON, Thomas Dewar (1896–1958). He took a BA from Magdalen College in 1921 and was Fellow and Tutor in Philosophy at Magdalen 1923–58. Lewis wrote of him:

"*Determined to be a villain.* He is a man of the melancholy complexion: his face very pale, his hair very black and streaked down with oil over his head without a parting: his mouth long and thin: the features clear cut, and very little flesh on the face. He is a frequent and loud laugher, but the expression of his face in repose is fierce and sullen. He carries a great deal of liquor without being drunk. His light talk is cynicism and bawdy: when he grows serious without anger (which is seldom) he likes to rap out his sentences very sharply and close his mouth after them like a trap. In anger – which always rises unless he is opposed – he is not at all hot, but grows paler, smiles a great deal and is powerful in dialectic. He is insolent by custom to servants and to old men, yet capable of kindliness, though not to be depended on. He showed himself courageous in the war and is so in peace. He has great abilities, but

would despise himself if he wasted them on disinterested undertakings. He gives no quarter and would ask none. He believes that
he has seen through everything and lives at rock bottom. He
would be capable of treachery, and would think the victim a fool for
being betrayed. Contempt is his ruling passion: courage his chief
virtue."

Index

Abercrombie, Lascelles: *Idea of Great Poetry*, 407; *Principles of English Prosody*, 433

Achilles: 122

Adam (the first man): 306, 361

Adamson, Robert: *Development of Greek Philosophy*, 16

Addison, Joseph: 235, 383

A. E.: *see* G. W. Russell

Aeschylus: *Prometheus Vinctus*, 438; men. 190

Agesilaus: 423

Aiken, Conrad: 47

Ainley, Henry: 93

Alexander, Samuel: *Space, Time, and Deity*, 301, 304, 394, 403; men. 403–4

Alfred, King: 119, 124, 128

Allan, Archibald: *Space and Personality*, 242; men. 248

Allchin, Basil Charles: *Aural Training*, 459; men. 30, 38, 75, 128, 137, 268, 271, 459

Allen, Carleton Kemp: 49, 53, 187, 222, 271, 273, 293, 303, 304, 328, 329, 349, 354, 355, 389

Allen, Sir Hugh: 34, 148, 268

Ancrene Riwle: 200

Anderson, John Edward: 197

Anglo-Saxon Chronicle: 124, 184

Anne, Queen: 39, 234, 381

Anthology (Greek): 297

Anthroposophical Quarterly: 339

Anthroposophical Society: 338, 465

Anthroposophy: 338–39, 431–32, 439, 449, 461, 465

Appleton, E. R.: 30, 286, 288

Archer, William: 37

Ariel: 131

Ariosto, Ludovico: 193, 236

Aristotle: *Metaphysics*, 440; *Nicomachean Ethics*, 432–33; *Politics*, 29, 36; men. 16, 48, 110, 187, 223, 383, 384, 385, 397, 398, 434, 435, 441–42

Arnold, Matthew: *Empedocles on Etna*, 159; "Tristram and Iseult," 15; men. 188, 328, 448

Artemis: 336

Arthur, King: 344

Ascham, Roger: *Scholemaster*, 136; *Toxophilus*, 398; men. 406

Askins, Charles (son of "Willie" Askins): 460

Askins, Edith ("Edie", sister of Mrs Moore): 3, 116, 229–30, 306, 308, 312

Askins, Frances (daughter of "Willie" Askins): 460

Askins, Jane King (mother of Mrs Moore): 3, 459, 460

Askins, Dr John Hawkins ("the Doc", brother of Mrs Moore): on Atlantis, 15; eloquent and characteristic figure, 31; talks about perversion, 41; philosophy of primal One, 72; his sail up the Amazon, 73; on Scripture, 75; on psychoanalysis, 116; talks of death, 135; vaccinates with a nail file, 154; talks about "the Titanic", 156; on Satanic badness, 191–2; his madness, 201–19; his spiritualism, 221; his death, 229–30; biography, 459–60; men. 3, 20, 33, 36, 38, 39, 40, 42, 48, 61, 74, 130, 140, 145, 152, 153, 166, 179, 180, 195, 224, 257, 301, 308, 317, 459–60

Askins, Mary Goldworthy (wife of Dr John Askins): 15, 31, 33, 38, 39, 42, 43, 58, 73, 74, 80, 116,

Askins, Mary Goldworthy (*continued*)
145, 152, 153, 156, 179, 191,
200, 202–19, 229–30, 290, 306,
308, 311, 459, 470
Askins, Mollie Whaddon (wife of
Dr Robert Askins): 460
Askins, Peony ("The Brat")
(daughter of Dr & Mrs John
Askins): 31, 153, 200, 459
Askins, Dr Robert (brother of Mrs
Moore): 3, 116, 202–18, 222,
229–30, 252, 279, 312, 324, 460
Askins, Sarah: *see* Mrs Sarah Horan
Askins, Rev. William James (father
of Mrs Moore): 3, 156, 459, 460
Askins, Rev. William James
("Willie", brother of Mrs Moore):
3, 229–30, 281, 306, 312, 460
Asquith, Herbert Henry: 34, 143–4
Asquith, Margot: *The
Autobiography of Margot
Asquith*, 124, 136; men. 27, 34
Austen, Jane: *Emma*, 66, 306; men.
132, 319
Atlantis: 15, 355
Ausonius: 109
Bach, Johann Sebastian: *Coffee
Cantata*, 389; men. 34, 148
Bach Choir: 135, 148, 329, 474
Bacon, Francis: 132, 146, 147, 244,
406
Baconian Theory: 132
Bailey, Cyril: 33–34, 135, 319
Baker, Leo: rehearsing for Wycherley
play, 26–27; Barfield on his past
life, 30; on first Canto of
"Dymer", 32–33; in ballet, 34; on
Myth in "Dymer", 35; audition at
Old Vic, 36–37; symbolism in
"Dymer", 42; on L being a junior
dean, 46; overworked, 47; nervous
breakdown, 54; Mrs Moore
looks after him, 56–57; lack of
kindliness, 57; more human, 58;
compared to Barfield, 67; his viva,
72; his horoscope, 73–74; meets
Vaughan Williams, 74–75;
tendency to caricature, 77;
entertains L in London, 93–95;

his lack of "chat", 78; living in
London, 156–57; conversation
contrasted with Harwood's, 253;
why L's friendship suspended,
301; writes to L about
misunderstanding, 317; L visits in
London, 336–37; biography, 460;
men. 29, 35, 38, 39, 40–41, 43,
49, 63, 76, 87, 99, 100, 101, 107,
112, 138, 154, 155, 163, 185,
234, 245
Baker, Miss: 391
Baldwin, Stanley: 384, 388, 389,
393, 395
Balfour, Arthur James: *Theism and
Humanism*, 283; *Theism and
Thought*, 283
Barbour, John: *The Bruce*, 216
Barfield, Mrs Matilda (Maud):
156–57, 228, 259, 277, 301, 438,
439, 455, 461
Barfield, Owen: sub-editor of
Beacon, 27; accepts L's "Joy" for
Beacon, 28; his holiday in Italy,
30; in ballet, 34; considers dancing
career, 37–38; on "Christina
Dreams", 39; his pessimism, 40;
his "Tower", 52–53; on fancy and
imagination, 59; dances in field,
60; meets Mrs Moore, 65–66; his
charm, 74; engaged, 156–57; on
L's poetry, 185–87; "when one is
afraid that one may not be a great
man after all", 194; meets his
future wife, 228; impressed by
Rudolf Steiner, 254; discussion
about women, 277–78; visits L in
Oxford, 299–301; his office at
Truth, 340; reads *Prometheus* with
L, 438–39; with his sisters, 455;
biography, 460–61; *Owen
Barfield on C. S. Lewis*, 461;
Poetic Diction, 461; *Romanticism
Comes of Age*, 461; *Saving the
Appearances*, 461; *The Silver
Trumpet*, 275; *This Ever Diverse
Pair*, 461; *Unancestral Voice*, 461;
Voice of Cecil Harwood (ed.), 53,
147, 339; *What Coleridge*

Thought, 461; *Worlds Apart*, 461; men. 29, 35, 56, 57, 61, 146, 190, 191, 192, 259, 276, 338, 368, 392, 431, 434, 465

Barrie, Sir James: *Admirable Crichton*, 37; *Mary Rose*, 352; *Shall We Join the Ladies?*, 107; men. 76

Barton, Rev. Arthur: 172

Bateson, Fredrick Wilse: 236–37, 240, 291, 320–21

Bateson, William: 128, 228

Battle of Maldon: 144, 230, 231

Bayliss, Lilian: 63, 72

Beacon, The: 27, 28, 29, 30, 185, 286, 311

Beardsley, Aubrey Vincent: 59, 410

Beattie, George Liddell Caruthers: 349, 351, 354

Beaumont, Francis: *see* under John Fletcher

Beckett, Sir Eric: 56, 84, 87, 102, 157, 191, 234, 274, 275, 304–6, 324, 325, 340, 461

Beethoven, Ludwig van: "Kreutzer Sonata", 94; *Mass in D*, 329; men. 134, 138, 259

Belial: 456

Bellock, Hilaire: *Mr Emanuel Burden*, 365

Benecke, Paul Victor Mendelssohn: 83, 383, 386, 389, 394, 412, 416, 417, 451, 452, 454, 475–76

Bennett, Arnold: *Human Machine*, 176

Bentham, Jeremy: 319

Bentley, Richard: 441

Beowulf: 135, 136–37, 138, 140, 176, 196, 230

Bergson, Henri: *Energie Spirituelle*, 285; *L'Évolution Créatrice*, 269; *Matière et Mémoire*, 349; men. 128, 132, 224, 278, 293, 439

Berkeley, George: *Principles of Human Knowledge*, 332; men. 185, 329, 350, 394, 400, 414

Berlioz, Hector: 177

Berners, John Bourchier: *Chronicles of Froissart*, 399

Betjeman, John: 380, 386, 394–95, 399, 401, 402, 406, 410, 411, 412, 427, 433, 434–35, 436, 437, 440, 442, 447, 448, 450–51, 453, 456

Bibesco, Princess: 27

Biggs, Joan: 46

Birkenhead, first Earl of: 389, 390

Bizet, Georges: *Carmen*, 95

Blackmore, Richard: *Lorna Doone*, 364

Blackwood, Algernon: 76, 327

Blake, Leonard: 458

Blake, William: 190

Blakiston, Rev. Herbert Edward: 319, 328

Blockley, Rev. Thomas Trotter: 451

Blunt, Henry Pyot: 25, 26, 29, 30, 33, 36, 41, 46, 47

Boccaccio, Giovanni: *Decameron*, 244; *Filostrato*, 120, 123

Boddington, Hubert Cecil: 384, 385, 397, 398, 400, 408

Boethius: 134

Borrier: 110

Bosanquet, Bernard: *Philosophical Theory of the State*, 41; *Suggestions in Ethics*, 323; men. 240, 415

Boswell, James: *Life of Samuel Johnson*, 164; men. 18, 44, 254, 336, 437

Botticelli, Sandro: 95

Bourdillon, Robert Benedict: 223

Bowen, Edmund John: 292, 329

Boyd, Mr: 170

Boyd, Molly: 163, 166, 168, 170, 171

Boyd, Molly (daughter): 170, 171

Boyd, Dot: 170, 171

"Boys' Names": x, 74, 278, 289

Bradley, Francis Herbert: *Appearance and Reality*, 74, 350; men. 50, 83, 240, 350

Bradley, Henry: *Making of English*, 432

Bradley, Kenneth Grenville (L's pupil): 350, 352, 355

Brett-Smith, Herbert Francis: 247, 256, 445

Bridges, Robert: *New Poems*, 442–43; men. 26, 137, 249, 352

Brightman, Rev. Frank Edward: *The English Rite*, 387; men. 387, 402, 408

British Museum: 335–36

Brontë, Charlotte: *Jane Eyre*, 359; *Shirley*, 350

Brontë, Emily: 408

Brown, John: 307

Browne, Sir Thomas: *Urn Burial*, 332; men. 332

Browning, Elizabeth Barrett: *Sonnets from the Portuguese*, 311

Browning, Robert: *Ring and the Book*, 272–73, 288, 297; *Sordello*, 53; men. 473

Bruce: see Barbour

Bryson, John Norman: 58, 358

Buchan, John: *Path of the King*, 415

Buchanan, Edward Handasyde: 350, 352

Buckley, Charles Douglas: 348, 354, 356

Buffalo Bill: 176

Bunyan, John: *Pilgrim's Progress*, 312, 327; men. 244

Burns, Gilbert Talbot: 211, 216

Burns, Robert: 125

Burton, Richard: *Anatomy of Melancholy*, 113, 456

Butler, Samuel ("Hudibras Butler"): 395

Butler, Samuel ("Erewhon Butler"): *Erewhon*, 276, 315; *Erewhon Revisited*, 426

Butler, Theobald: 1, 51, 55

Byrd, William: 34

Byron, Lord George Gordon: *Beppo*, 229; *Childe Harold's Pilgrimage*, 249; *Don Juan*, 44, 132, 235, 241, 286; *Vision of Judgment*, 229; men. 45

Cahen, Andrée: 78, 79, 80–81, 84–85, 87, 88, 89, 90, 91, 92–93, 95, 96, 98, 99, 100, 103, 232

Caird, Edward: 470

Calwell, Miss: 162

Campagnac, Ernest Trafford: *Cambridge Platonists*, 281

Campbell, Archibald Hunter: 414

Campbell, John Colquhoun (pupil at Magdalen): 436, 442, 448, 451

Campbell, John Edward (of Hertford College): 353

Campbell, Ralph Abercrombie: 350, 354–55

Cambellian, The: 467

Candide: see Voltaire

Capron, Robert ("Oldy"): 342, 343

Capron, Wynyard: 342

Carl Rosa Opera Company: 138

Carlyle, Alexander James: *History of Mediaeval Political Theory in the West* (with R. W. Carlyle), 461; men. 114–15, 117, 118, 125, 126, 150–51, 187, 222, 225, 291, 301–2, 328, 355, 398, 450, 461

Carlyle, Sir Robert Warrand: *History of Mediaeval Theory in the West* (with A. J. Carlyle), 461

Carlyle, Thomas: *French Revolution*, 262; men. 48

Carr, Herbert Wildon: trans., *Mind-Energy*, 285

Carritt, Edgar Frederick: *Ethical and Political Thinking; Philosophies of Beauty; Theory of Beauty*, 464; men. 25, 30, 33, 36, 37, 39, 40, 41, 43, 45, 46, 49–50, 51, 53, 55, 77, 83, 87, 107, 108, 127, 150–51, 184, 187–88, 222, 223, 229, 230, 234, 242–43, 271, 278, 280, 284, 292–93, 299, 301–2, 303–4, 311, 318, 320, 328, 329, 335, 348, 350, 398, 403–4, 461–62

Carroll, Lewis: *Alice's Adventures in Wonderland*, 359

Carter, Rev. Cyril Robert: 387, 409, 419, 420–21, 445

Carter, Nancy: 380

Catlin, Sir George: 330–31, 333

Cato: 134

Catullus: 192, 193

Cecil, Lord David: 413

Chanson de Roland: 74

Chaliapin, Fedor Ivanovich: 94

Chapman, George: *Bussy D'Ambois*, 155; *Iliads*, 221

Chaucer, Geoffrey: *Boke of the Duchesse*, 117; *Canterbury Tales*, 123, 124, 125, 126, 127, 453, 462; *Hous of Fame*, 122; *Legende of Good Women*, 123; *Troylus and Cryseyde*, 119, 120, 121, 123, 245, 462; men. 118, 125, 130–31, 134, 235, 241, 242, 243, 366, 452

Cherbourg School: 264

Chesterston, Gilbert Keith: *Bernard Shaw*, 420; *Browning*, 108, 297; *Club of Queer Trades*, 395; *Eugenics and Other Evils*, 412; *St Francis*, 297; *Lunatic at Large*, 400; *Magic*, 34, 35

Childe, Rowland: 149, 194

Childs, William Macbride: 54–55

Chopin, Frédéric: 134

Christ: 128, 141, 183, 355

"Christina Dreams": 20, 28, 57, 82, 84, 411, 418, 432

Chrysippus: 335

Churchill, Sir Winston: 389, 393

Chute, Rev. Anthony William: 384, 389, 390, 450

Cicero: *De Finibus*, 66; *De Natura Deorum*, 47; men. 468

Cinderella: 85

Clarendon, Edward Hyde: *True Historical Narrative of the Rebellion and Civil War in England*, 113

Clark, Leonard Ernle (L's pupil): 383, 389, 395, 399, 402, 407

Clarke, Rev. Alured George: 21, 41

Clarke, Studdert: 244

Coccles, H.: 75

Cochran, Sir Charles Blake: 337

Coghill, Sir Egerton Bushe: 462

Coghill, Sir Jocelyn: 194

Coghill, Nevill: trans., *Canterbury Tales*, 462; trans., *Troilus and Criseyde*, 462; men. 189–91, 192–95, 201, 211, 221, 236, 240–42, 243, 244, 245, 249, 257, 285, 329, 333–34, 357, 379, 410, 413–14, 453, 462

Colbourne, Joan Elizabeth: 380, 387, 394, 401, 409, 410, 414

Coleridge, Samuel Taylor: *Ancient Mariner*, 241, 253; men. xi, 128, 256, 432

Colvin, Sidney: *John Keats*, 225, 228

Conrad, Joseph: *Chance*, 372, 374; *Lord Jim*, 415; *Typhoon*, 226; men. 53

Corneille, Pierre: 144, 189

Coué, Émile: 50, 72

Courthope, William John: 402, 457

Cowie, Miss G. E.: 37

Cowley, Abraham: 184

Cowley, Arthur Ernest: 401, 437, 457

Cowper, William: *The Task*, 362, 366, 367; men. 238, 240

Cox, Harold Henry: 351, 353, 355, 400, 403, 414

Crabbe, George: 238, 240, 266

Craig, Edith: 26, 35

Craig, Edwin Stewart (of Magdalen): 384, 386, 388, 389, 391, 422, 423, 439, 444, 445, 450, 476–77

Craig, Sir James: 416

Craig, Lady: 416

Craigie, Sir William Alexander: *Icelandic Reader*, 440; men. 247, 256

"Cranny": *see* F. W. Macran

Crichton-Miller, Hugh: *New Psychology and the Teacher*, 62, 63

Criterion: 410

Croce, Benedetto: *Essence of Aesthetic*, 39; men. 36, 197, 304, 321, 404, 470

Cullen, Mary ("Witch of Endor"): 178

Cura Pastoralis: 128

Currie, John Alexander: 46, 49, 150

Curtis, Geoffrey William Seymour: 33–34, 53, 125, 126, 135, 150, 188, 197, 271, 293, 303, 328, 332

Dante, Alighieri: *Divine Comedy*, 126, 260, 342, 449; men. 40

Darlow, Rev. Thomas Herbert: 185

Darlow, Thomas Sherrock: 151, 185, 186, 190, 191, 192–94, 201

David, Rev. Albert Augustus: 442

Davie, Keith Maitland: 125

Dawnay, Alan Geoffrey: 408

Dawson, John Hill Mackintosh: 125,

Dawson, John Hill Mackintosh
(*continued*)
150, 188, 328, 335, 351, 352, 354,
355, 356
Day, Thomas: *Sandford and Merton,*
278
De Bergerac, Bernice: *Glorious
England,* 38, 72, 76, 78
De Burgh, William George: 54–55
De la Mare, Walter: *Ding Dong Bell,*
334; *The Return,* 135, 219; *The
Veil,* 52, 161; men. 60, 185, 186,
291, 317, 320, 379
De Natura Deorum: see Cicero
De Peyer, Eric Clarence Evelyn: 383,
389, 395, 399, 402, 407
De Selincourt, Ernest: ed.,
Wordsworth's *Prelude,* 381, 385,
386
De Villiers, Iris: 99, 100
Debussy, Claude: *La Cathédrale
Engloutie,* 57
Dee, Dr John: 244
Dekker, Thomas: 472
Delanges, Maurice: 261, 262–66,
267
Democrat: 20
Democritus: 423
Denham, Sir John: *Cooper's Hill,*
455
Dent, Joseph Malaby: 395
Descartes, René: *Meditations,*
399–400; men. 281, 401, 402
Deverill, John: 93
Dial: 410
Dickens, Charles: *David
Copperfield,* 310, 311, 312, 344;
Nicholas Nickelby, 15; men. 320
Dickinson, Goldsworthy Lowes: *The
Magic Flute,* 112
Dictionary of National Biography
(D. N. B.): 292, 416
Dill, Sir Samuel: *Roman Society,* 159
Dionysius of Halicarnassus: 109
Dionysus (the god): 55
Discussion Class: 151, 184–85,
189–90, 192–94, 200–201, 210–
11, 220–21, 236–37, 240–41, 464
Disney, Sydney Cecil William
("Diz"): 381, 382, 419, 421

Disraeli, Benjamin: 22
Dixon, Arthur Lee: 386, 477–78
Dobrée, Bonamy: 473
Dodds, Eric Robertson: 51, 54–55,
62, 108
Donald, Douglas Alexander: 335,
349, 351, 354
Donne, John: *Progresse of the Soule,*
181; *Second Anniversary,* 181;
men. 123, 167, 183, 185, 339, 456
Doughty, Charles Montagu: *The
Cliffs,* 249; men. 57
Douglas, Gavin: *Aeneid,* 394; *Palice
of Honour,* 395; men. 394, 405
Douglas Scheme: 277
Douie, Mrs: 277
Driver, Sir Godfrey: 387, 409, 417,
445, 449, 451
Driver, Mrs Godfrey: 450
Dryden, John: *Astraea Redux,* 196;
men. xii, 256, 457
Dublin Society for the Prevention of
Cruelty to Animals: 458
Dunbar, William: "Lament for the
Makaris", 141; men. 387, 388
Dunciad: see Pope
Earp, Thomas Wade: 149, 194
Edda (Younger) (Icelandic saga):
441, 448
Edward, Prince (later Edward VIII):
472
Edwards, John Robert: 335
Elgar, William: *Grania and Diarmid,*
135
Elgin Marbles, the: 335–36
Eliot, George: *Middlemarch,* 262
Eliot, T. S.: 409–10, 411, 413–14,
418, 470
Ellis, Havelock: *Kanga Creek,* 226;
Studies in the Psychology of Sex,
45, 75; *World of Dreams,* 44;
men. 285
Elton, Oliver: *Sheaf of Papers,* 288
Elyot, Sir Thomas: *Boke named the
Governour,* 404, 406, 416–17;
Titus and Gisippus, 405; men.
406, 422, 423
Emerson, Ralph Waldo: 133, 153
Emmet, Rev. Cyril William: 135, 187,
273, 329

English Review, The: 19, 50

Eothen: see Kinglake

Erasmus, Desiderius: *Institutio Principis Christiani*, 422; *Institutio Regis Christiana*, 416

Ervine, St John: *Alice and a Family*, 363

Ethics: see Aristotle

Euphorion: 131

Euripides: *Heracleidae*, 295; *Hippolytus*, 296, 299; men. 54

Evans, Valerie: 315, 345–46, 407, 411, 416

Eve: 361

Ewart, Charles Gordon: 168, 171, 173, 465

Ewart, Charlotte Hope: 465

Ewart, Isabella Kelso ("Kelsie"): 105, 158, 159–60, 174, 463

Ewart, Lily Greeves: 158, 165, 168, 171, 173, 463

Ewart, Lady Mary ("Cousin Mary"): 146, 159–60, 162, 462–63

Ewart, Mary Gundreda ("Gunny"): 105, 158, 159–60, 167, 463

Ewart, Robert Heard: 159–60, 162, 168, 463

Ewart, Sir William Quartus: 462–63

Ewing, Alfred Cecil: 108, 233, 235, 245, 271, 285, 293, 296, 299, 303, 322, 328, 351, 354, 379, 398

Fairfax, Edward: trans., *Jerusalem Delivered*, 267

Fairfax, Robert: 123

Fall of the Angels: 177, 231, 399, 436

Falle, Major: 342

Faranby, Giles: 34

Farquharson, Arthur Spenser Loat: 38, 43, 58, 80, 81, 117, 118, 187, 191, 222, 287–88, 292–93, 299, 318, 319, 320, 329, 353, 354, 398, 408, 450, 463–64

Fasnacht, George Eugène: 49, 53, 125, 135, 149–50, 189, 197–200, 293, 300, 303, 328, 335, 428

Fausset, Hugh: 429, 434

Featherstone, Miss: 15, 18, 21, 23, 29, 32, 47, 69, 110, 112, 114, 216, 217, 228, 234, 252, 253, 288, 322

Felix (the Cat): 391

Fell, Bryan Greg: 398, 409

Fiedler, Hermann George: 408

Fielding, Henry: *Amelia*, xii, 424; *Tom Jones*, 346–47

Firth, Edward Michael Tyndell: 351, 354, 355

Flecker, James Elroy: *Hassan*, 276, 278, 279

Fletcher, John: (with Francis Beaumont) *Faithful Shepherdess*, 172; *Maid's Tragedy*, 153; *Philaster*, 153

Fletcher, Rev. Ronald Frank William: 392

Flower and the Leaf, The: 235

Ford, John: *The Broken Heart*, 153

Forster, E. M.: *Passage to India*, 431

Forrest, John: 463

France, Anatole: *Revolt of the Angels*, 342, 344

Francis of Assisi, St: 303

Frazer, Sir James George: *The Golden Bough*, 170, 379

Frederick the Great: 34

Freeman, John: 398–99

Freud, Sigmund: *Introductory Letters*, 44; men. 41, 45

Friar Bacon: see R. Greene

G. K.'s Weekly: 436

Gadney, Mr: 291

Galsworthy, John: *Forsyte Saga*, 105, 419; *Loyalties*, 107; men. 188

Garrod, Heathcote William: *Wordsworth*, 273, 274

Gawain and the Green Knight: 200, 214

General Strike, the: 384–95, 397, 399, 402–3

Gentile, Giovanni: 351, 354, 470

George V, King: 472

Ghost Train: see A. Ridley

Gibb, Jocelyn: *Light on C. S. Lewis* (ed.): 462

Gibbon, Edward: *Decline and Fall of the Roman Empire*, 285

Gilbert and Sullivan operas: *Pirates of Penzance*, 402; *Ruddigore*, 400–401; men. 477

Giotto: 303

Girdle of Aphrodite: see F. A. Wright
Glasgow, Paul John Weade: 383, 399, 402, 407
Gnomic Verses: 177
Godley, Alfred Denis: *Unpublished Works,* 423, 424
Goethe, Johann Wolfgang: *Dichtung und Wahrheit,* 307; men. 115
Goldsmith, Oliver: *Citizen of the World,* 421; men. 115
Gonner, Sir Edward: 17
Gonner, Lady Nannie: 17, 21, 22, 33, 45, 48, 63, 69, 71, 97, 98, 114, 142, 203, 209, 210, 211, 220, 221, 284–85
Gonner, Sheila: 17, 23, 44, 247
Gorboduc: 189
Gordon, George Stuart: 131, 138, 139, 142, 147, 151, 181, 183, 184–85, 189–90, 192–94, 210–11, 216, 220–21, 236–37, 240–41, 274, 357, 392, 464
Gordon, M. C.: *Life of George S. Gordon,* 184, 464
Gordon-Clark, John Stanley: 350, 352, 355
Gower, John: *Vox Clamantis,* 130; men. 131, 452, 453
Grant, Violet Augusta: 380, 394, 414
Graves, Robert: *Poetic Unreason,* 394; men. 62, 399
Green, Henry: *see* H. V. Yorke
Green, John Richard: *Short History of the English People,* 113
Green, Roger Lancelyn: (with Walter Hooper) *C. S. Lewis: A Biography,* 6
Green, T. H.: 470
Greene, Robert: *Friar Bacon and Friar Bungay,* 380
Greeves, Arthur: L finds "tremendously improved", 57–59; meets Robert Graves, 62; interest in psychology, 63; sketches Barfield, 65; "incorrigible baby after all", 67; his painting, 68–70; punting on the Cherwell, 70–72; family baptism, 71; gluttony, 73; "mania for confession", 74; miserably changed by ideal of "being himself", 256–59;
biography, 464; men. 1–2, 4, 9, 16, 61, 62, 64, 106, 160, 164, 166–67, 169, 172, 177, 247, 252, 275, 463
Greeves, Florrie: 169
Greeves, John (Arthur's brother): 161, 163, 172
Greeves, Joseph (Arthur's father): 63, 69, 71, 161, 464
Greeves, Mary Margretta (Arthur's mother): 73, 105, 161, 166–67, 169, 170, 171, 172, 173, 174, 175, 176–77, 178, 464
Gregory I, Pope St: 449
Gregory, Lady Augusta: 26
Grey, Major: 345
Grundy, George Beardoe: *The Great Persian War,* 20
Haggard, Rider: 327
Haig, Douglas, first Earl Haig: 388
Haig, Edward Felix Gray: 25, 29, 33, 50, 350
Haldane, John Burdon Sanderson: *Daedalus,* 287, 330
Hallam, Arthur: 229
Hamilton, Anne: 159, 174
Hamilton, Augustus Warren ("Uncle Gussie"): 159, 174
Hamilton, Sir Ian: *Gallipoli Diary,* 113
Hamilton, Mary Warren: 462, 470
Hamilton, Robert William (pupil at Magdalen): 380, 386, 398, 401, 405, 410, 414, 442, 448, 451, 453, 456
Hamilton, Ruth: 174
Hamilton, Rev. Thomas Robert: 158, 163, 164, 467, 470
Hamilton-Jenkin, Alfred Kenneth: on Martlets, 31–32; his ill health, 38; on "having every experience", 44; on slang in "Dymer", 45; sees Sophocles in the rain, 55–56; "all roads lead to Cornwall", 56; Cornish mining, 66; "humanitarian" romantics after Rousseau, 67; work on B.Litt., 118; discusses chivalry, 121–22; "delight in the more elementary pleasures", 133–34; visit to

Binsey, 140–42; exhilarating ride to Elsfield, 219–20; dangers of being a scholar, 236; brings mother to tea, 247; on research degrees, 253; his and L's idea for "shocker" play, 266–67; on "homeliness", 272; trip to Switzerland, 329–30; loss of "intellectual gloss", 332–33; on bull fighting, 334; bid for better health, 417; biography, 464–65; men. 28, 35, 68, 119, 123, 125, 126, 133, 139–40, 147, 149, 150, 183, 194, 197–200, 205, 207–8, 209, 212, 218, 232–33, 238, 244, 271, 278, 285, 386; *Cornish Homes and Customs; Cornish Mines; Cornish Seafarers; Cornwall and its People; Cornwall and the Cornish; News from Cornwall; Story of Cornwall*, 465

Hampton Court: 276–77

Handel, George Frederick: *Messiah*, 148, 183

Hankin, Mrs: 113, 114, 115, 116–17, 120, 123, 124, 127

Hansel and Gretel: see Humperdinck

Hardie, Christian: 11

Hardie, Colin: 467

Hardie, William Francis Ross: *A Study in Plato; Aristotle's Ethical Theory*, 465; men. 379, 381, 383, 384, 386, 387, 389, 390, 391, 392, 393–94, 397–98, 400, 402, 403, 404, 405, 408, 411, 412, 413–14, 417, 418, 419, 444, 448, 450, 453, 465

Harding, George: 463

Hardy, Thomas: *Jude the Obscure*, 160, 161; *Tess of the D'Urbervilles*, 196; men. 44

Harper, Annie: 162

Harris, F. R.: 34

Hartmann, Eduard Von: 149

Harwood, Cecil: L visits at Bee Cottage, 38; "danced with joy" over "Dymer", 40; at Parson's Pleasure, 41–42; "original, quaint and catchy" poems, 52–53; discusses Doughty, 57; L visits, 59–60; distressed at leaving Bee Cottage, 65; his poetry, 147; Aunt Lily on his poetry, 148; Epithalamion for Barfield, 228; R. Steiner "made the burden roll from his back", 253–55; in love, 258–60; L visits in London, 274–77; visits L in Oxford, 278; with L to Stanton Harcourt, 304–6; visits L, 324–6; takes L to British Museum and Anthroposophical Society, 335–40; his son John, 405; biography, 460–61, 465; *Recovery of Man in Childhood*, 465; *Shakespeare's Prophetic Mind*, 465; *Voice of Cecil Harwood* (ed. Owen Barfield), 53, 147, 326, 339; *Way of a Child*, 465; men. 47, 56, 57, 61, 66, 117, 169, 185, 234–35, 288, 352, 392, 441, 452, 454

Harwood, Daphne (née Daphne Olivier): 274–75, 338–39, 405, 465

Harwood, George: 437

Harwood, John Oliver: 405

Hassal, Arthur: *European History Chronologically Arranged*, 129

Hassan: see J. E. Flecker

Hastings, John Maurice: 25, 29, 33

Hatton, W. K.: 436, 457

Havelock: 184

Havergall, Frances: 396

Hawes, Commander: 85–86, 94, 95, 96, 99–103, 170

Hawes, Maisie ("Moppie"): 85–86, 88, 91, 92, 93, 94, 95, 96–97, 98–104, 107, 108, 109, 110, 112, 113, 137–38, 157, 180, 181, 232, 262

Hawes, Mrs ("The Bitch"): 85–86, 95, 96, 98–103, 137–38

Hawker, Gerald Wynne: 348–49, 353, 354, 355

Hay, Ian: *A Man's Man*, 96

Hegel, Georg Wilhelm Friedrich: 112

Heitland, William: 43

Helen (of Troy): 238

Henderson, Kenneth David Druitt: 351, 353, 355, 414–15
Henry VI, King: 294
Henryson, Robert: *Testament of Cresseid*, 235
Herod: 157
Herodotus: *History*, 24, 25, 274, 276
Hesiod: 109
Hetherington, William Dixon: 380, 386, 392, 398, 401, 405–6, 410, 414, 436, 441–42, 448, 451, 456
Hewlett, Maurice: *Fool Errant*, 286; *Lore of Proserpine*, 411
Heyn, Maurice: 170
Hicks, Sir William Joynson: 390
Hilary, Sister: 102–3
Hillier, Bevis: *Young Betjeman*, 379, 437
Hinckley, Veronica: 68, 70, 71–72
Hinckley, Mrs: 68, 76, 427, 430
Hingley, R. H.: *Psycho-analysis*, 70
Hichens, Dr: 202, 203
Hobbes, Thomas: 189, 191, 343
Hobhouse, Leonard Trelawny: 354
Hoby, Sir Thomas: *Courtyer of Count Baldessar Castilio*, 416, 419, 420
Hoccleve, Thomas: 388, 398
Höffding, Harald: 352
Hogg, Robert Heuzé: 348, 354, 356
Holmes, Bobbie: 325
Holmes, Joy: 325, 340
Holmes, Mrs: 324–25
Holst, Gustav Theodore: 55
Homer: *Iliad*, 182; *Odyssey*, 104–5; men. 335
Honorius III, Pope: 303
Hood, John Douglas Lloyd: 441
Hooker, Richard: *Laws of Ecclesiastical Politie*, 406, 407; men. 429
Hooper, Walter: (with Roger Lancelyn Green) *C. S. Lewis: A Biography*, 6
Hope, Edward: 475, 478
Horace: *Satires*, 444; men. 147
Horan, Mrs Sarah (sister of Mrs Moore): 3, 17

House, Elizabeth: 380
Housman, Laurence: *Trimblerigg*, 451
Hudson, William Henry: xi
Hugo, Victor: 110
Hugon, Marianne Cecile Gabrielle: 71–72, 85
Hume, David: *An Enquiry Concerning the Principles of Morals*, 51; men. 185, 332, 350, 401
Hume-Rothery, Mrs: 220, 364
Humperdinck, Engelbert: *Hansel and Gretel*
Hurd, Richard: 235
Huxley, Aldous: *Antic Hay*, 329; *Crome Yellow*, 44
Huxley, Thomas Henry: "Ethics and Evolution", 282
Ibsen, Henrik: *Peer Gynt*, 37, 350–51
Inge, Rev. William Ralph: *Outspoken Essays*, 158, 168
Irish Statesman: 453
Isaiah: 327
Isocrates: 468
J. A.: *see* J. A. Smith
Jacks, Leonard Pearsall: 267
Jacks, Maurice Leonard: 59
James I of Scotland, King: *Kingis Quair*, 375
James, Henry: *Roderick Hudson*, 279; *Turn of the Screw*, 58, 62, 63, 66
James, William: *Varieties of Religious Experience*, 48, 49, 50
Jefferies, Richard: xi
Jeffrey, Mrs John: 103, 200, 252
Jellicoe, Rev. John Basil Lee: 390, 391, 392, 393
Joachin, Harold Henry: *Study of the Ethics of Spinoza*, 351; men. 33–34, 131
Joan of Arc, St: 190
Job: 221
Johnson, Harold Cottam (University College): 353, 355
Johnson, Patrick (Magdalen College): 454
Johnson, Dr Samuel: *Life of Waller*,

455; *Lives of the Poets*, 184, 235;
Rasselas, 110–11; men. 185, 244,
396

Johnston, Bridget: 379–80

Jones, Elias Henry: *Road to Endor*,
34–35

Jonson, Ben: *The Alchemist*, 144;
men. 121

Joseph, Horace William Brindley:
Introduction to Logic, 54; men.
76–77, 131, 234

Jowett, Benjamin: 32, 449, 474

Jowett Society: 300, 397

Joyce, James: *Ulysses*, 135

Judith: 149

Jung, Carl Gustave: *Analytical
Psychology*, 63

Juvenal: 47

Kalevala: 424–25, 437

Kant, Immanuel: *Ethics*, 353; men.
32, 33, 36, 96, 109, 299, 348,
349, 354, 355, 477

Kaufman, George Adams von: 338

Kaufman, Mrs George Adams von:
338

Keats, John: *Eve of St Agnes*, 228;
Isabella, 228; *To a Nightingale*,
198; men. 114, 135, 143, 225, 228

Keefe, Carolyn: 335

Keir, Sir David Lindsay: *Cases in
Constitutional Law;
Constitutional History of Modern
Britain*, 466; men. 150, 187,
197–200, 349, 350, 353, 354,
355, 385, 391, 397, 398, 400,
404, 409, 442, 444, 451, 465–66

Kemshead, Chaloner Thomas Taplin:
144–45

Ker, William Paton: *Essays on
Medieval Literature*, 123

Kilmore Cathedral: 460

King, Grace: 116, 229

King, Richard Henry: 150, 293, 303,
328, 335

Kingis Quair: see James I

Kinglake, Alexander William:
Eothen, 344

Kipling, Rudyard: *Puck of Pook's
Hill*, 341; 59, 96, 341

Kirk, Rev. Kenneth Escott: 320

Kirkpatrick, William Thompson
("Kirk"): xi, 249, 274, 307, 351,
432, 436, 466

Kolbitár (Icelandic Society): 440,
449, 453

Ku Klux Klan: 255

Lamb, Charles: 344

Lamb, Mary: 353

Landon, Philip Aislabie: 319

Langland, William: *Piers Plowman*,
134; men. 190, 242

Lawrence, Thomas Edward: 84, 305

Lawson, Frederick Henry:
*Constitutional and Administrative
Law; Negligence in the Civil Law;
Oxford Law School 1850–1965*,
466; men. 349, 350, 351, 353,
354, 385, 391, 397, 400, 404,
409, 417, 466

Lee, Margaret Lucy: 392

Lee, Stephen: 475, 478–79

Legouis, Emile: 123

Leibniz, Gottfried Wilhelm:
Monadologie, 321; *Sur
L'Entendement Humain*, 321;
Systeme Nouveau, 321; men. 352

Leonard, William Ellery: *Two Lives*,
418

Leslie, Gladys: 169

Lessing, Gotthold Ephraim: 147

Lewis, Albert (father of L): is told
about Mrs Moore, 2; on Mrs
Moore, 8–9; tells L "stay on" in
Oxford; 39; "at his best", 105–6;
Christmas 1922 with Warnie and
L, 157–78; offers to keep L in
Oxford "some years longer",
250–51; L's pleasant visit
September–October 1923,
270–71; L visits December 1923,
280; L asks for help, 287; offers
L what is necessary, 291; his
unhappy nature, 323; news of
L's appointment to Magdalen,
357–58; L's visit home in
September 1925, 378; last
Christmas with both sons, 425;
biography, 466–67; men. 4, 5, 6,
7, 16, 24, 36, 40, 52, 62, 69, 73,
76, 83, 84, 88, 121, 139, 143,

Lewis, Albert (*continued*)
155, 195, 223, 234, 246, 280, 288, 297, 407, 416, 430, 471
Lewis, Clive Staples (Jack): Owen Barfield on, ix–xiii; comes up to Oxford; 1; meets the Moores, 2, 3; promise to Paddy Moore, 4; in Battle of Arras, 5; return to Oxford, 6; shares home with Moores, 7; his friendship with Mrs Moore, 8–9; his diary, 10; preparing for exams in Greats, 15; begins *Dymer*, 15; revising Roman and Greek history, 16–21; talks theology with "Cranny", 22; return to Warneford Road, 23; more revision for Greats, 24–26; calls on Leo Baker, 26–27; walk with Hamilton-Jenkin, 28–29; on "l'art pour l'art", 29; talks to Barfield of *Beacon*, 30; a new version of "Psyche", 30–31; curses J. C. Squire, 32–33; sees Barfield dance, 34; myth in "Dymer", 35; tutors advise to "stay up another year", 36, 37; on Harwood, 38; discusses "Christina Dreams" and Barfield's pessimism, 39–40; asks for tutorial work, 41; erotic passage in "Dymer", 42; hopes for job tutoring, 43; reads Freud, 44; reads Havelock Ellis, 44–45; exams in Greats, 46–49; on the subconscious, 50; misery and depression, 51; Barfield "has forgotten more than I ever knew", 52–53; advertises for pupils, 53; sees *Antigone* in Greek, 54–56; finds Arthur Greeves "tremendously improved", 57–58; at Bee Cottage with Barfield and Harwood, 59–61; begins tutoring Miss Wiblin, 61; fails to get job at Reading, 62; walks with Arthur, 63–64; entertains Barfield, 65–66; "Barfield towers above us all", 67; dissertation on moral values, 68; with Arthur, 69–73; preparation for viva, 74–77; on outdoor theatrical, 78; the move to "Hillsboro", 79–80; a First in Greats, 81; Warnie meets the Moores, 82; Miss Wiblin in love with L, 82; Warnie's attempt to get L to Ireland, 83–84; Maisie Hawes's problems, 85–86; Warnie at "Hillsboro", 87–93; visits Leo Baker, 93–95; Baker's prediction that L's "chimney stack would turn into a spire", 94; trouble with Mr Raymond, 96–97; "no pleasure bad in itself", 98; helps Maisie Hawes escape, 99–104; visits father, 105–6; with Warnie in London, 107; tries for Magdalen fellowship in Philosophy, 108–10; "English language has completed its cycle", 111; "hungry for peace and quiet", 112; reads Milton for English School, 113–17; tutored by F. P. Wilson and E. E. Wardale, 118–19; first term of lectures in English School, 120–29; dislike of Percy Simpson, 130; visits Aunt Lily, 131–33; reads *Piers Plowman*, 134; hears Bach Choir, 135–36; house hunting, 137; hears Carl Rosa Company, 138; on "The Cad", 139–40; fear of death, 141–42; Aunt Lily, 143–44; "loathed female sex", 145; depression, 146; the rest of Michaelmas Term, 147–57; at Little Lea for Christmas 1922, 157–78; work on "Dymer", 179–80; John Donne and the poets, 181–84; T. S. Darlow and the English Discussion Class, 184–85; Barfield on his poetry, 185–87; Martlets, 187–88; meets Nevill Coghill, 189–91; Discussion Class, 192–95; Cranny's atheism, 196; a Martlets discussion, 197–200; the Doc's madness, 201–19; search for a job, 220–24; Aunt Lily's "abominable confession", 224–25; tries to borrow from Warnie, 226–27; Doc's death,

229–30; move to "Hillsboro",
230–34; a "modern Ariosto"
romance, 235; Discussion Class,
236–37; thinks of writing horror
play, 238–39; nicknamed "Heavy
Lewis", 240; on Nevill Coghill,
241–42; takes English Schools,
243–45; "rage against poverty",
246; discusses exams, 247–50;
Oxford houses he has lived in,
252–53; Harwood on Rudolf
Steiner, 254–55; viva in English,
255–56; First in English, 257;
Arthur Greeves tries "being
himself", 257–58; Harwood a
"real sunbeam", 259–60; on
Maurice Delanges, 261–65;
"creative years slipping past", 265;
"pleasures of death", 265; version
of the Cupid and Psyche story,
266; idea for shocker play,
266–67; Maureen's music,
268–69; visits father, Sept. 1923,
270–71; feels for Ireland, 270–71;
thinks of doing B.Litt., 272; Sir
Michael Sadler helps, 273–74;
visits Harwood, 274–77; visits
Barfield and wife, 277–78;
difference between men and
women, 278; visits Ireland, 279;
considers D.Phil. on Henry More,
280–88; chicken-pox, 285–86; on
Lord Byron, 286; college fees, 287;
visits from Pasleys, 289–90; Henry
More, 290–92; viva in English,
291; possibility of fellowship at
Trinity, 293–94; Aunt Lily
discovers secret of creation,
295–96; on G. K. Chesterton,
297; writes "Hegemony of Moral
Values", 298–99; visit from
Barfield, 300–301; reads
Alexander's Space, Time and
Deity, 301; visits Aunt Lily,
302–3; walk with Harwood and
Beckett, 304–6; family holiday in
Clevedon, 306–18; on George
Moore, 307–8; dines at Trinity,
319–20; offered teaching at
University College, 320–21;

personal element in poetry, 321;
Philosophical Society, 322;
nervous irritation, 323–24;
Harwood restores to sanity,
324–26; pains of animals, 325;
Christian idea of heaven, 327;
reading for Univ. job, 329;
Postgraduate Philosophical Society,
330–31; Wordsworth's Prelude,
333; H. G. Wells at All Souls,
333–34; the Elgin Marbles,
335–36; sees Leo Baker in As You
Like It, 336–37; The Valkyrie,
339; visits Warnie in Colchester,
341–44; on Anatole France, 344;
on Macaulay, 344–45; corrects
School Certificates, 344–45; on
Fielding, 346; on Tom Jones, 347;
tutorials and lectures at University
College, 348–56; made Fellow
of Magdalen, 357–58; family
holiday on Exmoor, 358–77; on
Evolutionary Theory, 361; dialects
in literature, 363; visits father,
378; tutorials at Magdalen and
Lady Margaret Hall, 379–83; has
John Betjeman as pupil, 380; the
General Strike, 384–95; meets
J. R. R. Tolkien, 392–93;
psychoanalytic principles, 394;
on self-examination, 396; Mrs
Moore's "raging temper",
396–97; John Freeman's poems,
398–99; on modern poets, 399;
Gilbert and Sullivan, 400–401;
ideas in "crumbling state", 401;
Betjeman in bedroom slippers,
401; visit from Warnie, 402–3;
hears Samuel Alexander, 403–4;
reads Renaissance writers, 406;
on jealousy, 407; humour of
J. A. Smith, 408; "Eliotic" poems,
409–11; invention of Rollo and
Bridget Considine, 413–14;
Conrad's Lord Jim, 425; meets
Sir James Craig, 416; beauty of
Magdalen, 418; Mrs Moore looks
at a house, 418–19; "sense of 'an
other'", 419; teaches Mrs Moore
badminton, 420; re-reads Well at

Lewis, Clive Staples (*continued*)
the World's End, 421–22;
Fielding's *Amelia*, 424; he and
Warnie have last Christmas with
father, 425; *Dymer* published,
425; reads for School Certificates,
427–28; review of *Dymer*, 429;
begins "King of Drum", 430;
thoughts in "unholy muddle",
431–32; on God and Satan in
Paradise Lost, 433; writes more
"King of Drum", 434; difficulty of
Old English, 435–36; Betjeman's
tea party, 437; reads *Prometheus*
with Barfield, 438; "playing the
devil" with his nerves, 439–40;
reads the *Younger Edda*, 441;
Paradise Lost—"wonderful stuff",
442; Aunt Lily's courage, 444;
hatred of Mermaid Club, 445;
Betjeman's essay a "pure fake",
447; Trench's *Study of Words*,
448; "passion for things Norse",
448; degrading of pure
imagination into facts, 449;
"whether God can understand his
own necessity", 450; on Laurence
Housman, 451; dislike of OUDS's
Lear, 452; meeting of Kolbítar,
453; college election, 454; meets
Barfield's sisters, 455; work on
"King of Drum", 455–56;
Mermaid Club "sons of Belial",
456–57; "Is there never to be any
peace or comfort?" and end of
diary, 457
BOOKS: *Christian Reflections*, 464;
Dymer, xii, 340, 425, 427, 429,
430, 436, 438, 444, 446, 453,
455; *English Literature in the
Sixteenth Century*, 475; *Letters of
C. S. Lewis*, x, 2, 3, 5, 6, 251, 287,
316; *Narrative Poems*, 456;
Poems, 403; *Preface to Paradise
Lost*, 433; *Queen of Drum*, 456;
Selected Literary Essays, 192;
Spirits in Bondage, 4, 21, 125,
222; *Surprised by Joy*, xi, 15, 249,
311, 342, 379, 458, 459, 461,
462, 463, 464, 465, 467–68; *They
Stand Together*, 2, 9, 464; *Till We
Have Faces*, 266; *Undeceptions
(God in the Dock)*, 469

Lewis, Florence Augusta (mother of
L): 62, 146, 246, 302, 466–67,
470
Lewis, Joseph (brother of Albert):
158
Lewis, Joseph ("Joey"): 158
Lewis, Martha (mother of Albert):
466
Lewis, Mary Anne: 245
Lewis, Richard (father of Albert):
466
Lewis, Warren Hamilton (Warnie):
his picture of Mrs Moore, x; on
relationship between L and Mrs
Moore, 2–3, 6–7, 8; edits *Lewis
Papers*, 10; home from Sierra
Leone, 24; arrives in Oxford, 81;
meets Mrs Moore, 82; returns to
Wynyard, 82; at "Hillsboro",
83–93; with L at Little Lea,
105–7; Christmas 1922 at Little
Lea, 157–64; visits L in Oxford,
225–27; his pleasant life, 234;
another visit to Oxford, 263–64;
with L to Belfast, 278–79; motor-
bike excursion with L, 315–18; L
visits at Colchester, 341–44; in
Belfast, 348; visits L, 402–3; last
Christmas with father, 425–26;
retires to the Kilns, 458; biography
of father, 466–67; portrait of Lily
Suffern, 471; men. 46, 62, 108,
111, 152, 167, 172, 175, 230,
246, 280, 303, 396, 412–13, 428,
450, 463; "Memoir" in *Letters of
C. S. Lewis*, x, 2–3, 5, 7
Ley, Henry George: 28, 350
Leyden: 273
Leys, Kenneth King: 329, 355
Liddell, Henry George: (with Robert
Scott) *Greek-English Lexicon*, 453
Lindsay, Alexander Dunlop: 33–34,
322, 334, 388
Little, William: 468
Lloyd, Harold: 391, 405

Lloyd-Jones, Harry Vincent: 189–90, 236–37, 255

Locke, John: *On Education*, 274; men. 235, 323, 327, 328, 437

Lodge, Thomas: *Rosalynde*, 180

Logue, Michael Cardinal: 160

London Mercury: 17, 19, 47, 56, 282

Longfellow, Henry Wadsworth: *Saga of King Olaf*, 448

Lord, Lionel: 83

Lorenz, Konrad: xi

Low, Marcus Warren: 353, 355

Lowell, James Russell: 49

Lucretius: 224

Lydgate, John: *Story of Thebes*, 375; men. 383, 398, 446

Lyly, John: *Endimion*, 152

Mabbott, John David: 62, 393, 412

Macan, Reginal Walter: 31, 37, 89, 107–8, 118, 128–29, 189, 217–18, 222, 329

Macan, Mrs Reginal Walter: 89

Macaulay, Rose: *Lee Shore*, 424; *Mystery at Geneva*, 455; *Potterism*, 397, 398

Macaulay, Thomas Babington: *Chatham and Clive*, 344; *Lays of Ancient Rome*, 255

Macdonald, Fiona: 451

MacDonald, George: *Lilith*, 362, 364, 413, 418; *Phantastes*, xii, 177, 456; men. 415

Macdonald, Robert: 200–201

Mackail, John William: 220

McKay, Roy: 31

MacKeith, Malcolm Henry: 449, 479–80

Mackenzie, Charles Wilfred: 46

McKisack, Audley: 125, 188, 197

Macmurray, John: 322

McNaughtan, Sarah: *Lame Dog's Diary*, 178, 179

MacNeice, Louis: *Blind Fireworks*, 437

McNeill, James: 467

McNeill, Jane Agnes ("Tchanie"): 45, 46, 160, 162, 165, 167–68, 169, 171, 174, 175, 353, 467

McNeill, Mrs Margaret: 45, 46, 162, 165, 168, 169, 171, 174–75, 467

Macran, Rev. Frederick Walter ("Cranny"): 22, 33, 69, 116, 122, 138, 139, 183, 196, 229–30, 252, 306, 467–68

Macran, Violet: 122, 139

Maeterlinck, Maurice: 76

Magdalen College Register: 424

Mallam, Ernest: 440

Mallock, William Hurrell: *The New Republic*, 18

Malory, Sir Thomas: *Morte d'Arthur*, 115, 270, 322

Manley, John Job: 444, 449–50

Manley, Mrs John Job: 449–50

Marchant, Stanley: 34

Marcus Aurelius Antoninus: 464

Marett, Robert Ranulph: 225

Margoliouth, Herschel Maurice: 409

Marlowe, Christopher: *Edward II*, 397; *Faustus*, 202; *Tamburlaine*, 197, 397; men. 243, 320

Marshall, Archibald: *The Eldest Son*, 272

Martineau, James: *Types of Ethical Theory*, 283

Martlets Society: 32, 53, 125, 142, 150–51, 184, 188, 191, 192, 197–200, 278, 328, 335, 352, 355, 398–99

Martley, Averell Robert: 194, 236–37, 240, 243, 249, 255

Masefield, John: *Daffodil Fields*, 279; *Dauber*, 19, 342, 419; *Everlasting Mercy*, 18–19; *Philip the King*, 332; *Reynard the Fox*, 19; *Right Royal*, 323; men. 17, 71, 240, 456

Masson, David: 110, 113, 116, 428

Master Builder: 352

Mawer, A.: 247

May, Lewis: 324

Mendelian Law: 163

Mendelssohn, Felix: 475

Meredith, George: *Beauchamp's Career*, 165, 166, 168, 169, 172–73, 256; *Egoist*, 256, 451; *Modern Love*, 241; *Ordeal of*

499

Meredith, George (*continued*)
Richard Feverel, 266; men. 303,
415
Mermaid Club: 409, 445, 456–57
Meynell, Alice: 312
Michael Hall School: 465
Middleton, Thomas: (with William
Rowley) *The Changeling*, 155;
Women Beware Women, 155
Miles, Sir John Charles: 329
Mill, John Stuart: 380, 442
Milton, John: *L'Allegro*, 113;
Apology for Smectymnuus, 440;
Comus, 114, 275, 433; *Doctrine
and Discipline of Divorce*, 113,
444, 445; *Lycidas*, 113; *Paradise
Lost*, 66, 112, 113, 116, 117, 241,
333, 392, 433, 440, 442, 451,
457; men. 441; Il Penseroso, 113;
Prelaticall Episcopacy, 429, 431;
Reason of Church Government,
431, 432; *Reformation Touching
Church Discipline*, 428–29;
Tractate of Education, 113; men.
xii, 57, 110, 147, 177, 189, 196,
243, 244, 268, 392, 428, 437,
439, 456
Moltke, Count Helmuth von: 408
Monro, C. K.: *Rumour*, 455
Montagu, John Eric: 25, 29, 33, 46,
47, 49
Moore, Canon Courtenay: 3
Moore, Courtenay Edward (husband
of Mrs Moore): 3, 8, 16, 17, 265,
458
Moore, Edward Francis Courtenay
("Paddy", son of Mrs Moore):
16, 45, 139, 253
Moore, George: *Confessions of a
Young Man*, 307–8
Moore, George Edward:
Philosophical Studies, 353, 354
Moore, Mrs Janie King: Owen
Barfield recalls, ix–xiii; comes to
know L, 1–9; making marmalade,
15; worried about husband ceasing
payments, 17; financial crisis
resolved, 18; exhausted by
"Cranny", 22; on being poor,
24–25; making "nighties", 26;

looks for good music teacher,
28; indigestion, 29; fear of
thrombosis, 40; on L's inability to
be a dean, 46; on ways and means,
48; on gulf between married and
unmarried, 49; is read L's diary,
54; nurses Leo Baker, 56–58;
anxious not to influence L, 62; "hit
it off splendidly" with Barfield,
65–66; on difference between
Baker and Barfield, 67; makes
petticoat for Lady Gonner, 68;
jam making, 70–71; Maureen's
schooling, 75; argument with Leo
Baker, 77; move to "Hillsboro",
79; on paying guest Andrée Cahen,
80; making jam for Mr Raymond,
95–98; rescue of Maisie Hawes,
99–103; L reads diary to her, 111;
Maisie tells "silent lie", 112–13;
on Mrs Hankin, a paying guest,
114–17; "too much work in the
sewing line", 123–24; search for
a house, 136–37; worried by
Moppie, 137–38; depressed by
Cranny, 139; collapses, 140;
"convinced she would never again
live in a house of her own",
144–46; hears more of L's diary,
151–52; sees Maureen confirmed,
152; lost confidence in Moppie,
180–81; her brother's madness,
201–19; his death, 229; moves
into "Hillsboro", 230–34; various
Oxford houses she's lived in,
252–53; "overworked, worried
and miserable", 259–61; on
paying guest Maurice Delanges,
261–67; very poorly, 278–79;
holiday in Clevedon, 306–15;
entertains Dotty Vaughan, 345–47;
"marmalading", 350; holiday on
Exmoor, 357–77; quarrel with
Maureen, 396–97; trouble with
Dotty Vaughan, 405; her temper,
430; reads *Passage to India*, 431;
finally has a house of her own,
458; men. 16, 19–21, 23, 27, 29,
31–35, 37–39, 41, 43, 48, 50–52,
54, 56, 59, 61–64, 69–70, 72–74,

76, 78, 104–17, 119–22, 125–28,
130, 133–35, 142, 147–49,
154–58, 160–61, 164, 166–73,
175, 177–79, 182–83, 186–87,
195–96, 200, 221–25, 227–28,
237, 242, 244–50, 254–58,
271–73, 281–86, 288–92,
294–96, 299, 301, 303–4, 306–7,
320, 322–25, 327–28, 331–34,
340, 351–56, 377, 381–82,
384–85, 387, 389–91, 394–97,
398–99, 403–7, 409, 411–12,
414–16, 418–37, 439, 441,
445–48, 450–52, 454–58,
459–60, 467

Moore, Jessie Mona Duff: 3

Moore, Maureen (daughter of Mrs
  Moore): in the Foreword, x; comes
  with mother to Oxford, 2; pupil
  at Headington School, 15; Miss
  Whitty finds music "hopeless", 25,
  26; "outbreak of feminism", 37;
  on possibility of L marrying,
  56–57; forgetfulness, 71; question
  of her schooling, 75; first
  impressions of Warnie, 82; L
  tutors in English, 108; L tutors in
  Latin, 109; confirmed, 152; uncle's
  funeral, 229–30; musical career
  discussed, 268–69; chicken-pox,
  283–85; holiday in Clevedon,
  306–15; and Dotty Vaughan,
  345–47; holiday on Exmoor,
  358–77; asks L to explain
  Evolutionary Theory, 361; quarrel
  with mother, 396–97; German
  measles, 426–27; becomes Lady
  Dunbar, 458; men. 3, 7, 16–17, 19,
  23, 28, 30, 33, 36, 38, 41, 43, 45,
  48, 51, 56–57, 62–63, 66, 68–69,
  73–74, 77–80, 83, 85, 87, 90, 92,
  97–98, 111, 113, 116–117,
  121–26, 128, 133–40, 145–49,
  153–56, 158, 179, 181–82, 184,
  186, 189, 202–3, 207, 209–13,
  221–24, 227, 231–33, 242, 244,
  248, 252, 254, 257, 259, 261–63,
  265, 267, 271, 273, 278–79,
  281–83, 289, 304, 328–29,
  332–33, 340, 350, 352, 377, 380,

383, 390–91, 393, 398, 400,
  406–7, 418–21, 425, 428–30,
  441–42, 445–47, 452, 458

More, Hannah: 396

More, Henry: Antidote against
  Atheism, 280; Defence of the
  Cabbala, 288, 290–91;
  Enthusiasmus Triumphatus,
  281; Explanation of the Grand
  Mystery of Godliness, 292, 296;
  Philosophical Works, 291–92;
  Theological Works, 292; men.
  280–81, 284, 285, 296, 297, 300

Morrah, Dermot Macgreggor:
  333–34

Morris, Albert: 252

Morris, Mrs Albert: 252

Morris, William: Earthly Paradise,
  241; "In Prison", 164; Life and
  Death of Jason, 164, 284, 297;
  Sigurd the Volsung, 449, 452; Well
  at the World's End, 421, 422; men.
  120, 190, 191, 297, 368, 420, 452

Morris, William Richard (Viscount
  Nuffield): 124

Mort, Arthur Basil Sutcliff: 126, 135

Moses: 355

Mozart, Wolfgang Amadeus: 112,
  115, 190

Munro, Hector Hugh: At Mrs
  Bean's, 276; Rumour, 455

Munroe, Helen: 83, 247

Murray, Basil: 87

Murray, George Gilbert Aimé: Rise
  of the Greek Epic, 299; men. 197,
  334, 388

Murray, J. A. H.: 468

Murray, Norah: 324–25

Murrell, Mrs James: 416

Mussolini, Benito: 255

Mussorgsky, Modest Petrovich: Boris
  Godunov, 94

Myers, John Linton: 76, 319

Mythology: 269

Nash, Eric Francis: 350, 352

New Arabian Nights: see R. L.
  Stevenson

Newton, Sir Isaac: 437

Nietzsche, Friedrich Wilhelm:
  Beyond Good and Evil, 314

Nightingale, Rev. Frank: 348–49, 353, 354, 355, 356

Nirvanah: 327

Noyes, Alfred: *William Morris*, 297

Officers' Training Corps: 1, 30

Olivier, Daphne: *see* Daphne Harwood

Olivier, Lord Sydney Haldane: 275

Omond, Thomas Stewart: *Study of Metre*, 61

Oneida Community: 75

Onions, Charles Talbut: *Oxford Dictionary of English Etymology*, 468; men. 122, 126, 184, 189, 408, 423, 436, 468

Osborne, Dr: 176–77

Osmond, Austin: 59

Otway, Thomas: *Venice Preserv'd*, 247

Ovid: *Metamorphoses*, 68, 237–38, 242, 251–52; men. 258, 477

Owl and the Nightingale, The: 206

Oxford Magazine: 474

Oxford Orchestral Society: 474

Oxford Poetry: 149, 237

Oxford Times, The: 34, 41, 53, 58, 134, 136

Oxford University Dramatic Society (OUDS): 288, 350–51, 414, 416, 452

Oxford University Officers' Training Corps: 1, 2, 459

Palestrina, Giovanni: 110

Paley, Frederick Apthorp: *Heracleidae*, 295

Panton Arts Club: 445

Panton Magazine: 446–47

Parker, Desmond: 174

Parker, Henry Michael Denne: 436, 439, 451, 454, 480–81

Parry, Edward Abbott: *What the Judge Thought*, 155

Parry, Hubert: *Jerusalem*, 135

"Parson's Pleasure": 39, 41, 43, 70, 253–54, 255, 258, 263–64, 421, 424

Parthenon, the: 336

Pasley, Aldyth ("Johnnie"): 19, 21, 79, 80, 81, 83, 88, 90, 93, 289–90, 292, 334, 468

Pasley, Sir Rodney: 19, 21, 42, 49, 57, 65–66, 68, 79, 80, 81, 83, 88, 89, 90, 92, 93, 149, 289–90, 292, 301, 305–6, 317, 334, 405, 416, 468

Pasley, Sir Thomas: *Private Sea Journals*, 289

Pater, Walter Horatio: 77, 321

Paton, Herbert James: 355–56

Patrizi, Francesco: *De Regno et Regis Institutione*, 416, 423

Patterne, Sir Willoughby: *see* Meredith's *Egoist*

Patterson, Melville Watson: 319

Patterson, William Hugh: 132, 143

Pattison, Mark: *Milton*, 110, 111

Paul, St: 122

Payne, Frederick Lewis: 200, 240, 243

Peacock, Conway John: 444–45

Peacock, Rev. Gerald: 174

Peacock, Mona: 174

Peacock, Thomas Love: 256

Peer Gynt: see Ibsen

Percival, David Athelstane: 380, 388, 399, 402, 406, 451, 455

Perham, Margery Freda: 379

Pericles: 335

Perrott, Daisy ("The Dud"): 90–91

Phaedrus: see Plato

Philological Society: 455

Philosophical Society (Postgraduate): 298, 322, 328, 330–31, 351, 450, 453

Philosophical Society (University College): 303–4

Philostratus: 46

Phipps, Mrs ("Phippy", the charwoman): 340, 351, 353, 398

Pickard-Campbridge, Mrs: 416

Pindar: 197

Pirates of Penzance: see Gilbert and Sullivan operas

Plato: *Dialogues*, 379; *Erastae*, 456; *Phaedrus*, 284; *Philebus*, 293; *Politicus*, 449; *Republic*, 18, 20, 21, 53; *Theaetetus*, 444, 448, 449, 450, 453; men. 26, 47, 48, 77, 110, 319, 446, 449

Plotinus: 128, 224

Ploughman, Mary: 28
Pocock, Guy: 395, 409, 410, 411, 412, 414
Poe, Edgar Allan: 267
Politicus: see Plato
Pollock, Sir Frederick: *Spinoza,* 352
Polonius: 131
Poole, Thomas: 256
Pope, Alexander: *Dunciad,* 402; men. 235
Poynton, Arthur Blackburne: *Cicero Pro Milone; Flosculi Graeci; Flosculi Latini,* 469; men. 35, 48–49, 59, 61, 63, 81, 117–18, 259, 271–72, 319, 329, 350, 354, 468–69
Price, Henry Habberley: 117, 296, 303–4, 322, 328, 419, 469
Prichard, Harold Arthur: *Kant's Theory of Knowledge,* 299; men. 301–2, 319, 403, 412, 453
Prichard, Mrs Harold Arthur: 412
Pringle-Pattison, Andrew Seth: *English Philosophers,* 281
Psychical Research, Society for: 469
Purcell, Henry: 34, 389
Pusey, Edward Bouverie: 31
Quarles, Francis: 448
Quiller-Couch, Sir Arthur Thomas: 220
Quinlan, Miss: 180, 181
Quo Vadis?: see Sienkiewicz
Rabelais, François: 162
Rackham, Arthur: 157, 448
Radice, Edward Albert: 440, 446, 450, 455
Ralegh, Sir Walter: 185
Raleigh, Sir Walter: *Milton,* 433, 441, 469; *Six Essays on Johnson,* 255; *Shakespeare,* 469; *Wordsworth,* 469; men. 35, 52, 130–31, 138, 184, 194, 416, 431, 464, 469
Rasputin: 50, 450
Raymond, Mr: 65, 79, 96–97, 100, 103, 115, 147, 154, 201, 222, 225, 227, 229, 234, 280, 295, 419
Raymond, Mrs: 26, 36, 92, 147, 154, 201, 222, 225, 227, 229

Repington, Charles à Court: *After the War,* 16, 17
Rice-Oxley, Leonard: 345
Richardson, Samuel: 132
Riddles (Anglo-Saxon): 121, 124, 128
Ridley, Arnold: *Ghost Train,* 430
Rink, George Arnold: 188, 197–200, 201, 240, 293, 300, 303–4, 328
Rivers, William Halse R.: *Instinct and the Unconscious,* 63, 67, 70
Robbins, Cherry: 71
Roberts, William: *Memoirs of the Life and Correspondence of Mrs Hannah More,* 396
Robertson, Miss: 162
Robinson, Edwin Arlington: "For a Dead Lady", 47, 56
Robinson, Heath: 64
Robson-Scott, William Douglas: *German Travellers in England 1400–1800; Goethe and the Visual Arts,* 469–70; men. 31, 53, 125, 126, 135, 142, 150, 151, 182, 184, 188, 189, 191, 197–200, 222, 233, 236–37, 242, 287–88, 291, 320–21, 469–70
Rochester, Mrs: *see* Charlotte Brontë, *Jane Eyre*
Rodin, Auguste: 275–76
Rogers, Ethel: 169
Rooke, Eleanor Willoughby: 410
Ross, James Alexander: 351, 353, 355
Ross, Martin: 241
Ross, William David: 298–99
Rossetti, William Michael: 120
Rostand: 110
Rousseau, Jean-Jacques: *Emile,* 274; men. 67
Rowell, Helen: 80, 261, 292
Rowley, William: (with Thomas Middleton) *The Changeling,* 155
Rowse, Alfred Leslie: *Memories and Glimpses,* 379
Royal Air Force: 460
Royal Army Medical Corps: 459, 460
Royal College of Music: 458, 459
Rübezahl: 251, 253
Ruddigore: see Gilbert and Sullivan operas

Ruskin, John: 368
Russell, Bertrand: *A.B.C. of Atoms*,
281; *Icarus*, 304; *Philosophical
Essays*, 281, 282; *Problems of
Philosophy*, 352; *Worship of a
Free Man*, 281, 282; men. 298
Russell, George William ("A. E."):
453
Sackville, Thomas: 197
Sade, Comte Donatien Alphonse
François de: 410, 411
Sadler, Sir Michael Ernest: 222, 233,
272, 273, 274, 278, 318, 320,
328–29, 355, 388
Saint Frideswide: 140–41
Saint Margaret: 140
Saint-Saëns, Camille: *Samson et
Dalila*, 138
Saintsbury, George Edward Bateman:
129, 156, 291
Saklatvala, Shapurji: 402
Salvesen, Harold Keith: 25, 125–26
Sandford, M. E.: *Thomas Poole and
His Friends*, 256
Santayana, George: *Reason in Art*,
182; *Winds of Doctrine*, 281; men.
224
Sassoon, Siegfried: 399
Saurat, Denis: *Milton*, 433, 439, 440
Savage, Richard: 235
School Certificates: 310, 344, 348,
349, 350, 427–28
Schopenhauer, Arthur: 128, 149
Scoones, Diana Dalton: 380, 387, 414
Scott, Robert: *see* Liddell
Scott, Sir Walter: *Bride of
Lammermoor*, 374; *Guy
Mannering*, 427, 428; *Quentin
Durward*, 423; *Waverly*, 244; men.
320
Sée, George: 92–93, 103
Seebohm, Henry: *Oxford Reformers*,
379
Segar, Robert: 388, 400, 406,
418–19, 448–49, 481–82
Selbourne, Lord: 109
Seth: *see* Pringle-Pattison
Seymour, Mrs: 266, 292, 409, 452
Shadwell, Thomas: 244

Shakespeare, William: *Antony and
Cleopatra*, 242; *As You Like It*,
143, 336; *Coriolanus*, 337, 409;
Cymbeline, 233; *Hamlet*, 131, 132,
288, 344; *Henry IV*, 95, 142;
Henry V, 144; *Henry VI*, 74; *King
Lear*, 189, 197, 243, 303, 344,
452; *Love's Labour's Lost*, 140;
Macbeth, 76, 120, 344, 428;
Measure for Measure, 233;
Merchant of Venice, 349; *Merry
Wives of Windsor*, 95, 107, 233,
243, 420; *Midsummer Night's
Dream*, 143, 175, 233, 414; *Much
Ado about Nothing*, 132; *Othello*,
224; *Phoenix and the Turtle*, 230;
Richard II, 344; *Richard III*, 230;
Romeo and Juliet, 38, 337;
Taming of the Shrew, 132;
Tempest, 131; *Timon of Athens*,
230; *Twelfth Night*, 230, 344;
Two Gentlemen of Verona, 124;
Troilus and Cressida, 123, 450;
men. 138, 139, 153, 155, 183, 200,
240, 243, 244, 248, 337, 428
Shaw, George Bernard: *Candida*,
178; *Irrational Knot*, 61
Shelley, Percy Bysshe: *The Cenci*,
139; *Prometheus Unbound*,
67–68, 125, 192, 194, 368; men.
59, 76, 127, 135
Shorter Oxford English Dictionary:
470
Sidgwick, Henry: *Ballads and Poems
Illustrating English History*, 427
Sienkiewicz, Henryk: *Quo Vadis?*,
24
Simon, Sir John: 87, 304, 389
Simon Magus: 238
Simpson, Percy: 120, 121, 130–31,
194, 247, 256, 296–97, 433
Simpson, Philip Overend: 25, 26, 30,
46, 47, 53, 150
Singh, Fateh: 189–90, 216–17
Slade, Humphrey: 451–52
Slade School of Fine Art: 464
Smith, Harry Wakelyn: 319
Smith, John Alexander (of Magdalen
College): trans., *De Anima*, 470;

men. 230, 393–94, 400, 401, 404,
405, 406, 407, 408, 411, 440, 442,
446, 450, 453, 455, 470

Smith, Logan Pearsall: *Trivia*, 185;
men. 188, 432

Socrates: 296, 450

Somerville, Edith Oenone: 241, 462

Somerville, Henry: 462

Somerville, Martin Ashworth: 45

Sophocles: *Antigone*, 52, 54–55, 78;
men. 119

Sorley, William Ritchie: *Moral
Values and the Idea of God*, 283

Sortes Virgilianae: 245, 324, 392

Sparrow, John Hanbury Angus: 437

Spencer, Charles Richard: 387, 388,
397, 398, 400, 409

Spengler, Oswald: 448

Spens, Janet: 410, 415

Spenser, Edmund: *Faerie Queene*, 40,
44, 119, 165, 167, 226; *Shepheards
Calender*, 404; men. 147, 151, 181,
191, 192, 193, 197, 238, 243–44,
248, 258, 267, 270, 286, 393, 406,
413

Spinoza, Benedict: *Ethics*, 352; men.
352, 353, 354

Squire, John Collins: 17, 20, 29,
32–33, 185–86, 282, 286, 300,
452

Stanford, Charles Villiers:
"Magnificat", 71

Stead, William Force: *Festival in
Tuscany*, 472; *Shadow of Mount
Carmel*, 409; *The Sweet Miracle*,
17, 26, 470; *Verd Antique*, 472;
men. 22, 34, 254–55, 409, 411, 472

Stead, Mrs William Force: 470

Steele, Sir Richard: 383

Stein, Gertrude: 413, 414, 418

Steiner, Rudolf: 254, 275, 277, 301,
339, 449, 452, 461, 465

Stephens, James: *Crock of Gold*,
105, 288, 303, 328; *Deirdre*, 279;
Insurrections, 222; *Irish Fairy
Tales*, 105; men. 335, 347

Sterne, Laurence: *Tristram Shandy*,
369; men. 115

Stevenson, Arthur: 21–22

Stevenson, George Hope (L's tutor):
Roman History; *Roman
Provincial Administration*, 470;
men. 25, 26, 29, 31, 33, 46, 48,
49–50, 83, 107, 108, 119, 183,
187, 222, 223, 242–43, 272,
273–74, 328, 351, 470

Stevenson, Mrs George Hope: 31,
119

Stevenson, Helen: 31

Stevenson, Mrs: 21, 24, 41, 80, 87,
90, 133, 221

Stevenson, Robert Louis: *New
Arabian Nights*, 242; *Travels with
a Donkey*, 349

Stevenson, Sydney: 21, 133, 195, 212,
214, 219

Stevenson, Sylvia: 21, 70

Stout, Alan Ker: 298, 299, 330

Strachey, Giles Lytton: *Adventure
in Living*, 176–77; *Eminent
Victorians*, 45; *Queen Victoria*, 41

Stravinsky, Igor: 57

Strick, Richard Boase Kelynack: 190,
193, 194, 240–41, 242, 244, 245

Studer, Paul: 436, 439

Studer, Mrs Paul: 432, 435, 436,
441, 457

Suetonius: *Life of Emperor
Vespasian*, 293

Suffern, Mrs Lily: 21, 52, 127–28,
131–33, 143–44, 148, 153–54,
224–25, 228, 234, 242, 246–47,
288, 291, 292, 295–96, 302–3,
329, 364, 444, 470–71

Suffern, William: 471

Sullivan, Arthur: 138

Surrey, Henry Howard: 197

Sutton, Alexander Gordon: 45

Sutton, W. H.: 330–31, 335

Swanwick, Michael Robert: 348,
349, 350, 351, 353, 354

Sweet, Henry: *Anglo-Saxon Reader*,
119, 123, 124, 167, 170, 176, 224,
435, 455; men. 473

Swift, Jonathan: *Battle of the Books*,
220, 347; *Gulliver's Travels*, 221,
426; men. 381, 399

Swinburne, Algernon Charles: 57

Sykes, Richard Laurence: 386, 401, 405, 409, 422

Symonds, John Addington: 321

Tacitus: *Agricola*, 113, 115; *Histories*, 23

Tagore, Sir Rabindranath: 151, 216–17

Tansley, Sir Arthur George: 442, 444, 448

Tasso, Torquato: *Gerusalemme Liberata*, 267–68, 356; men. 477

Taylor, Mr: 155, 229, 283, 306, 356

Taylor, Mrs: 144–45, 155, 356

Tennyson, Alfred: 135

Terence: *Heauton Timorumenos*, 257

Terry, Ellen: 26, 35

Terry, Philip John: 188, 197–200

Tertullian: 110

Thaïs: 238

Thackeray, William Makepeace: *Henry Esmond*, 364–65, 367; *Vanity Fair*, 285–86

Theaetetus: see Plato

Thomas, James Henry: 395

Thomas Aquinas, St: *Summa Theologica*, 450

Thompson, Edith: 176

Thompson, Rev. James Matthew (Magdalen College): 381, 416, 418, 420, 455

Thoreau, Henry David: 307

Thornton, Edna: 339

Thrasymachus: 352

Thring, J. R.: 258

Thring, Monica Rose: 380, 394

Thucydides: 28, 29, 32, 36

Titian: 95

Tolkien, John Ronald Reuel: *Hobbit; Lord of the Rings; Silmarillion*, 471; men. 392–93, 440, 471

Tolley, Mr: 231–32, 234

Tolstoy, Count Leo: *Anna Karenina*, 279; *The Godson*, 100; *Where God Is, There Is Love*, 100

Touche, George Lawrence Capel: 328, 351, 354

Tourneur, Cyril: *Revenger's Tragedy*, 456

Trades Union Congress: 384, 385, 388, 389, 390, 391, 393, 397

Traherne, Thomas: *Christian Ethics*, 325

Trajan, Emperor: 449

Trench, Richard Chenevix: *The Study of Words*, 448, 449

Trevelyan, George Macauley: *England in the Age of Wycliffe*, 452; *England under the Stuarts*, 382, 383

Trinity College Dublin: 459, 460

Troeltsch, Ernst: 298

Troilus and Cressida: see Shakespeare

Trollope, Anthony: *Autobiography*, 173, 174; *Warden*, 416; men. 477

Truth: 301, 338, 340

Tubbs, Mr: 37

Tupper, Martin: 447

Ure, Percy Neville: 55

Valentin, Deric William: 380, 386, 390, 397, 401, 404, 406, 408, 412, 413, 434–35, 436, 437, 441, 442, 447, 448, 451, 453, 455

Van Dyck, Anthony: 273

Vaughan, Dorothea ("Dotty"): 347, 351–52, 381–82, 383, 390, 400, 403, 405, 407, 409, 411, 412, 414, 416, 420, 422, 424, 427, 441, 445–46, 452, 455, 457

Vecchio, Palma: 273

Verdi, Giuseppe: 135

Virgil: *Aeneid*, 85, 109, 110, 117, 121, 123–24, 126, 153, 208, 235, 324, 327, 330, 344, 392; *Georgics*, 346, 392; men. 245, 303, 392

Volsunga Saga: 449, 452

Voltaire: *Candide*, 272

Voyages of Ohthere and Wulfstan: 380, 386, 440

Waddington, Thomas Elliot: 386, 401, 405, 409, 422

Wagner, Richard: *Ring of the Nibelung*, 128, 259, 339–40, 448; men. 131, 138, 148, 190, 366

Waller, Edmund: 454, 455

Wallis, Edward John: 30

Walpole, Hugh: xii, 188
Walsh, Mr (solicitor): 100, 101–2, 104
Wanderer, The: 133, 134, 135
Ward, James: *Realm of Ideas,* 282
Ward, Mrs Humphrey: *Lady Rose's Daughter,* 286
Ward, Richard: *Life of Henry More,* 291, 292, 296
Wardale, Edith Elizabeth: *Introduction to Middle English,* 472; *An Old English Grammar,* 140, 472; men. 118, 121, 123, 125, 126, 129, 130, 131, 133, 136, 137, 140, 149, 182, 184, 190, 195, 207, 214, 215, 219, 235, 247, 415, 471–72
Ware, Robert Remington: 303, 328, 351
Warren, Sir Herbert (President of Magdalen): *By Severn Sea; Death of Virgil,* 472; men. 107, 108, 118, 358, 378, 402, 416, 417, 439, 445, 453, 472
Warren, Lady: 416, 419
Warton, Joseph: 235
Waterfield, Thomas Edward: 380, 388, 399, 402, 406, 439, 441, 446, 450, 451, 453, 454
Waterhouse, Celia: 350
Watling, Edward Fairchild: 25, 29, 30, 32, 33, 45, 53, 55, 66, 82
Watson, John: *Philosophy of Kant,* 348
Watts-Dunton, Walter Theodore: 57
Webb, Clement Charles Julian: 447
Webb, Mrs Clement Charles Julian: 416
Webster, John: *White Divel,* 169, 445
Weldon, Thomas Dewar: 379, 387, 388, 390, 391–92, 401, 402, 408, 412, 417, 418, 434, 435, 445, 448, 450, 453, 480, 482–83
Wells, Herbert George: *Country of the Blind,* xii, 390; *Modern Utopia,* 106, 415; men. 57, 333–34
Whibley, Leonard: *Political Parties in*

Athens during the Peloponnesian War, 25
Whitman, Walt: 57, 76
Whitty, Kathleen: 25, 26, 209
Who's Who: 424
Wiblin, Christine: 182–83, 263
Wiblin, Maurice: 99
Wiblin, Vida Mary ("Smudge"): 42, 44, 50, 57–58, 61, 64, 65, 69, 75, 78–84, 86, 88–91, 97–99, 100, 104, 108, 112–15, 120, 122, 126, 134, 138, 152, 155, 181, 182, 183, 214, 218, 225, 255–56, 263, 472
Wilbraham, Mrs: 285, 381, 399, 420, 424
Wilkinson, Cyril Hackett: 310–11
Williams, Vaughan: *Shepherds of the Delectable Mountains,* 389; men. 74–75, 122, 135–36, 148, 383
Wilson, Cooke: 80
Wilson, Frank Percy: gen. ed., *Oxford History of English Literature,* 473; men. 118, 123, 126–27, 131, 142–43, 147, 181, 182, 196, 206, 217, 218, 233, 236, 240, 243, 248, 249, 251, 258–59, 272, 284, 357, 472–73
Wood, Arthur Denis: 439, 440, 441, 446, 450–51, 455
Wordsworth, William: *The Excursion,* 195–96; *The Prelude,* 110, 252, 333, 382, 385, 386, 427; men. 115, 222, 240, 251, 273, 329, 344, 362, 415, 432, 447
Wren, Sir Christopher: 277
Wright, Elizabeth: *see* Joseph Wright
Wright, Frank Arnold: ed., *Girdle of Aphrodite,* 297
Wright, Joseph: *Old English Grammar* (with Elizabeth Wright), 432, 434; men. 473
Wrong, Edward Murray: 388, 390–91, 406, 418, 419
Wulfstan: *Address to the English,* 174, 435, 436, 437, 441
Wyatt, Sir Thomas: 197
Wycherley, William: *The Country*

Wycherley, William (*continued*)
Wife, 245; *The Gentleman
Dancing-Master*, 33, 34
Wyld, Henry Cecil Kennedy ("The
Cad"): *Historical Study of the
Mother Tongue*, 387, 428–29,
431, 432, 433–34, 436, 473;
A Short History of English, 130,
473; *Studies in English Rhymes*,
473; *Universal Dictionary of the
English Language*, 473; men. 120,
124–25, 128, 130, 133, 137,
139–40, 142, 191, 195, 200, 291,
431–32, 433–34, 436, 473
Wyllie, Basil Platel: 25, 29, 33, 37,
39, 46, 47, 183
Wynn, George William Nevill: 195,
240
Wynyard School ("Belsen"): 15, 82

Yeats, William Butler: *Land of
Heart's Desire*, 15; *Two Kings*,
161; *Wanderings of Oisin*, 420;
men. 26, 167, 187, 255, 320
Yorke, Henry Vincent (pseudonym,
"Henry Green"): *Pack My Bag*,
380; men. 380, 381, 383, 395,
399, 402, 406, 407, 409, 410,
411, 413–14, 417
Younger Edda: see Edda
Youssopoff, Prince: 450
Youth: 36
Ziman, Herbert David: 31, 53, 150,
188, 291, 293, 299, 303–4,
321–22, 332, 351, 353, 355
Zoëga, Geir Tómasson: *A Concise
Dictionary of Old Icelandic*, 448
Zulueta, Francis de: 87
Zumagrinoff: 50

*Also by C. S. Lewis and available
in Harvest/HBJ paperback editions:*

Boxen: The Imaginary World of the Young C. S. Lewis
The Business of Heaven: Daily Readings from C. S. Lewis
The Dark Tower and Other Stories
The Four Loves
Letters to Malcolm: Chiefly on Prayer
Narrative Poems
Of Other Worlds: Essays and Stories
On Stories: And Other Essays on Literature
Poems
Present Concerns
Reflections on the Psalms
Spirits in Bondage: A Cycle of Lyrics
Surprised by Joy: The Shape of My Early Life
Till We Have Faces: A Myth Retold
The World's Last Night and Other Essays